CLEMENTINE
CHURCHILL

CLEMENTINE CHURCHILL

by her daughter
MARY SOAMES

CASSELL
LONDON

CASSELL LTD.
35 Red Lion Square, London WC1R 4SG
and at Sydney, Auckland, Toronto, Johannesburg,
an affiliate of
Macmillan Publishing Co., Inc.,
New York

First published 1979

ISBN 0 304 30321 6

Printed in Great Britain
by Richard Clay (The Chaucer Press) Ltd
Bungay, Suffolk

This book is dedicated to my children
NICHOLAS   EMMA   JEREMY
CHARLOTTE   RUPERT

CONTENTS

CONTENTS

ILLUSTRATIONS

ACKNOWLEDGMENTS

I wish first of all to acknowledge my gratitude to Her Majesty The Queen for her gracious permission to use letters which are in Her Majesty's copyright, and to quote from two of her speeches. I also wish to thank Her Majesty Queen Elizabeth The Queen Mother for graciously allowing me to quote from letters to and from Her Majesty.

My main sources of information for this book are my mother's – Clementine Churchill's – own recollections told to me at various times, and her own brief written account of part of her childhood and girlhood, entitled '*My* Early Life'. My parents' relationship to each other, their views on the events in their lives, and their opinions of other people, are for the greater part drawn from their massive correspondence, direct quotations from which, for reasons of space alone, I have had to curtail. I have also drawn on my mother's letters to my sister, Sarah Audley, and on my father's and my own personal diaries and papers.

For the events in my father's life I have depended in the main on his own published accounts (as listed in the bibliography), and on his official biography started by my brother, Randolph S. Churchill, and continued after his death by Mr Martin Gilbert, M.A., to whom I wish to record my special thanks for his ready help to me and my research assistant in all matters concerning this book on which we have sought his assistance.

Members of my family have given me much help, and I record my true thanks to my late brother, Randolph Churchill, for making copies of my parents' letters to each other which were in his possession available to me. I am very grateful to my sister, Sarah Audley, for permission to use extracts from her letters, and for making available to me our mother's letters to her. Sarah also read the whole script, and I was greatly helped by her comments, and by being able to discuss with her intimate family matters. I wish to thank the children of my late sister Diana, Julian and Edwina Sandys, for permission to quote from her letters, and Celia Walters for searching for photographs of her mother. And I am grateful to my nephew, Winston S. Churchill, for giving me permission to quote from his father's (Randolph Churchill's) letters to his mother, and for allowing me to use the photograph of the sketch portrait of her painted by Winston Churchill, which is in his possession.

I am indebted to my kinsman, the Earl of Airlie, for allowing me to read, and use extracts from, the diaries of his great-grandmother, Blanche, Countess of Airlie, and for allowing me to copy various family photographs. Lord Airlie also kindly read the early chapters of the book, and I am grateful to him for his comments on points of family history. I received valuable help from the late Lady Helen Nutting, who through her own recollections and family letters shed useful light on the relationship between Lady Blanche Hozier and her husband. Also, my thanks are due to Professor Jack Ogilvy of Boulder, Colorado, for writing to me his recollections of my grandmother, Lady Blanche.

I am grateful to my cousin, the late (10th) Duke of Marlborough for his account of the 'scene' at Blenheim described in Chapter 7 and for allowing me to have copied extracts from the Blenheim Visitors' Book; and I wish to thank his son, the present Duke of Marlborough, for supplying me with a photograph of the Temple of Diana at Blenheim.

I am indebted to my cousin, the late Giles Romilly, who furnished me with copies of Clementine Churchill's letters to her sister Nellie Romilly and to himself. And I wish to thank the Trustees of the Romilly Papers, who allowed me access to them after Giles Romilly's death, and from which I gleaned some valuable background detail for my mother's early years.

I wish to record my gratitude to my late cousin, Judy Montagu (Mrs Milton Gendel), who made available to me in the first instance the extracts concerning my mother in the H. H. Asquith/Venetia Stanley correspondence. And I am most grateful to the Hon. Mark Bonham Carter for assisting me to verify and correct Judy Montagu's transcripts through the good offices of the Warden of Nuffield College, Oxford, Mr Michael G. Brock, M.A., F.R.Hist.S. I also thank Mr Bonham Carter for his permission to quote these extracts, as well as extracts from *Winston Churchill As I Knew Him* by his mother, Lady Violet Bonham Carter, and from her letters to my mother.

I am indebted to Mr Donald Whyte, F.S.A.Scot., L.H.G., who compiled genealogical tables for me which have been invaluable, and who also supplied me with interesting information about the Ogilvy and Hozier families, and other related matters. Also to Mr P. L. Gwynn-Jones, Bluemantle Pursuivant of Arms, for advice and layout of the family pedigree.

I owe a special debt of gratitude to Sir John Colville, C.B., C.V.O., and to Mr Anthony Montague Browne, C.B.E., D.F.C., who have both read much of the manuscript, and whose advice and criticism have been of inestimable value.

The following people have also read and commented on parts of the manuscript, and I am most grateful to them: Miss Nonie Chapman; Lord Clark, O.M., C.H. (re the Sutherland picture); Mr Frank Giles; Miss Grace Hamblin, O.B.E.; the Hon. Mrs Henley, O.B.E.; Sir Robert Mackworth-Young, K.C.V.O. (Librarian at Windsor Castle); Mr Alan Philpotts (Literary Trustee); Sir Frank Roberts, G.C.M.G., G.C.V.O. (Clementine's journey to Russia); the late Mr Michael Wolff.

I would like to record my thanks to the following persons for sending me reminiscences and making information available to me, or for sending me letters and photographs: Sir Richard Barlas, K.C.B., O.B.E. (Clerk of the House of Commons); Miss M. R. Bateman, M.A. (Headmistress of Berkhamsted High School for Girls); the Marquess of Bath; the Dowager Countess of Bessborough; the Countess of Birkenhead; the late Margaret, Countess of Birkenhead; Mr E. H. Cookridge (for valuable information concerning Sir Henry Hozier's writings and military career); Col. R. O. Dennys, Somerset Herald (WSC funeral arrangements); Lord Duncan-Sandys, P.C., C.H.; the Hon. Mrs Averell Harriman; Miss A. M. Johnson; Sir Alan Lascelles; Viscount Montgomery of Alamein, M.B.E.; Mr A. H. Montgomery (Perseverance Trust – Howard House Appeal); Mrs Bryce Nairn; Lord Redesdale; Mr Sydney Reynolds (information concerning the Hoziers' house at Berkhamsted); Mr Kenneth Rose; Mr John Spencer-Churchill; Mr Peregrine Spencer Churchill; the Rev. C. N. White (former Rector of Ellesborough, near Chequers); the late Miss Maryott Whyte; Lord Zuckerman, O.M., K.C.B., F.R.S.

For enabling my research assistant to copy entries in the Chequers Visitors' Book I wish to thank Group Captain J. M. Ayre, C.B.E. (Secretary to the Chequers Trustees) and Vera E. Thomas, O.B.E., Wing Commander W.R.A.F. Rtd. (Curator at Chequers).

For permission to have photographed several family portraits at Chartwell, and for permitting my research assistant to copy entries from the Chartwell Visitors' Book, I wish to thank the National Trust, and Miss Grace Hamblin, O.B.E., and Mrs Jean Broome (the former, and present, Administrators at Chartwell).

I am most grateful for the help afforded me by Mrs Pat Bradford and Miss Clare Stephens, Archivists at Churchill College, Cambridge.

On matters connected with my mother's visits to air-raid shelters during the Second World War I am grateful for information supplied by the late Mrs Olive Prentice and by Mrs J. Fawcett, Archivist of the British Red Cross Society.

For information and reminiscences about both my parents covering the forty years Winston Churchill was the Member of Parliament for the Epping (later Wanstead and Woodford) Division, I wish to thank very particularly: Col. W. H. Barlow-Wheeler, D.S.O., M.B.E.;

Mr Donald Forbes, J. P.; Mrs Doris Moss, O.B.E.; Mr A. R. Pittman (Editor of the *Loughton and Woodford Gazette and Guardian*); and Mrs Vera Wilson. In the same connection I also want to thank Mr Gordon (Red) Allen, D.F.C.; Mrs Lilian Henderson; and Mr David A. Thomas.

For information concerning my mother's involvement with the Y.M.C.A. in the First World War (munition workers' canteens) I am indebted to: Mrs G. L. Clapperton; Dame Joan Marsham, D.B.E.; and Mr R. E. Roberts (former General Secretary).

I am very grateful to the following, who have helped to supply information about my mother's work for the Y.W.C.A. in the Second World War: Miss J. M. Nelson (formerly Personal Assistant to the National General Secretary); Miss Edna Rowe (Archivist); Miss E. Sharples (National General Secretary).

I wish to express my appreciation to Prudence Cuming Associates for photographing the pictures at Chartwell, and those in my possession which appear in the book. And to Marriotts Photo Stores of Tunbridge Wells, who have copied with care and skill many faded and damaged photographs from old albums. Also to the Viking Studios, Dundee, for copying pictures and photographs made available to me by Lord Airlie.

I wish to record my thanks to the staffs of BBC Written Archives; the British Library; Conservative Central Office; Hereford and Worcester Records Office; the House of Lords Record Office; and the London Library, who have helped either myself or my research assistant on various occasions.

I also wish to thank all members of the general public who kindly sent reminiscences in response to my appeals through the Press asking for material – even if their specific contributions do not appear in the text, all facts and reminiscences were valuable in building up the overall picture.

*

I am truly grateful to all those who, at various times and in diverse ways, have helped me with the preparation of this book.

Specifically I wish to thank Mr Robert Skepper, M.A., who got me started, and under whose direction Mr W. Allen, Mr C. Beauman and Mr de Bunsen did the first arranging and indexing of the material.

I am most grateful to Miss Heather Forbes-Watson, who was my secretary from 1963 to 1967, and who typed all the earlier chapters.

I wish to express my thanks to Mr John Hazelden, who with patience and tenacity recorded on tape all references in *The Times* to my mother; and my thanks too to Mrs Irene Thrower who typed out the tapes.

I am greatly indebted to Miss Ann Hoffmann of Authors' Research Services, who did all my research from 1966 onwards, which included interviewing many people on my behalf. She has housed and organised my archives, and typed the greater part of the manuscript; she has also compiled the index. I am deeply grateful to Ann Hoffmann, not only for her professional skill and hard work, but also for her unfailing enthusiasm and devotion to the task.

I wish to record my thanks to both Mrs Philippa Boland and Mrs Pat Hodgson, who have assisted Miss Hoffmann at various times.

I am very grateful indeed to Mrs Margot Levy, M.A., who has checked my manuscript and advised me on the historical and political background of the biography. When it became clear that the original manuscript was much too long, she gave me invaluable help in rearranging and cutting the material for the final draft.

I wish to record my gratitude to Sir Denis Hamilton, D.S.O., who, both while Editor of the *Sunday Times* and later as Editor-in-Chief and Chief Executive of Times Newspapers Ltd., demonstrated his confidence in me, and whose support and patience I have greatly appreciated.

To Mr Graham Watson of Curtis Brown Ltd. I owe a special debt of gratitude for his sympathetic and ever sensible advice. His constructive criticism and encouragement have throughout been of the greatest help to me.

I wish to express my warm thanks to Miss Anne Carter of Cassell Ltd. and to her assistant,

Miss Jannet Grant, who with great patience and meticulous care have seen me through the last stages of preparing the book for publication.

Finally, I want to say a heartfelt 'thank you' to my husband. Although, undeniably, the various events in his distinguished career have mainly served to hinder, rather than prosper, the progress of this book – yet without his belief that I was the person who should write Clementine Churchill's life, and his unwavering confidence in my capacity to do so, I would have lost heart on many occasions.

*

The author and publishers are grateful to the following authors, publishers, agents, literary executors and others for permission to quote copyright material not already mentioned:
Firstly, to C. & T. Publications Ltd., William Heinemann Ltd. and the Houghton Mifflin Company for permission to quote extensively from the Churchill Papers. Churchill's letters to his wife (the copyright of C. & T. Publications Limited) quoted in this book appear in full in the seven-volume official biography *Winston S. Churchill* by Randolph Churchill and Martin Gilbert (Heinemann: U.K., and Houghton Mifflin: U.S.A.). Next, to Lord Clark, O.M., C.H. and Sir Alan Lascelles for the use of extracts from their own letters to the Author; to Viscount Montgomery of Alamein, M.B.E. for two extracts from his father's letters to Lady Churchill and to the Author; to Lady Madeleine Lytton for two passages from the letters of Neville Lytton to Nellie Hozier; to Lady Diana Cooper for permission to quote from her book, *Trumpets from the Steep*; to the Hon. Mark Bonham Carter for the use of several extracts from the Asquith/Stanley correspondence; to the Beaverbrook Foundation for access to the Beaverbrook Papers, now in the custody of the House of Lords Record Office and reproduced by courtesy of the Clerk of the Records; to the Beaverbrook Foundation and William Collins, Sons & Co. Ltd. for a short extract from Beaverbrook, *Politicians and the War*; to the Director of Publishing at Her Majesty's Stationery Office for the use of Crown Copyright material from *Hansard*; to Times Newspapers Ltd. for permission to quote medical reports on Churchill signed by Lord Moran and Sir Russell Brain and one statement issued by Clementine Churchill also printed in that newspaper; to Mr Anthony Montague Browne, Mr Evan Davies and the executors of Mrs B. E. Moir (deceased) for extracts from letters to *The Times*; to the Hamlyn Group, for passages from Winston S. Churchill, *Painting as a Pastime* and from Lord Riddell, *More Pages from my Diary*; to the Hamlyn Group and Charles Scribner's Sons for *Thoughts and Adventures* and *The World Crisis* by Winston S. Churchill; to Cassell Ltd. and Houghton Mifflin for a number of quotations from Winston S. Churchill, *The Second World War*; to Curtis Brown Ltd. for extracts from Randolph S. Churchill, *Twenty-One Years*; to Sarah, Lady Audley and André Deutsch for a quotation from her book, *A Thread in the Tapestry*; to André Deutsch and W. W. Norton & Company Inc. for some short passages from Joseph P. Lash, *Eleanor and Franklin*; to the Hon. Mark Bonham Carter and Thornton Butterworth Ltd., the original publishers of Margot Asquith's *Autobiography*, for two short extracts; to the Hutchinson Publishing Group Ltd. for extracts from Mabell, Countess of Airlie, *Thatched with Gold*, E. Ashmead-Bartlett, *The Uncensored Dardanelles*, Lady Cynthia Asquith, *Diaries 1915–18* and Clementine Churchill, *My Visit to Russia*; to Weidenfeld (Publishers) Ltd. for passages from Harold Nicolson, *Letters and Diaries 1939–45*, and Robert Rhodes James, *'Chips': The Diary of Sir Henry Channon*, and *Churchill: A Study in Failure*; to Eyre & Spottiswoode (Publishers) Ltd. and William Collins, Sons & Co. Ltd. for 8 short extracts from Lady Violet Bonham Carter's *Winston Churchill As I Knew Him*; to George Allen & Unwin (Publishers) Ltd. for permission to quote a short passage from Lord Hankey, *The Supreme Command*; to Collins, Publishers and Curtis Brown Ltd. for one short extract from Tom Harrisson, *Living through the Blitz*; to Brandt & Brandt, Literary Agents Inc. and Harper & Row for permission to quote from Robert E. Sherwood, *The White House Papers of Harry L. Hopkins*; to the Estate of the late Dr Hewlett Johnson for the use of a short extract from *Searching for Light*; to the London School of Economics and Political Science for permission to quote from Beatrice Webb, *Our Partnership*; to the Secretary of the University Court of the University of Glasgow for an extract from the speech of the late Professor John Duncan Mackie; to Miss

E. Sharples, National General Secretary of the Y.W.C.A. for the use of letters of former officials of the Association; to Dr John G. Griffith, Public Orator of the University of Oxford, for both verifying the Latin text of the speech of a former Public Orator and clearing up the question of copyright; to the Editor of the *British Medical Journal* for a quotation from that publication; finally, permission to quote 8 lines from the song 'I'm Forever Blowing Bubbles' © 1919 by Kendis Brockman Music Co., sub-published by B. Feldman & Co. Ltd. and reproduced by permission of EMI Music Publishing Ltd.

Edward
2nd Baron Stanley
1802–69
=
Henrietta Maria
dau. of 13th Viscount
Dillon
1808–95

...uest
...aron
...orne
...–1914
=
Cornelia
1847–1927

Other
issue

James
Hozier
1791–
1878
=
Catherine
Feilden
1803–70

David
10th Earl of
Airlie
1826–81
=
Henrietta
Blanche
1830–1921

Henry
(3rd Baron)
1827–1903

Maude
1833–
1915

Edward
(4th Baron)
1839–
1925
=
Mary Bell
'Aunt Maisie'
1848–1929

William
Wallace
1st Baron
Newlands
1825–1906

Other
issue

Mary

Arthur
(5th Baron)
1875–1931
=
Margaret
Gordon

Other
issue

Anthony
Henley
1873–1925
=
Sylvia
1882–

Edwin
Montagu
1879–
1924

Venetia
1887–
1948

...ram
...rd
...aron
...sdale
...–1916
=
Clementine
1854–1932

David
(11th Earl)
1856–1900

Lady Mabell
Gore
1866–1956

Theodore
Whyte
=
Maude
1859–1933

James
Cheape
=
Griselda
1865–1934

Milton
Gendel
=
Judy
1923–1972

Lyulph
1861–
1947

...ozier
...–1921

Bertram
Romilly
1878–1940
=
Nellie
1888–1955

Other
issue

Maryott
'Cousin Moppett'
'Nana'
1895–1973

Giles Romilly
1916–1967
=
Mary Ball Dodd
1927–

Esmond
1918–
1942
=
Jessica Mitford
1917–

Vic Oliver
1898–1964
1st husband
(Marriage
dissolved)
=
Sarah
1914–
=
Antony
Beauchamp
Died 1957
2nd husband
=
Henry
23rd Baron
Audley
1913–63
3rd husband

Marigold
1918–21

Christopher
Soames,
created Baron
Soames 1978
1920–
=
May
1922–

...mes
...ton

Nicholas Soames
1948–

Emma
1949–

Jeremy
1952–
=
Susanna
Keith

Richard
Hambro
=
Charlotte
1954–

Rupert
1959–

...dolph
...ncer
...chill
...5–

Jennie
1966–

Marina
1967–

Jack
1975–

Jake Barton
1973–

Clementine Sylvia
1976–

PREFACE

It was my husband who suggested to me that I ought to write my mother's life. The idea at first startled me; but presently I broached the subject with my mother. She liked the idea, and with characteristic immediacy sent me, within a week, the tin boxes containing her archives. From the outset it was agreed between us that the book should not appear in her lifetime.

It would always have been a difficult task for me, since I have never before written so much as a pamphlet. A further dilemma was the sheer wealth of the material; and reasons of space alone made it imperative for me to cut severely quotations from my parents' prolific correspondence.

I have not always followed a strictly chronological arrangement: to have done so (without interrupting the flow of the narrative) would have prevented me from dealing in depth with such important aspects of my mother's life as Chartwell, her war work (1939–45), and her personal attitudes and relationships.

It has been a personally moving experience for me to delve back into my mother's long lifetime; and to trace through her spoken recollections, but above all in their letters to each other, the record of her loving and heroic partnership with my father, which lasted over half a century.

One curious effect of writing about my parents is that as time and the book go on, from being an observer in the wings I myself become involved as a witness in the story, and a background, 'incidental' participant in events which have shaped and shaken all our lives in the last forty years.

My mother herself took a great interest in the book, and read, or had read to her, all the chapters up to the early days of the First World War: and she was pleased with them.

Now that the book is finished, as in Parliament I must 'declare my interest': it is a labour of love – but I trust not of blind love.

MARY SOAMES
January 1979

FORBEARS AND EARLY
CHILDHOOD

WHEN IN 1878 Lady Blanche Ogilvy, the eldest daughter of the 10th Earl of Airlie, became engaged to Colonel Henry Hozier, her family acquiesced with relief rather than enthusiasm to a match which could not have been considered a brilliant, or even a very suitable one for the beautiful daughter of an earl. Henry Hozier was forty, and older by fourteen years than his intended bride. He was a gentleman, but he possessed only a modest fortune, and none of the four Ogilvy girls was well endowed. Moreover, Colonel Hozier had already been married, and only quite recently divorced, a circumstance which would, in those days, certainly have been regarded as a serious impediment. He had met Blanche Ogilvy on one of his visits to Cortachy Castle, Kirriemuir, Angus (the Ogilvy home), for he was a friend of long standing of Lady Airlie (although her husband always thought the Colonel was a bit of a bounder).

When Blanche Ogilvy was fourteen or fifteen, the famous artist G. F. Watts was staying at Cortachy painting the portraits of her parents, and he painted also a small and ravishing study of Blanche's head. She had the face of an angel: but this angelic countenance belied a very humanly passionate nature, and, as she grew older, she was to cause her parents grave anxiety by her wayward and capricious spirit. In 1878 she was moreover twenty-six years old, and Lord and Lady Airlie no doubt thought it high time she was 'settled'. Despite, therefore, the not inconsiderable disadvantages, they gave their consent to the engagement, and Henry and Blanche were married in the private chapel at Cortachy Castle, according to the forms of the Episcopal Church of Scotland, on 28th September 1878.

The Ogilvys are of ancient Scottish lineage, and their family has a stormy and romantic history. Their ancestors can be traced back to the middle of the twelfth century when the third son of the Earl of Angus assumed the name of Sir Patrick Ogilvy on being given the land and barony of Ogilvy for services to King William the Lion. His descendant, Sir James Ogilvy, was raised to the peerage in 1491 for services to his country as Ambassador to Denmark. The Lord Ogilvy of the day was one of those who signed the association in defence of Mary, Queen of Scots in 1568. The earldom of Airlie dates from 1639, and was granted to the 8th Lord Ogilvy for supporting Charles I against the Covenanters. This same Lord Airlie paid a high price for his loyalty: by way of punishment Airlie Castle was burnt by the Earl of Argyll. It was after this that Cortachy Castle became the family's home.

Earlier in the seventeenth century, another forbear, John Ogilvie, who was converted from Calvinism and became a Jesuit priest, was martyred for his faith at Glasgow Cross. In 1976 he was canonised – becoming the first Scottish saint since St Margaret, Queen of Scotland.[1]

Throughout the eighteenth century the Ogilvys were unwavering in their support of the Stuarts, and the Ogilvys of Airlie forfeited their land and titles after the defeat of the Jacobite supporters at the Battle of Culloden in 1745. These were not fully restored until 1826.

The character and career of David Graham, 10th Earl of Airlie, lacked the romantic and dashing aspects which had characterised the lives of so many of his ancestors, and during his life he departed from several family traditions. He was, for instance, the first Ogilvy ever to be educated at an English school – Eton College, from where he went up to Oxford. Unlike most of his forbears, soldiering had no attraction for him. As a child his health had been fragile, and his gentle nature, combined with scholarly tastes, led him along different paths. Along with intellectual predilections, the young Lord Ogilvy (as he then was) developed at university a passion for gambling; and both as a backer and owner of racehorses he was to lose large sums of money, thereby dissipating the family fortunes, which he was to spend much of his later life repairing.

He succeeded to the title in 1849 aged twenty-three, and two years later he was the first of his family to seek a bride across the English Border. In 1851 he married the Hon. Henrietta Blanche Stanley, one of the daughters of Edward, 2nd Baron Stanley of Alderley. She came from a family whose women in particular were renowned for their intellectual abilities and forceful personalities. Blanche Stanley's mother, Henrietta Maria (a daughter of Henry, 13th Viscount Dillon), was a pioneer of women's education, and was one of the founders of Girton College, Cambridge. Her sister, Rosalind, Countess of Carlisle, was a formidable woman, who took an active part in politics, combining radical Liberal views with aristocratic arrogance. Her brothers also demonstrated independence of mind – one of them becoming a Roman Catholic priest, and later Bishop of Emmaus, while another embraced the Mohammedan faith.

When Blanche Airlie first came to Scotland as a bride of twenty-one she was shocked by the crudeness of the manners, the limited conversation and the drinking habits of the new circle in which she found herself. With intrepid firmness, the young Countess ordained that after two glasses of wine the decanters were to be removed from the table; card-playing after dinner was banned, because it interfered with the conversation. Alarming and dictatorial to some, she charmed those who shared her tastes and outlook. Clever men enjoyed her company, and when she was a young woman Thackeray, Matthew Arnold and Thomas Carlyle were her friends. Gladstone, Disraeli, Lord Rosebery and John Ruskin were all guests at Cortachy at various times. A sincerely religious woman, her friendship and correspondence with Dr Jowett, the Master of Balliol, developed in her over the years a philosophical and catholic outlook on spiritual matters. Unlike her sister, Lady Carlisle, she took no part in public life herself although, with her family, she held Liberal views. But combined with these elevated qualities of mind Blanche Airlie also possessed a valuable fund of common-sense; and to an ancient family she brought the priceless gift of sturdy good health.

Throughout the thirty years of her marriage she governed her rather ineffectual husband, her children and her household with unquestioned authority. Persuading her husband to sell his stud, Lady Airlie sought to divert his interests and energies into less unprofitable and more useful channels. Although he never became prominent in politics (he was far too easy-going), through his wife's influence and encouragement he began to take an interest in political and social problems. And it was doubtless due to her influence that when he took his seat in the House of Lords as one of the Representative Scottish peers, he sat with the Liberals, thus breaking the Ogilvy family's traditional Tory loyalty.

In 1864 Lord Airlie went to North America and travelled widely on that great continent, being much impressed and excited by the golden opportunities it offered. When he returned home to Scotland his mind was full of schemes and new ambitions: selling his remaining bloodstock, Lord Airlie used the proceeds to expand and improve the small herd of Aberdeen Angus cattle which he already owned. Such was the success of this venture that he later invested extensively in ranching in America, settling one of his sons, Lyulph, on land in Colorado. It was on one of his visits of inspection, in 1881, that he was taken ill and died in Denver, Colorado.[2]

The Hozier family had grown from a very different root-stock from that of the Ogilvy clan. Their forbears had come into Glasgow from the Stirlingshire countryside at the close of the seventeenth century, and their name was originally McIlhose or McLehose. In the city the family prospered as maltmen or brewers, and William McLehose, the great-great-grandfather of Henry Hozier, became a Burgess and Guildbrother of Glasgow in 1717, through his first wife, Marion Leggat.

As time went on the family bought Partick, Newlands and other properties in the neighbourhood of Glasgow. William McLehose (born in 1760) was admitted Burgess and Guildbrother in 1786; he changed his surname to Hozier, which seems to have been suggested by a pun on the name: McLehose – 'Mak' the hose'. His son James (1791–1878), an Advocate at the Scottish Bar, purchased in 1850 part of the once extensive Barony of Mauldslie, near Carluke, Lanarkshire, including the Adam mansion, Mauldslie Castle. James Hozier married Catherine Feilden, daughter of a Lancashire baronet, and had eight children. Their eldest son, William Wallace, became the 1st Baron Newlands; and it was their youngest son, Henry Montague Hozier, who married Blanche Ogilvy.

The Hozier family history provides an interesting example of how, from humble and obscure beginnings, in the course of only a few generations the transition was made from the professional, city-dwelling class to that of the landed gentry. But lest the tale of the upward social progress of the Hoziers might seem too plodding and prosaic, an enduring gleam of fame and romance gilded a collateral branch of the family. James McLehose (1754–1812), a lawyer (and the first cousin to Burgess William who changed his name to Hozier), married when she was seventeen Agnes (called Nancy) Craig, the daughter of a Glasgow surgeon. Presently James went off to Jamaica to become the Clerk of Common Pleas there, leaving his wife and three children in straitened circumstances in Glasgow. Nancy moved to Edinburgh, and there she met the Ayrshire ploughman-poet, Robert Burns, who fell deeply in love with her and, calling her 'Clarinda', addressed to her some of his most beautiful and famous lyrics. Their love affair was never consummated; but despite other attachments, and Burns's marriage to Jean Armour, he continued his correspondence (which was later published by her grandson) with Nancy. Their last meeting, in December 1791, before she sailed to Jamaica to join her husband, was immortalised by Burns in the poem, 'Ae fond kiss and then we sever'.[3]

Henry Montague Hozier was born in 1838. He was educated at Rugby and Edinburgh Academy; going into the army, he carved out for himself a brilliant career. He showed early distinction by passing first in and first out of the Staff College. He served in China and Abyssinia, and was attached to the German Army during the Austro-Prussian war of 1866, which he reported for *The Times* as military correspondent. His account of that campaign, *The Seven Weeks' War*, was used by the German Army as a textbook. In the War Office Captain Hozier was associated with a group of progressively-minded young officers who supported reforming measures which were afoot at the time; he was also concerned with Intelligence matters, and was one of the pioneers of the Intelligence service. At the young age of thirty-two he was appointed an Honorary Lieutenant-Colonel, and Controller at Aldershot. During the Franco-Prussian War he was sent as Assistant Military Attaché to the Prussian forces, being subsequently decorated with the Iron Cross by the Emperor William I. He left the Army in 1874, and entered the City as Secretary to the Corporation of Lloyds of London, the great insurance under-writers.

Henry Hozier was a prolific writer. Drawing on personal experience and observation, he wrote *The Franco-Prussian War* and *The Rise and Fall of the Commune*. His other works were *The Russo-Turkish War*, *The Rise and Decline of the Ottoman Empire*, and a biography of the French Marshal Turenne. In addition to all these activities Henry Hozier also dabbled briefly in politics – he was an unsuccessful Liberal–Unionist candidate for Woolwich in 1885.

But his consuming interest was his career with Lloyds. The official historian of the company, D. E. W. Gibb, has written:

> At one time and another Lloyds has produced many able men and many interesting men, but in the combination of intelligence and personality few of them have surpassed Henry Hozier.[4]

During his thirty-two years as Secretary, this unusually able man was to become the driving and dominating force at Lloyds. Of a mathematical and scientific turn of mind, Henry Hozier was keenly aware of the possibilities offered by the science of radio-telegraphy (then in its infancy), and he exploited this invention to the great advantage and prestige of the Corporation he served. His name will always be particularly remembered at Lloyds in connection with the network of telegraphic signal stations linking their offices throughout the world, which were his creation.

In 1878, therefore, at the time of his engagement to Blanche Ogilvy, despite the fact that he was a divorced man, and much older than his bride, Henry Hozier had behind him an extremely distinguished military career; he had been Secretary to Lloyds for four years already, and a secure future lay before him. His maturity no doubt also helped to recommend him to the Airlie family as an acceptable match for their beautiful but flighty daughter.

With all the advantages of hindsight it is possible to feel their life together was destined for storms. The nearly middle-aged, experienced man with his forceful and determined character, allied to the wayward, passionate young woman throbbing with the desire to spread her wings, proved to be too explosive a combination. Moreover, they each possessed the power and, alas, the desire, to tease and taunt the other, and it was not long before their natures were in conflict. An early but profound rift between the two was revealed in their different attitudes to children. He was openly averse to the prospect of a family; she, on the other hand, was deeply maternal, and must have found the five years which elapsed before the birth of their first child a time of grievous frustration.

The Hoziers' first child, a girl, was born in 1883 in London at 18 Queen Anne's Gate: named Katharine, she was always called Kitty. She quickly seized and held pride of place in her mother's warm but uneven affections, and in the seventeen years of her life grew to be a dominating force in her family circle. Two years later, on 1st April 1885, at 75 Grosvenor Street (whence the Hoziers had moved in the interval), a second daughter was born, somewhat precipitately, in the drawing-room.

The new baby was called Clementine – an Ogilvy name recalling the family's historic loyalties: for 'Clementina' had been a popular name in Jacobite circles since the marriage of the 'Old Pretender' to Princess Maria Clementina of Poland.

*

Memories of early childhood are never continuous, but certain moments and incidents are retained with snapshot clarity. The only recollection Clementine had of the house in Grosvenor Street was of being carried downstairs by her nurse to her parents' bedroom, and of being deposited at the foot of their bed. She recalled:

> I was afraid to move from this position, because although my Mother, whom I remember looking lovely and gay, held out her arms to me, on the other side of the bed was my Father's sleeping form; even then I was frightened of him.[5]

But their parents were inevitably rather remote figures for the two girls, for Kitty and Clementine lived the ordered life of upper-class children of that period, in which their existence centred on the nursery (and later the schoolroom), with brief daily contacts with their parents when they were at home.

In 1888 the twins, Bill and Nellie, were born, and the family was now complete. The babies had their own domain, the nursery, and their life was made happy or miserable by the nurse or governess of the moment. All her life Clementine remembered that when Kitty was about six their mother took her for a visit to Holland, leaving Clementine at home with the twins in the charge of a cross, unkind nurse, whom she remembered as beating her unmercifully.

But there were other, kindlier reigns, the memory of which also endured. In the autumn of 1888 Mlle Elise Aeschimann, a Swiss nursery governess, aged sixteen at the time, came to take charge of the two elder girls. Of Mlle Elise there were only happy memories. She stayed for two years, starting the two elder children on their lessons, and laying the foundations of the good French Clementine was to write and speak all her life.

Both the children loved this charming, kindly young woman, who returned their affection. But in particular she showed tenderness to Clementine, 'Rosebud', as her mother called her, who was a somewhat timid child and prone to tears. She had a most sensitive conscience, and suffered untold miseries if the immaculate white of her lace-edged pinafore was marred by spot or stain. Clementine remembered that

> when I cried or was naughty she [Mlle Elise] used to carry me about in her arms, although I was quite a big girl. Mother used to tell her not to spoil me, but she did, just the same.

Perhaps Mlle Elise sensed that Kitty, the more buoyant of the two sisters, was already the star in her mother's firmament, and the perceptive governess sought to comfort and protect the somewhat fearful, tearful younger child. Mlle Elise recalled that Clementine was 'more sensitive, more affectionate, more spontaneous' than her elder sister.

Once, Clementine was discovered sobbing her heart out in bed, and the inconsolable child was brought to her mother. The girls' hair was (prior to special occasions) wound up in 'curlpapers' overnight, and between sobs Clementine managed to tell her mother that she was panic-stricken lest 'Prince Charming' should arrive in the middle of the night and find her in such a plain state. Blanche Hozier had many faults as a mother and was often unjust to Clementine, but she understood romance – the offending 'curlpapers' were laboriously undone, and a sleepy, calmed child returned to her bed.

The Hoziers also had a small house in Scotland, at Alyth, not far from Cortachy, called The Netherton. Clementine wrote of it:

> There was a lawn and a pretty garden just outside the drawing room windows, and beyond this a little wood. I have seen it since, so I know it is a little wood, but to me it seemed like a great forest.

The wood that rose, so forest-like to childish eyes, provided perfect hide-and-seek arrangements, and was full of fascination and mystery to the children.

Their social life consisted of visits to and from nearby relations. Their grandmother, Blanche, Countess of Airlie, a widow since 1881, had moved, soon after the marriage of her son David (11th Earl of Airlie) to Lady Mabell Gore in 1886, to the Cortachy dower house, Airlie Castle, which was within easy driving distance of The Netherton. Cortachy itself was only a little further away, and here a brood of young Ogilvy cousins was starting to make its appearance. Blanche Hozier had a 'tilbury and a cob', which she drove herself, and for nursery outings there was Ginger, the pony, and 'trap', with John, the stable-boy, in attendance.

The family spent regular periods each year in the house in Grosvenor Street. Life in London for the nursery child seems to have changed remarkably little over the years: walks-in-the-park, visits to museums or picture galleries on wet days, and – for treats – occasional expeditions to the Zoo were the main features, then as now, of a well-found child's daily life. Nor did the young Hoziers lack for companionship; their own close family circle provided them with a large mixed bag of contemporary cousins. Blanche Hozier was herself one of six; her brother, Lord Airlie, had the same number of children, while one of her three sisters, Clementine Mitford (whose husband later became the 1st Lord Redesdale), bore nine children, and Blanche's uncle and aunt, Lord and Lady Stanley of Alderley, had a family of eight. The Mitfords and the Stanleys were often in London, and there were frequent visits between the families.

But town life did not suit Kitty, who was not as strong as Clementine, so there were several seaside visits with Mlle Elise, to recover from chills and colds, and one whole summer was spent by all four children at Westgate. There were other more glamorous journeys with their mother. Clementine remembered an Easter visit to Paris, staying at a hotel in the Rue de Rivoli. The children spent many happy hours playing in the Jardin des Tuileries, diverted quite as much by a goat-cart in which they went for rides as by *Le Théâtre Guignol*.

In 1889, when Kitty was six and Clementine four years old, their portrait was painted by a young and gifted artist, Dampier May. It is an enchanting picture: the two little girls (their hair 'Eton-cropped' in the fasion of the day) in delightful lace pinafores are standing before a round looking-glass; Kitty stands in front, confident and assured, while peeping shyly round her shoulder is her younger sister. Clementine remembered quite clearly the portrait being painted; Kitty had enjoyed the sittings, and was 'cool and dignified', while 'I', Clementine recalled, 'wept and was tiresome'.[6]

On looking back, Clementine later sadly recognised that her parents probably never knew any true happiness together, and that from the beginning of their marriage their relationship was a stormy one. But, for the children, these early years were, on the whole, happy ones. Safe and secure in their nursery world, they were too young to feel the rising tension between their parents. But flashpoint was reached between Henry Hozier and his wife at the end of 1890, when (as is quite clear from family letters) Blanche was discovered to have been unfaithful to her husband. Her family stood by her loyally, but they were consternated at the prospect of the breakdown of the marriage and deeply shocked by the fact of what her brother described as Blanche's 'wrong-doing'.[7]

Early in 1891 Blanche and Henry Hozier separated for ever: he must have been an angry, strange man indeed, for his entry in *Who's Who* made no mention of either of his wives, nor of the existence of any children. Despite the fact that Henry Hozier had been divorced by his first wife on grounds of desertion and adultery, and that there were strong grounds for believing that he himself may have been less white than the driven snow since his second marriage, he was to show himself towards Blanche as hard and revengeful.

Both Blanche's brother and her brother-in-law (Bertram Mitford, later Lord Redesdale) tried to help her. And when it was quite evident that reconciliation was out of the question, they sought to ensure that proper provision should be made by her husband for herself and the children. However, on being pressed to provide more than he intended to supply, Henry Hozier rounded on the family, and made it quite clear that he would not have the slightest hesitation in publicly branding his wife as an adulteress. Whereupon the family settled for what Henry Hozier was prepared to give – which was very little indeed.

Blanche therefore became largely dependent upon her family for financial support. The Ogilvys had never been a very wealthy family – most of their fortune being tied up in their estates. Lord Airlie was a serving soldier, with a growing family of his own; and of his four sisters only two, Clementine Mitford and Griselda (married in 1897 to James Cheape of St Andrews), married reasonably well in a worldly sense. Notes at the end of Blanche Airlie's diaries show that she was consistently generous to her more impecunious children. But there is no doubt that, despite help from her family, Blanche Hozier was from now on very badly off financially.

The question of the care and custody of the children was, predictably, the subject of bitter disagreements between their parents, and they became helpless hostages in the ensuing tussle. The first arrangement was that the twins, Bill and Nellie, now aged three, were to remain with their mother, while the two elder girls, aged eight and six, went to live with their father, in the charge of a kind, elderly governess – Miss Rosa Stevenson.

The first memory Clementine had of their new life was when she and Kitty went with their father to Homburg, a fashionable watering-place in Germany. In order to prepare themselves for this journey, the two girls were taken by Miss Stevenson to the Army & Navy Stores, from where, among other things, two large trunks were bought, upon which their names were impressively inscribed. The trunks were also decorated with gay yellow and red painted bands for easier recognition. They had new best frocks of tartan silk with crochet lace collars. The little girls did not see a great deal of their father, and indeed stayed in a different hotel, but every morning they escorted him when he went to take the waters, breakfasting afterwards under the trees on deliciously sweet sultana bread and warm goat's milk.

Although Henry Hozier was determined to establish his right to his children, the two small girls were no doubt an encumbrance to him, and on their return home from Homburg, Kitty and Clementine went to stay with Miss Stevenson in her own home at Berkhamsted. For a short time they attended a Kindergarten, but for some reason this did not last for more than a week or two. Thereafter, instead of making paper mats or counting beads, the children spent the mornings watching Miss Stevenson do the housework, a labour she performed with the utmost care and attention.

At this time there loomed into the children's lives the formidable figure of 'Aunt Mary'. She was Henry Hozier's unmarried sister, and from time to time visited the children to inspect and supervise. She wore a black, jet-trimmed bonnet and a sombre, though richly embroidered cape and dress of bombazine; the final touch to this imposing (and reproving) presence being given by a châtelaine which rattled as she walked. Clementine was terrified of her, but Kitty did not mind her a bit and was cheerfully impertinent.

The pleasant days at Berkhamsted, however, were numbered; whether or not on the advice of the formidable Aunt Mary is not known, but Kitty and Clementine were now sent to a bleak school in Edinburgh kept by Herr Karl Fröbel and his three daughters (reputedly relations of the celebrated German educationalist).

It was situated in Moray Place, a roundel at the west end of Georgian Edinburgh.[8] Clementine remembered lessons in the dining-room, with crumbs on the floor and an all-pervading smell of finnan haddock. Here in this somewhat grim establishment, Kitty and Clementine knew the first pangs of unhappiness and homesickness.

There is something heartrending about these two doll-like creatures (for their photographs show them as such) contending with a stony world so early in life. The sisters clung together with a fierce loyalty, and developed a strong sense of dependence each upon the other. Kitty was the bolder, and the natural leader of the two, but Clementine, although two years younger, could already write a nice clear hand. And so when the children decided life was not bearable at the Fröbels' school, and Kitty had the idea that an appeal should be made to their father to take them away, she bullied the timorous Clementine into writing the letter. All letters to and from the pupils were scrutinised, so it had to be posted by stealth; this Kitty contrived to do, unperceived by the Mistress in charge of the girls, while they were out for their afternoon walk.

The two little girls waited with pent-up anxiety, and four days later Kitty found a letter on her plate, but before she could open it Fräulein Fröbel demanded to have it; she read it on the spot, and immediately burst into loud, hysterical sobs. However, she allowed the children to have the letter, which said:

My dear Children,
    If you are unhappy, I will take you away at once.

Your affectionate
Father

But, alas for parental honour, he did nothing, and Kitty and Clementine were put into Coventry by the whole school.

Meanwhile, Blanche Hozier had discovered the whereabouts of her two elder children. It seems that they had been sent to this school without her knowledge, and contrary to an agreement she and her husband had entered into as to the management of the children. Indignant and anxious as to the children's well-being, Blanche Hozier behaved with characteristic impetuosity and lack of convention. She hastened at once to Edinburgh, and one afternoon surprised Kitty and Clementine while they were on their weekly expedition to buy sweets. There was great excitement, tears and delight. Their mother then approached the Mistress in charge and asked if she could take the children out to luncheon. The Mistress demurred, but invited her back to the school to meet the Principal. After some discussion, the children were not permitted to go out with their mother, since Henry Hozier had already briefed Herr Fröbel on his matrimonial difficulties, and had expressly forbidden this. Disappointed, and no doubt angered by this embargo, Blanche Hozier promptly found lodgings immediately opposite the school, and used to wave out of the windows to Kitty and Clementine. She also took to attending the children's classes, thereby creating dismay among the staff, but giving great pleasure to the pupils, who all liked her very much and told the now gratified Kitty and Clementine they thought their mother very beautiful. Had the children been older, no doubt they would have been embarrassed by this unusual behaviour; but Clementine remembered they felt only joy and relief at being once more near their mother. Moreover, from being under a cloud of displeasure, they were now the objects of the open envy and interest of their contemporaries. The Fröbels apparently concealed their inner thoughts beneath a diplomatically benevolent aspect.

The Edinburgh episode brought about the negotiation of another arrangement between their parents, which was happier from every point of view for the children. Shortly after these happenings, Kitty and Clementine went to live once more with their mother. To mark their joint acceptance of this new policy, Henry and Blanche Hozier were both at the station to meet the children on their return from their northern exile; they all went at once to 97 Cornwall Road, in Bayswater, where Blanche Hozier was now living. The twins, who had been under three years old when they had last seen their elder sisters over a year before, not surprisingly showed no signs of recognising Kitty and Clementine, who, in their turn, felt acutely embarrassed, and were uncertain as to whether they should kiss them or not. Meanwhile their father once more took his departure. Thereafter he came once or twice to tea with his wife; the children were sent for on these occasions, which were uneasy and silent; and these visits soon ceased.

A more settled life now began for Kitty and Clementine – 'settled' that is in the sense that for the rest of their childhood and adolescent years they were to be in the care and company of their mother; but the family never had a fixed home for long. Even today life is full of problems for a woman living apart from her husband, and having to shoulder alone the responsibility and organisation of her family. In those days a woman left the protection of her own family and home for that of her husband, and she rarely had any experience of independence of life. Moreover, there was then a considerable degree of social stigma attached to a woman separated from her husband: it was altogether an unenviable situation. Blanche Hozier, with her four children and their governess, lived for much of the time in furnished lodgings; but this way of life may well have been dictated in part by her own restless and capricious nature, as well as by financial difficulties, or the stresses of her relationship with her husband.

Clementine remembered very clearly the distinctive imprint which her mother left wherever she lived. Although one presumes she rented furnished lodgings partly for reasons of economy, this did not deter Lady Blanche from often painting and papering the rooms in which she and her family were established. 'She had very simple, but distinguished taste,' Clementine wrote, 'and you could never mistake a house or room in which she had lived for anyone else's in the world.' Although surrounded by other people's furniture, she always had loose covers of her own made for the sofas and chairs: they were of pure white dimity. 'There were two sets, and these were always being changed. I remember dark green taffeta cushions, and in her bedroom pale blue ones.' The windows were hung with fine book muslin curtains – always fresh and snowy white, so that a friend said, 'I cannot remember the number of Lady Blanche's house, but it does not matter. All I have to do is just walk down the street and look at the windows.'

Nor was Blanche Hozier's fastidious taste confined to interior decoration; she was very much interested in food, and was an excellent cook. At one time (to help her precarious finances) she contributed a series of articles on food to the *Daily Express*. But Clementine remembered rather ruefully that as a housekeeper her mother was distinctly erratic; when she gave her mind to it, the food was delicious, but when she was bored or had other distractions, rations were often sparse.

There was nothing haphazard, however, about their educational arrangements. The Hozier children may sometimes have lacked food, but they never went short of learning. They always had a full-time governess, either French or German, and they also attended various courses from time to time given by other professors in various subjects, excluding always, however, arithmetic, which Blanche Hozier in her arbitrary way deemed an unnecessary and unseemly study for girls.

When Kitty and Clementine came to live once more with their mother in London, a Frenchwoman, Mlle Gonnard, made her appearance as governess to the four children. Clementine remembered her as 'vivacious, touchy, untruthful and tale-bearing'. But, whatever her shortcomings, the poor woman must have had her hands full with the four children aged between nine and four years old, headed by the saucy and rebellious Kitty. On one of their customary and seemingly interminable walks, while Mlle Gonnard was re-tying her shoe-laces (a frequent occurrence), Kitty, dragging the unwilling Clementine with her, ran away. Mlle Gonnard, anchored to the twins, could not give chase. The two girls ran quite a distance, and then became lost, and were eventually returned to their home by a policeman. Lady Blanche was away, but the outraged Mlle Gonnard threatened to report her daughters' iniquity immediately upon her return; whereupon, Clementine remembered a terrifying scene – Kitty seized a lighted oil-lamp and, holding it above her head, said to Mlle Gonnard: 'If you don't swear by God and the Holy Virgin that you won't tell, I shall throw the lamp across the room, and then we shall all be burned to death!' Terrorised by Kitty's violent and determined behaviour, Mlle Gonnard promised not to tell – but later broke her word.

About this time, perhaps because all four children were too much for Mlle Gonnard, Clementine was sent to a course of French lessons with a remarkable woman, Mlle Louise Henri. Clementine regarded these lessons as a special treat, and greatly admired Mlle Henri's powerful intelligence. But Kitty hated lessons and, being much indulged and spoilt by her mother, was not made to attend these classes, but had singing and guitar lessons instead. She had a lovely little voice, and sang 'A goldfish swam in a big glass bowl' and 'Click, click, I'm a monkey on a stick', and other popular songs.

From 1895 the Hozier family spent many months of the year in furnished apartments at Seaford, a small resort on the south coast near Newhaven in Sussex. They lived at Nos. 9 and 11 Pelham Place; the landladies were sisters – the Misses Rolls. Miss Caroline was severe, and did not like children, but her sister, Miss Emily, was large and cosy and far more amiable. Fortunately for the children, they and Mlle Gonnard lived under Miss Emily's benevolent rule in No. 11, while their mother occupied the first floor of No. 9 with her Griffons Belges dogs, 'Fifinne' and 'Gubbins' (mother and son), on whom she doted.

Blanche Hozier went away on frequent visits, and in her absence the children were alone with the Rolls' sisters, and under the care of Mlle Gonnard. She cannot have been over-vigilant, for during their mother's absence the two elder girls in-dulged in various escapades – in which Kitty was ever the leader and instigator and Clementine her anxious, but loyal lieutenant. They were the proud owners of bicycles, and played hectic games of bicycle-polo on the rough grass opposite the lodgings, although Mlle Gonnard greatly disapproved of such unrefined pursuits.

Kitty, now in her early teens, was a flirt, and she already had several admirers. One of these – more devoted and daring than the others – was in the habit of climb-ing up the garden wall, and crawling along the narrow parapet of the house – from where he could gossip with Kitty through her bedroom window. Clementine was made to mount guard in the passage outside the bedroom while these clandestine conversations were in progress. Although disapproving intensely, Clementine loyally paced the passage outside in an agony of apprehension. She asked Kitty one day what she would do if a grown-up came upstairs suddenly, for the young gentleman concerned would hardly have had time to retreat backwards along the narrow parapet in order to avoid discovery. 'Oh,' said Kitty airily. 'I'd just push him off.' She would have, too.

Despite the open preference their mother displayed towards Kitty, the bond of loyalty and affection between the two sisters remained quite unaffected. Clementine accepted the situation philosophically; indeed, she felt her mother's preference to be quite natural, for she too was dazzled by Kitty's prettiness, gaiety and impudence. Kitty adopted a somewhat patronising air towards her less favoured sister, but was full of affection, and the two girls would often discuss their mother's blatant favouri-tism. Kitty used to say, 'You mustn't mind. She can't help it.' But both of them felt a contempt for their mother's ungovernable partiality.

When their mother was at home, life was full of interest, uncertainty and amuse-ment. A variety of relations (including their grandmother, Lady Airlie) and friends came and went, staying either in one of the Seaford hotels, or in the lodgings in Pelham Place. One of Blanche Hozier's friends, Mrs Mary Paget, who lived not far from Seaford, was a frequent visitor, and, although of an older generation, became Clementine's firm friend. No doubt she observed the preference Blanche Hozier did not seek to hide for Kitty and, feeling sorry for the younger child, held out her hand in kindness and understanding. Mrs Paget took to 'borrowing' Clementine for quite long periods, to stay with her at her farm, West Wantley, near Storrington in Sussex. Kitty also was at first included in these invitations, but she was sent home on one occasion for being too naughty and tiresome. There-after the visits remained Clementine's personal and particular treat, and the weeks that she passed with Mary Paget and her family became gilded in her memory with the light that shines forever on remembered happiness.

When the time came for Clementine to return to the lodgings in Seaford which passed for home, after visiting the Pagets, she felt she was leaving paradise and used to shed many bitter tears. On one occasion her reddened eyes were noticed by her mother, who observed angrily, 'I believe you love Mary Paget more than me', to which Clementine, with more truth than wisdom, replied, 'Of course I do.' And after that, for some time, there were no more visits to Wantley.

*

When Blanche Hozier and her husband parted, The Netherton was given up, and thereafter a firm fixture in the family's life was the annual, month-long visit to their grandmother at Airlie Castle. This enchanting small castle stands on a precipitous rock, and in the gorge beneath flows the river Isla. It is a romantic, beautiful place and as, over the thirty years that she had lived at Cortachy as reigning Countess, Blanche Airlie had improved and beautified it, so in the long years of her widowhood she left the mark of her distinguished taste on the 'dower castle'. The watchful suspicion with which she had for a long time been regarded as a 'foreigner' by the local Scots had long since given way to a wry respect, and that affection which a sturdy, independent-minded people, slowly but finally, accord to real 'characters'; and in the neighbourhood the Dowager Countess was cordially known as 'Auld Blanche'.

After her husband's death, Lady Airlie led a retired life, her estate and public duties soon devolving onto her daughter-in-law, and her entertaining necessarily being on a smaller scale. She had a small, distinguished circle of friends, and divided her time between Airlie Castle, her house in London, and her villa in Florence. Her tastes were essentially intellectual, and she was extremely well-read. Among her friends she had a reputation for writing, but to the detached eye of her great-granddaughter her essays seem both pretentious and sententious. She also spent a good deal of time covering acres of material with beautiful, elaborate Queen-Anne-style embroidery.

Blanche Airlie was a loving mother and grandmother, and her diary is full of entries recording visits to and from various members of her family, and their births, illnesses, engagements, marriages and deaths. She had a particularly close relationship with her daughter, Blanche Hozier, and it is known that when apart, they wrote to each other nearly every day; unfortunately their correspondence has not survived. Several of her younger relations were devoted to her, but despite her love and concern for her family, old Lady Airlie, now in her sixties, was awe-inspiring, arousing feelings of respect rather than of spontaneous affection. Clementine was not one of her grandmother's favourites, and she herself never really came to love or appreciate this undoubtedly remarkable personage. As a child she was frightened of her, and as she grew older she dared to survey this matriarchal figure with a not wholly uncritical gaze.

It can hardly therefore be a cause for surprise that the annual holiday at Airlie was for the Hozier children a period they regarded with mixed feelings. The dates were settled months ahead, and any attempt to alter them was met with tight-lipped disapproval. Clementine's chief memories of these visits were of the devices whereby the children sought to circumvent the many restrictions placed on their activities by the wide range of their grandmother's prohibitions. Blanche Hozier, although strict in some ways, wanted her children to enjoy the liberty and opportunities for fun that life at Airlie offered, after the more confined life they perforce led at home. So she allowed her children to bring their bicycles with them, but they had to be kept out of sight, and used surreptitiously, for Lady Airlie (like Mlle Gonnard) disapproved of bicycles for young ladies. They used sometimes to bicycle to Lintrathen Loch, which is about three miles from Airlie Castle; here they would fish happily for hours with a kindly fisherman. On their return their grandmother would remark approvingly what excellent walkers the children were.

One year, Kitty and Clementine were given a croquet set, but their grandmother said it would spoil the appearance of her lawn in front of the castle, and ordered that it should be sent back immediately to Seaford. However, their mother persuaded the gardener's wife, Margaret Milne, to have the hoops put up on the small green patch at the back of her cottage, and here, out of sight of their grandmother's eagle eye, the children played croquet; although they were somewhat hampered by the length of the grass, and by having to dodge under kind Mrs Milne's washing when she hung it out to dry.

In November 1898 Clementine was confirmed in Kirriemuir Church, near Airlie, by the Bishop of St Andrews, who had also prepared her for confirmation. Present with her at this serious moment was, as well as her mother and grandmother, her beloved friend, Mary Paget. Clementine went through an emotionally religious phase at this time and, on one occasion, being deeply moved by a sermon on sacrificial giving, snatched off the pendant she was wearing and placed it in the offertory bag. After the service, however, she had some qualms, for the pendant was a precious one and had been given to her by a relation. When her quandary became known to the grown-ups, she was admonished for excess of zeal, and the pendant was retrieved – a more reasonable offering being substituted.

Kitty and Clementine also often visited their Stanley cousins, usually in their London house in Mansfield Street, but also at Easthope, their country home in Yorkshire. Great-aunt Maisie Stanley was kindness itself, and there was always a warm welcome for the Hozier children. Here they were thrown into the enjoyable hurly-burly of a large family, and here began friendships which were to endure throughout a lifetime. Venetia and Sylvia Stanley were the immediate contemporaries of Kitty and Clementine; both became and remained Clementine's friends. But it was she and Sylvia who had most in common, and Sylvia's loyalty, love and powers of companionship never wavered; in her Clementine was to find a tower of strength and a true friend to the end of her life.

But in the schoolroom days there were, of course, the special friendships, quarrels and larks, into which Kitty entered with zest, but Clementine, who was rather a prude and always full of anxious forebodings, came in for a lot of teasing. On the brink of adolescence, she showed little sign of beauty; she suffered from red eyes, and was prone to be timorous and tearful. In all things she was overshadowed by the fascinating, boisterous Kitty.

DIEPPE AND AFTERWARDS

THE SPRING AND SUMMER OF 1899 proved a harassing and difficult time for Blanche Hozier. In the first place she was in debt, and had to ask her brother for help. Henry Hozier had shown for the last six or seven years little concern for the children's welfare, and was at this time defaulting on the meagre allowance he had undertaken to pay his wife. Kitty was now sixteen, Clementine fourteen, and Bill and Nellie eleven years old. In addition to paying the wages of a governess and other teachers for the girls, the fees for Bill's schooling at Summerfields Preparatory School had to be found. Blanche Airlie helped her daughter with money on a considerable scale this year, and Lord Airlie, as well as paying some of his sister's bills, caused his lawyer to press Henry Hozier for the money he owed. In addition to these worries, Blanche was taken quite seriously ill with influenza and quinsy towards the end of March.

In the last week of July, with the unpredictable suddenness that marked so many events in their lives, the Hozier family moved at one day's notice (as far as the children were concerned) from Seaford to Dieppe, on the French coast. Blanche Hozier never discussed her personal life or difficulties with her children, but it seems that she had always thought her husband might some day try (despite his indifference and neglect) to regain the custody of the two older children, who were the only ones in whom he ever evinced any interest. And it may be that when she originally picked on Seaford as a place to live, she may have had this easy 'escape route' in mind. Dieppe was only four or five hours away and, indeed, the daily steamer from nearby Newhaven was a familiar sight to Seaford residents. When, therefore, during this summer of 1899, Blanche Hozier had reason to believe that her husband was about to take action of some sort, she quickly made her plans, and removed herself and her family from England by the quickest and nearest route.

The announcement by their mother that they were all to leave Seaford at once came as a complete surprise to the children, who greeted the news with shouts of glee. There must have been a flurry of packing, and hurried goodbyes to the Misses Rolls, and also to Mlle Gonnard, whose mediocre, although tenacious services were now dispensed with. Family legend has it that on her arrival in Dieppe with her four children (and of course Fifinne and Gubbins), Blanche Hozier spun a coin to decide whether they should seek lodgings in Puys or Pourville, two villages in the neighbourhood of Dieppe. The coin declared for Puys and, hailing a cab, Lady

Blanche told the coachman to drive there. Once in the village, she smote the driver on the back with her umbrella as they were passing a charming-looking farm – *La Ferme des Colombiers*; leaving her family in the cab, Lady Blanche disappeared into the farm, emerging triumphantly a short while later accompanied by a stout lady – Madame Balle – with whom she had concluded an agreement by which the Hozier family would stay there for two months.

There at Puys, which is by the sea, the family spent an idyllic summer; bathing, canoeing, picnics and blackberrying filled the happy days. With the coming of the autumn schooling had once more to be thought of, and Blanche Hozier took a furnished house in Dieppe itself: No. 49 rue du Faubourg de la Barre. Outside it is not an attractive house, the front door opening straight onto the narrow pavement, but it was most conveniently situated in the same street as the Convent of the Immaculate Conception, to which the three girls were sent. As the children already spoke good French, they quickly adapted themselves to their new life, and to the convent uniform of black overalls with brilliant green belts.

Dieppe is probably one of the most historic towns on the French Channel coast, and at the end of the nineteenth century it was a popular summer resort, being the nearest seaside town to Paris. It offered the lure of a Casino, and was one of the few places at that time to have a golf course. In the early 1900s Dieppe also was second only to Vichy as a musical centre; indeed, Saint-Saens adopted it as his home town. During the season, and before Deauville and Le Touquet exerted their rival and more powerful attractions, Dieppe was full of chic *Parisien* society, which crowded the sea-front hotels and paraded on the promenade in elaborate *toilettes*.

Apart from these seasonal visitors, there was a resident English community, such as was to be found in many French towns up to the Second World War. *La Colonie*, as the English inhabitants were collectively known, consisted largely of retired and, for the most part, impoverished military men, diversified by the presence of various writers and artists who either lived there, or were passing visitors to the picturesque town and the lovely countryside around, and whose presence lent a Bohemian and intellectual flavour to Dieppe society. The famous French painter Jacques-Emile Blanche had a house and studio there, where the intellectual and artistic *monde* met; and at various times Aubrey Beardsley, Oscar Wilde, George Moore, Arthur Symons, Max Beerbohm and Walter Sickert all frequented Dieppe.

French life and French people were much to Blanche Hozier's taste, and she soon made friends (and not a few foes) both among the French and *La Colonie*. Artists and writers, such as Jacques-Emile Blanche, Walter Sickert and George Du Maurier, found her company agreeable, and she quickly established an elegant manner of life. She also began to divert herself with frequent visits to the Casino, becoming an inveterate gambler, and thus further compromising her precarious finances.

Lady Blanche was soon recognised as *une vraie caractère*; her circumstances also no doubt aroused curiosity and speculation. At forty-seven she was still very beautiful, dressing elegantly, but quite independently of changing fashions. Instead of hats, she wore lace mantillas, and Clementine remembered being embarrassed by the way her mother would often wear her hair in a long thick plait down her back, instead of piled conventionally on her head, or in a bun. It appears also that her children's clothes were the cause of comment among local children, who expected to see the granddaughters of an earl attired otherwise than in check gingham.[1]

Kitty and Clementine were a noticeable pair as they went about Dieppe. Their looks and natures formed a striking contrast: Kitty with her long dark hair in plaits and deep blue eyes being ever in the fore, compared with Clementine, who was so much fairer and much less obviously pretty, and whose nature was shy and retiring. But if Kitty was already a beauty, to the discerning eye there were signs of dawning loveliness in her younger sister. And George Du Maurier, visiting Blanche Hozier at about this time, on seeing Clementine declared: '. . . she's my Trilby – she's come to life!' A comment which Blanche Hozier did not allow him to repeat in Clementine's presence, it being considered inappropriate in those days for young people to be 'noticed' or praised to their faces.[2]

Living at this time in Neuville-les-Dieppe was Walter Sickert, the painter. Although he had many friends in the fashionable, conventional part of the town, Mr Sickert found it more congenial to live in Neuville-les-Dieppe, which is on the far side of the harbour, and where, in houses which climb up a steep hillside, most of the seaport and fishing community lived. He had lodgings in the house of Madame Augustine Eugénie Villain, the acknowledged Queen of the Dieppe fish-market. *La Belle Rousse*, as she was known, was locally famous for her red hair and her fiery temper.[3] In Sickert's life she had the triple role of landlady, model and mistress.

Mr Sickert soon became a friend and frequent visitor of Blanche Hozier and her children. No doubt he enjoyed both her unusual, fascinating company, and the delicious food which was always to be found in her house. In 1899 he was about forty years old; he was then clean-shaven and had thick honey-coloured hair; his eyes were a piercing sea green. His mode of dress was generally eccentric, his most usual form of headgear being a workman's *casquette*. Clementine was deeply struck by him, and thought he was the most handsome and compelling man she had ever seen.

Her mother often sent her to do the shopping, armed with a large basket, and Clementine frequently came upon Mr Sickert sketching at the corner of one of the small narrow streets leading to the church of St Jacques. One day when she stopped to look at his painting he asked, 'Do you like my work?' Clementine, after a pause, replied, 'Yes.' 'What is it you don't like?' asked Mr Sickert, noting her hesitation. Clementine struggled between truth and politeness, but finally said, 'Well, Mr Sickert, you seem to see everything through dirty eyes.'

Evidently this frank criticism did not offend him, for he presently asked her mother if she could come to tea with him. Clementine wrote her own vivid account of this occasion. After toiling up the hill to Neuville-les-Dieppe, she presently found the right house.

The door was open, no bell, no knocker; so I rapped with my knuckles. After a long pause a magnificent commanding woman appeared, and I recognised Madame Villain. She was very big and tall, dressed in a black dress with a blue and white check apron tied tightly round her shapely waist, her hair stood out round her head like a golden red halo, her sleeves were rolled up, and she stood akimbo displaying beautiful white arms and hands like those in a Vandyck picture. They were covered with tiny freckles, and each almond-shaped nail with a perfect half-moon was (alas) bordered with black. 'Que voulez-vous?' she asked abruptly. I was terrified, but determined to keep my end up. 'Je viens prendre le thé avec Monsieur Sickert.'

'Eh bien, il n'est pas là.'

I was dumbfounded. She then said, 'Mais si vous voulez vous pouvez l'attendre.' She then flung open the door leading into a very dirty bedroom. The bed was unmade and on a rickety deal table were the remains of a herring. I was profoundly shocked and thought, 'Perhaps Mother can find Mr Sickert a better house-keeper.' I waited – no Mr Sickert – so then I decided to clean up his room. I made the bed, found an old broom and swept the floor, and finally seizing the skeleton of the herring by the tail flung it out of the window upon a rubbish heap just below. I then washed the plate and put it away. Just then I heard loud melodious singing and there he was, with a large bag of hot brioches under his arm.

'What have you been doing to my room?' he asked suspiciously.

'It was very untidy, so while I was waiting for you I cleaned it up; which I think your landlady might have done.'

'Where's my herring?'

'I threw it away.'

'You little interfering wretch, I was just going to paint it. And where, pray, is the handsome plate it was sitting on?'

'I have washed it and put it on the shelf.'

We then consumed the brioches, accompanied by tepid cider, after which Mr Sickert took me home.

That winter Mr Sickert executed Clementine's portrait with a sharp, red-hot poker on her hockey stick; she had just returned from playing in a match at school. Mr Sickert disapproved of such violent and aggressive sports for young women. 'I must show you what you look like,' he said, and burnt her silhouette along the length of her hockey stick. It was the very image of her, but Clementine was mortified, and covered her poker-work portrait with sticking-plaster. Shortly afterwards the hockey stick was anyhow broken, during a fierce bout with the opposing centre-forward.

During the late winter of 1899 an extraordinary and dramatic incident took place, which shows that Blanche Hozier was quite right in thinking her husband might try to get hold of the children. An entry in her mother's diary also reveals that Lady Airlie still had some contact with her strange and intransigent son-in-law, Henry Hozier, for on 16th December 1899 she recorded: 'Anxious about Blanche's children. HH wants to see them. Goes to Dieppe today.' She obviously had no time to warn her daughter, and the sequel is taken up in Dieppe.

It was a snowy evening, and Blanche Hozier, Mr Sickert (who often came to supper), Kitty and Clementine were all in the sitting-room, the window of which gave onto the street. The curtains were not yet drawn, and the room was lit only by the flickering flames of the log fire. Suddenly Clementine saw a man looking in at the window; her mother noticed him at the same moment, and instantly dragged both the children down onto the floor. The man continued to stare into the room for a few minutes, but then turned away, and then they heard the front door bell tinkle. Kitty got up to answer it, but she was immediately dragged down again by her mother. The bell rang several times more, no one moved, and they then heard something being thrust into the letter-box. The man reappeared at the window, peered again into the darkened room and then walked away. Clementine, besides being extremely frightened, was also acutely embarrassed by the presence of Mr Sickert, who was the astonished witness of this scene. However Blanche Hozier remained quite calm, and said simply, 'That was my husband; I expect he brought a letter. Kitty, go and see.'

Kitty returned with two letters, one for herself and one for Clementine. Both letters contained similarly worded invitations to dine and lunch on succeeding days with their father at the Hôtel Royal. Clementine was terrified by this prospect; Kitty was thrilled, and rushed out the next morning to buy a new pale blue sash to adorn her white net dress for the occasion.

Although Blanche Hozier must have been anxious and apprehensive, she made no demur about the girls accepting their father's invitations; but she sent with them on each occasion their stalwart French maid Justine, to accompany them to and from the Hôtel Royal. Kitty's dinner with her father was a great success: he had invited her to stay with him, and had promised to give her a dog and a pony. The next day it was Clementine's turn; again Justine acted as escort, with strict instructions to say to 'Monsieur le Colonel' that she would collect Mlle Clementine promptly at two o'clock; but on receiving this message Henry Hozier replied that Justine need not return, as he would bring Mademoiselle home himself. Clementine, hearing this, cast imploring looks at Justine, who replied with a reassuring wink. During luncheon (an omelette followed by larks *en brochette*), Clementine could hardly speak from shyness and anxiety. Henry Hozier asked numerous questions about the children's life and upbringing, and expressed strong disapproval when he learnt that they were being educated at a convent. Presently he said, 'I suppose your mother has told you that in future you will be living with me, or rather with your Aunt Mary.' Clementine was aghast at this information, and replied that she had heard of no such plan. Plucking up courage, she added that she did not think her mother would let her and Kitty go. All this time her eyes were on the clock, watching the hands creeping on towards the hour of deliverance. At five minutes to two, she started surreptitiously pulling on her gloves; at two o'clock exactly Justine reappeared. Clementine rose and bade her father goodbye, but he looked angry; and striding towards Justine, he thrust a gold coin in her hand and pushed her out of the door. Clementine felt trapped and wondered desperately what to do; but when her father went across the room to get a cigar, she saw her chance. Quick as lightning she rushed to the door, dashed down the passage and out of the hotel – and there was the faithful Justine waiting anxiously for her in the snowy street. They started to run as fast as they could on the icy pavements. Henry Hozier pursued them at a fast walk, swearing angrily, but he soon gave up the chase; nor did he reappear at their house. Later Blanche heard from the bank manager, and from the captain of the Dieppe–Newhaven steamer, that her husband had intended kidnapping Clementine, and taking her back to England with him that very afternoon.

The Boer War, which had started in October 1899, was now raging fiercely, and although personal friendships were maintained, England's role was viewed with hostility by the French. Kitty and Clementine were aware of the thinly veiled disapproval of their companions at school; nor did the nuns maintain too saintly a detachment from these worldly events and the prejudices aroused by them. In November the British forces in the town of Ladysmith were besieged by the Boers. The siege continued for four months, but rumours that the town had been relieved were circulating in January, causing great rejoicings among *La Colonie*, which were not shared by their French neighbours.

One morning the Mother Superior swept into the classroom, interrupting the lesson. 'I wish,' she said, 'to make an announcement. Despite many rumours to the contrary, Ladysmith has not been relieved.' On her withdrawal from the room, all the French children stood up and cheered. Kitty and Clementine burned with indignation and resentment. After a brief and whispered consultation they rose and, heads high, left the room. Once in the passage, a difficulty arose; all the doors were glazed halfway down to permit easy observation, so the two girls, determined to carry through their patriotic gesture of defiance, crawled on all fours along the passage to the entrance, where they also evaded the notice of the doorkeeper, and managed to reach the street unhindered.

But then what? Courage had now rather evaporated, and uncertainty set in as to their reception at home. They wandered down to the beach, and whiled away the time by playing ducks and drakes. At luncheon time they were of course missed at home, and Blanche Hozier sent her maid to enquire as to her elder daughters' whereabouts. Her messenger was somewhat coldly informed that 'les Mesdemoiselles d'Hozier' had removed themselves earlier in the day. When, eventually, the two (by now rather rueful, and very hungry) heroines returned home, they were received with a mixture of relief and reproaches. However, all in all, they were thought to have done rather well; and no more was said at school about this episode.

The two elder girls were now in their middle teens and, as when they were children, they were inseparable companions. Kitty was sixteen, and the naughty, fascinating, fearless child was fast maturing into a beautiful and alluring woman. She used often to sit in the open window of their house playing her guitar, the gaily coloured ribbons which were attached to it waving gently as she played and sang in her charming natural voice; she caused quite a sensation among old and young alike. But the pleasant life in Dieppe to which the Hozier family was so quickly becoming accustomed was soon to be darkened by tragedy.

In the middle of February 1900 Kitty fell ill, and typhoid fever was diagnosed. It soon became clear that she was desperately ill. She was submitted to the most drastic and primitive treatments (Mr Sickert was constantly in the house carrying great jugs of icy water upstairs). Lady Airlie sent a nurse out from England, following herself a short time later. Meanwhile Blanche Hozier decided to send Clementine and Nellie (Bill was already back at boarding school) to stay with their aunt, Lady

Griselda Cheape, at St Andrews, so that she could devote every ounce of her strength to the now grim battle for her adored Kitty's life. Hurriedly the girls' trunks were packed. They were to travel by themselves, but Mr Sickert offered to take them to the boat which left late at night, and see them safely on board. When they were all ready to go, Clementine and Nellie went upstairs to say goodbye. Their mother met them at the bedroom door, and peremptorily told them to take off their hats, so that Kitty should not guess they were leaving. The sisters said goodnight to the strangely still and silent figure in the bed – and did not know it must be for ever. Mr Sickert saw the two rather subdued girls off on the first stage of their long bleak journey to St Andrews.

Kitty died on 5th March, a little more than a month before her seventeenth birthday. The telegram bearing the dread news to her sisters in Scotland was somehow delayed or lost. A second telegram, telling them of the plans for the funeral was the only one they received. It read: 'Am taking Kitty to Batsford. Come at once.' Hope and joy were rekindled in the hearts of the family gathered at Strathtyrum. Surely this meant that Kitty must be better? – she must be convalescent, and well enough to travel to Batsford, their Aunt Clementine Mitford's home? The children were discussing this seemingly hopeful news with their Aunt Griselda when suddenly Mr Black, Lord Airlie's factor from Cortachy, was announced. His aspect was respectful and grave. 'I have come, m'lady, to offer my condolences upon the death of your niece . . .' The hope that had soared like a bright star was extinguished. Kitty, the bold, beautiful Kitty, was indeed gone for ever. Once more, the children packed up, and set out with sad and heavy hearts, to bury her at Batsford.

*

Kitty's death marks the end of a whole period in Clementine's life. Kitty, it is true, had caused her younger sister moments of embarrassment, and anxiety, but the sisters loved each other dearly, and together they had faced the sorrows and dramas of their childhood, and shared pleasures and secrets. Kitty had ever tempered her mother's injustice to Clementine, and had been her leader and champion. Clementine, in return, gave Kitty unwavering love, loyalty and admiration. And now that Kitty was gone, she was a lonely figure in the family scene; for the twins, at twelve, were still children and bound up in each other's lives.

Blanche Hozier was paralysed with grief by the death of her favourite child. There were bonds of affection and duty between her and Clementine, but not much understanding, and little ease. Kitty and her mother had been kindred spirits, but Clementine's nature and her own were too dissimilar. The unspoken knowledge that Kitty had been so much her favourite child added remorse to Blanche Hozier's bitter grief, and made a shyness in Clementine's approaches to her mother. They both sorrowed deeply and separately.

After Kitty died, Blanche Hozier and her three children came back to England, and settled for the next four years at Berkhamsted in Hertfordshire. The decision to live at Berkhamsted was governed by educational considerations – the town offered excellent schools both for the two girls and for Bill. Clementine and Nellie went to the Berkhamsted School for Girls, while Bill went to the Berkhamsted

Grammar School for Boys. By the middle of the summer Blanche Hozier had found a small but charming eighteenth-century house, No. 85 (now re-numbered 107) in the High Street, with a long narrow garden running uphill at the back. She soon made the house pretty, and imported a cook from Dieppe. And so once more, despite adverse circumstances and deep sorrow, Blanche Hozier created around herself a charming and civilised atmosphere.

As far as the girls were concerned, the family and economic circumstances which combined to make them Grammar-School pupils certainly meant that they received a superior and wider education than they would had they been taught by governesses at home, which was still the predominating pattern of education for girls of their class. Already accustomed to changes in their place and way of life, Clementine and Nellie became quickly acclimatised to their new school and companions. But for Bill this change was one that caused him bitterness of heart. At Summerfields he had been with boys who, almost without exception, were going on to one or other of the great public schools. By right and custom he should have done so too, but his mother was simply unable to afford the fees, and Henry Hozier showed not the slightest wish or intention of contributing more than he already grudgingly did towards his family's maintenance.

Clementine (now fifteen) and Nellie (twelve) started at the High School in the autumn, and Clementine's studious nature now came into its own. Despite so many years of governess teaching, she relished the competitive atmosphere of work, and the wider opportunities this larger community offered her. Starting in the Upper Fifth Form, Clementine was soon promoted to the Sixth for French, but suffered humbling demotion to a much lower form for mathematics (which was hardly surprising, since her mother had always prevented the girls from learning this subject). Nellie also settled in well and was happy at school, but she had a much more easy-going and carefree nature, and did not overburden herself with too much scholastic endeavour.

It was not only the work that Clementine enjoyed: she flung herself into school life with zest, and enjoyed it to the full. Many years later (in 1947), in a speech on Commemoration Day at the school, Clementine spoke of her time there:

> I began my school life in the old building in the High Street, and although it has been described as bare and gloomy, I loved it. I felt I was out in the world, and on my own, away from the fiddling little tasks of arranging the flowers, folding the newspapers and plumping up the cushions, and the tender (though I sometimes ungratefully thought) exaggerated solicitude of my Mother over wet feet, colds in the head, and difficult homework.

In 1901 Clementine distinguished herself by winning, in open competition with students from all over the country, a handsome solid silver medal for French, presented by the Société des Professeurs Français en Angleterre. She received it from the hands of Monsieur Jules Cambon, the French Ambassador. Partly as a reward for her Silver Medal, Blanche Hozier gave Clementine a special treat. She sent her to Paris for a fortnight, some time in 1902, in the care of Mlle Louise Henri, whose classes Clementine had so greatly enjoyed even when she was a child of nine or ten. They stayed at a modest hotel so as to spin out their money, and the days flew by, each one full of interest and pleasure. Museums, lectures and art galleries were interspersed with thrilling glimpses of other worlds and ways. Mlle Henri had procured tickets for a *Vernissage*. There Clementine's attention was distracted from the pictures by a most handsome and fantastic-looking woman; she had a wasp-waist, and her hour-glass form was encased in a white cloth dress; both her gown and large hat were trimmed lavishly with ermine tails. Mlle Henri, seeing that Clementine was riveted by this astonishing person, drew her aside and whispered to her that this vision was none other than Polaire, the most famous *demi-mondaine* and *cocotte* in Paris. No wonder Mlle Henri was so interesting and agreeable a companion, for her knowledge and interest were not confined merely to academic subjects.

Another delightful event in this magical fortnight was the sudden arrival, out of the blue, of Mr Sickert, who turned up one evening and announced his intention of taking Clementine out with him the following day. Mlle Henri was, not unnaturally, somewhat dubious as to the wisdom or propriety of this suggestion. However, she was soon won over by the Sickert charm and by Clementine's assurances that he was an old friend of her mother.

Clementine had a wonderful day: they started by breakfasting in a little café (Clementine noticed Mr Sickert did not pay the bill, but that it was chalked up on a blackboard). Thus sustained, he then took her to the Luxembourg Gallery, where he asked her to point out to him her favourite picture. Clementine chose John Sargent's '*La Carmencita*' (a sparkling Spanish dancer in yellow satin); Mr Sickert was much shocked by the vulgarity of her taste, and directed her attention to the gentle, dreamy painting, '*Le Pauvre Pêcheur*', by Puvis de Chavannes. They lunched in a bistro in a rather poor neighbourhood, and once again the bill was chalked up. During luncheon Clementine asked Mr Sickert, 'Who is the greatest living painter?' He looked astonished at the question, and answered quite simply, 'I am, of course.'

In the afternoon Mr Sickert took Clementine with him to call upon Camille Pissarro, who lived in a garret overlooking the Madeleine.

He was a magnificent old man, with a great silver beard and a black sombrero hat. There were at least ten people sitting in a small attic, and they were all drinking tepid beer, which we shared with them.[4]

To wind up the day, Mr Sickert took Clementine to dinner with Monsieur Jacques-Emile Blanche in his elegant house on the outskirts of Paris, a great contrast to the Bohemian flavour of their day so far. 'Everything was exquisite,' Clementine recalled,

the furniture, the food and Monsieur Blanche's manners, though I did overhear him enquiring from Mr Sickert how he came to be entrusted with the care of a *jeune fille bien élevée*.

After a most pleasant evening, Mr Sickert took Clementine home, exhausted but happy. She did not see him again for twenty years.

This wonderful, never-to-be-forgotten fortnight came all too quickly to its end, and Clementine had to come down to earth, and back to school.

The Headmistress of Berkhamsted High School at this time was Miss Beatrice Harris, whom Clementine greatly admired and described as an 'inspired and inspiring personality'. Miss Harris held advanced views on Women's Suffrage, and the school was imbued with the spirit of feminine advance and independence. Influenced by her, Clementine nursed dreams of going to university. This was an unusual thing for a girl to do then, and required a strenuous, single-minded dedication. Miss Harris, who wished to encourage Clementine in her ambition, offered to have her to stay during the holidays, so that she could the better continue her studies.

This helpful invitation was never taken up, for despite the fact that Blanche Hozier believed strongly in women being well educated, the idea of her daughter becoming an earnest 'blue stocking' never gained any favour with her. Indeed, when she saw how much engrossed by school life and studies Clementine was becoming, she deliberately set out in trivial and annoying ways to hinder her from doing her homework, and to distract her into less unfeminine interests and pursuits.

Clementine minded very much her mother's open or covert attempts to sabotage her educational progress and thwart her ambitions, and the conflict between their outlooks and wills increasingly produced abrasive encounters. Clementine was often reduced to tears by her mother, and now she had no champion (although Nellie was ever the loyal confidante and peace-maker). Their mother's curious and arbitrary notions forced the girls into subterfuges, arithmetic often being studied in secret on the flat tombstones in the graveyard which adjoined the top of their garden.

Clementine's character, so long eclipsed by Kitty's more dominating nature, now began to show its strength and fortitude. She had an unexpected ally in her great-aunt, Maude Stanley (Blanche Airlie's sister), a benevolent old spinster, who lived in Smith Square and of whom Clementine was very fond. Sharing the reforming zeal of so many of her family, Miss Stanley had started the first Working Girls' Clubs in London. She was a great supporter of women's education and emancipation, and was delighted to find in one of her younger relations a somewhat kindred spirit.

But Blanche Hozier was not to be so easily circumvented; she was quite determined that Clementine should not pursue her aim of going to university. Totally socially unambitious for herself, Blanche Hozier now pocketed her pride and approached an aunt of hers by marriage, Lady St Helier, and sought her help in launching Clementine into the world to which by birth and upbringing she properly belonged. It was not easy for Blanche to take this step, for not only was she averse from asking favours, but she did not like Lady St Helier personally, thinking her worldly and snobbish. It is difficult, however, to understand now how much Blanche Hozier and her children were cut off from the normal social life of their day by the fact of Blanche's separation from her husband, and her straitened financial circumstances.

Lady St Helier, a Miss Mary Mackenzie by birth, had first married Colonel John Stanley, one of Blanche Hozier's uncles. After his death, she married Sir Francis

Jeune, a distinguished judge, who became the first Lord St Helier. She was a remarkable personality, combining energetic and intelligent service with the London County Council and numerous good causes with a flair and taste for large-scale entertaining. A prominent London hostess, she pursued the lions of society, and always liked to have several of them roaring at her dinner parties.

But although Lady St Helier so much relished the company of the successful and the famous, her warm heart led her to many acts of kindness to young people not yet arrived in any conspicuous way upon the world's stage. And it was only some years before this that she had helped Winston, the adventure-seeking son of her friend Lady Randolph Churchill, by intervening on his behalf with Sir Evelyn Wood, the Adjutant-General, to get Winston attached to the British Army in Egypt. Now, when she was asked to help a beautiful, but obscure and poor young relation, with her usual warm-heartedness she agreed to do so.

Blanche Hozier's circumstances were such that a whole 'season' was out of the question; moreover, Clementine was still at school. However, from time to time she would go and stay with her Great-Aunt Mary, who would take her to a ball or invite her to one of her many dinner parties: and indeed she gave Clementine as a present her gown for her first ball.

During the summer of 1903, Clementine passed her Higher School Certificate in French, German and biology. There was no more talk now of her desire to go to university. Her mother's opposition, reinforced by the pleasurable and beguiling glimpses she had from time to time of the London scene, where she was already making a mark, had settled the issue. And so, after taking her examinations, Clementine left the High School. That summer, Bill too left school and, deciding on a naval career, took a cadetship in H.M.S. *Britannia*.

All her life, however, Clementine was to remember with happiness and gratitude her time at Berkhamsted School. She kept in touch over the years with Miss Harris, and visited the school on several occasions. Writing to Miss Harris in 1942, she told her:

> I want you to know how very happy I was during the four years I spent at Berkhamsted School. The older I get, the oftener I think about those days, and realize what an influence you and Miss Stephenson have had upon my whole life.[5]

Perhaps to tide over the break from school and the fading of Clementine's intellectual aspirations, Blanche Hozier took a house for the winter in Paris, in the rue Oudinot in the 7^{ml} *arrondissement*. Clementine attended lectures at the Sorbonne, which thrilled and absorbed her. She used to return home for luncheon between her lectures, but when the windows were being cleaned (a frequent happening in Blanche Hozier's house) or when her mother was bored with ordering meals, Clementine was given a franc and sent to have her luncheon at the *laiterie*. Here she sat up at the counter, her skirts and feet tucked up off the floor, which seemed always wet from frequent washings. Her franc bought her a lightly boiled pullet's egg, a glass of milk, a fresh roll and a pat of butter: marvellous value for money, but hardly a winter meal for a hungry girl of eighteen.

But, despite the straitness of the family finances, Blanche Hozier was not parsimonious, and she had the gift of providing unexpected, delectable treats. One day she took Clementine and Nellie to Voisin – an elegant, fashionable and extremely expensive restaurant. There they were regaled on *tournedos* and *pommes soufflées*, and excellent wine. Clementine was delighted, and enjoyed it all immensely, but nonetheless asked her mother if this was not a grossly extravagant treat, for they were, at the time, passing through a particularly lean time as regards money. 'My dear child,' replied her mother, 'to know how to order and enjoy good food is part of a civilised education.'

The following spring Clementine was sent for three months to stay with the Von Siemens family, who had a beautiful house on the Wannsee, near Berlin. Here she had an agreeable time taking a certain part in fashionable Berlin life; she also learnt to ride, and inevitably fell in love with the riding master.

The house at Berkhamsted having now fulfilled its purpose, Blanche Hozier thought it better for them all to live in London, and more 'in the world'. She accordingly took a house in Kensington – 20 Upper Phillimore Place.

When Clementine returned from her stay in Germany, in order to supplement her small allowance she started to give French lessons at 2s 6d an hour. Her moment of triumph was when she assured the success of a young boy sitting for an entrance examination by running him through various technical terms and data in French. The fact that he knew the correct word for 'ball-bearing' sealed the result, and called forth praise for his tutor – Miss Hozier – from the child's gratified parents.

The Hoziers lived in Upper Phillimore Place for only about a year, when they moved to a charming white-painted stucco house, No. 51 Abingdon Villas, just behind Kensington High Street, where they were to remain for several years. In addition to giving French lessons, Clementine now started to work for her cousin, Lena Whyte, who had a small dressmaking business in North Audley Street. Clementine was not gifted with her hands, but she toiled away with perseverance, and learned enough to make some of her own clothes and to do the endless refurbishing and repairing of her very limited wardrobe.

Although there were difficulties in Clementine's life, and her activities were considerably limited by her family's circumstances, she had all the resilience and hopefulness of youth, and she flung herself with zest into the pleasures and ploys that came her way. Admiration adds much to a woman's morale – and Clementine lacked neither admirers nor serious proposals of marriage. Nellie, three years younger than Clementine, watched all this with admiration, untinged with jealousy, and often, shared amusement. Indeed, she saucily suggested at one moment that a file of 'Proposals to Clementine' should be kept, with the headings: 'Discussed', 'Answered', and 'Pending Decision'.

Clementine had much to endure from her mother's unreasonable nature and capricious temper. Even when she was nineteen, her mother used to insist that she should return home by midnight: since no ball started before eleven o'clock, this rule was patently ridiculous, and, needless to tell, Clementine was often late. She would find her mother awaiting her on the doorstep, and was subjected to furious upbraidings. One morning, after a particularly stormy scene, Blanche Hozier, beside herself with temper, boxed Clementine's ears. What is endurable for a child, is a mortification not to be borne by a grown girl of nearly twenty. It was certainly too much for Clementine's proud spirit. She left the house, not waiting to put on her coat or hat, and ran all the way across the park to Harley Street, where lived Mrs Paget, her faithful friend of Seaford days. Here she poured out her woe and indignation. Clementine stayed the night there, and before she returned home, Mary Paget visited her old friend Blanche Hozier, and no doubt delivered herself of some words of warning and moderation.

At eighteen Clementine had met at one of her great-aunt's parties a man whose devoted love and friendship were to colour her life for the next few years. Sidney Peel was thirty-three when he met Clementine. The son of the 3rd Viscount Peel, he was a man of brilliance and distinction: he was a Fellow of Trinity College, Oxford, and sometime lecturer there. In the South African War he had served with the Imperial Yeomanry and had been decorated, and he afterwards wrote a book about his campaigning experiences. Now, in 1903, he was a barrister and in banking. Sidney Peel became deeply and devotedly in love with Clementine, whose serious nature and intelligence appealed to him as much as her great beauty. He courted her with a tenacity and grace which seems strange to a generation used to more casual, hurried ways. Clementine never left London but he was there to escort her to the train; he always met her on her return. He lent her books, took her to the theatre, and (fired by the example of the hero of a contemporary novel) sent her a bunch of white violets every single day, except during the month of August, when even his devotion and resource could not produce one white violet. During the winter the Hozier family spent in Paris, Sidney Peel would make the long journey from London every week-end in order to spend a day or two in her company.

Clementine was deeply fond of him; she valued his love, and rejoiced in his companionship. These were difficult, lonely years for her. She longed at times to escape from her circumscribed home life with its sadness and tensions to the spacious security that marriage to such a man could offer. Moreover, he loved her truly, and she might so easily have persuaded herself that esteem and affection are substitutes for love. Perhaps she nearly did, for twice she was secretly engaged to Sidney Peel. Those closest to her hoped she would marry him; her mother would have been happy to see her settled, and she was, herself, very fond of him. But although it would have been a good marriage, Blanche Hozier's own romantic nature prevented her putting any undue pressure on Clementine.

Not so Lady St Helier, who strongly recommended Clementine to accept this suitor, and subjected her great-niece to searching enquiries as to why she held back from so satisfactory a match with a man who loved her dearly, and who could offer her so much. Lady St Helier was not impressed by Clementine's explanations that she did not feel herself to be 'in love'. But despite all these pressures Clementine remained true to her own inmost instincts and feelings.

It was about this time that Clementine formed a friendship that was to prove life-long, with Horatia Seymour. Beautiful, brilliant, and poor herself, this young woman, a few years older than Clementine, always showed her warmth and kindness; to a mutual liking was added the understanding of each other's situation.

Clementine had many ardent admirers and true friends, but there were some sharp tongues and jealous, watchful eyes. Clementine was greatly touched by Horatia Seymour's friendliness to a newcomer on the scene, and valued her helping hand.

Now was the heyday of Edwardian times. Entertaining was on a scale of luxury, formality and elaboration unknown to the Victorians. Society had never been so brilliant or so mixed, and money set the pace in the smart world. Leisure was a common commodity; servants were plentiful, and large hospitable houses abounded both in London and the country. Spirits and confidence were undimmed by any premonition of the holocausts to come; nor had values in money and manners been changed by the social revolution which has transformed the face and form of society beyond recognition. Country house visits were a great feature of life. Week-ends were from Friday to Monday, but many house parties lasted for longer, centred round a coming-of-age, shooting or amateur theatricals (which Clementine loved), when the entire cast would stay for weeks at a time.

Dressing for women was time-consuming and intricate; hats, coiffures and gowns were beautiful and complicated, and needed hours of care and maintenance. Armies of personal maids (of varying degrees of grandeur, strictly related to their employer's status) washed, starched, goffered, ironed and stitched.

The clothes needed for a mere week-end visit usually fitted into several sizeable trunks, with at least one large unwieldy hat-box, for it was quite usual to change into three different ensembles during the course of the day. Ball gowns were beautiful, lavish creations with yards of frilling, flouncing or lace, and it took hours to repair the ravages of dancing. A great extra expense felt very much by poorer girls was the absolute necessity for long, spotless white kid gloves for all evening occasions. It is not surprising, therefore, that Clementine's social life was strictly rationed by sheer lack of money. But she was then, as later, immensely fastidious, and had simple good taste, and so despite the not inconsiderable difficulties, Clementine soon became remarked upon for her beauty, charm and natural elegance by her own, as well as the older generation.

Various contemporary memoirs contain references to Clementine's outstanding beauty, to which photographs, either then or later, rarely did justice. Lady Cynthia Asquith was to write of her: 'Queen she should have been; her superbly sculptured features would have looked so splendid on a coin.'[6] She had hazel-green eyes, with fascinating little brown flecks in them; her ash-blonde hair, which had been somewhat lank and wispy as a child, became thick and lustrous; she held herself well, and moved with grace. She was lively and enthusiastic, and one of her great charms was that, despite being an acknowledged 'beauty', she was completely lacking in self-consciousness.

Sir Alan Lascelles recalled most charmingly the first, and indelible impression Clementine made upon him:

My first glimpse of her was in the Xmas holidays, 1903, when, as a 16-year-old schoolboy, I was staying with old Judge Ridley & his wife at Crabbet. There was a largish party, for some private theatricals.

One day at luncheon, Lady Ridley announced, 'The beautiful Miss Hozier is coming tonight. She will be with us at tea-time.'

About 5 o'clock we were all sitting in the hall having tea. Suddenly the butler threw open the door, & shouted (as if he were on the stage at Covent Garden), 'Miss Clementine Hozier'.

There was an instant (& for her, poor girl, most shy-making) silence, for there in the doorway was a vision so radiant that even now, after 61 years, my always roving, always fastidious, eye has never seen another vision to beat it.[7]

TO THINE OWN SELF
BE TRUE

URING THE SUMMER SEASON OF 1904, when Clementine was nineteen, she met Winston Churchill at a ball given by Lord and Lady Crewe at their house in Curzon Street.

Winston Churchill was now thirty. He had been born in 1874 at his grandparents' home – Blenheim Palace – the elder of the two sons of Lord Randolph Churchill and the American beauty, Jennie Jerome. After schooldays which showed no surface sign of ability to come, Winston had opted for the Army, and passed (at his second attempt) into the Royal Military College at Sandhurst. His father died in January 1895 at the early age of forty-six, his tragic illness and death cutting short a political career of exceptional and meteoric brilliance. Shortly afterwards, Winston was commissioned as an officer in the 4th Hussars, a cavalry regiment. He yearned for excitement and action, and during his first prolonged period of leave he and a brother officer sought both in Cuba where the Spaniards were fighting a guerrilla uprising. Winston received his baptism of fire on his twenty-first birthday.

The following year the 4th Hussars were posted to India, where Winston discovered the beauty of butterflies, and became a keen and effective polo player. It was during his time in India that a great desire for knowledge seized him and he embarked on a prodigious programme of serious reading, his mother finding it difficult to keep him adequately supplied with books from home. Ever on the look-out for action and for a chance to distinguish himself, he took part (first as a war correspondent, and then as an officer) in the campaign of 1897 on the North-West Frontier, afterwards publishing his first book, *The Story of the Malakand Field Force*, which attracted considerable attention and some favourable comment.

Soon a new field of action caught Winston's impatiently roving eye – Egypt, where Lord Kitchener was fighting the Mahdi in the Sudan. Partly through the good offices of the benevolent Lady St Helier, a friend of his mother, he succeeded in joining the Army of the Nile, and in September 1898 he took part in the last cavalry charge of history at Omdurman. The *Morning Post* published his letters describing the battle, and on his return to India he wrote the greater part of his two-volume account of the Egyptian campaign, *The River War*.

In 1899 Winston resigned his commission in the Army, and made his first venture into politics by fighting a by-election in Oldham, Lancashire, in which he was narrowly defeated. In October of that year the Boer War broke out, and Winston sailed for Cape Town as correspondent for the *Morning Post*. He secured a commission in the Lancashire Hussars, and then made for Natal, where it seemed the serious fighting would be. Then followed a series of novel-worthy episodes, starting with 'Armoured Train' when Winston, exposed to fierce enemy fire, according to all reports acquitted himself with gallantry. During this foray he was captured by the Boers and was incarcerated in a prisoner-of-war camp in the State Model School in Pretoria. He made his escape from prison camp on the evening of 12th December 1899. After a series of adventures, he arrived in Durban on 23rd December, to find himself a popular hero – his capture, imprisonment, escape and subsequent speculation as to his fate having been widely reported in the press.

Winston returned home in July 1900, and in the General Election which took place that autumn, he stood once more for Oldham, and was this time elected. In the New Year of 1901 he made his maiden speech as a Conservative Unionist Member of Parliament. The House listened with sympathy and interest to the dashing and enterprising son of the brilliant, ephemeral Lord Randolph.

When, therefore, some three years later, Winston Churchill met Clementine Hozier for the first time, he had already packed a great deal into three decades and was a colourful public personality. And he had added to his dashing career as a soldier and war correspondent that of a successful author, with five books already published. Now, in this spring of 1904, he had also become politically controversial. He bitterly opposed the Conservative Party's drift towards Tariff Reform, and in defence of Free Trade he abandoned his father's party, crossing the floor of the House to sit on the Liberal benches.

The Liberals were, of course, enchanted by this new acquisition to their ranks, but in the eyes of his own party he was regarded as a renegade and a turn-coat. Moreover, success (especially if it is judged to be premature) makes many enemies. Although, at thirty, Winston Churchill had his friends and believers, he was also a controversial figure and, especially among his own class and contemporaries, was judged by many to be bumptious, an opportunist and generally insufferable. Politics were more vehement in those days, and permeated social life to a marked degree. Since Winston's defection, therefore, the doors of nearly all Conservative houses were closed to him. But he was welcome at Crewe House, since Lord Crewe was a prominent member of the Liberal Party.

Winston arrived at the ball with his mother: standing alone in a doorway he saw the girl of whom it was later to be written, '. . . her beauty needed no adornment. She looked like a lily.'[1] He asked his mother who she was – Lady Randolph* did not know, but said she would find out. Presently she returned with the news that, by coincidence, the admired being was Clementine Hozier, the daughter of an old friend of hers, whom, however, she had not seen for some years. In addition Lady Randolph's brother-in-law, Sir Jack Leslie, was Clementine's godfather. These links made it easy and natural for Lady Randolph to introduce her son to Clementine.

*She was now Mrs George Cornwallis-West since her marriage in 1900 to a man twenty years her junior. She divorced him in 1913. In 1918 she married again – once more to a man almost half her age – Montagu Porch. For convenience she will be referred to throughout as Jennie, or Lady Randolph.

Their first encounter was, however, brief and unpropitious. For upon his mother introducing him, instead of asking Clementine to dance, Winston stood rooted to the spot, staring at the vision which had so powerfully beguiled him. Clementine felt embarrassed and mortified, and, far from thinking this strange, intent young man had asked to be introduced to her, she imagined that Lady Randolph had noticed that she was, for the moment, without a partner and, taking pity on her plight, had out of kindness introduced her son.

Moreover, Clementine had heard about Winston Churchill; she had heard him discussed on several occasions, and she was not at all favourably disposed towards him on that account. And now his gauche, singular behaviour settled it. Luckily help was at hand; a beau of hers was standing nearby and, obeying a discreet signal, he came up and asked her to dance with him. During the course of the dance he asked Clementine what she was doing talking to 'that frightful fellow Winston Churchill'. Their paths were not destined to cross again for nearly four years.

This brief encounter only has significance in retrospect; it left no profound impression at the time on either Winston or Clementine. If she thought of the incident again, it was with amused disdain. As for Winston Churchill, on one of his rare excursions into purely social life, he had been struck by a girl's beauty and grace. But his life was not in ballrooms, nor even in the fashionable country-house parties where they might have met again far sooner, for already the world of politics was claiming him for its own.

During these last years he had had friendships with several beautiful and clever girls. Pamela Plowden, the daughter of the Resident at Hyderabad (whom he had first met in India as a young subaltern), was his first great love. She married the Earl of Lytton in 1902; but they were to remain friends always. A little later, an heiress (her family were Hull shipowners) and a great beauty, Muriel Wilson, held his attention; he thought of marrying her, but she rejected him; it is said she did not think he had much of a future; they too always remained on the friendliest terms. Winston also in his time proposed to the famous actress, Miss Ethel Barrymore, who later said she had been much attracted to him, but that 'she felt she would not be able to cope with the great world of politics'.[2]

But although he relished the company of beautiful, lively women, Winston was never – then, or later – a 'ladies man'; somewhat gauche and un-handy in his manner, he also neglected those charming but trivial small attentions which so often pave the way in gallant relationships. Politics were always to fill and dominate his thoughts – and now his star was in the ascendant.

The Conservatives had been in power for twenty years, but Mr Balfour's Government was by now seriously weakened by the split over Protection. In December 1905 Mr Balfour resigned, and the King sent for the Liberal leader, Sir Henry Campbell-Bannerman. The new Prime Minister offered the post of Under-Secretary at the Colonial Office to Winston Churchill. Parliament was dissolved, and early in 1906 the General Election took place. In a dramatic landslide the Liberals were swept into power with a large majority over all other parties.

Winston at once began to play a prominent part in affairs, for although he was only a junior Minister, his chief, Lord Elgin, the Colonial Secretary, sat in the House of

Lords. Winston, as Under-Secretary, was therefore the chief government spokesman on Colonial Affairs in the House of Commons.

*

In April 1906 Clementine's cousin and great friend, Sylvia Stanley, married Colonel Anthony Henley, and she was one of the bridesmaids. Shortly before the wedding Sylvia had broken her arm, but despite the necessity for a sling, and although still suffering considerable pain, she insisted that the plans should not be altered. Her fortitude made a deep impression on Clementine, who was at this time secretly engaged to Sidney Peel; she reflected that were such an accident to befall her on the eve of her marriage, she felt she would not have the tenacious devotion to go through with it; it made her realise that her feelings for Sidney Peel fell short of true love. Soon after Sylvia's wedding, therefore, she broke off her own engagement.

But Clementine must, all this time, have subconsciously been looking for an avenue of escape to a freer and more fulfilled life, for during the summer of this same year she became suddenly engaged to Mr Lionel Earle – a man nearly twice her age – whom she had met for the first time some six weeks before at a house party. Lionel Earle was forty: a distinguished Civil Servant, with intellectual tastes, he was very well off, and had a somewhat stiff nature and pompous manner.

They met for the second time at Castle Ashby in Northamptonshire during the brilliant party held at the end of July to celebrate the coming-of-age of Lord Compton, the heir to the Marquess of Northampton. During the festivities, which lasted for five days, Lionel Earle, who knew very well how to make himself agreeable to a beautiful woman, laid siege to Clementine's affections, and she fell in love with him. No doubt life and personalities assumed a rosy hue in the general atmosphere of gaiety and pleasure. Before the party broke up, Clementine had accepted his proposal of marriage.

Lady Blanche was not enthusiastic about the engagement; she may have felt that in the greyer light of everyday life Lionel Earle's sophistication and the somewhat formal side to his character would come to jar on Clementine's more spontaneous nature. Moreover, it may well have made her uneasy that Clementine should plunge so hastily into such a serious relationship, when only a short time before she had been engaged to Sidney Peel. But Blanche Hozier had learned to reckon with her daughter's determination and, after all, it was a good solid match for a penniless girl.

Clementine's engagement to Lionel Earle was announced on 15th August 1906. A few days after the announcement Lady Blanche and Clementine left for a pre-arranged holiday with old friends, Mr and Mrs Charles Labouchère, at their beautiful property at Bantam in Holland; knowing of Clementine's engagement, the hospitable Labouchères invited Lionel Earle to come as well. During the fortnight that ensued, when she was constantly in the company of her betrothed, Clementine began to have serious doubts. Later that year Blanche Hozier wrote to her brother Lyulph Ogilvy (who ranched in America):

I v. soon saw that Clementine was not happy – and I asked her what was amiss – told her that if she had made a mistake she must say so. She said she was frightened, would not dare – I told her she need not be frightened if I stood by her – so – the engagement was broken off.[3]

Blanche Hozier was in many ways difficult and unpredictable, but in matters of the heart her sense of priorities was clear and steady.

It was of course most tiresome and awkward: many wedding presents had already arrived, and these had all to be packed up and sent back; the family had to be told; and the disengagement announced. But through it all Blanche Hozier firmly and consistently supported Clementine.

Now was the time for the Hozier family's annual visit to Airlie. But this year, Clementine's heart failed her – she did not feel she could face her formidable grandmother's cold disapproval. For old Lady Airlie took a far from indulgent view of her granddaughter's conduct in this whole affair. In her estimation Clementine had behaved in a foolish and hysterical fashion. Fortunately for Clementine, just at this time Lena Whyte (the kind dressmaking cousin) was convalescing from an operation for appendicitis; she begged that Clementine, instead of going to Scotland, might keep her company. This was a happy solution. But this whole episode affected Clementine deeply. Her equilibrium and self-confidence were shaken, and she felt a sense of humiliation. For a month or two she was quite ill – no doubt a direct result of her mental and emotional distress.

At the end of February 1907 the news came of Henry Hozier's death in Panama, at the age of sixty-nine. He had resigned from being Secretary at Lloyds after thirty-two years in 1906. All his considerable talents and force of character had been devoted to this job; in 1903 he had been given a knighthood. Even after his resignation, Sir Henry had still busied himself with the Corporation's affairs, and indeed was visiting one of Lloyd's Signal Stations when he was taken ill and, after a short illness, died.

With Henry Hozier's death, an element of tension was removed from his family's life; and yet Clementine was deeply saddened. Although she had feared her father, she had always cherished the hope that in time she might come to know and to understand this strange, violent, yet most compelling man. After his attempt to take Kitty and Clementine from their mother in Dieppe in the winter of 1899, Clementine had seen her father only on one other occasion. It was in the summer of 1900, when the family had returned to live in England following Kitty's death. Henry Hozier had expressed a wish to see Clementine; this was duly arranged, and Blanche Hozier accompanied her fifteen-year-old daughter to his house in North Audley Street. She was taking leave of her on the doorstep when the door suddenly opened, and out came her husband. On seeing his wife, Henry Hozier flew into a rage, and upbraided her for daring to appear at his house. Blanche Hozier remonstrated that she had merely come to leave Clementine for the appointed meeting, but he was not to be pacified, and an angry scene took place between them in the street, of which Clementine was the unwilling and mortified witness. Presently her mother left, and Clementine followed her father into his house; the interview that ensued, not surprisingly, was not a source of pleasure or comfort to either of them and, saddest of all, though neither could know, it was to be their last encounter.

*

One evening in March 1908, Clementine arrived home rather bent and weary after giving French lessons to find a message from Lady St Helier asking her to dine that very evening, as one of her guests had fallen out, and she was in danger of being an unlucky thirteen. Clementine was reluctant to go; she was tired, she had no suitable gown ready, and no clean gloves. But her mother was adamant that she must brace up and go to the dinner party, reminding Clementine of the many kindnesses she had received at Aunt Mary St Helier's hands. And so, without any relish for the evening ahead, Clementine went upstairs to change.

Lady St Helier, in fact, was very lucky not to have another defection from her party: one of her other guests, Mr Winston Churchill, decided the whole evening was going to be a great bore, and told his Private Secretary, Eddie Marsh (who found him dawdling in his bath), that he did not intend to go. Eddie Marsh was shocked, and reminded Winston of Lady St Helier's efforts on his behalf when he was having such difficulty in getting out to Egypt in 1898. So, with none too good a grace, Winston hurriedly dressed and set out, already late, for the dinner party.

At Lady St Helier's house, No. 52 Portland Place, the assembled company, besides Clementine, included Mr and Mrs F. E. Smith (he was already a rising star in Tory politics and the law, and Winston's great friend); Lord Tweedmouth, the First Lord of the Admiralty; Sir Henry Lucy, a political journalist, who wrote for *Punch* under the name of 'Toby M.P.'; Miss Ruth Moore, who later married Lord Lee of Fareham; and Sir Frederick Lugard, the great West African explorer and colonial administrator, and his wife, Flora Shaw, herself an expert on colonial affairs. Winston Churchill being very late, they started dinner without him. Clementine in consequence had a gap on her right; on her left was Sir Henry Lucy. Halfway through dinner Winston Churchill arrived full of explanations and excuses, and took his place between Lady Lugard and Clementine.

Clementine and Winston's first meeting at the ball at Crewe House four years before had not been a signal success, and now this second encounter seemed to have got off to a bad start as well. But things went very differently this time. Since Winston was, at the time, Under-Secretary for the Colonies, he might well have been expected to devote a good deal of his attention to the distinguished and knowledgeable Lady Lugard; however, he turned almost at once to the ravishing young woman on his left, and monopolised her for the rest of dinner. Afterwards, when the gentlemen joined the ladies, Winston, who usually liked to linger behind, was first into the drawing-room, making straight for Clementine, in whose company he remained for the rest of the evening. His attentions were so noticeable that Clementine had to endure a little gentle teasing from the other ladies, when they all went to get their cloaks.

The romantic in Winston Churchill's nature sought in women beauty, distinction and nobility of character: Clementine Hozier possessed all three. On their first brief encounter he had recognised the first two qualities; now, after an evening spent in her company, he realised that here was a girl of lively intelligence and great character. Clementine, for her part, was enthralled by the brilliance, warmth and charm of his personality, which filled his whole being and made his attraction so irresistible, despite his forgetful, unpunctual and even at times un-gallant ways. During their conversation he asked Clementine if she had read the life he had written of his father, which had been published in 1906. She said she had not read it, but would like to. 'I will send it to you tomorrow,' he said. But he forgot!

Events were moving in Winston's political life as well. In early April 1908 Sir Henry Campbell-Bannerman, the Prime Minister, mortally stricken by an illness from which he died only a few weeks later, resigned and was succeeded by Mr H. H. Asquith. The new Prime Minister made few changes, but one of them was to move Churchill from the Colonal Office and to make him President of the Board of Trade, with a seat in the Cabinet. At that time, on being appointed a minister a Member of Parliament had to seek re-election. Winston was therefore faced with a by-election in his seat at N.W. Manchester, which he had won with a respectable majority for the Liberals at the General Election two years before.

Although there was so much afoot politically for Winston he was now in love – and he had no intention of allowing even weeks, let alone years, to slip by this time before he saw Clementine again. He therefore asked his mother to invite her, with Lady Blanche, to spend the week-end of 11–12th April at her house, Salisbury Hall, near St Albans in Hertfordshire. To her lasting credit, Lady Randolph from the first welcomed Winston's attachment to Clementine. It would clearly have been advantageous for him to have married a girl with some money, and Lady Randolph was a worldly woman. But she instantly recognised in Clementine those sterling qualities which were to make her the perfect wife for her brilliant son.

It was during this week-end that Mr Asquith announced his Cabinet, so that spring Sunday at Salisbury Hall must have been full of excitement at the present, as well as of unspoken hopes for the future.

The next day Clementine (most reluctantly now) left England with her mother, on a long-arranged journey to Germany. During the previous summer it had been discovered that Nellie had tuberculosis. She had therefore been packed off to a clinic at Nordrach to undergo a rigorous cure. The treatment, which took a year, but which was complete and lasting, was now in its last few weeks, and Lady Blanche and Clementine were going out to collect her. On their way home they all planned to visit old Lady Airlie in Florence, where she invariably spent the summer months.

At this juncture of her life it must have been agony for Clementine to contemplate such a long and distant separation from Winston, who now occupied her thoughts and, increasingly, her heart. As for Lady St Helier, who had got wind of the affair, she expressed herself strongly to Blanche Hozier – to the effect that she must be out of her mind to remove Clementine from the country for over a month just when it was clear that Winston Churchill was seriously interested in her.

As Clementine rested in Paris between trains, on Monday, 13th April, she wrote to Winston's mother:

Dear Mrs West,
I want to thank you very much for making me so happy during my visit to you.
At this moment your whole mind must be filled with joy & triumph for Mr Churchill, but you were so kind to me that you make me feel as if I had known

you always. I feel no one can know him, even as little as I do, without being dominated by his charm and brilliancy. I wish I could be with you in this stirring fortnight.

This is a poor scribble after a rough crossing, but I feel I want to write to you at once.

Yours affectionately,
Clementine Hozier

Three days later Winston wrote Clementine a long letter from his house, 12 Bolton Street (which he shared with his brother Jack). He had returned from the political battlefront to 'kiss hands' on his new appointment. He gave a lively account of the campaign in Manchester, and was full of confidence that he would have a 'substantial success'.

A considerable part of his letter was taken up by his account of Lady Dorothy Howard's electioneering activities and talents. Dorothy Howard was the daughter of Lord and Lady Carlisle, and was Clementine's cousin. She was beautiful, gifted and intensely politically-minded. Clementine had distinctly mixed feelings on reading Winston's enthusiastic recital of how Dorothy arrived 'of her own accord, alone and independent' to help him in his campaign. However she need not have worried – earnest women were never really to Winston's liking. Nor can Lady Dorothy's passionate advocacy of 'Votes for Women' and the 'Anti-drink' lobby have aroused in him much enthusiasm. Indeed, in this same letter Winston told Clementine how he had teased her

by refusing to give a decided answer about women's votes, she left at once for the North in a most obstinate temper. However on reading my answers given in public, back she came, and is fighting away like Diana for the Greeks.

But his letter was not wholly about the election or Lady Dorothy. Of his meeting with Clementine he wrote:

. . . what a comfort & pleasure it was to me to meet a girl with so much intellectual quality & such strong reserves of noble sentiment. I hope we shall meet again and come to know each other better and like each other more . . . Meanwhile I will let you know from time to time how I am getting on here in the storm; and we may lay the foundations of a frank & clear-eyed friendship which I certainly should value and cherish with many serious feelings of respect.[4]

On 23rd April Clementine replied to him from Nordrach:

Your letter found me here only yesterday – Seemingly, our maid at home thought there was no hurry in forwarding letters. If it were not for the excitement of reading about Manchester every day in the belated newspapers I should feel as if I were living in another world than the delightful one we inhabited together for a day at Salisbury Hall . . .

I feel so envious of Dorothy Howard. It must be very exciting to feel one has the power of influencing people, ever so little. One more day & we shall know the result of the Election. I feel as much excited as if I were a candidate. . . .

I don't know if wishing & hoping can influence human affairs – if so – poor Joynson-Hicks!

> Yours very sincerely,
> Clementine Hozier

Before he wrote his next letter on 27th April the battle in N.W. Manchester was over. Churchill was defeated by Mr Joynson-Hicks, the Conservative candidate, by 429 votes. The Tory press was beside itself with exultation. 'Winston Churchill is out, OUT, OUT!' wrote, or rather shrieked, the *Daily Telegraph*. Winston took his defeat philosophically, and wrote to Clementine:

> . . . If I had won Manchester now, I should probably have lost it at the general election. Losing it now I shall I hope get a seat wh will make me secure for many years. Still I don't pretend not to be vexed. Defeat however consoled explained or discounted is odious . . .

There was more – somewhat annoyingly – about Lady Dorothy (who had changed identity, style and century since his previous letter):

> [she] fought like Joan of Arc before Orleans. The dirtiest slum, the roughest crowd, the ugliest street corner. She is a wonderful woman – tireless, fearless, convinced, inflexible – yet preserving all her womanliness . . .

Is it possible that Winston could have been gently tantalising his true love? But the letter ends with a very special message for her:

> How I should have liked you to have been there. You would have enjoyed it I think. We had a jolly party and it was a whirling week. Life for all its incompleteness is rather fun sometimes.
>
> Write to me again. I am a solitary creature in the midst of crowds. Be kind to me.
>
> > Yours vy sincerely,
> > W

Towards the end of May Clementine, with her mother and sister, returned home. In the interval, Winston had fought and won Dundee at a by-election. He was to represent this constituency for twelve years. During the months of June and July he and Clementine met several times, but as unmarried girls did not in those days lunch or dine alone with men, they met in the main only on social occasions. Clementine was by now deeply in love, and in an agony lest their growing friendship should be remarked upon. Such was her anxiety on this count that when Winston invited her to a garden party he was giving in the gardens of Gwdyr House (then the Board of Trade) she declined to go. Presumably their closest family must have been aware that something was brewing, but their discretion was complete. More than most girls Clementine could keep her own counsel, so now at this crucial moment of her life even her few close friends were not aware of her feelings.

She spent part of these, for her, most trying summer months staying with her Great-aunt Maude Stanley, who once more proved to be a sympathetic refuge for her great-niece during a time which, for Clementine, was filled with alternating hopes and fears.

The parliamentary summer recess was soon imminent, and both Winston and Clementine were committed to prearranged visits, but they planned to meet at Salisbury Hall in the middle of August. In the interval, Clementine went to stay with Mrs Godfrey Baring at Nubia House in Cowes. She took part in the round of balls and entertainments, but she was a somewhat distracted guest, as her thoughts and heart were elsewhere.

Winston was staying with his cousin, Freddie Guest, and his American wife, Amy Phipps, at Burley Hall, near Oakham, a house the Guests had rented. During the night of 6th August, soon after everyone had gone to bed, a fire broke out, and a whole wing of the house was burned to the ground by daybreak. Rumours fly fast, and Clementine's heart turned over when she heard a garbled account of the disaster. She knew Winston to be one of the house party, and first reports were alarming about loss and injury. Fortunately *The Times* put her out of her misery: the damage had been great, but no loss of life or injury had occurred. Unable to contain her relief and joy, she rushed to the local post office and sent a telegram to Winston.

On 7th August he wrote her a long letter from Nuneham Park (Sir Lewis and Lady Harcourt's house, where some of the Burley Hall party had taken refuge), in which a lively account of the fire took third place to an alteration in plans for the visit to Salisbury Hall, and an account of his brother Jack's marriage to Lady Gwendeline Bertie (daughter of the Earl of Abingdon), which had taken place at Abingdon on 4th August.

The alteration in plans consisted of interposing a two-day visit to Blenheim Palace before going on to Salisbury Hall. Winston had arranged everything with his cousin Sunny, the Duke of Marlborough, who invited Clementine at Winston's urgent behest. Clementine jibbed at this, to her, somewhat alarming suggestion, but allowed herself to be persuaded by Winston's assurance that

Sunny wants us all to come, & my Mother will look after you – & so will I. I want so much to show you that beautiful place & in its gardens we shall find lots of places to talk in, & lots of things to talk about.

Of the fire at Burley Hall, he wrote:

The Fire was great fun, & we all enjoyed it thoroughly. It is a pity such jolly entertainments are so costly ... It was vy lucky that the fire was discovered before we had *all* gone to sleep – or more life might have been lost – than one canary bird; & even as it was there were moments of danger for some.

He ended his letter by asking her what she had been thinking of during her days at Cowes

& whether you would have thought of me at all – if the newspapers had not jogged your memory! You know the answer that I want to this.

Winston omitted in his letter to mention that he had taken a leading part in salvaging pictures and other valuables from the conflagration, and had escaped possible death or serious injury when, just as he left one part of the house carrying two marble busts, the roof, which had been blazing furiously, collapsed.

The following evening, 8th August, Clementine wrote from Cowes:

> I was so glad to get your delightful letter this morning. I retired with it into the garden, but for a long time before opening it I amused myself by wondering what would be inside. I have been able to think of nothing but the fire & the terrible danger you have been in – The first news I heard was a rumour that the house was burnt down – That was all – My dear my heart stood still with terror. All the same I did not need that horrible emotion to 'jog my memory'.
>
> We all went to a ball the next night which I hated. I was extremely odious to several young partners not on purpose, but because they would interrupt my train of thought with irrelevant patter about yachts, racing, the weather, Cowes gossip, etc. So I was obliged to feign deafness –
>
> Please do not think there is any real reason for my not at first wanting to go to Blenheim. It was only a sudden access of shyness . . .

Another reason for her hesitation in accepting the invitation was that Clementine was down to her last laundered and starched dress and, having no personal maid, she would have to make this one last the unexpected visit.

Winston's next letter, written also on 8th August, must have crossed with Clementine's, and in it he reproaches her for being an indifferent correspondent. However, he had tidings of her from his aunt, Lady Leslie, who had arrived at Nuneham Court from Cowes to attend Jack Churchill's wedding, and who, he wrote,

> brings me news from Cowes of a young lady who made a great impression at a dance four nights ago on all beholders. I wonder who it could have been!

Clementine had evidently telegraphed Winston that same Saturday morning to acquiesce in the plans to go to Blenheim. Winston hastened to reassure her that there would be no large party, and to introduce her, as it were ahead of the event, to his first cousin, the Duke.

> I hope you will like my friend, & fascinate him with those strange mysterious eyes of yours, whose secret I have been trying so hard to learn . . .
>
> He is quite different from me, understanding women thoroughly, getting into touch with them at once . . . Whereas I am stupid and clumsy in that relation, and naturally quite self-reliant and self-contained. Yet by such vy different paths we both arrive at loneliness!

His cousin's loneliness was due to the fact that since 1906 he had been living apart from his beautiful duchess. She was born Consuelo Vanderbilt of New York City, and her marriage to the Duke of Marlborough had been arranged by her domineering mother, in the manner of a bygone century, and in the face of her daughter's declared attachment to another man. The inner wishes of the Duke's heart also lay elsewhere, but the duty and desire to perpetuate the historical splendours of Blenheim were paramount to him. His well-dowered and beautiful bride came to the altar in tears, but she stayed at Blenheim for eleven years, fulfilling her duties as Duchess with grace and distinction, and providing her husband with two sons. But the differences between their natures were deep and irreconcilable, and finally they separated. Later the Duke married again, but now at this moment he was a solitary figure in a great setting.

Winston had a strong sense of consanguinity, and between him and his first cousin Sunny were not only bonds of blood, but also true liking and affection. Winston's Radical views were not those of the Duke's; but neither then nor later, despite some brisk verbal passages, did political differences interfere for long with their friendship.

Throughout his life Winston was a frequent visitor to Blenheim. It was in a special sense his home: there he was born; there he became engaged; there he spent the first few days of his honeymoon. Later, when Winston wrote his splendid life of the great Duke of Marlborough, Blenheim epitomised for him the triumphs and magnificence of England and of his hero. And so it seemed most right and fitting that in the end he should have wished to return there – to Bladon, the little churchyard just outside the park – to lie close to his parents and kinsfolk.

It seems certain from his letters that Winston had determined to ask Clementine to be his wife. He had taken his cousin, the Duke, into his confidence, and the Blenheim visit was undoubtedly arranged so that he could propose to this beautiful girl with whom he was so deeply in love in a setting which combined the romantic with the heroic, and where he felt so strongly the ties of family and friendship.

In the train travelling between Cowes and Blenheim, Clementine wrote to her mother, who was in London.

Darling mother,
Thank you so much for your letter. I shall get to Oxford at 5.20 where I shall be met by motor.

I feel dreadfully shy & rather tired . . . I will write to you tomorrow morning from Blenheim.

I shall see 2 of Winston's greatest friends there – the Duke and F. E. Smith. On Wednesday we go to Salisbury Hall . . .

I cannot write a good letter – I feel like in a dream & can do nothing more intelligent than count the telegraph posts as they flash by or the pattern on the railway cushions.

Much love from
Clem

The somewhat hastily arranged house party gathered at Blenheim Palace on Monday, 10th August. It was, as promised, a small one. Winston came with his mother, and a Private Secretary from the Board of Trade (for affairs of state must not be neglected, even at such an hour). The F. E. Smiths were the only other guests.

Before retiring to bed on the Monday evening Winston made an assignation with Clementine to walk in the rose garden the following morning after breakfast. Appearing punctually at breakfast was never at any time in his life one of Winston's more pronounced qualities; even on this day of days he was late!

Clementine came downstairs with characteristic punctuality, and was much discomfited by Winston's non-appearance. While she was eating breakfast, she seriously turned over in her mind the possibility of returning then and there to London. The Duke observed that Clementine was much put out, and took charge of the situation. He despatched a sharp, cousinly note upstairs to Winston and, deploying his utmost charm, suggested to Clementine that he should take her for a drive in his buggy. He whirled her round the estate for about half an hour, and upon their return there was the dilatory Winston anxiously scanning the horizon.

During the course of the late afternoon Winston and Clementine went for a walk in the garden; overtaken by a torrential rainstorm, they took refuge in a little Greek temple, which looks out over the great lake. Here Winston declared his love, and asked Clementine to marry him. When in due course, and the rain shower being over, they emerged from the temple – they were betrothed.

Clementine had enjoined absolute secrecy upon Winston until she had been to London to tell her mother their great news, and to seek her formal consent. But as they drew near the house they met the Duke and his other guests gathered on the lawn; whereupon Winston's triumph and joy were too much for him to contain – he started running across the lawn waving his arms with excitement, and, despite his promise to the contrary, told his assembled friends and relations his glorious tidings.

It was arranged that Clementine should go to London the next morning to see her mother. Early on that morning Winston and Clementine exchanged notes. He wrote:

My dearest,
    How are you? I send you my best love to salute you: & I am getting up at once in order if you like to walk to the rose garden after breakfast & pick a bunch before you start. You will have to leave here about 10.30 & I will come with you to Oxford.
    Shall I not give you a letter for your mother?

Always,
W

She replied:

My dearest,
    I am very well – Yes please give me a letter to take to Mother. I should love to go to the rose garden.

Yours always
Clementine

A few hours later Clementine left Blenheim with Winston, who was to accompany her to the station. She bore with her the following letter:

Blenheim Palace
12th Aug. 1908.

My dear Lady Blanche Hozier,
    Clementine will be my ambassador to you today. I have asked her to marry me & we both ask you to give your consent & your blessing.

You have known my family so many years that there is no need to say vy much in this letter. I am not rich nor powerfully established, but your daughter loves me & with that love I feel strong enough to assume this great & sacred responsibility; & I think I can make her happy & give her a station & career worthy of her beauty and her virtues.

Marlborough is vy much in hopes that you will be able to come down here today & he is telegraphing to you this morning. That would indeed be vy charming & I am sure Clementine will persuade you.

With sincere affection
Yours ever,
Winston S. Churchill

But in the event the letter was hardly necessary, as we see from the account Clementine gave of that whirlwind twenty-four hours. For she wrote a somewhat breathless and disjointed letter a day or two later to Nellie who, throughout these emotional and exciting days for her sister, was staying away with friends in the country:

Well it happened Tuesday evening – & on Wednesday morning I telegraphed mother to say I was coming to see her from Blenheim. The Duke telegraphed asking her to come & stay – Winston was by way of coming in the motor to the station only, as he had some work to do with his secretary at Blenheim, but when we got there we hopped into the train together. When we got to Paddington I went off alone to Abingdon [Villas] & told him to follow in $\frac{1}{2}$ an hour – I wanted to see the Min [the nickname the children used for their mother among themselves] alone first & also I was not sure if she would be dressed! However, my dear, she was! with her hair beautifully done by Miss Blount looking quite beautiful – much nicer than me – I have become very ugly & thin & I don't know what to do about it.

Well W arrived presently & I left them alone & everything was all right. Gubbins [Lady Blanche's dog] looked much disgusted. I tried to remove him from the room as I thought he was a disgrace to the establishment, but was prevented – When I am married I am going to have a dog. You must come and help to choose it – a Pekinese.

My dear, I have the most lovely ring – a fat ruby with 2 diamonds – I must tell you about it – When Lord Randolph married he gave her [Lady Randolph] 3 lovely rings – one all diamond, one sapphire & diamond & one ruby & diamond – she wears the diamond one, & Goonie [Jack's wife] has the sapphire & diamond & I have the twin ruby one – Lord Randolph said they were for his 2 sons to give their wives.

Well to return to the narrative – Min, Winston & I returned to Blenheim in the afternoon – We were all dog-tired, but no matter – Min was most delightful at dinner & looked lovely in her white lace arrangement . . .

Blanche Hozier must have expected the news Clementine brought her, and, as we have seen, much to her daughter's relief, had taken trouble with her appearance.

Perhaps she had hoped Clementine would marry a man who, as well as personal happiness, could offer her solid financial security. Winston Churchill was a poor man by the standards of the world in which he lived; his talents were his only prospects; and although he was undeniably brilliant, he was ill-regarded by many both on public and personal grounds. But in many ways, as we have seen, Blanche Hozier was an unworldly woman and, intuitive in all things concerning the heart, she probably recognised that now, for the first time, Clementine was truly in love.

Moreover, Lady Blanche had herself been captivated by Winston's personality and charm. Clementine wrote to Nellie:

> I am so afraid you will fall in love with Winston – Mother has already & he with her. He thinks she is the most delightful person almost in the world![5]

In a letter to her sister-in-law, Lady Airlie, Blanche Hozier wrote:

> Clementine is engaged to be married to Winston Churchill. I do not know which of the two is the more in love. I think that to know him is to like him. His brilliant brain the world knows, but he is so charming and affectionate in his own home life.[6]

And to an old friend – the poet and author Wilfrid Scawen Blunt:

> He [WSC] is so like Lord Randolph, he has some of his faults, and all his qualities. He is gentle and tender, and affectionate to those he loves, much hated by those who have not come under his personal charm.[7]

During the following day or two, notes flew along the corridors of the Palace. No more formality now, no veiled words – both could give rein to the love and spontaneous joy each felt.

From Winston:

> My dearest,
>
> I hope you have slept like a stone. I did not get to bed till 1 o'clock; for Sunny kept me long in discussion about his affairs wh go less prosperously than ours. But from 1 onwards I slept the sleep of the just, & this morning am fresh and fit. Tell me how you feel & whether you mean to get up for breakfast. The purpose of this letter is also to send you heaps of love and four kisses XXXX
>
> > from your always devoted
> > Winston[8]

Clementine replied:

> My darling,
>
> I never slept so well and I had the most heavenly dreams.
>
> I am coming down presently – Mother is quite worn out as we have been talking for the last two hours.
>
> Je t'aime passionément [sic] – I feel less shy in French.
>
> > Clementine[9]

From Blenheim, Winston and his mother took Clementine with them to Salisbury Hall for the week-end, and also Jack and his bride, Gwendeline (always known as Goonie): and they were all there when the engagement was officially announced on Saturday, 15th August. Close friends and relations were hurriedly told the great news, and to nearly everybody it came as a surprise, and was the cause of much excited comment. If Winston's name had been linked romantically, it had certainly not been with the beautiful, but obscure and penniless, Clementine Hozier.

To one person at least, the tidings brought bitter pain: Sidney Peel had always told Clementine that he would wait for her for ever, but in the event of her marrying someone else it would be the end of everything between them. While she was free he could endure anything, but once hope (however frail) was dead he could not transmute his deep devotion into terms of pallid friendship. So when Clementine wrote to tell him of her engagement she knew she was severing for ever a friendship she greatly valued, and in which she had found much comfort and happiness in bleaker days. Some years after her marriage Clementine met Sidney Peel unexpectedly in the street. 'Are you happy?' he asked. 'Yes – I'm happy,' replied Clementine. He turned on his heel and walked away. They were never to meet again.

The news, with various inaccurate embellishments, travelled to Dieppe, and caused much local interest. Madame Villain, still the reigning queen of the fish market, mounted a herring box and, clapping her hands for silence, announced to the assembled company: 'Voilà des nouvelles! ... Vous vous rappelez de notre petite Clementine? Eh bien, elle s'est fiancée ... avec un ministre anglais ... millionaire et décoré!'

Clementine's grandmother, Lady Airlie, noted in her diary for 13th August 1908:

I get news of Clem Hozier's engagement to W. Churchill sitting in the garden seeing the hedges clipt ...

She later wrote to her daughter-in-law, Mabell Airlie:

Winston is his father over again, with the American driving force added. His mother and he are devoted to one another, and I think a good son makes a good husband. Clementine is wise. She will follow him and, I hope, say little.[10]

It is evident that old Lady Airlie had not fully estimated her granddaughter Clementine's strength of character, nor her capacity to express strongly held opinions.

Winston would not brook a long engagement. Then as later, he saw no reasons for delay once a plan was decided upon; moreover, the dictates of the parliamentary year set certain time-limits.

In a letter to her Aunt Mabell (young Lady Airlie) Clementine wrote of their plans:

... I cannot describe my happiness to you. I can hardly believe it is true. I have been engaged nine days now. I cared very much for him when he asked me to marry him, but every day since has been more heavenly. The only crumpled roseleaf is the scrimmage getting ready in time. September 12th has now been settled for our wedding. We shall have only seventeen days away as Winston has to be back in London on October 3rd.[11]

Even today, when an elaborate trousseau is no longer a necessity, a month is scant time for a bride to organise herself. Clementine was soon swept up in a tidal wave of preparations and correspondence, which at moments seemed daunting. Writing from Abingdon Villas (in an undated letter), she told Winston:

> My darling,
>   Thinking about you has been the only pleasant thing today.
>   I have tried on so many garments (all of which I am told are indispensable) . . .
>   My tailor told me he approved of you & had paid 10/6d. to hear you make a speech about the war at Birmingham – After that I felt I could not bargain with him any more . . .
>   Goodbye my darling I feel there is no room for anyone but you in my heart – you fill every corner.
>
> Clementine

It is not an uncommon experience in the interim between betrothal and marriage for the sunshine of joy and confidence to be overcast by a fleeting cloud of doubt. Clementine had her moment of trepidation. Perhaps in part it was reaction to the excitement, the public interest and the exhausting bustle of the preparations. Maybe she even wondered if Winston truly loved her. Even during these few weeks of their engagement, public life laid constant claim to both his time and interest. Already she saw the face of the only real rival she was to know in all the fifty-seven years of marriage that lay ahead – and for a brief moment she quailed. She confided her doubts and fears to Bill, who showed himself in a firmly steadying role. He wrote to her saying that although he was younger than her, he was now the head of the family, and that as such, he must remind her that she had already broken off at least two engagements – one of them publicly announced; he told her that she could not make an exhibition of, and humiliate, a public personage such as Winston. But more than Bill's brotherly admonition, it was the warmth of Winston's swift reassurance, and the force of his own supreme confidence in their future together, which swept away the doubts that had beset her.

Their letters to each other during those short weeks of their engagement breathe love and hope and joy – long pent up – at last finding release and expression. In one of her letters to Winston, Clementine wonders

> how I have lived 23 years without you. Everything that happened before about 5 months ago seems unreal.[12]

Winston's underlying mood was one of wonder and thankfulness. 'There are no words,' he wrote to her,

> to convey to you the feelings of love & joy by wh my being is possessed. May God who has given me so much more than I ever knew how to ask keep you safe and sound.[13]

EARLY DAYS TOGETHER

THERE WAS much public interest in the marriage. It was an indication of how already Winston Churchill had captured people's imagination, by his exploits and his writings as much as through the name he bore. Moreover, the British public is incurably romantic, and in this match they found all their favourite ingredients: youth, courage, beauty, birth and, above all – true love.

As the day of the wedding, 12th September, drew near, many of the daily papers carried running commentaries on the progress the bride was making with her preparations, and published long lists of wedding presents. The bridegroom's status as a national figure received a measure of significant recognition on the day of his wedding, when his life-size model went on display at Madame Tussaud's.

Kind and hospitable Lady St Helier had offered her house in Portland Place for the reception, and since Abingdon Villas was small and would be full of relations and bridesmaids, it was arranged that Clementine should spend the night before her wedding at her great-aunt's house, and that she would leave from there for the church.

On the eve of her wedding, therefore, Clementine went to stay with Lady St Helier. The next morning – her wedding day – she awoke very early indeed. The bedroom seemed chill and vast, and in the grey dawn light her wedding dress glimmered remote and unreal. A sudden wave of panic and homesickness swept through Clementine, and she wished with all her heart that she was back in the familiar bustle of Abingdon Villas.

On the spur of the moment Clementine decided she would go home for breakfast; but this was easier wished than done, as all her everyday clothes had been swept away the night before by her great-aunt's lady's maid. In her dressing-gown, Clementine crept downstairs: the great rooms were still in darkness, but in the morning room a young under-housemaid was busily blacking the grate. Clementine confided to her the great longing she had to go home; the maid understood at once – probably she too found the house in Portland Place stiff and grand. Clementine seemed near enough the same size; the friendly girl ran upstairs and returned with a complete set of her own best, 'going out' clothes. Shortly afterwards Clementine was let out of the back door, attired in a pretty print dress, dark fitting coat and black-buttoned boots, with a neat bonnet and kid gloves. The early buses were running, and she caught one on the route she often used. As he gave her a ticket, the conductor eyed her narrowly. 'Ain't you going the wrong way, Miss?' he said.

Great was the astonishment and merriment when she appeared at home, and dressed so strangely. After a cheerful breakfast with her family she was packed off back to Portland Place, her spirits restored. The bride-in-disguise managed to slip in amid the general confusion of preparations before her absence had been reported to Lady St Helier.

Although September was a time of the year when many people were away from London, nonetheless St Margaret's, Westminster, was packed to the doors with wedding guests. For a day a truce was called between Radical and Tory, and indeed, one of the first guests to arrive was the Tory member for N.W. Manchester, Mr Joynson-Hicks, who had so narrowly defeated Winston earlier in that same year. Great crowds had assembled in Parliament Square, and both the bridegroom, with his best man (Lord Hugh Cecil), and bride were enthusiastically cheered as they arrived.

Clementine was – from all accounts – a glorious sight, as she came up the aisle on the arm of Bill, a handsome and devoted brother, now a Sub-Lieutenant in the Royal Navy. Her gown was of shimmering white satin, and her voluminous veil of tulle was held in place by a coronet of fresh orange blossoms; and she wore the diamond earrings given her by Winston. Her bouquet was of white tuberoses, and she also carried the white parchment Prayer Book which was the gift of her godfather, Sir Jack Leslie. Nellie was of course a bridesmaid, with Clementine's cousins Venetia Stanley and Madeline Whyte, Clare Frewen (Winston's cousin) and one dear friend – the exquisite Horatia Seymour. The bridesmaids wore gowns of biscuit-coloured satin with large romantic black hats wreathed in roses and camellias; they carried bouquets of pink roses.

St Margaret's was a bower of palms and ferns, with white lilies everywhere.

The Bishop of St Asaph conducted the service, and the address was given by the Dean of Manchester – Bishop Welldon, Winston's former Headmaster at Harrow. Lady Blanche's friend Wilfrid Scawen Blunt recorded in his diary:

> Winston's responses were clearly made in a pleasant voice, Clementine's inaudible.[1]

While the bridal party was in the vestry, the bridesmaids carrying wickerwork baskets distributed 'favours' of orange blossom to the guests. Mr Lloyd George, the Chancellor of the Exchequer, signed the register, and Winston immediately set to talking politics with him.

As the bride and bridegroom left the church they were cheered vociferously, and another crowd greeted them at 52 Portland Place. After being received by Lady Blanche and greeting the bride and bridegroom, the guests were able to review the wedding presents, which were many and splendid. These were still spacious times; the day had not yet come when tea towels, washing-up machines and ovenware are welcome presents. Clementine's present list was sprinkled with pendants, muff chains and a variety of ornamental boxes. Winston received several silver candelabra, wine coasters, pepper pots, and no fewer than seventeen silver inkstands. King

Edward sent him a gold-topped walking stick. Dundee Liberal Association weighed in with a large and beautiful Georgian silver dinner service; and his colleagues in the Government gave him a large scallop-edged silver tray, with all their signatures engraved on the back. While prominently displayed among these rich trophies was a glistening turbot with a lemon in its mouth – the gift of Mme Villain from Dieppe.

While the fine company admired the presents and toasted the bride and bridegroom, jollity reigned outside in Portland Place. The crowd of admirers and unknown friends included a contingent of 'Pearly Kings and Queens', their clothes resplendent with pearl buttons sewn in intricate patterns. As President of the Board of Trade, Winston had helped to protect the costermongers' rights to trade in the streets; so, on this his wedding day, many of them gathered in their splendid traditional finery to wish him well. Late in the afternoon the bride and bridegroom left Lady St Helier's house to start their journey to Blenheim, where they were to spend a day or two before going to Italy. With her grey cloth ensemble Clementine wore a large black satin hat adorned with one long sweeping ostrich feather. The Pearly Queens, whose own large hats are always decorated with waving ostrich plumes, were delighted. 'Ooh, wot a luv'ly fevver!' they cried, as Winston and Clementine got into their carriage.

The poor bridegroom, however, did not draw such favourable comments on his apparel – at least from the *Tailor and Cutter*, which described his wedding outfit as

'neither fish, flesh, nor fowl', and was one of the greatest failures as a wedding garment we have ever seen, giving the wearer a sort of glorified coachman appearance.

The bridal couple travelled to Woodstock by train, and were greeted at the station by an enthusiastic crowd, their cheers mingling with the bells of St Mary Magdalene. It had been a long and glorious day, and presently, amid the splendours of the past, and where their own present happiness had begun – Winston and Clementine were alone together.

*

After a few days spent at Blenheim recovering from the emotions and excitements of their wedding day, the honeymooners travelled to Italy, visiting Lake Lugano and Venice. From there they went to stay with Baron (Tuty) de Forest and his wife at Eichorn in Austria. Born in 1879 of Austrian extraction, the Baron had been educated and brought up in England, and both he and his wife had been friends of Winston from childhood. As his guest, Winston enjoyed some excellent shooting, but Clementine found the large house party rather grand, stiff and social, and was glad to begin the homeward journey. Winston wrote to his mother on 20th September 1908:

We have only loitered & loved, a good & serious occupation for which the histories furnish respectable precedents.

One of their first visits on their return to England was to old Lady Airlie at Airlie

Castle, where they stayed on 8th October on their way to Dundee, in order that Winston might present his bride to his constituents.

*

There had been no time for house-hunting in the weeks before their wedding, and so they had decided to start their married life in Winston's bachelor establishment in Bolton Street. Winston had entrusted the necessary rearrangements to his mother, and she had set about the house with characteristic energy and perhaps rather too much zeal, and on their arrival home in early October Clementine was greatly surprised to find her bedroom completely redecorated. To her simple and rather austere taste, the sateen and muslin covers trimmed with bows, which decked the chairs, dressing-table and bed, appeared vulgar and tawdry. She did her best, however, to conceal her lack of appreciation of her mother-in-law's well-meant efforts.

Clementine was never to have a really close relationship with Lady Randolph. This once supremely beautiful woman was still, in her fifties, remarkably handsome; but, accustomed all her life to attention and adulation, Lady Randolph had now to accept a long, cool look from her new daughter-in-law. Although as time went on Clementine came to salute her courage and her unfailing zest for life, now in these early years of her marriage she passed (in her heart) a fairly harsh judgment on her celebrated mother-in-law. She thought her vain and frivolous and, in her marriage to a man so much younger than herself, somewhat ridiculous.

As Jennie Jerome, she had been brought up one of the three beautiful daughters of a generous father – Leonard Jerome of New York City – who made, lost and recouped fortunes with surprising speed. Jennie was open-handed and a great spender, and Clementine was on many occasions to feel resentment (fully shared by Jack's wife) at Lady Randolph's extravagances, which often weighed heavily upon her two sons.

But Jennie was a celebrated character, and we see her through more indulgent eyes in Eddie Marsh's vivid sketch of her:

> She was an incredible and most delightful compound of flagrant worldliness and eternal childhood, in thrall to fashion and luxury (life didn't begin for her on a basis of less than forty pairs of shoes) yet never sacrificing one human quality of warm-heartedness, humour, loyalty, sincerity, or steadfast and pugnacious courage . . .[2]

Clementine knew how dearly Winston loved his mother, and she kept (for the most part) her opinions and reservations about Lady Randolph to herself. And mutual good manners, surface affection and a shared loyalty to Winston maintained a civilised relationship between these two very different women.

On their return from their honeymoon, while Winston plunged once more into politics, Clementine proceeded to arrange their domestic affairs. She started with the kitchen. Needless to say, Winston's bachelor establishment had not been run on economical lines. Clementine set to with energy to improve upon this state of affairs. Accustomed all her life to managing on very little money, she had a horror of extravagance, and from her mother she had learnt that delicious food is more a matter of taking trouble than lavish spending. And to assist her in these laudable endeavours, she was armed with a little booklet (given to her as a wedding present) entitled *House Books on 12/- a week*, which was considered to be a generous allowance per head in those days. Clementine also took up the cudgels for economy on the wardrobe front. Lady Violet Bonham Carter (Mr Asquith's daughter by his first marriage) recorded that soon after her marriage Clementine confided to her that

> Winston was most extravagant about his underclothes. These were made of very finely woven silk (pale pink) and came from the Army and Navy Stores and cost the eyes out of the head.[3]

Whether Clementine's campaign for cheaper chemises was successful is not recorded, but Winston protested that he had a most delicate skin (which was true) which necessitated such luxurious lingerie. The author's memory is that he always wore very fine silk underclothes.

But Clementine was not entirely engrossed by domestic affairs. Politics thrilled her, and she now flung herself with passion into Radical politics. The noble, puritan element in her nature responded naturally to the great reforming measures in which Winston, working closely with Lloyd George, was deeply involved. Old Age Pensions had been introduced earlier in that year, and Winston, who had taken up the cause of social reform with ardour and determination, was now pushing forward the schemes for Trade Boards, which would attack the exploitation of sweated labour, and of Labour Exchanges to combat the scourge of unemployment.

Clementine was proud to be the wife of one of the leaders of such noble causes. As Winston's wife, she moved naturally into the orbit of the young reformers such as Lloyd George and C. F. G. Masterman (then Parliamentary Secretary to the Local Government Board) and the higher echelons of the Liberal leadership, including the Asquiths, the Foreign Secretary, Sir Edward Grey, and the Secretary of State for War, Mr Haldane. Bitterness in politics had spread into social life, and there were certain Tory houses where Clementine was no longer welcome. Some die-hard Tory acquaintances would even cross the road rather than meet her in the street now that she was Mrs Winston Churchill. This only served to fan her crusading ardour, and was no impoverishment, for the young Churchills' friends included government colleagues, eminent Civil Servants, Radical politicians and writers and journalists drawn from the galaxy of talent surrounding the Government in these years before the Great War. And Winston maintained his links across the 'barricades' with such Tories as F. E. Smith, Lord Hugh Cecil and A. J. Balfour, whose friendship never faltered.

Wherever Winston took his bride, Clementine's beauty, charm and enthusiasm gained her friends and praise. She even earned the, albeit somewhat patronising, approval of that High Priestess of the Left – Mrs Sidney Webb, who wrote in her diary:

> On Sunday we lunched with Winston C. and his bride – a charming lady, well bred and pretty, and earnest withal – but not rich, by no means a good match, which is to Winston's credit.[4]

Clementine soon had a preoccupation, more personal, but quite as exciting as radical politics – she was expecting her first child. The lease of No. 12 Bolton Street was due to expire in February 1909, and in any case it was of doll's house proportions, so in the latter part of 1908 she was busy house-hunting. In the New Year they found and bought 33 Eccleston Square, a substantial family house in one of the large squares with tree-filled gardens behind Victoria Station, and most conveniently situated for the House of Commons. It needed, however, considerable alterations and complete redecoration, and to bridge the time between leaving Bolton Street and moving into Eccleston Square, Freddie Guest, Winston's cousin, lent them his house in Carlton House Terrace.

The baby was expected in July, and towards the end of April Clementine was invited to Blenheim, and stayed for nearly a fortnight. It was the first time in their married life that Winston and Clementine had been apart, for he had to remain in London, as the House was sitting, and much was afoot politically. Also staying at Blenheim was Clementine's sister-in-law, Goonie Churchill – she too was expecting her first child. It was during this visit that the two sisters-in-law cemented a liking that had been immediate. Quite different in nature, their mutual affection and loyalty was to be lifelong.

Winston was not too much embroiled with political affairs to fail to give Clementine a detailed report of the work being carried out in the Eccleston Square house. On 21st April he wrote to her:

> The marble basin has arrived. Your window is up – a great improvement. All the bookcases are in position. (I have ordered two more for the side windows of the alcove) The dining room gleams in creamy white. The Big room is papered. The bath room well advanced. Altogether there will be a fine show for you on Monday . . .

After her visit to London to inspect progress, Clementine wrote to Winston on 27th April 1909:

> . . . I had a long afternoon with Baxter & carpets. The green carpet is lovely & will do beautifully for library. It looks like soft green moss . . . I tried hard to make the red stair carpet do for the dining room, but it is really too shabby – The edges of the stairs have made ridges along it – & there are awful stains (not my dog this time!) . . . Green sickly looking carpet out of Jack's bedroom in Bolton Street does Puppy Kitten rooms. Another bit does the Cook's room – A big rug (from dining room in Bolton Street?) does my little sitting room . . .
>
> The whole house is now carpeted except one big servants room (which can be done with cheap linoleum for about £2) *and* the Dining room! for which new carpet will have to be got. I have written to the people who are making the blue stair carpet to ask what it will cost to cover dining room entirely with the blue – (4/6 a yard) . . .

These thrifty details show how much Winston and Clementine needed to economise and husband their capital resources, and how conscientiously Clementine tried to make-do with leftovers from Bolton Street. She must have been relieved to know her carpeting decisions met with Winston's approval, when he wrote in reply:

> You certainly have made a judicious selection of carpets & I entirely approve it.[5]

With the first appearance of the term 'Puppy Kitten' in Clementine's letter – the name by which she and Winston referred to their expected baby – it would seem to be the moment to describe the various soubriquets which they employed, and also the emblems and devices with which they adorned their letters and signatures.

From the earliest days of their marriage, Winston and Clementine conferred on each other honorary titles of affection. Clementine was always the 'Cat' or 'Kat', and her letters were invariably adorned with cats in various moods and poses. But although resembling more the drawings on a child's slate, they are full of character and meaning.

Winston was at first the 'Pug', then the 'Amber Pug'. And pugdogs rampant, joyful, fatigued or frivolous always accompanied his signature. In one letter Clementine wrote, 'I must have lessons in Kat-drawing as your pugs are so much better than my Kats.'[6] Gradually the Pug motif was replaced by the Pig symbol, and many are the pigs, expressive of every varying mood, which adorn Winston's letters to her throughout their correspondence; but Clementine's cypher always remained a cat. In due course their children, unborn or born, acquired 'pet' names, some of which stuck to them in the family for all time.

Meanwhile, events were moving swiftly at Westminster; the Liberal Government had determined upon the policy which was to plunge the country into one of the most dramatic periods of Britain's political history – the Budget of 1909, which provoked the conflict between the Liberal Government and the House of Lords. Winston had been much occupied with the passage through the House of his Trade Boards Act; he wrote to Clementine daily, and his letter of 27th April 1909 ends:

> . . . Tomorrow – Sweated Trades! Thursday – the deluge!!! [the Budget] Thus the world wags – good, bad, & indifferent intermingled or alternating, & only my sweet Pussy cat remains a constant darling . . .

The following day he could report that his Bill had been 'beautifully received & will be passed without division'. But there was doubt of the storms that lay ahead:

> Tomorrow is the day of wrath! I feel this Budget will be kill or cure. Either we shall secure ample funds for great reforms next year, or the Lords will force a Dissolution in September.

Writing from Blenheim the same day, Clementine mentions that 'Sunny is much preoccupied about the Budget. It will make politics vy bitter for a long time.' It did indeed.

Lloyd George introduced his Budget on 29th April 1909. A considerable increase in revenue was needed to sustain the Government's reforming legislation. And the 'People's Budget' – as it came to be called – aimed to secure this by increasing taxation, and introducing for the first time super-tax, a tax on motor-cars and petrol, and land value duties. The last of these, necessitating the valuation of all land by the Government, was luridly depicted as the thin end of a very sinister and odious wedge. The generation of the Welfare State, attuned to Budgets of astronomical figures, and accustomed to bearing taxation of penal proportions, may find it difficult to understand the passions aroused by these measures.

But deep and bitter was the gulf between those who believed they stood on the threshold of a brighter day when the wealth of the nation could be mobilised for the elimination of poverty, and those who felt their whole way of life was threatened by wild men with wild tongues, who showered wrath and contempt on property, place and privilege. And these latter determined to resist the Budget to the end.

*

Early in May 1909 Winston and Clementine moved into their new home, with some weeks to settle down before the arrival of their first baby. At the end of the month Winston took a few days' respite from political turmoil to take part in the annual camp of the Oxfordshire Yeomanry, in which he was an officer. He greatly enjoyed these military gallivantings, which often (as in this year) took place in the Park at Blenheim. Among the officers were also his brother Jack, F. E. Smith, and various other agreeable cronies. While the menfolk endured the rigours of camp life, their wives were entertained in the Palace – so a good time was had by all. But on this occasion Clementine did not feel up to a large house party, and chose to spend part of these last, and tedious weeks of waiting with her cousin, Dorothy Allhusen (who was the daughter of Lady St Helier by her first marriage) and her family at their house at Stoke Poges Court in Buckinghamshire.

In a letter dated 30th May 1909,* Winston wrote to her from 'Camp Goring' (the Yeomanry Camp); he was in buoyant form after a strenuous Field Day:

... My poor face was roasted like a chestnut ... We had an amusing day. There were lots of soldiers & pseudo soldiers galloping about ...

On 31st May, Goonie Churchill, Jack's wife, gave birth to her first child, John George. Winston wrote (in the same letter quoted above) to Clementine to give her the news, and taking pains to describe how expeditiously the event had been accomplished. 'It seems to have been a most smooth and successful affair.' He went on:

My dear Bird – this happy event will be a great help to you & will encourage you. I rather shrink from it – because I dont like your having to bear pain & face this ordeal. But we are in the grip of circumstances, and out of pain joy will spring & from passing weakness new strengths arise.

Clementine replied (1st June) that his letter found her

in the schoolroom here, playing games with my small cousins ...

It is wonderful Goonie having her Baby so easily – I feel it is nothing now & only wish there was not another month to wait.

*WSC must have made a mistake, as the latter part of his letter makes it clear that he was writing on 31st May.

Winston and Clementine's first child was born on 11th July 1909 at 33 Eccleston Square. The baby was a girl, and they named her Diana. In a letter later that summer Winston was to write:

Kiss especially the beautiful P.K. [Puppy Kitten] for me. I wonder what she will grow into, & whether she will be lucky or unlucky to have been dragged out of chaos. She ought to have some rare qualities both of mind & body. But these do not always mean happiness or peace. Still I think a bright star shines for her.[7]

These were strangely prescient words. Diana grew up to have an ardent, sensitive nature, and the capacity to give and to love largely, but life brought her much unhappiness and disillusion.

When Diana was about two weeks old, Clementine went to recuperate at 'Carpenters' at Southwater, near Brighton, a small house on the property of the poet Wilfrid Scawen Blunt, who was a great friend of Lady Blanche and her daughters (he was particularly fond of Nellie) and used to lend them 'Carpenters' from time to time. Clementine joined her mother and sister in this charming place, from where she wrote to Winston on 29th August that she found the countryside

quite wild, savage and altogether delightful . . . The butter is yellower, the cream thicker & the honey sweeter . . . than anywhere else in the world.

The baby remained in London with her father, who kept a vigilant eye on nursery matters. '. . . The P.K. is vy well,' he wrote on 31st August,

but the nurse is rather inclined to glower at me as if I was a tiresome interloper. I missed seeing her (the P.K.) take her bath this morning. But tomorrow I propose to officiate!

On 6th September he further reported:

. . . I have just seen the P.K. She is flourishing and weighs 10 tons!

During the ten days Clementine was recuperating at 'Carpenters', Winston managed two fleeting visits to her; in the intervals he made a speech at Leicester, and attended army manoeuvres at Swindon. During this time he wrote her four long letters; her health and strength were (now and always) a preoccupation to him: 'Dearest Clemmie do try to gather your strength,' he wrote on 6th September, in the train on his way back from Swindon –

Don't spend it as it comes. Let it accumulate. Remember my two rules – No walk of more than $\frac{1}{2}$ a mile; no risk of catching cold. There will be so much to do in the autumn & if there is an Election – you will have to play a great part . . . My darling I do so want your life to be a full & sweet one, I want it to be worthy of all the beauties of your nature. I am so much centred in my politics, that I often feel I must be a dull companion, to anyone who is not in the trade too. It gives me so much joy to make you happy – & often wish I were more various in my topics. Still the best is to be true to oneself – unless you happen to have a vy tiresome self! Good night my sweet Clemmie, give my love to your Mamma and Nellinita – and keep yourself the fondest wishes of my heart – now & always.

Although Clementine's confinements were generally straightforward and relatively speedy, the births of her children were always to leave her exhausted and low. The visit to 'Carpenters' did her a great deal of good, but to complete her convalescence she went almost at once to stay with her Aunt Maisie Stanley (now Lady Sheffield, since her husband's accession to the barony) at Alderley Park, Cheshire, this time taking Diana and her nannie with her.

Clementine loved her visits to her Stanley cousins, who had always received her from her earliest years with warmth and kindness. This time she joined an already large family party. 'There are six babies here,' she wrote to Winston on 11th September:

The eldest is 4 years & the youngest 4 days old! None of them are fit to hold a candle to our P.K. or even to unloose the latchet of her shoe.

A day later she had more grist for the mill of parental pride –

Our Nurse is purring with joy because of the compliments which are showered on our P.K. who is universally proclaimed (below stairs) to be the finest specimen ever brought within these walls.[8]

Despite her summer visits, Clementine's health was not fully restored, and in order to consolidate her strength, she spent a few weeks in the early autumn at the Crest Hotel at Crowborough, Sussex, taking with her Diana and her nurse. Here she played some golf, and took up her riding again; this gave her much enjoyment, and was greatly encouraged by Winston. When he came down at the week-ends they rode together, and on her return to London she kept up her riding in Rotten Row, and sometimes had lessons in the Riding School of Knightsbridge Barracks.

But the joys and triumphs of her maternal state did not lessen the attention Clementine gave to public events; and throughout her life, whether at home or away, she was an assiduous reader of the daily newspapers. One of her first letters to Winston from Alderley shows how she was following politics and making her own assessments with a keen eye and penetrating judgment. She noted that Lord Rose-bery's alternative to the Budget proposals – cutting down the Civil Service, spending less on Ireland and encouraging self-reliance and thrift in the working-classes – 'would seem hardly to provide the necessary cash . . .'. And his remark that 'being a Peer . . . I do not regard myself as a financier' drew from Clementine (in view of his marriage to Hannah Rothschild) the somewhat tart observation that

His delicate & refined nature has been kept aloof since early youth (by a thrifty marriage) from the sordid consideration of how to make both ends meet.[9]

The first anniversary of their wedding found Clementine still staying at Alderley, while Winston was on his way to attend the German Army manoeuvres at the personal invitation of the Kaiser. But their thoughts were of each other on 12th September, and from Strasbourg Winston wrote:

My darling Clemmie,

A year to-day my lovely white pussy-cat came to me, & I hope & pray she may find on this September morning no cause – however vague or secret – for regrets.

The bells of this old city are ringing now & they recall to my mind the chimes which saluted our wedding & the crowds of cheering people. A year has gone – and if it has not brought you all the glowing & perfect joy which fancy paints, still it has brought a clear bright light of happiness & some great things.

And from Alderley Clementine wrote:

... The year I have lived with you has been far the happiest in my life & even if it had not been it would have been well worth living.[10]

HOME OFFICE TO ADMIRALTY

I N THE SUMMER OF 1909 Winston had warned Clementine that she would need all her strength and energy later in the year, and he was proved right. Political tension was rising, and public meetings, which in those days drew large audiences, were held throughout the country to plead the rights or wrongs of the Budget. While staying at Alderley in September, Clementine travelled to Birmingham with her great-aunt Lady Sheffield to attend a large meeting addressed by Mr Asquith. These great political meetings never failed to thrill her, and she gloried in the popularity and affection engendered by Winston's reputation as one of the most energetic members of the reforming radical Government. 'The P.M. made a splendid speech,' she wrote the following day.

> The meeting was in a state of wild excitement – We came out by a side door. A steward said to the crowd 'There's Mrs Churchill' and they all cheered The Pug – Two boys leant into the carriage and said 'Give him our love.' Those poor people love and trust you absolutely. I felt so proud.[1]

After vehement debate, reflecting the passion which Lloyd George's proposals had aroused in the country, the Commons finally passed the Finance Bill on 4th November. The Conservatives were powerless against the enormous Liberal majority in the elected Chamber, but they had determined to use their built-in majority in the House of Lords against the Government. The Opposition benches in the Lords were swelled by the presence of 'backwoods peers', who arrived in Westminster in the last days before the crucial debate to take the Oath so that they could join in defeating the infamous 'People's Budget'. On 28th November the Lords rejected the Finance Bill by a large majority, thus shattering the centuries-old tradition that control over the raising and spending of revenue was the exclusive prerogative of the Lower House. The Government thereupon dissolved Parliament and appealed to the country – the Liberals' rallying cry being 'The Peers against the People'.

Winston at once set off, accompanied by Clementine, for a speaking tour in Lancashire and Cheshire. He addressed thronged meetings on the burning issues of the hour in eight towns. At nearly all of them he was constantly interrupted by shrill voices screaming 'Votes for Women!' At Bolton, a young woman hurled a heavy piece of iron, round which was wrapped a political message, at Winston's car. She chose to go to prison for seven days rather than pay the forty-shilling fine.[2]

From 1905 until the outbreak of the First World War, prominent politicians were subject not only to disturbances and interruptions at public meetings, but also to personal physical attacks of quite astonishing violence at the hands of the militant Suffragettes. Churchill never publicly opposed the principle of giving women the right to vote (unlike Asquith, who was unwavering in his antipathy to the idea). Clementine strongly supported the Suffragists, an organisation which sought by legal and constitutional methods to press for the right for women to vote, but which was opposed to the militant, law-breaking activities of the Suffragettes. Although the Suffragists commanded wider and more influential support both from men and women, the Suffragettes caused the greater stir. Clementine publicly declared that she was 'ardently in favour of votes for women'[3] and privately lobbied Winston, but she had ruefully to acknowledge that she was never able to make him support the cause, except in carefully qualified terms. Clementine's disapproval of the violent aspects of the Suffragettes' campaign was, not surprisingly, strengthened by the quite frequent attacks on Winston himself.

An alarming incident had taken place when Winston and Clementine arrived at Bristol Station in November 1909.[4] As they descended from the train and were being greeted by local Liberal notables, a young woman advanced on Winston and attempted to strike him in the face with a riding whip; in self-defence he seized her wrists, whereupon she started to manoeuvre him to the very edge of the platform. The train on which he had travelled was beginning to draw slowly out of the station. Clementine realised the danger instantly and, scrambling over a pile of luggage which was between her and the struggling Winston, seized him by the coat-tails and pulled him back with all her might. The Suffragette was then laid hold of and arrested, but there had been a moment of very real danger, when Winston could easily have been toppled under the train. Such incidents were the constant lot of all prominent members of the Government, and were difficult to guard against because of the fanaticism of the women involved, who courted arrest, and were indifferent to personal pain or injury.

Winston and Clementine (with baby Diana) spent the Christmas of 1909, as was their custom in the early years of their marriage, with a convivial family gathering at Blenheim. In the New Year the General Election campaign launched into full swing. It was Clementine's initiation into the excitements and fatigues of electioneering, and the first of fifteen electoral battles in which she was to take part with Winston over the years. Dundee must have been a somewhat bleak and bitter battleground at that season; but she was not a Scot for nothing, and the fight evoked all her enthusiasm and energy. But although Winston scored a handsome victory in Dundee, the Government overall lost 104 seats – the great Liberal majority of 1906 had vanished.

Mr Asquith now had to rely on the votes of the 82 Irish Nationalists and 40 Labour Members of Parliament in the hard struggle which lay ahead to secure the Budget, and the Government's programme as a whole.

The Prime Minister immediately reconstructed his Government, and appointed

Churchill Home Secretary. At thirty-five, he was the youngest holder of that office since Sir Robert Peel.

*

When Churchill went to the Home Office in February 1910, he took with him all his reforming zeal, and an essentially humane attitude towards those who lie in gaol. It had been his own experience to suffer imprisonment, and to his ardent temperament the loss of personal freedom seemed the blackest of all curses.

He was less than two years at the Home Office, but in that time he did much to forward the then comparatively novel idea that the reform of the criminal was more important than mere punishment. He sought to humanise conditions in the over-crowded gaols, and to improve the treatment of young prisoners. Although he was totally out of sympathy with the methods of the Suffragettes, he considered that they should be treated more as prisoners-of-war than criminals; he therefore instituted a new category of 'political prisoner', which carried with it certain amenities and privileges. But since 1909 the Suffragettes had adopted the new tactic of going on hunger strike as soon as they were arrested, and as Home Secretary Winston had to follow his predecessor in authorising forcible feeding (a brutal and disgusting process) to prevent women, bent on martyrdom, from dying of starvation.

One of the most onerous duties of the Home Secretary was the grim responsi-bility for the signing of death sentences. Clementine remembered how heavily this burden weighed upon Winston, and she recalled with what scrupulous attention he sifted every case. Of the forty-three cases which came before him, he recommended clemency for twenty-one persons.

The Home Secretary at that time held a wide brief: he was responsible for the well-being of seven million people in factories and workshops, and a million more in the mines. Churchill was able to effect major improvements in working conditions and safety in the mines; he tried (but failed) to limit the appallingly long hours then worked by shop assistants; and he shared the task of seeing through the House of Commons Lloyd George's National Insurance Act of 1911 – the apogee of the Liberal Government's social reforms.

But the prime duty of the Home Secretary is the maintenance of law and order, and these last years of peace on the international scene were marked in Britain by domestic strife. In the summer of 1910 the country entered upon two years of mount-ing industrial unrest, increasingly accompanied by violence. It was here that the Home Secretary had to take critical decisions to maintain order and to prevent loss of life.

It was against this background of swiftly moving events, dramatic incidents and political argument that Clementine led the first few years of her married life. At a time when most women are preoccupied with arranging their first home, and brooding over their first baby, her interest and energy had other pressing claims as well. Right from the start of her married life she learned to live with crisis and controversy. Looking back, one can see it was a fitting training for the more sombre, deadly days that lay ahead.

The hazards and excitements of political life, and the joys of marriage and motherhood, were not, moreover, unalloyed by anxieties. By the prevailing standards of the times, Winston and Clementine were by no means well off. Although when they moved into Eccleston Square, which was to be their home for nearly four years, they had a household of five, this was not, by any contemporary yardstick, a lavish establishment for their particular station in life; and they lived in a world of people who were, in the main, much better off than themselves.

Neither Winston nor Clementine possessed any significant personal fortune; Winston earned somewhat less than their keep by his ministerial salary, and by his writings. He could already command quite large sums as a writer, but politics and the demands of high office severely curtailed his activities as an author. In his bachelor days, Winston had constantly been short of money, but it is one thing for a young Cavalry officer to have debts, and quite another for a Cabinet Minister, with a wife and family to support and a position to keep up, to be encumbered financially.

Clementine had always been accustomed to manage on very little money for herself, but she soon discovered that it was a teasing problem housekeeping for an extravagant and – although loving – a most inconsiderate husband. Often at very short notice Winston would announce that he was bringing home several cronies to dinner. Few wives (and fewer cooks) will endure such behaviour. It made housekeeping not only exasperating, but also needlessly expensive, and very soon in their married life Clementine found herself beset with financial difficulties. She had a proud and independent spirit and was meticulous in all money matters; above all, she dreaded accepting favours from the very rich. Her mother, although always short of money and an inveterate gambler, had brought her children up to have an unmercenary attitude towards wealth. She despised money-grubbing ways and the asking of favours and, badly off though she was, she would never allow anxieties about money to dominate either her thoughts or her conversation. 'Never talk rich, never talk poor, never talk money,' she used to say.

But within a few months of her marriage, Clementine found herself preoccupied with money worries and struggling to make ends meet. Unpaid bills were a nightmare anxiety to her, but it was one which was to haunt her continually, and constant money troubles had a wearing effect on her health and spirits. Winston, of course, felt the burden of his financial difficulties too, but he was so deeply engrossed by other and larger problems that they only preoccupied him at intervals. Moreover, his confidence in his ability to provide by his pen, and his generally optimistic outlook, let him off more lightly.

Although Clementine had an inborn tendency to worry about many things, causing her anguish which a more carefree, happy-go-lucky spirit would have been spared, one cannot but be thankful, on looking back, for her sensitivity and watchfulness. The British public has always expected high standards of probity. from its public figures; had Winston married a feckless woman who could shrug off such inconveniences as unpaid bills, or who would easily have accepted favours from her husband's rich friends or admirers, who knows if some worldly catastrophe might not have left a tarnish, which might have forever hampered, if not ruined, Winston's political career?

Soon Clementine also discovered in Winston a trait which was to be a cause of deep anxiety to her throughout their life together – he loved gambling. Clementine was a good spender – when she had the money to spend – but she loathed gambling. To her it was a senseless, almost wicked waste of money, and it was her fate in life to be surrounded by gamblers. Her mother, her brother, her sister and her husband were all, to varying degrees, gamblers. Over the years, she schooled herself to display a tolerance of gambling which she did not feel, and she suffered both anxiety and unhappiness on this score.

By nature shy and reserved, all the circumstances of Clementine's childhood and youth had combined to accentuate these characteristics. Her shyness she soon conquered, and the civilised education she had received, and her lively intelligence, amply equipped her for the political and social world into which her marriage brought her. She could quickly break the ice of any conversation, and people warmed to her spontaneity, liveliness and charm.

But although Clementine's manner was warm and friendly, her inner reserve never left her, and, throughout her life, she fended off attempts to make intimate relationships. She never felt the need, as so many women do, for confidential gossipings; and she could keep her own counsel even with close friends. In these early years of marriage, as in later years, Clementine focused all her energy and interest upon Winston, his career and their home.

She had two staunch friends from before her marriage – Sylvia Henley (Stanley) and Horatia Seymour, both of whom were greatly liked by Winston – and it was happy and fortunate that Clementine and Jack's wife, Goonie, should have from the start made friends, for the brothers were devoted to each other.

Goonie Churchill's loveliness was of the sort that does not depend essentially on features or dramatic colouring – it was not easily definable. Lord David Cecil after her death recalled 'her subtle twilight beauty'. Cultivated and well-read, she had a puckish sense of humour which was devoid of any touch of malice, and she distilled a sense of enchantment. She had a rare power of sympathy, and in her Clementine found an affectionate, loyal and companionable sister-in-law.

At the start of their married life Winston and Clementine had few friends in common. This was not surprising, since their paths had rarely crossed, and Winston was ten years older than Clementine. She approached his close friends with understandable wariness. A great friend of Winston's was Violet Asquith, the Prime Minister's daughter by his first wife. Winston and she had first met in 1906, and they had established a close and confidential friendship. On his many visits to No. 10, Winston used to 'drop in' to see Violet in her sitting-room on his way to or from Cabinet meetings; he greatly enjoyed her company; she had a brilliant mind, and was as passionately interested as he was in the high politics of the day. When Winston married, she extended her friendship to Clementine and – as the years went on – increasingly her affection and esteem.

But now in these early days, Clementine felt an understandable reserve towards this well-ensconced friend of Winston's. Moreover, Violet's bosom companion was Venetia Stanley (Clementine's cousin, and Sylvia Henley's younger sister). Venetia had a strong personality, and her standards and outlook were in many ways the antithesis of Clementine's. In the Violet–Venetia combination Clementine sensed a threat; and she felt that in any difficulties between her and Winston, she would not find support from that quarter.

Clementine must have found it difficult at first to accept without question or uneasiness the frequent absences – short though they were – which Winston's work and pace of life made inevitable. No clue exists to the circumstances of the little tiff which drew from Winston the following vigorous and moving protestation. The reasons for it have long since vanished into oblivion; but it shows that Clementine could nurse jealous fears:

. . . Dearest it worries me vy much that you should seem to nurse such absolutely wild suspicions wh are so dishonouring to all the love & loyalty I bear you & will please god bear you while I breathe. They are unworthy of you & me. And they fill my mind with feelings of embarrassment to wh I have been a stranger since I was a schoolboy. I know that they originate in the fond love you have for me, and therefore they make me feel tenderly towards you & anxious always to deserve that most precious possession of my life. But at the same time they depress me & vex me – & without reason.

We do not live in a world of small intrigues, but of serious & important affairs. I could not conceive myself forming any other attachment than that to which I have fastened the happiness of my life here below. And it offends my best nature that you should – against your true instinct – indulge small emotions & wounding doubts. You ought to trust me for I do not love & will never love any woman in the world but you and my chief desire is to link myself to you week by week by bonds which shall ever become more intimate & profound.

Beloved I kiss your memory – your sweetness & beauty have cast a glory upon my life.

> You will find me always
> Your loving & devoted husband
> W[5]

As for Winston's men friends, Clementine viewed them too with shyness and caution. His closest political colleague was Lloyd George, whom she admired, but even now, vaguely mistrusted. But Winston's greatest personal friend was F.E. Smith. Their friendship had begun and prospered despite the party issues which divided them deeply; it was to endure, unwavering, until F.E.'s early death in 1930, at the age of fifty-eight. Clementine never took to this brilliant and unusual man, and from the first she disapproved of his influence upon Winston politically. Moreover, she thought F.E. encouraged Winston to gamble. They were fellow officers in the Oxfordshire Yeomanry, and Clementine learned to dread the camps, for they afforded opportunities for gambling. Winston often lost a good deal of money. F.E. could always recoup his losses by some brilliant brief, but no such means of replenishment was open to Winston. Conversely, however, Clementine greatly liked and admired F.E.'s wife, Margaret.

Winston's friendship with F. E. Smith was particularly remarkable in view of the bitterness of party strife at that time; and it was much disapproved of in some quarters. Both Clementine and Margaret Smith were approached on several occasions by Liberals or Conservatives and each asked to use their wifely influence to wean their respective husbands away from a friendship which was considered politically harmful.

Clementine had often to suffer the company of people she did not really like, either friends of Winston's or else relations to whom she never warmed. Into this category came Lord Wimborne (who had married Winston's aunt, Lady Cornelia Spencer-Churchill) and his sons Ivor and Freddie Guest, who were not only Winston's first cousins, but also his great friends; and more particularly Freddie Guest, who was his exact contemporary. Unfortunately Clementine could never abide them. Nevertheless, in the first years of their married life she was often in their company, for both Lord and Lady Wimborne and their sons invariably showed kindness and hospitality to both Winston and Clementine. She generally managed to conceal her feelings, but despite good and loyal intentions, her antipathy sooner or later revealed itself.

There was a scene on one occasion when Winston and Clementine were staying with the Wimbornes at Canford Manor. During bridge after dinner, Ivor Guest lost his temper, and threw his cards at Clementine's head; not surprisingly, she left the card table and went upstairs to bed. The next day, despite profuse apologies from the contrite Ivor, she insisted on returning to London, taking Winston (one suspects rather reluctantly) with her. Clementine undoubtedly took things too much to heart, and when she was aroused her reflex actions were swift and determined.

These difficulties which Clementine experienced with some of Winston's friends in these early days were to be a feature all through her life. Her highly developed critical faculty made it hard for her to accept and enjoy people at their face value. And this trait in her character, combined with her inborn reserve, was to be the cause of much loneliness in a life which, to the casual observer, would appear to be teeming with friends.

It was fortunate for Clementine (and indeed for Winston too) that purely social life held no charms for her. Immersed as Winston was in politics, it might well have led to a rift, if she had yearned for the bright lights of the ballrooms, or had wanted to swim with the tide of the social season. From time to time Winston would for a few days enjoy the life of the great country houses, and the sports and pleasures of the social world into which he had been born, and from which his ardent pursuit of politics had made him a cheerful exile. When he hunted, he enjoyed hunting; when he shot, he enjoyed shooting, and he did both remarkably well, for one who had so little practice.

One such occasion was in December 1910, when Winston stayed for a few days at Warter Priory in Yorkshire (the home at that time of the Nunburnholme family). Clementine had been kept at home by a cold. Winston wrote to her of his visit:

... A nice party – puissant, presentable, radical in preponderance – a rare combination. I wish you were here ... Nearly all men. Tweedmouth, Elcho, Lovatt, Cowley, daughters of the House, Granards. Tomorrow pheasants in thousands – the vy best wot ever was seen. Tonight Poker – I lost a little – but the play was low.

On the whole survey, how much more power and great business are to me, than this kind of thing, pleasant tho it seems by contrast to our humble modes of entertainment.

I expect I will have a headache tomorrow night after firing so many cartridges. All the glitter of the world appeals to me: but not thank God in comparison with serious things.

How naughty of the Kat to be enrhumed. Tell Beauchamp [the doctor] to telegraph fully and take the greatest care. I will be back on Weds. . .

The letter was signed, 'Your pug in clover, W.'[6]

Clementine wrote back on 20th December:

My Own Darling Pug,

Now that I feel better, I do so wish I was at Warter with you enjoying the Flesh Pots of Egypt! It sounds a delightful party and your frivolous Kat would have purred with pleasure . . . Dearest you work so hard and have so little fun in your life. I wish you had more of this sort of thing. But I would not have liked to marry a Cowley or a Granard, or Even a Lovat (tho' I should *then* have had porridge every morning and not only when I go to Dundee) . . .

One feels in these letters that although both Winston and Clementine could enjoy these fleeting distractions, they were more like spectators looking in on a brilliantly lighted scene. They gladly returned to the blustery weather outside.

*

In April 1910 the House of Lords finally passed the bitterly-contested 'People's Budget'. However, this brought no end to political strife, because the Liberals were determined to break the power of the Lords to veto legislation passed by the Commons, and they at once introduced the Parliament Bill designed to accomplish this purpose. King Edward died in May, but national mourning, which was deep and real, brought only a brief respite to the parliamentary struggle.

The atmosphere of clash and crisis was not confined to Westminster. The late summer saw mounting unrest in the country, and although Winston and Clementine were able to get away in late August for a cruise in Baron de Forest's yacht, they returned home early, and Winston was able to take part in the army manoeuvres with the Yeomanry. Clementine wrote to him from London:

I am thinking of you galloping about on Salisbury Plain in this delicious crisp weather & wishing you were Commander in Chief on the eve of war instead of Home Secretary on the brink of an Autumn Session. I hope your horse is good & I am sure my sweet Pug looks more amber than ever in his lovely new russet clothes . . .[7]

Winston had then to grapple with the mounting industrial strife: 30,000 miners went on strike in the Rhondda and Aberdare valleys. The strikes were accompanied by rioting and often looting, and proved beyond the power of the local police forces to control. The General Commanding Southern Command on his own initiative ordered troops into the area. Anxious to avoid the fearful possibility of armed troops clashing with civilians, Churchill sent in a strong force of Metropolitan Police, who restored order at Tonypandy by wielding their rolled-up mackintoshes among the rioters. Nevertheless, this aroused the fury of the Left wing, and the whole incident became grossly distorted, 'Tonypandy' throughout his career being used as a stick with which to belabour Winston. The Right, on the other hand, took him severely to task for doing too little – so he was roundly abused by both sides.

Drama and action seemed to attend Winston for most of his life – sometimes they were of his own making; and a good example of this is his own participation in an extraordinary incident which took place in early January 1911, which became known as the 'Battle of Sidney Street'. Some notorious anarchists barricaded themselves into a house, fired on the police, and were successfully resisting all attempts to dislodge them. Authority was sought of the Home Secretary for troops to be sent. Churchill gave the necessary permission, and characteristically hurried himself to the scene of battle to share the excitements and the responsibilities. After a fierce resistance by the cornered men, the house – No. 100 Sidney Street – caught fire; Churchill used his authority to prevent the Fire Brigade intervening, and two bodies were later found in the smoking ruins. He was sharply criticised in Parliament and trounced by the press for his presence and intervention during the affray. Clementine was early on receiving some sharp lessons in the vagaries and hazards of political life.

The All-Party Constitutional Conference called by the King in June 1910 had failed utterly to find a workable compromise. Mr Asquith therefore decided to hold a General Election specifically on the issue of the reform of the House of Lords. He had wrung from the uneasy King a secret pledge that if the Liberal Party won the forthcoming election, and the House of Lords obstructed the passage of the Parliament Bill, the King would create sufficient new peers to ensure the passing of the measure in the Upper House.

On 28th November 1910 Parliament was dissolved, and the country was faced with a second General Election within a year. Although Clementine was expecting her second child, she played her part in the campaign. Winston held his seat at Dundee with a slightly smaller majority than in the previous February. The overall result of the General Election was to leave the balance of power between the parties practically unchanged.

After the Election, Winston went for a few days' rest to Alderley, staying with Clementine's Stanley relations. But she herself had to remain in London, nursing a heavy cold which threatened to settle on her chest. Winston, although absent, was not forgetful, as Clementine's letter shows:

My Own Darling,
    After lunching with your Mamma today and doing a little Christmas shopping I again returned to bed – I dozed off – When I woke up, imagine my surprise and delight to see my room transformed into a Paradise of exquisite flowers and a lovely melon sitting near the bed. You are a sweet Darling Lamb Bird!! . . .[8]

Winston and Clementine's tender devotion for each other was plain for all to see,

and we have a charming glimpse of them lunching with Wilfrid Scawen Blunt in the
late summer of 1909:

> . . . We lunched in the garden, and sat on there after it till four o'clock, discussing
> nearly all the great questions of the day . . . I like him much. He is *aux plus petits
> soins* with his wife, taking all possible care of her. They are a very happy married
> pair. Clementine was afraid of wasps, and one settled on her sleeve, and Winston
> gallantly took the wasp by the wings and thrust it into the ashes of the fire . . .[9]

Mr Blunt gives us another peep into the young Churchills' connubial bliss when he
lunched with them later that same year:

> . . . we had a merry rattling hour and a half before he was obliged to go back to his
> office, with intervals of domestic felicity, his baby [Diana] being brought in with
> the coffee. There is no more fortunate man than Winston at home or in his
> political prosperity . . .[10]

During the spring of 1911, in the last month or two before the birth of their
second child (dubbed the 'Chumbolly'), Winston and Clementine spent Easter at
Blenheim together. Later that April Clementine went by herself to stay with Lord
and Lady Sheffield at Penrhos, Holyhead. She was always happy staying with Aunt
Maisie and her family, and this visit helped to while away the last weeks of waiting.
'I am counting the days till May 15th when the Chumbolly is due,' she wrote on
18th April, adding – 'I hope he will not have inherited the Pug's unpunctual habits.'
In the event, the baby kept her waiting a fortnight. But then all was rejoicing, for on
28th May their second child, and only son, Randolph, was born at their home in
Eccleston Square.

A few days after this exciting event in their family life, Winston had to go into
camp with his Yeomanry at Blenheim, but his thoughts were constantly with
Clementine. Writing on 2nd June from Blenheim Camp, he described the beauty of
the park in high summer, and the agreeable gay company assembled. He went on:

> Many congratulations are offered me upon the son. With that lack of jealousy wh
> ennobles my nature, I lay them all at your feet.
>
> My precious pussy cat, I do trust & hope that you are being good, & not sitting
> up or fussing yourself. Just get well & strong & enjoy the richness wh this new
> event will I know have brought into your life. The Chumbolly must do his duty
> and help you with your milk, you are to tell him so from me. At his age greediness
> & even swinishness at table are virtues . . .

Clementine wrote back the next day:

> Blenheim sounds gay & entrancing, & I long to be there sharing all the fun &
> glitter. But I am very happy here, contemplating the beautiful Chumbolly who
> grows more darling & handsome every hour, & puts on weight with every meal;
> so that soon he will be a little round ball of fat.
>
> Just now I was kissing him, when catching sight of my nose he suddenly
> fastened upon it & began to suck it, no doubt thinking it was another part of my
> person![11]

Winston hated to feel out of touch with family affairs:

A telephone message was received this morning that all was well with you: but no telegram from you. Tell the nurse to send one every day without fail . . .

he directed in his letter on 4th June.

Clementine's letters during this period breathe happiness and contentment.

33 Eccleston Square, S.W.
Whit Sunday Evening [4 June 1911]

My Sweet Beloved Winston,

The Chumbolly & I are both very well. It is a lovely calm evening after a most sultry airless day & I have been thinking of you with pleasure among the green trees & cool waters . . .

I am so happy with you my Dear. You have so transformed my life that I can hardly remember what it felt like three years ago before I knew you. Goodbye Dearest One.

Your own loving
Clemmie

Please be a good Pug & not destroy the good of your little open air holiday by smoking too many fat cigars. This recommendation comes rather late!

The Coronation of King George V was to take place on 22nd June, just over three weeks after the birth of her baby. Clementine had resigned herself some time before to missing the ceremony in Westminster Abbey, as she would not have been strong enough to endure the hours of waiting and standing which such an occasion entails; nor could she have left her precious new baby so long unsustained. However, during an audience some weeks previously the King had enquired of Winston how his wife was and, on hearing that to her great disappointment Clementine would be unable to attend the Coronation, with charming thoughtfulness and solicitude, His Majesty made special and exceptional arrangements, which enabled Clementine after all to be present at what is one of the most moving, grandiose and beautiful ceremonies – the crowning of the Sovereign. A royal brougham called for her at her house and drove her to Westminster Abbey, so that she arrived at the latest possible moment; she watched the ceremony until after the actual crowning of the King, then she slipped discreetly away and was driven home to the hungering Randolph. This was the first of three Coronations at which both Winston and Clementine were destined to be present.

The day after the Coronation Clementine was also able to go with Winston when he accompanied the King and Queen on the first of their Coronation State Drives through London. A day or two later she went with the children and their nurse to Seaford, where they all spent a happy sunshine month. As she had spent part of her childhood at Seaford, the neighbourhood was well known to her. Nor did she lack for company: her mother was there too, staying with an old friend, Mrs Jack, of whom Clementine also was very fond. There were other friends besides, and old acquaintances it gave her pleasure to find and see again. It was a restful, idyllic interlude.

Winston kept her regularly informed about his doings. He had accompanied the King and Queen on another of the Coronation 'royal progresses', and he gave Clementine a diverting account of his drive, his two carriage companions being the Duchess of Devonshire and the Countess of Minto:

. . . Of course all the whole route I was cheered and in places booed vigorously. It was rather embarrassing for these two Tory dames. They got awfully depressed when the cheering was vy loud, but bucked up a little around the Mansion House where there were hostile demonstrations.[12]

The King, Winston told Clementine, had been most friendly, and the Queen had asked solicitously after her and had 'urged the importance of a full rest before beginning gaieties . . .'

Winston had also given dinner to Lloyd George at the Café Royal; they had had a very good talk, and had 'renewed treaties of alliance for another seven years'. Lloyd George had been

full of your praises – said you were my 'salvation' and that your beauty was the least thing about you . . .[13]

But for Winston this summer of 1911 was a time of crisis. Despite the verdict of two General Elections, the Conservatives struggled on bitterly through the long sweltering summer to defeat the Parliament Bill. There were scenes of unparalleled hysteria in both Houses before the Government made public the King's pledge to create enough Liberal peers to ensure the passage of the Bill: only then did the Lords surrender.

Meanwhile, an ominous warning note was sounded from abroad. London society was in a whirl of Coronation celebrations when, in June, Germany galvanised Europe by sending a gunboat to Agadir, as a challenge to French claims to Morocco. On 21st July, in a speech at the Mansion House, Lloyd George in measured terms warned Germany that if she intended war she would find England against her. During those sultry weeks the threat of war crystallised as a reality: the moment of danger passed, but to those who could read the omens aright, this incident meant only one thing – that Germany was bent on trouble, and that her expanding economic vitality and growing physical power made her a grave threat to the peace of Europe.

Winston's mind ever roved over a wide field, and his interest and superabundant energy were never confined to matters relating solely to his office-of-the-moment. Even in his earliest days as a minister, at first concerned with Colonial Affairs, and then with various aspects of social reform, he had always shown a keen interest in military and naval affairs. Ever since the days of his childhood, when he passed hours at a time manoeuvring his armies of tin soldiers on the schoolroom floor, military tactics, movements and problems had always held an intense fascination for him. And later, the days he spent in camp with the Yeomanry always brought this inborn preoccupation to the surface. In a letter to Clementine from Camp Goring on 31st May 1909, Winston had confided to her:

. . . Do you know I would greatly like to have some practice in the handling of large forces. I have much confidence in my judgment on things, when I see clearly, but on nothing do I seem to *feel* the truth more than in tactical combinations. It is a vain and foolish thing to say – but *you* will not laugh at it. I am sure I have the root of the matter in me – but never I fear in this state of existence will it have a chance of flowering – in bright red blossom.

But if his pulses raced at the excitement of these exercises and the epic aspects of war – he saw clearly behind the wheeling columns the savagery and tragedy. When later that same summer he had attended the German manoeuvres, and received marked attention from the Kaiser, he had written to Clementine of the deep impression this display of military might had made upon him (15th September 1909):

This army is a terrible engine. It marches sometimes 35 miles in a day. It is in number as the sands of the sea . . . Much as war attracts me & fascinates my mind with its tremendous situations – I feel more deeply every year – & can measure the feeling here in the midst of arms – what vile and wicked folly and barbarism it all is.

In the winter of 1908–9, Winston had joined Lloyd George in heated denunciations of the greatly increased Naval Estimates, which provided for the building of extra Dreadnoughts (the most powerful battleships hitherto known), believing that Germany at that time did not constitute a threat to Britain, and that the country could not afford the extra battleships as well as the great social reforms they had at heart. Since then the Agadir crisis brought into sharp focus the need to consider in a different light all matters concerning the country's defence. And Winston's sense of priorities continued to change in direct relation to the altered international situation. The Navy and the organisation of the Admiralty caused him increasing disquiet; and his preoccupations over this were shared by the Prime Minister.

But his immediate concern and responsibility as Home Secretary was the preservation of law and order, which all through this summer were threatened as industrial disruption increased. In June there was a seamen's strike, and a dock strike which spread from Southampton to London and other ports.

These events prevented Winston from visiting Clementine and the babies at Seaford as much as he would have wished. He missed them very much: 'This house is vy silent without you; & I am reverting to my bachelor type with melancholy rapidity', he wrote on 29th June.

The dialogue of their letters continued with great regularity: his full of public happenings, hers on a quieter theme. Plans were made for the Chumbolly christening in the autumn. Winston suggested that they should invite Sir Edward Grey, the Foreign Secretary, to be a godfather; this shy, withdrawn and, since his wife's tragic death a few years earlier, sad man was touchingly fond of the young Churchills. In accepting their invitation he wrote on 28th June 1911:

. . . My best wishes will always be with him & I hope he will never cease to contribute to the happiness of your home which it always rejoices me to see.

The other godparents were F. E. Smith and the Wimbornes' daughter, Lady Ridley.

The Chumbolly was duly christened in the Crypt of the House of Commons on 26th October 1911, and given the names of Randolph Frederick Edward.

As Diana's second birthday approached, Winston was charged with the important task of procuring a suitable present for her. On 11th July he wrote to report progress:

My dearest one,

I bought some toys for the P.K. last night – but she is so little that it is vy difficult to know what will amuse her. Be careful not to let her suck the paint off the Noah's Ark Animals. I hovered long on the verge of buying plain white wood animals but decided at last to risk the coloured ones. They are so much more interesting. The Shopman expressed himself hopefully about the nourishing qualities of the paint & of the numbers sold – and presumably sucked without misadventure. But do not trust to this . . .

It is interesting, and touching, to see from these letters how much Winston participated in a most 'modern' way in the lives of his small children; it certainly was not typical of the time. Perhaps it shows how deeply he had felt the great distance which separated him as a child from his parents.

After nearly a month at Seaford with her nursery, Clementine returned home to London, where she stayed a fortnight before going off with Goonie to Garmisch, a resort high in the Bavarian Alps, to complete her convalescence after Randolph's birth. Various enjoyable projects for Winston and Clementine to go away together after the rising of the House feature in their letters to each other; but in the end none of these agreeable plans came to fruition, for events on the home front demanded his presence and attention. The strikes in the docks had been quickly succeeded by partial strikes by railwaymen, which in turn escalated into a general railway strike in August; there were stoppages in the London markets, and there was a serious threat that food supplies generally might be jeopardised. These grave troubles were the source of several violent incidents.

Clementine would certainly have accepted the scrapping of their holiday plans with a good grace; she must have shared the general anxiety over events and, indeed, preferred to be with Winston at a time when he bore such a burden of responsibility himself. This, however, must have been one of her early experiences of the uncertainties and inconveniences of political life in general, and of life with Winston in particular. In the course of years, over and over again some agreeable project, or carefully planned holiday, had to be abandoned, or drastically altered.

Fortunately Clementine had a highly developed sense of duty and an order of priorities in all matters concerning public affairs or Winston's political obligations, and invariably accepted last-minute cancellations and changes of plan philosophically. But she was to suffer many real disappointments, particularly when a little holiday à deux had been planned, or a cosy spell with the family at the seaside. Sometimes, however, her feelings of disappointment would have a tinge of bitterness, for although often it was a question of crisis or public duty, there were occasions when Winston simply changed his mind, or could not bear to tear himself away from the hub of events, even when he was not directly involved.

*

Late in September 1911, Winston and Clementine went to Scotland. It was customary, then as now, for senior Cabinet Ministers to be invited for a day or two to Balmoral Castle in Aberdeenshire, and Winston planned to combine his formal ministerial visit to the King with a descent upon Dundee to attend to constituency affairs. He and Clementine had also been invited by the Prime Minister and Mrs Asquith to spend a few days with them at Archerfield, on the East Lothian coast. While Winston was at Balmoral (it not being the custom for ministers' wives to be invited), Clementine paid a visit to her grandmother at Airlie Castle.

Once a source of awe to her, Clementine could by this time view her formidable grandmother (now eighty-one) with detached amusement. On 25th September she wrote to Winston:

I hope you are happy my sweet Pug and that you are being properly petted, & that you will secure a huge stag. I am very happy here – Granny is become much kinder with age tho' she points out all my defects for my 'good'. She, like you, finds my handwriting detestable and observes while looking at me severely and stroking her lace lappets, that 'a gentlewoman of consequence should not write like a housemaid'. She is going to give me samples of the handwritings she most admires so that I may try & copy them – Lord Melbourne and Lord Palmerston are her favourite guides in this.

She sends you her love & is looking forward to seeing you on Wednesday for luncheon which is at 1.30 *to the second by Greenwich time*. Afterwards we fly away to Archerfield in the new motor . . .

The 'new motor' was a great event in the family: a red Napier, it had cost £610, and in Winston's letters to Clementine while she had been in Austria he had expatiated upon its wonders and comforts. It was due to be delivered to him at Balmoral, whence he would drive to Airlie Castle to pick up Clementine.

During their stay at Archerfield with Mr and Mrs Asquith, there hung over Winston and Clementine the tantalising question of the designation of the new First Lord of the Admiralty. The need for a change at the Admiralty had been clear since the Agadir crisis. There were two obvious candidates for this glittering post – Lord Haldane, at present Secretary of State for War, whose reorganisation of that Ministry had been acclaimed – and Winston himself. In addition to other weighty recommendations, Lord Haldane was a close and long-time friend of the Prime Minister. Piquancy was lent to the situation when Lord Haldane (who lived in the neighbourhood) paid two long visits to Archerfield, and was closeted with Mr Asquith.

Winston was far from confident that he would be offered the post, and Lord Haldane's visits made him even more uncertain. One evening he confided his fears to Clementine. On a sudden impulse she opened the Bible which, as in most Scottish houses of the day, was in their bedroom and, after a brief pause, she said to Winston, 'I know it's all right about the Admiralty,' and she read him the passage she had lit upon at random. It was the verse from the 107th Psalm – 'They that go down to the sea in ships, that do business in great waters.'

Before the end of their visit, Mr Asquith offered Winston the post he so earnestly desired – First Lord of the Admiralty. Lord Haldane remained for the time being at the War Office, becoming Lord Chancellor in June 1912. It is agreeable to relate that Winston and he worked together at their vital posts closely and harmoniously.

Churchill's appointment was announced on 24th October 1911. He flung himself into this new and coveted job with ardour and confidence. Here was the work for which all his talents fitted him, the task for which he was destined – the defence of Britain.

AT THE ADMIRALTY

A NEW MINISTRY brings fresh contacts and a different sphere of duty and activity to the minister's wife as well as to himself. Agreeables must be exchanged between herself and the wives of her husband's new colleagues (and in those days more time and importance were devoted to those social amenities); there may be an official house to inspect and inhabit; and, apart from all these obligations, a minister's wife is always in demand to play her part in the good works, social functions and entertaining which automatically pertain to a government department.

Clementine had always thrown herself with energy and enthusiasm into whatever duties of this sort came her way. Whether it was visiting Labour Exchanges, attending socials, visiting prisons, or giving away prizes at police sports, it was all part and parcel of her day's work as Winston's wife. Her natural liveliness and the genuine interest she felt in all these different jobs made lighter work for her, and evoked warmth from the people she met.

But however interesting the work of civilian departments may be, there is no doubt that in the service ministries a dash of panache is added. There is not only the dignity of a government department to be upheld in a decorous manner, but the prestige and public image of the particular service is involved; and each looks after its own with meticulous care. None more so than the Navy which, as someone once remarked, 'always travels First Class'. And indeed, one of Clementine's first engagements as wife of the First Lord of the Admiralty was a glamorous and enjoyable one: she launched the battleship *Centurion* at Devonport on 18th November 1911.

Until the Great War the Lords Commissioners of the Admiralty, and in particular the First Lord, had at their disposal a steam yacht, the *Enchantress*, in which they could visit the British Navy, which in those days was large, prestigious, and far-flung. Winston made the fullest use of the Admiralty yacht for his naval business, and on many occasions business and pleasure could be combined. Writing of it himself he described how

the Admiralty Yacht *Enchantress* was now to become largely my office, almost my home; and my work my sole occupation and amusement. In all, I spent eight months afloat in the three years before the war. I visited every dockyard, shipyard and naval establishment in the British Isles and in the Mediterranean and every important ship.[1]

When Winston was in the *Enchantress* he was, and felt himself to be, in close touch with the men and ships whose destiny was his special charge.

Another agreeable adjunct to the historic and then still powerful office of First Lord was Admiralty House. Tucked between the Admiralty itself and the Horse Guards buildings, it faces onto both Horse Guards Parade and Whitehall, on which side a courtyard bounded by a stone screen (designed by the brothers Adam) protects the Admiralty and Admiralty House from the ever-increasing hurly-burly of the traffic. Now this beautiful eighteenth century house has been converted into convenient flats for ministers, some of the main rooms being used for government entertaining. But in 1911 it was still the residence of the First Lord of the Admiralty, and must surely have been one of the most desirable and grandly elegant 'tied' houses of all time.

It was entirely to Winston's taste, and indeed to Clementine's, but since they were considerably encumbered financially at this time even by the outgoings of the much smaller house in Eccleston Square, Clementine used all her powers of persuasion – on this occasion with success – to prevail upon Winston to remain in their more humdrum civilian house which could be managed with five servants, rather than to move into the agreeable splendours of Admiralty House, which would require a staff of eleven or twelve. She won a delaying action, for it was not until the spring of 1913 that they made the move and, in the interval, apart from the ground floor, where the reception rooms were kept for official entertainments, the rest of the house was used as offices.

With Winston deeply immersed in his new tasks, and spending much of his time on the *Enchantress*, Clementine took advantage of the opportunity which now presented itself to discover a new (to her) sporting activity – foxhunting. Lithe and lissom, but blessedly without a trace of heartiness, she loved sports and games. We have a romantic and vivid description of her bathing at the seaside from the pen of Neville Lytton, the artist. Visiting his brother and sister-in-law, Lord and Lady Lytton (she was Pamela Plowden – Winston's early love) at Broadstairs in September 1911, he had found Winston and Clementine also staying there. Through his wife, Judith Blunt, he already knew the Hozier family well, and he described beach life in a letter to Nellie Hozier:

> Winston went off to dig castles in the sands and the rest of us bathed. It was a broiling day and the water was heavenly. Clemmie came forth like the reincarnation of Venus re-entering the sea. Her form is most beautiful. I had no idea she had such a splendid body. She joined in a game of water-polo with Victor [Lytton] and me and then she and I swam out half way across the Channel, and had an animated conversation bobbing up and down between the waves . . .[2]

Perhaps in a different set of circumstances Clementine would have become a noted sportswoman; she played both golf and tennis, and of these she shone at the latter; and with her good eye and rock-like steadiness, she was much in demand as a partner.

Now, Clementine leapt at the chance to hunt, which was offered her by several of Winston's friends, and her descriptions of her hunting activities bubble over with the excitement and fun of it all. Her first sporting report was from Blenheim. She wrote to Winston on 3rd January 1912:

> My Darling,
>   I have just come back from a long day's hunting . . . It was the greatest fun – Sunny took charge of me and gave me a lead over the stone walls. We found at once, and had a lovely run over the vale . . . Sunny was most kind, he thinks the little bay mare is a splendid jumper. We went over some quite big places . . . I took all the fences after Sunny. No one was in at the death, but Captain Daly gave me the brush . . .

Below the signature to this letter are four rough drawings – a fox's brush, a couple of fences, and an excited-looking feline labelled 'Kat about to leap'.

Later that winter she paid several visits to Freddie and Amy Guest at Burley-on-the-Hill (the scene of the great fire). Here she had some highly enjoyable hunting, of which she wrote long and entertaining descriptions to Winston. But she missed him and wanted his news:

> Do write to me my darling – I feel a long way off from my Pug down here with the Fox hunting Squires.[3]

Although appreciating their kindness and hospitality, Clementine was never quite on the same wave-length as her hosts, and one of her letters contains the pithy comment,

> Amy is kind, but more Suffragetty, Christian Sciency and Yankee Doodle than ever. Poor Freddie is a sheep in Lion's clothing.[4]

Winston was delighted that she was having so much fun, but it caused him some anxiety, and he expected daily reports, writing on 23rd January 1912:

> I hope you have had a good day – no telegram! bad Cat – but no news is good news. Do not do foolish things.

Clementine replied on the 24th, assuring Winston that she had sent two telegrams the previous day, and adding:

> . . . Lovely hunting yesterday with the Belvoir – lots of fences & a long run. Today I was too tired. But I hope tomorrow to hunt with Mr Ferney's. But Alack it looks like freezing.

Clementine's hunting activities became so important to her that Sir Edward Grey, with whom she used to bicycle energetically whenever Winston and she visited him at his home at Fallodon in Northumberland, wrote to her at about this time:

> I hear such accounts of your prowess in hunting that I fear you will despise a bicycle, & I shall never see you on one any more.[5]

But although she had taken so enthusiastically to this sport, and was to hunt again the following season and on isolated occasions from time to time in the future, these two brief hunting seasons were not to be repeated – sterner days lay so soon ahead.

Although Churchill's prime preoccupation was now with the Navy, his attention and interest roamed over the whole field of domestic and foreign affairs. National security was his over-riding concern, and the prospect of violence and civil war in Ireland now loomed ever closer. Home Rule for Ireland had been an explosive ingredient in British politics ever since Mr Gladstone had espoused the cause in 1886. Lord Randolph Churchill himself had rallied the Protestant North with the cry 'Ulster will fight and Ulster will be right'. In 1912 the Liberals introduced the third Home Rule Bill; because of the Parliament Act, the House of Lords could now only delay, but not prevent, its passage, and the militant Ulstermen thereupon determined that they would resist it by force.

Winston was one of the Government's chief spokesmen on the Irish question, and early in 1912 plans were made for him to address a rally in Belfast, the very heart and centre of the Unionist North, where was focused all the passionate determination of the Protestants never to submit to rule by a Catholic parliament in Dublin. The Ulster Hall, the only building suitable for a large gathering, had been booked by the Orangemen * for the night before Winston was due to speak, and it was known that they intended to remain in the Hall overnight and, if necessary, to hold it by force. The Ulster Liberal Association retaliated by hiring the Celtic Football Ground on the outskirts of Belfast, where they proposed to erect a vast tent to accommodate the meeting.

The situation was so tense that the civil and military authorities tried to dissuade Winston from going, but he was determined upon it: ' "coute que coute" ', he wrote to Clementine on 23rd January 1912, 'I shall begin punctually at 8 o'clock on 8th February to speak on Home Rule in Belfast.' Clementine approved his determination, and decided to accompany him, even though the organisers of the meeting were doubtful of the wisdom of her coming, and several people tried to dissuade her – Winston warned her (24th January), 'Do not be too venturesome hunting. Keep some of your luck unused.' But her courage was equalled by good sense, for she believed that her presence at the meeting would probably discourage violence.

Winston and Clementine set out for this momentous occasion on the evening of 7th February 1912, crossing from Stranraer on the night ferry. They hardly had a wink of sleep because some Suffragettes who were on board ran round and round the decks all night shrieking 'Votes for Women'. When they berthed at Larne at half-past seven on the morning of 8th February, they found the walls surrounding the quay placarded with anti-Home Rule slogans and a large hostile crowd who hooted at them as they disembarked and sang 'Rule Britannia' and the National Anthem. Another unfriendly reception from a great crowd awaited them at the station in Belfast.

They spent the several hours before the meeting at the Grand Central Hotel,

*Orangemen are members of a Protestant political organisation originating in the eighteenth century. They were and are noted for their vigorous and intolerant Protestantism.

and by the evening the crowd outside – Unionist to a man – had swelled to some 10,000 people.

As they started on their long drive to the Celtic Football Ground, the crowd surged round the car and, despite the strong escort of police, very nearly overturned it. As the cars in the cortège slowly made their way through the milling mass, men thrust their heads through the windows, uttering menaces.[6]

This was Clementine's first experience of mass hostility and must have been extremely frightening to her. But despite her initial natural alarm, she remained steadfastly at Winston's side throughout the day. She later told George Riddell (later Lord Riddell, newspaper proprietor and diarist) that when they were in the car with the crowd pressing round them,

> . . . she was not afraid of being killed, but feared she might be disfigured for life by the glass of the motor being broken or by some other means . . .[7]

She also observed Winston's calm, remarking that 'the opposition and threats seemed to "ginger him up" '.[8]

It must have been a bewildering sensation to experience the dramatic change in the emotional climate as the cars crossed the boundary line into the Falls (the Nationalist Roman Catholic area of the city), where the yells of angry resentment turned to cheers and cries of greeting, as their car was suddenly surrounded by ardent supporters.[9]

After these dramatic preliminaries, the meeting itself passed off surprisingly peacefully. Despite deluging rain 5,000 people crowded the stands of the Football Ground and the huge marquee; they gave an ecstatic welcome to Winston and Clementine, shouting and waving sticks, hats and handkerchiefs. Winston then addressed the meeting for over an hour. Having well and truly carried out his advertised intent to speak on Home Rule in Belfast, he accepted the advice of the city authorities to return by a different route. And so, after leaving the Nationalist quarter, where they were once more cheered enthusiastically, he and Clementine were driven back to the railway station through quiet back streets.

Some months afterwards a deputation from the Liberals of Ulster called at the Admiralty and presented blackthorns (hefty walking sticks) to Winston and Clementine as souvenirs of their stormy visit to Belfast. The gentleman making the presentation spoke 'enthusiastically of the pluck shown by Mrs Churchill in accompanying her husband to Ireland'.

*

Whether it was hunting or their visit to Belfast, Clementine had a miscarriage at the end of February 1912. She appeared to make a swift recovery, and towards the middle of March went to Brighton for a short visit to recuperate. But when she returned to Eccleston Square, she was still obviously far from well. She wrote to Winston, who was away on the *Enchantress*:

My Own Darling,

Yesterday was such a soft spring day, that I longed to be out in the sunshine instead of lying flat on my back looking at the tops of the sooty trees in the square.

It is so strange to have all the same sensations that one has after a real Baby, but with no result. I hope I shall never have such another accident again . . .[10]

After a short while she again seemed recovered, and certainly she was 'taking notice', for in a letter to Winston dated 1st April 1912, Mr Asquith wrote:

Much the best thing that I have read for a long time on the Woman Question is a short but very pointed letter in *The Times* today signed C.S.C. Have you any clue to the identity of the writer?

The letter referred to was in reply to one over 3,000 words long of exceptional pomposity and tedium written by an eminent physician, Sir Almroth Wright, which had appeared in *The Times* on 28th March, opposing the granting of votes to women on psychological and physiological grounds. The reply which had attracted Mr Asquith's attention appeared under the heading:

'Ought not women to be abolished?'

and read as follows:

To the Editor of *The Times*. March 30th.
Sir,
    After reading Sir Almroth Wright's able and weighty exposition of women as he knows them the question seems no longer to be 'Should women have votes?' but 'Ought women not to be abolished altogether?'
    I have been so much impressed by Sir Almroth Wright's disquisition . . . that I have come to the conclusion that women should be put a stop to.
    We learn from him that in their youth they are unbalanced, that from time to time they suffer from unreasonableness and hypersensitiveness . . . and . . . Later on in life they are subject to grave and long-continued mental disorders, and, if not quite insane, many of them have to be shut up.
    Now this being so, how much happier and better would the world not be if only it could be purged of women? . . . Is the case really hopeless? . . . Cannot science give us some assurance, or at least some ground of hope, that we are on the eve of the greatest discovery of all – i.e., how to maintain a race of males by purely scientific means?
    And may we not look to Sir Almroth Wright to crown his many achievements by delivering mankind from the parasitic, demented, and immoral species which has infested the world for so long?
                                        Yours obediently,
                                        C.S.C.
                                        ('One of the Doomed')

About a fortnight later, Clementine seemed well enough to go for a few days to Paris, where she stayed at the Hotel Bristol with Mrs Beatty (the American wife of the Rear-Admiral, later of Jutland fame), and Lord Ridley and his wife Rosie (Guest, Randolph's godmother). But after a few days Clementine felt so tired and ill that the kind and watchful Rosie Ridley sent for a French gynaecologist. His report was disconcerting, as it cast grave doubts on the the treatment of her miscarriage by her English doctor who, in the French specialist's view, had allowed her to get up far too soon, and in consequence of which she must now lead an invalid's life for a month, if she was to avoid becoming really ill and having to have an operation. He counselled her to return home at once. Poor Clementine arrived home therefore a bare four days after she had set out on this potentially enjoyable jaunt. She found that Winston had had to go away in the *Enchantress* for several days of meetings and inspections, but flowers and anxious enquiries awaited her.

During the whole of the summer of 1912, Clementine was in poor health and undergoing treatment on and off from her doctors. She wrote Winston debonair letters, but she had spells of great depression, for she hated to be out of things and longed to take up her active life again.

In May, however, despite her indifferent health, she went with Winston in the *Enchantress* for a cruise in the Mediterranean. The party included the Prime Minister and Violet Asquith, Goonie Churchill and Nellie Hozier, as well as the Second Sea Lord (Prince Louis of Battenberg), and Winston's Private Secretaries, Eddie Marsh and James Masterton-Smith. They all embarked at Genoa on 22nd May and visited Naples, Syracuse, Malta, Bizerta and Gibraltar, before returning to Portsmouth.

Violet Asquith wrote a lively account of how the journey provided diversions and interest for all the members of the party; from her father, whose bent was classical and intellectual, to Winston, who, apart from his naval inspections and conferences at every port of call, tended to see the ancient scenes of bygone conflicts in modern strategic terms; while the rest of the party partook of all the various pleasures – sightseeing, bathing, parties ashore and on board, according to their various temperaments. In the evenings there was bridge, to which game the Prime Minister was an addict. Clementine played a socially sufficient game, while (in the words of his own daughter) Mr Asquith was 'an eager and execrable player' and 'Winston was even more dangerous, for he played a romantic game untrammelled by conventions, codes or rules.'[11]

Although generally she throve on sea air, Clementine was dogged by ill-health on this otherwise perfect holiday, and on their return home her condition deteriorated further – so much so that she began to be really alarmed lest her health was permanently undermined. Winston also was greatly worried by her continuing illness, and himself took matters in hand, seeking further medical advice. During his tours on the *Enchantress* he demanded not only reports from Clementine, but daily telegrams from her doctors.

She seemed to be responding to the new treatment, and Winston wrote encouragingly and tenderly on 30th June 1912:

> Aarons' [the doctor] telegram yesterday was vy satisfactory. I really believe you are going to have a new lease of health & vigour. I do trust he did not hurt you at all this morning.
>
> I love you so much & thought so much about you last night & all your courage and sweetness . . .

But the better news which was evidently signalled by the doctors was again followed by a relapse. From the *Enchantress*, he wrote on 9th July:

My poor darling one,
I am most grieved to find that the rosy views of Parkinson's [another doctor]
earlier telegrams have not been confirmed, & that you have had a return of the
pain & only 'a fair night' . . .
  My dear darling I am so distressed to think of you in pain & in discouragement.
Hope deferred makyth the heart sick. Always to be expecting that you are going
to get well & then one thing after another. It is a cruel trial for you. But you will
bear it bravely – my own darling & emerge triumphantly into the sunlight . . .

While she was ill, Clementine seems to have relied chiefly on telegrams as her
means of communication with Winston – fortunately they were then much cheaper
than they are today! But although she was so unwell at this time, she would not
allow her thoughts to be dominated by her ill-health. She was much enthralled and
excited when the National Insurance Act, which Winston had helped to draft, came
into operation on 12th July; and she wrote Winston a long letter:

My own Darling,
  . . . it [the Insurance Act] is a real triumph. I suppose it is almost the first time
in the world that every single person in the country will have to perform a
definite action as the result of a single act of Parliament. Every single person must
be affected by it as everybody must be employed or else employ someone . . .[12]

Clementine's excitement over the implementation of this measure may well seem
exaggerated to a later generation, who have long become accustomed to their everyday actions being governed by Acts of Parliament. But her enthusiasm is a reminder
of how those who viewed the Liberal reforms as the dawn of a new day felt at that
time. Although the great wave of radical legislation had now lost much of its early
force, and although Winston's whole interest had shifted to the field of national
defence, Clementine had lost none of her reforming zeal.
  During these politically charged years Clementine had worked up a healthy
hatred of the Tories, and her radical enthusiasm made her deeply distrustful of
Winston's Tory friends. In the same letter in which she saluted the implementation
of the National Insurance Act, she made a passionate outburst, prompted no doubt
by her fears that the wicked Tories might cast their toils around her shining,
progressive Winston:

My dear Darling Amber Pug – Do not let the glamour of elegance & refinement
& the return of old associations blind you. The charming people you are meeting
to-day – they do not represent Toryism, they are just the cream on the top.
Below, they are ignorant, vulgar, prejudiced. They can't bear the idea of the lower
classes being independent & free. They want them to sweat for them when they
are well & to accept flannel & skilly as a dole if they fall ill, & to touch their caps
& drop curtsies when the great people go by – Goodbye my Darling. I love you
very much.

                                                    Your Radical Bristling
                                                    [diagram of cat]

Many years later, when asked what she regarded as the happiest time of her life, Clementine was to point without hesitation to these – the first early years of her life with Winston. She had embraced not only the man, but also his cause, with whole-hearted fervour. When in the early twenties Winston left the Liberal Party, and by stages eventually rejoined the Conservatives, Clementine too shifted her public allegiance. She followed his transition with her reason, but she never made a good Tory. And from time to time her natural radicalism would burst through the layers of reasonable compliance like a volcanic eruption, often to people's astonished bewilderment.

*

By the late summer of 1912, the new course of medical treatment recommended by her doctors was at last producing satisfactory results, and Clementine's health was really on the mend. To establish the cure, she spent a few seaside weeks with the children at Sandwich, staying at Rest Harrow, a charming house lent to them by Waldorf and Nancy Astor (his American wife, who was later to become the first woman to take her seat in Parliament). The House was sitting, and Winston was therefore only an intermittent visitor; and, moreover, he was deeply engaged in introducing his Supplementary Estimates to Parliament. These had become essential in order to maintain the superiority in strength of the British Navy over the German fleet; but they were strongly contested.

During the debate, which lasted over several days, Winston spoke several times. Clementine was disappointed she could not be in the Gallery to hear his main speech on 22nd July, and her first letter from Sandwich starts a little wistfully:

> All this afternoon I was thinking of you making your speech. I am so jealous of Goonie and Nellie hearing you & not your Kat.[13]

However, she read avidly the reports of the debate in the newspapers and commented:

> . . . I must own that I should like a handful more dreadnoughts – 23 to 29 [British to German ships] is certainly a close shave, especially as we have come off so badly in the Olympic Games!! . . .[14]

Meanwhile she had established a happy holiday life with the children:

> I have had a delicious blowy afternoon on the Beach with the Babies. You would have laughed if you had seen Randolph eating his pap for supper. If ever the spoon contained too much milk & not enough solid he roared with rage & insisted on solid food being scooped up. Diana says her prayers so sweetly & with great dignity. God keep Papa & Mama & little Randolph & make Diana a good little girl for Jesus Christ's sake, Amen. Randolph goes to sleep holding his Nurse's hand & gurgling & cooing like a Ring Dove. Tomorrow comes George [John George, later always called Johnny, Jack and Goonie's elder son; the same age as Diana]. Thursday Goonie & Saturday Oh Joy my Pig. Come early not late dear one.[15]

The following day she wrote again:

My Darling,

Another speech! I cannot follow you in my thoughts more swiftly than you fly from one scene to another thro' space, like a glorious star shedding comet. And all the time your lazy Kat sits purring & lapping cream & stroking her kittens &, after these exhausting operations, sleeps soundly . . .[16]

Life was not all halcyon calm, however; Clementine had to report to Winston that the kitchenmaid had become demented, threatened to commit suicide, and tried to murder the cook. The poor girl had been returned to her own home in the custody of the children's nurse.

Usually such a faithful letter-writer, Winston had told Clementine in a letter from the yacht on 25th July,

I have been too busy and too tired to write these last two days. But I hope my telegrams have kept you appraised of my violent movements.

But despite being constantly on the move between London and the *Enchantress*, he managed to spend the week-end after the Estimates debate with his family at Rest Harrow.

After he departed back to his toil once more, Clementine continued her account of her seaside life:

Two windy days since you departed, but tonight I think the weather is abating. Neville Lytton & Nellie turned up yesterday evening late, just before dinner & we had a merry evening – singing songs, dancing one-steps & flute playing by Neville. This morning Neville, Bill & Nellie bathed, but your Kat was good & sat looking on with her tail just dipping enviously in the water. This afternoon we motored to Ramsgate & sat on the sands . . . Come down soon my dear one. I think it is going to be lovely & hot & I am longing to talk with you, walk with you, bathe with you, sing with you.

Your own
Clemmie[17]

But there were quiet spaces for Winston in his hectic life, and he looked forward to them. On 1st August he told Clementine:

I have made no plans for Sunday next except to come down quietly and see you. We ought to find a really good sandy beach where I can cut the sand into a nicely bevelled fortress – or best of all with a little stream running down – You might explore and report . . .

They stayed at Sandwich until the middle of August, and Winston was able to make several visits to them during that time. However, even ministers' holiday retreats were not free from disturbance by the ubiquitous Suffragettes. Returning to Rest Harrow on the afternoon of 13th August, Winston found the road to the house blocked by two women about a hundred yards from the house, who had wheeled their bicycles in front of the car; the driver was however able to circumvent them.

And a day or two later, several parties of Suffragists gathered on the high road, hoping to intercept his car; but Winston had already left his lair before they arrived.[18]

In mid-August Winston and Clementine, with a family party, went for a cruise in Scottish waters in the *Enchantress*. This was a perfect plan, combining pleasure with Winston's visits to naval establishments, and it added an ideal postscript to Clementine's convalescence. The *Enchantress* was comfortable and beautifully run, involving the hostess in the minimum amount of planning and domestic preoccupation – an aspect of holiday life which greatly appeals to all women.

The party, which apart from other members of the Board of Admiralty included Lady Blanche and Nellie, embarked at Chatham Dockyard on 19th August, and they sailed up the east coast, stopping at various ports and harbours for Winston to make his inspections, to the Tyne and Aberdeen Bay, from where Winston and Clementine were bidden to dine at Balmoral. They then cruised round the wild and beautiful Scottish coastline to the west coast.

In mid-September they broke their holiday to visit Winston's constituency in Dundee, where he held several meetings. These were constantly subject to noisy interruptions by Suffragettes, and at one meeting at least there was considerable disorder, and several women were forcibly ejected. Clementine herself in a short speech, referring to the interruptions, said: 'All women must feel a sense of humiliation and degradation at the scenes we have just witnessed.'[19]

Although basically in sympathy with the campaign for women's suffrage, Clementine was appalled by the outrageous methods employed by the militant Suffragettes whose campaign of violence was reaching its zenith. Their attacks were becoming increasingly dangerous; they included setting fire to railway stations, and planting bombs (one of which exploded) in a house being built for Lloyd George. At the Derby in 1913 Miss Emily Davison flung herself in front of the horses at Tattenham Corner, dying later from her injuries, and becoming a martyr to the cause.

Dining with the Asquiths in November 1913, Clementine heard from them of an unnerving attack on the Prime Minister, of which she wrote to Winston:

> The suffragette affair on the road to Stirling was horrible & upset poor Violet a good deal. One of the women slashed Mr Asquith 4 times with a crop over the head, before she was seized. Luckily his face was saved (like yours at Bristol) by the brim of his stiff hat. He never seems to defend himself on these occasions but remains calm & stolid & unshrinking! About two pints of pepper were thrown into the car, but luckily no one's eyes were injured . . .[20]

The measures which individuals in the public eye were forced to take will have an all too familiar ring to the modern reader; Winston had to warn Clementine not to open

> suspicious parcels arriving by post without precautions . . . These harpies are quite capable of trying to burn us out . . .[21]

And following letters threatening to kidnap the children, Diana and Randolph had to be escorted by plain-clothes detectives on their walks in the parks.

It was not until 1918 that women over thirty were given the vote, and it was the general view that this was in recognition of their unstinted contribution to the war effort, rather than the campaign of disruption and violence. But Clementine's opinion in after years was that, although most rational opinion was affronted by the excesses of the Suffragette movement – nonetheless, the day would not have been won when it was, had not the cause of 'Votes for Women' been championed with a passion which exceeded constitutional and legal bounds.

THE SANDS RUN OUT

T HE 'delaying action' fought and won by Clementine at the time of Winston's appointment as First Lord, to defer their move to Admiralty House on grounds of economy, now ended in reluctant, but graceful, defeat for her; and they moved from Eccleston Square to Admiralty House in early April 1913. Clementine, however, still succeeded in winning a compromise victory: in order to diminish the number of staff they would need, they decided to seal off the main first floor with its large suite of grand and beautiful rooms. In this way Clementine could run the house with nine servants instead of the twelve needed if four floors were used.

The main rooms were already furnished by the Government, but the wife of the First Lord could exercise her personal choice when it came to the sitting-rooms, bedrooms and nurseries. 'I have spent yesterday & today morning in grapple with the Admiralty installation & the Office of Works officials,' wrote Clementine on 31st January 1913

I am afraid altho' we are allowed to 'choose' our bedroom furniture it will be difficult to get anything attractive as the 'choosing' is to be done out of a grim catalogue; so far I have *avoided* but not chosen anything.

I really think they ought to have a woman at the head of the Office of Works – someone like your Mama . . . [1]

Winston had been champing to move from the start, and was looking forward to their installation at Admiralty House with undisguised relish. House-moving being an essentially female occupation, Clementine was no doubt relieved that he had a programme of visits and inspections over the days of the move, leaving her free to conduct operations.

From the *Enchantress* he wrote to her on 6th April:

. . . It will be nice coming back to the Admiralty. I like the idea of those spacious rooms. I am sure you will take to it when you get there. I am afraid it all means vy hard work for you – Poor lamb. But remember I am going to turn over a new leaf! That I promise – the only mystery is 'What is written on the other side'. It may be only 'ditto ditto'!

Although even now the move was against her better judgment, Clementine was in good spirits, and not weighed down by the rigours of house-moving. From a forlorn and dismantled No. 33, she penned a hurried note to Winston on Saturday, 5th April:

My darling,

House moving is going on & there is no resting place for the soles of my feet. I am now sitting in a desolated library (ink-pots & pens gone) . . .

Clementine spent the week-end with the Asquiths at their riverside house, The Wharf, at Sutton Courtenay, and wrote to Winston on the Sunday:

My darling Winston,

A very pleasant Sunday here. The Prime & Violet picked me up yesterday morning at Eccleston Square & as I was whisked away, I felt it was the end of a chapter in my life. Leaving a house where one has lived nearly 4 years is as much of an event in a 'Kat's' life, as changing from Home Office to Admiralty for a statesman!

We stopped on our way to Huntercombe [golf course] & lunched at 'Skindles' where we had 'all the delicacies of the season' – Plover's eggs (I hope you will not have had a surfeit of them on the yacht, as they are to smile at you on your return), salmon, lamb, asparagus, rhubarb. Then we proceeded on our way & played very badly. We said it was the wind, but I suspect it was Skindles.

This morning we played again, a 3 ball match – I halved with Violet & was badly beaten by the Prime, but defeated him in the bye . . . Tomorrow I fly back by the early morning train as I am longing to take possession of our Mansion . . .[2]

Any anxieties Winston and (especially) Clementine might have had about their treasured first home in Eccleston Square must have been allayed by their good fortune in finding an ideal tenant – their friend and Winston's colleague, Sir Edward Grey.

An amusing story arises from his tenancy of their house. One day he entertained the French Ambassador, and during the course of his visit showed him over his new abode. The Ambassador was greatly startled by the decor in Sir Edward Grey's bedroom (formerly Clementine's room). In the main, Clementine had lovely, unaffected taste and particularly disliked decorators' effects, but while she was planning her first house she had fallen under the influence of the 'art nouveau' movement, and although the main rooms at 33 Eccleston Square excited no undue comment, she had thoroughly let herself go in her own bedroom (perhaps in revulsion from the 'sugary' muslin-and-bows decoration which her mother-in-law had so kindly, but indiscreetly, prepared for her as a surprise in their first home in Bolton Street). At any rate, Clementine's bedroom in the Eccleston Square house was decorated in shades of green, brown and orange, with a large orange-tree laden with oranges appliquéd all over the walls. The Ambassador was transfixed with undisguised amazement and horror. When, shortly afterwards, he lunched at Admiralty House, he remarked to his hostess that he had been astonished by what he considered 'un drôle de décor pour la chambre à coucher d'une ravissante jeune femme'.

*

Clementine soon established her own domestic life at Admiralty House. She spent much time and thought on her housekeeping; and then, as always, the food in her house was delicious. Winston was exacting in standards of comfort and hospitality: 'I am easily satisfied,' he would say disarmingly, 'with the very best.' Clementine herself had perfectionist standards and tussled willingly, but sometimes wearily, to produce a perfectly run house and elegant and plenteous hospitality on too little money.

The menu book was never 'sent up' to her for approval, as was the custom in many similar households; she always saw the cook herself, usually at about half-past eight, when a conference would take place between them both in her bedroom, every detail being gone over with care and interest. These morning interviews were always a feature of the day – Clementine sitting up in bed, looking ravishing in a lace cap and bedjacket, the cook, clad in a dazzling white apron, bearing the menu book, and probably a child sprawled on the bed or rampaging round the room. Sometimes their deliberations would be interrupted by Winston, who would come stumping in in his dressing-gown to say 'Good morning' or to draw Clementine's attention to something in the newspapers. 'Let's have Irish stew,' he would say, 'with lots of onions.'

Winston and Clementine invariably breakfasted in their respective rooms; he had usually worked late the night before and woke up later than Clementine. She was a habitual early bird, and was ravenous by eight; indeed, by that time she had probably written several letters, curled her hair and read several chapters, for it was not unusual for her to wake between five and six o'clock. In some ways this early morning pattern was a handicap to her, for by the evening her energy had waned, and, especially as she grew older, she yearned for an early bedtime. At this time, she often went up to bed hours before Winston, sometimes leaving little 'Kat'–signed notes for him. One found among her papers reads:

My darling,
    When your business is finished do come to bed as early as you can. You look weary from want of sleep & tomorrow you will need all your cool brain & judgement.

[sketch of a cat]

Another note reads:

    Mrs Grimalkin [an old she-cat] presents her compliments & would appreciate a little visit with the Speech.

[sketch of a cat] Miaow, but sitting tight

One of Clementine's most attractive characteristics was her vitality – but it was not accompanied by an equal stamina, and she was dogged all her life by feeling strain and fatigue to a marked degree. Even as a young woman, it was a necessity for her to rest during the afternoon if she was to be equal to her evening's activities.

Since Winston and Clementine rarely partook of fashionable social life, those who frequented their house, or with whom they lunched and dined, were for the most part either relations or government and ministerial colleagues, and their close friends were all in the political world.

The Prime Minister found pleasure and relaxation to a very great extent among the younger members of his Government such as the Churchills, preferring small dinner parties, after which he liked to play bridge. Mr Asquith's affectionate regard for Winston had grown with his appreciation of his abilities, although he regarded his rampageous enthusiasm and loquacity with ironic amusement. Since Winston's marriage, Clementine's beauty, good manners and sufficiency at bridge had made them, as a couple, welcome in the fairly small circle of the Asquiths' private social life; Winston's friendship with his daughter Violet also was a further link. Winston and Clementine were frequent guests both at Downing Street and at The Wharf at week-ends. Included also in many of these invitations were Goonie Churchill (whom the Prime Minister greatly admired) and Nellie Hozier (known as 'the Bud' or 'Mlle Beauxyeux').

Margot Asquith, a Tennant before her marriage to Mr Asquith as his second wife, was a most eccentric woman, famed and feared for her whiplash tongue. But she was fond of both Winston and Clementine, although she frequently criticised the former, very often to his wife. For Clementine she had a rather touching admiration, writing once to Winston, 'I have a great feeling for Clemmy, she is *so* rare not to be vain of her marvellous beauty.'[3] This was generous praise from an older woman, among whose attributes it was impossible to include beauty.

For Winston's part, he had strong reservations about Margot Asquith: for one thing, ugly women rarely appealed to him. But he was probably more put off by her aggressive manner and overbearing personality. His attempts to avoid her did not go unobserved; in a rather naïve postscript to a note to Clementine on 2nd April 1912, Mrs Asquith wrote: 'Whenever I meet Winston he sits out of range – such a bore!'

Although she was treated with much kindness by the Asquiths, Clementine was not really in her element with them; their world was one of high intellectual peaks (as well as not very good bridge), and although Clementine was intelligent and well-educated, she was not an intellectual, and never had any pretensions as such. The austere side of her nature made her dislike Mr Asquith's predilection for peering down 'Pennsylvania Avenue' (the contemporary expression for a lady's cleavage) whenever he was seated next to a pretty woman. Moreover she was uncomfortable in the company of Violet Asquith and Venetia Stanley, in whose close friendship she had always sensed a latent threat, despite an outward show of smiling affection.

The lack of self-confidence which had been a feature of Clementine's character right through her childhood and adolescence had not yet been exorcised by the depth and abiding strength of Winston's love for her. Although kindly received, Clementine felt in a sense an 'outsider' in this small, brilliant circle to which she was a late-comer, with its criss-cross currents and watchful eyes.

Nor was her discomfiture without foundation. In January 1912, Mr Asquith and Edwin Montagu (a junior minister in the Government) were in Sicily, and were joined there by Violet and Venetia. The friendship which had already existed for several years between Mr Asquith and Venetia, in these holiday weeks began to become a very close and important one. He was then fifty-nine years old, and she was twenty-four. Venetia was handsome, clever and worldly, and Mr Asquith became infatuated by her. Their relationship developed virtually unremarked, camouflaged as it was by the already existing friendship between Violet and Venetia.

Mr Asquith and Venetia Stanley wrote constantly to each other – he often doing so during the course of Cabinet meetings. Only a few of her letters to him survive, but she kept the greater part of his letters to her; and it is from them that one learns details of state affairs, many of them of a highly secret nature at the time. In addition, Mr Asquith expressed his private opinions of people, including those in the close circle of his friendship.

Clementine rates quite a few mentions in these letters, but one sentence sums up Mr Asquith's opinion of her: 'Clemmie, of whom I am quite fond, is *au fond* a thundering bore!'[4] His view is comprehensible, for their characters and outlook could not have been more different. Mr Asquith was supremely sophisticated, erudite and worldly. Unlike Winston, who lived and breathed politics in all his waking hours, Mr Asquith, having dealt with affairs of state, preferred to put them aside, and to distract himself with golf, long motor-car drives, bridge and intellectual pursuits – preferably in the company of beautiful, easy-going, clever women. Clementine was earnest, enthusiastic, highly moral and, although he never actually used the word, obviously – in Mr Asquith's view – a prig.

His descriptions of Clementine in his letters to Venetia were generally critical. As a motoring companion, for instance, Clementine appears to have been defective: after a wet week-end in March 1914 he complained to Venetia:

> The weather was vile, and we could not golf – only trundle about at snail's pace (in deference to Clemmie's fears) in a shut up motor.[5]

During another week-end party, both Clementine and Goonie came under criticism:

> The critical among us don't think either Clemmie or Goonie quite in their best looks. In spite of her excellent manners & many good qualities, I think the former would rather try one as 'yoke-fellow' & perpetual companion. It is by no means a deep well.[6]

Soon afterwards Mr Asquith sat next to Goonie, dining with the Wimbornes; he reported to Venetia:

> Goonie & I had a delightful talk about you. She is a loyal & devoted & appreciating friend of yours – worth (I think) 100 Clemmies – not that I am the least anti-Clemmie . . .[7]

Of the two sisters, Clementine and Nellie, the latter with her gayer and more easy-going temperament appealed (although not without evaluation) more to Mr Asquith: 'The Bud herself is rather a curious study,' he wrote to Venetia,

> . . . I like her (not vehemently) and she is really much cleverer and more original than Clemmie. But her pose of a sort of simple fatuity is apt to take one in and sometimes one is not quite sure whether it is a pose or the real person . . .[8]

Mr Asquith's geniality and good manners, however, must have concealed his reservations about her, for Clementine felt quite able to confide in him, while walking in the grounds of Walmer Castle, an incident that had occurred a few days previously when Mrs Keppel (the beautiful and amiable friend of King Edward VII) had warmheartedly offered to give her a dress from some fashionable couturier, which Clementine had declined to accept. Her scrupulous rejection of a lovely present, however, earned her no marks at all: 'Clemmie tells me,' Mr Asquith wrote to Venetia,

> you were present at a curious scene . . . when Mrs Keppel offered her a dress, wh. she was too proud & 'well brought up' to accept, notwithstanding your advice to the contrary. Clemmie is very 'particular', isn't she?[9]

One cannot but feel a little sorry for Clementine – surrounded as she was by such critical eyes, and at the mercy of such a sharp pen.

Given the puritan streak in Clementine's nature, her highly developed critical faculty, and the shyness which made her so reserved and withdrawn at times, it is not surprising that worldly sophisticates should not have found her totally to their liking. And some people, at first introduction anyway, preferred the ebullient and light-hearted Nellie, though they might warm to Clementine on further acquaintance. Such a one was Neville Lytton, who subsequently was so much struck by Clementine's 'Venus'-like appearance at the seaside, and who was to become both an admirer and a friend. He had written to Nellie:

> It is only right and just that I shld write and tell you how immensely I liked your sister yesterday. I have always been the one to say disagreeable things about her, but I am quite wrong . . . there is something so natural and impulsively light-hearted about your sister as well as such far greater claims to beauty than the stars [fashionable women] I have been seeing lately . . .[10]

Throughout her life Clementine was not easy to know well; and at times she never lowered the barriers of her reserve, leaving people baffled, and often with a false impression of her nature. A woman she liked and trusted once told me that she found Clementine 'very un-even' – one day she would be completely approachable and ready to confide her thoughts, and the next, her defences would be up, and they might have been distant acquaintances. But if people found it difficult to establish real and intimate friendship, she was not shy in terms of daily social intercourse, or in the contacts she had with Winston's colleagues.

During 1913 Clementine led an increasingly active social life, quite frequently attending dinner parties and other functions on her own, since Winston was so often away on naval business. And her letters to him during that summer are full of her goings-about in London, and plans for their own entertaining at home.

While Winston was on manoeuvres with the Fleet towards the end of July, Clementine wrote to tell him that she had met Lord Kitchener (at this time a member of the Committee of Imperial Defence) at Lady Crewe's, and that he had expressed a desire to see Winston; she suggested that they should invite him to luncheon. 'By all means ask K [Kitchener] to lunch,' he answered. ' . . . Let us be

just *à trois*. I have some things to talk to him about.'[11] This is an interesting indication that Winston had already acquired the habit he practised throughout his life
of talking 'shop' at meals. For this reason, when he was in office he very much deplored merely 'social' meals, as he then naturally felt inhibited from discussing
many confidential subjects. And from this letter we also see that Clementine is
accepted into his full confidence, and that he had no secrets from her. She never in
fifty-seven years betrayed that trust by deed, or sign, or word.

Winston, in marrying Clementine, had found an equal in spirit and temperament.
But in her character was also a super-sensitivity and a proneness to worry which
were to cause her moments of great anxiety and unhappiness all through her life.
'It may never happen,' Winston would say consolingly, when she was fretting about
some vexing possibility. 'Cast care aside,' he would enjoin when worries were
threatening to spoil some enjoyable plan. One must observe that these wise and
kindly meant injunctions did not always have the soothing effect he desired. Clementine was not quarrelsome, but she could easily become vehement and agitated. And
it was hardly strange that the union of these two highly-charged natures sometimes
generated flashes of lightning.

In retrospect one sees that they shared a very important characteristic, which is a
vital ingredient in a long-enduring marriage – namely the ardent wish to make up
any quarrel without delay. 'Let not the sun go down upon your wrath,' was a Biblical
precept which Winston often quoted, and which he practised in all his relationships.
Clementine, too, was always swift and ready to make up any quarrel, but she tended
to suffer inner 'bruising' for longer than Winston.

There is an exchange of letters at the end of January 1913 which is illustrative.
They had evidently had a sharp disagreement just before Winston left home to go
aboard the *Enchantress*, which was in Scottish waters, for on 30th January he
wrote to her about their prospective move into Admiralty House, continuing:

> I was stupid last night – but you know what a prey I am to nerves and prepossess-
> sions. It is a great comfort to me to feel *absolute* confidence in your love & cherish-
> ment for your poor P.D. [Pugdog].

In a postscript he added:

> . . . Don't be disloyal to me in thought. I have no one but you to break the lone-
> liness of a bustling and bustled existence.
>
> Write to me at Queensferry on receipt of this. It will reach me Satdy morning,
> and tell me how much you care about your W. XXX Here are three kisses one for
> each of you. Don't waste them. They are good ones.

This letter, with its moving avowal of how much in five years of marriage Winston
had come to depend upon Clementine as his sure refuge, received a swift reply:

'My Sweet Darling Winston,' she wrote on 31st January,

> I love you so much & what I want & enjoy is that you should feel quite comfort-
> able and at home with me – you know I never have any arrière pensée that does
> not immediately come to the top and boil over; so that when I get excited &

cross, I always say more than I feel & mean instead of less. There are never any dregs left behind.

The only time I feel a little low is when the breaks in the 'bustling & bustled existence' are few & far between. I suppose they are not *really* few, but I am a very greedy Kat and I like a great deal of cream . . .

One of the causes of worry and tension which they both shared, but which Winston cast off more easily than Clementine, was money – or rather, their lack of it. Admiralty House was proving the burden Clementine had always feared it would be. In April 1914 she was in Paris for a few days on her way home from a holiday with Winston in Madrid (he had returned ahead of her). In a letter which also gave her good news of 'the Kittens', Winston reviewed their financial situation and found that:

Our finances are in a condition wh requires serious & prompt attention. The expense of the 1st quarter of 1914 with our holiday trip is astonishing. Money seems to flow away . . .[12]

A few days later he wrote again, and returned to their money situation:

I . . . am preparing a scheme which will enable us to clear off our debts & bills & start on a clean ready money basis. We shall have to pull in our horns. The money simply drains away.

But even when oppressed by these concerns, Winston was not stingy:

If you have anything left out of the £40, spend it on some little thing you like in Paris.[13]

It may have been after this financial crisis that the sad and touching episode of the ruby necklace occurred. When Winston and Clementine were married, his Aunt Cornelia Wimborne had given her a muff chain. It was very pretty, and at first Clementine had supposed the gems composing it to be moonstones – however, they turned out to be diamonds! Winston had given Clementine as a wedding present a beautiful ruby and diamond-cluster necklace, which she proceeded to have combined with the 'moonstones' to make an even more ravishing possession. But, sad to relate, during a moment of financial panic Clementine sold this exquisite necklace to pay the house-books. On discovering her precipitate action, Winston rushed to the jeweller to try to retrieve her treasured possession, but – alas – he was too late.

In the last eighteen months before the war engulfed personal life and enjoyment like so much flotsam and jetsam in its overwhelming tide, Winston and Clementine had a series of delightful holidays. In February 1913 they went to Cannes for a short break, and in May there was yet another sunlit cruise on *Enchantress* in the Mediterranean, when Winston inspected the naval establishments in Malta. The Asquiths were once more members of the party.

They all embarked at Venice, and on the way to Malta they visited Athens, and saw the Acropolis by moonlight. It was on one of these voyages that Clementine, paying a visit to the galley to talk to the cook, found a large and beautiful turtle confined in a tin bath; it had, she said, 'such beautiful eyes', and with sinking heart she enquired what it was proposed to do with the turtle. The answer was obvious: 'Which evening would Madam prefer turtle soup?' Clementine fled aloft and besought the Captain for a dinghy and a party of men sufficient to grapple with a baby's bathful of live turtle. She herself accompanied this expedition, and, after rowing a little distance from the yacht, the turtle was carefully decanted into the crystalline Mediterranean. Winston, who, although very fond of turtle soup, was always tender-hearted towards animals, fully supported her deed of mercy. The cook's reaction is not recorded.

Once at Malta, where they arrived on 22nd May, private pleasures and romantic sightseeing were succeeded by official receptions, inspections and conferences on shore. At sea there were firing exercises, and a mock submarine attack. Only too soon were these dress rehearsals to become real-life drama, and the sunlit holiday interludes to acquire a strange unreality – faint echoes from a life and a world that was to vanish in the smoke and thunder of a thousand guns.

In September 1913, as in the previous year, there was a cruise up the west coast of Scotland. Among other calls, they visited Mr and Mrs Lloyd George at their home at Criccieth Castle, overlooking Cardigan Bay, and then sailed on up the coast to Greenock. Clementine stayed on the *Enchantress*, with Goonie and Nellie for company, while Winston made his annual ministerial visit to Balmoral.

One day they all drove to Ayr for the races; and Clementine wrote to Winston that she was astonished at the gaiety of the scene: 'It was like a miniature Ascot.' Mrs Keppel was also at the races, 'looking very prosperous';[14] however, she gave Clementine several wrong tips.

The chief interest of this occasion for Clementine and Nellie lay in the presence of their brother Bill and his 'young lady'. Clementine described her to Winston:

> Her tiny little frame seems to have been constructed for the sole purpose of carrying the most enormous & lustrous eyes I have ever seen. Her hair is soft & silky. It will not break my heart if she does not marry Bill, tho' his, poor boy, will take a long time to mend. I fear she is a minx & a puss . . .

Clementine's sisterly fears that Bill might marry this pretty minx were groundless; indeed, he died unmarried.

The cruise wound up with a ministerial conference, which gathered at Castle Brodick on the Isle of Arran (the home of Mr Illingworth, the Government Chief Whip). Several other ministers' wives were there, and the gathering, which lasted two days, had a social as well as a political flavour. On the last evening the entire party dined on board *Enchantress*. It made a fitting climax to this autumn cruise; it was destined to be the last of those glamorous enjoyable holiday voyages, which would always glow in Clementine's memory of those Admiralty days.

*

Although Winston and Clementine were part of the small but brilliant world at the heart of events, and were totally preoccupied by their crowded and demanding life, there is an interesting passage in one of Winston's letters which shows he was aware of the social isolation in which they found themselves. Winston was always particularly anxious to maintain the links which bound him to his family; but it was not always easy for Clementine to meet his wishes, for, despite her reserve, dignity and graceful ways, she found it difficult to overcome or conceal her feelings about people. From the *Enchantress* at Newcastle, Winston wrote to her at Alderley on 19th October 1913:

> Here is a letter from Cornelia [Wimborne]. I want you to write & accept. I have a great regard for her – & we have not too many friends. If however you don't want to go – I will go alone. Don't come with all your hackles up & your fur brushed the wrong way – you naughty.

Clementine's dislike of the Wimbornes was centred on Ivor and Freddie Guest, rather than on their generous and amiable mother, Winston's aunt, and she answered dutifully:

> ... I will write tomorrow to Aunt Cornelia – I would like to go, & I will be very good I promise you, especially if you stroke my silky tail.[15]

There were no political differences with the Wimbornes, who were Liberals; nor had politics ever interfered with Winston's friendship with his cousin, Sunny Marlborough. Despite real differences in point of view, they had maintained a cordial relationship. Since their marriage Winston and Clementine had often stayed (together and separately) at Blenheim. But about now politics were the cause of an incident between Clementine and Sunny Marlborough which resulted in a distinct chill between the cousins for nearly two years.

It is hardly surprising that the controversies surrounding the People's Budget and the Parliament Bill should have caused tension between the ducal and radical branches of the family. Lloyd George had pilloried the dukes in his famous Limehouse speech in July 1909; and Winston too had had fiery things to say about peers and primogeniture which did not pass unnoticed, and must have been exceedingly irritating to Sunny Marlborough, despite his tolerant and hospitable ways.

But in the autumn of 1913, Clementine, Goonie Churchill and Nellie were all staying at Blenheim. Also among the guests was Margaret Smith (Mrs F. E. Smith) who, like Clementine and Goonie, was there without her husband. Apart from the Duke himself, Lady Norah Churchill, one of his sisters (thirty-eight, and still unmarried), and his elder son, Blandford, a boy of sixteen, made up the family side of the party.

On 22nd October Lloyd George made an important speech at Swindon, in which he outlined the Government's proposals for Land Reform, which, as can be imagined, held no joy for the land-owning classes who, in addition, were roundly castigated and held up to ridicule in the more inflammatory passages of the Chancellor of the Exchequer's oration. The following morning, in the Great Library, Clemmie and Nellie were observed to be reading reports of the speech, not only with interest, but with loud expressions of admiration and approval, which cannot have failed to have caused displeasure to the Duke, already ruffled by his own perusal of the morning's papers. That same day Clementine wrote to Winston:

How splendid Lloyd George's Swindon Speech is! I think it is the greatest speech I have ever read. Nellie read it aloud to me this morning & we were both moved to tears. Sunny is '*au fond*' broad-minded about the land, but he does not let it appear on the surface & indulges in the sourness & bitterness of a crab apple! But he works it all off at tennis . . .[16]

The Duke also relieved his feelings at meal-times by teasingly referring to Mr Asquith's drinking habits, which were the subject of comment at the time; this greatly offended Clementine's sense of loyalty to Winston's chief, and she begged Sunny to refrain from these unseemly jokes (particularly while the servants were in the room): whereupon he repeated them in a clearer tone. Tempers were clearly rising, but flash-point was reached when a telegram was handed to Clementine while they were all at luncheon – it was from Lloyd George and concerned some arrangements in which Winston and she were involved. Declaring that the message was most important, and that she must answer it at once, Clementine got up, and proceeded to write a reply at one of the writing tables which were in the Green Room where the family lunched when they were few in numbers. Sunny Marl-borough said to her, 'Please, Clemmie, would you mind not writing to that horrible little man on Blenheim writing-paper.' Upon which Clementine left the room, went straight up to her bedroom and rang for the maid, whom she instructed to pack her cases; she then ordered a 'fly' from Woodstock to take her to the station.

Presently Goonie came upstairs with Norah Churchill. 'You're not really going?' she asked. Upon Clementine assuring her that she most certainly was, Goonie loyally said she would go too, but Clementine dissuaded her from doing this; Lady Norah watched with consternation (possibly not unmixed with admiration). When the packing was done, Clementine descended to the front hall, where she was met by Sunny Marlborough, who begged her not to leave, and apologised for upsetting her. But Clementine, once roused, was not easily calmed, and despite this proffered twig of olive, left the house and took a train from Woodstock to London.

When Winston heard of it, he thought the whole affair a storm in a teacup, and only took Clementine's part rather half-heartedly, which caused her deep mortifica-tion, for she felt she had nobly defended his colleagues against Tory malice. The incident upset her very much, and not long after the quarrel, when she was alone with Margaret Smith, and they were talking about it, she became very agitated and burst into floods of tears. In after years Clementine said she thought she had been wrong not to have accepted Sunny Marlborough's apology.[17]

It may have been this scene at Blenheim, or perhaps some other passing cause of friction, which accounts for a letter she wrote to Winston on 2nd November 1913:

My sweet and Dear Pig, when I am a withered old woman how miserable I shall be if I have disturbed your life & troubled your spirit by my temper. Do not cease to love me. I could not do without it. If no one loves me, instead of being a Cat

with teeth & Claws, but you will admit soft fur, I shall become like the prickly
porcupine outside, & inside so raw & unhappy.

In his reply Winston made a touching avowal of his sense of his own inadequacies:

I loved much to read the words of your dear letter. You know so much about me,
& with your intuition have measured the good & bad in my nature. Alas I have
no good opinion of myself. At times, I think I cd conquer everything – & then
again I know I am only a weak vain fool. But your love for me is the greatest
glory & recognition that has or will ever befall me: the attachment wh I feel
towards you is not capable of being altered by the sort of things that happen in this
world. I only wish I were more worthy of you, & more able to meet the inner
needs of your soul.[18]

'Thank you my darling for your dear letter,' she replied the next day, 'I feel *so*
good now, as if I could never be naughty again!' The storm clouds had rolled by,
and once more the sun burst out over a wide and verdant landscape.

*

As the year 1914 opened, the sands of peace were fast running out: but even to
those who saw clearly the growing menace of a European conflagration, the day and
the hour, and the immediate cause, were all hidden. The dominating issue for Great
Britain was the Irish Question. Passions were fanned white hot when the Home
Rule Bill had its third reading in the House of Commons, while gun-running and
military drilling in Ulster emphasised the danger of a descent into civil war.

Despite these convulsions, Winston and Clementine were able to take a short
holiday abroad together at Easter: it was to be the last for a long time. They went
to Madrid as the guests of Winston's old friend and patron, Sir Ernest Cassel;
also in the same party were Mrs Keppel and her daughter Violet (later Trefusis).
After Winston had to return home, Clementine stayed on to visit Seville and Granada.
She was once more expecting a child, and since the mishap she sustained in 1912,
she was observing all sensible precautions and did not join the party at the Great
Bull Fight in Seville, from which she recounted that Mrs Keppel and Violet returned 'ashy grey & dreadfully upset'.[19]

Sir Ernest also had to return home ahead of the party, and he generously suggested
that they should, on their homeward journey, all spend a few days in Paris as his
guests; which they gratefully did. It was probably during these pleasant holiday
weeks that Mrs Keppel made to Clementine the startling, if well meant, suggestion
that she could greatly assist Winston in his career by finding herself a rich and well-
placed lover! Mrs Keppel indicated her willingness to assist in the search for a suitable candidate, and inferred that it would be positively selfish of Clementine to
neglect to help Winston forward in this way! It is a measure of her affection for
Mrs Keppel that Clementine was much amused by this quaint suggestion.

But although Clementine enjoyed her time in Spain and, as was usual with her,
was in good health during her pregnancy, there had been for many months a constant fear which gnawed away at her: Winston had taken up flying.

Churchill was the chief inaugurator of the Royal Naval Air Service, the purpose of which was for the Navy to have its own independent means of defending our harbours and other vital naval installations. He believed passionately in the role of this new arm for the Navy, and took a keen and close interest in its development. And, of course, quite soon he was not content to watch from the ground. Flying was still in its infancy; it was only in 1909 that Blériot had flown the Channel; now both the Army and the Navy were exploring the immense possibilities the aeroplane presented as a war machine. But aircraft were in a rudimentary state of development, and these early machines took their toll of the daring men who experimented with them.

During 1912 and 1913 Winston made many flights, and this new activity was a cause of deep anxiety to Clementine. She felt he took unnecessary risks and that flying was for him 'above & beyond the call of duty'. Her view was shared by Sunny Marlborough, who on 12th March 1913 wrote Winston a letter starting:

> I do not suppose I shall get the chance of writing you many more letters if you continue your journeys in the air . . .

and he went on to tell Winston that he owed it to his 'wife, family and friends' to desist from this hazardous occupation.

But flying thrilled and fascinated Winston. In October 1913, while he was in the *Enchantress*, he visited the airfield at Eastchurch, near Sheerness, and flew in a seaplane, a bi-plane, and finally in a naval airship. On 23rd October he wrote Clementine a high-spirited account of it all:

> Darling, We have had a vy jolly day in the air . . . It has been as good as one of those old days in the S. African war, & I have lived entirely in the moment, with no care for all those tiresome party politics & searching newspapers, and awkward by-elections . . .
>
> For good luck before I started I put your locket on. It has been lying in my desk since it got bent – & as usual worked like a charm.

Clementine was much alarmed by this casual account of Winston's exploits, and at once sent him an imploring telegram, which she followed up with a letter:

> I hope my telegram will not have vexed you, but please be kind & don't fly any more just now.[20]

Her entreaties fell on deaf ears, for on 25th October (when he would have certainly received her telegram) he flew again – and continued to do so whenever the opportunity presented itself.

Winston was aware of the immense urgency for Great Britain to develop this new science, with all its far-reaching implications for both war and peace. And not only did flying grip him, but also he came to know and admire many of the men who were developing and testing these new machines, and he loved to share some of the risks taken by them; and he always found in physical danger a release from mental care. That winter, Winston, no longer content to be merely a passenger, started receiving instruction in the art of flying. Of course this only served to increase Clementine's fears for him, and he wrote somewhat apologetically on 29th November:

I have been naughty today about flying. Down here with twenty machines in the air at once and thousands of flights made without mishap, it is not possible to look upon it as a vy serious risk. Do not be vexed with me.

Three days later Captain Wildman-Lushington, with whom Winston had spent such a happy day on 29th November, was killed in his 'plane. This tragedy only served further to alarm Clementine, and fanned the anxiety already felt by many of his friends. 'Why do you do such a foolish thing as fly repeatedly?' wrote F. E. Smith on 6th December 1913. 'Surely it is unfair to your family, your career & your friends.'[21] Winston, however, continued to be deaf to all reasonings and entreaties.

Even while she was enjoying her Easter holiday in Spain in 1914, Clementine's fears were not asleep, and she wrote:

I have just been seized with a dreadful anxiety that you are making use of my absence to fly even more often than you do when I am there – I beg of you not to do it at all, at any rate till I can be there.[22]

Her anxieties were not ill-founded, for on the very day she wrote to him, Winston not only made a flight in a seaplane, but was involved in a minor mishap, when engine-failure forced the pilot to make an emergency descent on the water close to Clacton jetty. But Winston was completely undeterred, and made a further flight a day or two later.

At the end of May, Clementine took Diana and Randolph (now aged five and three) to stay with her mother in Dieppe. Despite the tragedy of Kitty's death, Lady Blanche had retained agreeable memories of Dieppe life, and she had acquired a few years previously a charming house, St Antoine, 16 rue des Fontaines; across the small garden was an old converted coach house, which was known as the Petit St Antoine, and served as an annexe to the main house.

Winston's first letter to Clementine at Dieppe on 29th May must have caused her an agony of worry:

I have been at the Central Flying School for a couple of days – flying a little in good & careful hands & under perfect conditions. So I did not write you from there as I knew you would be vexed.

By the time she replied, the papers had been full of accounts of the loss over the Channel of Gustave Hamel, a famous aviator, known to both Winston and Clementine. All this naturally added to Clementine's anxiety, and her first letter from Dieppe on 30th May has a note of despair in it:

St Antoine
16 Rue des Fontaines
Dieppe
30th May [1914]

My Darling,
I began writing to you, but was nipped in the bud by reading of your exploits & of your determination to repeat them the next day! . . .

I felt what you were doing before I read about it, but I felt too weak & tired to struggle against it. It is like beating one's head against a stone wall . . .

The babies are well & very happy & I think are a pleasure to mother. She & they inhabit the large house while Nellie & I conduct our establishment in the dower house [the coachhouse] opposite! Everything is minute but very comfortable. We go out every morning with a large basket and do our marketing which is very engrossing, altho' not on a large scale. Goodbye my dear love. Perhaps if I saw you, I could love and pet you, but you have been so naughty that I can't do it on paper. I must be 'brought round' first.

Your loving
Clemmie
[Sketch] ears down.

Two more letters in swift succession from Winston kept Clementine in touch with his plans; but in neither of them did he mention the sore subject of flying. Perhaps he felt no explanations could remove her fears, which now were undoubtedly beginning to prey on her spirits, and she was now nearly five months with child. On 1st June 1914 she wrote again:

Life here is so tame and uneventful that the days slip by without being noticed – almost too easily, for one might grow old without having felt any acute sensation of either pain or pleasure. The Daily Mail keeps me in touch with the outside world where things happen such as ghastly shipwrecks, & pigs flying & other events; when the Times arrives at 6 o'clock I am too lazy to open it . . .

Clementine was obviously feeling a little neglected; the letter goes on:

Meanwhile I have had much leisure to play with & observe the 'kittens'. You will be surprised to hear that they are getting quite fond of me. I am finding out a lot of things about them. They ask occasionally with solicitude & respect about you . . . When shall I see you again!!! Mother & Nellie have gadded off to the Casino to have a little flutter at Chemin de Fer, but I feel apathetic about that too.

I shall go quite to sleep unless someone takes a lot of trouble soon. I am making *such* good salads & coffee & even roasted a chicken tho' the stove is so tiny here it would hardly go inside.

I shall walk out & post this letter & then I think I shall have done very well for one day.

Goodbye absent & wandering Pig!
Your loving
Clemmie
[sketch of cat with two kittens]

Winston was able to spend one day with them all on 3rd June, the *Enchantress* dropping him off at a point near Dieppe early in the morning, and picking him up that same evening, to continue his naval peregrinations. The children were enchanted by this sudden appearance, but, as Clementine wrote the next day,

> The Babies were sad when they found the Enchantress had sailed away in the night & there was no 'Papa' in the Bed in the Day Nursery.[23]

They must have talked about the flying, and Clementine seemed to have resigned herself to the fact that Winston meant to continue his exploits, for she wrote in the same letter:

> I cannot help knowing that you are going to fly as you go to Sheerness & it fills me with anxiety. I know nothing will stop you from doing it so I will not weary you with tedious entreaties, but don't forget that I am thinking about it all the time & so, do it as little, & as moderately as you can, & only with the *very best* Pilot. I feel very 'ears down' about it . . .

A very long letter she wrote the next day shows how much it preyed on her mind, and how overwrought her nerves had become. Nellie and she had made an expedition to Puys, the little village about three miles along the coast where the Hozier family had spent the summer of 1899, before they moved into Dieppe itself. They had a delightful day visiting old haunts, and prospecting possible seaside houses. 'We got home very late,' wrote Clementine,

> But after this pleasant day I have had a miserable night haunted by hideous dreams, so this morning I am sad & worn out.
>   I dreamt that I had my Baby, but the Doctor & Nurse wouldn't show it to me & hid it away. Finally after all my entreaties had been refused I jumped out of bed & ran all over the house searching for it. At last I found it in a darkened room. It looked all right & I feverishly undressed it & counted its fingers & toes. It seemed quite normal & I ran out of the room with it in my arms. And then in the Daylight I saw it was a gaping idiot. And then the worst thing of all happened – I wanted the Doctor to kill it – but he was shocked & took it away & I was mad too. And then I woke up & went to sleep again *and dreamt* it a second time. I feel very nervous and unhappy & the little thing has been fluttering all the morning.
>   Your telegram arrived last night, after we were in bed. Every time I see a telegram now I think it is to announce that you have been killed flying. I had a fright but went to sleep relieved & reassured; but this morning after the nightmare I looked at it again for consolation & found to my horror it was from Sheerness & not from Dover where I thought you were going first – so you are probably at it again at this very moment.
>
> Goodbye Dear but Cruel One
Your loving
Clemmie[24]

Every woman who has borne a child will surely recognise in Clementine's vivid description of her ghastly nightmare the sudden panic-fear that no logic can dispel. Winston may have talked and reasoned down her pleas and arguments and discounted her fears up to now – but his reaction to this letter was instantaneous.

'My darling one, I will not fly any more until at any rate you have recovered from
your kitten,' he wrote to her on 6th June. He went on:

> This is a wrench, because I was on the verge of taking my pilot's certificate. It
> only needed a couple of calm mornings; & I am confident of my ability to achieve
> it vy respectably. I shd greatly have liked to reach this point wh wd have made a
> suitable moment for breaking off. But I must admit that the numerous fatalities
> of this year wd justify you in complaining if I continued to share the risks – as I
> am proud to do – of these good fellows. So I give it up decidedly for many months
> & perhaps for ever. This is a gift – so stupidly am I made – wh costs me more than
> anything wh cd be bought with money. So I am vy glad to lay it at your feet,
> because I know it will rejoice & relieve your heart . . .
>
> You will give me some kisses and forgive me for past distresses – I am sure.
> Though I had no need & perhaps no right to do it – it was an important part of
> my life during the last 7 months, & I am sure my nerve, my spirits & my virtue
> were all improved by it. But at your expense my poor pussy cat! I am so sorry . . .

Winston was as good as his word: he abandoned flying at once.

With this gnawing anxiety removed from her mind, Clementine was able to relax
and enjoy the summer. The sisters-in-law had arranged to spend the best part of
July and August by the sea at Overstrand, near Cromer, with their respective
nurseries. Clementine, Diana, Randolph and their Nanny installed themselves in a
little house called Pear Tree Cottage, while five minutes away Goonie Churchill
and her two sons, Johnny and Peregrine, aged five and one, had taken Beehive
Cottage. Here Clementine passed some happy sunshine weeks, garnering her strength
for her new child, and enjoying the last carefree days she, and many others, were to
know for four long dark years.

The Home Rule Bill had its third reading and was passed by the House of Commons on 26th May 1914, and during the ensuing weeks tension over the Irish Question seemed to be reaching breaking-point. In a last-minute attempt to avert an explosion, the King called a Home Rule Conference at Buckingham Palace on 21st July.
The next day Winston, under a heading *Secretissime*, reported to Clementine that
'the conference is in extremis'; two days later it broke up, having failed to reach
agreement.

While the country's attention was engrossed by these bitter domestic struggles, an
event occurred in central Europe that passed almost unnoticed by the mass of the
British people – on 28th June the Archduke Franz Ferdinand and his wife were
murdered at Sarajevo (in Serbia), setting in train a sequence of events which was to
prove fatal to Europe's peace.

But despite troubles at home and menacing news from abroad, Winston managed
to spend several Sundays with his family at Pear Tree Cottage, where Clementine
declared to him in a letter, 'I am very happy perched among its branches . . .'[25]
After his second visit to them on 12th July, Winston left by sea (being taken off by
Enchantress), writing the next day to Clementine:

> It was quite forlorn leaving you last night. I don't know why a departure to the

sea seems so much more significant, than going off by train. We watched your figures slowly climbing up the zigzag & slowly fading in the dusk; and I felt as if I were going to the other end of the world.

The kittens were vy dear & caressing. They get more lovable every day. Altogether Pear Tree is a vy happy, sunlit picture in my mind's eye. Tender love my dearest – I must try to get you a little country house 'for always'.[26]

Early in 1914 it had been decided by the Cabinet that, as an economy measure, the customary Grand Manoeuvres of the Fleet (involving the wide deployment of many ships) should not take place, but would be replaced by a test mobilisation of part of the Fleet. This took place in July, and was followed by a grand review of the ships of every Fleet passing in front of the King in the Royal Yacht at Spithead. 'It constituted,' Churchill later wrote, 'incomparably the greatest assemblage of naval power ever witnessed in the history of the world.'[27] The ships of the Third Fleet, having completed their test mobilisation, were about to disperse to their various ports, when it was learnt that Austria had delivered an ultimatum to Serbia.

After attending a Cabinet meeting on Friday, 24th July, Winston wrote to Clementine:

. . . Europe is trembling on the verge of a general war. The Austrian ultimatum to Serbia being the most insolent document of its kind ever devised. Side by side with this the Provincial govt. in Ulster wh is now imminent appears comparatively a humdrum affair.

But despite the gravity of the situation, there was no positive feeling in government circles that England would be involved, even if there were to be a conflict on the European continent, and Winston was able to spend the week-end at Overstrand.

On Sunday, 26th July, between telephone calls to and from the Admiralty, Winston played with the children on the beach:

We dammed the little rivulets which trickled down to the sea as the tide went out. It was a very beautiful day. The North Sea sparkled to a far horizon.[28]

However, this idyllic and domestic day was to be cut short. After speaking on the telephone to Prince Louis of Battenberg (the First Sea Lord) at midday, Winston decided that events demanded his presence, and he returned to London, where Prince Louis had already given orders to halt the dispersal of the Fleet.

During the ensuing days Winston kept Clementine in touch with events both by letter and telephone. Pear Tree Cottage had no telephone, but kind neighbours, Sir Edgar Speyer and his wife (rich Liberal German Jews), offered Clementine the use of their telephone. From there at pre-set times, and talking in veiled language, she was able to keep track of the increasingly menacing course of events. On returning to the cottage after talking to Winston one night, she wrote:

. . . Goodnight my Dearest one. I trust the news may be better tomorrow. Surely every hour of delay must make the forces of peace more powerful. It would be a wicked war.[29]

But Austria rejected Serbia's conciliatory reply to her ultimatum, and the prospect of Russian intervention on Serbia's side, which would draw in France and Britain, grew more likely every hour. At midnight on 28th July Winston wrote to Clementine from the Admiralty:

> Everything tends towards catastrophe & collapse. I am interested, geared up & happy. Is it not horrible to be built like that? The preparations have a hideous fascination for me. I pray to God to forgive me for such fearful moods of levity. Yet I wd do my best for peace . . .

Despite the imminence of catastrophe, he could still turn his attention to small and peaceful things:

> The two black swans on St James's Park lake have a darling cygnet – grey, fluffy, precious and unique. I watched them this evening for some time as a relief from all the plans & schemes.[30]

The next day, Clementine replied:

> My Darling,
>
>   I have just returned from telephoning you & find your letter. I am glad that you are 'cap à pied' but how I do pray that the perfection of your plans may not be brought to the test in this foreign quarrel. I am sad that I shall not see you this week (last Sunday was so delicious) but I fear it is far for you in these critical times, in spite of the Speyers' splendid telephone.
>
>   While I am waiting for the connection in Sir Edgar's 'study' I contemplate a lovely Madonna over the mantelpiece who gazes with melancholy eyes at the piles of Business Books on the writing table . . . [31]

Two days later, on 31st July, Winston told her: 'There is still hope although the clouds are blacker and blacker.'

Happy though she was with her seaside life and in the company of her babies Clementine longed to be with Winston:

> . . . I much wish I were with you during these anxious thrilling days & know how you are feeling – tingling with life to the tips of your fingers . . . [32]

On Sunday, 2nd August the Cabinet sat almost continuously; there were deep divisions among its members at this agonising hour of decision. In the early hours of that morning Winston had written a hurried note to Clementine to tell her the latest, fateful piece of news.

2nd August 1914   Admiralty,
1 a.m.   Whitehall.
>   Cat – dear,
>
>   It is all up. Germany has quenched the last hopes of peace by declaring war on Russia.

Events now took charge of men, and rolled them forward relentlessly towards the terrible abyss. Following on Germany's ultimatum, the King of the Belgians appealed to France and Great Britain to protect his country's neutrality. On 3rd August Germany declared war on France and invaded Belgium. At eleven o'clock on the night of 4th August the British ultimatum to Germany expired, and Great Britain was at war. As the first strokes of Big Ben sounded the fatal hour, there flashed from the Admiralty to every British ship and naval establishment throughout the world the signal: 'Commence hostilities against Germany.'

ALL OVER BY CHRISTMAS

RITAIN'S DECLARATION OF WAR against Germany was greeted by a gale of patriotic hysteria and flag-waving, in strong contrast to the country's quiet dogged acceptance of war twenty-five years later. The spectre of civil war with Ireland, which had loomed so large, was, for the time being, exorcised; and despite bitter divisions between the parties, the Conservatives gave the Government their wholehearted support. The outbreak of war unified all classes and shades of opinion throughout the country. Conscription was not to come till much later, and in this autumn of 1914 men flocked to the recruiting stations – among them many Irish volunteers. Guarded by the Navy, the British Expeditionary Force was transported safe and sound across the Channel during the first weeks of August. The general feeling throughout the country was one of elation and excitement, and a confident certainty (shared even in some well-informed quarters) that it would all be over by Christmas.

All Churchill's efforts since his appointment to the Admiralty to put the Navy on a war footing had culminated in the swift and efficient mobilisation of the Fleet. But the dramatic speed at which the final crisis had developed meant that many decisions concerning the High Command had to be taken without delay. One of these decisions, which Winston found a painful one, was to relieve Admiral Sir George Callaghan of the Supreme Command of the Home Fleets, replacing him by Sir John Jellicoe. Sir George was due to retire on 1st October 1914 but Churchill was doubtful whether his health and physical strength were equal to the immense strain that would now be cast upon him, and this was no time to consider individuals. Winston told Clementine of the decision on 31st July, when he wrote to her:

> I have resolved to remove Callaghan & place Jellicoe in supreme command as soon as it becomes certain that war will be declared.

Clementine's reply provides an example of the sage and perceptive advice she was to give Winston many times during their long life together. Often he did not take it, and sometimes he regretted he had not. In this case she did not doubt the wisdom of the decision, but she expressed concern about the manner in which Sir George Callaghan should be relieved of his command. On 4th August she wrote to Winston:

> I have been cogitating for an hour or two over the 'Callico Jellatine' crisis, which, Thank God, is over as far as essentials are concerned.

There only remains the deep wound in an old man's heart.

If you put the wrong sort of poultice on, it will fester – (Do not be vexed, when you are so occupied with vital things my writing to you about this, which, in its way, is important too). An interview with the Sovereign and a decoration to my mind is the wrong practice – To a proud sensitive man at this moment a decoration must be an insult.

Please see him yourself & take him by the hand and (additional) offer him a seat on the Board, or if this is impossible give him *some* advisory position at the Admiralty. It does not matter if he 'cannot say Bo to a Goose' – His lips will then be sealed and his wife's too. Don't think this is a trivial matter. At this moment you want everyone's heart & soul – you don't want even a small clique of retired people to feel bitter & to cackle. If you give him a position of honour and confidence, the whole service will feel that he has been as well treated as possible under the circumstances, & that he has not been humiliated.

This will prevent people now at the top of the Tree feeling 'In a few years *I* shall be cast off like an old shoe' – Jellicoe & Beatty & Warrender & Bailey, now the flower of the service, are only a few years younger than Callaghan.

Then, don't underrate the power of women to do mischief. I don't want Lady Callaghan & Lady Bridgeman* to form a league of retired Officers' Cats, to abuse you. Poor old Lady Callaghan's grief will be intense but if you are good to him now it will be softened; if he is still employed she is bound to be comparatively silent.

Anyhow I beg of you to see him.

If I were doing it – if he refused the appointment I would earnestly urge him again & again . . . to accept it, saying you need his services – then he will believe it & come round & there will not be any disagreeableness left from this difficult business.

[sketch of a cat]

In the crash of war, molehills retain their proper proportions; but Clementine's perception and awareness of people's feelings were over and over again to be a help to Winston, who in striding towards the main goal was often totally oblivious of the side-effects of his actions, or of other people's reactions to them. No immediate appointment was announced for Sir George Callaghan, but in December 1914 he was appointed Commander-in-Chief at the Nore.

Another example of Clementine's moderating and sage advice is to be found in an undated letter of hers, which must belong to this period. Winston formed the habit of making frequent short visits to see Sir John French, the Commander-in-Chief of the British Expeditionary Force, at his Headquarters in France. From these visits Winston gained much useful information, and was able to form a wide and general view of the military situation; but they were criticised by some of his colleagues. One of these expeditions was in the offing towards the end of September, when Clementine wrote to Winston:

. . . Now please don't think *me* tiresome; but I want you to tell the P.M. of your

*The wife of Admiral Sir Francis Bridgeman, who had prematurely retired as First Sea Lord in 1912, to make way for Prince Louis of Battenberg.

projected visit to Sir John French. It would be very bad manners if you do not & he will be displeased and hurt.

Of course I know you will consult K [Lord Kitchener, now Secretary of State for War]. Otherwise the journey will savour of a week-end escapade & not of a mission. You would be surprised and incensed if K skipped off to visit Jellicoe on his own. I wish my Darling you didn't crave to go. It makes me grieve to see you gloomy & dissatisfied with the unique position you have reached thro' years of ceaseless industry & foresight. The P.M. leans on you & listens to you more & more. You are the only young vital person in the Cabinet. It is really wicked of you not to be swelling with pride at being 1st Lord of the Admiralty during the greatest War since the beginning of the World. And there is still much to be done & only *you* can do it . . .

Be a good one & rejoice & don't hanker. Great & glorious as have been the achievements of our army, it is only a small one, ⅛ of the allied forces. Whereas you rule this gigantic Navy which will in the end decide the War . . .[1]

Winston paid heed to Clementine's advice; he wrote on 26th September to Lord Kitchener, who made no objection. 'How right you were about telling K.,' Winston acknowledged, in a letter written aboard the ship taking him to France.[2]

Although she must have longed to be at his side and at the centre of events, Clementine, now in the seventh month of pregnancy, wisely stayed on at Pear Tree Cottage with the children. She gleaned what news she could from Winston's letters and the veiled conversations she was able to conduct over the Speyers' telephone. Winston had left their car with her; in the back of his mind lurked the fear that the east coast might be the objective for a German raid, and he wished her and the children to have a ready means of flight if necessary. However, the car gave trouble: 'The motor is a lame duck till Wednesday at least,' Clementine wrote on Saturday, 8th August, 'so I hope the Germans won't arrive before that date. I have taken I hope efficient measures to have it seen to . . .'

But in any case the future of the 'motor', it seems, was uncertain, for her next letter on the following day puts forward a delightful suggestion:

. . . I have had such a good idea. Later on, in the spring . . . let us instead [of the motor] have 2 chestnut horses 'with nice long tails' & ride for an hour every morning. It would be far more value to you than a motor & I should enjoy it so much. It would not cost so much surely? . . .[3]

It is interesting that even she, living so much in touch with affairs, had not grasped, at that moment, the severity of the ordeal that lay ahead.

Most of the summer visitors to Cromer were packing up and leaving for their homes, to the great distress of the local landladies and shopkeepers. Clementine described to Winston in the same letter how

Yesterday the local authorities in a frantic effort to stem the ebbing tide of tourists had the following pathetic appeal flashed on the screen of the local cinema show. (I am not sure of the words, but this is the gist.)

'Visitors! Why are you leaving Cromer? Mrs Winston Churchill and her children are in residence in the neighbourhood. If it's safe enough for her, surely it's safe enough for you!'

In his letter of 9th August, Winston reverted to his fears for her safety:

It makes me a little anxious that you should be on the coast. It is a 100 to one against a raid – but still there is the chance, and Cromer has a good landing place near.

I wish you would get the motor repaired and keep it so that you can whisk away at the first sign of trouble . . .

His anxiety over a possible raid was not merely fanciful, for that very December the east coast towns of Scarborough, Whitby and Hartlepool were bombarded by German ships, with considerable loss of life.

Clementine thirsted for news; Winston must have alerted her (on the telephone) to the arrival of a letter from him, for in her letter of 9th August she goes on:

I am longing to get your letter with the secret news. It shall be destroyed at once. I hope that in it, you tell me about the expeditionary force. Do I guess right that some have gone already? Be a good one and write again & feed me with tit-bits. I am being so wise & good & sitting on the Beach & playing with my kittens, & doing my little housekeeping, but how I long to dash up & be near you and the pulse of things . . .

The same day Winston sent her a document to put her in the picture, with strict instructions to burn it at once. Replying to him on 10th August, she assured him:

The Secret document has been read & burnt before my eyes in the kitchen fire! It was most interesting but I was disappointed because I hoped you were going to tell me about the Expeditionary Force. Do send me news of it. When it is going, where it will land, which regiments are in the first batch, etc. I long for it to arrive in time to save the Liège citizens from being massacred in their houses.

On 11th August Winston wrote a very short note, which revealed how tired he was; it contained also a very gentle rebuke regarding her undeniably indiscreet questions about the Expeditionary Force.

My dear one,
    This is only a line from a vy tired Winston. The Expedy Force about wh you are so inquisitive is on its road & will be all on the spot in time. I wish I cd whisk down to you & dig a little on the beach. My work here is vy heavy & so interesting that I cannot leave it.
                                            Now I am really going to knock off.
                                            Ever your loving
                                                    W

The note of fatigue in Winston's letter produced a reply the next day, full of practical suggestions as well as sympathy:

Now are you doing everything you can not to be too tired?
1) Never missing your morning ride.

2) Going to bed well *before* midnight & sleeping well and *not* allowing yourself
to be woken up every time a Belgian kills a German. (You *must* have 8
hours sleep every night to be your best self.)

3) Not smoking too much & not having indigestion.

Now shall I come up for a day or two next Monday & tease you partly into
doing all these things? Or are you being a good one all by yourself? . . .

The golden sands are too delicious & long to have fortifications made on them,
& there is a little stream that really *ought* to be dammed. But Alas it is too far.
Goodbye my sweet one. I am so proud of you & love you very much . . .[4]

Although removed from the hub of affairs, life at Pear Tree and Beehive Cottages
was not without its diversions and excitements. Out of the blue a Mr Robert
Houston, a wealthy ship-owner and Conservative M.P., although unacquainted with
either Winston or Clementine, sent her, enclosed in a letter of praise of Winston, a
huge emerald and diamond ring. Clementine of course returned this generous, but
unsuitable present with an appreciative letter. But during the brief time she had this
lovely jewel in her possession it caused a sensation. 'Goonie was struck all of a
heap,' she wrote to Winston, and 'Lady Speyer who is a "connoisseur" says she
thinks it is an antique. She is covered with emerald rings . . . none of them come
anywhere near it!' Clementine went on to philosophise on the unfairness of things:

What an illogical world it is. Becos' I have a Pig who is a Genius and a 'Poodle-
Ching' I am given a costly jewel, whereas if I had an inferior husband & needed
consolation I should get nothing! for nothing.

Winston wrote back on 13th August, full of praise for his high-minded 'Kat':

How right you were not to hesitate to send back the ring, & what a good thing it is
to have high & inflexible principles! You are a dear & splendid Kat. I am vy
proud of you. What you have done for me no one can measure.

Both Clementine and Nellie thought it unwise for their mother to go on living
in Dieppe, and Nellie was therefore despatched to bring her home; Clementine
invited her to join them at Pear Tree Cottage, where she arrived around the middle
of August. Her arrival coincided with Overstrand's local attack of 'spy-mania' –
an epidemic of highly-coloured (and generally not well substantiated) stories of
spies and their alleged activities, which swept through the country just then.

Clementine reported a local incident to Winston on 13th August 1914:

Yesterday one of the cottager's wives saw two men walking along the cliff. Their
coats were bulging & she thought they were carrying some puppies. It was rather
a lonely part of the cliff & they looked annoyed when they saw her, & spoke to
each other in a foreign tongue. When they had passed, she hid herself & then
followed them at a distance. She then saw them open their jackets & let fly 4
carrier pigeons! She kept them in sight for some time but eventually they disappeared into a lane. Luckily on her way home she met 2 officers in a little car.
She told them about it, & they pursued the men & caught them . . .

Mother is much alarmed at the 'carrier pigeon story' & insists that the message carried by the pigeons was that 'the wife of the First Lord is at Overstrand, & that the Germans are to send an aeroplane to kidnap me & that then I am to be ransomed by the handing over of several of our handsomest ships.'

If I *am* kidnapped I beg of you not to sacrifice the smallest or cheapest submarine or even the oldest ship . . . I could not face the subsequent unpopularity whereas I should be quite a heroine & you a Spartan if I died bravely & unransomed . . .

But although Clementine recounted the 'spy' incident with such verve and gaiety, she was in fact in a highly agitated, almost hysterical state of mind, engendered by what she considered to be Nellie's inconsiderate and wrong-headed behaviour. She poured out the whole story in great detail to Winston, in a letter on 14th August which covered pages and pages of writing paper.

Nellie had escorted Lady Blanche back to England, and Clementine had expected that she would deliver their mother herself to Pear Tree Cottage. However, in the event, Lady Blanche arrived alone, in a feeble and exhausted state, bearing a letter from Nellie telling Clementine she had gone to Cliveden (the Astors' house in Buckinghamshire) to help in its conversion into a convalescent home.

Clementine was displeased by this news, as she had arranged with Nellie that she would come with their mother to Overstrand, and remain to look after her, so that Clementine could go up to London to spend some time with Winston. She was made even more angry when another letter arrived from Nellie announcing that she was going immediately to Belgium as part of a nursing unit headed by her friend Angela Manners, whose parents, Lord and Lady Manners, and their friends were financing the team, which was to consist of a surgeon, six nurses and Nellie, who was to act as secretary and interpreter.*

Clementine was outraged – at this distance of time it seems rather unreasonably so. She wrote to Winston:

It is all cheap emotion. Nellie is not trained, she will be one more useless mouth to feed in that poor little country which in a few days will be the scene of horrible grim happenings.

Nellie's obvious and natural duty is to look after Mother whom she has brought over from Dieppe and 'dumped' down thus leaving her responsibilities without a thought to others.

I feel quite ill this morning, as I have had a very bad night & this on top of it has really upset me. I long to see you & put my arms round your neck. You are always so sane and sensible my darling one, & you would calm my hurt and angry feelings . . .

But my Dear, in the midst of your work it is wrong of me to bubble over like this, but my heart is full & I can't help it.

Goonie is sweet & placid & I have confided my indignation to her . . .[5]

In a long sequel to this stormy letter, written a few hours later, Clementine, now

*This is an interesting example of what scope there was in the First World War for 'private enterprise' schemes. There were many similar teams and organisations.

somewhat calmed, attempted to be 'reasonable and calm & to analyse why I was so upset'. She had to admit it was because she felt she had been left in the lurch by Nellie:

> ... just now when I am not feeling very well & would appreciate comfort & support she has left me to cope with Mother alone, which she knows, even when I am feeling very brisk & well is a tax on the nerves![6]

It must be remembered that Clementine was now within six weeks of her confinement and was, of course, feeling her long separation from Winston. Having got it all off her chest in this tempestuous outburst, however, she avowed:

> I feel better since writing to you my Darling. Do not misjudge me for being so garrulous.
>
> > Your loving very tired
> > Clemmie

But despite her elder sister's disapproval the impetuous and intrepid Nellie lost no time in carrying out her intentions, and she left for Brussels on 14th August with the nursing unit, as she had intended. She and her friends were in Brussels when it was occupied by the Germans on 20th August, but they managed to get to Mons a few days after the battle, and in the confusion of the retreat which followed their unit was taken prisoner by the Germans. Nellie's spirits were undaunted, however, and her natural impudence unquenched. While locked in the waiting-room of a railway station with her companions, she scrawled upon the walls the following jingle:

> Our good King George is both
> Greater and wiser,
> Than all other monarchs,
> Including 'der Kaiser'.

The nursing unit, however, was eventually allowed to continue its work with the British wounded, and several fascinating letters from Nellie survive, giving a lively and moving account of daily life in the little hospital, and the horrors and ordeals to which the Belgian civilian population were subjected by their conquerors. Clementine and Lady Blanche were able to communicate with her occasionally, but their anxiety was intense, not only because of Nellie's proximity to the fighting line, but also on account of her impudent tongue and plucky spirit which could easily have got her and her fellow prisoners into trouble with their captors.

At the end of the summer Clementine left Pear Tree Cottage and returned with the children to Winston in London, where she spent the last month before the birth of her child. This joyous, natural event was deeply overcast by the news of the terrible events which were sweeping over Europe like relentless waves. As the weeks went by, more and more people bore the burden of bereavement as the armies came to grips, and the remorseless harvesting of a whole generation began on the battle-fields of Flanders and France.

The early sunlit seaside weeks of the war must now have seemed like a dream for

Clementine who, in addition to feeling national events and the sorrows of her friends, had personal and family preoccupations. As well as anxiety for Nellie, Bill was now commanding H.M.S. *Thorn*, a torpedo destroyer, and Jack Churchill was in France with the Oxfordshire Hussars. And these worries were much increased by Winston's sudden departure on 3rd October to take part in the defence of Antwerp.

The Germans' plan had been to take the Allies by surprise – to sweep through Belgium and then destroy the French army in a single mighty onslaught. This plan was foiled by the Allies' desperate resistance on the River Marne. The opposing armies became locked in bitter conflict, and on both flanks a race for the sea began, to gain possession of the strategic ports on the Belgian coast. Of these, one of the most vital was Antwerp, which was not only important to the strategy and safety of the British Army but was made also the heart and stronghold of Belgian resistance by the presence there of the King and Queen of the Belgians and their Government.

On 2nd October a telegram had been received from Antwerp announcing the intention of the Belgian Government and the King and Queen to leave Antwerp the following day. This was grave news indeed; and at a midnight conference Sir Edward Grey, Lord Kitchener and Churchill agreed that someone of standing and authority should be sent immediately to the beleaguered fortress city. This task was confided to Churchill, who, needless to say, was an eager volunteer. Very early on the morning of 3rd October he was on his way to Antwerp. It was a situation which appealed to his every instinct: a desperate struggle; action in which he himself could play a decisive role; and, above all, the chance to share dangers with brave and patriotic men.

On learning that reinforcements were to be sent and that Winston Churchill – a Cabinet Minister – was on the way to join them as the emissary of the British Government, the Belgian Council of War suspended the order to evacuate Antwerp.

During the few hectic and dangerous days Churchill remained in the now closely besieged city, he became deeply and emotionally identified with its fate, and on the morning of 5th October he telegraphed to the Prime Minister asking that he might be permitted to resign as First Lord of the Admiralty and take formal charge of the British forces in Antwerp. This extraordinary request, which Mr Asquith described as being received by his colleagues with a 'Homeric laugh'[7], was firmly refused. The Cabinet decided to send out Lieutenant-General Sir Henry Rawlinson, and Churchill was asked to hold the fort as best he might until Sir Henry's arrival. Churchill handed over to him on the evening of 6th October, and travelled back to London overnight. It was clear that Antwerp could not hold out much longer, and the city in fact capitulated on 10th October.

Clementine had been startled by the suddenness of Winston's departure for Antwerp, and during the ensuing days her fears for his safety were mingled with deep doubts as to the wisdom of his action. In her heart, she thought his impetuous intervention – albeit as the official representative of the Government – unwise. She was even more disconcerted when she learnt of his wild telegram: to her it smacked of an almost frivolous approach to this affair. Both to his wife and his colleagues it seemed crystal clear that Winston's sense of proportion had deserted him. The

siege of Antwerp was a dramatic incident; the prolongation of the city's resistance
was certainly of vital importance at that moment, but in the whole scale of events it
could not compare in significance with Winston's own ministerial responsibility for
the overall direction of the maritime power of Great Britain. Politically astute,
Clementine realised also that Winston's rash and ill-conceived request would harm
him both in the opinion of his colleagues and in the eyes of the general public.

It was towards the end of these days of doubt and sharp anxiety that, early on the
morning of Wednesday, 7th October, Clementine gave birth at Admiralty House
to their third child – a red-headed daughter. During the course of the same day
Winston arrived home, and the Court Circular records that he was received at
Buckingham Palace by the King. He also was received 'in audience' by his Clemmie
and the new Sarah (as the baby was to be called) – and great were the relief and
the rejoicings.

But in after years, Clementine was always to speak of the Antwerp incident with
a tinge of resentment. She never really accepted that Winston's inescapable public
duty was there, and amid her anxieties for his safety, and her apprehensions over
the wisdom of his actions, was mingled the very understandable wish for her husband
to be near her for the birth of their child.

Although Churchill's impetuous intervention at Antwerp brought him discredit
in many quarters, and was attacked by most of the Press, he was given a warm
reception by his colleagues on his return. Whatever reservations they may have felt,
they appreciated the heroic efforts he had made to prolong Antwerp's resistance.
One of them, Sir Edward Grey, wrote Clementine this warm and charming letter:

> Committee of Imperial Defence,
> 2, Whitehall Gardens, S.W
> October 7, 1914
>
> Dear Mrs Churchill
> I am so glad to hear that you & the new baby are well.
> I am sitting next Winston at this Committee, having just welcomed his return
> from Antwerp.
> And I feel a glow imported by the thought that I am sitting next a Hero. I
> cant tell you how much I admire his courage & gallant spirit & genius for war.
> It inspires us all.
>
> Yours very sincerely
> Edward Grey

Later this incident, or 'escapade', as many regarded it, was used to brand Winston
as an irresponsible adventurer; but in retrospect two things emerge quite clearly:
Churchill's presence in Antwerp undeniably stiffened the resistance of the Belgians, and in delaying the capitulation of the city, a signal service was rendered to
the Allies. But it was Violet Bonham Carter's measured opinion that 'No event in
his whole career, with the one exception of Gallipoli, did him greater and more
undeserved damage.'[8]

*

In order to recuperate after the birth of Sarah, Clementine spent a few weeks in November at Belcaire, Lympne, in Kent, the house of Sir Philip Sassoon, where she and Winston were often to be guests in the years to come. Winston was not able to visit her much during this time, the pressure and gravity of events being too great. Although Clementine longed to see him, she completely understood the reason for his absence. 'I am sure you ought not to leave London just now even for a few hours,' she wrote on 18th November 1914, 'so don't even *think* of coming next Sunday . . .'

Happily she was not without company, as Goonie was able to be with her for part of the time. 'Poor Goonie is in a great state of anxiety about Jack,' she wrote to Winston on 19th November,

> as the 2nd Division was in action on Tuesday, and she calculates from his last letter that Jack would that day have been in the trenches.

Many, many women must have been making these agonising calculations. But before she had finished this letter, Winston had telephoned that Jack (quite coincidentally) had been posted to Sir John French's staff, and so Clementine was able to finish her letter on a brighter note:

> Goonie is *so* happy about Jack being on the staff. She has been so sad all day, but now she is overjoyed. We have both been sitting completely buried by papers all the afternoon paying our bills. Outside the snow is falling thick and fast.

Later that same month, to all her family's relief and joy, Nellie arrived home; the Germans having apparently decided to repatriate the whole nursing unit, after they had gone on strike and refused to nurse German wounded. Evidently the authorities felt they had enough troubles on their hands without being encumbered by a small party of non-combatants, imbued with a saucy and rebellious spirit. Nellie and her companions were therefore bundled home; they were routed through Norway and arrived safe and sound, but shivering, as they were still in the thin summer uniforms in which they had set out the previous August.

In the first months of the war, the Navy had sustained some severe blows. But in early December cheering news of a splendid victory at sea warmed British hearts when Admiral Sturdee's ships sank four out of five of a German squadron near the Falkland Islands. The British Navy was now supreme, and our supply lines across the world were (for the time being) free from the fear of surface raiders.

As 1914 drew to its close, such good news was indeed welcome, for all hope of a quick victory had faded from even the most sanguine heart. From the Channel to the Swiss frontier the armies faced each other, locked in the pattern of trench warfare whose grim grip was to hold them fast for four long years. By the end of December, on the western front alone, 95,654 British soldiers of all ranks had been killed.[9] And this was a mere tithe of the grisly harvest other years held in store.

THE DARDANELLES

S THE RIGIDITY AND HORROR of the trench-bound 'slogging match' established itself on the western front, the War Council cast about for some alternative and more hopeful strategy, and a division of opinion developed between those – the 'Westerners' – who believed the war could be more swiftly won by a diversionary thrust across the North Sea from the west, and the 'Easterners', who believed in a breakthrough from the Eastern Mediterranean.

Of the Easterners' stratagems, the forcing of the Dardanelles Straits (between the Turkish mainland and the Gallipoli Peninsula), with the capture of Constantinople as its objective, soon gained promoters – and from the first caught Churchill's attention and imagination. The particular relevance of this scheme to the needs of the moment was vividly underlined when on 5th November 1914 Turkey entered the war as Germany's ally.

The original Dardanelles project involved the necessity of a considerable military force to take, and to hold, the Gallipoli Peninsula, as well as the naval forces required to force the Straits, pushing through into the Sea of Marmara, where Constantinople, which held the key to many doors, would lie within our grasp.

The search for an alternative strategy continued all through the winter months of 1914, and at least four possibilities were seriously considered. Although from the first convinced of the virtues of attacking through the Dardanelles, Churchill, at the New Year, was pressing for the Borkum plan (a scheme to invade Schleswig-Holstein from the island of Borkum off the Dutch coast), Lord Kitchener having told the War Council that no troops could be made available for a Mediterranean operation from the western theatre of war. But early in January 1915 there came a desperate appeal to the Allies from the Grand Duke Nicholas for some major demonstration to be made against the Turks, who were pressing the Russians hard in the Caucasus. The way to help them swiftly and effectively was by attacking the Turks through the Dardanelles.

Meanwhile a vitally important change had taken place in the considerations governing the Dardanelles plan. Admiral Carden (the Commander in the Eastern Mediterranean) had given it as his considered professional opinion that the Dardanelles could be forced by ships alone, and on 12th January 1915 his detailed scheme was received at the Admiralty.

The strategic situation had thus been transformed. When Churchill eloquently presented this scheme to his weary colleagues the following day, Sir Maurice Hankey (Secretary to the War Council, later Lord Hankey) recalled how

The whole atmosphere changed. Fatigue was forgotten. The War Council turned eagerly from the dreary vista of a 'slogging match' on the Western Front to brighter prospects, as they seemed, in the Mediterranean.[1]

And the Council resolved that the Admiralty should forthwith prepare for a naval expedition in February to bombard and take the Gallipoli Peninsula, with Constantinople as its objective.

*

One of Churchill's first actions on going to the Admiralty had been to persuade Admiral of the Fleet Lord Fisher (then aged seventy) to abandon his retirement by the Lake of Lucerne and to return to England to act as his unofficial adviser on naval matters. Lord Fisher had always been a controversial character; but his single-minded devotion to the Navy, and his undoubted brilliance, had placed him in a special position of power and influence. When in 1910 he retired after six years as First Sea Lord, he had become a legend – admired by many, and detested by not a few: for, to use his own words, he was 'ruthless, relentless and remorseless'[2] in regard to anyone who opposed or gainsaid him.

Churchill had first met Admiral Fisher in 1907, and over the succeeding years had come to know and esteem this strange, volcanic character. For three years after he was appointed to the Admiralty, the youthful First Lord and the veteran Admiral worked in the closest co-operation and warm friendship, and Churchill had shown unusual patience and tact in handling his eccentric, but invaluable colleague. When at the end of October 1914 the First Sea Lord, Prince Louis of Battenberg, was forced to resign as the result of a shameful campaign of vilification, based on his German extraction, Churchill pressed for Lord Fisher to be his successor. The appointment was duly made. It was to prove to be of ill-omen to Churchill himself.

From the time the Dardanelles project was first mooted, Clementine knew about it, and became well acquainted with the arguments which surrounded the concept, and the rival schemes which were propounded. Winston then, as later, had complete confidence in her discretion, and to her he confided his hopes, his fears, and his frustrations. She knew how deeply he believed in the strategic plan for the forcing of the Dardanelles, a belief he never abandoned – neither in the overturn of his most sanguine hopes and careful plans, nor afterwards, in the shambles of his own fortunes.

Many errors of judgment, both by the commanders on the spot and the War Council in London, contributed to the failure of Churchill's grand strategy. Since an immediate success was expected after the first naval assault, there was no prior agreement on the number of men and ships which might ultimately be committed in the Eastern Mediterranean. And when there was no easy victory, the field was open to those whose opposition to the plan Churchill had so eloquently persuaded away. And this applied most particularly to Lord Fisher, whose changing views had swung during the weeks of discussion and preparation from violent opposition to wild enthusiasm, and back again to grumbling disapproval.

These dramatic tergiversations in the old Admiral's views caused Clementine increasing uneasiness. Winston had told her that although Lord Fisher's original preference had been for the 'Borkum' plan, he had been won over, and had thrown himself enthusiastically into the preparations for the Dardanelles operation. Nevertheless, Clementine was anxious. She knew how changeable and chancy 'Fisher weather' could be, and she realised that his real feelings and instincts had been overruled by Winston's passionate enthusiasm, and by his capacity to put a case with irresistible force.

It had meanwhile been decided that a military force should be sent to the Dardanelles, and at the end of February the King reviewed the Royal Naval Division (who had received their baptism of fire at the siege of Antwerp) before their embarkation for Gallipoli. The review was held on the downs above Blandford Camp in Dorset. Clementine went with Winston, and Mrs Asquith and Violet were there, for one of Violet's brothers was among those on parade. It was a day of brilliant sunshine sparkling with frost; Clementine and Violet were on horseback, and before the King's arrival they cantered along the lines of the battalions drawn up on the sweeping downland. It was a stirring sight, and although hopes were high, it must have had a poignant touch, for among those 'standing like rocks before their men'[3] were faces dear and familiar to Clementine and Violet, and to many of those who had gathered to watch the review. They were a fair pattern of the generation of gifted young men, so many of whom the war was to sweep away.

From the outset the Dardanelles force was ill-equipped; it was discovered at the last moment that the Hood Battalion was without doctors or drugs, and, Mr Asquith wrote to Venetia, 'Clemmie showed a good deal of resource, with the result that they will pick up some necessary "details" at Malta.'[4]

A week or two later there was another 'farewell', when Winston and Clementine went to Charing Cross to bid Godspeed to Major-General Sir Ian Hamilton, who was leaving with his staff to take command at the seat of operations. Among his officers was Jack Churchill (now a major). The little band was full of hope and confidence in the enterprise. They did not guess – happily could not know – the disasters that lay ahead.

During these anxious, fateful months of the spring of 1915 even the nursery-world at Admiralty House, cocooned and sheltered in its upstairs existence, was aware of some threatening cloud which seemed to brood over their parents' life. Hanging round the dining-room table, or crawling on the drawing-room floor, the children heard snippets of conversation. Diana remembered clearly sensing the atmosphere of anxiety, and every night she ended her prayers with an earnest plea: 'God bless the Dardanelles' – whatever they might be.

On 19th February the bombardment and reduction of the outer defences of the Dardanelles began, and although operations had to be suspended owing to bad weather, they were resumed a few days later, and were progressing well. But as time went on, Churchill became concerned that Admiral Carden did not seem to be pressing the attack with sufficient vigour. The Admiral was in fact ill, and in the middle of March he had to resign his command; his place was taken by his second-in-command, Admiral J. N. de Robeck.

On 18th March British and French ships entered the Straits and bombarded the Turkish forts. It is now known that the ammunition in these forts was exhausted in this onslaught, and that further supplies were not at hand. Unfortunately two British battleships (expendable, inasmuch as they were both out of date and due to be scrapped) and a French ship were sunk by mines. But instead of driving on, Admiral de Robeck, after consultation with Sir Ian Hamilton, called off the naval attack. It was never to be renewed.

The commanders at the scene of these events decided to withdraw and to prepare an amphibious landing with reinforcements on the Gallipoli Peninsula. It was not until 25th April that the landings were made by British and Anzac troops. In the five weeks' interval between the main attack on the Straits and the amphibious assault on the Peninsula, the enemy had not been idle, and the landings were made in the face of blistering fire from the Turks. At the cost of heavy loss of life, our forces gained a precarious foothold along the southern tip of the Peninsula. The Turks held the higher ground, and no further advance was possible; our forces dug themselves lines of trenches – it was a touch of bitter irony that the same hideous pattern was repeating itself.

Churchill was consternated and did his utmost to get orders sent for the resumption of the attack, but there was general reluctance both at the Admiralty and at Downing Street to overrule the 'man-on-the-spot'. Lord Fisher obstructed all his efforts to send naval reinforcements, being determined that the British Navy should not be endangered in the Dardanelles. Churchill was to write later:

> The 'No' principle had become established in men's minds, and nothing could ever eradicate it.[5]

Events at home now started to move towards crisis point. Gallipoli was not the only source of disturbing news; in France the Second Battle of Ypres had begun on 22nd April. During the course of it the Germans used poison gas for the first time, adding a new and terrifying ingredient to life at the front. Sir John French complained of a shortage of shells: the shell 'scandal' was thereupon taken up by Lord Northcliffe, who fanned the trouble in his newspapers. Lord Kitchener, the hero of Omdurman and of the Boer War, hitherto beyond criticism in the eyes of the British public, was the principal target of his attacks, but blame and discredit fell upon the whole Liberal administration. There was a political truce in force, but many Conservative back-benchers were restive and critical; and above all, their hostility was directed upon that renegade Tory – Winston Churchill. Every naval disaster was laid at his door. They had blamed him for his part in the siege of Antwerp, and now as the news made clear bit by bit the miscarrying of the Dardanelles plan, the volume of criticism directed personally against him increased every hour.

It was at this moment of rising political tension at home and bad news from abroad that Lord Fisher abruptly resigned as First Sea Lord.

In these last few months Churchill's relationship with Lord Fisher had been particularly difficult and explosive. Soon after the 'go ahead' had been given to the Dardanelles operation, rumblings of dissent and dissatisfaction began to emanate from the First Sea Lord; but he never voiced his objections in open council. Moreover, the disagreements between the two men were not confined to the Dardanelles, and on more than one occasion Lord Fisher had resigned (or threatened to resign) on other issues, but he had always, in the end, been persuaded to stay.

Clementine's doubts and anxieties about the old Admiral had meanwhile increased. She noticed that whenever Winston was away from the Admiralty for a few days, the First Sea Lord seemed profoundly uneasy at being 'in charge of the shop'. Despite his frequently expressed contempt for politicians, he showed every sign of nervousness when the moment-to-moment responsibility was his. Furthermore, a curious incident took place, which left a strong and unfavourable impression upon her.

Sometimes, when Winston was going to be away, he would say to Clementine, 'Just look after "the old boy" for me.' And so Clementine would invite Lord Fisher to have luncheon with her from time to time, during Winston's absences.

Early in May 1915, Winston went to Paris to take part in the delicate negotiations to bring Italy into the war; Clementine had advised him not to go, because she doubted whether Fisher could bear the strain of being in charge of the Admiralty. While he was away, Clementine invited Lord Fisher to luncheon, which passed very agreeably, and he took his leave of her in cheerful mood. A short while later she herself left the sitting-room and, to her astonishment, found the old Admiral lurking in the passage. She asked him what he wanted, whereupon, in a brusque and somewhat incoherent manner he told her that, while she no doubt was under the impression that Winston was conferring with Sir John French, he was in fact frolicking with a mistress in Paris! Clementine was much taken aback, but treated this interesting piece of information with the scorn it deserved. 'Be quiet, you silly old man,' she said, 'and get out.' He went.

Clementine of course told Winston about this extraordinary episode, and of her deep-seated doubts of Lord Fisher's mental steadiness and loyalty – but he just brushed them aside. He was fully confident of his firm relationship with the Admiral and oblivious to anything except that agreement between them had always been reached.

But on 14th May the final outburst occurred: at a meeting of the War Council to discuss further reinforcements for Gallipoli, Lord Fisher's long-standing, but hitherto suppressed, opposition to the campaign exploded. Interrupting the Council's proceedings, he announced that 'he had been against the Dardanelles operations from the beginning, and that the Prime Minister and Lord Kitchener knew this fact well.'[6] This statement was received in silence. Outraged by Lord Fisher's statement, Churchill wrote in a letter to the Prime Minister on the same day:

> ... The First Sea Lord has agreed in writing to every executive telegram on which the operations have been conducted ...[7]

But Churchill was so accustomed to Lord Fisher's erratic behaviour that when he saw him that same evening at the Admiralty, the two men had a long talk in which they came to an agreement on all outstanding points, and parted amicably. Early the next morning, 15th May, however, Churchill received a letter from the Admiral containing his resignation. He immediately went to the Prime Minister, who had received a similar missive. Mr Asquith was furious, and wrote out an order to Lord Fisher to return at once to his post. Winston wrote him a moving personal appeal – but it was all to no avail: Lord Fisher steadfastly refused to work any longer with Churchill. The end of their road together had been reached. It was a stunning blow, but Churchill did not waste time lamenting, and speedily reconstituted his Board of Admiralty, the other Sea Lords remaining firm and steady. On the Sunday afternoon of this most harassing week-end, Winston and Clementine drove down to The Wharf. Winston described to the Prime Minister his proposals for the new Board of Admiralty, which seemed to have his approval. Violet Bonham Carter wrote that

> Clemmie was naturally very upset and as ever very brave. We had quite a happy dinner and they both drove away in better spirits.[8]

But the crisis was not over – it was only just beginning. And, moreover, what none of them knew then, was that Mr Asquith himself was reeling from a shattering personal shock. On 11th May, Venetia Stanley had written to tell him that she intended to marry Edwin Montagu. 'This is too terrible; no hell could be so bad,' he had written to her a few days later.[9] At a moment, therefore, of deep personal distress, when his powers of judgment may have been temporarily impaired – he was, as Prime Minister, confronted with a grave and complex crisis.

Early on the morning of Monday, 17th May, Mr Bonar Law, the Leader of the Opposition, called on Mr Lloyd George at No. 11 Downing Street, to seek confirmation that Lord Fisher had in fact resigned. He made it clear that a combination of the 'shell scandal' with this latest development would make it impossible for him to restrain his followers; that if Lord Fisher resigned Churchill could not stay as First Lord of the Admiralty, and that the Opposition was prepared to make the issue the subject of a full-scale parliamentary challenge.

Mr Lloyd George begged Mr Bonar Law to wait, and went through the communicating door to see Mr Asquith in No. 10. During his talk with the Prime Minister, Lloyd George argued forcefully in favour of a Coalition Government, and the Prime Minister acquiesced in his view. Lloyd George returned to No. 11, and brought Bonar Law back to join the discussion. In the period of about a quarter of an hour, the idea of a coalition grew from an idea to a possibility, and from a possibility to a probability. The price to be paid was the removal of Churchill from the Admiralty and Haldane from the Government (this last demand arising from a despicable smear campaign based on the Lord Chancellor's life-long study of German thought and letters).

Churchill had always strongly supported the idea of a Coalition Government, but he hoped that such a large question could wait until he had dealt with the immediate crisis, and had announced his new Board of Admiralty. But when he saw Mr Asquith in the afternoon he was consternated to learn that the Prime Minister intended to form a National Government, and that in the course of such a wide reconstruction, he would have to leave the Admiralty. In the midst of this conversation, which became at moments vehement, a message arrived from the Admiralty asking Churchill to return there at once – the German Grand Fleet was putting to sea.

This news put all considerations of the political crisis, and of his own fate which was so closely involved with it, to the back of Churchill's mind. Returning at once to the Admiralty and gathering around him the Senior Naval staff, he prepared to supervise what promised to be a major encounter between the two great naval powers. During the night, as he watched the development of this dramatic situation, Churchill received a letter from the Prime Minister (similar to those sent to all ministers) announcing to him Mr Asquith's intention to form a National administration. Replying to his Chief, Churchill wrote that he would gladly serve in the new Government, but would only accept a military department, and, if that were not convenient, he would prefer to be found a post in the field.

During the morning of Tuesday, 18th May, it became clear from signals that the German Fleet was turning for home – the crisis at sea was resolved.

For a week more there followed a period of behind-the-scenes activity and tension, while the mandarins of the political parties conferred, attended by a buzz of intrigue, public speculation and gossip. Churchill made no secret of the fact that he earnestly hoped to stay at the Admiralty, to see through much of what he had initiated, and above all to have a powerful say in the matter of the Dardanelles, for which he bore so much responsibility. As the week wore on, it became clear that too many voices in public, in the Press, and in private, in high governmental and administrative places, were against him. On Friday, 21st May, in answer to an emotional, deep-felt appeal from Churchill to be allowed to stay at his post, the Prime Minister replied kindly, but briefly, that he 'must take it as settled that you are not to remain at the Admiralty'.[10] Churchill bowed with stoicism to this, for him, bitter decision. The next day Mr Asquith saw him briefly, writing afterwards to Venetia Stanley that it was 'a most painful interview to me: but he was good and in his best mood . . .'[11] Churchill drew some consolation from the fact that his successor was to be Mr Balfour, one of his few friends among the Tories, and who, as a member of the War Council, had always supported the plan for the Dardanelles.

Of his own feelings at this bitter hour, Churchill wrote:

> The more serious physical wounds are often surprisingly endurable at the moment they are received. There is an interval of uncertain length before sensation is renewed. The shock numbs but does not paralyse: the wound bleeds but does not smart. So it is with the great reverses and losses of life.[12]

Many years later, looking back over her life with Winston, Clementine was to say that, of all the events they had lived through together, none had been so agonising as the drama of the Dardanelles. During these days of 1915, and for long weeks and months thereafter, she shared with Winston every anxiety, every brief hope, every twist and turn of the devious course of the crisis. Half a century later, Clementine was to tell Martin Gilbert, Winston's biographer: 'I thought he would die of grief.'[13]

Clementine was always at her best when things were going badly, and we may be sure she rose to the level of these dire events. But as she watched them, as a helpless spectator, bitterness and anger welled up in her heart. Winston's sense of his betrayal was slow in developing: utterly loyal himself, and always courageous in the defence of his own friends or colleagues, it took him some time to grasp that the Prime Minister, although he had supported and approved the Dardanelles plan all along, had sacrificed him to Tory prejudice and hatred with scarcely a struggle. Mr Asquith's abandonment of Haldane was even more chilling, for the two men had been close and lifelong friends: but he let him go without a word.[14]

Unable to contain her feelings, Clementine wrote a remarkable letter to the Prime Minister on 20th May 1915. Her love for Winston, and a burning sense that he was being shabbily treated, made her both brave and eloquent:

My dear Mr Asquith,
    For nearly four years Winston has worked to master every detail of naval science. There is no man in this country who possesses equal knowledge capacity & vigour. If he goes, the injury to Admiralty business will not be reparable for many months – if indeed it is ever made good during the war.
    Why do you part with Winston? unless indeed you have lost confidence in his work and ability?
    But I know that cannot be the reason. Is not the reason expediency – 'to restore public confidence'. I suggest to you that public confidence will be restored in *Germany* by Winston's downfall.
    There *is* no general desire here for a change, but it certainly is being fostered by the press who have apparently made up their minds. I trust they are not making up yours for you . . .
    If you throw Winston overboard you will be committing an act of weakness and your Coalition Government will not be as formidable a War machine as the present Government.
    Winston may in your eyes & in those with whom he has to work have faults but he has the supreme quality which I venture to say very few of your present or future Cabinet possess – the power, the imagination, the deadliness to fight Germany.

Mr Asquith never answered her letter. Some of his family showed affront for a brief period on his behalf, but the Prime Minister evidently did not take it much amiss. Indeed, Clementine was later told that on several occasions he read her outburst aloud at the luncheon table, with amused relish. To Venetia Stanley he commented that 'she wrote me the letter of a maniac . . .'[15]

There is a poignant description of Clementine at this time in a letter to Venetia Stanley from Edwin Montagu (to whom she was now engaged). Montagu had called at Admiralty House on 26th May.

She was so sweet but so miserable and crying all the time. I was very inarticulate, but how I feel for her and him.[16]

Later he wrote Clementine a moving and prophetic letter:

My dear Mrs Winston,

My heart bled to see you so unhappy and I came back from your house to write a line in the hope of atoning for my lack of capacity to express myself verbally.

It is a hard time and it is true that Winston has suffered a blow to prestige, reputation and happiness which counts above all. All that is not worth arguing.

But it is also indisputably true that Winston is far too great to be more than pulled up for a period. His courage is enormous, his genius understood even by his enemies and I am as confident that he will rise again as I am that the sun will rise tomorrow . . .

Be as miserable as you must about the present; have no misgivings as to the future; I have none, Winston I am sure has none and I know that in your heart and amid your gloom you have undaunted confidence in the man you love . . .[17]

In the Coalition Government announced on 26th May Winston was made Chancellor of the Duchy of Lancaster: a sinecure with no executive power, but in this case it was coupled with a place in the Cabinet, and a seat on the War Council. This proviso alone made the offer of such an otherwise derisory post acceptable to Winston. He felt he would still be able to influence the course of the Dardanelles operation.

That morning, as he left the Admiralty in gloom and despair, he could not guess that twenty-four years later, when Britain once more was in mortal peril, the message would be flashed to the Navy: 'Winston is back.'

A mundane consideration, but nevertheless a very real one, was that in going to the Duchy of Lancaster Winston's salary as a minister was more than halved. Mr Balfour thoughtfully assured the Churchills that they need be in no haste to move out of Admiralty House. But Clementine could not wait to be gone from a scene which was now so painful to her. Their own house in Eccleston Square was still let to Sir Edward Grey, but Ivor Guest (now Lord Wimborne) offered the homeless pair his house in Arlington Street, to which they moved in the middle of June. Here Winston and Clementine paused for a short space while they made more permanent plans.

These were hard, bleak days for both of them. The sting of public obloquy was added to their feelings of humiliation, and sense of personal betrayal. Clementine had faced social ostracism and public criticism of Winston from the earliest days of their marriage – indeed, she had gloried in them. But this was different. There was the haunting knowledge that lives had been lost, and that many more must yet be sacrificed before the end of the story. This was an anguishing burden for Winston to sustain. So much could not be told now; so many voices that later would speak out loudly and fearlessly in defence of the Dardanelles plan, and of Churchill's role in it, were at this fateful time perforce silent. Only the critics were unbridled, and the continual lash of criticism, much of it envenomed and ill-informed, had to be borne in silence.

As the weeks went by, their feelings of bitterness grew towards those who, in their eyes, had betrayed Winston, and above all the 'plan' at the moment of greatest trial. Nevertheless, Winston was still a member of the Government, although his colleagues now numbered men whom he knew disliked and mistrusted him, and the chief he still served with loyalty and friendship had, in the event, proved supine in his defence.

But whatever passed between Winston and Clementine in these desolate days and nights, to the world they displayed a proud, courageous and dignified aspect. It was a sore trial enduring the curiosity or even the sympathy of strangers, but the outside world had to be faced, and Clementine summoned up all her pride and fortitude to meet this ordeal.

On 30th June she honoured an engagement to open a new wing at her old school, at Berkhamsted. Her former headmistress, Miss Harris, still reigned and received her with kindness. In her speech to the girls, Clementine spoke of the many women whom the war had bereaved, but some of her words had a poignantly personal ring:

. . . At this time I think one of the most wonderful things is the stoic fortitude with which women bear the most agonising sorrows . . . I think people are able to put aside their private griefs because the thoughts and energies of everyone are concentrated on one idea – how to win the war: how to make victory sure and safe in the end . . .

After due thought and consultation within the family, the 'Winstons' and the 'Jacks' decided to pool their resources. Both families were under financial strain, and so it seemed a good arrangement all round. Jack and Goonie were living at 41 Cromwell Road, in South Kensington, but it was really too big for them, particularly now that Jack was serving abroad.

It was quite a task amalgamating the two households, and especially combining the nurseries under the command of one nannie, who had the charge of the five cousins: three boys, John George, aged six, Randolph, four, and Peregrine, two, and the two girls, Diana, now six, and the baby, Sarah. Winston and Clementine with their brood moved into Cromwell Road at the end of June.

★

One of the first actions of the new Coalition was to endorse the vigorous prosecution of the Dardanelles campaign. As a member of the War Council (now reconstituted and known as the Dardanelles Committee), Winston did all in his power to sustain and further the plan, in which he still wholeheartedly believed. But with no great department to administer, he suddenly found time on his hands; and it hung sad and heavy. It was during these months of gloom and despair that Winston first discovered the charm of painting.

At the end of May, Winston and Clementine had rented for the summer a small house, Hoe Farm, near Godalming, as a week-end and holiday refuge. One day, wandering, brooding, in the garden, Winston came upon Goonie sketching with water-colours; watching her, he became fascinated, demanded a brush, and tried his hand. Goonie, delighted with this development, lent him John George's paintbox. After experimenting briefly with water-colours, however, Winston became convinced that '*La peinture à l'huile est bien difficile, mais c'est beaucoup plus beau que la peinture à l'eau.*'[18] Clementine was so thrilled that Winston had found a distraction from his worries that she rushed off to Godalming and bought every variety of oil paints available. Alas, she was not aware that turpentine is essential to painting with oils, and the ensuing results were most unsatisfactory!

But help was at hand. John Lavery, the celebrated painter, and his beautiful wife, Hazel, lived round the corner from the Churchills in Cromwell Place, and they had made friends. Clementine, in a quandary with the oil paints, telephoned John Lavery, who was so overjoyed to hear of Winston's new ploy that he leapt into a hired car and drove immediately to Hoe Farm, bringing not only turpentine, but all his knowledge and skill. Hazel Lavery, too, was a gifted painter, and between them they gave Winston his first lessons in painting, an occupation of which he was never to tire, and a companion who kept him company almost to the end of the road.

It was during this summer that Sir William Orpen painted a remarkable, full-length portrait of Winston. At the time Clementine did not care for the picture; it showed all too painfully the ravages wrought upon Winston by these days of crisis and personal torment. She minded the almost 'beaten and finished' look of the portrait. That it was a truthful portrayal is borne out by Ashmead-Bartlett, the war correspondent, who, returning home from Gallipoli in the early summer of 1915, noted in his diary:

> I am much surprised at the change in Winston Churchill. He looks years older, his face is pale, he seems very depressed and to feel keenly his retirement from the Admiralty . . .[19]

Among the many vexations and frustrations which were Churchill's lot at this time, none embittered him more than the occasion when in July 1915 he was prevented, on the very eve of his departure, from visiting Gallipoli. It was Lord Kitchener who had suggested that he should make an official visit, and Mr Asquith and Mr Balfour both gave their approval. When, however, other Tory colleagues got wind of the proposal, they opposed it tooth and nail. Mr Asquith bowed before the storm, and Churchill's proposed journey was cancelled. It was probably with this expedition in view that Winston wrote a letter which was found among his papers, dated 17th July, 1915, and marked 'To be sent to Mrs Churchill in the event of my death'. In it he explained the financial provisions he had been able to make for her and the children – they would have been dismally slender. The letter shows what deep faith he had in her judgment and resolution, for he appointed her his sole literary executor, with the request that she should get hold of all his papers, especially those dealing with his work at the Admiralty.

> . . . There is no hurry; but some day I shld like the truth to be known. Randolph will carry on the lamp. Do not grieve for me too much. I am a spirit confident of my rights. Death is only an incident, & not the most important wh happens to us in this state of being. On the whole, especially since I met you my darling one I have been happy, & you have taught me how noble a woman's heart can be. If

there is anywhere else I shall be on the look out for you. Meanwhile look forward, feel free, rejoice in life, cherish the children, guard my memory. God bless you.

Good-bye

W

With Winston's departure from the Admiralty, Clementine was relieved of the task of running a large official house, and of the obligation to entertain extensively. As soon as she had reorganised her family and household, she looked around for some form of war work. As a result of the 'shell scandal', which had contributed to the downfall of the Liberal Government, a Ministry of Munitions had been set up, with Mr Lloyd George at its head. New factories were started; many hitherto occupied with peacetime production now turned over to making munitions, and a vast civilian army of men and women was daily growing in numbers to produce the arms. From the outbreak of the war a variety of organisations had devoted themselves to sustaining the fighting soldier and sailor, but now the needs of the civilian war workers were also pressing. The arms factories worked day and night, and for the most part the canteen arrangements organised by the managements were totally inadequate. In June 1915, therefore, the Young Men's Christian Association formed the Munition Workers' Auxiliary Committee, for the express purpose of providing canteens for the munitions workers. Clementine was invited to join this committee, and undertook the task of organising canteens in the north and north-eastern Metropolitan area of London. During the ensuing months she became responsible for the opening, staffing and running of nine canteens, each one feeding anything up to five hundred workers at a time.

Clementine, like many other women who then undertook quite large administrative jobs, had no previous experience or training; nonetheless she plunged into the work, undaunted and full of enthusiasm. Her new task was a challenge, and more than that for her at this moment, it was an anodyne against the bitter thoughts and gnawing anxieties which beset her.

Driving herself, Clementine toured her area, enlisting helpers and persuading factory managers to give the necessary co-operation and provide suitable accommodation. Once on its feet, each canteen had to be visited often, to encourage the staff (ninety per cent of whom were unpaid volunteers), deal with troubles and complaints, and to ensure that high standards of food and service were maintained.

Such a novelty was it for women to be employed on a large scale, side by side with men in industry, that one of the first difficulties Clementine had to deal with was a general complaint from the men that they objected to the women workers smoking in the canteens and recreation rooms! A special committee meeting had to be called to consider this point. After due deliberation, a ruling was given that, where and when smoking was allowed, women should be on a par with their male colleagues. This dictum was rather reluctantly accepted by the men, and another barrier in the sex war demolished.

As the summer of 1915 wore on, the ill-starred campaign in Gallipoli ran into further difficulties. At home, the new Coalition was proving to be a worse war-machine than the Government it had superseded. Within the Cabinet there were animosities and tensions which vitiated its power of decision, and the enlarged Dardanelles Committee was too big for effective action. Early in August British forces launched an attack at Suvla Bay: it was a disastrous failure, whose repercussions extended beyond the blood-soaked beaches to Greece and the Balkan States; and in October 1915 Bulgaria threw in her lot with Germany and Austria.

As the weeks went by and events moved from bad to worse, the idea of evacuation and abandonment was, inevitably, mooted. And in November the Cabinet decided to reduce the size of the Dardanelles Committee in an attempt to make it a more effective instrument. The smaller team did not include Churchill.

For many months the thought of resignation had been in Churchill's mind. The honourable alternative of taking up his commission (he was a major in the Oxfordshire Yeomanry) and joining his regiment in France was always open to him. As the weeks had gone by, he had found himself in the invidious position of bearing responsibility without the power to act according to his deeply held convictions. Increasingly frustrated, Churchill had sent a letter of resignation to the Prime Minister at the end of October; but Mr Asquith had persuaded him to stay on. But now that he found that (although continuing in the Cabinet) he was to be excluded from the newly constructed Dardanelles Committee, the one condition which had made tolerable to him his acceptance of the Chancellorship of the Duchy of Lancaster was removed.

On 11th November 1915 Churchill wrote to the Prime Minister, once more, and finally, tendering his resignation. He told Mr Asquith:

> I could not accept a position of general responsibility for war policy without any effective share in its guidance and control . . . Nor do I feel in times like these able to remain in well-paid inactivity. I therefore ask you to submit my resignation to the King. I am an officer, and I place myself unreservedly at the disposal of the military authorities, observing that my regiment is in France.
>
> I have a clear conscience, which enables me to bear my responsibility for past events with composure.
>
> With much respect and unaltered personal friendship, I bid you good-bye.

Four days later, on 15th November, Churchill made a statement to the House of Commons, as he was by custom entitled to do as a resigning minister. There was much he could not say – either for reasons of security, or through loyalty to friends and former colleagues.

He then went home to Cromwell Road to prepare for his departure for France.

THE PLACE OF HONOUR

T HE DECISION TAKEN and the deed done, Winston made haste to be gone. Sir Max Aitken (later Lord Beaverbrook), who visited the house on the eve of his departure, found

The whole household was upside down while the soldier-statesman was buckling on his sword. Downstairs, Mr 'Eddie' Marsh, his faithful secretary, was in tears ... Upstairs, Lady Randolph was in a state of despair at the idea of her brilliant son being relegated to the trenches. Mrs Churchill seemed to be the only person who remained calm, collected and efficient.[1]

Even had she felt inclined to do so, Clementine had little time to brood or repine, for there were only a few days to gather together all the equipment and uniform Winston would need in France.

On Tuesday, 16th November there was a farewell luncheon at 41 Cromwell Road. Violet Asquith and her stepmother, Margot Asquith, were present, and Eddie Marsh; otherwise it was the family – Winston, Clementine, Nellie Hozier and Goonie. In the circumstances it may seem surprising that any Asquiths should have been present. But Violet was a close friend and political confidante, and despite the fact that Winston and Margot Asquith never really got on together, there was a long story of liking, shared endeavour and loyalty between the Asquiths and the Churchills. Whatever thoughts and feelings brewed beneath, the surface calm of the relationship between the two families remained unruffled. Violet Asquith described what must have been a somewhat dismal occasion:

Clemmie was admirably calm and brave, poor Eddie blinking back his tears, the rest of us trying to 'play up' and hide our leaden hearts. Winston alone was at his gayest and his best . . .[2]

On Thursday, 18th November, 'Major Churchill' left for France. on arriving at Boulogne he found the Commander-in-Chief, Sir John French, had sent a car to meet him. After reporting briefly to his own regiment (The Queen's Own Oxfordshire Hussars), Winston went to GHQ, where Sir John welcomed him with the utmost cordiality. Winston stayed a night or two at GHQ while his immediate future as a soldier was decided upon.

Sir John offered Winston the alternative of remaining at St Omer as an ADC, or the command of a brigade; Winston unhesitatingly chose the latter, but with the proviso that he should gain some experience of trench warfare as a regimental officer before taking up his command; and so it was arranged. Winston wrote to Clementine:

> I am staying tonight at GHQ in a fine chateau, with hot baths, beds, champagne & all the conveniences . . . I am sure I am going to be entirely happy out here & at peace. I must try to win my way as a good & sincere soldier. But do not suppose I shall run any foolish risks or do anything wh is not obviously required.[3]

The following day it was arranged that Winston should at once join a battalion of the Grenadier Guards in the line, and he wrote to Clementine at midnight on Friday, 19th November:

> My dearest soul – (this is what the gt d of Marlborough used to write from the low countries to his cat) All is vy well arranged . . . I cannot tell the rota in wh we shall go into the trenches. But I do hope you will realise what a vy harmless thing this is. To my surprise I learn they only have about 15 killed & wounded each day out of 8000 men exposed! It will make me vy sulky if I think you are allowing yourself to be made anxious by any risk like that . . .

He himself had no backward-looking thoughts:

> I am vy happy here. I did not know what release from care meant. It is a blessed peace. How I ever cd have wasted so many months in impotent misery, wh might have been spent in war, I cannot tell.

Clementine's first letter already showed how acutely she felt their separation: 'Altho' it's only a few miles you seem to me as far away as the stars, lost among a million khaki figures.' She ended on a note of almost pathetic yearning: 'Write to me Winston. I want a letter from you badly.'[4]

Happily she did not have long to wait, for by Sunday she had received his first letter telling her of his intention to go into the line before accepting a brigade, and she lost no time in answering it:

41 Cromwell Road

My Darling,

   I was very much relieved when your letter reached me yesterday morning, but the news in it makes me terribly anxious. I feel very proud of you my Dear.

   I long for you to have a Brigade & yet not too soon for fear of partly dimming the 'blaze of glory' in which you have left the country.

   Wherever I go I find people awestruck at your sacrifice . . .

   I have had a charming letter from Sir John French, telling me that he was going to look after you . . .

   Quite apart from the danger, I do wish you had not gone at once into the 'line' – I fear so much that you may get pneumonia or an internal chill unless you get gradually hardened.

Your loving lonely
Clemmie
[sketch of a cat][5]

On Sunday, 21st November Winston joined the 2nd Battalion of the Grenadier Guards, stationed at that time near Laventie. His sense of history and romance was gratified by the coincidence that John, Duke of Marlborough, had once served in, and commanded, the same unit. The officers were suspicious and even resentful of his presence, and he was received with reserve and coldness, the commanding officer, Lieutenant-Colonel Jeffreys, remarking: 'I think I ought to tell you we were not at all consulted in the matter of your coming to join us.'[6] Winston knew that only time and his own bearing would break down their hostility.

His equipment was evidently very deficient, for he sent Clementine a long list of urgent requirements, namely:

1 A warm brown leather waistcoat.
2 A pair of trench wading boots . . .
3 a periscope (most important) . . .
4 a sheepskin sleeping bag . . .
5 2 pairs of khaki trousers . . .
6 1 pair of brown buttoned boots –
7 three small face towels

'Voila tout!' he added cheerfully at the end of this list. But one comfort he had with him was much appreciated: 'Your little pillow,' he wrote, 'is a boon & a pet.' Clementine hastened to gather all these much-needed items, and she wrote on 25th November (7.30 a.m.) to report progress:

I went yesterday & sent you all the things you ask for in your letter from the trenches with the exception (Alas) of the trench wading boots. London seems to be emptied of these, but I am going to make a fresh try this morning & if I fail I shall send you pro tem, a pair of rubber waders which they say is the next best thing. I wake up in the night & think of you shivering in the trenches; it makes me so miserable (You know how warm the Kat has to be before she can sleep) I fear I should never sleep in a trench even in a sheep skin bag. Randolph wishes to come with me to choose the wading boots. He wishes to send you as personal presents from himself a photograph of himself & a spade. He says you must have a spade 'to dig out a little sideways, so if a bomb comes in the trench Papa won't be killed.' Don't you think it rather wonderful for a child of 4 to have thought of this. On Monday I dined with Venetia [Montagu] where everyone was thrilled at your having joined the Grenadiers . . . Nellie met a young soldier from a line regiment (a former partner) who said that it was common knowledge that you had refused a brigade & wished to go in the trenches – He said Everyone thought this splendid as the General Expectation among the rank & file of officers was that you would join your regiment for a week or a fortnight; that you would then be put on some staff while the regiment was given some interesting work & that you would then be given a Brigade . . .

My darling I think of you constantly & I do hope that when you think of me, it is not a picture of a harsh arguing scold, but your loving & sad Clemmie. I love you very much more even than I thought I did – for seven years you have filled my whole life & now I feel more than half my life has vanished across the channel. I have cut out of the Daily Mirror a delightful snap-shot of you in uniform taken just as you left the house. There was a thick fog & the figure is misty & dim & so I feel you receding into the fog & mud of Flanders & not coming back for so long . . .

Apart from her anxieties for Winston on account of obvious dangers from bullets and shells, Clementine was fearful lest he should neglect some elementary health precaution, such as inoculation, and so fall a victim to typhoid or enteric. She begged him to be inoculated:

. . . you ought to be *done twice running* (the interval between the 2 inoculations must not be more than 10 days) *as soon as possible* . . . Please be done as soon as you come out of the line. Every officer in France & Flanders has been inoculated twice.[7]

As soon as Winston finished his first forty-eight hours' spell in the trenches on 23rd November he wrote to Clementine from the 'billets in support' where he and his comrades were resting. He described the trenches:

It is a wild scene . . . Filth and rubbish everywhere, graves built into the defences . . . feet and clothing breaking through the soil, water & muck on all sides; & about this scene in the dazzling moonlight troops of enormous rats creep & glide, to the unceasing accompaniment of rifle & machine guns & the venomous whining & whirring of the bullets wh pass overhead. Amid these surroundings, aided by wet & cold, & every minor discomfort, I have found happiness & content such as I have not known for many months.

But on his return to the trenches a few days later Winston had a near escape from death. He had received a peremptory telegram summoning him to meet the Corps Commander at a certain point about three miles away on the main road late in the afternoon. Arriving at the rendezvous after walking across wet fields under spasmodic fire, Winston waited vainly for the General. Finally a staff officer turned up, who informed him there had been a mistake, that it was too late now, and that the General had returned to his Headquarters. Winston, highly indignant at this cavalier treatment, returned the long wet way he had come. By this time darkness was falling over the dismal countryside; it was pouring with rain, and it took him over two hours to reach his unit. When he finally arrived back in his own lines, he discovered that shortly after he had left in the morning, the dug-out in which he would have been sitting had been struck by a shell. The whole structure had been smashed, and the mess orderly who was in it had had his head blown off. 'When I saw the ruin,' Winston wrote to Clementine,

I was not so angry with the General after all . . . Now see from this how vain it is to worry about things . . . One must yield oneself simply & naturally to the mood of the game, and trust in God wh is another way of saying the same thing.[8]

Winston had thought for Clementine's peace of mind: he did not send her his letter describing this incident until he was safely returned to GHQ.

Resting with his unit after his second spell in the firing line, Winston wrote to Clementine on 27th November:

We came out of the line last night without mishap, & marched in under brilliant moonlight while the men sang 'Tipperary' and the 'Farmer's Boy' and the guns boomed applause. It is like getting to a jolly good tavern after a long day's hunting, wet & cold & hungry, but not without having had sport.

His peace of mind and feeling of release from care still prevailed despite the dangers and physical discomforts of his daily life; and he had a feeling of detachment from the hurly-burly of politics and the machinations of government. Lloyd George, McKenna and Asquith seemed very far away and looked to him 'like the mandarins of some remote province of China'.[9]

But despite this feeling of distance he now had from the political scene, Winston nonetheless urged Clementine to keep in touch with politicians and the Press:

Show complete confidence in our fortunes. Hold your head vy high. You always do. Above all don't be worried about me. If my destiny has not already been accomplished, I shall be guarded surely . . .

In practical ways Winston was not remiss, sending through his man of business £100 for any urgent bills and later £300 as 'a reserve in case of accidents'.[10] He urged Clementine and Goonie not to deny themselves any reasonable comfort:

Keep a good table . . . entertain with discrimination, have a little amusement from time to time . . . With £140 a month there should be sufficient.[11]

That winter, Lady Randolph let her own house, and came to join the throng at 41 Cromwell Road. Clementine wrote appreciatively, 'Your Mother is being very generous & is contributing £40 a month to the upkeep of this establishment until she comes to live with us.'[12] Lady Randolph was writing literary articles to help 'keep the home fires burning'; she sent Winston gossipy letters full of gay courage. Like Clementine she kept up her contacts with the political world, giving and attending luncheons and dinners, helping to keep open the links for Winston.

Clementine's work with the YMCA was getting into its stride, and she spent long days touring her own north-easterly sector of London, where the number of canteens over which she presided eventually rose to nine. When Winston resigned and the two Churchill households amalgamated, as a further measure of economy Winston and Clementine decided to dispense with their car: this made her work even more tiring, as her canteens were widely scattered. Writing to Winston, Clementine said:

Without a motor it's harder to get to Enfield than to France – $\frac{1}{4}$ of the day has been spent in tube, tram, train, the remainder grappling with committees . . .[13]

Clementine was, at this time, much concerned about Nellie, who in August 1915 had become engaged to Bertram Romilly, a Lieutenant-Colonel in the Scots Guards. Romantically good-looking, charming, and a gallant soldier (he had won the D.S.O.), he had suffered a severe head wound, and his health was fragile. He and Nellie had met after he had been invalided home.

Clementine feared for her sister's happiness, married as she would be to a semi-invalid. Moreover, as she wrote to Winston:

> I don't believe she loves him at all but is simply marrying him out of pity . . . She vacillated (for the last week) between breaking off entirely, postponement, & immediate marriage with every hour of the day, but now she has hardened into a sort of mule-like obstinacy & says with a drawn wretched face that she loves him, is divinely happy & will marry him on the 4th. She is now furious with me for my former support of her postponing intentions, & says that if I say one word against her marriage on Dec. 4th she will leave the house & never come near me when she is married. Goonie thinks the marriage ought not to take place, but we can do no more.[14]

Winston was devoted to Nellie – 'The Nellinita', as he called her – so he shared Clementine's anxiety, but agreed that nothing could be done to stop the marriage.

Another wedding was causing a stir in London society: Violet Asquith was to marry Maurice Bonham Carter, her father's Private Secretary. In a long letter, in which she tried to sew up every bit of news for Winston's diversion, Clementine commented somewhat acidly

> . . . rumour whispers darkly but insistently that we have sustained a very damaging defeat & have lost many men. But for comfort & confidence we all look on the P.M. & McKenna both looking happy, sleek & complacent & for distraction on Violet's forthcoming marriage which is turning the town topsy-turvy with excitement . . .[15]

On 1st December she wrote an account of this great occasion:

> Yesterday was Violet's marriage – Great throng of crowds everywhere – Randolph officiated as one of the pages & looked *quite* beautiful in a little Russian velvet suit with fur. His looks made quite a sensation & at Downing Street afterwards he was surrounded & kissed & admired by dozens of lovely women . . .
>
> The great feature at yesterday's wedding was the re-appearance of K [Lord Kitchener] who, while everyone still imagined him to be receiving the plaudits of the Italians stalked into the Church & afterwards signed the register. I am told that in his absence the W.O. had begun to be swept & garnished & that his sudden return caused some dismay.

But full as her letters were of news from all aspects of the home front, Clementine's deep and continual anxiety and concern for Winston's health and safety leaps up again and again throughout her long and frequent letters. From Cromwell Road on Sunday, 28th November, she wrote to him:

> My Darling,
>
> I miss you terribly – I ache to see you. When do you think you will get a little leave? Shall I come & spend it with you in Paris or will you come home?

I don't like to make any request which might worry or vex you, but it makes me very anxious to feel that you are staying longer in the trenches than your duty requires. All the other officers & the men have been hardened to the wet & cold by their training but you have gone at one swoop from an atmosphere of hot rooms, sedentary work & Turkish baths to a life of the most cruel hardships & exposure. And besides thinking of me & the babies think of your duty to yourself & your reputation. If you were killed & you had over exposed yourself the world might think that you had sought death out of grief for your share in the Dardanelles. It is your duty to the country to try to live (consistent with your honour as a soldier)...

Tell me some more about your life – Have you a nice servant – What do you have to eat & do you eat it in a trench or in a farm or where? I shd mind the rats more even than the bullets – Can you kill them or wld that be wasting good ammunition? ...

The Daily Mail rings me up nearly every day & asks if I have had any news from 'Major Churchill'. Major Churchill has a strange sound, but I am prouder of this title than of any other ... when I think of you my Dearest Darling, I forget all disappointment, bitterness, or ambition & long to have you safe & warm & alive in my arms. Since you have re-become a soldier I look upon civilians of high or low degree with pity & indulgence. The wives of men over military age may be lucky but I am sorry for them being married to feeble & incompetent old men.

I think you will get this letter on your birthday & it brings you all my love & many passionate kisses.

I find my morning breakfast lonely without you so Sarah fills your place & does her best to look almost exactly like you.

I'm keeping the flag flying till you return by getting up Early & having break-fast down-stairs ... Goodbye my Darling. I *love* your letters. I read them again & again.

On 28th November Lord Cavan (the Commander of the Guards' Division) had invited Winston to luncheon with him; he suggested that until he was offered a command of his own, Winston should remain at Brigade HQ. Winston refused. 'I said I wouldn't miss a day of it. Nor did I,' he wrote to Clementine two evenings later.

I also scorned the modest comfort of Battalion HQ & lived in the wet & the mud with the men in the firing line.

My physique is such that I support these conditions without the slightest ill effect. Of course I have seen vy little, but I have seen enough to be quite at my ease about all the ordinary things.[16]

On 30th November – Winston's forty-first birthday – his company came out of the trenches for an eight-day break; his unit had been subjected to a three-hour spell of shelling, but despite splinters and debris falling very close, there had been only two men hurt in the company. They were all glad to be relieved and had cele-brated his birthday behind the lines with a convivial dinner party.

Winston had received Clementine's 'dear letter' of the 28th. 'I reciprocate intensely the feelings of love & devotion you show to me,' he wrote back to her:

> My greatest good fortune in a life of brilliant experience has been to find you, & to lead my life with you. I don't feel far away from you out here at all. I feel vy near in my heart; and also I feel that the nearer I get to honour, the nearer I am to you.[17]

*

With his company at present relieved from duty in the line, Winston now took leave of the Grenadiers. He described to Clementine, with pardonable satisfaction, the warmth and friendliness of the farewells which surrounded his departure, coupled with pressing invitations 'to return whenever I liked & stay as long as I liked'.[18] It was in strong contrast to the icy nature of the welcome he had received on his arrival among them two weeks before. Winston then returned to GHQ at St Omer, to see Sir John French, for the next step for him as a soldier had now to be determined.

When Winston had visited the Commander-in-Chief just over two weeks before, on his arrival in France, Sir John had offered him the command of a brigade; Winston also had Mr Asquith's private assurance (given him when he left the Admiralty) that the Prime Minister would support such an appointment. But when he arrived at GHQ he found that Sir John French had been recalled to London for consultations, and it was by now fairly general knowledge that his days as Commander-in Chief were numbered. Discontent with his direction of strategy had been growing since the failure of the British offensive at Loos in the early autumn.

While waiting for Sir John's return, Winston lunched again with Lord Cavan; he had a long talk with him about his affairs, and Lord Cavan's advice was that he should take a battalion before accepting command of a brigade. This advice accorded with Winston's own thoughts and wishes at this moment. He added:

> He [Lord Cavan] spoke of my having high command as if it were the natural thing, but urged the importance of going up step by step.[19]

One piece of news must have reassured Clementine: while Winston was at GHQ he took the opportunity of being inoculated, and was 'consequently teetotal and housebound'.[20] Winston ended his letter of 4th December on a buoyant note:

> They all say I look 5 years younger: & certainly I have never been in better health & spirits. Christmas in Paris – I think for you & me. I shall probably be in the collar then; but 2 or 3 days shd not be an impossibility.

During these days, Winston was able to visit different parts of the front line, and he had long conversations with friends and officers in command, among whom he found a general impression of the

> utter inability to take a decision on the part of the Government . . . The able soldiers there are miserable at the Government's drifting. Some urge me to return and try to break them up. I reply no – I will not go back unless I am wounded; or unless I have effective control.[21]

But the effect of his visit to GHQ was to unsettle this calm detachment from political affairs. As Winston watched from afar the march of events, his special knowledge and experience enabled him to sense the drift of affairs, and his feelings grew daily more contemptuous and bitter against those with the power to act, whose hands should have been gripping and directing the situation. He poured out all his thoughts and feelings to Clementine, reminding her 'These letters are for you *alone*', but adding that she might read or copy out for his mother and others anything 'not purely for us two'.[22]

For all the months Winston was to be in France, for the greater part of which he was in or near the front line, he and Clementine wrote to each other almost every day. Their letters form a uniquely interesting and deeply moving correspondence. For the most part the letters were concerned with matters of deep import to themselves personally, and with details of public figures and events which engrossed their interest and attention. Their biographers – and indeed posterity – must ever be thankful that both Winston and Clementine were able to take advantage of a special privilege: their letters were sent through GHQ, and were not subject to censorship. Had they been, much fascinating information, and frankly expressed opinions, would, perforce, never have been committed to paper.

Winston's letters nearly always included an urgent demand for food or other comforts, much like a schoolboy's letters home.

> Will you send now regularly once a week a *small* box of food to supplement the rations. Sardines, chocolate, potted meats, and other things wh may strike your fancy . . . Send me also a new Onoto [fountain] pen. I have stupidly lost mine. Send me also lots of love and many kisses.[23]

And two days later:

> Will you now send me 2 bottles of my old brandy & a bottle of peach brandy. This consignment might be repeated at intervals of ten days.[24]

> I want 2 more pairs of thick Jaeger draws [sic], vests & socks (soft).
> 2 more pairs of brown leather gloves (warm) 1 more pair of field boots (like those I had from Fortnum & Mason) only from the fourth hole from the bottom instead of holes there shd be good strong tags for lacing quicker. One size larger than the last. Also one more pair of Fortnum & M's ankle boots only with tags right up from the bottom hole (the same size these as before).
> With these continual wettings and no means of drying one must have plenty of spares. I am so sorry to be so extravagant . . .[25]

> Also send me a big bath towel. I now have to wipe myself all over with things that resemble pocket handkerchiefs.[26]

In conditions of real hardship small comforts and luxuries acquire a vast significance; moreover, food parcels were shared out among the Mess, and Winston was anxious to make a suitable and generous contribution. A minor inconvenience was the non-arrival of the food parcels and various items of clothing and equipment he had asked Clementine to procure and send to him. Naturally she was much distressed when she learnt that none of the parcels she had hastened to send off had arrived by the end of the first week of December, but this had arisen because she had mistakenly sent them to the Grenadiers instead of to GHQ. She earned a mild scolding for this:

> How naughty of you not to send everything to G.H.Q. as I said. Now I do not know whether the boots have reached the Guards or not – or what has happened to the food. However, it will all come right – I daresay.[27]

However, Winston retrieved the first food parcel on 10th December from Grenadier Headquarters, and two days later he announced with satisfaction that

> . . . the most divine & glorious sleeping bag has arrived, & I spent last night in it in one long 11 hours purr. Also food boxes are now following steadily; & I get daily evidences of the Cat's untiring zeal on my behalf.[28]

So all was now well on the 'Parcels Front'!

Apart from this brief period, when the non-delivery of parcels arose from a misunderstanding as to where they should be sent, the postal services available to Winston and Clementine appear to have been nothing short of miraculous. Small parcels took only about three days to arrive, and letters were often received within forty-eight hours, although obviously these timings varied according to the conditions of warfare on the spot at any one time; and a special privilege available to them was that their letters were often carried by King's Messenger from the Admiralty.

On the night of 3rd December Sir John French returned to his own GHQ from his consultations with the Prime Minister. Winston and two or three others in his confidence dined with him that night and learned the latest developments concerning the command of the armies. Asquith evidently wanted Sir John to go, but without any inconvenient commotion; French was reluctant to relinquish his command, but determined to behave with dignity. The result was a sort of agreed stalemate which could only have an ill-effect at a time when decisions and actions were required daily if not hourly. Winston commented to Clementine: 'For three weeks no one has thought of the enemy.'[29] His understanding and sympathy for his friend in these last days of uncertainty were profound:

> I am so sorry for him. No man can sustain two different kinds of separate worries – a tremendous army in the face of the enemy: a gnawing intrigue at his back.[30]

Winston's own future was also discussed that same evening, and in this same letter to Clementine, dated the day after the dinner, he wrote:

> I proposed to French that I shd take a battalion; but he rejected it, & said 'no a brigade at once' & that he wd settle it quickly in case any accident shd happen to him. I have acquiesced . . .[31]

There is no mention in this letter of Sir John having discussed the question of Winston's military future in specific terms with the Prime Minister; but he told Winston that Asquith had spoken 'with emotion' about him. Winston remarked to Clementine that 'Asquith's sentiments are always governed by his interests. They are vy hearty & warm within limits wh cost nothing.'[32] This somewhat harsh judgment was to be amply borne out by future events.

Clementine meanwhile had received Winston's letter describing his lucky escape from almost certain death, owing to the General's caprice. She wrote to him on 4th December (as usual, early in the morning, at 6.30 a.m.).

It is horrible to sit here in warmth & luxury while danger & suffering are so close to you. That dreadful walk across the fields there & back among falling shells was on Nov: 24th & now it is 10 days later & Heaven knows what narrow escapes you may have had since.

But she had strong views on the subject of Winston's promotion:

My Darling, altho' I ache for you to have a brigade so that you may be in less danger I admire you so very much for taking a battalion first. I am sure it is the right & wise thing. General Bridges came to see me last night; (what a tremendous fellow he is to look at). He told me he had seen you & that you were then in high spirits. He said 'I suppose Winston is going to get a brigade.' I said I thought you would rather take a battalion first. His face lighted up & he said 'I am *so* glad'. It is nectar to me to feel & see generous admiration & appreciation of you, which for so long have been denied unjustly . . .

I am so glad that you & Lord Cavan are friends – He seems to be a fine soldier & one of the few unblighted generals in the general mildew.

What you tell me of Sir John F. grieves me but not really for your sake, for I prefer you to win your way than to be thought a favourite of the C. in C. I *feel* confidence in your star my Dearest & I know all soldiers who meet you will love you . . .

There was plenty of news from the home front as well:

Margot & Elizabeth [Asquith] came here yesterday to tea & were very friendly. The 'Block' [nickname for Mr Asquith] I have seen only at Downing Street after Violet's wedding; he ran across me & Lord Haldane(!) together in the hall, muttered a few civil words & shuffled off sniffing nervously. Goonie & I have been bidden for luncheon there on Sunday which is most unusual as they are generally away; I don't expect the old boy will be there . . .

To-day is Nellie's marriage, but the whole house is still asleep. For the last few days the rooms have looked very odd, full of Nellie's presents & cardboard boxes & new clothes & tissue paper . . .

Since Clementine had confided her anxieties about this match to Winston, Nellie had become much calmer and more settled in her mind; and she and Bertram Romilly were married at the Guards' Chapel on 4th December. It was a marriage which was to last the test of time and divers tribulations. Two days after the wedding, Clementine described it all to Winston in one of her early morning letters:

My Darling,
Nellie was married on Saturday – I feel much happier now about her, as from several people I have heard good reports of Bertram . . .

I wish you could have been here – Nellie looked really lovely; her long train was carried by Diana, Johnny & Randolph. After the wedding we all went to Aunt Mary's house in Portland Place & many people came there to see the last of her as Miss Nellie Hozier! It is 7 years & nearly 3 months since you & I drove away from there to Blenheim.

Yesterday Goonie & I lunched at Downing Street. No 'Block' (he had gone down to Munstead after attending a conference at Calais on Saturday). But Violet & Bongey appeared from their honeymoon on their way to the Italian Riviera where they are to spend a month. They both looked rather dreary & blue-stockingey.

I long for more news from G.H.Q. where you have now been for 6 days. I suppose the conference at Calais was partly about the possible change there. I cannot get used to not knowing what is really going on . . .[33]

Being 'out of the know' was a deprivation Clementine felt very much. At the end of November she had written to Winston:

. . . For the first time for seven years besides being parted from you I am cut off from the stream of private news & have to rely upon the newspapers & *rumour*, so that I am in a state of suspended animation . . .[34]

And now she told him:

I can send you so little news Darling only my love & thoughts. I'm completely cut off from secret information – you at GHQ know far more than I do.[35]

Quite apart from any source of private news, a general shortage of information for public consumption was a curious feature of the First World War, and in the absence of official news, every kind of rumour and speculation ran rife.

When Clementine received the letter in which Winston told her that he had allowed Sir John French to persuade him to take a brigade, she was greatly disturbed. She saw clearly the adverse comment and hostility such an appointment would arouse. Her love for Winston was ardent, but not blind, and she used all her powers of persuasion and argument to dissuade him from accepting such promotion at this moment.

I hope so much my Darling that you may *still* decide to take a battalion first, much as I long for you to be not so much in the trenches. I am absolutely certain that whoever is C. in C., you will rise to high commands. I'm sure everyone feels that anything else would be wasting a valuable instrument. But everyone who *really* loves you & has your interest at heart wants you to go step by step whereas I notice the Downing Street tone is 'of course Winston will have a brigade in a fortnight'. Thus do they hope to ease their conscience from the wrong they have done you, and then hope to hear no more of you . . . Sir John loves you & wants *himself* to have the joy of doing something for you, but I believe in Lord Cavan's advice – you & he should make a very strong combination & if he gets a corps I feel sure you wld soon get a division under him. Do get a battalion *now* & a brigade later.[36]

After this eloquent plea for second (and wiser) thoughts, Clementine turned to her second preoccupation on his behalf – his comforts.

I am so distressed about the food, & to-day I have despatched a big box to G.H.Q. . . . I have also sent boots (3 pairs) vests, pants, socks, gloves, sleeping cap, onoto pen.

If you go back to the trenches shall I send you a trench stove – I saw a lovely one in a shop quite portable & takes to bits – You are meant to have it in your dug-out. It burns charcoal . . .

Clementine took a more detached view than Winston of the impending change of command:

I feel so grieved for Sir J's anxieties, but I am sure a change is inevitable & tho' I am sure he is a good soldier if I were Prime Minister I would make the change; but I hope swiftly & with decision not wavering towards it in the way he does about everything. Do not my Dear be shocked & angry with me for saying this. I know he is your friend & I too feel much warmth, affection & gratitude towards him, but with the 2 disasters impending in the East, I would like a fresh un-tortured mind in the west.

Goodbye my Darling – I feel sad to-day & as if we could not win the war. But perhaps this is becos' I long for you very much & I feel the reaction after Nellie's wedding & rain is falling in buckets. But in your star I have confidence.

Your loving
Clemmie
[sketch of cat][37]

She added an endearing P.S. 'Do Majors or Colonels command battalions?'

During the next few days Winston remained at GHQ, passing the time in visiting units of the French Army, where he was received with warmth. On one of these occasions he was presented with 'a fine steel helmet . . . wh I am going to wear, as it looks so nice & will perhaps protect my valuable cranium'.[38] During part of this time French was away in Paris, and so Winston's own personal affairs hung fire. His busy mind, however, played on the role he relished, and now with reason entertained – that of a brigadier in active command of a fighting brigade. When Clementine's letter of 6th December arrived, with its earnest plea to be guided by Lord Cavan's 'step by step' advice, Winston brushed her objections aside, writing:

You must not suppose that anything that I can do will enable me to 'win my way'[39]. Rising rapidly through the grades cd only be accomplished by favour, i.e., by a view being taken of my personal qualities apart from military services or local experience.[40]

With so much uncertainty still prevailing about his personal future, Winston wrote that, failing a definite decision, he would return to his Grenadiers the next day for another cycle in the trenches. That same evening, he succeeded in speaking to her on the telephone; this, and a few other conversations, were arranged through GHQ and the Admiralty, where chivalrous feelings still burned for the erstwhile First

Lord. Clementine described how when she went to the Admiralty to speak to Winston on the telephone,

Everything there [was] very quiet & solemn except old Page [a Messenger] . . . who frisked about like a faithful old dog & plied me with tea & arm chairs near the fire. Masterton [James Masterton-Smith, First Lord's Private Secretary] very nice & amiable – I think he manages the whole show. Colonel Hankey came out of 'your' room where he had been speaking to Mr Balfour & was then wending his way to Downing Street. He said to me 'In these moments of anxiety & difficulty I miss your Husband's courage & power to take a decision.'[41]

She told Winston:

It was wonderful yesterday to hear your voice on the telephone, But very tantalising, as there is so much I want to say to you which cannot be shouted into an unsympathetic receiver!

It must be thrilling to see all the famous positions along the French line. I feel that you have had an interesting & happy week which consoles me for your absence. Here everyone is downcast & gloomy & there are rumours of a very bad reverse to our troops at Salonica . . . Mrs Greville, dining at Cassell's [sic] last night sat next to the P.M. who she said was very depressed about Salonica; perhaps however his spirits were merely dashed by his neighbour being of mature years! My dear if only you can escape death or injury, how well out of all this you are . . . Goodbye my Darling. Think of me often – During this last week I feel as if I had missed your thoughts – or is it fancy?

Clemmie
[sketch of cat][42]

Clementine's 'antennae' were not out of tune; during this time Winston's train of thought and hers were not in harmony. She was in an agony of mind – if he were given a brigade he would be safer, but she felt deeply it would harm him both in the eyes of his enemies and in the estimation of his true friends. But despite her counsels, the die was cast.

On 10th December Winston wrote that he was to be given the command of the 56th Brigade. He had lunched the previous day with Lord Cavan and had talked the whole question over with him. He assured Clementine that Lord Cavan seemed quite content with the arrangement. Winston was of course aware that his appointment would arouse 'criticism & carping'. But he pointed out to Clementine that even had he taken a battalion for a short period, he would still have been assailed for using this as a stepping stone to higher things.

I am satisfied this is the right thing to do in the circumstances, & for the rest my attention will concentrate upon the Germans.[43]

In this same letter Winston asked Clementine to order him a new khaki tunic, with the insignia of a brigadier-general; he enjoined secrecy, suggesting she could pretend it was for Bertram Romilly. Whatever their differences of point of view, the bond of tenderness between them was not weakened: he ended this letter:

You have been much in my thoughts this week my darling. I rejoiced to hear
your voice over the telephone . . . I cd not say much & even feared you might
think I was abrupt. One cannot really talk down it. But nevertheless we will try
it again.

With tenderest love,
Your devoted
W

Winston had sent Clementine a letter and papers of a highly confidential nature
from Lord Curzon, who was now Lord Privy Seal, instructing her, after she had
herself read them, to keep them under lock and key. Lord Curzon had now emerged
as the strongest advocate in the Cabinet of a renewed effort in Gallipoli, and
Clementine read the papers with passionate interest; on 12th December she told
Winston that they had thrown her

> into a state of agitation and mild hope that at last for the first time since you left
> the Admiralty a courageous & bold decision was going to be taken . . . How
> clear & able Lord C's 2 papers are – I wish he could be Scty of State for War
> instead of that cowardly & base old K . . .

Clementine also was much concerned at this time because Sarah, now just over a
year old, was suffering from acute bouts of neuralgia:

> She becomes rigid & screams with agony for about 20 minutes & when the pain
> ceases she is quite done & exhausted & falls asleep. She has lost her lovely pink
> cheeks and is losing weight. Parkinson has been called in & has prescribed (as
> the last resort) bromide, but we have not yet opened the bottle. It is on the
> mantle piece [sic] & I'm putting it off as long as I can. Today she is a little better.

It is hardly surprising that this letter ended on a somewhat melancholic note:

> Meanwhile I toil away at my working-men's restaurants. After Christmas I am
> opening 2 to seat 400 men each . . . It is snowing hard and makes me fear that
> you are wet & cold. Write & tell me what everyone thinks about Sir John's
> retirement. I fear you will perhaps not go to GHQ so often now? Do you know
> Haig & is he a friend

Your own Clemmie
[sketch of cat][44]

Meanwhile Winston returned to the Grenadiers, and he wrote to tell Clementine
that he would stay with them rather than wait about at GHQ. Lord Cavan had
arranged for Winston to be instructed in the supply system, in preparation for
his new appointment; 'I am to follow the course of a biscuit from the base to the
trenches etc.'[45]

Once Clementine knew that the decision was taken, she did not continue her
protestations, or indulge in warnings of the ill results which might flow from this
step, which she still nevertheless deeply deplored. She knew how much Winston
yearned for a command in keeping with his capacity, and, accepting this outcome

of events, she tried to share in his satisfaction. This was to be her attitude on the many occasions in the years to come when she differed strongly from Winston on various issues. Earnest, even passionate in the advocacy of her point of view, once Winston had taken a decision she would swallow her objections, and loyally support him through thick and thin, only revealing to her most intimate friends or closest relations that her instincts and advice had all been to the contrary.

Now, downing her true feelings, Clementine wrote bravely on 15th December:

My Darling,

I am thrilled to hear that you are to have a Brigade, but I should rejoice more if I thought that in that position you would be in less danger than you are now. I suppose the danger from rifle fire will be less & that from shells greater.

The greater part of her letter, however, was finished later that day, when she had some interesting news to impart:

Later. Goonie has just returned from lunching at Downing Street where she sat between the P.M. & K. She reports that K looked very thin; he told her that he had seen your paper on Trench Warfare which he thought very good & he is having it circulated to the Staffs. The P.M. sniffed & asked after you & asked if you were happy to which Goonie replied acting according to consultation (for we had discussed it beforehand) that you said in all your letters that you were very happy. The old Boy looked rather uncomfortable & then passed on to me 'Why don't I ever see Clemmie, why doesn't she come here?' Goonie enquired if I had Ever been invited to which he replied I ought to propose myself. I think he feels thoroughly sheepish & uneasy, or perhaps he just pretends to be as he thinks it good taste! . . .

I am so relieved that at last the things I ordered are beginning to arrive. Now Christmas congestion is beginning, so if there is anything very special you want, let me know quickly & I will send it out by F. E. I spoke to him this morning on the telephone & he said he would come and see me before starting. The government attitude is that everything is now going splendidly at Salonika. Rumours of the Dardanelles Evacuation are of course all over London (the usual W.O. leakage I suppose) but the rumours differ. The latest Society canard is that the Government will fall this week & that for the duration of the war the Speaker will be made P.M.! This is the very newest, last week it was Lord Derby –

Christmas is coming very soon – shall we meet then?

Goodbye my Darling Winston. I think of you constantly especially at night. I hope you are not very cold.

Your
Clemmie
[sketch of cat]

Meanwhile, events which were to have direct and dramatic repercussions for Winston were moving fast. On 15th December French returned to London to surrender his command, and his replacement by Sir Douglas Haig was announced the following day. During his farewell interview with the Prime Minister Sir John

told him that he had given Churchill a brigade, and 'Asquith said he was delighted.'[46]
But a few hours later the Prime Minister wrote a note to French, saying that 'with
regard to our conversation about our friend – the appointment might cause some
criticism' and should not therefore be made – adding: 'Perhaps you might give him
a battalion.' It is probable that, during the interval between Asquith's conversation
with French and the writing of this note, he had been told of the question tabled
for the House of Commons on the following day by Sir Charles Hunter, a Conservative M.P., asking the Under-Secretary of State for War

> if Major Winston Churchill has been promised the command of an Infantry
> brigade; if this officer has ever commanded a battalion of Infantry; and for how
> many weeks he has served at the front as an Infantry Officer?[47]

Rather than face a parliamentary challenge in defence of Churchill's promotion,
Asquith bent before the prospect of a storm and vetoed the brigade. Naturally
French was astonished and dismayed; astonished no doubt by the lack of loyalty
and firmness shown by the Prime Minister, and dismayed because he had told
many people that Winston was to have a brigade. His hour of influence and power
was gone, however, and he could but acquiesce in a decision which caused him
profound distress and must inflict mortification on his friend, to whom he hastened
to communicate the distasteful news.

While these events were taking place in London, Winston had come out of the
line with the Grenadiers and had repaired to GHQ, from where he wrote a brief
note to Clementine early on 15th December to tell her that he was safe and sound,
and he remained at GHQ to bid farewell to 'my poor friend who returns to pack up
tomorrow'.[48]

Although he knew nothing as yet of Asquith's *volte-face*, Winston realised that the
changeover in command might have an effect on his personal affairs. 'Believe me,'
he wrote to Clementine, 'I am superior to anything that can happen to me out here.
My conviction that the greatest of my work is still to be done is strong within me.'[49]
And, significantly, he suggested for the first time that it might be his duty to return
early in the following year to take his place in Parliament, 'to procure the dismissal
of Asquith and Kitchener' whose lack of direction and ineptitude provoked his
rising contempt.

His long letter was closed up, but not sent, when 'stop press' news of an urgent
character arrived. Another sheet of paper marked 'later' was slipped into the envelope. It read:

> My darling,
>
> I reopen my letter to say that French has telephoned from London that the
> P.M. has written to him that I am not to have a Brigade but a Battalion. I hope
> however to secure one that is now going into the line. You will cancel the order
> for the tunic!
>
> Do not allow the P.M. to discuss my affairs with you. Be vy cool & detached
> and avoid any sign of acquiescence in anything he may say.
>
> > Your devoted
> > W

On this crucial Wednesday, 15th December, Clementine knew nothing further than that Winston was to be given command of the 56th Brigade. But during the next two days various events were further to disturb her peace of mind. On Thursday, 16th December she met Lord Esher (who had just returned from France, where he had seen Winston) in the Berkeley Grill at luncheon; he had expressed himself of views which greatly perturbed her, the more so as they echoed her own inmost feelings.

That same afternoon Sir Charles Hunter asked his 'loaded' question in the House of Commons. It brought into the open, once more, the hostility and malice of Winston's enemies. In answer to the question, the Under-Secretary of State for War replied:

> I have no knowledge myself, and have not been able to obtain any, of a promise of command of an Infantry brigade having been made to my right hon and gallant Friend . . .

Clementine would of course have read the report of the Question and the exchanges it produced. It can only have confirmed her fears that Winston's promotion would arouse fierce criticism and opposition.

The following morning she wrote to Winston and confined herself to generalities, giving only a partial account of her conversation with Lord Esher:

> . . . I met Lord Esher at a restaurant yesterday fresh from France. He said you looked like a boy, all the lines of care gone from your face. He seemed to think there was going to be a row over your Brigade. I pointed out to him that if you had a Battalion first & then a Brigade there would have been 2 rows instead of one.
>
> Jack Tennant denied knowledge of it in the House yesterday. When will it be announced? I feel very anxious & long for a sight of you.
>
> Do you know Sir Douglas Haig? Did he agree to your appointment or was it finally settled before he supervened? He looks a superior man, but his expression is cold & prejudiced, & I fear he is narrow . . .

She ended her letter:

> Randolph asks every day about you & also asks every day when the war will be over. I fear he's a peace crank. I feel like that too![50]

But later that day Clementine was in touch with Eddie Marsh (now one of the Prime Minister's Private Secretaries), and what he told her prompted her to write a second letter to Winston, in which she gave him not only a full account of her meeting with Lord Esher, but no longer hid from him her state of heart-broken anxiety.

> 41 Cromwell Road
> 17th December [1915]
> [Letter 2]
>
> My Darling,
>   Since writing to you I have been wondering whether I ought not to have told you exactly what Lord Esher said. I did not do so becos' I thought your appoint-

ment was absolutely fixed; but now I hear from Eddie that you say that the recall of Sir John may affect your private fortunes. So I will tell you (for what it is worth) what Lord E. said. Of course you will know better than I can whether he is in touch with feeling in the Army or not & whether to attach importance & weight to his opinion. He said 'Of course you know Winston is taking a Brigade & as a personal friend of his I am very sorry about it; as I think he is making a great mistake. Of course it's not his fault, Sir John forced it upon him. All W's friends are very distressed about it as they hoped he would take a batallion [sic] first.' He said how tremendously popular & respected you had become in the short time you had been there & repeated to me the story you told me of the Colonel of the Grenadiers receiving you so disagreeably & then being entirely won over. This interview took place in the crowded grill-room of the Berkeley. I preserved a calm & composed demeanour, but I was astonished & hurt at his blurting all this out to me. He repeated again & again that the thing was a mistake; I tried at last to head him off by asking him personal questions about you, how you were looking, if you were well. He then launched forth again, saying that you had been in the greatest danger, in more than was necessary etc & that French had determined to give you this Brigade as he was convinced you wld otherwise be killed.

After this I crawled home quite stunned & heart-broken.

My Darling Love – I live from day to day in suspense and anguish. At night when I lie down I say to myself Thank God he is still alive. The 4 weeks of your absence seem to me like 4 years – If only My Dear you had no military ambitions. If only you would stay with the Oxfordshire Hussars in their billets –

I can just bear it – feeling that you are really happy. I have ceased to have ambitions for you – Just come back to me alive that's all.

Your loving
Clemmie

But the events and cares of that long day were not yet over. During the course of the evening F.E. Smith (now the Solicitor-General) telephoned to say he was going over to France and would see Winston the next day; he offered to act as messenger or postman. Later still she received the letter from Winston written from GHQ on 15th December, with its last-minute enclosure telling her he was not, after all, to be given the promised brigade.

At one o'clock on the morning of Friday, 18th December, Clementine wrote her third letter to Winston in the last twenty-four hours. It is jumbled and disjointed. One senses her stunned dismay, as she sat wearily writing in those dark hours:

My Darling,

Late in the evening I had a telephone message from F. E. saying he was going to see you tomorrow. I would like to have sent you some delicacies but the shops were closed so all this letter brings is my tender love. My Dear – your letter has just come telling me that your hopes of a Brigade have vanished. I do trust that Haig will give you one later. If he does it may be all for the best – but if not it is cruel that the change at G.H.Q. came before all was fixed. You will receive later by King's messenger 2 letters written earlier in the afternoon [of the 17th]. Do not pay any attention to No. 2 written at a moment of sadness, uncertainty & agitation. Your letter with its firm & confident tone has restored me. I telephoned to F. E. where he was dining & he very good naturedly came round & saw me. He is your true & faithful friend & I felt so glad that you will now see each other . . .

I must say I am astounded at the P.M. not backing you for a brigade but I cannot help hoping that he has asked Haig to give you one later on after you have commanded a battalion for a little while.

My own Darling I feel such absolute confidence in your future – it is your present which causes me agony – I feel as if I had a tight band of pain round my heart.

It fills me with great pride to think that you have won the love & respect of those splendid Grenadiers & their austere Colonel.

In happier times you must let me see them all. Perhaps if any of them come home on leave they would come & see me.

> Your loving
> Clemmie
> [sketch of cat]

When Sir John French returned to GHQ to pack up and take his leave he gave Winston a full account of his conversation with the Prime Minister and the events that flowed therefrom, and he showed him Asquith's note. Its tone, and particularly the last phrase – 'Perhaps you might give him a battalion' – rankled deeply. In giving Clementine all the details of the sorry affair, Winston commented: 'The almost contemptuous indifference of this note was a revelation to me.'[51] He went on to recall the sequence of events: when he left the Admiralty, Asquith had offered Winston a brigade in the event of his going out to France; in the following September Winston told the Prime Minister of offers of command made to him by French, and the Prime Minister had assured him of his support in any advancement thought fitting by the Commander-in-Chief. Winston called to mind the long tale of his connection, work and friendship with Asquith.

> Altogether I am inclined to think his conduct reaches the limit of meanness & ungenerousness . . . Personally I feel that every link is severed: & while I do not wish to decide in a hurry – my feeling is that all relationship shd cease.[52]

Winston then discussed the question of whether in these changed circumstances he should accept command of a battalion; his mood was one of uncertainty and depression; he expressed himself as reluctant to accept the responsibilities of such an appointment unless it were under 'a C-in-C who believes in me . . .' He realised clearly that he would be an easy target for criticism. Winston was as yet uncertain of what his relationship with the new Commander-in-Chief would be, although he had known him in days gone by when Haig was a major and he, Winston, a young M.P. In this gloomy hour, one bright vista gleamed ahead, he could always return to his Grenadiers – 'This at any rate is the place of honour.'[53]

Winston ended his letter with an urgent request; he had written two letters to

Clementine on the previous day, he now asked her to burn them – 'I was depressed & my thought was not organised. It is now quite clear & good again & I see plainly the steps to take.' Clementine faithfully did his bidding: the letters do not survive.

But these distressing events had a more cheerful sequel. Later that day he was able to tell Clementine of his first interview with Sir Douglas Haig, who had received him with the 'utmost kindness of manner & consideration'.[54] In the course of their conversation the new Commander-in-Chief had assured Winston of his sympathetic support, and Winston felt reassured that even under the new regime he would get a fair chance. 'In these circumstances I consented to take a battalion.' Altogether the meeting was a great success, and Winston endearingly commented: 'So I am back on my perch again with my feathers stroked down.'[55]

Winston had received Clementine's letters written on 17th December, and his ire was roused by her account of Lord Esher's outburst –

Esher talks foolishly. It wd not have been a great mistake for me to take a Brigade. There was something to be said either way . . .[56]

As to her relationship with Asquith, Clementine received explicit instructions: she was to make no change, but was to show an unwillingness to discuss him or his affairs. And 'Don't you tell me he was quite right – or let him persuade you,' he added.

Two days later, Clementine, who must have been eating her heart out for news, wrote:

20th December [1915]

My Darling,

Your two letters of the 17th [destroyed at his request] made me so sad & if your happier one of the 18th, (describing your interview with Haig) had not come at the same time I would have been absolutely heart-broken.

I will write to you fully tomorrow, but can now only send a scrawl to send you a thousand kisses & to assure you of my undying love for you. You must not beat your poor Kat so hard; it is very cruel & not the right treatment for mousers.

I am absolutely worn out to-night.

I gave F. E. a letter for you which will I hope soon arrive.

Your loving
Clemmie

Large posters just out:—
TROOPS WITHDRAWN FROM DARDANELLES
OFFICIAL

Pending his posting to a battalion, Winston moved two hundred yards down the street to a house occupied by Sir Max Aitken – 'a sort of Canadian war office'[57], as Winston described it – from where Sir Max operated as a Canadian Eyewitness at the Front. Here the two men's lifelong friendship was cemented.

Winston awaited the outcome of events with surprising patience. 'It is odd to pass these days of absolute idleness,' he wrote. '. . . It does not fret me. In war one takes everything as it comes . . .'[58] He watched from afar the irresolution and incompetence of the men in power, and turned himself with relief to the 'tremendous little tasks wh my new work will give me'. He looked forward to this new experience and to building a good relationship with the men he would soon command; he hoped to come to them '. . . like a breeze . . . I shall give them my vy best.'[59]

He was at GHQ when French took his departure; it moved him very much. After seeing many generals and other commanders, Sir John had sent for Churchill, saying '. . . it is fitting my last quarter of an hour here shd be spent with you.' After that he had departed '. . . with a guard of honour, saluting officers, cheering soldiers & townsfolk – stepping swiftly from the stage of history into the dull humdrum of ordinary life . . .'[60]

In their letters a possible reunion in Paris had been canvassed, but in the event – and better still – Winston came home for Christmas. He arrived on Christmas Eve, and paid a visit to the Prime Minister: it cannot have been a comfortable interview.

But great were the rejoicings at 41 Cromwell Road, where the two families were packed in. The two elder children must have sensed the strain of the last weeks: but now it was Christmas-time, and Papa was home to make it all quite perfect. As for their parents – neither the bitter disappointments and dramatic events of the last year, nor the anxieties and perils which loomed ahead, could dim the joy and thankfulness that they were together again.

But Winston's leave was painfully short: he had arrived home on Friday, and he left for France again on the following Monday. Now, as always, his wife and family had to share him with events and people, for he did not omit to look up some of his political friends. During those three brief days, however, we may be quite sure Winston and Clementine found time to open their hearts to one another. They had many things to discuss: past griefs and mortifications; present political preoccupations, and the prospect before them, of long, grey months of separation.

Then Winston went back, like so many more, to danger and squalor and, in his case, frustration too. Clementine saw him off; they cut it rather fine – 'I could not tell you how much I wanted you at the station,' she wrote in a short note on 28th December – 'I was so out of breath with running for the train.'

WAITING IN SILENCE

WHEN CHURCHILL went back to France at the end of December 1915 he was politically down-and-out; many people thought he was finished forever – and some hoped he was.

He turned to soldiering, as we have seen, with relief; but there too the way to further advancement was temporarily barred. He had the worst of both worlds: he was at once too junior (in a strictly military sense), and too formidable in another. But Churchill found real solace and satisfaction in the zealous performance of his duties as an officer in the field; and he devoted to his regiment the energy and thought he had once applied to larger matters. He enjoyed the company of his fellow officers, and soon won their respect and friendship, sharing with them to the full the daily hazards and discomforts of life at the Front.

At this low ebb in his fortunes Winston turned more and more to Clementine as the one person to whom he could express himself freely, and on whom he could unload himself of the bitterness and even hatred he felt for those who had seen him sink unaided. She was also his link with the political world, whose hold upon him continued to be strong. And again and again in his letters he was to urge her to keep in touch with events and people, and to go about in society for that purpose. Clementine rose valiantly to the occasion, but her days were already long and full. Apart from her family and household, she was committed to her canteen work, which at this time was increasingly demanding and arduous. It required a supreme effort on her part to find the time, and to summon up the extra energy for social life. But she was zealous in following Winston's instructions to move in political society, sending him long accounts of her conversations and impressions.

In all Clementine's letters during these early months of 1916 one is struck, not only by her faith (at times prophetic) in Winston's star, but also by her wisdom. No one had shared more keenly his disappointments and mortifications. We know she could feel things passionately, and express herself even violently; but she seems to have set herself out to deflect and moderate Winston's wrath and bitterness against Asquith. Partly she feared Winston might blunt his talents, and sour his normally warm and generous nature by too much brooding over past wrongs. But perhaps more than that, she did not want him to fall too much under the spell of Lloyd George, about whom she had some rough and penetrating things to say.

Winston's brief Christmas leave had left Clementine worn out with emotion and excitement; so she went to stay with her Stanley cousins for a few days to recover herself. But before she left for Alderley, Lloyd George had lunched with her on 29th December, and had told her about the crisis then rending the Cabinet over the introduction of a limited form of compulsory military service, an issue over which three ministers were threatening to resign. Clementine had duly regaled Winston with all the intricate details in a long letter to him later that same day. From Alderley she wrote again on 30th December, having further pondered upon the crisis, and some of the personalities involved in it.

I came here last night & intend to stay till Monday. I hope the change will cure the melancholia which was dispelled by your return, but which has now settled on me again! . . . I suppose that if compulsion is carried without a single resignation (which seems likely) it will be a feather in the P.M's cap & a vindication of his slow statecraft. I am very much afraid this is going to be a 'personal triumph' for him.

I think my Darling you will have to be very patient – Do not burn any boats – The P.M. has not treated you worse than Ll. G has done, in fact not so badly for he is not as much in your debt as the other man, (i.e. Marconi).* On the other hand are the Dardanelles. I feel sure that if the choice were equal you would prefer to work with the P.M. than with Ll. G. – It's true that when association ceases with the P.M. he cools & congeals visibly, but all the time you were at the Admiralty he was loyal & steadfast while the other would barter you away at any time in any place – I assure you he is the direct descendant of Judas Iscariott [sic]. At this moment altho I hate the P.M, if he held out his hand I could take it, (tho' I would give it a nasty twist) but before taking Ll. G's I would have to safeguard myself with charms, touchwoods, exorcisms & by crossing my-self –

I always can get on with him & yesterday I had a good talk, but you can't hold his eyes, they shift away –

You know I'm not good at pretending but I am going to put my pride in my pocket & reconnoitre Downing Street.

Even this one night in the country has done me good & I feel able to sit up & take an interest in life. Yesterday I was bitterly dejected & could not quench an endless flow of tears . . .

'You are a vy sapient cat to write as you do,'[1] Winston commented when he received this letter with Clementine's dissection of Asquith and Lloyd George. But he felt deeply that the former had shown himself to be a 'weak and disloyal chief', and that their days of working together were over. Whereas, although Winston conceded (somewhat reluctantly) that Lloyd George 'is no doubt all you say', yet he had always been against the Dardanelles, and not, like Asquith, a 'co-adventurer', who had ruined the policy by his slothfulness and procrastination.

*Churchill had done much to help Lloyd George during the Marconi Scandal of 1912–13, when the revelation that Lloyd George owned shares in the American Marconi Company and had concealed this information from the House of Commons had nearly forced him to resign.

At the dawn of this New Year, Winston's greetings were tinged with subdued optimism:

All my tenderest wishes for a Happy New Year. I think it will be better for us than the last – wh after all was not so bad. At any rate our fortunes have more room to expand & less to decline than in Jany last.

But his forecast for world affairs was less sanguine.

I do not see how any end will be reached in 1916: and the probability is that 1917 will dawn like this new year in world wide bloodshed & devastation . . .[2]

Clementine's New Year letter was rather depressed in tone. Everywhere at home people were now feeling the weight of the war. Bereavement, separation, shortages and toil had changed the almost ecstatic atmosphere of endeavour and sacrifice of the first few months to a grim and dogged spirit of 'Carry on'. The family gathered at Alderley was no exception to the prevailing mood:

. . . The household here . . . is very subdued in spite of seven grand-children. Three daughters of the house, Margaret Goodenough & Blanche Serocold & Sylvia Henley look patient but war worn. Margaret has seen her Admiral 4 times since the beginning of the war (he is still cruising around in the Southampton). Blanche is going to have her 3rd child & her husband recovered from his serious wound has his brigade in the line somewhere – Antony Henley is moderately safe on a Divisional Staff – Venetia* the prosperous and the happy, arrives this evening to enliven us & to lift us out of the Doldrums – We expect to hear from her 'the latest' concerning the crisis – she entertained the P.M. on New Year's Eve to Beer & Skittles . . .[3]

Clementine was much depressed by a temporary absence of news from Winston, and two days later she wrote this pathetic note:

> Alderley Park,
> Chelford, Cheshire
> 3rd January [1916]

My Darling,
    Still no letter & you have been gone a week to-day.
    I wonder where you are.
    I have no news of the great world, the little intimate things are starved – So my pen runs dry –
    I return home to-day hoping rather hopelessly to find something from you.

> Adieu
> Clemmie

I send you some timid & tentative kisses.

In fact Winston had not been neglectful, he had written every day (save one) long and newsful letters of his daily doings and reflections, and when Clementine reached home, two of these letters had arrived, '. . . so I feel revived, but not yet

*Married July 1915 to Hon. Edwin Montagu M.P., Financial Secretary to the Treasury.

nourished,' she wrote in a letter marked '5 a.m.' on 5th January. But later that day two more letters arrived to assuage her hunger.

Winston's immediate future as a soldier had now been settled: he was appointed Colonel of the 6th Battalion Royal Scots Fusiliers, in the IXth Division under the command of General Furse. The battalion was at present in the village of Moolenacker (not far from Armentières), licking its wounds after being severely mauled in battle. Winston made much of joining a Scots regiment, and asked her to send him a copy of Burns' poetry:

> I will soothe and cheer their spirits by quotations from it . . . You know I am a vy gt admirer of that race. A wife, a constituency, & now a regiment attest the sincerity of my choice![4]

He also asked her to send him a new tunic with the insignia of a lieutenant-colonel and 'a Glengarry cap'[5]. Although always much addicted to dashing hats, Winston in the event very rarely wore his 'bonnet' – he rightly opined it did not become him, and he reverted to his French *poilu*'s helmet. This was greatly to Clementine's relief – since steel was safer than tartan.

Soon Clementine had some 'Downing Street' news to impart. On 7th January she had tea with Margot Asquith:

> . . . She was in a very good mood, there being I am sure great relief in that quarter that the division on compulsion went so well . . . I met the P.M in the hall. – He looked shy when he first saw me, but thought better of it & I had a little talk to him – He looks as if he had been thro' a good deal. He asked after you with compunction in his voice.[6]

The following Sunday she lunched with the Asquiths. It was the first time since Winston's resignation that she had talked at any length with the Prime Minister.

> . . . He talked a great deal about you & asked a great many questions. I was perfectly natural (except perhaps that I was a little too buoyant) & he tried to be natural too, but it was an effort. I think it is a good thing to keep up civil relations & it is always interesting to follow the Block's train of thought.[7]

When Winston received her letter he was not satisfied with her account:

> . . . You do not tell me in yr letter what the P.M. said. You only say he said a lot. But I shd like a *verbatim* report of the Kat's conversation with the old ruffian.[8]

So Clementine duly sat down to write an amplified version of her original account:

> . . . If you received the impression from my letter that the P.M. 'said a lot' about politics and the situation I gave you a wrong impression – He talked a great deal about trivialities & femininities which you know he adores and he asked a good many questions about you & about the detail of your life out there – He *wanted* the answers to be reassuring, & my good manners as a guest forbade me making him uncomfortable which of course I could easily have done. He seemed grateful

to me for sparing him –! He is a sensualist & if I had depicted you in a tragic & sinister light it would have ruined his meal & I shd probably not be bidden again . . .[9]

Winston's almost daily letters told her of his first experiences with his new battalion. He found the work absorbing, and a challenge. Practically every regular officer had been killed in recent actions, and the regiment was, in consequence, officered by very young men 'vy brave & willing & intelligent: but of course all quite new to soldiering'.[10] He had been allowed to bring with him as his Second-in-Command Sir Archibald Sinclair, a young Scottish baronet, and a regular officer in the Life Guards. Winston had got to know him in the last few months, and had formed a high regard for him both as an experienced soldier, and a friend in whom he could confide. Their friendship forged in these hard times was to be an enduring one. But despite the absorbing preoccupations of his new command, Winston had moments of deep depression, and these he confided only to Clementine:

I do not ever show anything but a smiling face to the military world: a proper complete detachment & contentment. But so it is a relief to write one's heart out to you. Bear with me.[11]

Her letters to him were a source not only of news, but also of comfort and strength; and, like her, he became depressed and agitated if the flow of her letters was for any reason interrupted.

You cannot write to me too often or too long – my dearest & sweetest. The beauty & strength of your character & the sagacity of yr judgment are more realised by me every day. I ought to have followed yr counsels in my days of prosperity. Only sometimes they are too negative. I shd have made nothing if I had not made mistakes . . .[12]

On 11th January Clementine wrote in answer to several letters which had arrived simultaneously. Winston had dwelt on the conscription crisis, which had raised the possibility that the Government might fall:

. . . I knew my Darling that you would be feeling the political excitement of the last 10 days. Everybody here seemed rather thrilled, but I could not get worked up over it as it seemed impossible to me that the anti-compulsionists would face the racket. I'm afraid I can't agree that the P.M's position is only temporarily strengthened – He will always in the end tip down on the side of strong measures after delaying them & devitalising them so as to try & keep everybody together.

His method of defeating the enemy is not by well-planned lightning strokes but by presenting to him a large stolid gelatinous mass which he the enemy is supposed to pommel in vain.

I am afraid the war will drag slowly to its end with him & K still at the helm. No one trusts Ll-G. & Bonar is light metal. These are only my own reflections as I have seen no-one of consequence for some days – Yesterday I was very sad, the end of Gallipoli & a fine battleship gone down . . .

She also had practical and sagacious views on Winston's intention to press the Prime Minister for the publication of the papers relating to the Dardanelles:

> If you ask the P.M to publish the Dardanelles papers let me know what happens. If he refuses or delays I beg you not to do anything without telling me first & giving me time to give you my valuable(!) opinion on it. It is an unequal match between the P.M. & an officer in the field in war-time – If he dissents I fear you will have to wait. If you insisted on publication agnst his wish you would have agnst you all the forces of cohesion & stability including every member of the Cabinet.
>
> On the other hand when the papers are eventually published his refusal to do so earlier will have a very bad effect for him.
>
> But of course the P.M. may consent – Are you quite certain however that this is the best time for publication, when you are away & not able to speak in the debate which is bound to take place. I am very anxious that you should not blunt this precious weapon prematurely . . .[13]

But her letters were not all views and political advice. The following day she wrote again; perhaps in the night she had brooded over the sad and depressed passages in his letters, and she sensed his feelings of frustration, bitterness and isolation.

41 Cromwell Road
Jan. 12th, 1916

My own Darling,

I long so to be able to comfort you. Later on when you are in danger in the trenches you will be equable & contented, while I who am now comparatively at ease will be in mortal anxiety. Try not to brood too much; I would be so unhappy if your naturally open and unsuspicious nature became embittered. Patience is the only grace you need. If you are not killed, as sure as day follows night you will come into your own again. I know *you* don't fear death, it is I who dread that. But I am almost glad to be suffering now, becos' I am sure no single soul will be allowed to live thro' this time without sorrow, so perhaps what we are enduring now will be counted & we shall be spared the greatest pain of all.

I remember quite well when we were at the Admiralty during those wonderful opening weeks of the war we were both so happy, you with the success of the Naval preparations & with the excitement of swiftly moving events and I with pride at the glamour surrounding you & the Navy – I remember feeling guilty & ashamed that the terrible casualties of those first battles did not sadden me more. I wondered how long we should continue to tread on air –

When it is all over, we shall be proud that you were a soldier & not a politician for the greater part of the war. Soldiers and soldiers' wives seem to me now the only real people.

I am glad you tell me all you feel my Darling, I want to know it all. I too shew a detached & smiling face to the world.

I have Goonie for a safety-valve & you must make use of Archie who is safe & loyal – Do not tell curious acquaintances your opinion of the P.M's character or policy . . .

We hope now that Cape Helles has been evacuated that Jack may come home on leave, but we have had no news.

You will see that Edwin Montagu is restored to the Duchy of Lancaster but keeps his work as financial secretary to the Treasury which saves him from the slur of well-paid inactivity –

I will try and see Lloyd-George again –

I wish I had some interesting news for you.

Goodbye my Darling. I send you many kisses –

Your letters are very precious.

> Your loving
> Clemmie
> [sketch of cat]

Do you want any more cigars yet??

'Your letter of 12th is splendid,' Winston replied. 'I run in and out of moods; but I do not doubt the wisdom & necessity of my coming out here: nor do I repent at all my decision . . .'[14] He was insistent that Clementine should maintain contact with his political confidants: 'Now mind you keep in touch with Garvin, Scott & Dalziel, & don't let them drift off or think I have resigned the game,' he had commanded her in a long letter on 16th January.

Tell them I am taking time to consider, method & occasion, but that in principle I have decided. Also I think you might have a talk with Cawley – & even with the Fiend himself [Fisher].

Although the declaration of Winston's decision presently to return home and re-enter the political arena must have struck a chill note for her, Clementine carried out his instructions – baulking only at Fisher, whom she flatly refused to contact. It must have been a source of reassurance to her that Archie Sinclair – Winston's closest confidant – agreed with her: 'Archie is a strong advocate of my staying here . . .', he wrote in the same letter. 'It is odd how similar are the standpoints from wh you and he both view my tiresome affairs.'

The reserve billets in which Winston's battalion found itself for the time being were a series of '. . . squalid little French farms rising from a sea of soppy fields & muddy lanes'.[15] He told Clementine, however, that he was quite comfortable in his little farmhouse.

. . . The guns boom away in the distance, & at night the sky to the Northward blinks & flickers with the wicked lights of war.[16]

His whole thought and activity was concentrated on the detail of his new command: he attended a Machine Gun School, conducted drilling periods, practised bomb-throwing, and, by night, accompanied by the faithful Archie, patrolled the regimental area. About four days before the battalion was due to move forward to start taking over its position in the Line, Churchill organised a combined sports day and concert for the men, which was a tremendous success and did much to raise their spirits. 'Poor fellows –', Winston wrote, 'nothing like this has ever been done for them before. They do not get much to brighten their lives – short though they may be . . .'[17]

A red-letter day was when the hamper Clementine had despatched him for Christmas suddenly arrived on 13th January. '. . . I never saw such dainties & such profusion,' Winston wrote appreciatively the same day. 'We shall eat them sparingly keeping the best for the trenches . . .'

But although Winston's letters gave lively and detailed accounts of his military activities, and he was immersed in plans for his battalion's organisation and welfare, there is scarcely one in which his feeling of injustice, nor his sense of Asquith's betrayal, does not emerge; and through them runs the burning thread of constant anger at the utter squandering of men, opportunity and materials by reason of the failure to carry through the strategy of the Dardanelles operation. His feeling of frustration was sharp:

> . . . I have no means of expression. I am impotent to give what there is to be given – of truth & value & urgency. I must wait in silence the sombre movement of events. Still it is better to be gagged than give unheeded counsel.[18]

Although he was out of sight, Winston was determined that he should not be out of mind, and he never ceased to adjure Clementine to keep in touch with his friends, and even 'pseudo-friends'[19]. 'Don't neglect these matters,' he wrote,

> I have no one but you to act for me. I shd like you to make the seeing of my friends a regular business, like your canteens wh are going so well. It is fatal to let the threads drop . . . There is nothing to ask of them – only represent *me* in their circle.[20]

Clementine, like many others, was feeling the burden and plod of life on the home front. Her work for the YMCA was ever on the increase, and she was just now greatly occupied with a new canteen for a big munitions factory which was to be opened on Hackney Marshes, where a thousand men would have to be fed at one sitting. In her own family circle she had worries also: her mother had hurt her leg and was laid up, while the formidable old Lady Airlie seemed at point of death; she in fact recovered, but Clementine at the time wrote to Winston:

> . . . She is having a long struggle, the light flickers & burns quite low and then burns up brightly again. It is a strange contrast to the swift deaths of strong young men.[21]

In another letter she reported that everyone seemed rather war worn, and she apologised that her account was not more amusing.[22] A tempting suggestion arose in her mind: 'If I came to Dieppe could you get 2 days' leave? I do long to see you. I'm very very lonely.'[23]

Many women would have found a real consolation in such days of trial and separation in the company of their children. Clementine loved her children, and was devoted to their welfare, but it is marked how small a part they play in her letters. Her whole life's centre was out there in France, and all her thoughts and actions revolved around Winston, his welfare and his interests. 'I hope you love me very much Darling,' she wrote at the end of one letter –

I long for you often – I wake up in the night & think of you in your squalid billet & of all the women in Europe who are lying awake praying for safety for their men.[24]

The 6th Battalion The Royal Scots Fusiliers was due to go into the trenches on 27th January, and they would move into 'support' positions a few days before. Earlier Winston had visited the part of the line to be occupied by his battalion, near Ploegsteert (which had instantly been re-christened 'Plugstreet' by the Tommies), a village a mile or two over the Belgian border. He had been impressed by the condition of the trenches and defences, and had reported favourably upon them to Clementine. As Battalion Commander he would live alternately in two places, the Hospice (Support HQ) and Laurence Farm (Advance Battalion HQ):

... in fact I shall only move back about $\frac{3}{4}$s of a mile from the front line when we are in support and supposed to be 'resting'. Therefore for the next 2 or 3 months we shall all dwell continuously in close range of the enemys artillery.[25]

He hastened to reassure Clementine by saying that the houses in that neighbourhood had not been much knocked about, and that losses had been small.

But the knowledge of the exact date that Winston was to move into the front line threw Clementine into a panic: 'Oh my dearest, I can't get used to the idea,' she wrote on 21st January. A few days later he tried to calm her fears:

Don't worry I beseech you. Women & children will be living under exactly the same conditions within a quarter of a mile of my advanced HQ: & 2 nuns are still residing in the support HQ.

It is splendid having you at home to think about me & love me & share my inmost fancies. What shd I find to hold on to without you. All my gt political estate seems to have vanished away – all my friends are mute – all my own *moyens* are in abeyance. But there is the Kat with her kittens, supplied I trust adequately with cream & occasional mice. That is all my world in England . . .[26]

Clementine was conscientious about Winston's instructions for keeping in touch with people. But she wrote:

I will try & see your friends, but everyone 'in office' seems to be unbelievably smug – Were we like that when you were in power? There is an atmospheric non conductive barrier between those whose men are in danger & those whose men are in powerful security at home.[27]

She gave him some penetrating appraisals of political figures. Lloyd George was temporarily weakened by his unpopular views on labour questions and compulsory service, and she commented:

... I think it will take Ll-George (even allowing for his marvellous recuperative powers) a long time to recover – If tomorrow the P.M disappeared Bonar Law would be the successor. He has made a great impression in the House during these last weeks by his skilful handling of delicate topics & this impression will spread to the country. Myself I think Bonar is not a big man, but he is a very skilful one & does not miss his markets. I think Ll-George will remain 'perdu' for a bit & then gradually slide away from his 'compulsion' attitude towards the working men. Montagu after an absence of 6 months from the Cabinet finds very little change except a greater disinclination to action, the only Warrior is Curzon.

God bless you my Darling and keep you safe

Your loving
Clemmie [28]

Clementine had been for a long time wary of Lloyd George, and her suspicions were not alleviated by his charm:

... I get on so well with him & I know he likes me, but he is a sneak – I would never like you to be intimately connected becos tho' he seems to recover again & again from his muddles & mistakes I am not sure his partner would; he would instead be saddled with the whole lot while Ll-G skipped off laughing . . .[29]

Earlier on she had written of him:

... He is a barometer, but not a really useful one as he is always measuring his own temperature not yours![30]

But Winston continued to differ with her on this subject, writing:

I am sorry for what you tell me about L.G. he has been vy faithless & is now friendless.

But in justice he reminded her: 'Still he has been more on the true trail than anyone else in this war.'[31]

It had obviously occurred to Winston that he had been somewhat peremptory in his tone when urging Clementine not to lose touch with his friends and the political world generally, and he wrote almost apologetically:

My beloved, I wrote a miauling letter yesterday, and I expect the Kat will be flustered by my directions to keep in touch with so many people. Do only just what comes easily & naturally to you my darling. On the other hand don't simply vanish out of the political circle & plunge into bed & canteens.[32]

Clementine had responded vigorously to his 'miauling' letter:

... Now don't scold your Kat too much for being a hermit. Here in two days I have hob-nobbed with Montagu, Birrell, Lloyd George & a South African potentate [Sir Abe Bailey]! Tomorrow night I am dining with Cassel. Please send me home the Distinguished Conduct Medal at once & much praise . . .[33]

But she found most of the politicians she met cynical and remote. On 29th January she wrote a long letter:

My darling,

I dined with F.E. & Lady F.E. on Thursday night . . . F.E. was most pleasant & mellow, but like Lord Robert Cecil has become an absolute mandarin & is enamoured of the Government & all its machinery – I suppose that a dignified position & heaps of money have inevitably a sedative effect. After dinner we dropped in for 5 minutes at the Empire & so to bed – Yesterday I put on 3 layers of armour & went to luncheon with the McKennas [he was now Chancellor of the Exchequer]. There I met Sir Ernest Cassel & my sense of humour was tickled by the contrast in their attitude towards the war, the red-hot patriotism of the German & the tepid counter-jumping calculation of the Englishman – McKenna's candour is astonishing – He wld reduce the size of the present army if he had the power. His plan is to pay our allies to do all the fighting while we do all the manufacturing here. He reeled out strings of figures none of which I was in the position to question; he really is a most noxious creature. Sir Ernest & I walked away from the house much depressed. I expressed myself rather forcibly which rather shocked him; (altho' he agreed) he is much impressed by the purple of authority & office. I am afraid the war will go on forever at this rate.

Winston was much delighted by these accounts of Clementine's social activities and showed his appreciation: 'You have indeed been active seeing all those people . . . Persevere, the D.C.M. is yours.'[34]

Enclosed in nearly all Clementine's letters were any newspaper cuttings she thought would interest him: she never sheltered him from the slings and arrows of public comment, any more than Winston spared her details of the dangers through which he passed. Commenting on one batch of cuttings, she wrote:

I keep sending you the press-cuttings – It is quite out of the common to come across a sentence that is not ignorant & prejudiced.

She then added a remark which reveals her good and clear understanding in these matters:

But all this does not really influence the public against you becos' the public is very fond of your personality.[35]

Through all the ups and downs of his long life this dictum remained true.

Her faith in Winston's future was unwavering, and she sought to reassure him:

Do not fear, your political estate has not vanished, it is all waiting for you when the right moment comes which (Alas for the country) may not be till after the war – If only you come safely thro' . . .

To-day is your first day in the trenches & how I pray you may be protected. I hope you wear a steel helmet always & not the Glengarry.

It seems so hard that I cannot come & see you – It would be so easy & I cld live with the poor French women in a ruined cottage & hoe turnips . . .[36]

The nuns, who were so gallantly sticking it out and keeping up the little chapel in the Hospice, received Winston and his colleagues 'most graciously' when they marched in. That evening, 26th January, Winston wrote:

I am extremely well lodged here – with a fine bedroom looking out across fields to the German lines 3,000 yards away . . . On the right & left the guns are booming, & behind us a British field piece barks like a spaniel at frequent intervals. But the women & children still inhabit the little town & laugh at the shells wh occasionally buff into the old church.

On the eve of their going into the trenches Churchill delivered a short homily to his young officers, counselling them, among other sensible precautions, to have a spare pair of boots, and reiterating his theme that 'War is a game that is played with a smile' – to which maxim he added the rider: 'If you can't smile grin.'[37]

The next day the battalion moved up into the trenches for a tour of forty-eight hours (future spells of duty were to be of six days' duration). The two days turned out to be relatively calm and uneventful, but Winston wrote:

> . . . You know a Colonel's day in the line is almost the greatest personal demand on a man's qualities – vy like being a Captain of a vy big ship in submarine infested waters.[38]

The battalion was relieved on 29th January, and he reported that it had all gone off with clockwork precision – the changeover being completed without casualties. He had been delighted with the bearing of his officers and men. When they got safely back some of them had attended Mass in the chapel, where the old priest, despite a shattered church and a house frequently under shell-fire, was still at his post. But when Clementine wrote on 30th January, she did not know that Winston and his comrades were back in their support billets, and her letter breathes anxiety:

My darling

Today the newspapers contain very alarming news of a German attack – I wish I knew for certain that it was nowhere in your neighbourhood – No letters from you lately, the last is dated Jan: 24th. – The communiqué is brief but we have had them brief before and a very long casualty list to follow . . . I long for the return of Lloyd-George & F.E. for personal news of you – I pray this attack of the enemy may not lead to a foolish counter offensive on our part. The air is thick with rumours that *our* push is to be made quite soon . . .

The mood at home was subdued, and people were weighed down by the long and weary course of the war. Many people's lives had changed, and Clementine gave an account of a former gilded socialite, Irene Lawley, 'rather pretty & fluffy & used to be rather silly', who under the harrow of war had become a person of consequence and endurance. '. . . now,' wrote Clementine,

she gets up at crack of dawn & nurses all day at a hospital & in her off time she drives herself in a little open car – She took me home last night thro' the pitch black streets driving most skilfully . . . She wears white fur clothes & the car is pale blue & altogether she looked rather attractive but very overworked and unhappy & I then recollected that Lord Vernon whom she loved and Charles Lister who loved her are both dead –

The atmosphere here is very bleak & gloomy & chills my heart in the spare moments of my work – The Government people are unbelievably smug – I am seeing them occasionally to please you my Darling but I cannot take any interest in these soul-less cold blooded tortoises & I have ceased to feel any curiosity about them . . .

One feels in this long letter that Clementine had reached a still centre of depression and sadness. In it she opened her heart about her religious feelings – a subject she rarely spoke or wrote about:

. . . I fear this trivial letter will be no good to you my Darling; I am rather in the rut to-day & can see only miles & miles of uphill road – Are your men and officers religious? Tell me if being near danger makes you think of Christ. Being unhappy brings Him to my thoughts but only, I fear, becos' I want to be comforted not becos I want Him for Himself . . .

Goodbye my Dearest love I send you tender kisses & fervent wishes for your safety. Your loving

Clemmie

Enclosed with this sad letter, copied out in her own hand, was this poem by Christina Rossetti:

UP-HILL

Does the road wind up-hill all the way?
　　Yes, to the very end.
Will the day's journey take the whole long day?
　　From morn to night, my friend.

But is there for the night a resting-place?
　　A roof for when the slow, dark hours begin.
May not the darkness hide it from my face?
　　You cannot miss that inn.

Shall I meet other wayfarers at night?
　　Those who have gone before.
Then must I knock, or call when just in sight?
　　They will not keep you standing at [that] door.

Shall I find comfort, travel-sore and weak?
　　Of labour you shall find the sum.
Will there be beds for me and all who seek?
　　Yea, beds for all who come.

For the most part Clementine kept her anguish and anxiety to herself; but fortunately she had a loyal confidante in her sister-in-law, Goonie; and on many evenings during these dark months she would slip round the corner to No. 5 Cromwell Place, where the Laverys lived. They were staunch and understanding friends, and it soothed Clementine to sit quietly in John Lavery's studio while he painted. He did a portrait of her at this time, which seems to distil sadness and stillness. It hangs now, in its accustomed place, in Winston's study at Chartwell.

But the news that Winston was once more out of the line, and in a situation of comparative safety, revived her spirits. Moreover, she was now deeply engrossed with the arrangements for the official opening by Lloyd George of the new canteen for which she was responsible. She had some anxieties about it:

> I am feeling rather nervous about Lloyd George addressing my Munition Workers; the *skilled* men are growling about his visit; they are angry about the 'diluted labour'*. It will be very disagreeable if there is an uproar especially if it makes my nice canteen unpopular![39]

Clementine was also somewhat concerned

> ... if the Meeting gets widely reported, that people will think you & he are working together. You may *have* to work with him but never trust him – If he does not do you in he will at any rate 'let you down'.[40]

Clementine (whose claws were evidently fully extended at this moment) also sent Winston a barbed account of a meeting she had with Mr Balfour.

> I saw Mr Balfour yesterday playing tennis, looking more like a shabby maiden aunt's tabby cat than ever. He said 'remember me to Winston & tell him that Jacky Fisher is on the rampage.' I would have asked him to be more explicit but he took himself off – to rest before dinner I should think! I wish I had had your letter telling me of the German aeroplanes visits behind our lines (it arrived this morning). He was discussing the Foker [sic] machine & said it never ventured off its own ground but only attacked us when *we* raided. He is like the rest of them smug, purblind, indifferent, ignorant, casual! . . .[41]

During the last days of January Winston was cheered by seeing F.E. and Lloyd George, who visited GHQ during this time and made contact with him. He enjoyed meeting them, but these encounters had not aroused in him any feelings of envy or discontent:

> I must say I felt vy strong & self-reliant meeting these two men today: & did not envy their situation or regret at all my decision to quit them.[42]

On 1st February his battalion again moved into the trenches, this time for a period of six days. He described to Clementine some of the 'disagreeables' they had exchanged on the first day, and broke off suddenly to ask her if such detailed accounts of these incidents caused her too much anxiety – 'But I think you like to know the dimensions of the dangers & what they are like.'[43]

On 4th February the opening of the canteen at Ponders End, the arrangements for which had been such a preoccupation for Clementine, took place; it was a resounding success. 'The great meeting is over & the whole thing went off brilliantly,'[44] Clementine began a long and lively letter to Winston that evening. The proceedings had started with a reception in the canteen:

> There was my Head Cook, Mr. Quinlan resplendent in white coat & hat, the paid

*The employment of women and unskilled men in the munitions factories. Vehemently opposed by the Trades Unions.

staff in brown holland overalls & my voluntary workers (about 150) looking like
blue and white angels. There was a great crowd of people from the neighbourhood & some from London and all the Y.M.C.A. swells . . . your mother &
Violet Bonham Carter & Lady Horner & Lady Henry Grosvenor who runs
Woolwich etc as I do north London . . .

Violet's presence had intrigued Clementine, because she had invited herself:

. . . she rang me up & insisted on coming. I think she came to see (on behalf of
Downing St) what was up between you & Ll-G. She was very pleasant & agreeable . . .

Clementine escorted Mr and Mrs Lloyd George round the whole establishment,
introducing them to numerous people, and they all then proceeded to the new
workshops for the meeting, where the men were gathered:

. . . 2000 of them packed like sardines standing very silently. They did not cheer
when they saw Ll-G but looked at him with interest & curiosity, (but don't say
I said so), they gave me a beautiful cheer.

In fact, the Manager of the Works had told Clementine that the previous day 300
men had threatened to file out of the meeting in silent protest against Lloyd
George's labour policies, and had only promised not to do so when the Manager
had pointed out that such an act would be a great discourtesy to Clementine, whose
guest Lloyd George was. 'Of course Ll-G does not know this,' she wrote, 'but I
must say it made me feel very superior & protective towards him!!'

The General Manager paid a warm tribute to Clementine and her band of
workers, and then Lloyd George addressed the meeting. 'Ll-G made a quite un-
distinguished speech,' Clementine wrote to Winston, 'and the shabby little tike
altho' he said he had just returned from the Front never mentioned your name.'
However, 'He was *very well* received but *not* enthusiastically.' For her own part,

I was simply deluged with presents a bouquet, a cheque from the Directors of
the firm for 100 guineas, (not for myself! but to spend as I like on canteens)
sleeve-links for you from the men *and* a little brooch in the shape of a shell from
the men enclosed in a *really* lovely gold box studded with turquoises, pearls &
diamonds for me. I nearly fainted with emotion & my speech was wrecked as I
had not expected these gifts – (except the cheque). But I just read out your message & the men were delighted – Don't tell anyone about all this as it sounds
vain, but I want you to know about my small success. I really have worked hard
but now I shall have to redouble my efforts to deserve all this. I feel I must give
the men fat chickens every day to eat!

The events of the day had strengthened her contempt for Lloyd George:

On the way home he said quite casually 'I'm so surprised, Curzon wants the "Air",
I thought perhaps Winston might have done it – Do you think he would have
liked it?' I said 'Winston would do it better than anyone else.' He did not reply –

I don't hate him, but I feel contempt & almost pity for him. This ungenerous cautious streak in his nature will in his old age which is fast approaching leave him lonely & friendless – Ishmael! I do not think *you* will ever need him, *he* will need you when he is on the down gradient – & of course you will help him and he knows it. As we drove home silently in the dark he was very white shabby & tired & I felt young strong & vital & felt you out there young & strong & vital & I thought & I know he felt me thinking 'If only Winston is not killed you will need us both' – Meanwhile you won't strike a blow or speak a word for him becos' you know it won't make any difference to his attitude later – You can always rely on him in any 'Marconi' affair . . .[45]

The triumphant success of the canteen opening had completely dispelled her depression and gloom of a short while before.

My Darling Dear One, to-day I feel happy & hopeful about you & your future. I know (D.V.) that you will come back rejuvenated & strengthened from the War & dominate all these decrepit exhausted politicians. Don't close your mind to the P.M. entirely. He is lazy but (or perhaps therefore) healthy & anyhow he is not a skunk tho' a wily old tortoise. I must meet him this week and tweak his ear – I feel full of beans as if you were Commander-in-Chief and not merely Lt. Colonel . . .

God bless you & I send you a thousand kisses.

Clemmie
[sketch of cat][46]

But her day of joy and triumph might well have ended in heartbreak, for on that same day Winston, Archie and some others were just finishing luncheon at Laurence Farm (Battalion Advanced HQ) when a shell burst close by. They were just discussing the prudence of repairing to a dug-out when

. . . there was a tremendous crash, dust & splinters came flying through the room, plates were smashed, chairs broken. Everyone was covered with debris and the Adjutant (he is only 18) hit on the finger. A shell had struck the roof and burst in the next room – mine & Archie's. We did not take long in reaching our shelter – wh is a good one! My bedroom presented a woe begone appearance, the nose of the shell passing clean through it smashed the floor and cut a hole in the rear wall. Luckily vy few of my things were damaged . . . The wonderful good luck is that the shell (a 4.2) did not – & cd not have – burst properly. Otherwise we shd have had the wall thrown in on us – & some wd surely have been hurt.

I have made them put up another still stronger dugout – quite close, on wh they are now hard at work. I slept peacefully in my tiny war-scarred room last night, after a prolonged tour of the trenches . . .[47]

Three days later, Winston was summoned to Brigade Headquarters to take over command in the temporary absence of the Brigadier, and he had a long talk with Lord Curzon (Lord Privy Seal), who was paying a visit to the front. The possibility had been mooted in some quarters (indeed Lloyd George had made reference of it to Clementine) that Winston might be called home and made responsible for Air Affairs. Clementine wrote about this to Winston on 7th February:

> Before this letter reaches you, you will have seen Garvin's appeal in the Observer for you & Lord Fisher to return. You as Air Minister, Fisher as First Sea Lord. If only you had been given the 'air' last May something substantial might by now have been accomplished.
>
> Oh my Darling I long so for it to happen, & I feel that it would except for the competition for the post inside the Cabinet – There are, Alas, 12 Ministers with minor officers who probably all think themselves competent. I have been invited to stay at Walmer* next Sunday. How wonderful it would be if by then you had returned.

In the same letter she gives him some news of the children:

> You will be surprised when you see Diana. I have cut off her hair & she now looks like Peter Pan – A great improvement! Sarah is on the verge of voluble speech & is only waiting for some teeth.

A few days later she took Diana and Randolph to a children's party. Clementine reported, all aglow with maternal satisfaction, that 'They both looked quite beautiful, quite different from the other children. I felt very proud to have produced 2 such delicious beings.'[48]

Winston's letter telling her that he was temporarily in command of his Brigade,[49] and a remark made by Lord Curzon led Clementine to nurse a further false hope. On 12th February (at 5 a.m.) she wrote:

> ...Do you think that perhaps you will be made Brigadier almost at once & that you have been made 'caretaker' for practice? I feel it must be so...
>
> Yesterday Goonie & I lunched with Lord Curzon at his handsome Mansion which (to indicate war economy even among the highest in the land) was swaddled with dust sheets – He was very affable & talked a great deal about you & also & especially a great deal about himself & his experiences in Flanders! He told me you were well & in high spirits & said he thought you would soon be a Brigadier – But he did not as I should have liked express indignation and surprise that you should be commanding a battallion [sic], but seemed to think it very natural, suitable & proper – What short memories these people have –! He discussed the possibility of your being made a Brigadier from the point of view that Brigadiers have £1000 a year whereas Colonels receive but £500 & expressed the opinion that as I must be feeling rather poor the promotion would no doubt be a very welcome one to me! Altogether he was most superior & patronizing tho' genuinely friendly & Goonie & I laughed at him a good deal as we drove home in his motor which he kindly lent us for the afternoon – He gave me 3 bottles of brandy for you which I will despatch by a tame messenger.

*Walmer Castle, on the Kent coast. Official residence of the Lord Warden of the Cinque Ports, which office was, at this time, held by Mr Asquith.

Winston himself was under no illusions, however, either as to office at home (remarking that Asquith regarded him now more as a critic than as a colleague) or promotion in the field, about which last prospect he wrote:

> ... Neither do I expect any speedy promotion here. The kind of work I am doing is being done equally well by many others ... Haig will no doubt eventually – if I survive – give me a Brigade. But he will be chiefly concerned at the impression such an appointment wd produce in the army: & he will certainly run no risks on my account.[50]

Clementine spent an agreeable week-end with the Asquiths at Walmer Castle, and on Sunday, 13th February she wrote to Winston:

> My Darling,
> The journey here yesterday was terribly long & tedious; we took four hours & the train stopped at each station.
> But I am glad to have come as I think it is useful & also I am having a pleasant Sunday. A perfect day, glorious sunshine, the sea blue & without a ripple & no wind –
> I sat in the garden most of the morning & found growing out of doors a pink rose, a white violet & a sprig of cherry pie!

Sitting on the bastion they had been able to hear the rumble of heavy guns. Clementine had played golf with

> the Prime who was very pleasant & mellow ... at one moment [I] thought I was going to give the old boy a good beating (which I shd have relished) but Alas! I fell off towards the end & he won by a short length ...

Winston upbraided Clementine mildly when he replied to this letter (as on a previous occasion) for giving him so few details of her conversations with Mr Asquith. To which Clementine answered that her exchanges with Mr Asquith had been of the most frivolous and trivial nature:

> You know what the P.M. is – He loathes talking about the War or work of any sort – He asked anxiously if you were happy.[51]

In this same letter Clementine gave Winston some sage advice about his relationship with the Prime Minister. It shows how well she understood the workings of the minds of the powerful:

> I think if you could do it, you might write to him occasionally private interesting friendly letters. With him it is so much out of sight out of mind – I am sure that he feels affection for you & that he would like you to be in the Government again, if it could be done without a row. This sounds very cowardly, but few Prime Ministers would do more. Anyhow nothing is gained by letting him see that you consider he has behaved badly; he only waddles off as quickly as possible & avoids you in future –

On 16th February she told Winston that 'Three letters from you arrived in a covey'. One of these had been written in a sombre mood. Clementine wrote:

... Do not I pray of you let this mood deepen & permanently tinge your heart & mind. There are only two things that can prevent you from being again the heart of action in this country – I mean your death or a serious wound. But I *will* not believe that either of these terrible things are going to happen. I am sure you will return to power after the war with increased prestige.

But while she looked forward with ardent hope to the brilliant future she was confident lay before him, Clementine made a heartfelt plea for a real place in his life for her and the children:

[They] are becoming so grown up & intelligent – They will be very sweet companions & I look forward with longing to the time when you come back to me & we will have a little country basket & in the intervals of your work we will all curl up together in it & be so happy. Only you must not become too famous or you won't have time for these pastoral joys! You will have to promise me that in future however full of work & ideas you are you will keep out of every day an hour & every week a day & every year 6 weeks for the small things of Life. Things like painting ... playing grizzly-bear, sitting on the grass with me & generally Leisure with a big L ...

Although in their life together *LOVE* never failed, *Leisure* was always to be at a premium.

On 13th February Winston had gone back into the line for another tour of duty of six days, and every day he wrote a long letter home, usually writing in the evening before setting out on his nightly patrol of the trenches with Archie Sinclair.

... I sit in a battered wicker chair within this shot scarred dwelling by the glowing coals of a brazier in the light of an acetyline lamp.[52]

After two relatively quiet days the headquarters was again the victim of a direct hit, when both the 'dining room' and Winston's and Archie's bedroom were battered, and the signal office next door completely shattered, but rather than move their headquarters they were busily piling sandbags inside all the walls on the upper floor. 'We have been hunted by shells during these last two days in "rest billets",' Winston wrote a little later; three times in a fortnight his bedroom (three different ones!) had been pierced by shells, and the church steeple which had withstood sixteen months of fighting had come down under shell-fire. 'One lives calmly on the brink of the abyss,' he wrote, but he now appreciated how people wearied under the strain, the excitement dying away leaving only a feeling of 'dull resentment'.[53]

The dream of a few days together in Dieppe had faded, but Winston now knew he would be able to take a week's leave at the beginning of March. He told Clementine that he would cross to Dover in a destroyer, and suggested she should meet him there at the Lord Warden Hotel. He gave her precise instructions for the plans for the short and precious time he would be at home:

You must parcel out the days as well as possible. I will have one dinner at my mother's, at least 3 at home, 2 plays alone with you & one man's dinner out somewhere.

He added that he hoped she would try to 'work in all my friends' at lunches, and that he wanted to have at least one day's painting in John Lavery's studio. Even on paper it did not look as if seven days could hold all he eagerly hoped to cram into them; but he assured her he would be 'vy good & keep all my engagements punctually'. He stated a distinct preference for inviting friends to dine with them at home rather than going out; he asked her to have a servant ready to look after him, but, finally: 'I put it all in your hands my dearest soul.'[54]

During these last days he had been in the line, Winston had complained of lack of news from home, for he hungered for every crumb of news from Clementine. But there had only been a short hold-up in the delivery of her letters. She had continued to be a faithful correspondent, writing him lively accounts of all her doings.

By far the greater part of Clementine's time during these months had been dedicated to her canteens. Energetic and conscientious, she also found (perhaps to her surprise) that she was also highly efficient. She told Winston with pardonable pride:

> I must tell you that from living with you & watching you for 7 years I have assimilated (in a small way) your methods & habits of work. In this Canteen work I find people who do it with me are surprised that I do things quickly & that I expect them to drive along too, & altho' I get very tired I find the others get tired first. When I am in full swing I begin work at 9 a.m. & finish at 7.30 p.m. It's no use scolding me becos' it's all your fault – You have taught me to work outside office hours . . .[55]

The Ponders End canteen was to be enlarged with another wing added for the men; in addition she was also to be responsible for feeding an extra 500 girls. Soon her canteens would be feeding 1800 people.

While he was proud of her devotion and ability, Winston, like many (if not most) men, tended to regard any time not spent in wifely or maternal duties as mere occupational therapy to pass away surplus time. While Winston and his affairs always commanded the cream of her heart and energy, Clementine now was experiencing for the first time the challenge and satisfaction of a job, and her thoughts were as much engrossed by its daily demands and problems as by the political events of the hour. Her days must have been very long. Letter after letter is marked as being written around five or six o'clock in the morning.

This demanding work gripped her, not only because she had a strong desire to serve, but also because it gave her an insight into the new phenomenon of the employment of women in heavy industry working alongside men. She had visited Woolwich Arsenal with Lady Henry Grosvenor, from whom she learnt a great deal. She gave a vivid account of her visit to Winston:

> . . . Very soon 90,000 workers will be employed in the Arsenal & if the war goes on long enough I should think you could bury the Germans with the hail of Munitions – But Alas! the same thing is going on in Germany . . . I was much interested in the girls at one big dining room – They earn between 18/- & 25/-

weekly. They are nearly all quite young very fresh and pretty & rather hoydenish –
Some of them were snowballing with boys outside the canteen. The fore-women
have their meals in a separate room. They are of course older & they belong to the
professional & suffragetty classes & some of them look as if they had seen 'life' –
They were nearly all smoking & playing Bridge & nap after their meals! The quiet
ones were reading rather advanced books, translations from the Russian Authors
& such-like.

I understand the prejudice of the skilled male worker against diluted female
labour. The women are full of beans & become terribly skilful very quickly.

They want good money too, but of course nothing like the men – A woman
earning 35/- a week feels like a millionaire. They don't mind paying properly for
their food now. They used, a few months ago to grudge 6d for a good dinner.[56]

Shortly after this Clementine was sent for by Dr Addison (the Parliamentary
Secretary to the Office of Munitions) to discuss hostels and canteens for munition
workers. While waiting for her appointment, she had the chance to observe the
difference between women munition workers and the girl clerks who now abounded
in government offices. She wrote to Winston:

. . . I waited in the hall a little time for my interview & while I was sitting there I
think I must have seen most of the people employed in the building, as there was
a constant stream backwards & forwards. Three quarters of the clerks seem to be
girls of a very inferior type. Curled fringes, paper cuffs, giggles – They were walking about some of them with their arms round each other's waists.[57]

Clementine was overjoyed when she got Winston's letter with the first inkling
that he might soon have leave. 'My Darling,' she wrote on 19th February (at 5 a.m.),

Your last letter brings the joyful news that very soon you will be home on leave.
This makes me very happy & I am now beginning to count the days. To-day you
come out of the trenches so for a few days I feel more at ease – This last week has
been a very anxious one, as although you have not been in the thick of the onslaught the Germans seem to have plenty of every sort of ammunition to spare
for other parts of the line. You seem to have had a tremendous dose. Please do
not become rash & prowl too much in the moon-light – I am sure it is a great risk.

The burden of anxiety was heavy during those days when Clementine knew that
Winston was in the line, and earlier she described the sense of release from tension
when she knew one such period of acute danger was safely over:

. . . Till I got your letter yesterday I had not realized you were now in rest-
billets – The relief I feel is quite extraordinary – One doesn't realize how high the
tension is until it is suddenly lowered.[58]

Now she had to endure one more anxious stretch of days while he was again in the
trenches, and then, God willing, she would have him home again.

Meanwhile she was going about quite a bit, and promised she would report to
Winston 'how the London world is wagging . . .'[59] In one week she had been out

to dinner or entertained at home each evening. Her own guests had included Lord Rothermere and the F. E. Smiths. But her most ambitious social undertaking was a dinner for the Asquiths, when she had to

> work like a beaver to get together the 8 indispensible [sic] bridge players which are necessary for their comfort & happiness . . . the party is: – P.M., Margot, Ivor Wimborne, Lady Mainwaring, Bogey Harris, Goonie, Mr. Cazalet, myself, Sir E. Cassel. Nine people becos' Lady Mainwaring refuses to play bridge as she always bunny-hugs & fox-trots after her meals! . . . We invited her as we thought the P.M would like something quite new! [60]

The evening turned out a great success:

> . . . the old sybarite [Mr Asquith] thoroughly enjoyed himself – Sunny turned up at the last minute & made himself very agreeable & as Ivor was there too, the Churchill family presented a solid & prosperous appearance. The food was good & afterwards there were 2 tables of bridge – I sat between the P.M. & Sir Ernest Cassel – The P.M won a little money & went home in high good humour. Ivor remained behind & philosophised & moralised. [61]

Meanwhile, less than a week now remained until Winston's eagerly awaited leave. There was a last-minute scare that the threat of a new German offensive might lead to all leave being stopped – but all was well, and on 2nd March Clementine went to Dover to meet Winston.

One can conceive a more romantic setting than the Lord Warden Hotel on Dover Pier. But it would be churlish indeed to criticise the scenery, when, despite the malice of the enemy and the dislocation of war, 'journeys end in lovers' meetings'.

Blanche, Countess of Airlie, Clementine's grandmother

1884

Lady Blanche Hozier, Clementine's mother, in 1884, the year before her daughter's birth

Kitty and Clementine, 1887

At The Netherton, 1888: Kitty (*left*) and Clementine with their father, Sir Henry Hozier

Kitty – April 18 1883 – March 5 1900.

Kitty on her death-bed

Horatia Seymour

Clementine Ogilvy Hozier. August. 1901.

Clementine aged sixteen

Clementine aged twenty

51 Abingdon Villas, where Lady Blanche and her family were living at the time of Clementine's engagement

The Temple of Diana at Blenheim where Winston Churchill proposed to Clementine Hozier on 11th August 1908

WINSTON'S LATEST LINE—
"HOZIERY."

12TH SEPTEMBER 1908

The bridegroom with his best man, Lord Hugh Cecil

The bride arrives at St Margaret's, Westminster

Lady Randolph Churchill (Mrs Cornwallis-West) at the period of Winston's marriage. Seen here with Sir Hubert Parry, she was an accomplished pianist

Goonie and Jack Churchill c. 1908

Winston and Clementine with their first baby, Diana, 1909

Nellie Hozier in 1914

Bill Hozier, Lieutenant, R.N. 1914

Winston, a portrait by John Lavery. Painted while he
was commanding the 6th Battalion the Royal Scots
Fusiliers in Flanders in 1916, and wearing a French
poilu's steel helmet

Clementine, a portrait by John Lavery, 1915/16

The opening of the munition workers' canteen at Ponders End by Lloyd George, 4th February 1916. *From left:* Lady Violet Bonham Carter, Clementine, Lloyd George

Clementine with Marigold *c.* 1920

Sarah

A visit to the Sphinx. The Cairo Conference, March 1921. *From left:* Clementine, Winston, Gertrude Bell, Col. T. E. Lawrence ('Lawrence of Arabia')

Clementine with Randolph at Eton 'Fourth of June' celebrations, 1926

Electioneering. Epping, 1924

Chartwell Manor as it was in 1922

Chartwell reborn

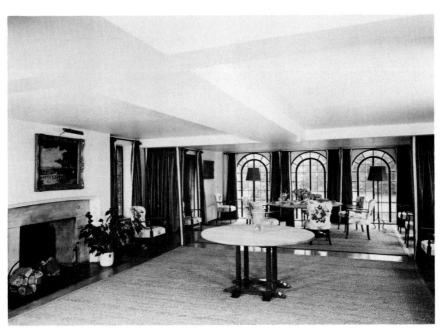

The dining-room at Chartwell

Winston with his bricklayer's mates Sarah and Mary, Chartwell late 1920s

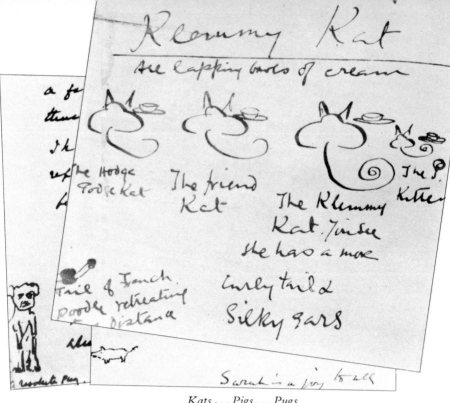

Kats ... Pigs ... Pugs

In Nassau, January 1932. Winston was convalescing from his road accident in New York, hence his scarred forehead

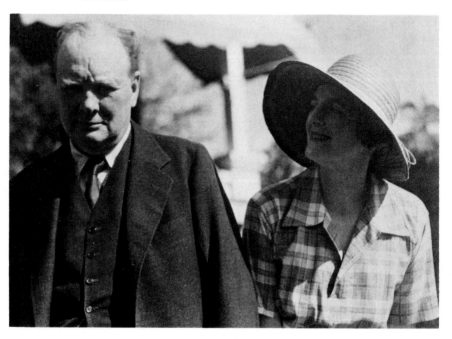

DAY MUST DAWN

WINSTON'S leave in March 1916 lasted ten days, and at the end of it both he and Clementine were physically and mentally exhausted and in a turmoil. Many of the plans she had made for him – and so skilfully dovetailed so that no precious minute would be wasted – had to be abandoned or changed, for almost as soon as he arrived home, Winston became embroiled in political machinations, as a result of which he decided to take part in the debate on the Navy Estimates. Several friends and confidants he saw during his first few days at home took the view that the time was now ripe for him to intervene actively once more in politics. Among those whose views he sought were F. E. Smith, J. L. Garvin of *The Observer*, and Max Aitken.

Clementine had never taken to Max Aitken, the dynamic Canadian who was shortly to acquire the *Daily Express* and become the 1st Lord Beaverbrook. And she viewed with uneasiness his steadily growing friendship with Winston. Her lifelong mistrust of him may well date from this period when Aitken was plying him with political advice with which she profoundly disagreed.

She was also dismayed that Winston was once more in close touch with Lord Fisher, who had been the immediate cause of his downfall at the Admiralty. The terrifying old man was once more on the rampage over the affairs of his beloved Navy, and urging Winston in his usual immoderate terms to attack the Government head-on about their mismanagement and ineptitude, assuring him that he alone could lead a united opposition, powerful enough even to topple the Government.

Clementine's heart must have sunk when she saw Winston so deeply involved with people she neither liked nor trusted, and whose advice ran contrary to her deepest instincts. One day, during a luncheon at Cromwell Road at which Lord Fisher was present, she could contain herself no longer, and suddenly burst out: 'Keep your hands off my husband. You have all but ruined him once. Leave him alone now!'[1]

But these persuasive counsellors lent their weight to Winston's already awakened desire, and he determined to speak in the debate. The night before, the Asquiths dined with the Churchills, and Winston was perfectly open as to his intention of speaking the following day. After dinner Mr Asquith, in a private conversation, sought to dissuade him from a step he felt sure would be unwise, and do Winston nothing but harm. But it was to no avail.

On 7th March Churchill rose in the House of Commons and launched a broad-side attack on Balfour's ineffectual tenure at the Admiralty. He deplored the inactive role played by the Navy and called for a new shipbuilding programme. He made a powerful case, was listened to with serious attention, and his speech might have done much to repair his political fortunes had he not flung all away by his conclusion, which was nothing less than an ardent appeal for the recall of Lord Fisher as First Sea Lord to supply the driving force and mental energy which were so patently lacking. This appeal was greeted with derision and hostility, and Churchill was stunned by the violence of the reaction he provoked and the lack of any general support.[2]

While he was out in France Winston had ever been pondering the question as to where his duty lay. Now active participation once more in politics, and discussion with his friends and colleagues brought the issue to a point where a decision seemed inevitable, and immediate. But there were two views on it, and, as on the 'Brigade' question, Clementine found herself in opposition to Winston's line of thought. She felt there were many reasons why his return to home politics should be postponed until a more opportune moment, reasons she was to beg him to consider in the following weeks. However, his view prevailed, and when she bade him farewell on the pier at Dover, on 13th March, she had in her charge a letter from Winston to the Prime Minister, asking to be relieved of his military duties so that he could return home to take part in public affairs.

Clementine spent that night at the Lord Warden Hotel, from where she wrote to the Prime Minister, enclosing Winston's letter, writing also to one or two other colleagues who had been involved in the anxious discussions of the last few days, telling them what was afoot. 'I then crept into bed & thought about you and prayed for happier days & calm waters.'[3]

She was up early the next morning to go and see Sir Edward Carson, the Unionist Leader and Attorney-General in the Coalition Government, who was ill at his home at Birchington in Kent, bearing a letter in which Winston sought this brilliant man's advice in his personal dilemma. She had a long and difficult time locating his house, but finally arrived, and was received by Sir Edward, who was still confined to his bed. They had a long talk, and that same evening she wrote Winston a full account of it. Carson took a grave view of Winston's course of action, and said of his part in the debate:

Winston has probably done the country & the government a service by his intervention last Tuesday, but he has not done himself any good . . .[4]

Clementine felt strongly the wisdom of Sir Edward's view:

I wish so much that we had planned things better & that you had seen him before sending the P.M. your letter – I am sure that tremendous decisions require *time* to resolve & a quiet atmosphere. The inferno of last week was not a favourable atmosphere. I hope I have not given the impression that Carson does not think you would be an asset here – He does but would like the asset in an undamaged condition. I feel sure that nothing will be lost by waiting . . .[5]

Clementine did not leave Sir Edward's house until half-past one, and she had a long and weary drive home through blinding rain, and with the tedium and frustration of a puncture. She arrived back home at Cromwell Road in the evening, worn out, to find a letter from Mr Asquith's Private Secretary telling her that Winston had telegraphed the Prime Minister, asking him to disregard the contents of the letter forwarded by Clementine from Dover. Although Clementine was taken aback by this turn of events, she was also deeply relieved:

I am anxiously waiting to hear further, but in the meanwhile if it means you are taking more time for consideration, I am sure my Darling that you are wise,

she wrote in a note she dashed off as soon as she had read the letter from Downing Street.

... My Darling I wish now I were near you. I feel that perhaps now you are in France you may revise your judgement. I long for you to come back, but I want you to come back welcomed & acclaimed by all, as you *ought* to be and as I know you will be very soon. Whatever you finally decide I loyally agree to ...[6]

But she was suddenly gripped by fear for the reason which might have prompted Winston to change his mind and added:

A dreadful anxiety has just seized me. I have recollected that you said that the only thing that would make you pause would be the knowledge that we are going to attack. Please God it is not the reason. Surely we are not going to make a counter-offensive? Let me know quickly the truth.

My Dearest own Winston thro these tumultuous days we have been together I have never been able to tell you or shew you how deep & true my love is for you & how I know that ultimately what you decide will be right & good.

God bless you
Clemmie

Clementine spent the better part of the following day seeing various people who had knowledge of Winston's decision, and in putting them in the now somewhat altered picture, as best she could. After the visit of Sir Henry Dalziel (the owner of the *Pall Mall Gazette*) she wrote:

He stayed some time and I think he is personally very friendly – But when I am re-incarnated and go into 'Public Life' I have determined with great courtesy to hold *all* newspaper men at arm's length, so that at a distance they may gaze at me with curiosity interest & respect – If they came closer they might observe the flaws in my armour![7]

Although writing half in jest, Clementine maintained this very policy when, in later years, she was eagerly sought after for interviews, which she rarely gave. Her relations with the Press were invariably courteous but distant.

Very early (5.30 a.m.) on 16th March, Clementine wrote off to Winston again:

My Darling
Every time the post came yesterday I ran down to the hall for the letter explaining your telegram to the P.M. Every time I was disappointed – Late in the after-

noon I retired to bed as my cold had gone down to my chest – I fell into a deep sleep & woke up only a few minutes ago – I immediately realized that while I had been sleeping, the best post of all (10 p.m) for letters from the front, had been & gone – I crept downstairs thro' the sleeping house & there on the hall table was the much wished-for blue envelope . . . I expect that my letters about the Carson interview will have seemed equally long in coming to you! . . .

The anxiously awaited letter had been written on 13th March, and in it Winston explained that he felt he needed a little more time for thought 'in this vy different atmosphere' before committing himself to an irrevocable step. He had therefore telegraphed the Prime Minister to delay any action on the letter he had written at the end of his leave. There was no doubt that Winston found the choice before him a hard one to make and he wrote,

My dearest soul –
You have seen me vy weak & foolish & mentally infirm this week. Dual obligations, both honourable both weighty have rent me . . . I cannot tell you how much I love & honour you and how sweet & steadfast you have been through all my hesitations & perplexity.[8]

Clementine was deeply relieved that Winston had changed his mind, and she wrote an eloquent and moving explanation of her own thoughts and feelings in relation to the anguishing dilemma which confronted him:

I think there are some solid qualities which English men & women value very highly – Virtues such as steadfastness & stability – After your speech in the House of C in which you placed yourself 'unreservedly at the disposal of the Military Authorities' it seems to me that more than your own conviction is needed that it is your duty to return to Parliament – I am convinced that sooner or later the demand will be made & that once made it will become insistent – Your speech has certainly animated & vivified the Admiralty but it has done you personally harm – I mean if you had been silent or put it differently the demand for your return would perhaps come sooner – But come it will – It must.
   I pray therefore my Darling Love that you may decide to bide the time – We are living on such a gigantic scale that I am sure everything ought to be simplified – our actions too, so that without explanation or justification they & their motives can be understood and grasped by all – You have assumed the yoke of your own free will like many other men, tho' none of them are in your situation. The others, having assumed the yoke cannot dis-engage themselves. You, owing to your exceptional circumstances have received the written promise of the head of the Government that in your speaking the word you shall be free. But that word must be spoken by others, if when free you are to be effective as an instrument to help the movement of events. Please forgive me my Darling if I express myself clumsily . . .

On 22nd March, Archie Sinclair arrived at Cromwell Road. Winston had confided him to Clementine's and Goonie's care, writing beforehand: 'I want him to stay at

Cromwell & you & Goonie to cherish & nourish him. He is all alone in the world, & vy precious as a friend to me . . .'[9] Clementine found that he looked pale and care-worn, and both the sisters-in-law did their utmost to look after him, and to give him a good time. Archie brought with him on his arrival only a short note from Winston, written in a somewhat morose vein: the battalion was back in the trenches; the weather had worsened; and he was losing his boon companion. During these last days Winston's intentions about his future had been hardening, and the letter ended with this firm admonition to Clementine:

> Be careful not to use arguments or take up an attitude in conflict with my general intention, & do nothing to discourage friends who wish for my return. On the contrary labour as opportunity serves to create favourable circumstances.[10]

Various friends and colleagues of Winston's called on Clementine just now, with letters or messages for him, and she loyally transmitted his views to them. Among the callers was C. P. Scott, the Editor of the *Manchester Guardian*, of whom she wrote to Winston: 'He is a valuable champion becos' of his great integrity – & incorrupti-bility – but he is not a man of the world . . .'[11] She doubted whether he was a good judge of effective political action, [12] and she also wondered whether Mr Garvin, the Editor of *The Observer*, was a sound counsellor.[13] Clementine was meticulous in reporting their arguments, but adjured Winston to 'Keep a level mind my Darling, & a stout heart.'[14]

Although Winston's friends at home held differing views as to whether the time was ripe for his return, Clementine was convinced that he should wait. And in the early hours (4 a.m.) on 24th March she wrote this long letter, once more advancing her own passionately-held point of view, and showing her keen awareness of his present political isolation:

> My Dearest Love you know that you can rely upon my steadfastness & loyalty, but the anxiety & grief at the step you are about to take sinks deeper into my heart day by day. It seems to me such an awful risk to take – to come back just *now* so lonely & unprotected with no following in the House & no backing in the Country. Please do not be angry with me for writing plainly –
> I think I know you very well & it seems to me that you are actuated by 2 motives – 1) You want to be in the place where your powers for helping to win the War will have fullest scope 2) You have a devouring thirst for 'War Direction' – Now I do beg you to reflect on this 2nd point – The war is (D.V.) ¾ over, the corner is nearly turned – (Perhaps you will disagree) The end is a long way off but still I think we are going to win in spite of slowness & hesitation – In your present weakened condition shall you recover prestige & the necessary power in time to be of real use? I think perhaps you may if you wait a little longer – But it is a great risk – It is *indeed* a gamble – If you do not succeed you may gradually decline in the public opinion (tho' a speech would always attract attention). If that happened then your return from the battlefield in the middle of the War might be a serious handicap to you in the future. The Government is nerveless & helpless but it represents all there is practically in public life – If you come back & attack them

they are bound to defend themselves & try to down you – And just *now* you are very defenceless. The Government may not wage war very vigorously but when on the defensive they are very strong.

Do not be anxious about my attitude – I do not tell my thoughts to any but you. When you were here last week I did not feel that there were any great or good elements of strength surrounding you. Fisher is a powerful but malevolent engine; you think him unimpaired by age but when the break-up comes, as soon it must it will come with a damaging explosion to all near him – Garvin and Scott, good time men & personal friends, but often wrong-headed, Dalziell [sic] curious & interested but corrupt & time-serving – *in* the Cabinet that Judas Lloyd-George never staunch in times of trial, always ready to injure secretly those with whom he is publicly associated . . .

Could you have the courage & the self denial if you returned to see *no one*, to help & not merely to criticize to refrain *absolutely* from personal attack. (You are vulnerable & your enemies would hope that you would indulge in this), to refrain also from *all* recriminations & attacks upon the *past* but only to apply your mind to the future – Not only the immediate future, but the great future beyond the war of which everyone is now (perhaps it is only the hopefulness of spring-time) perceiving the dawn.

I reflect upon you my Dear for hours together & lately I have had the time as I have had a little attack of bronchitis of which I have had to take care.

I was going away to the country for 3 days to try and shake it off when Archie was announced & so I put it off. I am not much fun for him as I can't go out.

The atmosphere here is wicked & stifling out where you are it is clean & clear – I fear very much that you will be very sad & unhappy here.

You must forgive me for this letter. If I did not tell you my thoughts I could not write at all.

The War is a terrible searcher of character. One must try to plod & persevere and absolutely stamp self out. If at the end one is found grimly holding on to one's simple daily round one can't have failed utterly . . .

This long letter was followed only a few hours later – at 8.30 a.m. – by another one, which enclosed a letter from Sir Edward Carson, which she had read. 'You see how anxious he is that you should not blunt or break yourself as an instrument by a premature return,'[15] she wrote. Clementine again showed her concern for Winston's public image:

When you do return the reason should be apparent to the man in the street, tho he need not necessarily agree with it.

It would be damaging for instance if it got about that you had returned becos' you were dissatisfied with your prospects of promotion & irked by the smallness of your duties in your present position . . .

But whatever the counsels Winston received, for or against the wisdom of his coming home, he was now firmly fixed in his own mind that his duty and his destiny lay in once more taking part in the political life of his country. The only point which remained to be decided was at what moment he should take this step. There had recently been a change of command at brigade level, which shut the door on any hopes he might have nurtured in that direction; but he did not want to leave his battalion while it was in contact with the enemy, and he also watched for an opportune moment as far as home affairs were concerned.

Winston's own analysis of the situation was that the broad facts concerning his resignation and return could confidently be submitted to the judgment of the public. And he set them out for Clementine when he wrote to her on 22nd March: he had resigned his ministerial office and salary rather than hold a sinecure; he had served in France for nearly five months 'almost always in the front line, certainly without discredit . . .'; he had a recognised position in British politics acquired over the years 'enabling me to command the attention . . .' of my fellow countrymen in a manner not exceeded by 3 or 4 living men', and in the present critical period of the national fortunes he felt he could not exclude himself from his responsibilities. 'Surely,' he wrote, 'these facts may stand by themselves in answer to sneers & cavillings.'[16]

But Clementine was not convinced by his argument: 'The facts you mention in support of your immediate return are weighty & well expressed,' she wrote in reply, 'but it would be better if they were stated by others than yourself . . .'[17]

Meanwhile the bronchitis she had already mentioned had worsened, and, as soon as Archie's leave was over she intended to go to the sea for a few days to recover. This was a low moment for Clementine. Many women would have found unbearable the claims that politics made on Winston's whole existence. From the first she had realised, and soon accepted, that they would always come first, but every now and then the desire that any woman might feel, to own a larger share of her husband's life, broke through. Now, lonely, tired, ill and beset with anxiety, she made an almost anguished plea:

My Darling these grave public anxieties are very wearing – When next I see you I hope there will be a little time for us both alone – We are still young, but Time flies stealing love away & leaving only friendship which is very peaceful but not stimulating or warming.[18]

Nor was Winston oblivious to the extent to which his public life jostled their private relationship, for in a letter which must have crossed with hers, he wrote:

I reproach myself so much with having got so involved in politics when I was home that all the comfort & joy of our meeting was spoiled. I had the share of events wh took an oddly exciting turn. And then the difficulty of reconciling two different kinds of lives & obligations or choosing definitely between them!

But he promised (one is sure with all sincerity),

. . . next time I come home it will be with a set purpose & a clear course, & with no wild & anxious hurry of fleeting moments & uncertain plans. I am going to live calmly.[19]

And Clementine's heartfelt outburst drew from Winston a declaration of the depth of his feelings for her, and a rare (very rare) admission that he too knew a longing for tranquillity:

> Oh my darling do not write of 'friendship' to me – I love you more each month that passes and feel the need of you & all your beauty. My precious charming Clemmie – I too feel sometimes the longing for rest & peace. So much effort, so many years of ceaseless fighting & worry, so much excitement & now this rough fierce life here under the hammer of Thor, makes my older mind turn – for the first time I think to other things than action.

He went on to paint in his mind's eye the picture of an idyllic holiday: they would go to Spain or Italy

> & just paint & wander about together in bright warm sunlight far from the clash of arms or the bray of Parliaments . . .
>
> Sometimes also I think I wd not mind stopping living vy much – I am so devoured by egoism that I wd like to have another soul in another world & meet you in another setting, & pay you all the love & honour of the gt romances . . .[20]

Clementine received this letter in time for her birthday on 1st April.

> Your delicious loving letter arrived last night & warmed & comforted me. To-day is my birth-day & it is like the 1st of May in a poetry-book – so blue & sunshiny . . I am 31, but if the war were nearly won & you were safe & had peace of heart I should not feel more than 20 . . .[21]

In order to recover from her bronchitis, Clementine spent four agreeable days staying with Sir Ernest Cassel at his house, Branksome Dene, in Bournemouth. She sat in the sun and took long walks along the beach, often in the company of Mrs Keppel, who was also recovering from an illness. Clementine always liked her, but on this occasion she (rather touchingly) complained to Winston, '. . . she tries me by long political discussions about you & by arguing against your coming home – She is very fond of you personally –'[22]

On her return to Cromwell Road, Clementine found a number of letters Winston asked her to forward, including one for Lord Northcliffe, which he expressly told her to read first. Her cautious attitude to the Press was again illustrated by her reply:

> I have dispatched all letters you sent me to forward with the exception of one that reached me this morning for Lord Northcliffe (which you said I might hold up for a couple of days) & which I earnestly beg you not to ask me to post, but to destroy. If it goes it will form part of your biography in after times and after the way Lord N has flouted you I cannot bear that you should write to him in that vein. Besides I do not think it is as well expressed as some of your letters.
>
> I am sure it is no use writing private letters to great journalists – Even if they do, in consequence decide to run you, they feel patronizing & protective about it & the support then lacks in genuine ardour.[23]

Clementine's arguments must have played their part in Winston's decision to hold back indefinitely his letter to Lord Northcliffe.[24]

Clementine now knew that Winston was definitely determined, beyond any per-suasion, upon returning home, and was only waiting to choose the moment to do so. Believing his best course was to remain for the time being at the Front, she found herself in an agonising dilemma, and she wrote on 6th April:

My Darling own Dear Winston I am so torn and lacerated over you. If I say 'stay where you are' a wicked bullet may find you which you might but for me escape . . .

If I were sure that you would come thro' unscathed I would say:– 'wait wait have patience, don't pluck the fruit before it is ripe – Everything will come to you if you don't snatch at it' – To be great one's actions must be able to be under-stood by simple people. Your motive for going to the Front was easy to under-stand – Your motive for coming back requires explanation.

That is why your Fisher speech was not a success, people could not understand it. It required another speech to make it clear. I do long to see you so terribly – Your last visit was no help to me personally – I must see you soon . . .

Darling Don't be vexed for me for writing so crudely – If to help you or make you great or happy I could give up my life it would be easy for me to do it. I love you very much. By doing nothing you risk your life, by taking the action you con-template you risk a life-long rankling regret which you might never admit even to yourself & on which you would brood & spend much time in arguing to your-self that it *was* the right thing to do – And you would rehearse all the past events over & over again & gradually live in the past instead of in the present and in the great future . . .

If you will only listen a tiny bit to me I know (barring all tragic accidents) that you will prevail & that some day perhaps soon, perhaps not for 5 years you will have a great & commanding position in this country, you will be held in the people's hearts and in their respect. I have no originality or brilliancy but I feel within me the power to help you now if you will let me. Just becos' I am ordinary & love you I know what is right for you & good for you in the end.

Clementine's often expressed hope that Winston should wait to return until he was summoned by a call from a large body of public opinion was somewhat over-optimistic in the political circumstances of that moment; but her faith in his ultimate destiny – for which she ever strove to keep him untarnished – was not to be con-founded. The fulfilment of her hopes expressed in these dark days took more than the five years she hazarded as a guess. But the day came when she saw Winston indeed called by the voice of the people to a 'great and commanding position . . . held in the people's hearts and in their respect.'

*

Winston meanwhile was still closely involved with his army life and regular tours of duty in the front line. Clementine had been concerned lest his growing preoccupation with affairs and events at home should distract his interest and attention from his duties as a soldier, and she had written:

I hope my Darling that you are giving your battalion as much care & thought now as you did before you had resolved to come home – I hope they don't feel that your interest in them has waned – I want them to miss you terribly.[25]

Winston reassured her on this point:

I am doing my duty here vy thoroughly, and am touched often by small evidences of the partisanship of these young officers . . . The men put up my photograph in the trenches, & I am sure they will make an effort if I asked them and some big test came upon us.[26]

Although Clementine knew that Winston had taken the decision she feared might so adversely affect his future, she nonetheless deployed yet once again both logic and emotion, in begging him to wait. In a letter on 12th April she argued that if the Government fell – as seemed possible in view of the renewed agitation for universal conscription – he would be included in any reconstructed administration, but that if Asquith survived, Winston would be at the mercy of his political enemies. 'The present Government may not be strong enough to beat the Germans,' she wrote, 'but I think they are powerful enough to do you in & I pray God you do not give the heartless brutes the chance –'[27]

To disagree with Winston on this issue caused Clementine untold anguish, and in her earnestness and distress her sense of reality seems for once to have deserted her:

My Darling Love – *For once only* I pray be patient. It will come if you wait. Don't tear off the unripe fruit which is maturing tho' slowly or check its growth by the frost of a premature return –

I could not bear you to lose your military halo I have had cause during the 8 years we have lived together to be proud & glad for you so often, but it is this I cherish most of all. And it is this phase which when all is known will strike the imagination of the people: The man who prepared & mobilized the Fleet who really won the war for England in the trenches as a simple Colonel. It would be a great romance.

You say you want to be where you can help the war most – If you come home & your return is not generally accepted as correct soldier-like conduct you will not be really able to help the war. You *are* helping it now by example. You are always an interesting figure, be a great one my Darling – You have the opportunity.[28]

By entrusting her with the letters to his various confidants and political allies, Winston had laid a distasteful task upon her; Clementine ended her long letter with a cry of protest:

Oh Winston I do not like all these letters I have to forward – I prefer Charlotte Corday – Shall I do it for you?

Do not be alienated from me by what I write – If I hide what I feel from you the constraint wld be unbearable.

Your loving
Clemmie

These were indeed dark days for Clementine; she knew she was fighting a losing battle; and yet she dreaded the possible consequences if in the end he were to change his mind. On 14th April she wrote a heart-rending letter:

My Darling

It is a long while since I have had real news of you – Your last letter contained only instructions & enclosures. Keep me going with something more. These last weeks since you returned to France have been sad & cruel & I have not been well which always makes anxiety harder to bear. Sometimes when I have been out all day canteening I dread coming home to find a telegram with terrible news. And now if the telephone rings it may be the War Office to say that you have been killed. And yet in spite of this I keep on writing urging you not to leave the scene of these awful dangers.

I am very unhappy.

But despite her anxiety and unhappiness, Clementine continued to go out and to keep herself in touch with the political world:

I saw Rufus Isaacs [Lord Chief Justice] the other day at a party after dinner at Downing Street – He was very friendly & I had a long talk to him. He fears coming back unless sent for would be injurious to your reputation. Nearly all the Ministers were there. Grey terribly aged & worn looking, Kitchener thinner & sad, A.J.B. [Balfour] wan & white, but still purring away.[29]

Another night she had dined with the Asquiths:

The P.M. seems quite unconcerned. The Pall Mall last night had an inspired article saying he had got a united Cabinet on recruiting measures. Can it be true? He is like morphia.[30]

There was one more letter from Winston in this remarkable series – written after he had received Clementine's further bid to make him reconsider his decision. But he was not prepared to argue the case any more – his mind was made up – and further discussion would be fruitless, and perhaps painful. He dismissed the tortured subject in one sentence: 'Well there is no use going over the old ground again, nor in darkening this page with my reflections.'[31]

Winston came home on leave in the middle of April, and on 28th April he returned to France to go into the line with his battalion for the last time. He had always hoped he would find the opportunity for finally returning home because of some military reason, and in the event this hope was to be fulfilled. Because of the heavy losses in the Scots regiments, it was decided to amalgamate several of the battalions; in this reorganisation Churchill had to give way to a senior colonel; his connection with the Royal Scots Fusiliers came therefore naturally to an end. Early in May 1916 Churchill returned home to England, where his true destiny awaited him.

*

Whatever Clementine's feelings had been about the wisdom of Winston returning to politics in April 1916, they were eclipsed by the joy and relief of having him safe at home once more. In the House of Commons Winston took his seat on the back benches, where, allied with others both in and out of Parliament, he was part of a now vociferous, and increasingly strong, patriotic opposition, bent on achieving a more vigorous and efficient prosecution of the war. The Prime Minister now not only faced formidable opponents outside his Government: within the closest council of ministers Lloyd George was bent on achieving power, and took every advantage offered him by the increasing weakness of the administration.

Churchill was determined to clear his name from the ignorant and unjust accusations which had been continuously levelled at him ever since the debacle of the Dardanelles. He sought no other defence for his conduct than the revelation of the truth. But although Asquith would not agree to the publication of the official papers, he appointed a Commission to investigate the Dardanelles operations. The Commission started its sessions in August 1916, and for nearly a year Churchill found himself involved in a continued and harassing defence of his own responsibilities.

This year of 1916 carried its share of portentous events on all war fronts. In May the indecisive Battle of Jutland saw the only engagement between the two Grand Fleets; and on 1st July began the Battle of the Somme. It dragged on until November, and the appalling casualty lists increased the volume of protest against the inefficient direction of the war, and in December Lloyd George successfully manoeuvred Asquith from power and succeeded him as Prime Minister.

Throbbing with energy and feeling himself equal to great tasks, Churchill confidently expected office under the new regime, and he felt once more the pangs of bitter disappointment and frustration when his hopes were confounded. But he had under-estimated, as Clementine had not, the tenacious hostility of some of his Conservative opponents, who had stipulated on joining the Cabinet that Churchill would not be given office. Moreover, although the Dardanelles Commission had been sitting for some months, it had so far published no report, and so, in the eyes of many, the responsibility for that disastrous episode still lay heavily upon his shoulders.

But temporary distraction at least from brooding and bitter thoughts was however near at hand. Both Churchill families had been bidden to Blenheim for Christmas with their united nurseries. The chill of the quarrel between Sunny and Clementine had long since been forgotten, and it must have been a marvellous party, for in addition to the Duke's own family he had invited the F. E. Smiths with their three children. And so, if for Winston and Clementine the winds blew chill outside, and the leaden clouds seemed to hold no promise for the future, the interior scene was warm and glowing.

On the home front, 1917 was to prove the hardest year of the war. There was scarcely a home that had not suffered bereavement, and inexorably the war was penetrating everyday life. But for Clementine the anguishing tension and anxiety of the previous year were mercifully eased. She had Winston at home once more, and in politics his fortunes began to revive. During the spring months of 1917, Churchill was constantly active in Parliament, and by his knowledge of affairs and fearless, forceful advocacy he was a formidable element to be reckoned with. In March 1917 the Interim Report of the Dardanelles Commission was published and part, at least, of the truth was told. Churchill's reputation was cleared of the damaging charges which had up to then been voiced without official contradiction; and it was furthermore clear to what extent others had been involved in decisions whose responsibility he had been made to bear almost alone. Lloyd George was now strong enough to defy Conservative objections, and on 17th July 1917 Churchill was made Minister of Munitions.

As was still the custom, he had, on being appointed a minister, to seek re-election in his constituency. Clementine campaigned energetically for him at Dundee, addressing meetings on his behalf when his ministerial duties kept him in London. It was a stormy battle, and at one meeting she had the unpleasant experience of being shouted down. But interruptions do not seem to have affrighted her:

... Rain was falling heavily, but under the shelter of an umbrella she stood wrestling with the hecklers, one of whom she invited to 'come closer so that she might hear what he had to say.' At least two accepted her invitation, and while the audience, or a portion of those present, engaged in a wrangle on their own, Mrs Churchill listened to their stories.[32]

Winston was safely returned with a majority of over 5000. He took up his new appointment with enthusiasm. It marked a new start, and once more his volcanic energy could be harnessed to a challenging task.

*

For some time after his return from the Front, Winston and Clementine had continued to share 41 Cromwell Road with Jack and Goonie, but presently they moved back into their first home, 33 Eccleston Square, which had been let. Clementine's dream of 'a little country basket'[33] was now revived. Both of them felt the need to retreat from the hurly-burly of London, and Winston was so enthralled with painting that he sought every opportunity of being in the countryside.

They presently found a charming house, Lullenden, near East Grinstead. It was a low building, built in grey stone, with a large barn nearby, and a small farmery. Downstairs, running the full length of the house, was a big high room with a large open fireplace, which made a delightful 'studio-like' nursery, from where a staircase led to a gallery, off which were the children's bedrooms. There was a good deal to be done to the place, including the laying on of piped water, and as the house was not over large, Clementine set about converting the barn for the children's use as well.

Although at first the children remained in London, going down to Lullenden for week-ends and holidays, it was later decided, on account of the air raids, that it was better for them to be permanently based in the country. Not that the raids had alarmed the children; Randolph recounted that they were

tremendously exciting, since we children would be woken up in the middle of the night, wrapped up in blankets and carried down to the basement where there would be a lot of grown-ups having supper and drinking champagne. We liked

Zeppelins very much indeed and thought it a great treat to mix with grown-ups in the middle of the night.[34]

It must have been a lively nursery party, for the cousins, Johnny and Peregrine, also moved down to the freedom and safety of the country. Despite the lack of entertainment provided by the air raids, the children were all very happy at Lullenden. The elder ones went to school in the nearby village of Dormansland.

Churchill's work as Minister of Munitions took him a great deal to France, for it was of prime importance for him to be in close touch with the commanders in the field, who knew at first hand the needs of the armies. During the summer of 1918, Lord Haig put at his disposal Château Verchocq, near St Omer, to facilitate his operations. At home the pressure of his work was so great that for a time Winston actually moved into rooms in the Ministry of Munitions in Northumberland Avenue. Any week-ends he was not in France, Winston spent at Lullenden, which was conveniently near the airfields of Penshurst and Godstone.

With the children now permanently in the country, Clementine made Lullenden her main base. Moreover, a country life was particularly suitable for her, as she was once more with child. During this summer she gave herself over to country life, finding real pleasure and interest in it. After making the house habitable and comfortable, she addressed her attention to the small farm (on which two German prisoners-of-war worked), and she also became very garden-minded. Writing to Winston, she asked him

> to take me to Crawley in the motor (about 10 miles) to see Cheal's Nursery Gardens. I want to buy some little rock plants to put in the chinks everywhere. This cannot be done before the autumn but the point is to see them all in bloom before they fade for the effect.[35]

During Winston's absences, the family depended for their transport on a pony and trap – a means of travel not without its own hazards, however, for in August Clementine described to Winston how their horse panicked at a steam roller, the trap being badly damaged. The horse escaped injury, and Clementine sustained only a badly bruised knee, but she wrote:

> 'The Chumbolly' (we have not got a new name for this one) objected & said that if he was disturbed again like this from his broodings he should come out & see what the matter was. He has however dozed off again & like Mahomet's coffin is suspended between 2 Worlds . . .[36]

But Clementine was not completely rusticated; despite her pregnancy she still continued her work, and made long, tiring expeditions to London to grapple with her canteens. Her ability and devotion to this work were officially recognised when, in the New Year's Honours, she was made a Commander of the British Empire.

During the summer of 1918 the Germans made their last desperate bid on the Marne, but the Allied counter-offensive soon gained momentum and everywhere now the blood-red flood tide of victory rolled forward.

As ever, Winston and his work took prime place in Clementine's thoughts, and she followed in minutest detail the progress of the war. From Mells in Somerset,

where she was staying with old family friends, the Horners, she wrote to him on
13th August:

> The War news continues good, but it seems to me that 'the Victory' is now
> complete & that for the present nothing more is to be expected? I do hope we
> shall be careful not to waste our men in pushing now that the spurt is finished . . .

For these thoughts she was presently praised by Winston as showing herself to be
'a vy wise & sagacious military pussy cat'.[37]

Clementine relished once more hearing and reading all the news from him:

> . . . How much better you describe things than the most brilliant Newspaper
> Correspondent. But I forget! You were one once – but that was before I knew
> you . . .[38]

She loved her visit to Mells, but she felt strongly the sadness and melancholy which
underlay the peace and beauty of the place:

> Both the sons dead, one lying in the little Churchyard next to the House carried
> away at sixteen by Scarlet Fever, the other sleeping in France as does the Husband
> of the best loved daughter of the House Katherine Asquith. Both their swords
> are hanging in the beautiful little Gothic Church beside long inscriptions com-
> memorating long dead Horners who died in their beds . . .[39]

Winston's letters to her at this time were (not unnaturally in view of his task as
Minister of Munitions) full of plans and details of weapons and engines of destruction. Clementine understood the necessity of this, but with the feeling that at last
the war was drawing to its close, and the bright personal preoccupation of a new
baby, her mind dwelt on the future, and on the role she longed for Winston to play
in the reconstruction of peace-time life. '. . . do come home and look after what is to
be done with the Munition Workers when the fighting really does stop,' she wrote
to him.

> Even if the fighting is not over yet, your share of it must be & I would like you to
> be praised as a reconstructive genius as well as for a Mustard Gas fiend, a Tank
> juggernaut & a flying Terror – Besides the credit for all these Bogey parts will be
> given to subordinates . . .

Her Utopian ardour was thoroughly aroused, for she continued:

> . . . Can't the men Munition Workers build lovely garden cities & pull down
> slums in places like Bethnal Green, Newcastle, Glasgow, Leeds etc & can't the
> women munition workers make all the lovely furniture for them Baby's cradles
> cupboards etc . . .
> Do come home & arrange all this.[40]

12th September marked the tenth anniversary of Winston's and Clementine's
wedding. He was in France, and wrote to her:

> Ten years ago my dearest one we were sliding down to Blenheim in our special
> train. Do you remember. It is a long stage on life's road. Do you think we have

been less happy or more happy than the average married couple. I reproach myself vy much for not having been more to you. But at any rate in these ten years the sun has never yet gone down on our wrath. Never once have we closed our eyes in slumber with an unappeased difference. My dearest sweet I hope & pray that future years may bring you serene & smiling days, & full & fruitful occupation. I think that you will find real scope in the new world opening out to women, & find interests wh will enrich yr life. And always at yr side in true & tender friendship as long as he breathes will be your ever devoted, if only partially satisfactory, W.[41]

It was during this absence that Clementine was found for the first time seriously wanting as a correspondent. For a whole week Winston received no word from her, and on 15th September he wrote her a reproachful letter:

. . . Up to this moment I have not had a single letter. Really it is unkind. Mails have reached me with gt regularity & swiftness by aeroplane or messengers. They have comprised all manner of communications, but never one line from the Cat . . .

His letter continued with much interesting news, and was signed: 'Your ever devoted though vilely neglected Pig.'

No explanation exists for the temporary lapse of the 'Cat'. But it warms the heart to sense the relaxed and humorous vein of the letters. They had both been through so much, and now sunshine once more gave its benediction to their lives.

On Armistice Day, Clementine joined Winston at the Ministry of Munitions, to be with him at this historic moment, and when they left to call on the Prime Minister at No. 10 on this day of triumph and rejoicing, their car was surrounded by a wildly cheering crowd.

*

The lease of 33 Eccleston Square expired during this year, and so with the approach of autumn and the new baby's arrival, a London home had to be found. The ever kindly Aunt Cornelia let Winston and Clementine her house: 3 Tenterden Street, near Hanover Square. And here on 15th November, four days after the Armistice had been signed, Clementine gave birth to her fourth child, another red-headed girl – whom they named Marigold Frances.

BLEAK MORNING

THE GENERAL ELECTION which was held immediately following the end of hostilities was characterised by hysterical patriotism and extravagant demands for vengeance against Germany. Churchill did not share the feelings which engendered such slogans as 'Hang the Kaiser', 'Squeeze them till the pips squeak'. His watchword then, as later, was 'In Victory – Magnanimity: in Peace – Goodwill'. At the Armistice, when he learned that Germany was at the point of near-starvation, his immediate reaction was that ships 'crammed with provisions'[1] should be sent immediately to Hamburg. Even before the fighting ended Churchill had spoken of the importance of not seeking the utter ruin of Germany[2], and during the election campaign he stressed that war reparations should not be pressed to the point where the German working classes would be reduced to 'a condition of sweated labour and servitude'[3], which could only have malign repercussions in our own country.

Lloyd George and Bonar Law had issued a joint manifesto, and the result of the election was a sweeping victory for the Coalition, in which the Conservative Party was the dominant partner. But it saw the final and fatal breach in the Liberal Party: Asquith and many of his followers lost their seats, and those who survived sat on the Opposition benches.

Clementine could take no part in this electoral battle, for Marigold was barely a month old on Polling Day, but Winston was re-elected at Dundee with a handsome majority.

That Christmas the Churchill family gathered once more at Blenheim, and Randolph, who was seven, had a vivid recollection of it:

Christmas 1918 coincided with the end of the War and with the delayed celebrations of the twenty-first birthday of the son and heir, Lord Blandford . . . There was a paper-chase on horseback and a whole ox was roasted. The day concluded with a gigantic bonfire on top of which was placed an effigy of the Kaiser.[4]

In the newly-formed administration, Churchill was made Secretary of State for War, an office he was to hold for two years. The Air Ministry, which had first come into being in 1917, was now combined with the War Office under his aegis. This arrangement aroused criticism in several quarters, and Clementine herself thought the duality of the ministries unwise. After she had sat next to an eminent airman at dinner one night, she wrote to Winston:

> Darling really don't you think it would be better to give up the Air & continue *concentrating* as you are doing on the War Office. It would be a sign of real strength to do so, & people would admire it very much. It is weak to hang on to 2 offices. You really are only doing the one. Or again if you swallow the 2 you will have violent indigestion! It would be a tour de force to do the 2, like keeping a lot of balls in the air at the same time. After all, you want to be a statesman not a juggler.[5]

However, the two offices continued to be combined until Churchill left the War Office in 1921 to become Colonial Secretary. During his term as Air Minister he did much to forward the building up of this branch of defence, whose vital role and powerful future he saw with penetrating clarity.

When Winston had abandoned flying in 1914 at Clementine's anguished and repeated requests shortly before the birth of Sarah, he had already completed many of the flying hours required to obtain a pilot's licence. Since his appointment to the Ministry of Munitions he had frequently flown to and from France, and now in the summer of 1919, he began once more to take flying lessons.

Flying was still a precarious business, and on 18th July Winston narrowly escaped death while piloting a dual-control aeroplane over Croydon airfield. The plane was 70 to 80 feet above ground and travelling at about 60 mph when the controls failed and the plane plunged towards the ground, striking it with terrific force. In the few seconds before impact Colonel Scott, his instructor, had the presence of mind to switch off the engine, thus preventing an explosion. Miraculously neither of the men was killed, although Colonel Scott suffered severe injuries (from which, happily, he recovered). Winston himself was badly shaken, his forehead scratched, and his legs covered with bruises. Nevertheless, two hours after this misadventure he presided at a dinner in honour of General Pershing, and made a speech. But despite his debonair demeanour, this accident shook him severely, and to the intense relief of Clementine and his friends, he abandoned further attempts to qualify as a pilot.

Churchill's work for the Army and Air Force, together with the demands of the Peace Conference which had opened early in 1919 at Versailles, continued to make his presence in France often necessary. Clementine therefore had much to cope with on her own including the running of their small farmery at Lullenden. In March of that year she had engaged a new gardener/bailiff, whose very energy and determination caused her anxiety. She wrote to Winston:

> If we sell Lullenden we can pass this tyrant on with the place! . . .
>
> What I feel about him is that either he will save Lullenden for us or we shall be positively forced to sell . . .
>
> I feel very anxious about our private affairs. It's clear we are far too much extended –[6]

In this same month a most tragic event took place in their domestic life, during the virulent influenza epidemic which swept across the world during the winter after the war, claiming 150,000 lives in England alone. Winston was away in France when their Scottish nannie, Isabelle, who had been with them for several years, was struck by this horrible illness. Its course was swift and violent; in her delirium the poor girl seized Marigold from her cot, taking the child into her own bed. Clementine took Marigold down to her own room, but because so many people were ill her efforts to get a doctor were unavailing. She spent a fearful night going up and down stairs between the dying Isabelle and Marigold, who was frightened by these inexplicable events.

Isabelle died in the early hours. Clementine herself sickened for the influenza, and had a high temperature, but mercifully her own attack was not so serious. But this experience affected her deeply, for she had been very fond of Isabelle. For days also there was acute anxiety lest Marigold should have caught the fell disease; however all was well. Winston on his return to England was made to stay with Sunny Marlborough until all fear of infection was past.

In August 1919 Clementine accompanied Winston when he visited the British Army on the Rhine, where he inspected many British units in the occupied zone. In Cologne there was a great parade and march past, and Winston addressed the troops. Clementine was unfavourably impressed by the arrogant manner of some of the senior army wives to the German population.[7]

September saw them once more apart, but the letters they exchanged on their eleventh wedding anniversary remain as a moving witness to their feelings for each other. Winston wrote from France:

11 Sept. 1919

My darling one

Only these few lines to mark the eleventh time we have seen the 12th Sept. together. How I rejoice to think of my gt good fortune on that day! There came to me the greatest happiness & the greatest honour of my life. My dear it is a rock of comfort to have yr love & companionship at my side. Every year we have formed more bonds of deep affection. I can never express my gratitude to you for all you have done for me & for all you have been to me.

Yr ever loving & devoted
W

Clementine, who had evidently not remembered the actual day in time, replied:

Sept. 14. 1919
Lullenden,
East Grinstead

My Darling Winston

At Wynyard [in Co. Durham. home of Lord and Lady Londonderry] early in the morning of Sept. 12th I woke up & remembered suddenly the importance of the day, & I had not written to you! And then your dear letter appeared upon my breakfast tray. It made me very happy and illumined my day.

I love to feel that I am a comfort in your rather tumultuous life. My Darling, you have been the great event in mine. You took me from the straitened little by-path I was treading and took me with you into the life & colour & jostle of the high-way. But how sad it is that Time slips along so fast. Eleven years more & we shall be quite middle-aged. But I have been happier every year since we started . . .

For nearly two years after they gave up their house in Eccleston Square, Winston and Clementine had no fixed London home, but lived in a series of borrowed or rented houses. Despite the 'new broom' tactics of the bailiff at Lullenden, the property continued to be a heavy financial burden, and towards the end of 1919 they sold it to General Sir Ian and Lady Hamilton, and for the next three years they had no 'country basket'.

Indeed, for a few months after the sale of Lullenden they had neither a town nor a country house, but while Clementine house-hunted, they all stayed with the Freddie Guests at their house, Templeton, at Roehampton, the families sharing the expenses. Soon, however, the Churchills found a house to their liking, No. 2 Sussex Square, which was admirably suited to the needs of their now considerable family. It was a high, handsome house (now demolished) just north of the Bayswater Road and within easy reach of Hyde Park. They also acquired the mews buildings at the back of the house, which provided a splendid studio for Winston. They still had no country home to retreat to, but Lullenden had proved a costly pleasure, and for the time being the altering, fitting and furnishing of their new London home fully occupied their needs, and financial means.

Not all Winston's expeditions to France were for working purposes only. Through his letters to Clementine we have delightful accounts of a spring holiday he took in France towards the end of March 1920, with General Lord Rawlinson, with whom he shared a taste for hunting and painting, Lord Rawlinson being a water-colourist. The Duke of Westminster put his charming house at Mimizan, south of Bordeaux, at their disposal, and there they spent some happy, carefree days 'en garçon'. Clementine was busy with the children's spring holidays, during which she supervised the kitting out of Randolph for his preparatory school: 'He looks such a thin shrimp in trousers & an Eton collar!'[8] she wrote to Winston. She enjoyed the vivid descriptions he sent her of his hunting, particularly as she knew Mimizan, and had hunted there herself.

But although absorbed by hunting and painting, Winston did not forget April the First, writing to her a day or two before:

My darling one, this is a line & only a line (as the sun is shining bright) to wish you many many happy returns of the day. Twelve times now I have seen yr birthday come, & each time yr gracious beauty & loving charm have made a deeper impression on my heart. God bless you my darling in the year that now opens & give you happinesses wh fill yr life. Always yr devoted loving husband
W[9]

In the summer term of 1920, when he was nine, Randolph went to Sandroyd, a preparatory school near Cobham in Surrey. It appears that both Randolph and Diana were extremely naughty children, and in the early years nannies and nursery-maids came and went with inconvenient frequency. Perhaps the two older children were just full of super-abundant animal spirits. Randolph recalled that 'Diana was more docile than I was' but that he 'could never brook authority or discipline'[10]. During the greater part of the war, Winston and Clementine's nursery was amalgamated with Jack and Goonie's, and Goonie's nannie commanded (with varying degrees of success) the combined force of children. After the war, there was a nannie for the two little ones, and Diana and Randolph had a series of governesses, the most remembered being Miss Kinsey, who was amiable and tenacious, and who even after the children had started school used sometimes to come back to the family during the holidays.

After Randolph had gone to Sandroyd, Clementine decided that school would be more satisfactory for both Diana and Sarah than being taught at home (she had not forgotten how happy she had been at Berkhamsted High School), and in the autumn of 1920, soon after they had all moved into their new home in Sussex Square, the two elder girls went as day pupils to Notting Hill High School, where they both stayed for a number of years.

*

In the opening days of 1921 Blanche, Countess of Airlie, Clementine's majestic and austere grandmother, died at the age of ninety. Clementine had been too much over-awed by her as a child to love her, and when she was grown-up she had not come to like her much as a person. But the resilient, magnificent old lady was a landmark in Clementine's life, and her death brought back thoughts of long-ago summer holidays at Airlie Castle, when she and Kitty were children.

Lady Airlie's death was the first of a series which were to darken the year that lay ahead. But mercifully unconscious of what the coming months had in store, Winston and Clementine were able to enjoy a sunshine holiday in Nice during January. They stayed in a hotel with Sir Ernest Cassel and his niece, Edwina Ashley, who the following year was to marry Lord Louis Mountbatten.

This was the first real holiday Winston and Clementine had had together since the beginning of the war, and Clementine was both physically and mentally in need of it. After the years of tension and anxiety, of arduous war work, the birth of Marigold, and last but not least, the effort of moving into Sussex Square, this new year found her reserves of strength low, and her spirits depressed. Winston was much concerned about her, and when he returned to London, leaving her behind to continue her holiday, adjured her again and again to take great care of herself, to avoid over-fatigue and to follow the doctor's instructions. 'I do hope you will soon see sunshine & preen yr poor feathers in it,' he wrote on 1st February; and in another letter, 'I do hope you are having fun & tennis & *above all* recharging yr accumulators.'[11]

Clementine's letters must have reassured him, for they bubbled over with animation and enjoyment. Perhaps the most important feature of this much-needed holiday, and the most effective therapeutic remedy, lay in the fact that she was simply enjoying herself. All her life her overpowering sense of duty, and the conscientious performance of whatever that entailed, again and again dominated her existence to the exclusion of fun and pleasure. Now, in these few sunlit weeks she gave herself over to doing what she liked, and in being what she was – a young and beautiful woman of thirty-six at the height of her vitality and powers.

As her health revived, which it quickly did, she played tennis with increasing zest and ability. Winston was somewhat concerned lest she should overstrain herself, and thus retard her complete recovery; after talking to her doctor he wrote on 9th February:

> Please my darling think of nothing else but this, subordinate everything in yr life to regathering yr nervous energy, and recharging yr batteries. Don't throw away yr gains as you make them.
>
> Don't play in any tournament. If you play tennis – play for pleasure – not to excel.

However, as the weeks went on she felt so much stronger that she disregarded Winston's prudent counsels and took part in several high-class amateur mixed doubles tournaments, writing him long and excited accounts.

After her visit to Sir Ernest Cassel, Clementine went on to stay with Lady Essex at her villa, Lou Mas, at St Jean Cap Ferrat. Imbued with a carefree holiday spirit, she even went to the Gaming Rooms several times, observing the characters who frequented them with a mordant wit. Although no real gambler herself, she dabbled at the green baize tables lightheartedly (but ever cautiously), writing to Winston with great glee, that she had learned a new 'system' for roulette, which she proceeded to describe in minute technical detail, remarking, somewhat disarmingly, that

> It did not work at all well but I think it is better than playing without a system as one certainly loses one's money more slowly –[12]

During her progress along the coast, Clementine also met several well-known personalities, and she duly described these meetings to Winston. Lady Essex had invited Mr Garvin (the veteran editor of *The Observer*) to luncheon: 'He has a great belief in you,' Clementine wrote; later in the garden 'he released about ⅓ of an Observer Article on me.'[13] A less pleasant encounter was when she saw Ashmead-Bartlett, the war correspondent, who had taken a hostile view of Winston's role in the Dardanelles campaign:

> Ashmead Bartlett is at Beaulieu. I saw him playing tennis & could not remember whether his conduct merited 'the cut direct'. While I was revolving this he came up & nodded so I bowed coldly & as there was a rabbit wire fence between us I did not have to shake hands. He has a mean odious face & is the sort of creature who would haunt the Riviera.[14]

And as always when they were apart Winston was a good correspondent, and kept her up to date with life at home.

Randolph was back at Sandroyd, and Winston twice visited him at school, reporting to Clementine that he had 'found him very well and very sprightly' and that the Headmaster seemed to be quite pleased with him, but 'described him as

very combative'[15]. The two elder girls, who had been afflicted during most of the
winter by a series of coughs, colds and other minor ailments, had been sent off by
Clementine for a recuperative visit to Broadstairs in the charge of the nice cosy maid
Annie, and this was so successful as to their health that Winston authorised a
third week for them there.

Marigold had not gone with the seaside party but stayed at home keeping house
with her father, who would have hated a solitary house denuded of all 'kittens'. She
was now in her third year, and full of fascination and vitality. She loved to run, full
pelt, round and round the dining-room table while the grown-ups were at luncheon,
so that Clementine, fearing she might slip and crack her head against the sharp
corners of the table, had soft pads affixed to them. Marigold had a sweet, true little
voice, and learnt the popular song:

> I'm forever blowing bubbles,
> Pretty bubbles in the air,
> They fly so high, nearly reach the sky,
> Then like my dreams they fade and die.
> Fortune's always hiding,
> I've looked ev'rywhere,
> I'm forever blowing bubbles,
> Pretty bubbles in the air.

She was always singing it, so that it became her signature tune. During this winter,
and the spring that followed, she was particularly prone to catching coughs and
suffering from sore throats. Twice during Clementine's absence in France Marigold
was thus afflicted, and on one occasion the doctor had to be called.

It is touching to see how much pleasure, care and interest Winston took in his
children, despite his manifold preoccupations, and how conscientiously he took his
role of parent-in-charge. Of the elder girls he wrote appreciatively:

> The children are vy sweet. Diana is shaping into a beautiful being. Sarah full of
> life & human qualities . . .[16]

Warmth, vitality, and the free (and often noisy) expression of their mutual affection,
was always the prevailing atmosphere of Winston's and Clementine's family life.
All the children had their pet-names: Randolph was 'The Rabbit' (a somewhat
mystifying pseudonym for such a 'combative' character!); Diana was most aptly
and charmingly called 'The Gold-cream kitten'; Sarah, with her cloud of hectic red
hair, was 'Bumble-bee'; and the darling Marigold 'Duckadilly'.

In January and February of 1921, two events of major significance in Winston's
life and career took place. On 26th January his first cousin once removed, Lord
Herbert Vane-Tempest, was killed in a railway accident in Wales; as he was child-
less, an estate in Ireland known as Garron Tower, and a considerable sum of money,
passed to Winston through the devious processes of entail and inheritance.

And on 13th February his appointment as Colonial Secretary was announced.
This was a notable and upward step in Churchill's career for the office of Colonial
Secretary was particularly important, at this period. Winston stayed for the first

week-end in February with the Prime Minister at Chequers, which had just been presented to the nation by Lord and Lady Lee of Fareham as a country home for British Prime Ministers for ever. From there he wrote to Clementine:

> Here I am. You wd like to see this place – Perhaps you will some day! It is just the kind of house you admire – a pannelled [sic] museum full of history, full of treasures – but insufficiently warmed – Anyhow a wonderful possession.[17]

It is worth remarking in passing that of course Clementine did see Chequers later-nearly twenty years on; it was still 'insufficiently warmed', and her taste for gloomy Elizabethan houses stuffed with 'treasures' had, in the intervening years, waned.

In the midst of her sunshine holiday Clementine thought constantly of Winston and of all the events which so closely touched their life. From Lou Mas on 7th February she wrote him a long letter:

> . . . I can imagine all the various things which are filling your mind, i.e. your new post, your inheritance, the painting, Chequers, the P.M., the re-arrangement of the Government . . . the Book [*The World Crisis*], the poor old worn out War Office – make this little peninsula seem a pin point in the sea while you are soaring in an aeroplane above the great Corniche of life . . . I wish I were with you spinning round & round instead of sitting lazily here in the sun.

The unexpected windfall brought about by the death of his kinsman was of immense and immediate consequence to Winston's financial affairs. He was now assured of an income of around £4,000 a year. This meant that for the first time in his life he had an income independent of any parliamentary or ministerial salary, or from what he could earn by writing. Although Clementine was the least money-grasping of women, she rejoiced with all her heart at this unsought, unawaited shower of golden security. Their financial difficulties had been from the earliest days of their marriage a source of wearing anxiety to her, and she had struggled constantly between maintaining elegant and fastidious standards and the (to her) embarrassing horror of unpaid bills. Overnight, this situation had been changed. She wrote to Winston, on 8th February:

> I can't describe the blessed feeling of relief that we need never never be worried about money again. (Except thro' our own fault of course!) It is like floating in a bath of cream.

And then a fortnight later Winston told her that the legacy was in fact appreciably smaller than he had been led to suppose. She wrote:

> I am so sorry my Dearest that you have had a deception as to the amount of the inheritance – It is certainly very disappointing after you had worked it out so carefully & thought about how to lay it out to the best advantage; but don't let a 'crumpled rose leaf' like this spoil the really glorious fact which rushed on us so suddenly a little time ago – that haunting care has vanished for ever from our lives –
>
>   It's so delicious to be easy – I hope I shall never take it for granted, but always feel like a cork bobbing on a sunny sea . . . [18]

One of Clementine's constant worries in the past had been that, in order to make ends more likely to meet, Winston might accept unworthy or unsuitable contracts for 'pot-boiling' newspaper and magazine articles; and even if the offers were above reproach, the work involved in fulfilling such contracts was an extra load on top of his ministerial and parliamentary work. Now, in the light of recent events, Clementine tried to dissuade Winston from writing an article for the *Strand Magazine* about his painting. She developed her arguments in a letter to him on 10th February:

> . . . if *you* write the Article what are you going to write about
>   1) Art in general? I expect the professionals would be vexed & say you do not yet know enough about Art –
>   2) Your own pictures in particular? The danger there seems to me that either it may be thought naif or conceited –
> I am as anxious as you are to snooker that £1000 & as proud as you can be that you have had the offer; but just now I do not think it would be wise to do anything which will cause you to be discussed trivially, as it were.
> If there *is* to be an argument let it be as to whether you are going to be a good 'Imperial Minister' or not . . . I have a sort of feeling that the 'All Highest' [Lord Curzon, the Foreign Secretary] rejoices every time you write an Article & thinks it brings *him* nearer the Premiership, tho' I think that a man who has had to bolster himself up with two rich wives to keep himself going is not so likely to keep the Empire going as you who for 12 years have been a Cabinet Minister & have besides kept a fortuneless Cat & four hungry Kittens.
> I think one of the reasons that your friends rejoice in your new fortune is that it frees you from the necessity of earning money from writing at inconvenient moments . . .

Winston promised to consider Clementine's views, but added:

> An article by Mr Balfour on golf or philosophy or by Mr Bonar Law on chess would be considered entirely proper. I think I can make it very light and amusing without in any way offending the professional painters.[19]

Eventually two articles, illustrated by reproductions of his paintings, were published in the *Strand Magazine*, in December 1921 and January 1922, under the title 'Painting as a Pastime'. Although in this case, as in so many others, Winston's view prevailed, it is a striking example of Clementine's vigilance and sensitivity to anything that might harm his reputation or dim his lustre.

With characteristic warmth and generosity, Winston did not confine the benefits of his good fortune solely to himself and Clementine. Nellie Romilly was at this time in very difficult financial circumstances, with a severely war-wounded husband and two small children; and, to help provide for them all, she was proposing to open a hat shop. At the end of January, Winston wrote to tell Clementine that Nellie had found suitable premises for her shop, and that he had lent her £500; and a little while later, when Nellie was still beset by worries, Winston assured her that he would help her through. He also looked into Lady Blanche's financial arrangements, and Clementine wrote on 13th February:

> I am so glad you are looking into Mother's affairs for her.
> I do hope you will be able to improve matters for her, & anyhow I would like her to have £100 a year out of the increased allowance you are so kindly making me.

Towards the end of February 1921 a new and enjoyable project took shape. Winston had to go to Cairo, where there was to be a Middle Eastern Conference to try to arrive at a working settlement for the affairs of that turbulent part of the world. The British delegation were travelling out by sea, and Winston proposed to Clementine that she should come with him, getting on board at Marseilles, where the ship, the *Sphinx*, was due to call. Clementine had by this time moved to the Hôtel Bristol at Beaulieu, and she wrote from there on 21st February:

> ... I am living in blissful contemplation of our smooth and care-free future; (I mean from a money point of view) & I am laying up stores of health by staying a lot in bed. The last two days I have been thinking chiefly of the great pleasure and excitement of going with you to Egypt & Palestine. I am thrilled by the idea & so so longing to see you.

Winston wrote to her with fuller details of their journey and programme: they would probably stay ten days in Cairo, and then go to Jerusalem; she would be able to sight-see, and probably play some tennis, 'so do not forget your racquet'. But he issued a sober warning about her health:

> It will be above all things necessary that you should not fatigue yourself on this expedition ... It would indeed be foolish if we returned without your having got quite strong and well.[20]

In order to see the two older girls before leaving for his journey, Winston sent for them to return from Broadstairs two days early. 'They were in the pink,' he reported to Clementine on 27th February,

> .... The Duckadilly received them with joy & is quite free from cold ...
> We are going down to see Randolph today. I gave the children the choice of Randolph or the Zoo. They screamed for Randolph in most loyal & gallant fashion. So we arranged for the Zoo too ...

Of their forthcoming travels together he wrote:

> ... I am looking forward eagerly to seeing you again. We shall have a beautiful cabin together, if only it is not rough – then I shall hide in any old dog hole far from yr sight ... If it is fine, it will be lovely & I shall write & paint & we will talk over all our affairs ...

Among their travelling companions were to be Archie Sinclair (who had followed Winston into political life and was now his Private Secretary), and the famous romantic Colonel Lawrence – Lawrence of Arabia, with whom during these next weeks Winston and Clementine formed a firm friendship.

This journey to the Middle East was, in personal terms, a great success and, on a wider canvas, at the Cairo Conference, Churchill was instrumental in bringing about a political settlement in Iraq and Transjordan. In intervals between sessions Winston found time to paint, and he and Clementine paid a visit to the Pyramids and the Sphinx, escorted by Colonel Lawrence and Gertrude Bell. In Jerusalem, Churchill reasserted the British Government's policy of allowing a Jewish National Home to be established in Palestine.

*

A few days after their homecoming a tragic event took place. On 14th April Bill Hozier was found shot dead in a hotel bedroom in Paris: he had killed himself. He was only thirty-four – debonair, good-looking and gallant. After the war he had retired from the Navy and gone into business, but, like his mother and Nellie his twin, he had a weakness for gambling, which inevitably had led him into financial difficulties. Some little time before Bill's death, Winston, who was extremely fond of him, had extracted from him a solemn promise that he would never gamble at cards again. Now Winston was filled with remorse as well as grief, for he feared that Bill's promise to him might have contributed to the reason for his suicide. But no evidence was found that Bill had in fact gambled again; nothing was known of any losses or heavy debts, and indeed he had just paid 10,000 francs into his bank account. His death was ever to remain a tragic mystery.

Clementine and Nellie travelled over at once to Dieppe, where Lady Blanche had several years since once more established herself. On Sunday, 17th April Clementine wrote to Winston:

Your beautiful letter has come –

My poor Mamma is so brave and dignified, but I do not think that she will recover from the shock & the grief. She sits in her chair shrunk and small. When we saw her she did not yet know that Bill had killed himself, but I saw by the look of agony & fear that she half guessed . . .

There was some doubt as to whether Bill could be buried in consecrated ground, or the body allowed to rest before the funeral in the church. The British Vice-Consul rallied round and went to see the clergyman, and all was decently and compassionately arranged.

The funeral was to take place on Monday, and the body would lie from that morning in the church. Clementine had the service delayed until four o'clock, in the hope that Winston might be able to come. 'Oh Winston my Dear do come tomorrow,' she wrote, '& dignify by your presence Bill's poor Suicide's Funeral.' She had sent Winston's letter to the clergyman for him to see,

. . . as I wanted him to realize what we all felt for Bill & that he was not a mere scapegrace disowned by his family . . .

Despite the very short notice, Winston managed to arrive in time for the funeral. In his will Bill had bequeathed him his elegant malacca gold-topped cane: Winston used it for the rest of his life.

*

At the end of June Winston's mother died at her home in Westbourne Street: she was sixty-seven. Her marriage to George Cornwallis-West had (perhaps predictably) ended in divorce in 1913, and he had promptly married the famous actress, Mrs Patrick Campbell. Four years later, Lady Randolph (then sixty-four) was married for the third time, and again to a man over twenty years younger than herself – Mr Montagu Porch, a member of the Northern Nigerian Civil Service. They had met several years before, and not unnaturally Lady Randolph's family had tried to dissuade her from this marriage. But Montagu Porch's devotion was very real, and Jennie Churchill was very lonely, and in June 1918 they married. Soon afterwards, Montagu Porch resigned from the Nigerian Civil Service to live in London, and despite the many forebodings they were happy together.

Now, in the summer of 1921, Lady Randolph had tripped in a perilously high-heeled pair of shoes, and fallen down the staircase while staying in the country at Mells, with her old friend Lady Horner. The local doctor diagnosed a broken ankle, and Lady Randolph was taken back to her house in London. But then gangrene set in, and her leg had to be amputated.

Sussex Square was just round the corner from Westbourne Street, and in these weeks of painful illness Clementine would often go and sit with her mother-in-law. Although Clementine and Lady Randolph had never been very close – indeed both she and Goonie had been exasperated many times by 'Belle-Maman's' (as they called her) extravagances – understanding and a real affection had grown over the years. The sisters-in-law had hated to see her humiliated by George Cornwallis-West's vagaries, and had been warmly sympathetic to her. Now, as Clementine witnessed the indomitable courage with which this vital, worldly woman faced the ordeal and pain of amputation, she felt a new admiration for her.

Montagu Porch was away on business in Africa when his wife had her accident; Winston kept him in close touch, and on 23rd June had cabled him to say that she was out of danger. But early on the morning of 29th June, Lady Randolph had a sudden, violent haemorrhage. Winston was sent for, and came running through the streets to his mother. But when he arrived, she was already dead.

Moving letters of condolence poured in – Jennie had come to be a legend in her lifetime. Winston was deeply grieved, for he had loved his mother dearly. He always spoke of her with uncritical admiration and devotion. Of all the tributes to her, perhaps his own words in his answer to Lord Curzon's letter strike the truest note:

> ... I do not feel a sense of tragedy, but only of loss. Her life was a full one. The wine of life was in her veins. Sorrows and storms were conquered by her nature & on the whole it was a life of sunshine.[21]

*

The plans for the summer holidays of 1921 promised to be agreeable and fun for all the family. All four children went into lodgings, 'Overblow' at Broadstairs, for the first half of August, in the charge of Mlle Rose, a young French nursery governess. It was planned that about the middle of the month the elder children would go up to Scotland, to join their parents, who would then be staying with the Duke and

Duchess of Westminster at their beautiful and remote estate in Sutherland. In the meantime, Clementine went on her own to stay with the Westminsters at Eaton, near Chester, to take part in a tennis tournament. She planned to join the train on which the children would be travelling from the south, and they would all journey on to Scotland together: Winston was to join them a few days later.

Clementine received happy news from the children, but in retrospect there are references in their naïve letters which sound a warning note. On 2nd August, Randolph wrote to his mother:

> Dear Mummie,
>
>   I hope that you are quite well. My legs are suffering from the sun, it has made them go all red. The other day Falkner lent us his big shrimping net, so we went out and caught lots of shrimps for tea. On Sunday we went out in a little rowing boat, which was great fun! Marigold has been rather ill, but is ever so much better today. We are all quite well here except for our legs.
>
> With much love
Randolph
>
> XXXXXXXXXXXXXXXXXXXXXXXXXXXXXXXXX

Sarah also wrote to her mother:

> . . . Baba is very sweet and quite well now We are enjoying ourselves very much here. We bathe every day . . . [22]

So from the start of their seaside holiday Marigold had not been very well; and since in the last year she had been subject to 'throats' and coughs, perhaps not enough significance was attached at first to what was the onset of a mortal illness. The local doctor was very good, but, alas for the 'Duckadilly', the age of antibiotics had not yet dawned, and her painful sore throat progressed into a fatal septicaemia. The child became really ill about 14th August, but it was a day or two before Mlle Rose, stimulated into action by the kind and watchful landlady of 'Overblow', sent for her mother. Clementine left Eaton at once and rushed to Broadstairs; the three elder children travelled to Scotland according to plan, with Bessie, Clementine's maid. By the time her mother arrived, Marigold was gravely ill. Winston came down from London; a specialist was sent for, but he could do nothing. Clementine wrote to the children in Scotland to tell them of the gravity of Marigold's illness. Diana replied:

> 20.8.21
>
> My darling Mummy,
>
>   We received your letter last night and I was very sorry to hear poor little Marigold is so ill. We have had a very unlucky year . . .
>
>   Yesterday we went to an Island called Handa, and we took our tea with us. We all go riding every day. I do wish you could be here; but it is impossible.
>
> Much love and kisses from
Diana

On the evening of 22nd August, Clementine was sitting by Marigold's bedside;

the child was sinking; suddenly she said to her mother: 'Sing me "Bubbles".' Clementine, summoning all the control she knew, began the haunting, wistful little song that Marigold loved so much; she had not struggled very far, when the child put out her hand and whispered, 'Not tonight . . . finish it tomorrow.' The next day Marigold died; she was two years and nine months old; both her parents were with her. Clementine in her agony gave a succession of wild shrieks, like an animal in mortal pain.[23]

After the funeral, Winston and Clementine got on the night train in a silent stupor of grief and went up to join the children at Lochmore. They stayed there for nearly a fortnight, at the end of which Winston went on to Dunrobin to stay with the Duke and Duchess of Sutherland, and Clementine took the children home, to make the necessary preparations for their return to school.

Margot Asquith wrote in her memoirs that 'No true woman ever gets over the loss of a child.'[24] It was certainly so with Clementine. But she did not indulge her grief: rather she battened it down, and got on with life with all its persistent, trivial demands.

At Dunrobin, a very large party of 'swells and notabilities' was gathered: Winston found some beautiful scenes to paint, but painful thoughts persisted:

Many tender thoughts my darling one of you & yr sweet kittens. Alas I keep on feeling the hurt of the Duckadilly. I expect you will have all made a pilgrimage yesterday . . . [25]

They had; and Clementine wrote:

I took the children on Sunday to Marigold's grave and as we knelt round it – would you believe that a little white butterfly . . . fluttered down & settled on the flowers which are now growing on it. We took some little bunches. The children were very silent all the way home.[26]

But she made heroic efforts to distract them, and made Randolph's return to Sandroyd the occasion for an excursion and picnic.

Yesterday we hired a car . . . & we all escorted Randolph in triumph back to school . . . We stopped on the road and had a splendid pic-nic & arrived torn & dishevelled at Sandroyds.[27]

In late September, Sir Ernest Cassel died at his London house; his secretary telephoned Clementine and asked her to tell Winston the news. She wrote:

. . . I have been through so much lately that I thought I had little feeling left, but I wept for our dear old friend; he was a feature in our life and he cared deeply for you . . . I feel the poorer becos' he is gone. He was a true & loyal friend & a good man.[28]

The end of this heavy year found Clementine on the edge of exhaustion, and she and Winston planned a Riviera holiday after Christmas at home. Winston went on

ahead of her to the South of France, in company with Mr Lloyd George, and
Clementine was to join him a little later.

Winston had hardly left the house on Boxing Day when, one after the other, the
children and servants started going down with influenza, of which there was currently another epidemic in London (but fortunately not of so violent a nature as the
so-called 'Spanish Influenza' which had been so devastating two years before).
Within twenty-four hours Clementine had four patients with roaring temperatures
and one with pneumonia on her hands. Diana and Sarah, who at first seemed unaffected, were given asylum by their Great-Aunt Maude (Lady Maude Whyte, one
of Lady Blanche's sisters); Diana developed the illness the following day and was
returned to Sussex Square, which now, with two nurses, resembled a private
nursing home. Indeed, Clementine remarked in a long letter she wrote to Winston
on December 27th:

> . . . I feel quite calm as now we are thoroughly organised, & could in fact with
> the same personnel deal with 2 more patients. Am thinking of advertising '2
> empty beds for rich patients at 2, Sussex Square 50 guineas a week' – This would
> pay for the whole thing!

But although she wrote in such a debonair fashion (Winston described her conduct
and letter as 'Napoleonic'[29]), Clementine herself, after organising the sick hordes,
collapsed; on examination her blood pressure was found to be dramatically low, she
was suffering from breathlessness, and in a state of utter nervous exhaustion, and
the doctor ordered her to bed for a week. From there, she continued to give bulletins on all the patients to Winston.

Clementine's plan to join him had to be postponed until everyone, herself
included, was once more on their feet. Meanwhile Winston urged her to come out to
France as soon as she was well enough 'to recuperate in this delicious sunshine, and
let me mount guard in yr place over the kittens'[30]. He was having an agreeable holiday: painting, writing, and, as he confessed to Clementine, he 'played' a little.
' . . . It excites me so much to play – foolish moth,' he wrote, adding – 'But I have
earned many times what I have lost by the work I have done here on my book . . . '[31]

But both Winston in the bright sunshine, and Clementine in her bed of sickness,
had thoughts of the dark year through which they had just lived. Clementine wrote:

> . . . the week that I was in bed I wandered in the miserable valley too tired to
> read much & all the sad events of last year culminating in Marigold passing and
> re-passing like a stage Army through my sad heart . . . [32]

And on New Year's Day, 1922, Winston had written:

> What changes in a year! What gaps! What a sense of fleeting shadows! But your
> sweet love and comradeship is a light that burns. The stronger as our brief
> years pass.

THE TWENTIES

THE YEAR 1921 had been one of grief and strain for Clementine, but the New Year brought fresh hope. Towards the end of January she joined Winston in Cannes for a much-needed holiday, and she remained there for some weeks after he had to return to his parliamentary and ministerial duties in London. Venetia Montagu was with her for a time, which made agreeable company.

While she was in Cannes, Clementine's expectations were confirmed: she was once more with child. Nevertheless, it was such early days that she continued to play tennis. This caused Winston some anxiety, but she wrote reassuringly to tell him that she was

> ... *really* very well considering ... I am playing a little tennis. There is a mild Club Tournament going on here & I am playing in it ... Don't think I am doing too much. On the contrary since the sun has come out & I have been playing I feel better & after playing I go to my Bunny & eschew the Casino & its heat & tobacco smoke, not to speak of its financial danger. The poor Cat has lost £10 at Chemin de Fer & is much annoyed –

She was evidently in good health and spirits; her letter ends on a gay note:

> Goodbye Darling – Kiss the two red haired kittens for me. I wonder if the new one will have red hair. Shall we have a bet about it 'Rouge ou Noir'?[1]

Clementine's tennis season ended in triumph, for she and her partner won the Mixed Doubles Handicap in the Cannes Lawn Tennis Tournament, and she returned much revived to London.

A source of recurring disappointment in Clementine's life was that, fond though Winston was of the children, she never could lure him to spend more than a few days with them all during the summer holidays. It was understandable, since many fathers who are neither statesmen nor geniuses do not take kindly to rented holiday houses or lodgings at the seaside. Winston felt cooped up after a very few days, and now that painting was such a joy and occupation to him, he continually felt drawn to 'paintatious' (his own adjective) places, where the sun might be expected to shine brightly and continuously. But Clementine was forever trying to find somewhere which would be fun and suitable for the children, and where also Winston would be content to stay.

Hoping to achieve this very end Clementine had taken one of the school houses at Rugby School, in the summer holidays of 1920, despite the fact that she greatly preferred to be by the sea. Rugby, however, was near Ashby St Ledgers, the Wimbornes' country house, and the plan was that Winston would stay with them all, and be diverted by polo with his Guest cousins. In the event, however, Winston made only spasmodic appearances: to do him justice, there was a political crisis on the brew. But the children were bitterly disappointed, and Clementine did not conceal her disgust. Her sole purpose had been to try to reconcile everyone's pleasures, and she found herself stranded 'inland', in a neighbourhood she did not particularly like, and in close proximity to the Guests, for whom she did not care.

However, the holiday plans for the summer of 1922 were arranged to everybody's satisfaction: a large house was taken at Frinton-on-Sea, where Clementine installed herself with the staff and children. She was expecting her child in September, and had no wish to go abroad. Winston was to go to France for the first part of the holidays, coming to join them all at Frinton during the later part of August; and this time he did not defect. Clementine was perfectly content meantime and wrote to him happily on 8th August:

I *am* so happy here – It's so comfortable & delicious. I hardly ever go outside the garden but just bask. The children scamper all over the place but I am not (just now) nimble enough to chase after them.

The children had plenty of companions on the beach and at the tennis club, where Randolph and Diana competed as partners in the tournament; Clementine sent photographs of them playing:

Randolph *looks* like a young champion but I'm sorry to say that playing together the children secured the Booby Prize! which I had the humiliation of presenting before a large crowd![2]

The holiday was such a success that Clementine pressed on Winston the idea of buying a house there:

I do love this place & if we had a 'permanent' little bug walk here we could use it for my tennis week-ends and children's recovery from illnesses at odd times . . . & be sure of always letting it well for the summer holidays if we fancied Deauville . . .[3]

Winston was glad she was so happy, but lukewarm about buying a house at Frinton.

Thoughts of the new baby occupied both their minds, but they were inextricably and painfully intertwined with memories of their beloved Marigold, the anniversary of whose illness and death fell in these days. 'I feel quite excited at the approach of a new kitten,' wrote Clementine on 8th August,

Only 5 weeks now & a new being – perhaps a genius – anyhow very precious to us – will make its appearance & demand our attention. Darling, I hope it will be like you.

Three days from now August the 11th our Marigold began to fade; She died on the 23rd.

Winston was particularly tender and understanding of her feelings in these days:

I think a gt deal of the coming kitten & about you my sweet pet. I feel it will enrich yr life and brighten our home to have the nursery started again. I pray to God to watch over us all.[4]

Again, a few days later, on 14th August, Winston wrote from Mimizan, where he was staying with Bendor (the Duke of Westminster):

My darling, I have thought vy often of you all & most of all of you. Yes I pass through again those sad scenes of last year when we lost our dear Duckadilly. Poor lamb – It is a gaping wound, whenever one touches it & removes the bandages & plasters of daily life. I do hope & pray all is well with you . . .

Your own adventure is vy near now & I look forward so much to seeing you safe & well with a new darling kitten to cherish . . .

Winston joined Clementine and the children on 24th August, and they were all very happy together during the last lap of the holidays. Assisted by the children, their nannie and his detectives, Winston organised a large and imposing sand fortress, which was the admiration of all on the beach, and which made a long and gallant stand against wind and tide. Presently Clementine returned to London to await the birth of her baby. Their fifth and last child, a girl, was born early on the morning of 15th September; they named her Mary.

It was in this summer that Winston first saw Chartwell, near Westerham in Kent. He was immediately captivated by it, and the story of its purchase and their life together there belongs to another chapter. It is enough to record here that Chartwell was bought in September 1922, and that it was to be Winston and Clementine's home for over forty years.

★

During the summer of 1921 a truce was signed with Sinn Fein, which at last marked the possible beginning-of-the-end of the fruitless deadlock in Ireland. Violence and bloodshed had been rife on both sides since the previous spring. Clementine, who as ever watched public affairs with vigilance, had written to Winston in February 1921 on the agonising situation:

Do my darling use your influence *now* for some sort of moderation or at any rate justice in Ireland. Put yourself in the place of the Irish – If you were their leader you would not be cowed by severity & certainly not by reprisals which fall like the rain from Heaven upon the Just & upon the Unjust . . .

It always makes me unhappy & disappointed when I see you *inclined* to take for granted that the rough iron-fisted 'hunnish' way will prevail . . .[5]

Despite continuing strife, events moved towards a settlement, and Churchill took a prominent part in these negotiations, establishing close and helpful contacts with several of the Republican leaders; and he was one of the signatories of the Treaty which was signed in December 1921. Ireland was granted Dominion status, and partition accepted, with separate parliaments in Dublin and Stormont (for the six Northern counties). There was immediate opposition to the Treaty from the Irish Republican Party, which determined to attempt to secure the complete independence of a united Ireland, and a period of civil war ensued before the terms of settlement were imposed, by Irishmen themselves, upon their distracted country.

With the granting of Dominion status, Ireland became part of Churchill's responsibility as Colonial Secretary, and, in consequence, he himself stood in danger of his life. As he was known to be on the 'list' for assassination, he was for some time guarded by armed detectives. For many months he always slept with a revolver at hand, and an armchair in his room was reinforced with metal, so as to afford him protection should he have to 'fight it out'. These precautions, and the necessity for them, added a constant tension to their everyday existence; but Clementine never made much of it, either at the time or afterwards.

Throughout 1922, dissatisfaction with Lloyd George's leadership had been growing among the Conservatives, who formed the majority in the Coalition Government. Plot and counter-plot were the order of the day in high political circles, culminating in the now famous meeting at the Carlton Club on 17th October, when the Conservatives voted by a large majority to withdraw from the Coalition. The King sent for Mr Bonar Law; a Conservative Government was formed, and a General Election took place forthwith.

In the midst of all this, on 16th October, Winston was taken gravely ill, and two days later he was operated on for appendicitis. In those days this was a serious operation, and although he weathered it well he was not sufficiently recovered to take part in the early and crucial stages of the election campaign in Dundee, which opened on 30th October. Although Clementine was still feeding their new baby, Mary (only seven weeks old), she was determined to do what she could in the fight, and travelled to Dundee, arriving on 5th November with (as the local press somewhat spitefully put it) 'her unbaptised infant'. Clementine stayed with supporters whose house was in a street ominously named Dudhope Crescent. Dundee was a two-member constituency, and there were six candidates: two National Liberals, one Labour (E. D. Morel), one Communist (W. Gallacher), one Liberal, and a 'Prohibition' candidate, Mr Scrymgeour, who had already contested the seat on five previous occasions.

Clementine flung herself into the campaign with energy, and in the course of the following week addressed at least six meetings, making spirited speeches on Winston's behalf. Although she was frequently shouted down, she was undaunted by the general uproar. General Spears (a friend of Winston's since the western front days), who had come to help out in the campaign, described how, when she appeared at one meeting wearing a string of pearls, women spat on her. He commented admiringly: 'Clemmie's bearing was magnificent – like an aristocrat going to the guillotine in a tumbril.'[6]

At one meeting, when she was consistently interrupted, the *Dundee Courier* reported:

In the course of further efforts to destroy her speech Mrs Churchill appealed, 'Do be kind and let me get on.' She then treated the whole affair laughingly, and her smiles won the interrupters to comparative silence once again.[7]

On 9th November, Clementine wrote Winston a long letter, telling him candidly, 'The situation here is an anxious one . . .' She went on to give him detailed information about the campaign and some advice:

If we win (which I pray & believe we will) we really must put in some time & work here & *re-organise* the whole organisation which was in chaos. Of course I feel the minute you arrive the atmosphere will change & the people will be roused. If you bring Sergeant Thompson etc tell him to conceal himself tactfully as it would not do if the populace thought you were afraid of them. The papers are so *vile*, they would misrepresent it & say you have brought detectives because you were afraid of the rowdy element. They are capable of anything.

If you feel strong enough I think besides the Drill Hall Meeting which is pretty sure to be broken up you should address one or two small open meetings. Every rowdy meeting rouses sympathy & brings votes & will especially as you have been so ill. Even in the rowdiest foulest place of all the people tho' abusive were really good-natured . . .

I am longing to see you & so is Dundee – I shall be heartbroken if you don't get in. I find what the people like best is the settlement of the Irish Question. So I trot that out & also your share in giving the Boers self government. The idea against you seems to be that you are a 'War Monger' but I am exhibiting you as a Cherub Peace Maker with little fluffy wings round your chubby face. I think the line is not so much 'Smash the Socialists' as to try with your great abilities to help in finding a solution of the Capital & Labour problem & I tell them that now you are free from the cares & labours of office you will have time to think that out & work for it in the next Parliament.

My darling, the misery here is appalling. Some of the people look absolutely starving. Morel's Election address just out *very moderate* & in favour of only constitutional methods. So one cannot compare him with Gallacher.

Your loving
Clemmie

On 11th November Winston himself arrived in Dundee for the last few days of the battle; he was barely convalescent, and delivered the greater part of his speeches sitting down. The meetings which he attended in these last stages of the campaign were particularly violent and noisy; the tide was flowing inexorably against him, and when the poll was announced on 15th November, Winston's massive majority had been swept away – Morel and Scrymgeour were overwhelmingly the victors. The national result gave the Conservatives a strong majority: in the Liberal Party there was a decisive verdict against Lloyd George but, more significant, the Labour

Party polled over four million votes compared with five and a half million for the Conservatives.

Winston and Clementine returned wearily to London. Freed from all public responsibilities, he could now at least plan a long convalescence; they took a villa in Cannes, and the whole family moved out there for Christmas and the New Year.

Winston was once again at a turning-point in his career, and while he painted in the winter sunshine, he no doubt pondered it all deeply. He had been a whole-hearted Coalitionist, and during the last months of the Lloyd George government he had striven unavailingly to perpetuate the Coalition spirit in the formation of a Centre Party, which would fuse together liberal/radical opinion to form an effective movement against the rising threat of Socialism. He now found himself a wanderer in a sort of political 'No Man's Land' between die-hard Conservatism and an enfeebled and disunited Liberal Party, whose faith and purpose seemed to have vanished. As the New Year opened Churchill was, as he later wrote of himself: '. . . without an office, without a seat, without a party, and without an appendix.'[8]

The dismal condition of the Liberal Party after the First World War was a source of bewilderment and dismay to many of its ardent supporters. The chasm between the two wings of the party could not be bridged, and after the fall of Lloyd George and the end of the Coalition, the Liberals found their popularity waning, while the Labour Party grew in strength. Winston continued to hope that the forces of anti-Socialism might be welded together effectively, and Clementine strongly approved of all his efforts to this end; but there was no way of preventing the new polarisation of Right and Left.

Churchill stood for the last time as a 'Liberal Free Trader' at West Leicester in 1923: he was defeated, and Asquith's subsequent decision to maintain a Socialist Government brought him to breaking-point with the Liberals. He could not, however, actually bring himself at this moment to re-join the Conservatives, and in March 1924 he stood as an 'Independent anti-Socialist' in a by-election in the Abbey Division of Westminster. Many prominent Conservatives supported him, and the campaign aroused much excitement. But it ended with Churchill being defeated by 43 votes. In the following June, Stanley Baldwin publicly abandoned his party's pledge to introduce Protective Tariffs; this removed the last great obstacle to Churchill's reconciliation with the Conservative Party.

In September 1924 Churchill was adopted by the West Essex (Epping) Conservative Association, and at the General Election following the fall of the Labour Government a month later, he won this seat with a handsome majority. He was to represent this constituency – later re-named the Wansted and Woodford Division for Essex – for forty years. The return of the Conservatives to power saw Standley Baldwin as Prime Minister, and the immediate return of Churchill to high office as Chancellor of the Exchequer from 1924 to 1929.

In all this logical sequence of thoughts and events, Clementine, dismayed by the plight of the Liberals, found herself broadly at one with Winston. But she did not want the Tory Party to win him back too easily. In February 1924, when his candidature for the Abbey by-election was being mooted, she was in the South of France, and Winston kept her closely informed about the situation at home.

Clementine was excited at the prospect of this new contest for him, assured as he would be of solid Conservative support. But in a letter on 24th February she sounded a note of warning:

> Do not however let the Tories get you too cheap – They have treated you so badly in the past & they ought to be made to feel it.

Later in the same letter she begged him not to stand

> unless you are reasonably sure of getting in – The movement inside the Tory Party to try & get you back is only just born & requires nursing & nourishing & educating to bring it to full strength. And there are of course counter influences as none of the Tory Leaders want you back as they see you would leap over their heads . . .

But in the by-election Clementine campaigned energetically for Winston, sending a personal letter to all the electors describing his twenty years of public service, and proudly proclaiming:

> With the single exception of Mr Lloyd George, no public man alive has been responsible for more important acts of social legislation than Mr Churchill . . .

In the three General Elections which took place between 1922 and 1924 Clementine also was ever in the thick of the fight. And when Winston reunited himself with the Conservative Party, she understood his political evolution, and followed his line of thought. Indeed, thereafter (as my mother told me) she herself did not vote Liberal again. But if with her reason Clementine may have 'crossed the floor of the House' with Winston, in her heart of hearts she remained to the end of her days a rather old-fashioned radical.

Winston recognised and respected this, and there is a charming story of how, in the late spring of 1924, when he was still in a transitional stage between parties, he addressed a purely Conservative rally in Liverpool; Clementine accompanied him and sat on the platform. After the meeting Winston told his hosts: 'She's a Liberal, and always has been. It's all very strange for her. But to me, of course, it's just like coming home.' [9]

It is interesting that despite the fact that Clementine was intensely politically aware and well-informed, and would have had ample opportunity to do so, she did not choose – either now or later – to play a more active or prominent role in politics than do most dutiful wives of Members of Parliament. She, in the main, confined her activity to Winston's own constituency, and rarely engaged in party politics at national or area level. This may have sprung in part from her natural shyness – all her life she was a very 'private' person; but one feels that her underlying radicalism and a latent, almost subconscious, hostility to Tories were also contributive reasons.

But within the bounds of the Epping Division Clementine worked hard, and was frequently in the constituency, opening bazaars, visiting schools for speech days, attending Conservative women's meetings, and taking a most active part in the work of the constituency Women's Advisory Committee. She nearly always accompanied Winston on his tours and visits, and her charm, her genuine interest in people and their lives, and her capacity for remembering names and faces (not one of Winston's conspicuous talents) endeared her to his supporters and workers and, over the years, built up a fund of love and loyalty for them both.

But although the support Clementine gave Winston in his public life was of great value, the real sphere of her influence and usefulness to him politically was in private, for the most part unseen, although not unrealised, by those who knew them both well. Her keen interest; her somewhat detached point of view and highly developed critical faculty; her lofty integrity – all made her a valuable counsellor. Winston trusted her completely, and although he might disagree with her views, he always wanted to know what they were. He showed Clementine the drafts of his speeches, although frequently her criticism caused him irritation, but the fact that he did not always (or even often) take her advice, was immaterial; the very fact that Clementine had the will, courage and capacity to battle with Winston in argument was an element throughout their life together of incalculable importance.

In one of Clementine's letters to Winston while he was at the front in 1916 she had described how Sir Ernest Cassel was 'much impressed by the purple of authority & office'.[10] This was never the case with her. She was no respecter of persons: indeed, she had a streak of 'inverted' snobbishness, and she was generally much warier, and much less trusting of people, than was Winston. But these characteristics were of immense relevance in her role as the wife of a man with a brilliant public career, lived in the main among the great and the powerful.

An example of Clementine's 'wariness' occurred in 1925 when Winston, as Chancellor of the Exchequer, was about to be involved in a struggle with Lord Beatty, the victor of Jutland, and now the First Sea Lord, over the Navy Estimates. She wrote warningly from Lou Sueil, where she was staying with the Balsans (Consuelo Balsan had previously been married to the Duke of Marlborough):

Now my lovely one – stand up to the Admiralty & don't be fascinated or flattered or cajoled by Beatty. I assure you the country doesn't care two pins about him. This may be very unfair to our only War Hero, but it's a fact. Consuelo tells me that he lunched here a little time ago. . . . & that he said 'I'm on my way home to fight my big battle with Churchill.' Consuelo said: 'Oh, I expect Winston will win all right –' to which Beatty retorted: 'I'm not so sure –' Of course I think it would be *not good* to score a sensational Winstonian triumph over your former love, but do not get sentimental & too soft hearted. Beatty is a tight little screw & he will bargain with you & cheat you as tho he were selling you a dud horse which is I fear what the Navy is.[11]

Winston in the event failed to win this tussle, for in 1927 Baldwin decided to accept Beatty's demands.

On one occasion, however, Clementine's judgment seems to have gone astray. While she was staying at the British Embassy in Rome in the spring of 1926, with Sir Ronald and Lady Graham, she briefly met Mussolini, who was then the leader of the Italian Fascist government, but was to become absolute ruler of Italy in November of that year. Clementine was at once aware that she was in the presence of a considerable personality; she wrote to Winston:

He is most impressive – quite simple & *natural*, very dignified, has a charming smile & the most beautiful golden brown piercing eyes which you see but can't look at. When he came in everyone (women too) got up as if he were a king – You couldn't help doing it. It seemed the natural thing to do . . . I had a few minutes talk with him – He sent you friendly messages & said he would like to meet you.[12]

After this tea-party, Mussolini sent Clementine a signed photograph, and she reported: 'All the Embassy ladies are dying of jealousy.'[13] Winston commented rather dryly on her description of this meeting:

> What a picture you draw of Mussolini! I feel sure you are right in regarding him as a prodigy. But as old Birrell says 'It is better to read about a world figure, than to live under his rule.'[14]

The photograph of the Duce stood for a short time in the drawing-room at Chartwell; but it was not long before it was banished for ever.

*

When Winston became Chancellor of the Exchequer they had moved into No. 11 Downing Street, selling the house in Sussex Square. 'Number Eleven' was then a charming house for a family, with the discreetly shared use of the 'Number Ten' garden. Clementine loved the house, and always remembered with pleasure the five years they lived there. The three elder children were passing through their teens; Diana made her debut and 'did' the London season from No. 11, and Chartwell provided the ideal solution for week-ends and holidays.

Churchill's tenure as Chancellor of the Exchequer was principally remembered for the Budget which returned Britain to the Gold Standard in April 1925. Although in retrospect Churchill was severely criticised for this policy, and various ills which subsequently afflicted Britain's economy were laid at its door, at the time the doctrine of the return to the Gold Standard found general acceptance among financial and economic pundits in all three parties.

In the following year a national crisis – the General Strike – brought Britain very near the precipitous edge of civil strife, when for nine days in May there was a nation-wide stoppage in transport, printing, heavy industry, gas and electricity. Hundreds of thousands of mainly middle-class volunteers kept the essential services and supplies going. There was amazingly little violence: but the General Strike shook the country to the core.

Churchill's principal role in this upheaval was to keep the nation informed, and a small team headed by himself and J. C. C. Davidson, a junior minister, produced an emergency newspaper called *The British Gazette*. It was the only newspaper to be published during the period of the Strike, and its circulation reached 2½ million. The tension and excitement of those days must have been intense, and once more Clementine found herself at the hub of the crisis. Her own role was to help to organise, with a group of friends, canteen arrangements for the teams of *British Gazette* workers at the printing office.

*

At the end of March 1925 Lady Blanche died; she was seventy-seven. Clementine was staying at Lou Sueil with the Balsans when she was sent for in haste, as her mother had been taken seriously ill. Both her daughters hurried to Dieppe to be with her, and kept vigil for the last days of her life. At Easter the previous year Clementine had spent two weeks with her mother, and had written a long letter to Winston, full of melancholy reflections:

> This is a sad old place & to me it is extraordinary that Mother should make it her home. To me it is haunted & decayed & melancholy. My sister Kitty died here of typhoid fever, & Bill is buried here in the cemetery at the top of the hill . . .
>
> It is extraordinary to reflect that if Mother had not on that first occasion come to Dieppe both Kitty & Bill might be alive today.
>
> I say Bill as well as Kitty, because it is here that Mother first began her regular gambling habits & it is here that Bill saw gambling from his childhood & used to come after he was grown up when on leave from his ship on week-end gambling expeditions.
>
> I went with Nellie to the Casino the other night & I was astounded at the reckless manner in which both Mother & Nellie gambled. Nellie very intelligently & dashingly, Mother in a superstitious and groping manner. It made me feel quite ill & ashamed to watch them & I went home to bed . . . Bill's grim & lonely end has not made the slightest difference – I don't feel I ought to criticize because gambling is not a temptation to me. It just seems to me a morbid mania . . .
>
> Mother who is getting very old & very feeble totters down every afternoon & plays – I believe only for an hour – But Bancos 2000 francs again & again without turning a hair . . .[15]

For the twenty-five years during which Lady Blanche had lived for the greater part of the time in Dieppe, she was one of the most colourful members of the British colony there, and many stories survive of her eccentric and sometimes malicious ways, though her charm and originality earned her many friends. Her gambling propensities aroused much speculation, for although she was known to be badly off, she never borrowed money from her friends. She owned two charming houses in the rue des Fontaines: St Antoine and Petit St Antoine (which was the converted coach house across the small garden), but Lady Blanche economised by letting the St Antoines, herself living for months on end in a modest hotel or pension. In this way she spent only about half of her income, leaving the rest for gambling. Indeed, when she died she was living in a hotel on the sea front, within easy walking distance of the Casino.

Despite the many difficulties which beset her, Lady Blanche had an unquenchably gay and gallant spirit, and throughout her life she was fascinating to men. Nellie shared many of her mother's characteristics, but Clementine, although inheriting much of her mother's elegance and fastidiousness, was too unlike her in character and temperament for there to have been any real degree of closeness between them. Also in earlier years the knowledge that Kitty had been her mother's idolised favourite came between them, albeit unbidden, like a shadow. But with her marriage to Winston, her relationship with her mother had improved; Lady Blanche had taken to him from the start, and between her and her son-in-law there grew up a mutual regard and affection, and she believed unwaveringly in his ability and destiny. Now, as she lay dying, Winston wrote warmly and movingly of her to Clementine:

> Yr Mamma is a gt woman: & her life has been a noble life. When I think of all the courage & tenacity & self denial that she showed during the long hard years when she was fighting to bring up you & Nellie & Bill, I feel what a true mother & grand woman she proved herself, & I am the more glad & proud to think her blood flows in the veins of our children.
>
> My darling I grieve for you . . . the loss of a mother severs a chord in the heart and makes life seem lonely & its duration fleeting. I know the sense of amputation from my own experience three years ago . . .
>
> I greatly admired & liked yr mother. She was an ideal mother-in-law. Never shall I allow that relationship to be spoken of with mockery – for her sake. I am pleased to think that perhaps she wd also have given me a good character. At any rate I am sure our marriage & life together were one of the gt satisfactions of her life.[16]

★

In May 1929 there was a General Election, and Clementine as usual took an active part in the campaign, enthusiastically assisted by her children – Randolph, aged eighteen, speaking at a meeting, and Diana, Sarah and I (now nearly seven) sporting our father's election colours in our hats. At this election the Conservatives failed to achieve an overall majority, and Mr Baldwin resigned, preferring to go into opposition rather than form a coalition with the Liberals, who held the balance between the Labour and Conservative parties; Mr Ramsay MacDonald formed his second Labour Government, depending upon the Liberals for survival. Winston therefore ceased to be Chancellor of the Exchequer early in June, and they had yet again to move house; but now they had Chartwell as a base to which to retreat.

Clementine had been gravely ill with mastoid in 1928, and since then she had suffered recurring bouts of ill-health; and only a month after the General Election, she had to undergo another operation – this time for tonsils. She had her operation in the first week of July, full of hope that she would be able to go with Winston a month later on a tour of Canada and the United States, which he had planned to make now that he was freed from ministerial office. It would have been a cheerful party, for as well as Winston and Clementine, Randolph, and Jack Churchill and his elder son Johnny were also to go on the journey.

But to Clementine's bitter disappointment she was not sufficiently recovered to go, and was left behind in a low and forlorn state. From the *Empress of Australia* on his first day out at sea, Winston wrote to her:

> . . . All departures from home even on pleasure are sad. The vessel drifts away from the shore & an ever-widening gulf opens between one and the citadel of ones life & soul. But most of all I was distressed to think of you being lonely & unhappy & left behind. My dearest it wd have been madness for you to face this rocketting

journey until you had regained full normal strength. This I trust & pray may be the result of 6 or 7 weeks of real quietness & calm . . .[17]

A few days later, one day out from Quebec, he wrote her a lively account of the voyage, but ended:

My darling I have been rather sad at times thinking of you in low spirits at home. Do send me some messages. I love you so much & it grieves me to feel you are lonely.[18]

Clementine was not quite deserted, however, having her three daughters at home – two of whom were of a highly companionable age. Diana (now twenty) spent much time with her mother this summer. They paid a visit to Dieppe, staying with Nellie, to whom Lady Blanche had bequeathed the St Antoines. Gradually both health and spirits improved, and Clementine made plans to go to Italy later in October.

The news from the travellers in Canada and then America had been good, Randolph and Winston sharing the task of keeping Clementine and the family at home fed with accounts of their movements and doings. Interspersed among the lively accounts Winston gave of their travels were mentions of money matters.

The markets were booming, and even before he left England Winston had (on very sound advice) been indulging in speculation in the American stock market. These operations had reaped a most satisfactory harvest, and he reported all this to Clementine when he wrote to her from Santa Barbara, California on 19th September. In addition, advance payment on his life of Marlborough, royalties from his other books and fees for various articles and lectures, all combined to make the financial horizon brighter than it had been for some years, despite the loss of his ministerial salary. Winston set it all out for his careful 'Kat' on a single page, adding: 'So we have really recovered in a few weeks a small fortune . . .'

Since his departure, Clementine had been making arrangements for their London life that autumn and winter, and the current idea was that they should rent Venetia Montagu's house. In the same letter in which Winston set out their finances so clearly for Clementine, he wrote approvingly of the plans she had been making:

I am glad you are taking Venetia's house for the session. Do not hesitate to engage one or two extra servants. Now that we are in opposition we must gather colleagues & M.P.s together a little at lunch & dinner, also I have now a few business people who are of importance. We ought to be able to have lunches of 8–10 often, & dinners of the same size about twice a week. You should have a staff equal to this.[19]

The outlook seemed rosy.

Winston and his party spent three weeks in California, and then they continued their journeyings through Arizona, and via the Grand Canyon to Chicago. From there they went to New York, where they were the guests of Bernard Baruch, the American financier and speculator who became an elder statesman, and whose long friendship with Winston had started in 1918 when he was Minister of Munitions and Baruch a Commissioner on the American War Industries Board.

Clementine had fulfilled her holiday plan to go with Diana to Italy; they had a lovely time staying both in Rome and Florence. Clementine was in good spirits and fully restored in her health and looking forward to the return of the other travellers. Early in October Randolph and Johnny left Winston to return to Oxford, and they brought her good news from New York. Winston's letters and cables continued to be couched in buoyant terms. He sailed for home on 30th October.

It had been a long separation, and Clementine went to the station to welcome Winston home on 5th November. But the joy of their meeting was marred. Nothing had prepared her for the bad news he bore, and could not withhold from her for an instant. There and then, on the platform, Winston told her that he had lost a small fortune in the Great Crash of the American Stock Market, which had taken place during the last week of October.

It must have seemed a long, long cry from the elation and excitement they had both felt when Winston had received his windfall inheritance in 1921, and Clementine had written of the 'blessed feeling of relief that we need never be worried about money again . . .'[20] Through the succeeding years, the inheritance had been eroded – by Chartwell, which so typically turned out to cost much more than had been calculated, and also by their ample way of life.

But although this financial disaster had befallen him in the markets, Winston had, during his stay in the United States, signed contracts for articles in weekly magazines which would earn him £40,000. He could, as he had always done, keep them all by his pen and his prodigious industry, but the loss of such a capital sum was a body blow. They retreated to lick their wounds at Chartwell, where a regime of stringent economies was promulgated. As for their London life, for a year or two they either took furnished houses for a few months at a time, or, with more economy and convenience, stayed at the Goring Hotel near Victoria Station.

CHARTWELL

EVER SINCE they had sold Lullenden at the end of 1919, Winston and Clementine had cherished the hope of once more possessing a 'country basket'. Winston's inheritance from his Vane-Tempest cousin in 1921 brought the dream within the realm of possibility. They both kept their eyes and ears open, and studied details of houses and even small estates coming on the market. Winston's ideas were braver and larger than Clementine's, envisaging a farm as well as a house and garden. But although she too longed for a country retreat, she was more cautious, and their only experience of farming at Lullenden had frightened her off another such venture. She had put her point of view to Winston in a letter in July 1921:

> . . . Darling let us beware of risking our newly come fortune in operations which we do not understand & have not the time to learn & to practise when learnt. Politics are absolutely engrossing to you really, or *should* be, & now you have Painting for your Leisure & Polo for excitement & danger.
>
> I long for a country home but I would like it to be a rest and joy Bunny not a fresh preoccupation.
>
> I do think that if we really *lived* in the country it would be the greatest fun & also a life occupation to own & develop so varied a property. I should simply love it, but it would be engrossing & to make a success of it would need real hard work & concentration & just now I am for relaxation –
>
> I want to lie in the sun & blink & wake up now & then to eat a mouse caught by someone else & drink a little cream & doze off again . . .[1]

In July 1921 Winston saw a property near Westerham in Kent, about twenty-five miles from London, called Chartwell Manor. It had belonged to the Campbell Colquhoun family since the middle of the nineteenth century.

The house itself was unprepossessing and dilapidated, but it stood on a hill commanding wide and beautiful views over the Weald of Kent. Before it to the southward a valley falls dramatically away, and in the bottom is a lake, fed by a spring – the Chart Well. Winston was at once captivated by the beauty of the view, and quickly grasped the possibilities of the lie of the land, and of the private source of crystal water. On the far side of the valley the park-like fields slope up to a wide belt of beeches which mark the boundary of the property and cast sheltering arms about the valley to the north and east. This beautiful place, which combines a feeling of space and liberation with a sense of almost secret seclusion, cast at once and forever its spell over Winston.

Thrilled with his discovery, he hastened to show it to Clementine, whose first reaction was enthusiastic. From Fairlawne (which was in the same neighbourhood), where she was staying with the Cazalets for a tennis party, she wrote:

> I can think of nothing but that heavenly tree-crowned hill – it is like a view from an aeroplane being up there.
>
> I do hope we shall get it – If we do I feel we shall live there a great deal & be very very happy.[2]

But a closer and more thoughtful inspection of the house and property quickly moderated her first impression. The house frankly appalled her. It was a grey Victorian mansion, built round, and on the site of a much older house; hemmed in by noisome laurels, it was damp, dreary and ugly. These surface defects, however, she could have coped with, but she had detected a major, and unalterable fault. Although to the south lies such a wide and pleasing prospect, the house had been built facing west, on the extreme edge of the property, and only eighty yards from the public road. From the other side of this road rose up a steep, wooded bank, which dominated the house, and effectively screened it from the afternoon sunshine. The bank was a mass of wild rhododendrons, which in the spring formed a cataract of mauve and purple. Unfortunately, these were colours which Clementine particularly disliked; moreover, neither the overshadowing trees nor the rhododendrons could ever be banished, as they were not part of the property, but were on common land. Another disadvantage which Clementine spotted was that a public right of way ran right through the garden, slicing it inconveniently in two, and diminishing its privacy.

Clementine saw at once that in order to correct (for to cure was impossible) the faults inherent in the siting and aspect of the house, it would be necessary to all intents and purposes to rebuild it. But Winston was blind to the drawbacks, and deaf to reason. It was as effective to point out to him these radical faults, and to calculate the enormous cost and difficulty of correcting them, as it is to tell a man who is in love that the object of his affections has bandy legs or rabbit teeth.

However, Clementine's strong and sustained opposition to buying Chartwell had a delaying effect. Indeed, for some time nothing more was said about the project, and she assumed that, however unwillingly, he had accepted her arguments and abandoned the whole project. But he had done no such thing: he had merely 'gone to ground' for the time being. Winston was absolutely determined to acquire Chartwell. He was sure the difficulties could be dismissed or surmounted, and that Clementine would come to see this beautiful valley as the place of enchantment it was for him, and that together they would make there a home where they and their children would find happiness and contentment.

During the course of fifty-seven years of marriage, Winston and Clementine often had disagreements. On many occasions he disregarded her advice, or took a course which was contrary to her wishes, but the purchase of Chartwell was the only issue over which Clementine felt Winston had acted with less than candour towards her. The subject was hardly mentioned again between them during the ensuing year, which was to prove full of events which obliterated other thoughts and plans. It was the year of heavy tidings, culminating with the death of Marigold; and then, after those desolate days, came the hope and expectation of another child.

It was about the middle of September 1922, just after the birth of Mary, that Winston suddenly swept the three elder children off for a 'mystery' expedition to the country. On the way down in the car he told them that he was taking them to see a house he was thinking of buying, and he wanted to know what they thought of it. Sarah has described their first impressions:

> Chartwell was wildly overgrown and untidy, and contained all the mystery of houses that had not been lived in for many years. We did a complete tour of the house and grounds, my father asking anxiously – it is still clear in my mind – 'Do you like it?' Did we like it? We were delirious. 'Oh, do buy it! Do buy it!' we exclaimed. 'Well, I'm not sure. . . .' He kept us in anxious suspense.[3]

It was not until they had nearly reached home that Winston told them that he had already bought it. The children were ecstatic.

Perhaps he thought their unbounded enthusiasm would carry the day with Clementine; but when he confessed to her that he had, without further consulting her views, made an offer for the house – she was frankly devastated. After short negotiations the house and eighty acres were bought for £5,000.

Winston was not indifferent to Clementine's feelings in this matter – on the contrary, he longed for her approval over this major step in their life. But he never doubted that he could bring her to share his enthusiasm for the place which had so captivated him, and which he was sure would make a perfect home for them all. Everything, he assured her, would be done to transform the house according to her wishes; difficulties and defects would melt away like morning dew: his confidence and enthusiasm were boundless and touching.

But he made a long-term strategic error. In all the forty years Chartwell was to be their home, Clementine never came to love the place as did Winston. For her, the beauty of the valley, the eventual charm and comfort of the house, and the possibilities of the garden, never outweighed the worries and difficulties of running the house and property. Moreover, her gloomy prophecies of the cost of making it the delightful home it became were more than fulfilled.

Clementine's fundamental and continuing disapproval of the whole Chartwell project form a very important factor in her life from this time on. She accepted the *fait accompli*, and, indeed, tried very hard to love the place which so enthralled Winston. She worked like a Trojan to make it the home and haven for us all that he dreamed of. But it never acquired for her the nature of a venture shared; rather, it was an extra duty, gallantly undertaken, and doggedly carried through.

Had Clementine come to love Chartwell, and had it been the fulfilment of some of her dreams and wishes, she might have found, despite all the drawbacks, contentment and release from pressure there, and found pleasure in all those domestic and garden pursuits which hold a compelling charm for so many Englishwomen. But although Chartwell was to be her principal home for the next forty years, she never became deeply attached to the place; although she devoted time, thought and energy on both the house and the garden, making both charming, and leaving her own 'stamp' upon them.

But for Winston, Chartwell represented sheer pleasure, occupation and happiness: from the very first days when he was slaughtering laurels and building dams, or later when he was constructing walls and cottages. It became his workshop – his 'factory' – whence poured his books and articles, which alone kept Chartwell and the whole fabric of our family life going. Here he found endless subjects to paint; here his friends and colleagues, and emissaries from afar foregathered. Here he planned his political forays, and here he retreated to relish his victories, or to lick his political wounds.

Chartwell never failed him in good times or in bad. Not even in the last sad years when, silent and remote from us all, he would sit for hours in the golden sunshine of the summer days, gazing out over his enchanted valley and lakes; down over the lushly green and tufted Wealden landscape beyond, which melts at last into the faint blue-grey line of the South Downs.

*

Once Clementine had accepted the situation, she determined to make the very best of it, despite her deep-seated foreboding that they had bitten off more than they could chew. The first essential was to find a good, practical architect, combining withal an imaginative approach. Their choice fell upon Mr Philip Tilden, who was well recommended to them. He had worked for Sir Philip Sassoon at Port Lympne in Kent, and also for Winston's aunt, Lady Leslie; and he was currently working upon a house at Churt in Surrey for Lloyd George.

Mr Tilden's opinion of the house was much the same as Clementine's. His trained eye saw the disadvantages of its natural aspect, but he was at one with them both in admiring the setting and the prospect. However, his greatest concern (which was amply justified) was the sinister presence of dry rot. But even his professional skill did not estimate how deep were its inroads upon the oldest part of the building.

It is sad to record that although they worked (or struggled) together for a number of years, the Churchills' intercourse with Mr Tilden became increasingly strained and acrimonious. One cause of dissatisfaction was the recurrence of the dry rot which had so permeated the original fabric that its total eradication proved a lengthy and expensive affair. It would be unprofitable to recite the tale of reproach, sufficient perhaps merely to recall that the history of the relationship between architects and their patrons is a notably stormy one. A precedent certainly existed in the Churchill family in the explosive exchanges maintained over a long period of years between Sarah, Duchess of Marlborough and Sir John Vanbrugh over the building of Blenheim Palace.

The autumn and early winter of 1922 had been singularly exhausting for both Winston and Clementine. But after the General Election, liberated as he then was from both ministerial and parliamentary obligations, Winston determined to make the most of this unexpected lease of freedom and he swept the whole family off to the South of France. They let Sussex Square and took a delightful house, the Villa Rêve d'Or, perched high on the hillside above Cannes.

There for several months they enjoyed a sunlit and carefree existence. Winston wrote and painted to his heart's content, fully recovering his health after his operation for appendicitis; and Clementine, recovered from baby Mary's birth, indulged to the full her enthusiasm for playing tennis; indeed, she and her partner won the local tournament. The older children had to return to England for school, but came out to France again for the Easter holidays. Winston made several journeys to London to attend to his personal affairs, and to visit Chartwell to discuss with the architect the plans which were now taking shape.

After one such visit at the end of January, Winston wrote a full report to Clementine. The chief challenge confronting the architect was to turn the whole 'sense' of the house through ninety degrees, so as to have the full benefit of the wonderful view and the southern aspect. It was proposed therefore to build out on the southern side of the original house a large four-storeyed wing. The west frontage of the house was to be extended on both sides of the core of the old house. It was proposed to make full use of the good interior features of the oldest part of the former house, which, when later additions had been stripped away, revealed some fine beamed ceilings.

Reporting to Clementine, Winston described in detail how these plans were taking shape; he mentioned an improved pantry-kitchen arrangement, the plans for the linen and box rooms, and other important domestic features. Tilden had conceived an idea for an additional reception room, which would be

in the direct line of the drawing room and the boudoir. When the doors are opened all through, the length of these three rooms will be over 80 feet. Tilden is very keen on this. It undoubtedly makes a very fine sweep,[4]

wrote Winston. 'The Chartwell plans sound charming,' Clementine replied a day or two later.

I hope in the new Tower arrangement the 'sewing room' has not been eliminated? . . . Tell Mr Tilden the Sewing-room should be as large and *nice* as the Lingerie here as 2 or 3 maids will sit and sew there every day.

The extra Reception room making a vista of 80 feet sounds very lovely and grand. We must have a State Festival there![5]

(Can one detect a gentle note of irony in the last sentence?)

It must have been somewhat frustrating for Clementine to be out of direct control of the plans, and she was evidently pondering over them in a good deal of detail. 'I have been thinking about that extra sitting-room,' she wrote a few days later,

. . . It is *most* tempting to do this, but I fear the result will be to introduce into modern Chartwell the inconveniences of so many lovely old houses i.e. a wrong balance of living & sleeping accommodation. Without this extra room we already have ample living accommodation for ourselves & our potential 5 or 6 guests. We each of us have our private sitting-room, the children have Day Nursery & Schoolroom, there is an office for business, and for the entertainment of the few guests there are 2 very beautiful rooms, the Drawing-room & the Library . . .

Also an extra sitting-room means more furniture, more fires, more flowers & *more* housemaiding. I do not want to have more than 2 housemaids at Chartwell . . .[6]

Clementine's eloquent plea won this particular argument, and the additional sitting-room was not embarked upon.

All these details read somewhat curiously half a century later, when even wealthy people are constantly preoccupied with 'shrinking' their houses, and diminishing their way of life. The plans for Chartwell as discussed in these letters sound dazzling, not to say grandiose. But then, even the cautious Clementine thought the possible five or six guests 'a few', and while counselling against any *folie de grandeur*, accepted as quite normal the proposed basic accommodation.

When they left the Villa Rêve d'Or and returned home in the early summer, Clementine went down to Chartwell to wrestle with the problems on the spot. In order to be able to supervise the work constantly, and to provide some country life for them all during the summer holidays, Winston took a house on the outskirts of Westerham called 'Hosey Rigge' (soon, of course, re-christened 'The Rosy Pig'). The children spent most of their time at Chartwell, and were blissfully happy discovering the glorious possibilities for every kind of activity and game which the wild and open gardens and grounds provided; Winston made a wonderful tree house for them in the great lime in the front drive. Although the house was far from ready for occupation, the stables were in action, and Winston's polo-ponies had taken up residence, so the children could ride as well.

As the work on Chartwell progressed, the inevitably mounting cost of the alterations and the prospect of how much it would cost to run the house and garden preyed heavily on Clementine's mind. Winston sought to reassure her:

My beloved, I do beg you not to worry about money, or to feel insecure. On the contrary the policy we are pursuing aims above all at *stability* (like Bonar Law!) Chartwell is to be our *home*. It will have cost us £20,000 and will be worth at least £15,000 apart from a fancy price. We must endeavour to live there for many years & hand it on to Randolph afterwards. We must make it in every way charming & as far as possible economically self contained. It will be cheaper than London . . .

Eventually – though there is no hurry – we must sell Sussex [Square] & find a small flat for you and me . . . If we go into office we will live in Downing Street!

He was confident that the literary projects he had under way would see the work at Chartwell finished and leave them with six or seven months living in hand, and he ended with an endearing plea:

Add to this my darling yr courage & good will and I am certain that we can make

ourselves a permanent resting place, so far as the money side of this uncertain &
transitory world is concerned.

But if you set yourself against Chartwell, or lose heart, or bite your bread &
butter & yr pig then it only means further instability, recasting of plans & further
expense & worry.[7]

Progress on the house seemed maddeningly slow during the winter, but after the
usual delays and discouragements which always seem to attend house-building
operations, the alterations and additions to Chartwell gradually neared completion.
But it was not until the Easter holidays of 1924 that they were able to move in, and
then only in 'camping' style. Winston and the children formed the advance guard
who first took possession of Chartwell, for Clementine was staying with her mother
in Dieppe.

Winston had persuaded her to spend a restful Easter with Lady Blanche, as she
was thoroughly exhausted, not only by the constant prodding over a long period that
had been required to get Chartwell to an even barely habitable state, but also by the
efforts and excitements of the Abbey Division by-election which had just taken
place. Nonetheless her absence at a moment which most women would regard as
crucial, and requiring their personal participation and close supervision, seems highly
significant. One cannot but feel that the real reason for her absence from the move-in
to Chartwell lay deeper than fatigue, however genuine. Somewhere deep down, her
basic mistrust and disbelief in the 'Chartwell dream' must have played its part in
allowing Winston to persuade her to have a holiday at this moment.

Winston himself slept at Chartwell for the first time on 17th April, and that night
he wrote to Clementine:

My Darling,
    This is the first letter I have ever written from this place, & it is right that it shd
be to you. I am in bed in your bedroom (wh I have annexed temporarily) & wh
is sparsely but comfortably furnished with the pick of yr two van loads.

They had had two glorious days moving in, and he reported that the children had
'worked like blacks'. He went on to describe the various activities which were in
progress both in the house and garden and, bursting into verse, declared:

> Only one thing lack these banks of green –
> The Pussy Cat who is their Queen . . .

Winston was thrilled by the spaciousness of the rooms.

You cannot imagine the size of these rooms till you put furniture into them. This
bedroom of yours is a magnificent aerial bower. Come as soon as you feel well
enough to share it.

Clementine's visit to Dieppe was not a happy one. She was utterly exhausted; she
found Dieppe full of unhappy memories, and her mother was now ageing visibly.
And part of her must have longed to be sharing with Winston and the children the

first moments in their new home, into which she had poured so much thought and energy. On 21st April she wrote to Winston rather wistfully:

16 rue des Fontaines
Dieppe
April 21st [1924]

My Darling Winston

I was so much delighted to get your long letter describing all that you are doing at Chartwell. I read it again & again & it made me long to be with you there.

If we are able in the future to live happily & peacefully there it will make up for all the effort you have poured out for it.

I have had sweet letters from all the children. They are blissfully happy. They will get to love it very much & it would be sad to have to part with it. I will do everything I can to help you to keep it . . .

I am not enjoying this, but I am resting – I find I am enormously & unbelievably tired & the strong air makes me drunk with sleep . . .

Despite Clementine's avowal of regret for her absence from Winston and the Chartwell scene at this moment, and the hope she expresses for a long and happy future there, and her touching pledge of personal endeavour, one seems to detect almost a feeling of detachment from it all – as if she herself was a mere onlooker in this important new aspect of their life together.

*

Despite the deep-seated reservations Clementine had from the first about Chartwell, she was never one to 'drag her feet', and there are few women who do not enjoy 'doing-up' a house. Clementine relied on her own good taste and straightforward sense of practicality, rather than employ a professional decorator, which she would have regarded as a gross extravagance. Even when she could afford them, she always loathed contrived effects. The rooms on view at Chartwell today faithfully reflect her simple, unaffected taste, which relied on clear, clean colours, chintzes with bold flower designs, which well suited the large, rather gaunt rooms, and charming pieces of furniture either inherited or picked up 'for a song'. An exception to this was the long, low dining-room with its arcaded windows looking out over the valley and lakes, where the unstained oak tables and chairs were made to special order by Heal's; while the great rush carpets were also specially woven. The curtains here were a brilliant plain green.

The fashion then was for plain painted walls (the era of dizzy and dazzling wall-papers belonging to a later generation, and at that time one found them – ravishing dimity and flowery ones – in the servants' bedrooms). At Chartwell in the early twenties there were acres of palest cream paint (which went very well with the old beams), a pale blue for the sitting-room, and exquisite cerulean blue for Clementine's barrel-domed bedroom, where her four-poster bed covered in tomato-coloured moiré silk looked lovely and sensational.

The scale of the garden always somewhat daunted Clementine, and shortage of labour was a perennial problem. She had a destructive element in her approach to trees – no trees were better than trees she did not like; and the Chartwell valley was never planted or re-planted to a consistent plan. But her taste in shrubs and flowers was exquisite: occasionally she became ambitious and launched out on a glade of *Lilium giganteum*, or a great planting of meconopsis: but these did not survive, and no trace remains. In the grey-walled rose garden, however, her taste and preferences are faithfully preserved. It was originally drawn up by the orderly-minded Venetia Montagu (a very good gardener herself), and the pattern of the beds has hardly changed. A central feature were the four standard wistarias. Round the sides of the rose garden were borders which were a jumble of plants and shrubs in soft colours; cherry-pie, pentstemons, catmint, *Lilium regale*, ceanothus and fuchsias, and paeonies. The walls everywhere were clad with roses and clematis; while the pergola leading from the stone loggia to the rose garden was draped with vines.

But Clementine had no pretensions to be a plants-woman; she only liked beautiful or fragrant plants, and was totally uninterested in obscure rarities. And the vogue for old-fashioned roses, grey-leaved plants and one-colour borders had not yet arrived.

Beyond the water garden was an azalea glade – which smelt heavenly, and in which there was not one distressing puce or orange. Above the goldfish pool was perhaps her one 'contrived effect' – a mass planting of blue anchusa and white foxgloves. It is still faithfully perpetuated.

*

'Living off the land' and 'being self-sufficient' are phrases which have a compelling charm to many, and more especially to those with the least practical experience of country life. Winston was no exception, and no sooner were they installed at Chartwell than he launched out with enthusiasm upon farming activities. They were to prove (as they had done at Lullenden) on the whole unsuccessful and very costly. Neither Winston nor Clementine knew the first thing about farming or stock, and she regarded all this with the utmost apprehension. Cows, sheep, pigs and chickens were all tried in turn, and Winston's letters to her were full of accounts of the births and deaths of the livestock and the other events, mostly dramatic and disastrous, which attended the obscure lives of these domestic animals.

And apart from livestock which might be deemed useful, and hopefully profitable, there was an ever-changing population of pets. The black Australian swans were much prized by Winston, and he went to endless trouble (and expense) to protect them from the depredations of foxes, as he did the ruddy sheldrakes and the exquisitely enamelled Carolina ducks. One of my bottle-fed lambs remained on into dreary and bad-tempered adulthood, and was only banished when it tactlessly butted Winston himself (to our secret delight). The marmalade cat was greatly beloved, and when he died in a week of heavy news during the war, Clementine would not allow Winston to be told until things looked brighter. The golden orfe lurked mysteriously in the water garden – a luscious prey for herons, and the subject of one of Winston's most beautiful pictures.

The expense of the original alterations to Chartwell, and the cost of living there, fully justified Clementine's gloomiest prognostications. Rather less than a year after

they moved into Chartwell they were seriously discussing the advantages of letting
it for a few months every year. Winston was offered eighty guineas a week to rent
the house, and Clementine suggested that they could

> establish the children in a comfortable but economical hotel near Dinard, go
> there ourselves for part of the time & travel about painting for you, sight seeing
> for me, or we could go to Tours & do the 'Chateaux' again – And we could go to
> Florence & Venice.[8]

It seems unlikely that this would have been an economically sound project, and
probably for that reason Chartwell was never in fact let, although the idea was mooted
again the following year.

In 1926 a crisis point was reached in the economy of Chartwell, and two long
memoranda survive, one from Clementine and one from Winston, proposing
economies. Winston had been toying with the idea of building a dairy and 'going
into milk'. Clementine viewed this idea with the utmost dismay, and in April she
wrote seven pages of cogent argument which not only covered the undesirability of
changing from beef to milk but reminded him of the troubles they had already
experienced.

> . . . you will remember that the chickens and the chicken houses got full of red
> mite and vermin; and you will also remember that one sow was covered with
> lice.[9]

Winston himself was alarmed by the general level of expenditure, and in September 1926 he addressed a memorandum to Clementine containing fourteen points
covering every aspect of household and farm administration. Chartwell was to be let
the following summer; the cattle and pigs and all but two of the ponies were to be
sold; the family was to remain in one place for longer periods, and during the winter
would only visit Chartwell for 'picnics with hampers'.

'Item 14' was headed 'BILLS', and covered everything domestic from the wines
and cigars to be offered at meals and the number of courses, down to the amount of
boot polish used and the number of clean evening shirts Winston should wear each
week. Visitors too were to be rationed: 'We must invite visitors very rarely, if at all,
other than Jack and Goonie . . .'

Like all dogmatic manifestos which fly in the face of natural desires and instincts,
this ruthless document was considerably modified. The family, it is true, spent the
greater part of that winter in London, but over Christmas and the New Year eleven
people signed the Visitors' Book at Chartwell. Some of the 'reforms' were carried
out, however; no more was heard of dairy cattle, and the ponies and the groom
disappeared. The pigs diminished in number (only to increase again shortly through
natural causes). Henceforward the farming activities at Chartwell were on a more
modest scale.

There were to be other years of acute economic strain, notably after the Wall
Street Crash in 1929, when Winston suffered such a great financial loss. To meet
this crisis, Chartwell was run down to a very low ebb that winter; Winston's study
being the only room left open in the house, so that he could work at week-ends.

Clementine mostly stayed in London (they had taken Venetia Montagu's house). Winston would come down mostly alone at week-ends and join me and my governess in the small house he had recently built overlooking the kitchen garden. Originally intended for a married butler, this charming house (Wellstreet) became a useful retreat in this 'slump' period. Later it was let until the war to Horatia Seymour, Clementine's great friend, and now it belongs to the National Trust and is the home of the Chartwell Administrator.

But Winston found it very difficult to economise for long, and lean times were followed by expansionist periods. From the day he bought Chartwell he engaged on operations of various kinds, a large number of which he aided or achieved with his own hands. Starting with damming a small stream to make two lakes connected by a waterfall, he progressed to make a swimming-pool. These ambitious works were the cause of endless vexation, with leaking dams and slipping banks; for Winston had a propensity for constructing lakes or pools on the sides of hills or slopes, thus ever contradicting the law of nature – that water flows downhill. Between 1929 and 1932 he built, largely with his own hands, the greater part of the red-brick wall which enclosed the vegetable garden, including in it a charming one-roomed cottage for Sarah and me. He also constructed a vast woodshed, the filling of which gave him extra employment in the form of cutting down and uprooting trees.

But all these wonderful works required extra manpower at one stage or another. Since Clementine greatly deplored her gardeners being whisked off to assist in these labours, the extra help had to be hired – at additional expense. A letter from Clementine to Margery Street ('Streetie'), their secretary for many years, who went to Australia in the spring of 1933, gives a rather rueful account of expensive constructional works later that year:

> Mr. Pug as usual is working hard not only at his Book but he is rapidly converting the whole valley at Chartwell into a Rock Garden. It's rather alarming & the 'outdoor economies' have gone West as you can imagine. The fat boy now earns 35/- a week & Kurn is a permanence & there are 2 other men who have been there 6 weeks.[10]

Kurn, who had originally been engaged on a temporary basis, had indeed 'become a permanence' – he was still employed at Chartwell twenty-five years later!

*

Winston and Clementine's first recorded house-party was in late June 1924, when Nellie and Goonie were the 'guinea-pigs'. Thereafter week-end parties of three to five people became the usual pattern, and since Chartwell was only an hour's drive from London, guests frequently came down for luncheon, returning during the late afternoon. Winston and Clementine were on the best of terms with their immediate neighbours whose properties marched with Chartwell, and the family had agreeable contacts with the Astors at Hever, where Winston often painted, with the Sidneys at Penshurst, and the Cazalets at Fairlawne near Tonbridge.

Looking through the Chartwell Visitors' Book one is immediately struck by the constant repetition of the same names. The 'stayers' were nearly all from the close family circle of the Jack Churchills and the Romillys, with their respective children, and Venetia Montagu and her sister, Sylvia Henley; or from that tight little band of faithful friends and colleagues (past or present) whose composition altered so little over the course of years.

But if it was, on the whole, a small, select group who came and went at Chartwell – it was an intensely brilliant and diverse one. Centred on politics, it included such varied personalities as the Birkenheads, Brendan Bracken, Bob Boothby, the Duff Coopers, the Archie Sinclairs, the Cranbornes (later Salisbury), Max Beaverbrook, the Camroses (he was proprietor of the *Daily Telegraph*), the Bonham Carters and Lloyd George. Bernard Baruch, the American financier-cum-statesman, never failed to pay a visit when over in Europe.

Among the regulars, science was represented by 'The Prof' (Professor F. A. Lindemann, erstwhile Director of the Physical Laboratory of the Royal Aircraft Factory at Farnborough). And letters and learning by Eddie Marsh – of the bushy eyebrows and the slate-squeak voice – whose appearances as a perennial and faithful Private Secretary heretofore in this account have masked his qualities as a delightful companion, and his brilliant achievements in classics and in belles lettres (notably his translations of the Odes of Horace and the Fables of la Fontaine). Through all these years he was building up an astonishing collection of pictures, which plastered the walls of his tiny house in Walton Street. He was a Trustee of the Tate Gallery, and a Chairman of the Contemporary Art Society. On his death he bequeathed his pictures to the National Gallery, the Tate, and other collections.

The classics, romance and adventure came, all three, in the person of the intense and strange Lawrence of Arabia. He would arrive on his (alas fatal) motor-bicycle as Aircraftman Shaw, and descend to dinner – to the amazed wonderment of my childish eyes – in the robes of a Prince of Arabia.

Over the years Winston's growing and enduring passion for painting brought artists. The Laverys who had started him off came quite often in the earlier Chartwell days. And then, after twenty-five years, an old friend of Clementine's – Mr Sickert – made a sudden reappearance in her life. In June 1927 she had the misfortune to be knocked down by a bus in the Brompton Road; although she only suffered from shock and severe bruising, the mishap was reported in the newspapers, and a few days afterwards Mr Sickert called at No. 11 Downing Street anxious to know how she was faring. Clementine was delighted to see him again after so many years, and Winston and he took instantly to each other. The Sickerts thereafter came on several occasions to stay at Chartwell, and he took a lively and most helpful interest in Winston's painting.

Paul Maze, the ebullient and well-known French painter, who had met Winston first on the western front, and who had the distinction of holding the D.C.M. and the M.M., as well as the Croix de Guerre and Légion d'Honneur, came a good deal to Chartwell in the mid-thirties.

Dearly loved by us all was William Nicholson, a most charming companion and friend; dubbed the 'Cher Maître', he was a family favourite. He had been commissioned by some of their friends to paint a conversation piece for Winston's and Clementine's Silver Wedding in 1933. He paid many visits to Chartwell, and painted some enchanting studies of the swans, the lakes and the valley. Apart from his immense charm, William Nicholson's influence on Winston's painting was thoroughly approved of by Clementine, chiefly for its softening and lightening effect on his palette.

Almost always present was a (usually young, and always exceptionally clever) literary researcher/assistant working with Winston on whatever major tome was on the stocks at the time. Of these, Bill Deakin, a Fellow and lecturer at Wadham College, came to Chartwell on and off from 1936 for three years; he was to reappear after the war to assist him with his War Memoirs. Always admired and liked by both Winston and Clementine, Bill and his wife 'Pussy' became close friends of Clementine. And among this Chartwell galaxy from time to time 'shooting stars' from other spheres would appear: Charlie Chaplin; Einstein; Tilly Losch; Ethel Barrymore.

But by far the most regular visitor outside the family was 'The Prof'. From 1925 until the outbreak of the Second World War, when his signature was transferred to the Chequers Book, he signed the Visitors' Book at Chartwell 112 times. This brilliant scientist and curious personality, of American/Alsatian extraction, was for nearly forty years Winston's close friend and his guide on all scientific matters, becoming during the Second World War his 'Personal Adviser' in an official scientific capacity.* It was a strange friendship, for on the surface the men could not have been more different. 'The Prof' was a teetotaller, a non-smoker and a strict vegetarian; his nature was enclosed rather than out-going. Nevertheless, he was a constant guest at Chartwell, welcomed as much by Clementine as by Winston. Fully self-occupied, he was an easy guest, and she found his company soothing; he also played very good lawn tennis. Clementine took endless pains with his food. He said he liked eggs, but we would watch with dismay as the yolks were removed from the specially prepared eggs, as he consumed only the whites! Winston, to whom the eating and drinking habits of 'The Prof' were an unfathomable mystery, would always press upon him a 'cubic centimetre' of brandy after meals; which 'The Prof' would imbibe, without much relish, to be obliging.

But whoever was staying at Chartwell, Winston's programme of work and play was independent and undisturbed. He usually worked in his room all the morning, leaving Clementine to entertain the company. Many of the men guests had work to do of their own, but there were plenty of diversions. There was an excellent golf course nearby, and in the summer tennis and swimming. During the afternoons Winston would paint or attend to whatever works of construction (or destruction) were to hand; and in all these activities there was scope for appreciative spectators or volunteer unskilled labour, and guests and children alike would heave to.

In the winter afternoons and evenings Winston very much enjoyed playing cards. Bridge was never a Chartwell game, but mahjong, bezique, backgammon, and later Oklahoma and gin rummy all had their vogue. Bezique and backgammon were the most enduring, and until the very last years he enjoyed playing these companionable games, both of which Clementine also played well enough and with pleasure. But when others were thinking of going to bed, Winston would retreat to his study and, summoning his secretary, might well dictate for two or three hours.

* Created 1st Baron Cherwell, 1941.

But meal-times were the highlights of the day at Chartwell, both from the point of view of food and entertainment. The 'basic' house-party, enlarged by other guests, usually formed a gathering it would be hard to beat for value. There was little warming up; the conversation plunged straight into some burning or vital question. But the talk was by no means confined to politics; it ranged over history, art, and literature; it toyed with philosophical themes; it visited the past and explored the future. 'The Prof' and his slide-rule were much in demand on all scientific problems. Sometimes the conversation was a ding-dong battle of wits and words between, say, Winston and Duff Cooper, with the rest of the company skirmishing on the sidelines and keeping the score. The verbal pyrotechnics waxed hot and fierce, usually dissolving in an instant into gales of laughter. General conversation usually dwindled, as nearly everyone wanted to share the main 'entertainment', whether it was a discussion, or a dramatic and compelling mono-logue from Winston. Perhaps most enjoyable of all, particularly to us children (who from an early age partook of dining-room life) were the days when the Muse of Poetry and of Song held sway: when from the incredible store of our father's memory would flow verse sacred and profane, heroic and frivolous, in glorious profusion. Many a time a luncheon party broke up only after the completion of a near word-perfect recitation of 'Horatius'. (Very popular with the children, as we could join in 'the brave days of old' bits.)

If 'high thinking' could be said to be a feature of life at Chartwell, it did not go hand-in-hand with 'plain living'; the hospitality was lavish and the food delicious. Clementine rarely had a highly-trained cook, she could not afford one; more often than not she had a talented kitchen-maid, whom she would 'develop' herself. This was long before the period when cook-hostesses became a commonplace, but Clementine knew a great deal about delicious food and the theory of cooking, and she was highly successful in imparting her knowledge, never grudging time or trouble spent on planning and discussing the food with her cook. Naturally, what with the food and the talk, mealtimes tended to prolong themselves far into the afternoon or evening. It was unusual at a week-end to leave the dining-room after luncheon before half past three or even four o'clock, and in the evenings the men stayed on endlessly after the women had gone to the drawing-room. Clementine found this habit increasingly trying as the years went by, and on one or two occasions marked her displeasure by taking the women off to bed, leaving a deserted drawing-room to greet the men when they eventually appeared, headed by Winston, full of guilty apologies.

Clementine rarely tried to compete against Winston in conversation during these long, verbose meals. However riveting the topics, she was always alert and attentive to the food and the service. She was, fortunately, a good listener, and for the most part enjoyed the arguments. But she sometimes tired of the monologues and would firmly try, with varying degrees of success, to resurrect some form of general con-versation. She could herself be a sparkling talker, with a sense of wit, and she laughed uproariously at times. In argument she often waxed passionate and partisan, and when the talk took a tone or direction of which she disapproved, she would after a time suddenly 'erupt', and could maul most savagely those of whose views or characters she either temporarily or habitually disapproved. The fact that they were her guests at the time afforded them no protection. Very occasionally, having delivered herself of her opinion, she simply rose and swept out, leaving her children puce with embarrassment, and any women guests flustered and uncertain as to whether they should 'sweep' too.

When Clementine was really roused, even Winston could not restrain her; and although these violent outbursts embarrassed him at the time, he would often recount the incident afterwards with a sort of rueful pride: 'Clemmie gave poor —— a most fearful mauling.' Or after one such occasion: 'She dropped on him like a jaguar out of a tree!' Her victims were never the timid, however tedious; but the brash and powerful, and those whose influence on Winston she deplored, were at sure risk, and Clementine's basic and undying radicalism also made high Tories and most very rich people potential targets for her scorn.

*

But this wonderfully agreeable and enriching life, enjoyed equally by Winston, his family and his guests, was only made possible by his prodigious literary output. Chartwell was exceedingly expensive to run. For life there to be easy and comfortable, eight or nine indoor servants were needed: two in the kitchen; two in the pantry; two housemaids; a personal maid for Clementine (who also did a good deal of family sewing); a nursery-maid; and an 'odd-man' (boots, boilers, dustbins) – these made up the tally of personnel necessary to run this enlarged manor house in the twenties. In addition there was a nannie or governess and always two secretaries, one being available for late-night work whenever necessary.

Outside they employed a chauffeur, three gardeners, a groom for the polo ponies (until they were sold), and a working bailiff for what passed as a farm. Although most of the outdoor staff stayed for long periods, the turnover in the house was fairly constant – one reason certainly being the remoteness of the house from any bus-stop. The process of procuring, and initiating, a stream of new servants was expensive, tiring and frustrating. To these problems, Winston, like so many men, was not particularly attentive or sympathetic. In September 1928 he wrote somewhat breezily to Clementine:

> . . . do not worry about household matters. Let them crash if they will. All will be well. Servants exist to save one trouble, & shd never be allowed to disturb ones inner peace. There will always be food to eat, & sleep will come even if the beds are not made. Nothing is worse than worrying about trifles. The big things do not chafe as much & if these are rightly settled the rest will fall in its place.[11]

It is doubted whether these Olympian sentiments had the cheering and calming effect intended.

The problem of running Chartwell efficiently and economically would have daunted even a woman with less exacting standards than Clementine. Over the years she was assisted in all these matters by two successive secretaries – Margery Street, and then Grace Hamblin, a local girl who came to 'help out' in the office over a holiday period in 1932, and succeeded 'Streetie' when she returned to Australia the following year. More than anyone else 'Hambone' (as we children early nicknamed her) helped Clementine to grapple with the ups and downs of Chartwell life. With the outbreak of war she came to London to be Clementine's personal Private Secretary, returning again to Chartwell after 1945. Depended upon, and beloved not only by Clementine but by Winston and all of us children, she became and remained a close personal friend. No account of Chartwell or of Winston's and Clementine's life would be complete without a prominent 'Mention in Despatches' for Grace Hamblin. After Winston's death, when Chartwell was handed over to the National Trust, she became its first Administrator.

From the first, Chartwell for Clementine had spelt anxiety and difficulty. Their precarious financial state had a wearing effect on her nerves, and the perpetual back-log of bills, and the struggle she had to get even the local tradesmen paid, were the cause of gnawing worry and mortification. Winston's optimism and the fertile flow of new and money-consuming projects which he was always considering, had an abrasive effect on her disposition, and were the cause of many arguments which sometimes waxed hot and angry. On one occasion she became so enraged that she hurled a dish of spinach at Winston's head (she missed, and the dish hit the wall, leaving a tell-tale mark). She sometimes abandoned the unequal struggle of arguing with Winston, and resorted to writing calmly considered minutes or memoranda setting forth her point of view. It was a method she was to pursue hereafter, for she found she often succeeded in making her case in this way, when verbal argument utterly failed.

But by 1937, the burden of Chartwell was telling, and Winston was definitely contemplating selling the property. He told Clementine that if he were offered a good enough price (in the region of £25,000), he would accept it; but that if no such offer were forthcoming, 'we can quite well carry on for a year or two more. But no good offer should be refused . . .'[12]

But despite all these cares and worries, which persisted throughout the fifteen between-the-war years that Winston and Clementine lived at Chartwell, the manner of the life they led belied the insecurity and fragility of their financial situation. They lived and entertained elegantly; they travelled; they brought up and educated their four surviving children handsomely. But had Winston's diligence, health or genius failed, the whole fabric of their life would have crashed, for they literally lived from book to book, and from one article to the next.

Of course, we children were aware from time to time that 'Papa and Mummie were economising': we were lectured about the necessity for turning off lights, and the older ones were very much scolded for lengthy telephone conversations. But when we took refuge in Wellstreet Cottage, I thought it was great fun, and very cosy. And when on another occasion the house was partially shut up to save on heating and servants, and the big ground-floor rooms swathed in dust-sheets, the dining-room downstairs divided perfectly into a charming sitting room-cum-dining room, and it seemed an excellent 'winter' arrangement with only a few of us at home.

It was only as I grew older, and my mother began to confide some of her troubles and anxieties to me, that I came to understand that Chartwell was not – and had never been – the joy and refuge it was for my father. At first I found this difficult to grasp, and I almost resented her critical unappreciative attitude to what was, for me, a Garden of Eden. And it was only when I read my mother's letters and papers that I really began to understand: then I realised how fragile was the raft which supported that seemingly so solid way of life.

*

But it is not the memory of the lean times that springs to my mind on looking back. Much more I recall the spaciousness of our life; the comfort and prettiness of the rooms; the masses of flowers (always clear, soft colours, and always arranged with great simplicity); the crackling log fires, and the delicious comfort of a warm, scented house on bleak winter days. And in the summer, all the joys of life in the garden, voices calling up from the tennis court, long happy hours by the swimming-pool, and tea in the loggia with strawberries and cream.

But no times glow so vividly in my own memory as the wonderful Christmases. I remember, as if it were yesterday, the exquisite, tantalising thrill of walking past a poky closet (known as the 'Genii's cupboard') which was strictly 'out of bounds' for weeks before, where my mother and Nana (my governess) rustled about with paper, and held whispered conferences. I used to watch with mounting excitement as the gardeners transformed the house; Clementine was never very 'tinsel' minded, and although modern Christmas decorations are exquisite in their glittering sophistication, I still recall how beautiful were the more sombre, mysterious effects produced by the different textures of the leaves, and the gradations of the lustrous greens of the ivy, laurel, yew and holly with which the house was hung. The centrepiece of the decorations was always a large and beautiful Della Robbia plaque depicting the Christ-child, who, swaddled and pensive, gazed down on us all.

Part of the potency of the Christmas magic lies in its unchangingness, and every family seems to evolve its own particular ritual, usually fiercely guarded from change by the children. It was certainly so with our family, and year after year the same party gathered at Chartwell: Jack and Goonie Churchill, with their three children, Johnny, Peregrine and Clarissa; Clementine's sister, Nellie, with her husband, Bertram Romilly, and their two sons, Giles and Esmond (curiously known as 'The Lambs'). One or other of the two lonely bachelors, 'The Prof' or Eddie Marsh, were the only two members of the party outside the family. The crowd of young cousins were close in age, and provided the necessary raw material for the jollity, special friendships, and in-fighting inseparable, and indeed, indispensable, on such occasions. Trailing far behind this closely knit group came myself, the 'baby', the 'Benjamin', at once petted or excluded according to moods and circumstances.

When we were all assembled on Christmas Eve, the double doors between the drawing-room and the library were flung open to reveal the Christmas tree, glowing with light, and radiating warmth, and a piny, waxy smell from a hundred real white wax candles. Electric lights can never distil for me the magic cast by the glimmering, sputtering beauty of the Christmas trees of my childhood days. Not surprisingly, one year the tree caught fire, and only Randolph's presence of mind, and speed in fetching an extinguisher, saved us from catastrophe.

Amusements and occupations were not hard to come by; in the year of the 'great snow', 1927, the bigger children built a wonderful igloo; there was skating on the lakes, and the lane below the house was so deep in snow that a tunnel had to be dug to allow the traffic to pass.

Amateur theatricals were a great ploy; the dining-room made a natural theatre, as there were dividing curtains. My mother greatly enjoyed these dramatic activities, and threw herself into them with enthusiasm. She wrote a lively account of it all to Streetie in January 1934:

> We all acted at Christmas – even me! You will hardly believe that. We (Sarah Mary & myself) acted a short play by Gertrude Jennings called 'Mother of Pearl' ... I took the part of a dirty old tramp & I enjoyed it enormously ... Mr. Gurnell the Chemist came & made us all up. Then there was a thriller called 'The Hand in the Dark' in which Mrs. Romilly, Sarah & Esmond performed. They wrote it themselves & it was really quite gruesome.
>
> We gave 3 performances 3 days running & you can imagine the disorder of the house. Nana prompted & produced & was very severe! Mr. Pug was too sweet. He said it was all lovely & that I was so tragic that I made him cry![13]

The Christmas of 1933 saw the last of the glorious family parties at Chartwell; time was spinning on, and all the cousins were growing up, and beginning to go their own ways. Of the five peacetime Christmases which remained, only one more, 1936, was to be at Chartwell. For all of the others the family for one reason or another was divided, either Winston or Clementine being on their travels. But the stay-at-home section received warm hospitality at Blenheim. 'Sunny' Marlborough died in 1934, and his son Bert, and Mary Marlborough, with their younger family, continued the tradition of friendship and hospitality to Winston and Clementine and their children.

As the years went on, inevitably threads of anxiety, sorrow, disappointment and misunderstanding crept here and there into the tapestry of our family life. But when one contemplates the finished piece, it is not these muted and sombre tones, but the glowing, happy colours that predominate. There was so much laughter, activity, and high spirits, and, above all, the golden skein of warmly expressed love and loyalty gleams throughout, strong and unfailing.

HERSELF AND OTHERS

FROM THE EARLIEST DAYS of their family life a conflict developed in Clementine's life between wifehood and motherhood. Many women today find themselves involved in a somewhat sterile competition between marriage, motherhood and a career, and politicians' wives particularly are nearly always unwilling participants in a sort of domestic 'tug-of-war', in which purely economic factors usually play a decisive role. Since Clementine and Winston nearly always had a London house, and always a nannie or a governess for the children, the cause of the conflict between her two roles lay, not in economics, but partly in her own character, and largely in the nature of her husband. The demands he himself made upon her, and the extraordinary circumstances of his career, created a sharp division between her two vocations. There was probably no single moment when Clementine made a conscious choice between her wifely and maternal interests, but a study of her life leaves one in no doubt as to what that declared choice would have been.

From the day she married him until his death fifty-seven years later, Winston dominated her whole life, and once this priority had been established, her children, personal pleasures, friends and outside interests competed for what was left. That she never lost her own individuality, despite the vocational quality of her devotion to her husband, and the demands his overpowering personality made on her, is a measure of Clementine's strength of character. Devoted and fiercely loyal, she never became a 'yes-woman' or lost her capacity for independent thought. But it supplies the answer to why a woman, whose social conscience had been so thoroughly aroused in the great radical reforming days, and whose organising ability was twice proved in wartime, did not in the intervening period of peace take up, to any marked degree, some form of community service, or develop any independent personal interest or occupation. She herself commented in a letter to Winston in 1920:

The Canteens – I sometimes wonder now if it was all a dream. One thing is certain, I couldn't manage them again. I began to think I had real organising ability, but it died with the war – if there ever was any![1]

This self-deprecating remark was to be proved wrong many times over in another testing time.

Unlike many women in a similar situation, Clementine showed no desire to play a great part in charitable work. She was not ungenerous to good causes, but she fought shy of fund-raising committees, and her name was rarely to be found on the patronage or committee lists of charity balls or play and film premieres. It was not 'her scene', and she had no desire for a platform to project either a cause, or her own personality. The considerable amount of work she did in Winston's constituency seems to have absorbed most of the energy and time she had for public work.

However, in 1934, Clementine was made a 'Guardian' for Maternity and Child Welfare by the Kent County Council, and she attended meetings of the Public Health and Housing Committee for several years. She also became the County Council's representative on the Management Committee of the Alexandra Hospital at Swanley. A fellow committee member said that, although she was assiduous in all matters relating to her particular subject, he never felt Clementine really relished this sort of work. It never gave her the feeling that she was achieving any concrete results. Moreover, she found the attitude of many of the other committee members hard and unsympathetic to the human problems involved. Since one of her chief characteristics was to react quickly to any situation, and seek a direct solution, it is easy to understand that public committee work did not appeal very much to her.

Winston was to be Clementine's lifework. Her concentration on him and his career consumed the cream of her thought and energy. She said to me once: 'It took me all my time and strength just to keep up with him. I never had anything left over.'

Clementine was a devoted and conscientious mother, but her priorities were never in doubt: Winston came first – always. It was not unusual in those days for upper-class children to lead much of their lives apart from their parents, but Winston's demanding nature, combined with the claims of his career, meant that even the school holidays had to take second or third place. When the children were babies, the competition between Clementine's nursery world and Winston's life was not so keen but she always tried to share their seaside holidays, and suffered some un-happiness and much frustration that Winston could not be persuaded that lodgings at Westgate or Frinton-on-Sea were just as enjoyable as the Riviera.

When the children had to have different arrangements, Clementine was always at pains to make suitable and enjoyable plans for them, but, to her own great sadness, time and again she could not share treats or expeditions with them. In later years, she realised what a 'missing factor' this had been in her relationship with her children. It would also have been a fortunate circumstance if, particularly in those early nursery years, there had been an enduring nannie or governess. But Clemen-time was not lucky enough to find such a treasure until much later on, and the three older children experienced many changes of rule in the nursery.

To her children, Clementine was a mixture of tenderness and severity. She loved her babies with a fierce physical relish, and she enjoyed them tumbling about in her room while she dressed, or conducted the business of the household. As a small child I was vividly aware of her beauty and fastidiousness; of the velvety texture of her skin, the softness of her lingerie, and of how delicious she smelt. But as her children grew older, the same shyness and reserve which inhibited her friendships with her own contemporaries formed a barrier between her and her children, tending to make the relationship between them somewhat unspontaneous and formal.

Clementine had no real understanding of the childish mind or outlook, and applied her own perfectionist standards not only to manners and morals, but to picnics or garden clothes. Consequently, although all her children loved and revered her, they did not find in her a fun-maker, or a companion for their more untidy, knock-about activities. Both the circumstances of her life and her own nature combined to place her goddess-like upon a pedestal. But on any big issue, once the courage was screwed up to broach the subject, her children could be sure of her attention, astonishingly quick action, and, if justified, the championing of their cause.

Winston was more relaxed and indulgent, greatly enjoying his children in the brief moments he could spend with them. His letters show a touching interest and concern for his nursery. His children, and later his grandchildren, were always conscious that he loved to have them around. 'Come to luncheon,' he would say to someone, extending an invitation to Chartwell, adding with obvious relish: 'You'll find us all bunged up with brats.' But the burden of bringing up and disciplining their brood was always left to Clementine.

When Chartwell was bought, school holidays together at last became a reality. Diana was then thirteen, Randolph eleven, and Sarah nearly eight. The three elder children revelled in the opportunities and freedom their new home offered them, and they unreservedly shared their father's enthusiasm for the place. Moreover, as they were able to help with the outside constructions and improvements, it brought them many hours of relaxed companionship with their father. Clementine's time and energies were chiefly concentrated on the house and its problems, and so she missed out on these enjoyable companionable occupations. Earlier than many children, however, we were promoted to dining-room meals, enjoying our parents' company, and mingling freely with their guests.

From a very early age public events played their part in nursery life. Diana, aged five, had been conscious of the feeling of impending disaster which permeated the house in the spring of 1915. The two older children had vague memories of walks in the park escorted by detectives to protect them from the suffragettes. The Irish troubles had brought armed detectives into the house. Randolph remembered how he and Diana, on returning one day (22nd June 1922) from roller skating in Holland Park,

> . . . found the house surrounded by policemen. Indoors all sorts of tough-looking men were running up and down the stairs, looking in cupboards, attics and cellars. It was explained to us that earlier in the afternoon Sir Henry Wilson* had been assassinated by Irish gunmen on the steps of his house.[2]

It was feared by the authorities that Winston might be next on the list, hence these alarms and excursions.

From our earliest years we were all passionate partisans of our family's electoral fortunes. Diana's and Randolph's childhood letters, in particular, show a keen

*Sir Henry Wilson. A prominent Ulsterman, and recently Chief of the Imperial Staff. Assassinated 22nd June 1922.

awareness of political affairs. In the General Election of November 1923 Diana, then fourteen, kept her parents (who were fighting West Leicester) well informed about the course of the campaign in their home constituency of Paddington, reporting that one of the candidates 'has not the slightest chance of getting in, & he is quite willing to pay the fine if he does not get a certain number of votes'.[3] In the same series of letters, she informed her father:

> ... I have got to write an essay for the 'Chick Memorial Essay Competition'. There were twelve subjects to choose from, & the one I have chosen is 'The advantages and disadvantages of Tariff Reform as opposed to Free Trade'. Perhaps when you come home & are not so busy, you will give me a few hints.[4]

During the General Strike, when Randolph was at Eton, he was determined to keep himself abreast of events, writing to his mother:

> At the beginning of the Strike I asked the 'Sheep' [Colonel Sheepshanks, his Housemaster] if I could install a wireless set, in order to hear the news bulletins. However he would not let me. So I have fitted up a secret one in the bottom of my armchair. It works extraordinarily well and I can hear London quite easily ...
> I am so glad the 'British Gazette' was such a success. I found it impossible to secure a copy down here.[5]

As children, we soon became aware that our parents' main interest and time were consumed by immensely important tasks, besides which our own demands and concerns were trivial. We never expected either of our parents to attend our school plays, prize-givings or sports' days. We knew they were both more urgently occupied, and any feelings of self-pity were overborne by a sense of gratification that their presence was so much required elsewhere. When our mother did manage to grace any of these (to children) important occasions, we were ecstatically grateful. Her elegance and beauty were a source of great pride to us, as her high standards in all things were a cause of anxiety, lest we should fall short of her expectations.

Once the school years were over, Clementine was able to establish a closer relationship with her daughters, taking them, each in their turn, on various journeys and holidays. It was at these times that we saw our mother at her gayest and best, for she loved travelling and sightseeing. And such expeditions were always pleasurable in her company, for she never made visits to galleries or museums too long or tedious.

In the autumn of 1926, when Diana was seventeen, she spent some months with a French family in Paris. Before leaving her there, however, Diana and her mother had a week's holiday together in France, of which Diana wrote a happy account to her father. Four days at Dinard were followed by three 'delightful days together' in Paris, mainly spent in sightseeing. 'One day we went and lunched at Voisin's, which I believe you sometimes frequent,'[6] wrote Diana. This was history repeating itself, for Lady Blanche had also taken Clementine as a girl to this same restaurant. Diana was very happy during the winter and spring months she spent in Paris, and she wrote a series of charming and lively letters to her parents. Among all the items of news from home, one in particular seized her attention, and she was swiftly to turn it to her own advantage. On 15th November 1926 Diana wrote:

Darling Mummy,

I have just had a letter from Randolph, and he sends me a very interesting piece of information; namely that you have shingled your hair again!!!

Well, Mummy, you really must let me cut mine off now, as it is quite absurd for me to have mine long and you to have yours short. Besides every one that I have met in Paris so far has advised & persuaded me to cut it off; as they nearly all say that my hair is much too overwhelming for my size. Also, I do really still suffer agonies with my hats, even with the new one.

Everyone here has got shingled hair (except Madame B.) [Madame Bellaigue, with whose family Diana was staying], and I am very démodé and old fashioned.

Do write & say that I can have it shingled, Mummy Darling, and then Madame Bellaigue, who is as anxious as anybody, will take me to a good coiffeur immediately. It would be better to have it off immediately, and then it will have a chance to settle down in time for Xmas.

As for Papa, I am sure he does not really mind. I would write and ask him, only I am sure that your arguments will have more weight than mine.

Do say yes, and I will try and be very good and tidy & work hard; – I will any how, but if I did not have so much hair to carry about with me it would be easier. Do not bother to write a letter in reply; because a post card will be quite large enough to write an immense YES.

All my love – in anxious expectation –
Your loving Diana

Such winning advocacy could not be resisted, and evidently Clementine must have sent the earnestly-sought-for permission, because four days later Diana wrote again to her:

I have just had my hair shingled; and I don't regret it a bit. I thought I had better have it off at once, as if Papa comes over to Paris with you, he might have changed his mind. As it is, I am sure he will like it much better, when he sees it. Everyone here says it is a great improvement.[7]

Winston, it seems, like so many fathers, had a sentimental attachment for the long and lovely burnished tresses of his 'gold-cream kitten'. Even Diana did not say goodbye to them without a pang, for in the same letter she wrote:

I have just said Good-Night to my cut off tail, and when I look at it, I feel quite poetic. I have just composed a poem which begins; 'Good-bye my golden glory!'

*

With Randolph, Clementine never established a close relationship; perhaps it would never have been possible to do so, for as his personality developed, it produced features of character and outlook too dissimilar from his mother's whole nature and attitude to life. This lively boy manifestly needed a father's hand; but the main task of controlling him fell almost entirely upon Clementine, and so right from the early days Randolph and she were at loggerheads. Winston was ever conscious of how remote and cold a figure his own father (greatly though he had loved and admired him) had seemed to him, both as a child and as a young man. He was determined it should not be the same with him and his son, and throughout Randolph's boyhood and early manhood Winston spoilt and indulged him, lavishing affection and praise upon his attractive and precocious only son.

Winston had never been happy at any of the schools to which he had been sent, nor, with very few exceptions, had he formed a high opinion of any of the masters who taught him. His school reports had been far from satisfactory and had earned for him Lord Randolph's anger and frigid contempt. Winston was therefore apt to take lightly any disagreeable comments in his own son's reports, and was wont to regale Randolph with tales of pedagogic folly and ineptitude, and generally encourage him in saucy opinions about his pastors and masters.

Clementine greatly disapproved of this line of talk, for she was well aware that Randolph needed no encouragement in impertinent or rebellious behaviour. Randolph soon realised that his mother disapproved in general of the attitudes in which he was encouraged in the manly world to which his father's indulgence soon admitted him. Moreover, Randolph must have felt that his mother did not share his father's uncritical admiration of his character and childish achievements. Thus early on a lasting barrier was formed between them.

Randolph greatly admired his brilliant godfather, Lord Birkenhead (F. E. Smith), and was brought up by his father 'on all the famous anecdotes illustrating his wit, brilliance and arrogance'.[8] Clementine, who ever deplored F.E.'s influence on Winston, feared even more for its heady effect on their immature son. During his formative years Randolph had many opportunities of seeing his godfather, both in his own parents' house and in Lord Birkenhead's home near Oxford, for the latter was always most kind to Randolph and undoubtedly had a strong influence upon him. But as Randolph himself wrote with objective perception:

> Without F.E.'s learning or his majestic command of the language, I sought to emulate his style of polished repartee. It didn't work in my case. I did not have my godfather's shining abilities and could not aspire to his brilliant gift of repartee.[9]

Winston himself had doubts, as time went on, about certain aspects of Randolph's character. Writing to Clementine, who was in Florence, in April 1928, he forwarded on to her Randolph's school report. Randolph was now in his seventeenth year and nearing the end of his Eton days; the report was evidently most satisfactory, but Winston remarked:

> There is no doubt he is developing fast, & in those directions wh will enable him to make his way in the world – by writing & speaking – in politics, at the bar, or in journalism. There are some vy strange & even formidable traits in his character ... He is far more advanced than I was at his age, & quite out of the common – for good or ill.[10]

Clementine's response was a mixture of immediate pleasure and future foreboding:

> Your delightful letter (with Randolph's report) arrived to-day & I read it with joy – I am so glad about Randolph. He is certainly going to be an interest, an anxiety & an excitement in our lives. I do hope he will always care for us –[11]

After he left Eton, Randolph went to Christ Church, Oxford, but remained there only four terms, when, on being offered a contract to give a series of lectures in the United States, he obtained a term's leave from the university and accepted this unexpected invitation. He disarmingly acknowledged that the idea of 'teaching, rather than learning, appealed to me strongly'.[12] Since he was at this time considerably encumbered with debts, and as the contract appeared highly advantageous financially, he eagerly grasped at this opportunity. Everyone, except Winston, thought the scheme a harebrained venture. Clementine feared it would, in fact, mean the end of his studies at Oxford, and that he would never get his degree. In this she was proved perfectly right, for he never returned to Christ Church. Randolph was of course aware once more of his mother's opposition to his wishes and intentions, which were, as on so many other occasions, encouraged by his father.

Strangely enough, however, this lecture tour, of which his mother so much disapproved, provided an interlude in which she and Randolph were for some time in each other's company, and upon which both in after years looked back with pleasure. Randolph left for the United States at the beginning of October 1930; he was nineteen years old, and combined with his unusual character and budding abilities stunning good looks.

Although there are several exchanges of letters between Clementine and Randolph full of news, views and affection, by Christmas Clementine was feeling out of touch, and perhaps a little uneasy as to what Randolph was up to in the brave new world. Winston had just given her some money to buy herself a car: she had a brainwave, and wrote to Randolph:

> . . . if you liked it I would spend the money on paying you & New York a flying visit?
>
> Shall I hop on a boat one day at the end of January or beginning of February & come to New York for a week . . .?[13]

On receiving a swift and enthusiastic reply in the affirmative, Clementine booked her passage and set off in early February 1931 for New York in the *Europa*.

Soon after her arrival, she wrote a long letter to Winston; it started with an account of the heart-warming welcome she had received from Randolph:

> The Europa docked early on Saturday & before 8 Randolph was on board looking splendid and beaming. His joy at seeing me was really sweet & I felt much moved.[14]

They had not been together two hours before Randolph told his mother that he was in love with a young lady from Cleveland, Ohio and that he hoped to marry her. Clementine was somewhat taken aback, but soon had the opportunity of meeting her, and she reported favourably on her to Winston. But in the course of several long, heart-to-heart talks with Randolph, she pointed out the possible disadvantages of marrying so young, and before he had in any way established himself in the world. These cogent maternal arguments were, needless to say, discounted by Randolph, who said he meant to marry the young lady if she would have him. In fact they never married, but remained life-long friends. Meanwhile reports began appearing in the American Press about Randolph's romance, and Clementine's arrival was directly linked with it. Several newspapers reported that she had arrived from England to put a stop to the whole thing.

From the moment she set foot in New York, Clementine was swept up in a whirl of plans by Winston's or Randolph's friends, and her intention of staying for only a few days was soon abandoned. Randolph persuaded her to go with him on part of his lecture-tour. She gladly agreed, as she was unreservedly enjoying herself. But the key to her happiness lay in Randolph's warmth and kindness; she wrote to Winston:

> He [Randolph] is a darling. He has quite captivated me. He is a most sweet companion & he seems to enjoy my company . . . It is quite like a honeymoon . . .[15]

For the best part of six weeks, Clementine travelled about with Randolph, visiting Palm Beach, Washington and Cleveland (where she met, and liked, Randolph's intended's family).

During this journey she kept a day-to-day diary, which tells how she and Randolph were welcomed and entertained wherever they went, as only the Americans know how. Far from being exhausted or bored by the succession of parties and entertainments, Clementine seems to have loved every moment of this happy and unexpected episode in her life. As time went on, this American interlude acquired a golden glow, and in after years, when the relationship between Clementine and Randolph had deteriorated, she would recall it with wistful nostalgia.

Randolph was determined to blaze his own trail, both as a journalist and as a politician. He was an aggressively loyal protagonist of his father's views, and was constantly drawing public attention to the scandalous exclusion of his father from office. Randolph's political skirmishings, however, were nearly always the cause of parental dismay or embarrassment – and sometimes both – and a constant source of noisy rows, for he would brook no moderating counsels, and forged ahead on his warpath regardless.

In 1934 in particular Randolph had set cats among the political pigeons by twice taking a prominent part in by-elections – the first at Wavertree, where he actually stood as an Independent Conservative candidate, thereby splitting the Tory vote and letting the Socialist candidate in, and a few months later at Norwood, where he espoused the cause of the Independent Conservative candidate there. But this time the 'official' candidate, Duncan Sandys, won hands down, Randolph's protégé losing his deposit. The main topic of controversy in both campaigns was the Government's India policy, and although Winston was firmly and openly opposed to them over this, he was much embarrassed by Randolph's actions, which only served to divide Tory support. Clementine was far from home on a Far Eastern cruise at this time, and so she only had the news from the electoral battle fronts in batches of letters from home. But she understood immediately how awkward Randolph's interventions must be for Winston. From Auckland on 22nd February 1935, she wrote:

How anxious & agonising & thrilling Wavertree must have been. I wish I had been there to help – Darling Winston, I hope it has not queered the pitch at Epping. I do think the Rabbit ought to have consulted you before rushing into the fray. However he seems to have done very well –[16]

Although Winston had disapproved of Randolph's candidature at Wavertree, he had spoken for him at his eve-of-poll meeting, but Randolph's renewed activity barely a month later at Norwood had been the cause of a violent row between him and his father, all of which the latter duly recounted to the absent Clementine. Winston did not lend Randolph his support in any way on this second occasion, nevertheless it was suspected in party circles that he had his father's approval. Altogether it was very tiresome: and Winston commented ruefully to Clementine: 'I shall of course have nothing to do with it, except to bear a good deal of the blame.'[17]

In the same letter Winston told Clementine how he had met up with Mr Baldwin about this time in the House of Commons, who remarked sympathetically that Mrs Baldwin had said: 'One's children are like a lot of live bombs. One never knows when they will go off, or in what direction.'[18]

*

During her childhood years Sarah caused her parents much anxiety on account of her health. Later on she developed an exceptionally strong constitution, and was able to stand up to all the rigorous demands of professional dancing and acting. But when she was five or six she alarmed everybody by producing tubercular glands in her neck, necessitating an operation. Too young and nervous to accept or understand soothing explanations, Sarah panicked when the chloroform mask was held over her face; becoming hysterical, she fought like a demon, and ran round and round the operating theatre until she was caught and subdued by sheer force. Neither she, nor Clementine (who was the horrified witness of the scene), ever forgot this harrowing experience. The operation left a scar on Sarah's neck which she has borne all her life, and it also made a deep impression on her inner being, making her dread all forms of physical restraint.

Sarah's seemingly frail health during these years caused Clementine much worry and concern, haunted as she was by Marigold's death and the memory of her sister Kitty. It also enhanced her tenderness towards Sarah. She confided many of her thoughts and feelings about her children to Margery Street, who had known them all so long. Of her fears for Sarah (then nineteen) she wrote:

I get fonder of her every day & sometimes I am terrified that something will happen to her.

I don't know why I have this feeling (which Thank God is not with me very often) I think it must be her likeness to my sister Kitty who died when she was 17. Also Sarah is not really strong which makes me anxious.[19]

When she was thirteen, Sarah left Notting Hill High School and went to North

Foreland Lodge, a boarding school by the sea, at Broadstairs in Kent, which Clementine selected very largely on the grounds of its bracing situation. After her time there, Sarah, like Diana, went to Paris for about a year, to a finishing school kept by the Mesdemoiselles Ozanne. After this she completed the programme for girls at that time by making her debut in the social world, and 'doing the season'. Sarah was beginning to be strikingly lovely, with her auburn hair, green eyes and ivory complexion. But Clementine was candid about her appearance, writing to Streetie: 'Sometimes she looks absolutely lovely – but on the other hand she can look like a moping raven.'[20]

Sarah was very shy and, with her dreamy temperament, did not really enjoy the endless succession of dances. In June 1933, Clementine, again writing to Streetie, told her:

Sarah is sweet & very good to me.

We are half-way through the so-called 'Season' & she and I are really longing for it to be over.

She is slowly overcoming her shyness & has plenty of partners but she makes few friends – She is nearly always ready to come home by two o'clock, so that I do not have very late nights.[21]

For Clementine, with her un-social nature and early-to-bed habits, bringing out her daughters must have been a real test of maternal devotion; she also confided to Streetie her views on her fellow mothers:

They are really rather a depressing back-biting tribe & I have to sit for hours with them on the Chaperons' Bench. I'm thinking of taking a cookery book to Balls. I could be hunting up tasty dishes for Margaret & Elizabeth to try, instead of listening to their gossip.[22]

The end of Sarah's first season saw also the end of her compliance with a conventional programme. She begged and persuaded, until her parents reluctantly gave her permission to train to be a professional dancer and actress. No doubt they hoped her passionate longing to 'go on the stage' would melt away. Diana had for a time studied at the Royal Academy of Dramatic Art; but she had no real gift for acting, and after a while she gave up any dramatic aspirations. But Sarah had real talent and her desire to act or dance professionally became an enduring passion, which dominated all others. Nevertheless, although Sarah's ambition to make the stage her career did not please her parents, it did not make a serious rift between them, and once Clementine saw how much in earnest she was, she took trouble to see that Sarah went to an efficient and reputable school of dancing, and also insisted that she should have a rigorous medical examination to make sure that physically she was up to the demands of the training.

But Clementine's fundamental lack of sympathy with either of her daughters' histrionic ambitions was expressed when she wrote somewhat testily to Streetie in September 1934:

It's very strange that both she [Sarah] and Diana should have this passionate wish to go on the stage without the slightest talent or even aptitude.[23]

Between Sarah and her mother there grew up a loving and companionable under-standing, which as time wore on survived some major emotional crises. But sadly, the relationship between Clementine and Diana, which was so sunny and open in the early days, became clouded by misunderstanding. The chilling of their relationship seems to date roughly from 1932. In December of that year Diana, who was twenty-three, married John Bailey, the son of Sir Abe Bailey, a wealthy South African, and a friend of long standing of Winston. The match however did not arouse much enthusiasm in Diana's family, although there was a brilliant wedding at St Margaret's, Westminster, where Winston and Clementine had themselves been married nearly twenty-five years before.

Any happiness between Diana and John Bailey was short-lived, and they separated after barely a year, and were divorced early in 1935. Diana thereafter lived alone in London; but although she came very often at week-ends to Chartwell, an element of strain was present between her mother and herself. Differences in their emotional make-up and misunderstandings marred their friendship from now on. Both were thereby the losers.

Diana mercifully, however, was not to be solitary and sad in her personal life for long. During the summer of 1935 she met Duncan Sandys – the victor at Norwood earlier in that year. He was a diplomat who had left the Foreign Office in order to go into politics. While she was helping Randolph with his disastrous campaign at the by-election, Diana had observed Duncan from afar, across the political barricades. And towards the end of August Clementine wrote to tell Streetie of their engage-ment. Both Winston and Clementine had obviously been taken by surprise:

Mr Pug & I were rather staggered at first but now we rather like him (no money) & *HOPE* all is for the best . . . they are to be married quietly on Sept. 16th.[24]

A few months later she was more enthusiastic:

I like my new son-in-law. He & Diana are very much in love.
    That is all a great relief.[25]

In the autumn of that same year, 1935, Sarah started her stage career by becoming one of Mr C. B. Cochran's 'Young Ladies' and taking part, as a member of the chorus, in a revue called *Follow the Sun*. The show opened in Manchester in December, and Clementine travelled up to see the first night; afterwards she wrote to Winston, who was in North Africa:

You really would have been proud of Sarah. The dancing performed by the chorus was difficult & intricate & she was certainly in the first flight. She looked graceful & distinguished.[26]

To Streetie she avowed: 'I'm really very proud of her 'tho I would rather she were not on the stage.'[27] Neither Winston nor Clementine could ever really reconcile themselves to Sarah's stage career, and as to her being 'in the chorus' – they both belonged to the generation of which several ladies of the chorus became duchesses but, on the other hand, ladies simply did not become chorus girls.

It was while she was in *Follow the Sun* that Sarah met the principal male star of the show – the comedian, Vic Oliver. He was thirty-seven, of Viennese and probably Jewish extraction, and was seventeen years older than Sarah; he had already been married twice. Vic Oliver was a man of great charm, and of many parts; he and Sarah fell deeply in love, and it was not long before Winston and Clementine were confronted with the to them unpalatable fact that they wished to be married. An unhappy and unsettled year followed, during which time her parents used every means within their power to dissuade her from this marriage. But Sarah did not earn the nickname 'Mule' for nothing, and she clung tenaciously to her point.

In September 1936, without prior warning, convinced she would never win her parents' approval (their consent was not necessary as she was over twenty-one), Sarah bolted off to New York to join Vic Oliver, who was working there. Great was the dismay of her parents, for she had promised them to wait a year. The inevitable publicity attracted by her sudden flight added to the general pain and embarrassment, and public interest was further fanned by Randolph following hot on Sarah's heels at Winston's behest to see what he could do even yet to put a stop to a marriage they were sure would lead to much unhappiness for Sarah.

This was a bitter period: both Winston and Clementine felt deeply wounded and ill-used; Sarah felt misunderstood and, not unnaturally, resented the various legal devices which were employed to delay or prevent her marriage. But through all the bitterness the bond of love between Sarah and her parents, though strained, never broke. Sarah and Vic Oliver were finally married on Christmas Eve, 1936, in New York. Christmas that year at Chartwell was very quiet; but a cheerful note was struck by the presence of Diana and Duncan, who brought their three-month-old son, Julian.

*

Meanwhile, a long way behind the others, I was also growing up. Apart from the preoccupations of her life with my father, my mother was naturally more taken up with the varied needs and demands of the three elder children. But I was blessed in having throughout my entire childhood and girlhood the same steady, loving presence and influence of one Nannie-cum-governess.

After Marigold's death, Mlle Rose, their young French nursery governess, had departed. No actual blame was ever laid at her door, although Clementine always felt she should have been sent for sooner. But her confidence was utterly shaken, and since her life was such that she would spend much of her time away from her children, Clementine looked round for someone to be with them in whose judgment and reliability she could have complete trust. She did not have to look far: her own first cousin, Maryott Whyte (Lady Maude's daughter), then aged twenty-two, was a trained Norland nurse.

Called variously 'Cousin Moppet', Nana and (by a later generation) Grandnana, she came to rule over the schoolroom and, soon, the new nursery. She stayed with our family for over twenty years, giving a blessed sense of security to Clementine, and a stability and orderliness in the children's lives, which had been greatly lacking through the constant change-around of nurses and governesses up to this time.

I was very much the 'Chartwell child' – indeed, it was the only home I could remember. I spent nearly all my time there, going to a local day school, and looked after at home by Nana. Eight years separated me from Sarah, and my life and up-bringing were in some ways like that of an only child. But I can just remember Sarah having some connection with nursery and schoolroom life, and this link became a bond of lifelong love and loyalty between us. Diana and Randolph were god-like beings, inhabiting a different world altogether, and I never really caught up with them.

I had a lovely life, designed by my mother, but administered in all its details by the faithful (and sometimes fierce) Nana, to whom as a child I turned for everything. I lived chiefly among grown-ups, with whom I was on the whole more at ease than with children of my own age. The lack of such companionship was largely supplied by a procession of pets: orphan lambs, chickens, bantams and goats. (These last were a great trial to my long-suffering mother, as they were wont to escape from their tethers and in their brief spell of liberty always managed to do to death some valu-able tree or shrub by 'ringing' the bark.) I also at one time or another possessed a monkey, budgerigars and two tame foxcubs. After my father gave up his polo, there was no 'pony' life at Chartwell, but I rode very often at a nearby riding school.

My mother found a wonderful Frenchwoman, Madame Gabrielle l'Honoré, who from 1929 for nearly ten years came every summer during the school holidays to teach me French. She was minute, vivacious, talented and chic, and, as my mother wrote to my father: 'She looks like Madame de Pompadour, takes away all Diana's young men from her & would lure a deaf & dumb orang-outang to speak French.'[28] We all loved her, and certainly she did teach me a great deal of French. My mother encouraged us all to play tennis, providing us with private tennis coaching at home, and spending much time unselfishly playing with us herself. In 1934, when I was twelve, I evidently promised well athletically, for my mother wrote to Streetie: 'I think if we concentrate on any one accomplishment that she could become a champion rider, lawn tennis player or swimmer!'[29] This somewhat over-optimistic and partisan prophecy was, I must add, never fulfilled in any respect.

Clementine was still full of physical energy, although somewhat lacking in stamina. She had loved with energy and passion the riding and hunting that had come her way earlier on in her married life, and still enjoyed boar-hunting from time to time when staying with Bendor Westminster. But since they only had for the briefest period of time a stable of their own, riding was supplanted by tennis, at which she shone. At Chartwell, tennis became a great feature of life, and although Clementine gradually gave up playing in tournaments, she enjoyed the game and played it well, right up to the War. Diana's and Sarah's young men were much in favour if they were good players; 'The Prof' was keen and proficient, and among tennis-playing neighbours Victor and Peter Cazalet from Fairlawne were much in evidence.

But in 1936, when she was fifty, Clementine suddenly became attracted by, and then positively addicted to ski-ing. Several of her friends were winter-sports' enthusiasts, and they fired her with the desire to learn to ski. Clementine also saw in this occupation an opportunity to make 'contact' with me: it was something we could do together, away from home.

I was now fourteen, and entirely engrossed by my work at school (where I was a persevering plodder) and with my life at Chartwell, which was centred round my animals and my riding, and was dominated by Nana.

My relationship with my mother was respectful and admiring rather than close. If she made a suggestion my natural reaction was to say: 'I must ask Nana.' My mother not unnaturally felt the time had come to change the orbit of my loyalty and to try to make a closer relationship with me. It was of course a great thrill for me when she announced we were going to Austria in the Christmas holidays of 1935–6. Up to that time I had hardly ever been alone with her for any period of time: for Nana even took me away to Scotland or the seaside for my summer holidays. This was to be, therefore, a new experience for us both.

We went to Zürs in the Arlberg mountains in Austria, in a party that included Goonie Churchill and Clarissa, and Venetia Montagu and her daughter Judy. It was a great success, and Clementine threw herself into this strenuous and hazardous sport with zeal and perseverance. For three years running, this Christmas holiday treat was repeated; twice we went to Zürs, and once to a Swiss ski-ing resort, Lenzerheide. Clementine simply loved it, and, considering that she was already fifty when she first set foot on a ski slope, she became remarkably proficient. Speed was never a characteristic of her ski-ing, but she was the epitome of the maxim 'dogged does it'. On her first visit to Zürs, she wrote to Winston that: 'The difficulties of ski-ing seem to me insurmountable! Perhaps I shall feel differently in a week.'[30]

Ten days later, we all ventured on our first expedition (as opposed to classes in the ski-ing school), and my mother reported:

> We had a charming guide who carried our food our coats 1st aid apparatus & poor fellow, in the end almost had to carry me! . . . Mary fell down 19 times . . . Today I am going in a sleigh as I am really bored with tumbling down![31]

This letter was signed: 'Your bruised & struggling but undaunted Clemmie'.

Each year my mother stayed on after I had to go back to England to return to school. She usually joined up with a friend, and persevered for a week or two more with this pleasurable if exhausting new-found sport.

It was chiefly during these lovely ski-ing holidays that I started to know her more as a person than a deity, and that the foundation was laid for a long and loving relationship which was to be precious to us both. I not only began to understand her better, but also to enjoy her companionship. She was delightful to be with, and during the long *après ski* evenings, she would regale me with accounts of her childhood: I loved to hear about Kitty and the Twins, and her fascinating, unpredictable mother, and Mr Sickert and terrifying old Lady Airlie. And I thought Sidney Peel's long and faithful courtship unbearably romantic, and found it hard to believe anyone could resist such delicate attentions and so much love.

But most vividly of all I recall the long reading-aloud sessions we had when, concentrating chiefly at that time on poetry, we would take it in turns to choose and read from anthologies or collected works. Thus were opened to me the beauties of Keats' 'St Agnes' Eve', Shelley's 'Witch of Atlas', and Milton's 'Ode on the Morning of Christ's Nativity', and so many more abiding joys. As time went on my mother's taste veered away from poetry to prose. Her preference was for memoirs, histories, and classical novels. Long books of several volumes never daunted her. She drew me to many books I doubt I should ever have discovered for myself, such as Renan's *Vie de Jésus*, and the long *Tale of Genji* translated from the Japanese by Arthur Waley, to mention only two.

But the development of our new relationship was not always easy, and there were tempestuous passages between us from time to time. I often found my mother most difficult to understand, and immensely demanding: I dreaded her displeasure, and the emotional, electric storms that could brew. And from her point of view, I must have been excessively tiresome, graceless and priggish. I was right in the middle of the 'terrible teens', or, as the French more elegantly put it, *L'âge ingrat*.

While my mother and I were away disporting ourselves in the snow, my father remained at Chartwell, totally engrossed in his writing, or went to seek warmth and sunshine on the Riviera, where, of course, he continued to work. Clementine longed for him to join her on her sunny, snowy Alps. '. . . I wish you liked the snow,' Clementine wrote wistfully on 11th January 1937. 'If you saw it glistening under a royal sun & a limpid blue sky, I think you might.'

The highlight of Clementine's ski-ing career was when, with caution and dignity, she negotiated the Parsenn Run. Afterwards she wrote to Winston that it was

Quite easy from a professional point of view, but the excitement & the beauty were almost too much for me & I did long for you to be with me.

Do you know, I believe you would *love* this. I wish you could try. Only I'm afraid you would be too bold & come the most frightful purlers.[32]

From St Moritz about a week later, she telegraphed:

Heavenly if you could come here. Lovely colours in the snow for painting. Love. Clemmie.[33]

But Winston was not to be lured, and the only snowscapes he ever painted were views of the garden at Chartwell, mostly as seen from the windows of the house.

*

One of Clementine's great contributions to Winston was her assessment of people. Both Sylvia Henley (a close friend and observer over many years) and Violet Bonham Carter agreed on this, the latter writing of Clementine:

His cause was her cause, his enemies were her enemies, though (to her credit) his friends were not invariably her friends. Her appraisal of people was often more discriminating than his own.[34]

Like many women, Clementine formed swift, instinctive judgments, which she often could not justify in words. In the long run she was hardly ever wrong about some-body's character or capacity, and she rarely changed her mind, but time sometimes modified her views, and this was certainly the case with Brendan Bracken.

This extraordinary man, who shrouded his origins in mystery, appeared on the scene of Churchill's life in 1923, and determinedly attached himself to Winston's wagon. Robert Rhodes James has given a vivid picture of him: 'He was a big man, with flaming carrot-red hair in a tousled mop, with gig-lamp spectacles . . .'[35] He talked with a polyglot Irish-Australian-Cockney accent, and words would cascade from him in a torrent. Bracken's undeniable charm competed with a superficial toughness and brashness, which from the first aroused Clementine's antipathy and suspicion; and she took an instant dislike to him. She thought him an adventurer – which he was – and she mistrusted his influence on Winston. So little was she able to conceal her feelings of dislike and irritation that for a time Bracken rationed his visits, and arranged to meet Winston away from his home.

A further cause of Clementine's dislike of Brendan Bracken was, almost certainly, her knowledge of the rumour which persisted for many years that he was Winston's illegitimate son. Brendan did nothing to contradict this totally unsubstantiated theory, and Winston treated it with amused indifference. It was not, however, the sort of 'joke' that appealed to Clementine. The mystery surrounding Bracken's origins was only finally resolved by Andrew Boyle in 1974 in his biography, when he established beyond all doubt that he was the son of a builder-stonemason and his wife, born in 1901 in Templemore, Tipperary.[36]

Barely two years after the beginning of their friendship, Churchill and Bracken quarrelled over the publication of a magazine article. It coincided in time with Churchill's appointment as Chancellor of the Exchequer, and for the next few years Bracken's place as political acolyte and confidant was largely taken by Bob Boothby, who was his Parliamentary Private Secretary. But in 1929 the breach was healed: Brendan Bracken had by this time established himself both financially and socially, and in 1929 he had also become a Member of Parliament. From then on he moved into the close circle of Winston's friendship, fixing his political fortunes on Churchill's star, in good times and in bad.

Slowly Clementine's hostility was softened. In January 1931, we find her writing to Randolph:

Mr Bracken has been here once or twice.

I am giving up my vendetta against him & shall probably end by quite liking him. I'm not sure if this is broadmindedness or old age with its tolerance creeping in.[37]

It is much more likely that the 'sea-change' which took place in her feelings over the next years was due to Brendan's unusual qualities of heart and mind, and her appreciation of his passionate loyalty to Winston; although she was nearly always to doubt the wisdom of Brendan's political advice. But slowly he won her regard and affection – and later her abiding gratitude – for after the war, Brendan was to become a member of the Chartwell Trust, and an adviser on whom Clementine learned to lean.

Another of Winston's friends whom Clementine had viewed with disfavour from the first was Lord Birkenhead – F. E. Smith: and in his case the passing of time brought no alteration to her feelings. He had become Winston's closest friend, and Clementine's perennial dislike of him did not affect the relationship. She never could 'take' to his personality, and moreover she deeply mistrusted his influence with

Winston generally. As we have seen, she disapproved strongly of the effect of F.E.'s arrogant brilliance on Randolph.

But Clementine had always liked and admired Margaret Birkenhead, and their children, Freddie, Eleanor and Pamela, were contemporaries and friends of Diana, Randolph and Sarah. Moreover, Freddie and Pamela both married children of Lord and Lady Camrose – Sheila and Michael Berry. The Camroses were friends of long standing of the Churchills, and so these links made easier and more natural a *modus vivendi* as far as Clementine and F.E. were concerned.

When F.E. died aged only fifty-eight in 1930 Winston was deeply grieved, and felt a real and abiding sense of loss. Clementine's warm and feeling letter to Margaret Birkenhead shows sensitivity and understanding.

> Chartwell Manor,
> Westerham, Kent
> October the 1st 1930
>
> Dearest Margaret,
>
> Last night Winston wept for his friend. He said several times 'I feel so lonely'.
>
> I think of the tension, the fatigue, the pain, the disappointed hopes of your long agonising vigil. But also of the pride you must feel.
>
> Margaret Dear – I am sure Life still holds much joy for you. It must, for you have been – and are gallant and brave.
>
> I am sure he must like you to think of that.
>
> Your affectionate
> Clementine S. Churchill

The third among Winston's close friends whom Clementine regarded with the utmost distrust and, at times, dislike was Max Beaverbrook. And as with Brendan Bracken, she nearly always disagreed with the political advice he gave Winston.

Despite many differences of political view, and several periods of 'chilliness', the friendship between Winston and Max Beaverbrook was to prove long and enduring, despite Clementine's unyielding attitude. She was not unconscious of Beaverbrook's gnomish charm but, apart from her fears for his political influence, the puritan streak in her was affronted by certain aspects of his life. From Grantully Castle in Perthshire, where she was staying with the Balsans in September 1926, she wrote to Winston concerning a luncheon party at Chartwell to which he had invited Lord Beaverbrook and his great friend, Mrs Norton:

> Please do not allow any very low conversation before the Children . . . & I hope the relationship between him & Mrs Norton will not be apparent to Randolph & Diana's inquisitive marmoset-like eyes and ears . . .[38]

Max Beaverbrook was perfectly aware of Clementine's hostility towards him, and the situation must have appealed to his sense of irony: he may even have found a challenge and a piquancy in it. The amenities of surface friendship were always maintained between the two adversaries, and Max throughout the years was most attentive in all the little ways so dear to womankind – showering Clementine with fruit, flowers and sympathy when she lay ill. And during the Second World War he never failed to contribute generously to her charities. Clementine was not insensible to all this, and there is a series of charming letters from her expressing warm and genuine thanks for all these kindnesses.

There were also times of truce. Nobody admired more than Clementine the prodigies Beaverbrook achieved at the Ministry of Aircraft Production in 1940-1. And in political storms she was the first to acknowledge in Max a true 'foul weather friend'.

As the years rolled by, her dislike of him diminished. But as long as Winston continued in public life, so long did Clementine fight Max Beaverbrook's influence over him. But in the last years she laid aside her arms: they were all old, and anyway by then Max could neither help nor harm Winston.

It grieved Winston very much that three of his closest friends should meet with so little approval or appreciation from Clementine, and he would ever try to bring about a better measure of liking and understanding of them on her side. There is no doubt that Clementine was hyper-critical, and possibly over-protective where Winston's career or reputation were concerned: for all their life together, she was to be the scabbard to his sword. But with hindsight one can see that these three men: Bracken, Birkenhead and Beaverbrook – 'The Three Terrible B's', as Clementine called them – all shared to some extent similar characteristics. In all of them there was a touch of the buccaneer, and a streak of brashness and vulgarity, which jarred with Clementine and made her fear for the influence they might have with Winston.

Clementine's highly strung nature made her capable of rising to the level of the demands of her exacting life, and the heroic streak in her enabled her to meet undaunted the challenges, the triumphs and disasters of Winston's career. But she paid a high price in nervous wear and tear. Although she gave for the most part an impression of cool poise, Clementine was both shy and passionate. The face of serenity and calm she presented to the world at large over the years was an artefact of self-control. And when that control cracked – tempests could rage.

Clementine was a perfectionist, and at times she sacrificed too much on the altar of that stern goddess. The timid, tearful child who had sobbed over the dirty marks on the dazzling white of her pinafore was truly the precursor of the immaculate woman who strove for perfection in all departments of her life, driving others hard – but herself hardest of all.

For most of her life Clementine suffered from anxiety: anxiety for Winston; anxiety for her children; and an almost continual anxiety over money matters. Again and again she suffered from feeling over-burdened by the demands life made upon her: two houses to run; four high-spirited children; a role to play politically and socially. Yet other women have contended with as much, and more. But only she – Clementine – was married to Winston Churchill. But if the sheer weight of trivial troubles could lay her low, crises – whether personal or national – found her robust, resourceful, and possessed of astonishing reserves of stamina.

Clementine was not unconscious of these facets of her character, and she would sometimes recite, in wry exasperation, lines from an elegy written for a hard-pressed governess, but which she said would do very well as her own epitaph:

Here lies a woman who always was tired,
For she lived in a world where too much was required . . .

And there is this touching admission in one of her letters to Winston (obviously written after they had had 'words'), of her tendency to create mountains out of molehills:

My dearest Love I hope you have forgiven me for being such a scold when you were here.

When I arrived & saw you a flood of happiness spread through my being. It is a great fault in me that small things should have the power to harass & agonise me. I do not think Voronoff monkey glands would do me any good! What I need is to be inoculated with vegetable marrow or cucumber juice![39]

Although Winston had a more optimistic nature than Clementine, he too had known times of depression and deep frustration. 'Black dog' (as he had called them) had been his companion too often in earlier years for him not to know the power of such feelings. But for him the security and loving companionship of marriage had banished 'Black dog' to his kennel. Moreover, all his 'Chartwell based' activities, his writing and, above all, his painting, were sovereign antidotes to the depressive element in his nature.

Sadly for Clementine, she rarely found relaxation or peace of mind in all that Chartwell had to offer, and she had no outlet for tension and anxiety in some form of creative work, such as gardening, painting or needlework.

Although Clementine took real pleasure in the company of many of the guests who came to Chartwell, and apparently had many friends, there were, in fact, very few people in whom she confided. Ever since she was a young woman she had shunned intimate friendships, and even with those truly close and trusted friends such as Goonie, Sylvia Henley, and Horatia Seymour, she was loath to discuss her most besetting worries. Consequently she denied herself the relief of 'unburdening', which is such an essential safety-valve for most people.

Winston and his life filled Clementine's whole existence, and when she was well and in good form, she neither desired nor needed other companions or distractions. But when she was low and fretted, and her 'batteries needed re-charging', it was often difficult to find a good solution. As her daughters grew up, she turned to each one and found company and companionship. But daughters soon have their own lives, careers, husbands and children. Clementine's diffidence in personal relationships made her hesitate to propose herself to people, who would probably have been delighted to see her. All through her life Clementine missed chances with people, because she was too shy, and could not bring herself to be a little more natural and carefree in her approach. Thus, in a life full of people, she knew much loneliness.

Although Winston was endowed with a superb constitution himself, and supplied with an immense store of stamina, he was always most understanding and solicitous in all physical illness. Swift to initiate action, and always seeking the best advice, he insisted that 'doctor's orders' should be strictly carried out. Although Clementine carried and bore her babies with relative ease and lack of complication, Winston readily accepted that child-bearing entailed, both before and after the event, much care and rest, and his letters to Clementine and the 'new kitten' were always full of tender solicitude and care.

Indeed, illness always evoked all Winston's capacity for sympathy and understanding. Early in 1928 Clementine was gravely ill with mastoid. As was quite common in those days, the operation was performed in her own home; for some weeks thereafter she was in great pain and very low in spirit. Winston was alarmed and deeply concerned for her; he spent much time at her bedside, and used to read passages from the Psalms to her. This time of pain and anxiety brought them very close: from Lou Sueil, where she went to convalesce, Clementine wrote to Winston:

My Darling One – I do not regret my illness for it has brought you so close to me . . . you are always deep down in my heart and now your tenderness has unlocked it.[40]

Winston replied:

I loved to read what you wrote . . . I am always 'there'; but I am afraid that vy often my business & my toys have made me a poor companion. Anyhow my darling I care for no one else in the world but you – & the kittens; & in spite of the anxiety of yr illness I was glad to feel that you relied on me & that I cd help & comfort you a little.[41]

But Winston found it difficult to understand illness which was rooted in nervous or psychological origins. Although 'Black dog' had haunted him as a younger man, the beast had never undermined his power of action, and with his essential resilience, it genuinely puzzled him that the mere wear and tear of daily life should be able to lay his valiant and spirited Clementine low. Indeed, since the apparent causes of her periods of fatigue and tension were nearly always in themselves relatively trivial, Winston had to force himself to accept – even when he could not understand – that Clementine's bouts of mental and physical exhaustion were as much 'illnesses' as influenza or measles.

Nor was he oblivious to the fact that he himself (however unwittingly) somehow contributed to her troubles. And although he hated her leaving him, he ruefully recognised that a 'let-up' away from home – and away from him – was from time to time necessary for her poise and health.

Winston's letters to Clementine on these occasions express not only his solicitude and an element of self-reproach, but also they reveal the extent to which he missed Clementine, and how much he depended upon her. 'When do you think you will return my dear one,' he wrote when she was staying with the Balsans in the South of France in March 1925.

Do not abridge yr holiday if it is doing you good – But of course I feel far safer from worry and depressions when you are with me & when I can confide in yr sweet soul. It has given me so much joy to see you becoming stronger & settling down in this new abode [Chartwell]. Health & nerves are the first requisites of happiness. I *do* think you have made great progress since the year began, in spite of all the work & burdens I have put on you . . .

This letter ends with a moving avowal of all that Clementine meant to him:

The most precious thing I have in life is yr love for me. I reproach myself for many shortcomings. You are a rock & I depend on you & rest on you . . .[42]

When, many years later, I, their youngest child, read this passage, not a word jarred. It was true when it was written, and it remained true for all the forty more years Winston and Clementine were to be together.

HOLIDAY TIME

ONCE THE FAMILY HAD SETTLED at Chartwell, Winston and Clementine tended to stay away from home less. Their own pattern of week-end entertaining became established and, particularly in the summer, they enjoyed having their friends down to visit them.

Nevertheless they paid short visits together from time to time within a small circle of friends and relations. Among their ports of call were the Marlboroughs at Blenheim; Sir Philip Sassoon at Trent Park or Lympne; and Lord and Lady Desborough at Taplow. For several years they visited Lord and Lady Pembroke at Wilton House for Whitsun; and in the Visitors' Book there, the week-end was labelled 'Winstontide'. And many were the visits to the Duke of Westminster – Bendor – at one or other of his homes in England, Scotland or France.

But when the question of holidays or travel abroad arose, it revealed a wide distance in Winston and Clementine's tastes and temperaments. Winston was happiest of all at Chartwell, but the charm of landscapes lit by a brilliant and more constant sunshine was also strong. The South of France, with its wonderfully 'paintatious' scenery, both by the coast and in the hinterland, provided him with endless subjects, with all the amenities offered by hospitable friends in splendidly comfortable villas.

Miss Maxine Elliott, a former actress, and a considerable figure in late and 'neo-Edwardian' society, was consistently hospitable at the Château de l'Horizon at Golfe Juan. Mrs Reginald Fellowes – Daisy, the daughter of the Duc de Decazes, who had married a Churchill kinsman of Winston – also offered agreeable entertainment at Les Zoraides. And Lord Rothermere made them welcome at La Dragonnière at Cap Martin.

Winston was happy at all these places. The greater part of his days was filled with painting or writing, and he almost invariably took a secretary with him. He loved swimming in the translucent water, and in the evenings he briefly enjoyed the gay, gilded company which always congregated along that sunshine coast. And of course the lure of the 'green baize' of the gaming tables was always, for him, potent.

Small talk or social chit-chat bored Winston profoundly – but he rarely suffered from it, since he completely ignored it, resolutely pursuing his own themes. And although he greatly liked the company of beautiful, lively women he quickly tired of their conversation, and would always prefer to talk (or even shout!) 'across' them, to some man, if one happened to be present. If he was trapped with no relief in sight, he tended to sink into a total and daunting silence.

Since Clementine did not write books or paint she found herself imprisoned in these luxurious cages with very little to do, and surrounded by people whom, for the main part, she found shallow, vulgar and boring. The expeditions to the Casino, too, were for her a combination of boredom and acute anxiety. She did not enjoy gambling herself, and she was always consumed with anxiety lest Winston should lose a lot of money – which he quite often did. There is, however, this charming story: Winston and Clementine were staying in the South of France, and she, tired and bored, had left the tables early and gone to bed, leaving him hard at it. When she awoke in the morning, she found every inch of her counterpane covered with bank notes. Winston had been in a lucky vein, and had bestrewn her bed with his winnings – as the birds covered the Babes in the Wood with leaves!

But there was one place that Clementine went to, often and with real pleasure: Lou Sueil, the beautiful home, perched high above Eze, of Consuelo and Jacques Balsan. A Vanderbilt by birth, Consuelo had been the first wife of Sunny Marlborough; they were divorced in 1920, and the following year she had married this charming and gentle Frenchman. The life and company at Lou Sueil were rather different from those in the other houses along that coast to which Winston and Clementine were so often invited. Although the Balsans also had a beautiful house at Dreux in the north of France (St Georges Motel), they led a settled and 'rooted' existence in both places. Consuelo had a lively social conscience, and wherever she lived she took an active interest in local community affairs. Both she and her husband were persons of culture and distinction, and Clementine found herself in an atmosphere in which she was at ease. Writing to Winston from Lou Sueil on 24th February 1924, Clementine told him:

> Nothing could be kinder & more charming than Consuelo & Balsan. They love each other very much & it is a most peaceful & restful atmosphere . . .

Although Winston and she sometimes stayed together at Lou Sueil, it became the custom for Clementine to pay an annual visit to the Balsans, usually in February, on her own. She also used to stay with them in the summertime in Scotland, where they had leased Grantully Castle, near Aberfeldy in Perthshire.

Clementine had greatly enjoyed the winter months of 1922–3 which they had all spent in Cannes as a family, in the Villa Rêve d'Or. Then she had not been a guest, but able to lead her own life; and she had been much diverted by the local tennis life. But as time went on she opted out of the Riviera invitations (except those to Lou Sueil), and preferred to make plans of her own, or simply to stay at Chartwell, often quite alone if the children happened to be dispersed.

Her favourite holiday was to stay in a modest but comfortable hotel in some beautiful and interesting place, with either a woman friend, or a party of congenial people, or, as the children grew older, a child, and spend a week or two sightseeing and gallery-visiting in an unhurried fashion. Winston did not really enjoy sightseeing. He could enjoy a brisk expedition to some glorious panorama, or the scene of dramatic historical events (particularly if they afforded subjects to paint), but galleries and museums were not for him.

Winston could never really understand Clementine's antipathy to the South of France, and he would always try to persuade her to go there with him, deploying all his skill to depict this, to him, delightful region in the most tempting guise. But she rarely relented; only occasionally making brief visits of *acte de présence*, lest his hospitable hosts and hostesses should be offended by her continual absence.

But there were occasions when they achieved highly enjoyable and successful holidays together, such as when they visited Florence in 1925, and Venice two years later, in the autumn of 1927. Both these places afforded pleasures and occupations for each of them: Winston painting to his heart's content, while Clementine roamed the sights and galleries.

Two major expeditions on which Winston and Clementine embarked together were marred, one by an accident and the other by a serious illness. The first was in the winter of 1931, when Winston contracted to make a lecture tour, comprising forty lectures, in the United States. This he undertook largely to help recoup some of the money he had lost in the Great Crash two years before. To make this formidable and exhausting enterprise less severe, Clementine and Diana went with him. They sailed to New York in the *Europa* on 5th December, staying on their arrival at the Waldorf Astoria.

On the night of Sunday, 13th December, Winston was knocked down by a car while crossing Fifth Avenue to visit his friend Bernard Baruch and was taken at once to the Lennox Hill Hospital. When Clementine was told the news she was just going to bed; in her alarm she dressed so quickly that she arrived at the hospital in her stockinged feet.

Had Winston not been wearing a heavy fur-lined overcoat he might well have been killed, as the car was travelling at speed. As it was, he suffered severe shock and bruising, and developed pleurisy. He was released from hospital after about ten days, but he had to spend a further fortnight in bed in the hotel, where they all passed a somewhat muted Christmas.

In the New Year Clementine and Diana took their invalid to convalesce in the sunshine of Nassau. Clementine wrote a long letter to Randolph after they had been there about ten days. Winston was terribly depressed by the slowness of his recovery, and suffering from severe pains in his arms and shoulders. He really needed three or four months of relaxation, but this was not possible; as soon as he was at all fit, he was determined to finish the series of lectures, of which he had delivered only one before his accident – although he himself was seriously worried he might not be able to stay the course. Clementine wrote wisely to Randolph, 'I hope however they may *actually* help his recovery, especially if he starts off with a big success in New York . . .'[1]

But Winston was very low, Clementine told Randolph:

Last night he was very sad & said that he had now in the last 2 years had 3 very heavy blows. First the loss of all that money in the crash, then the loss of his political position in the Conservative Party* and now this terrible physical injury – He said he did not think he would ever recover completely from the three events.

You can imagine how anxious I am & I often wish you were here to help & advise me . . .²

They remained for three weeks in the Bahamas, and then sailed for New York. Winston was much better, but still weak. Nevertheless he gave his first lecture since his accident on 28th January 1932, before two thousand people in Brooklyn. Thereafter, for the first three weeks in February, he travelled throughout the United States, lecturing every day in a different place. He had galvanised himself into action, and dominated his lassitude and weakness. Clementine stayed long enough to see that Winston was standing up to the tempo and strain of the tour, and then returned home to England ahead of him. When Winston arrived home on 17th March in the *Majestic*, he was greeted by a small group of friends who presented him with a beautiful Daimler as a gift to celebrate his recovery.

In August of this same year Winston, Clementine and Sarah set out on what promised to be a fascinating journey. Accompanied by 'The Prof' and Colonel Pakenham-Walsh, the military historian who was helping Winston with his life of Marlborough, they toured the battlefields of his campaigns, and followed the course of the long and fateful march of Marlborough's army, which had culminated in the Battle of Blenheim.

Winston then intended to go to Venice with his family, but during the first week in September he became afflicted with a persistent fever, which was diagnosed as paratyphoid. He was at once admitted to a clinic in Salzburg, where he remained for over a fortnight, when, although he was still rather weak, he was allowed to return home to Chartwell. Only four days after his homecoming, Winston suffered a severe haemorrhage, and had to be rushed by ambulance to a London nursing home. He took some little time recovering from this illness.

*

In the late summer of 1934, Winston and Clementine went for a month's holiday aboard Lord Moyne's yacht, ss *Rosaura*. A former Financial Secretary to the Treasury, Lord Moyne (Walter Guinness) was a most agreeable, intelligent and unusual friend. Sailing from Marseilles, they visited Athens and Cyprus and the southern coast of Turkey. At Beirut they left *Rosaura*, and drove to the ruins of Palmyra, and from there to Damascus and on to Nazareth and Nablus, eventually meeting up again with their host in Jerusalem. Before rejoining *Rosaura* at Alexandria, Winston and Clementine visited Jericho, Amman, Petra, Akaba, and Cairo. It was a wonderful holiday, combining all the things they both enjoyed.

But the active and enterprising element in Clementine's nature was not wholly satisfied with visits to places that had known civilisation for thousands of years. And this cruise was to prove the prelude to another, and much longer journey which would take her literally to the ends of the earth.

*Churchill had resigned from Mr Baldwin's Business Committee in January 1931 over the Conservative Party's Indian policy.

Lord Moyne had undertaken to try to capture alive for the London Zoo specimens of the species of strange dragon-like 'monitor' lizards which inhabit the island of Komodo, one of the Lesser Sunda Islands of Indonesia (then the Dutch East Indies). Both Winston and Clementine were invited to go with him in *Rosaura* on this thrilling and interesting journey, which would last at least four months.

Winston saw how much Clementine longed to go, but he himself did not really enjoy sea travel for long periods of time, and he was, moreover, engrossed by the successive volumes of *Marlborough*, the first of which had been published the previous year. He was loath to let her go so far, for so long without him. But perhaps he recognised that again and again in their life together her plans or preferences had been subordinated to his needs and wishes, and here was a chance for her which would not be likely to occur again. And so, somewhat ruefully, he agreed that she should accept Lord Moyne's invitation.

This journey was to be one of the great events of Clementine's life. She recorded it all in long and vividly descriptive letters to Winston, the journalistic portions of which he had copied and circulated round the family. But the tender passages he kept for himself alone. Winston too was a faithful correspondent: his long, minutely detailed 'Chartwell Bulletins', consecutively numbered (there were twelve in all), were invariably dictated and typewritten. They covered not only Chartwell news, but also gave brief accounts of parliamentary happenings, and, of course, news of the children. Each missive had its covering letter, written in his 'own paw', with any 'stop press' news, and with his own private thoughts.

Clementine could not know it then, but looking back over the span of her years one realises that this odyssey through tropical seas and coral-fringed islands comes as a sunshine interlude before the darkening, anxious ending of the decade ushered in a period when, yet again, the utmost effort and commitment would be demanded of her.

Clementine left London by train on 17th December 1934, travelling overland to join the *Rosaura* at Messina. As the train rumbled across Europe, she wrote on the 18th:

> My darling. As my train steamed away from Victoria and I saw you all collected on the platform, I thought how much I love you all, and above and more than them all *you* my sweet and darling Winston. You all looked so sweet and beautiful standing there, and I thought how fortunate I am to have such a family. Do not be vexed with your vagabond Cat – She has gone off towards the jungle with her tail in the air, but she will return presently to her basket and curl down comfortably . . .

Happily installed in the *Rosaura* a few days later, she wrote:

> As I lie in bed I contemplate the photographs of my family erected on the chest of drawers against the opposite wall. I don't generally take photographs away with me, but this time is such a long absence I felt I could not do without them.[3]

In the same letter Clementine also reported that she was

> . . . beginning an enormous piece of needlework which Venetia [Montagu] made

me bring. I have got 144 reels of silk with which to quilt it & I calculate that even if I sew all day & never catch a butterfly or a dragon I could not finish it before my return!

It was, in fact, to remain forever incomplete.

Until they reached Rangoon, the party on board the *Rosaura* consisted, apart from Clementine, of Mr and Mrs Lee Guinness (he was a cousin of Lord Moyne) and Mr Terence Philip (a very personable and agreeable man in his forties). At Rangoon their host, Lord Moyne, and Lady Broughton (Vera, the wife of Sir Delves Broughton, from whom she was later divorced), were to join the yacht, having flown out from England; a flight of such length in those days being considered quite hazardous. But from Messina to Rangoon, a distance of some 6,000 miles and twenty days' steaming, the Guinnesses, Terence Philip and Clementine were *à quatre*, and they all combined most agreeably. On New Year's Day 1935, Clementine's thoughts turned homewards. 'Oh my Darling,' she wrote,

> I'm thinking so much of you & how you have enriched my life. I have loved you very much but I wish I had been a more amusing wife to you. How nice it would be if we were both young again.

It was three weeks before Winston replied to this letter, for the distances were now immense and mails slow; but when she at last received his letter, her heart must have been warmed by his grateful, touching recognition of all she meant to him:

> In your letter from Madras you wrote some words vy dear to me, about my having enriched yr life. I cannot tell you what pleasure this gave me, because I always feel so overwhelmingly in yr debt, if there can be accounts in love. It was sweet of you to write this to me, & I hope & pray I shall be able to make you happy & secure during my remaining years, and cherish you my darling one as you deserve, & leave you in comfort when my race is run. What it has been to me to live all these years in yr heart & companionship no phrases can convey. Time passes swiftly, but is it not joyous to see how great and growing is the treasure we have gathered together, amid the storms & stresses of so many eventful & to millions tragic & terrible years?[4]

When Lord Moyne and Lady Broughton arrived safely as planned at Rangoon, they brought more letters with them from home. On the Chartwell front the bulletin was, on the whole, satisfactory: the family was well; and Winston was continuing his wall-building activities. But the principal news in this New Year's Day letter was the arrival of a mechanical digger to perform two major landscaping jobs. The first was the creation of a ha-ha to the north of the swimming-pool, so that 'Your eye will plunge, as you desire, across a valley of unbroken green.'[5] The second task for the monster was to make the peninsula on the bottom lake into an island. Winston was evidently delighted with his new toy. The plan was that the digger should complete these two tasks in a week, at the cost of £25. 'In this one week he [the digger] will do more than forty men do,' Winston reported with enthusiasm. 'There is no difficulty about bringing him in as he is a caterpillar and can walk over the most sloppy fields without doing any harm.'

Unfortunately, these splendid plans went somewhat awry, and successive letters from Winston described the 'digger drama' in all its prolonged horror. On 31st January, he admitted that

Making the island has proved a bigger and longer business than I expected. It will take a fortnight in all. But the results will be pleasing . . .

Nearly a month later, the digger was not only still at Chartwell, but was hopelessly bogged. On 23rd February Winston wrote:

. . . for the last three weeks it has done nothing as its works broke, and further, it got itself into a hole from which the greatest efforts have been necessary to extricate it.

On 2nd March he owned disconsolately, 'The digger has involved me in a chapter of accidents and I doubt if I shall get out of it under £150.' The weather had been appallingly wet, and the digger

sunk deeper into the mud and finally wallowed himself into an awful pit. It became necessary to bring four hydraulic jacks . . . However after nearly a week the animal emerged from his hole and practically finished the job, though there is still a fortnight's tidying up for five men.

The ill-starred digger had obviously acquired all the characteristics of a live animal with a perverse personality. Winston explained the creature's difficulties with great understanding:

This animal is very strong with his hands but very feeble with his caterpillar legs, and as the fields are sopping, they had the greatest difficulty in taking him away. They will have to lay down sleepers all the way from the lake to the gate over which he will waddle on Monday. I shall be glad to see the last of him.[6]

But as Clementine approached Singapore, she only knew of the arrival of the marvellous monster which was to perform such wonders in so short a time at so small a cost. 'What tremendous works you are doing at Chartwell,' she wrote,

I'm *delighted* about the Ha-ha. Please do *not* throw back *too* much earth on the garden side or the slope *might* look too sudden . . .
How lovely it will be when your beautiful wall reaches the end.[7]

Winston was able to report the departure of the 'Monster' on 8th March, and one can almost hear his sigh of relief: 'The digger has gone, thank God.' And he was also able to reassure Clementine, who must certainly have had some twinges of anxiety about the depredations of the 'Monster'.

We have had a successful week tidying up. The island will look delightful when all is green again and the lake refills. Next week we shall finish the haha, in a way which I am sure you will like . . .

This news, however, did not catch up with her until she reached Batavia on 1st April.

Another faithful correspondent was Cousin Moppet, who acted as 'Fort-holder-in-Chief' during any prolonged absence of Clementine. She kept the wanderer up to date with all the minutiae of domestic and family life. The school holidays were coming to an end, and I was spending the last lap working in a nearby livery stable learning stable work; I had been to the circus, a pantomime, and several parties. Sarah had been in Wales hunting, but was soon to return to her theatrical dancing training. Diana, who was living in London, was waiting rather bleakly and sadly for her divorce case to be heard. When that grey day came in mid-February, the staunch Moppet accompanied her to court.

We get a vivid glimpse of Winston in one of Cousin Moppet's letters:

Winston has so many irons in the fire that the day is not nearly long enough – what with the new wall & the wonderful mechanical digger which does the work of 40 men – rebuilding Howes' [the chauffeur's] cottage, films & India, and when there is nothing else Marlborough so you see we are very busy.[8]

Sarah's letters were very loving and gay:

DARLING, DARLING Mummy,
  While I imagine you, with blue sky above your head gaily chasing after butterflies and dragons, with Mr Terence Phillips – panting 'Hi, not so fast, I can't keep up' life goes on here at Chartwell much the same, except of course that we miss you very much, and in all the hundreds of little ways that you would like being missed . . .[9]

And a month later:

Don't forget to come home sometime. Papa is miserable and frightfully naughty without you! Your children however are model in every way – and Mary is getting prettier and terribly horsey – and Cousin Mop is getting fat again . . .[10]

A later batch of letters, waiting for her when she arrived at Auckland on 20th February, were full of accounts of Randolph's exploits in the Wavertree by-election.

At Singapore, where they arrived on 17th January, Clementine took the opportunity of going round the Dockyard. She gave Winston a remarkably detailed account of its construction, and the reduction of its scope and facilities due to the Government's cheese-paring in defence spending.[11] Despite the torrid heat, Clementine called at the principal bookshop to ask

if there were a brisk demand for your books. They said that the compressed World Crisis had gone very well. The second volume of Marlborough was doing better than the first. They had sold 12 sets of Marlborough & had 5 more on order. I think that this is rather good when you realise how expensive it is.[12]

After leaving Singapore, they visited Borneo briefly, and called in at the Celebes and the Moluccas, eventually reaching Amboina, from where they were to explore the south coast of New Guinea. On 30th January, Clementine wrote a thrilling account of an adventurous expedition they had made up the estuary of the Eilanden River, in an area where, for a thousand miles, the coast was practically unknown.

'This is the "genuine article"!' she wrote, 'unchartered [sic] seas, unexplored territory, stark naked savages.'

Leaving New Guinea, they steamed down the eastern coast of Australia along the Great Barrier Reef and reached Sydney early on 6th February, where Clementine had a happy reunion with Margery Street – the faithful and much-loved 'Streetie'.

The yacht sailed on to Wellington, and around 21st February they were at Deep Water Cove in the Bay of Islands, where Clementine had her first and last experience of deep-sea fishing. She and Terence Philip were in one fishing boat, while Walter Moyne and Vera Broughton (old hands at the game) were in another. They spent hours trying to catch bait in a choppy sea before they even started 'really fishing'. After three hours of this, Clementine said she felt faint and wanted food, so they hove to in a little bay and had luncheon. 'But I felt so sick I could only drink claret and suck some very strong peppermints.'[13] In the afternoon, despite torrents of rain they tried again, but with no success; they got home to the yacht drenched and exhausted.

After this stern experience Clementine and Terence Philip gave up fishing, and on one day when there was a gleam of sunshine they picnicked on an uninhabited island instead. Undeterred, however, by either the weather or the heaving seas, Walter Moyne and Vera Broughton persevered, catching a couple of swordfish and two or three sharks. Of her host Clementine wrote:

Poor Walter caught 1 shark only. But *he* did not mind – He is the most unselfish man in the world and thinks the whole time of making pleasure & fun for his guests . . .[14]

Clementine had one rather frightening experience: the whole party were on a small uninhabited island hunting for lizards called 'tuataras', a few of which Walter Moyne hoped to capture for the Zoo. The island was in reality a sheer cliff, with only one side which was accessible, by climbing up from rock to rock and tree root to tree root; where the hill flattened out at the top it was densely covered with jungle growth.

Writing about her adventure to Winston, Clementine described how she enjoyed the first part of the expedition:

. . . I love rock climbing; and you know I always start with zest any excursion or expedition – Where I fall short is that I soon get physically exhausted. Scrambling on hands and knees thro' the Bush soon tired me out & I thought I would go back & wait in the dinghy at the foot of the cliff . . . I was *sure* I could retrace my steps. But presently I realised that I was hopelessly lost.

She tried shouting, but there was no answer; so she then tried to retrace her footsteps, but became exhausted struggling with the thick undergrowth. Presently she was deluged by a tropical rainstorm, and she was soaked despite the thick canopy of vegetation. Tired and disconsolate, she suddenly realised she was not alone:

Suddenly I saw one of the lizards, quite close looking at me with his agate eyes. He was motionless. I sat down near him & we watched each other – Then I started shouting again & thought, Now the lizard will scuttle off but he did not move. They are stone deaf. But my voice did not carry far . . . Presently the lizard moved off and left me. Suddenly I heard Walter's voice far away . . . I called back but I felt he could not hear – Still I felt comforted – Presently I heard a loud crackling of branches & there was the second officer – I almost kissed him. He blew a whistle which was the signal Walter had arranged for whichever found me first. There were about 8 looking for me by now. Presently Walter appeared white with anxiety – I was really lost for only 1 hour, but it felt like much more in that dense enchanted wood – Of course there was no danger really I suppose but I thought of lying there & dying of hunger as far away from you as I can be on this earth.[15]

The *Rosaura* continued on her voyage, heading northwards now from New Caledonia to the New Hebrides, the Solomon Islands and New Britain. From the wastes of the Pacific Ocean, Clementine wrote on 7th March:

Since Nouméa [the capital of New Caledonia] we have been crossing the trackless ocean calling at various islands. We are quite out of touch, the waters round some of these islands are uncharted, they are surrounded by cruel coral reefs and often no bottom can be found. Captain Laidlaw is a tower of strength for which I magnify and praise the Lord daily.

The sense of the distance that separated them was very real also to Winston, who earlier had written:

. . . it makes one gasp to look at the map & see what enormous distances you have covered since I saw the last of your dear waving hand at Victoria Station; and it depresses me to feel the *weight* of all that space pressing down upon us both. How glad I shall be when you turn homewards, & when the mails will be closing up together, instead of lagging & widening apart![16]

On 18th March they arrived off the island of Komodo – the home of the huge monitor lizards, the capture of which was the object of the entire journey. The large trap was landed in sections, and a goat caught to act as bait. The dragons' lair was presently located:

Half way up a green velvet hill is a huge upended rock about 40 foot square – At the base are 2 cavernous holes & we could in the dust at the opening distinctly see the track of the monster's tail. So he was at home!

wrote Clementine on 18th March, in her first instalment of her account of the great hunt.

On 26th March she again took up the tale:

This has been an enchanting bewildering & exciting week – I meant to keep this letter in the form of a diary adding to it day by day but failed to do it – In this way I could have made you feel the excitement the suspense the heat the repeated disappointments the fearful smell of the decaying baits – (which of course had always to be approached and watched with the wind blowing towards

one). Side by side with all this 'big game' 'Boys own Annual' world is the enchantment of this island which is the most beautiful thing I have ever seen & is perhaps
one of the loveliest wildest strangest spots in the world. It is deeply indented with
bays and lagoons. It has innumerable paradise beaches – some of the finest sand
(there is a pink one of powdered coral) some of wild rocks with coral gardens far
lovelier than at Nassau, & accessible. That is if you are not afraid of being
observed by a giant polyp or tickled by a sea snake 12 foot long . . .

The total result of the week's hunt was five small lizards, of which two were
liberated; the longest was about six feet long and, wrote Clementine, 'they have not
yet developed a very dragon like appearance. This comes with hoary age . . .'
Apparently it was very difficult to trap a real monster, they being few, and very
cunning, but the Expedition's photographer had managed to photograph a twelve-
foot lizard going off with half a pig in its jaws.

He & Vera Broughton have lain in wait for hours in the long grass in the blazing
sun near the traps, and near dead exposed & rotting animals to get good pictures.
I spent one hot morning watching & decided upon the other life – But I did see
one prehistoric peep of a dragon on a stony beach looking for crabs . . .[17]

On his return, Lord Moyne presented two Komodo dragons to the London Zoo;
they both lived until 1946, which is considered quite a good survival rate. Of the
several tuataras that were captured, only one survived the voyage home, and was
duly given to the Zoo; but it only lived five or six months.[18]

For all this time, and on all these thrilling expeditions to strange peoples and
enchanted islands, Clementine's constant companion was Terence Philip. She was
in her fiftieth year, but she was still exceptionally beautiful, and slender and graceful.
Terence was about seven years younger; he had been born in Russia, of British
parents, his father being a wealthy merchant there. Much of his youth was spent in
Russia, and Terence spoke the language fluently. His family returned to England
when the Revolution broke out in 1917, and Terence made a career in the art world.
At the period when he knew Clementine he was working for Knoedler's Art Gallery
in Bond Street, and was much sought after by London hostesses. Suave, good-
looking, charming and cultivated – it is hardly surprising to relate that Clementine
fell romantically in love with him.

For a brief period in her long life, which for the most part was rooted in obligations and reality, she lived in a dream world of beauty and adventure. She tasted the
always heady elixir of admiration, and knew the pleasures of companionship in
trivial doings and sayings. Looking back in after years on these five months of her
life, she viewed it all with detached amusement, in which one could detect only the
faintest nostalgia. Acknowledging that Terence Philip had never really been in love
with her, she added: 'But he made me like him.'[19]

After the voyage was over, their friendship continued for a little while. Terence
Philip came several times to Chartwell in the following two years: but then he came
no more. There was no quarrel: there was nothing to quarrel about – only agreeable
things they had shared to be remembered. But their relationship was like a fragile

tropical flower which cannot survive in greyer, colder climes. Once home, Clementine's real life, and the one and only great love in it, claimed her back entirely, as his cosmopolitan, worldly life – so different from hers – claimed him. Terence Philip soon went to New York, where he worked at Wildenstein's Gallery until his early death during the war.

Perhaps it was the very difference in their ways of life and outlook which had been as much part of the magic spell as were the blue seas, waving palms and tropical islands. Both had to awake from the unreality of a dream. The French nearly always have the right words for these matters of the heart, and Clementine summed it all up in a saying which seems to breathe the Edwardian world of her youth: '*C'était une vraie connaissance de ville d'eau.*'[20]

★

There was one more great treat in store before the *Rosaura* and her company turned towards home; they spent two days in Bali. Clementine was entranced:

> [It] is an enchanted island. Lovely temples embedded in green vegetation in every village. Lovely dancers. The inhabitants lead an Elysian life. They work for about 2 hours a day— The rest of the time they play musical instruments dance make offerings in the Temples to the gods attend cock fights & make love! Perfect? Isn't it?[21]

At Batavia, the capital of Java, where they arrived on 1st April, Clementine's fiftieth birthday, there were letters from home to greet them. Winston's enclosed a handsome cheque, which presently bought a beautiful pair of diamond clips. He wrote of her return:

> This has been a vy long separation for us; but now that 'Your nose is turned homeward', we can look forward to the end of it . . .
> Now on yr return journey you will be meeting yr mails, instead of them lagging behind you.[22]

This letter was decorated with a charming pig, labelled 'On guard & waiting'. Clementine's letter in reply was signed 'Your loving Homeing Clemmie'.[23]

Winston's letters continued to bring her all the news from home. The digger had departed, the orchard had been grubbed up and re-turfed, and the chauffeur's cottage renovated. In the 'big house' new bookcases had been installed in the drawing-room, which had also been redecorated.

The news on the animal front was varied: a black swan sitting on six eggs; the prudent bird had made her nest on the new island, and therefore escaped the fate of an unfortunate goose, which had been devoured by a fox. In the house the dog population had been exceedingly troublesome; my pug was the chief culprit. 'He commits at least three indiscretions a day . . .'[24] and this set a bad example to Trouble, Sarah's chocolate spaniel (the present of an admirer) and Harvey, Randolph's wire-haired terrier, who was also a guest at this time. In early April Winston could bear it no longer, and in an exasperated postscript announced that he had 'banished all the dogs from our part of the house . . . I really think you will have to buy a new strip of carpet outside my landing.'[25] Despite all these other pre-occupations, Winston worked away at building his wall, and he promised it would be finished by her return.

> How paltry you must consider these domestic tales of peaceful England compared to your dragons and tuataras. But I think it is very important to have animals, flowers and plants in one's life while it lasts.[26]

Familial tribulations were also weighing upon Winston. After the efforts and excitements of the election at Norwood, the children proceeded to cause some anxiety in matters of health. Randolph had a severe bout of jaundice; Mary caught whooping-cough; and Sarah was reported by a family friend to be looking tired and pale, which was not surprising considering she was, her father reported,

> dancing practically four hours a day as well as going to balls . . . I have therefore told her that she must not go to a ball on any night when she practises her dancing.[27]

Although Winston grappled with all these situations gallantly, he nevertheless looked forward to Clementine being able to resume her control of such matters.

But Winston's letters were not only concerned with 'domestic tales of peaceful England'. Each one contained an account of the political affairs which daily occupied his mind. During the whole of Clementine's absence, Winston had been embattled and battling with the India Bill. The debates tired him so much that he often could not face the drive to Chartwell late at night, staying instead at the flat which they had acquired a few years before in Morpeth Mansions, near Westminster Cathedral. On 1st January 1935 he had described how, in a debate in the House of Lords before Christmas:

> The poor old Tory Lords came up in hundreds from the country and voted as the Government Whips directed. They would certainly have much rather voted the other way but they know their place since the Parliament Act.

Now, three months later, they were still at it: 'I have had a very hard time with the India Bill,' he wrote on 5th April.

> They have taken it four days this week, and there are to be four days next week. I have to be there practically all the time and the only time I was away the Government got sixty clauses through in a twinkling.

Quite apart from the India question, the political cauldron was brewing. There were at this time continuous rumours that Ramsay MacDonald would shortly resign, and that his successor, Baldwin, would wish to include Churchill in a reconstructed Government. He wrote to Clementine:

> I am not at all keen on this, and there is a very desperate General Election which lies ahead. One would simply have to take the disgrace of the Government for all the opportunities they have missed.[28]

But lowering over all other issues was the growing might of Nazi Germany. On 8th March, Winston told Clementine: 'The German situation is increasingly sombre.' A month later, he wrote:

The political sensation of course is the statement by Hitler that his air force is already as strong as ours. This completely stultifies everything that Baldwin has said and incidentally vindicates all the assertions that I have made.[29]

As the distance slowly diminished between them, Clementine's thoughts turned more and more towards Winston and home. From Suez, on 20th April, she sent a short note:

Oh my darling Winston
    The Air Mail is just flitting & I send you this like John the Baptist to prepare the way before me, to tell you I love you & that I long to be folded in your arms. . .

Winston's last letter had told her how much he had missed her:

I think a lot about you my darling Pussie . . . and rejoice that we have lived our lives together; and have still some years of expectation in this pleasant vale. I have been sometimes a little depressed about politics and would have liked to have been comforted by you. But I feel this has been a gt experience and adventure to you, & that it has introduced a new background to yr life, & a larger proportion; and so I have not grudged you yr long excursion; but now I do want you back.[30]

Clementine arrived home on 30th April 1935: and great were the family rejoicings. She had traversed in all 30,000 miles of water.
    The Silver Jubilee Celebrations of King George and Queen Mary were very shortly to begin, and Winston and Clementine had been bidden to all the great occasions. Fortunately for her, she had lost a good deal of weight, and so she was able to step easily into model-sized dresses.
    Evidently the 'wander-lust' had entered Clementine's blood, for in a letter to Margery Street later in the summer she wrote:

It's very nice to be back but Oh Dear I want to start out again very badly! Mr Pug is very sweet but now he says 'NO' . . .[31]

And like all travellers, Clementine returned with a cargo of strange bric-à-brac, some of which found a place at Chartwell, like the giant shells, which formed exotic-looking cups for the smaller waterfalls (although in time they became a rather depressing shade of greeny-yellow).
    But the most charming of her mementos of the East was a Bali dove, an enchanting pinky-beige little bird with coral beak and feet, who lived in a beautiful wicker cage rather like a glorified lobster-pot. He was a great pet, and would crou-crou and bow with exquisite oriental politeness to people he liked. He survived for two or three years, when, no doubt homesick for his enchanted island home, he died. Clementine

had him buried under the sundial in the centre of the walled garden. Round the base are carved the following lines:

HERE LIES THE BALI DOVE

It does not do to wander
Too far from sober men,
But there's an island yonder,
I think of it again.[32]

THE THIRTIES

THE TEN YEARS that Churchill spent out of office in the political wilderness have been regarded by many, in retrospect, as the continued working of that guiding hand of destiny which seems to have been with him throughout his life, although during all that time Churchill himself was far from being resigned to his exclusion from the exercise of power. But his gradual estrangement from the Conservative Party's leadership, due to his disagreement over their Indian policy, and then his campaign for rearmament and confrontation of the growing power of Germany, made the probability of his being offered office increasingly remote.

This can now be seen as providential, for when the hour struck which Churchill had so long and so eloquently foretold, he was in an unrivalled position, and untarnished by involvement in policies he might well not have been able either to change or to moderate, given the prevailing mood of the country in the thirties.

Even at the time Clementine understood this, for she wrote in one of her letters from Austria in January 1936:

> The political situation at home is depressing. I really would not like you to serve under Baldwin, unless he really gave you a great deal of power & you were able to inspire and vivify the Government. But as you say we are in it up to our necks & that cannot be altered now. All you could do would be to organise our armed forces.[1]

When the Conservatives left office in 1929, Churchill had been, at first, a member of Mr Baldwin's Business Committee (or 'Shadow Cabinet'), but he had become increasingly disturbed by the Conservative Party's proposals for Indian self-government, which he regarded as rash and premature, and he had resigned from the Committee in protest in January 1931. This step excluded him from office when later that year a National Government of all three parties was formed with Ramsay MacDonald still as Prime Minister.

During the next few years the Indian question continued to occupy much of Churchill's thought and activity, and he was vigorous in opposing a policy with which he strongly disagreed. Despite Clementine's inherent radical tendencies, she agreed in the main with Winston's point of view on the matter of India's self-rule.

Indeed it was on this subject that she made one of her rare speeches in a controversial vein. At the Annual Conference held by the Central Women's Advisory Committee of the Conservative Party in May 1933, she spoke in support of an amendment to a motion from the platform congratulating the Government 'on the success of the policy of maintaining law and order in India, while continuing constitutional reform . . .'[2] The Duchess of Atholl, a Scottish M.P., and an outspoken supporter of Churchill's views, moved an amendment incorporating these words: '. . . but would view with grave anxiety proposals to transfer at the present time responsibility at the Centre of Government in India . . .' etc. etc. The amendment was debated, and Clementine made a short but effective speech in its support. Despite a powerful intervention by Lady Iveagh (one of the Party's 'big guns') urging the conference not to accept the amendment, it was carried by a clear majority. Clementine returned home flushed and triumphant from her foray, to be much congratulated by Winston.

This same year of 1933 was in many ways full of fateful events: at home, unemployment figures reached the peak of three million; in January, Hitler became Chancellor of Germany, and in October, Germany withdrew from the League of Nations. Churchill had the previous year criticised the Government's inadequate defence programme, particularly with regard to air defence; now he attacked their proposals to accelerate disarmament, when he knew Germany was secretly re-arming.

Soon the threat of the growing power of Nazi Germany, and this country's unprepared state, came to dominate Churchill's thoughts, and he concentrated all his powers to the task of warning and awakening. His warnings fell largely on deaf ears. But there were a band, both in and out of Parliament, who fought this unequal fight with him. It was unequal, because not only was Churchill at odds with the hierarchy, and most of the rank and file of his own party, but also, in the main, people did not want to hear his message, which was delivered at a time when pacifism was growing both as a mood and a policy throughout the country. But this did not daunt him, and around him gathered politicians of different parties, Civil Servants, and servicemen (as far as their position allowed) who supported his views. Chartwell was their meeting-place, and here also came from time to time harassed-looking Germans, Austrians, Poles and Czechs who, often at great personal risk, came to urge Churchill on in his efforts to awake the British people to the danger, which yearly loomed larger, before it was too late.

In all this, Clementine was heart and soul with Winston; and she sometimes waxed very fierce in argument with those who maintained the official party line, or took a 'pussy-foot' (pacifist) view of these matters. But on one major issue Clementine found herself at variance with Winston – the question of the abdication of King Edward VIII.

Early in December 1936 the British public were made aware of what the world's Press at large had known, and commented upon for many months past, namely that King Edward (who had succeeded his father in January of that same year) was deeply in love with an American, Mrs Ernest Simpson. The British Press, by common agreement, had not made any mention of this romantic situation, but it had been the subject of discussion and grave speculation in Court and government circles after Mrs Simpson's divorce from her second husband, Ernest Simpson, in October 1936. When the news broke, people of all classes and all shades of opinion joined in the great argument as to whether a twice-divorced woman could be Queen Consort of England.

There was a large body of opinion, chiefly among the young and romantically minded, which saw no reason why the King should not marry the woman he loved. There was a larger but less vocal section of the public which thought, quite simply, that King Edward should sacrifice his personal happiness to his royal duty. During the series of interviews between the King and Mr Baldwin (who had succeeded Ramsay MacDonald in June 1935), the Prime Minister had to tell him that Mrs Simpson would not be acceptable as Queen. The possibility of a morganatic marriage was canvassed, but after Baldwin had consulted opinions both in this country and in the Dominions (none of whose governments were prepared to accept Mrs Simpson on any terms), it became quite clear that either the King must renounce his plan to make her his wife, or he must abdicate his throne. He chose without hesitation to do the latter.

During the course of these harassing and painful days, the King turned for advice to (among others) Churchill, who was a friend of long standing, and who sought by every means within his power to play for time. He felt this momentous decision was being resolved with wanton haste, and that given more time and consultation, a happier issue might be devised. Churchill espoused the King's cause with loyalty and vigour; always a monarchist, every instinct of personal loyalty and chivalry was aroused by the dilemma of his Sovereign, for whom he had always had a true regard. Moreover, Churchill tended to take the romantic view, and felt that some arrangement could have been devised whereby the King could marry Mrs Simpson, and the country be spared the convulsion of the crisis which would be caused by his abdication. Furthermore, Churchill was certain the King commanded wide sympathy among the people of this country, who would rally to support him.

Clementine disagreed profoundly with Winston, both in his view of the problem and in his estimation of what public feeling really was. She thought Baldwin had correctly interpreted public opinion, and that in no circumstances would Mrs Simpson be acceptable to the British either as Queen Consort or even as merely the wife of the King. Clementine saw something else very clearly too: she realised that Winston's championship of the King's cause would do him great harm, and that he would be accused of making political capital out of this crisis. In all this she was proved right. Churchill's intervention aroused a wave of hostility towards him, both in Parliament and in the country. When he rose in the House of Commons after the Prime Minister had made a statement on 7th December, Churchill had barely begun his plea that 'no irrevocable step should be taken' before he was silenced by cries from all sides of 'No' and 'Sit down'; it was described by an observer as the 'most striking rebuff of modern parliamentary history'.[3] Four days later, King Edward VIII abdicated.

Although Clementine took the view that, as King, Edward VIII should have sacrificed his happiness to his duty, she was wholeheartedly at one with Winston in his anger against those (many of them in high places) who had turned against their Sovereign in his hour of anguished decision. And she was particularly scornful of those in the social world who had been only too willing to entertain King Edward and Mrs Simpson during the months that led up to the final crisis, but who turned cool when the day of reckoning came. In the February following the Abdication the Churchills dined with Henry Channon, M.P. ('Chips' Channon, a great society host and diarist); among the other guests were Lord and Lady Granard (he had held several royal appointments and had been Master of the Horse). Channon wrote in his diary:

> . . . Perhaps my guests were a little too Edward VIII for the Granards? It was, I admit, a thoroughly 'Cavalier' collection. Lord Granard tactlessly attacked the late King and Mrs Simpson, to his neighbour, Clemmie Churchill, who turned on him and asked crushingly, 'If you feel that way, why did you invite Mrs Simpson to your house and put her on your right?' A long and embarrassed pause followed . . . [4]

There is also an interesting and rather moving postscript to Winston's attitude towards King Edward and Mrs Simpson. On 12th May 1937, he and Clementine were in Westminster Abbey attending the Coronation of King George VI. At the moment when Queen Elizabeth was crowned as Consort, after making vows of the utmost solemnity, and receiving tokens of grace for her special task, Winston turned to Clementine and, his eyes full of tears, said: 'You were right; I see now the "other one" wouldn't have done.'

*

The period following the Abdication was probably the lowest point of Winston's political fortunes since the dark days immediately following the Dardanelles disaster. His warnings of the national peril ahead had been practically unheeded, and now discredit was cast on him by the feeling that his support of the King sprang from ulterior motives, and was largely prompted by antipathy to Baldwin. To those who knew him well this was malicious nonsense: Churchill had reacted to the King's plight spontaneously and naturally, as one would expect of someone possessing his instincts of loyalty and chivalry. Nevertheless this unjust appraisal blunted, at a most critical moment, his power to act and to persuade. Clementine had argued fiercely with Winston at the time of the Abdication and, privately, she now grieved at the price he had to pay for his intervention. In public, her attitude was robust and loyal, but realistic as always. Asked at this period if she thought Winston would ever be Prime Minister, she said: 'No, unless some great disaster were to sweep the country, and no one could wish for that.'[5]

Winston himself suffered at this time from feelings of almost fatalistic depression; in a letter discussing with Clementine the possibility of having to sell Chartwell, he wrote that:

> . . . no good offer should be refused, having regard to the fact that our children are almost all flown, and my life is probably in its closing decade.[6]

These words read strangely indeed: Churchill had nearly three more decades to live, and his life's supreme task and achievement lay ahead.

But if Winston's star was burning dimly in his own country, he had a strong and admiring following in France; and this was demonstrated at the time of the State Visit of King George and Queen Elizabeth to Paris in July 1938. Although holding no official position whatsoever, and despite being out of favour with his own Government, the French Government invited the Churchills to attend all the splendid functions which had been arranged to entertain the royal guests. Moreover, at all these elegant occasions, for which the French have such exceptional genius, Winston and Clementine were remarkably *bien placés*. This did not escape the notice of other English guests, and interested observers from the British Embassy. Faded programmes still remain in Clementine's album, and one in particular catches the eye – it is the menu for the great luncheon given at Versailles on 21st July. It was signed for her by her neighbours at the luncheon: one was the distinguished author Monsieur Gabriel Hanotaux, the other the Maréchal Philippe Pétain, both of whom made themselves exceedingly agreeable. This golden visit remained long in Winston's and Clementine's memories. In retrospect it seemed like the last gleaming of sumptuous hospitality, of elegance and finesse, before the gloom and squalor of war engulfed all Europe.

Meanwhile from 1935 onwards events full of portent and doom followed fast one after another. The invasion and subsequent annexation of Abyssinia by Italy was followed the next year, in 1936, by the occupation of the Rhineland by Germany. That same year came the outbreak of the Spanish Civil War in which both Germany and Italy intervened, and the bombing of civilian populations was seen for the first time in all its brutality and horror. And in the spring of 1938 the Anschluss saw the swallowing up of Austria. Not before time, and in a half-hearted way, Britain started to re-arm in 1935 – the year that Hitler announced that the German Air Force was at least equal to that of Britain. In 1937 Stanley Baldwin retired as Prime Minister, and was succeeded by Neville Chamberlain.

In September 1938, after the now familiar propaganda campaign of lies, semi-truths and threats, Hitler demanded the incorporation in the Reich of those parts of Czechoslovakia where the population was predominantly German. Each successive act of aggression had found the democracies divided and futile, but now it was generally realised both in France and Britain that the moment had come when they must at last make a stand. Moreover France was bound by treaty to support Czechoslovakia if she were attacked, and although Britain had no direct obligation to Czechoslovakia, we were pledged to support France. War seemed inevitable. In Britain, preparations began: the Fleet was mobilised; air-raid trenches were dug in the London parks; gas-masks were issued. Chamberlain had been twice to parley with Hitler, now on 29th September he flew once more to Germany, this time to Munich, where he met both Hitler and Mussolini, with Daladier, the French Prime Minister. Chamberlain concluded with Hitler the Munich Agreement by which the greater part of Hitler's demands was conceded, and Czechoslovakia sacrificed. Britain and Germany entered into a solemn agreement never to go to war with one another again.

Chamberlain, with tragic naïveté, genuinely believed he had come to terms with Hitler. When he returned to England, he was received with hysterical relief, joy and gratitude; he said he had brought with him on that scrap of paper 'Peace with honour . . . Peace in our time'. It was neither. Nearly everyone joined in the rejoicings, feeling only the terrible moment of peril had passed, and not caring or choosing to count the cost.

But to Winston Churchill, and those who followed him, the Munich Agreement was an act of shame and betrayal; it represented the final, fatal grovelling to the insatiable appetite of the dictators. Looking back, it is difficult to describe the feelings of anger, shame and bitterness felt by those who opposed the Munich Agreement. Most people shared in the general sense of relief, or joined the chorus of praise and adulation, which for a short period surrounded Mr Chamberlain; but the little world of like-minded friends and colleagues which centred around Churchill throbbed with anger and emotion. It was almost impossible for those taking the opposing views in this fierce argument to meet without there being high words. Clementine felt this crisis with passionate indignation, and I well recall her setting upon one quite formidable lady, who had expressed pro-Chamberlain views during a luncheon at Chartwell, and reducing her to tears. But whether people supported Munich or not, only the most purblind thought it was anything more than time dearly bought.

*

The year of 1938 had not been a good one for Clementine's health; and in early July she had gone, alone, to a watering-place at Cauterets near Lourdes, in the French Pyrenees, where she took the cure for nearly three weeks before joining Winston in Paris for the very enjoyable State Visit. During her short stay in Paris she stubbed and broke her toe against the claw foot of an Empire table; although not a serious injury, this small accident was for many weeks the cause of considerable pain and hindrance. On top of this came the tensions and emotions of the Munich crisis, and by the autumn Clementine was low and debilitated again. However, at this moment a delightful invitation came her way: Lord Moyne once more invited her to go for a voyage in the *Rosaura*, this time to the Caribbean. The Government had set up a Royal Commission to enquire into the social conditions of the West Indies, and Lord Moyne had been appointed the Chairman; he proposed to take his yacht, and as well as accommodating about half the members of the Commission in turn, he also invited his son, Murtogh Guinness, Vera Broughton and Clementine, who gratefully accepted this chance to restore her health and spirits.

Although Clementine enjoyed this journey, and found it deeply interesting, it was not as carefree or idyllic as the long cruise she had made to the East Indies some three years before. In the first place, the whole purpose of this voyage was to carry out the exhaustive enquiries of the Royal Commission, and all purely pleasurable considerations were of secondary importance. Moreover, the enjoyment of the beauty of the islands and the pleasures of the cruise was to some extent tempered, even for the guests, by the depressing effect induced by a study of the social conditions which existed among the native populations, which had given rise to the demand for an official investigation.

Clementine felt keenly the contrast between the beauty of the island scenery and the squalor of the human conditions. From Barbados, she wrote to Winston:

... soon I think I will come home. These islands are beautiful in themselves but have been desecrated & fouled by man. These green hills covered with tropical bush & trees rise straight out of the sea, & fringing the coasts are hideous dilapidated crazy houses, unpainted for years with rusty, corrugated iron roofs – Trade stagnating, enough starchy food to keep the population alive but under nourished – Eighty per cent of the population is illegitimate, seventy per cent (in several islands) have syphilis and yaws. The homes of the labourers are small sheds full of holes stuffed with rags or patched with old tin – There is no sanitation of any sort, not even earth latrines; in some places the women have to walk 3 miles to get water – In many places the proportion of doctors to the population is one doctor to 30,000 persons. Labourers' wages are 1/- a day for men & 6d. for women – There is much unemployment & no system of Insurance – And this is a sample of the British Empire upon which the Sun never sets . . .[7]

Writing to Margery Street in a similar vein a month or two after her return home, she told her that

... the Commission disagreed bitterly among themselves, the Tories wanting to do nothing but introduce birth-control & even sterilization, & the Labour members stirring up trouble wherever we went (All the same, I felt much more sympathy with their point of view) . . .[8]

Clementine's thoughts had constantly turned towards home during her Far Eastern journey, but on this voyage there is a note of almost poignant homesickness in her letters. Although she was half the world away under blue skies, events in Europe cast their long cold shadows even there. Bound up closely as she was with Winston's frustrating battle to awake people to reality, and caring passionately for the issues involved, Clementine pined to be with him in these anxious, fateful months.

While staying in Jamaica for a few days with the Governor and his wife (Sir Arthur and Lady Richards) Clementine had a rather strange and moving experience. The Governor had invited her to come with him and his wife on a tour of the island which he was about to make as he was newly arrived there himself. 'I must tell you,' wrote Clementine,

that in a tiny highland village where the Foundation Stone of a school was being laid the Chairman welcomed me as the wife of the future Prime Minister of England upon which the whole pitch black Audience burst into 'loud & prolonged cheers'. The Chairman told me that they all know about you & follow your doings in the Jamaican Press. I was thrilled & moved but rather embarrassed, as this rather took off from the Welcome to the New Governor who had never been to the spot before.[9]

Half the world away at home, Winston thought a lot about Clementine; but much though it interested him to hear about her doings, and the politics and problems of the Commission, what he really yearned to hear was news about her own health and well-being, and in his first letter on 19th December he wrote:

I send you telegrams frequently: but in yr answers you do not tell me what I want to know – How are you? Are you better & more braced up? How is the voice? Have the rest & repose given you the means of recharging yr batteries. That is what I want to know. And even more – do you love me? I feel so deeply inter-woven with you that I follow yr movements at every turn & in all circumstances. I wonder what you are doing now. Yr dear letter from the ship arrived after my chiding telegram had been sent off. Do cable every few days, just to let me know all is well & that you are happy when you think of me.

But Clementine's thoughts also turned to him, for two days after Winston wrote asking so lovingly about her health, she cabled him:

My Darling. My thoughts are with you nearly all the time and though basking in lovely sunshine and blue seas I miss you and home terribly. Tender love. Clemmie.

Clementine spent Christmas in the Leeward Islands, and once again this year, the family at home was somewhat depleted. Diana was happily ensconced in London with her second baby, Edwina, born on 22nd December, and Sarah and Vic were away. So just three of us, Winston, Randolph and myself (now sixteen) repaired to Blenheim, where a large and gay party of cousins and friends was gathered.

On Christmas Eve, although she had only been away a month, Clementine con-fessed to Winston:

It feels much more. I miss you & Mary & home terribly; & although it is a boon to miss the English Winter & to bask in this warmth; I really think I should come home – only that I hope this prolonged voyage in warm weather will really set me up in health – I do not yet feel very strong, but I am sure I shall . . .[10]

On 1st January 1939, Clementine was in Antigua, where she visited Nelson's old dockyard:

There is an historic & romantic old Naval Dockyard set in a beautiful little bay called English Harbour. Rodney, Hood & Nelson all were here. It is not deep enough for modern ships and the Navy gave it up 50 years ago. Nelson served here as a young Captain of 25 . . . It is a beautiful but sad and eerie spot with the deserted Dockyard Buildings falling to pieces. The old capstans are there rotting into the ground, & huge iron rings. There is a tiny dock for small ships and great stone pillars which used to support the roof of a gigantic boathouse, all blown away in a Hurricane. I was alone for a while . . . and I wondered if I should see the shades of departed heroes & hear the men in the Stores and Workshops.[11]

The Dockyard made a lasting impression upon Clementine, and years later, in 1954, she became President of an appeal which raised enough money to restore this beautiful and historic place.

Although Winston sent frequent telegrams, almost for the first time in all their life together he was found wanting as a correspondent. It must have been the sheer volume and pressure of work, for he was in the throes of writing *The History of the English-Speaking Peoples* – and it absorbed him completely. His first letter to Clementine, a month after she had left home, told her how intensively he had been working: 'I have been toiling double shifts . . . It is laborious: & I resent it & the pressure.'

But poor Clementine was feeling thoroughly neglected: Winston had taken to dictating most of his letters – even personal ones, for he found it burdensome writing in his own hand. Clementine had always resented this now established habit, and he nearly always wrote a long Post Scriptum, or a covering note in his 'own paw' to mollify her. But now on New Year's Day 1939 she begged him:

Do you think you could dictate a few words every day to a secretary & she could send it off twice a week. Never mind about writing yourself – I used to mind about that, but I'm accustomed to type written letters now & I would rather have them than nothing. I feel quite cut off.

Your loving but sad
Clemmie

The series of telegrams Winston had sent had been a further cause of frustration to her, for she added in a rather cross postscript:

Please don't telegraph – I hate telegrams just saying 'all well rainy weather Love Winston'.

But even before he could have received this ruffled letter, Winston had resumed his habit of writing often, and his next letter bore a piece of news which deeply moved her: Sir Sidney Peel, her faithful lover of so long ago, had died. In a post-script in his own hand to his letter on 29th December, Winston wrote:

My dearest Clemmie, You will be saddened to know that Sidney Peel has died. I do not know the cause. Many are dying that I knew when we were young. It is quite astonishing to reach the end of life & feel just as you did fifty years before. One must always hope for a sudden end, before faculties decay . . .

But Clementine had already learned this news, and from Barbados on 19th January 1939 she wrote:

My darling. Four days ago I was sitting in the Public Library at Dominica (this was before getting your last letter[12]) reading up the back copies of the 'Times' and suddenly there was Sidney Peel looking at me from the middle of the Obituary page – A young photograph, as I used to know him – I closed my eyes; Time stood still, fell away, and I lived again those four years during which I saw him nearly every day – He was good to me and made my difficult rather arid life interesting – But I couldn't care for him & I was not kind or even very grateful – And then my Darling you came and in that moment I knew the difference –

I am glad you wrote to me about it because at that moment I longed for you – I wanted to put my arms round you and cry and cry.

Scanning the newspapers Clementine sensed that the whole political situation was deteriorating from day to day, and she felt deeply for Winston in his lonely battle:

I have been reading Prescott's Conquest of Mexico – At the end of his life Cortez was treated with coldness & ingratitude by the Spanish Government. 'He found like Columbus that it was possible to deserve too greatly.' So you see you are in good company. And Oh Winston are we drifting into War? without the wit to avoid it or the will to prepare for it – God bless you my Darling.[13]

One can plainly see from Clementine's letters that this holiday had not the quality of enchantment or the sense of escape from reality of her other voyage, when times were less harassing and anxious. Moreover, she now felt herself somewhat strained by tensions on board the yacht arising from political differences. There was a real blow-up one evening while they were in Barbados: the company was listening to a broadcast from England, in which Winston (and the anti-Government point of view in general) was attacked. Vera Broughton exclaimed in a loud voice, 'Hear, Hear!', which angered Clementine, as it was evidently intended for her benefit; but what really wounded and enraged her was that Walter Moyne remained ostentatiously silent – thereby inferring his tacit agreement with Lady Broughton. Clementine was already yearning for home, and her mind was particularly full of Winston and of his embattled position, and this was the last straw. She decided on the spur of the moment to return home. She went at once to her cabin and wrote a letter of explanation to her host; the next morning she went ashore and booked herself a berth on the Cuba, which was leaving Barbados the very next day bound for England. On her return aboard the Rosaura Lady Broughton came to her cabin, and although they had a somewhat heated exchange, she begged Clementine not to leave. But Clementine was not to be moved: she had made her plans, and politely but firmly she stuck to them. Accordingly, the next day she sailed for home. Despite her sudden departure under these strained circumstances, her long friendship with Walter Moyne remained unaltered.

There were seven months left to run of uneasy peace, and although one could not know the day or hour, all of us knew that time was short. Despite the feeling that the great storm was gathering on the near horizon, from a family point of view the spring and summer of 1939 were particularly happy months, and my mother, who was in much better health, felt in a mood to relish life at home. She spent a lot of time at Chartwell with me: I was basking in the glow of parental praise and approval at this time, having, to everyone's astonishment (including my own), managed to pass my School Certificate with considerable success. This normal and modest achievement was rewarded by the present of a horse of my own, which caused me ecstatic delight. My mother dug out her own old hunting clothes, and we went out with the Old Surrey and Burstow hounds together on several occasions that season. A further treat was when she took me for a wonderful week-end to Paris at my summer half-term, where we packed into three lovely days an orgy of sightseeing and several plays.

In August my father made a tour of the Maginot Line at the invitation of the

French Government, and afterwards he and my mother and I went to stay with Consuelo and Jacques Balsan at St Georges Motel, near Dreux. Conscious that the sands of peace were fast running out, one's appreciation of those halcyon summer days was heightened: there was swimming and tennis (so greatly enjoyed by Clementine) and *fraises des bois*; Winston painted a lovely picture of the exquisite old rose-brick house; we visited Chartres cathedral and were drenched in the cool blueness of the windows: 'Look thy last on all things lovely every hour.'[14]

On 23rd August Russia and Germany signed a pact of mutual non-aggression; Hitler, his Eastern frontier now made safe, could turn on Poland, but Chamberlain had issued a solemn warning that in this eventuality Great Britain would stand by her guarantee to Poland. We had to go home: my father left at once for London by air. My mother and I followed the next day, and as we passed through Paris on that golden summer evening the Gare du Nord teemed with soldiers: the French Army was mobilising.

YEAR OF DESTINY

CLEMENTINE arrived home with ten days of peace to run. War preparations were now afoot in earnest. Many people still believed that some miraculous, last-minute happening might yet stave off the terrible reckoning, but in the early hours of 1st September Germany fell upon Poland with all her might by land and air. The next day the mobilisation of British troops was ordered, and, acknowledging that war now seemed certain, the Prime Minister sent for Churchill and invited him to be a member of his small War Cabinet.

The final ultimatum to Germany expired at 11 a.m. on Sunday, 3rd September 1939, and at 11.15 a.m. on that bright, breezy morning Chamberlain broadcast to the country and to the world that Great Britain was at war. Winston and Clementine listened to this dread, yet, to them at least, long-expected news at Morpeth Mansions. The Prime Minister had hardly ceased speaking when the banshee wailing of the air-raid sirens, soon to become so familiar, was heard. Winston described how Clementine 'came into the room braced by the crisis and commented favourably upon German promptitude and precision . . .'[1] They went up onto the roof to see what was going on, and noted thirty or forty anti-aircraft barrage balloons slowly rising.

> We gave the Government a good mark for this evident sign of preparation, and as the quarter of an hour's notice which we had been led to expect we should receive was now running out we made our way to the shelter assigned to us, armed with a bottle of brandy and other appropriate medical comforts.[2]

However, this dramatically timed alarm proved to be a false one, and the 'All Clear' sounded about ten minutes later.

The House of Commons assembled briefly, and afterwards the Prime Minister again sent for Churchill, and offered him the office of First Lord of the Admiralty with a seat in the War Cabinet.

Winston reported to the Admiralty at six o'clock that evening. It was a moment fraught with emotions and memories of which Winston wrote: 'So it was that I came again into the room I had quitted in pain and sorrow almost exactly a quarter of a century before . . .'[3] The Admiralty saluted his return as First Lord in the terse signal sent to the Fleet: 'Winston is back!'[4]

Clementine now found herself with much to do: Winston was once more in high public office, and after so many years Admiralty House was again to be their home. When they had last lived there, reasons of personal economy had dictated that they only used part of this beautiful and rather grand house; now the exigencies of war made it prudent that they should once more inhabit only part of it. The Office of Works speedily made ready the top two floors of Admiralty House, and there Winston and Clementine were soon installed, in the nurseries and attics. Indeed, their drawing-room still had the chintz curtains with the gay design of red and blue sea-horses hung by Diana Cooper to divert their young son, during Duff Cooper's tenure as First Lord a year or two earlier.

Not only had the flat in Morpeth Mansions to be disposed of, but a decision had soon to be taken about Chartwell. At the end of August the evacuation of women and children from London had begun, and a few days later Chartwell received its party of evacuees – two mothers with seven children between them, from the East End. Like nearly all those families who left their homes in the first official evacuation these drifted back to London after about three weeks, preferring home and familar scenes, notwithstanding the risk of bombing, to the loneliness and intolerable boredom of country life. It was obviously impracticable to keep the big house open now, but the three-bedroomed cottage which Winston had been building in the orchard during the last two years, with this situation partly in view, was nearly finished; he and Clementine therefore decided to shut up the big house, and were soon able to use Orchard Cottage for fleeting week-ends. Cousin Moppet was put in charge of the property, and she moved into the former chauffeur's cottage with Diana's two small children, Julian and Edwina, who with their Nannie had been evacuated from London.

When war was declared people braced themselves for sudden and terrible events to overtake the country. From afar we witnessed the grim annihilation of Poland; and then there ensued months of almost uncanny inactivity on land and in the air, causing this period to be be known as the 'twilight war'. At sea, however, war began at once: on the night of 3rd September, a German U-boat torpedoed the outward-bound liner *Athenia*, which sank with heavy loss of life; in October the *Royal Oak* was torpedoed as she lay in supposed safety in Scapa Flow, and by the middle of November 60,000 tons of British shipping had been sunk by deadly magnetic mines. These dire events focused attention on the man who headed naval affairs. At the end of September, Clementine wrote to her sister Nellie:

> The war news is grim beyond words. One must fortify oneself by remembering that whereas the Germans are (we *hope*) at their peak, we have only just begun.
> Winston works night & day – He is well Thank God & gets tired only if he does not get his 8 hours sleep – He does not need it at a stretch but if he does not get that amount in the 24 then he gets weary.[5]

Winston's need for sleep to recoup his energies, and his capacity for going off quickly into a deep sleep, formed from the earliest weeks of the war a habit which he was to continue throughout the crisis years, namely, his insistence upon taking an hour's rest some time during the course of every afternoon or early evening; he undressed and went right to bed, and awoke a giant refreshed. He was then able to work after dinner long into the night. This system undoubtedly contributed to Winston's ability to survive the strains and support the burdens of five long years of war. It enabled him, as he wrote himself, 'to press a day and a half's work into one'.[6] But what was for him a life-saver, placed many of those who worked closest to him under fatigue and strain. Most of those affected by this unusual habit accepted the inconvenience to themselves with understanding and loyalty, and Clementine and his close entourage protected his rest hours with determination.

With really remarkable speed Clementine seemed to get our new home running smoothly and comfortably. From the first days there was a constant stream of people for lunch or dinner; very few of them were social acquaintances or friends, nearly all of them political and service colleagues. For Winston, meal-times were merely a convivial extension of working hours; he saw them as a golden opportunity to get to know a new personality, or to pursue a line of thought.

But now over all conversations hung the shadow of 'security'. The servants had to be vetted by the security service; and the presence of strangers, however charming, or most friends, however close, put a stop to nearly every subject. Clementine consequently had to plan any social entertaining with particular care, and, indeed, it was reduced to the bare minimum, with 'outsiders' grouped together. There was the small golden circle of trusted colleagues, and nearest relations known to be 'padlock', and to whom, of course, that trust was sacred.

Our domestic life, perched on the top two floors of Admiralty House during the opening months of the war, was very close and happy. Diana was serving in London as an officer with the Women's Royal Naval Service (W.R.N.S.), and her husband, Duncan Sandys, a Territorial Officer, was stationed with his Anti-Aircraft Regiment in the London area. Sarah and Vic had a flat in Westminster Gardens, and were busy and happy acting. I was seventeen and, having just left school, was revelling in my first taste of London and 'grown-up' life. While continuing my education part of the time, I also worked in a canteen and a Red Cross workroom. Living at home, I was able to help with the entertaining, and to be a companion and confidante for my mother.

In late September Randolph became engaged to Pamela Digby, the elder daughter of Lord and Lady Digby. Randolph was in his father's old regiment, the 4th Hussars. Since they might be ordered abroad at any time, the marriage took place very quickly, on 4th October, in London. The wedding reception was held at Admiralty House, where the state rooms were opened up for this joyous family occasion.

During the eight months Winston was at the Admiralty Clementine took a close interest in matters concerning naval welfare, and shared in much of the work encouraged and organised by the Navy wives. In January 1940 she made a public appeal for contributions to a Minesweepers and Coastal Craft Fund. These small ships, hurriedly commandeered to meet the emergency, and collected in large numbers in small ports, had few of the comforts on board or the amenities ashore that were available to bigger, regular service ships. Clementine's appeal touched the particularly warm spot in the British public heart reserved for the Navy, and considerable sums flowed in; she kept a close personal interest in the work of the Fund, and Diana Cooper recorded, after a visit to Winston and Clementine in the early months of 1940, 'She makes us all knit jerseys as thick as sheep's fleeces, for which the minesweepers must bless her.'[7] In November 1939 Clementine also began her work for the Fulmer Chase Maternity Home for the wives of officers of all three services, with which she became deeply involved.

During all these autumn and early winter months, Britain had been slowly adjusting herself to the new conditions of life. People had expected action, violence and suffering; instead, they had to stumble around in the darkness of the black-out and were asked to conform every day to more and more instructions from Whitehall; they complied with considerable goodwill, and an astonishing degree of self-discipline. No one doubted that sterner days would come, but in the meantime people tried to remember to carry their gas-masks and identity cards and to 'Talk Victory', as recommended from the hoardings. The news from the only real scene of action – the war at sea – was almost unrelievedly disastrous and depressing. But as the first year of the war drew to its close, the anxious dreariness was dramatically interrupted by the Battle of the River Plate, which ended with the scuttling of the German battleship *Graf Spee*, after a fierce encounter with three British cruisers. The suspense at Admiralty House was intense, as we followed the battle message by message. It was a glorious victory, and brought a gleam of light into a dark December.

Winston and Clementine spent this first Christmas of the war in London, gathering around them quite a number of the family, and two old and valued friends and 'Chartwell regulars', Brendan Bracken and 'The Prof'. The New Year of 1940 opened quietly, and towards the end of March Winston was able to go with Clementine when she went up to Barrow-in-Furness to launch an aircraft carrier, the *Indomitable*. There are few more moving, thrilling sights than the launching of a great ship. One of the best photographs ever taken of my mother was of her waving the newly named ship away; it became my father's favourite one of her, and after the war he painted a charming sketch-portrait from it.

*

The trance-like atmosphere of the 'twilight war' was abruptly shattered on 9th April, when Germany leapt upon Denmark and Norway. Denmark succumbed at once, but the Norwegians fought the invader with desperate heroism, appealing to Great Britain for help. A naval and military force was hurriedly despatched, but they could make no impact on the German defences, and were exposed to the deadly harassment of the Luftwaffe. The fateful consequences of the failure to heed Churchill's warnings about the might of Germany's air power were tragically clear. Within three weeks all British troops had been evacuated except those carrying on a desperate but doomed struggle to seize the port of Narvik.

The disastrous campaign in Norway brought home dramatically the consequences of irresolute leadership and inadequate planning. When on 7th May Chamberlain opened a two-day debate in the House of Commons on the Norwegian campaign, bitter and damaging speeches were made against the Government and the Prime Minister from all sides of the House. Churchill, who felt he bore a major responsibility for the events in Norway, asked to be allowed to wind up the debate, and made a spirited defence of the administration, although it included many who had turned a deaf ear to his warnings and had opposed him with determination and sometimes hostility for many a long year. The closing stages of the debate were passionate and noisy; the Conservative back-benchers came out in open revolt and, when the House divided, the Government's majority slumped from 240 to 81.

Faced with the loss of the confidence even of his own party, Chamberlain sought to discover whether the Opposition parties would be prepared to serve in a National Government; the answer was that both the Labour and Liberal parties were ready to join a National administration – but only under a new Prime Minister. Chamberlain's first hope was that his Foreign Secretary, Lord Halifax, might succeed him, but it became manifestly clear as the hours wore on that Churchill was emerging as the only acceptable leader around whom all parties would rally in this dire crisis.

On the night of 9–10th May, German forces invaded Holland and Belgium. These events clinched the political situation at home. At six o'clock on the evening of the 10th May Chamberlain went to Buckingham Palace to tender his resignation; half an hour later the King sent for Churchill and asked him to form a Government, and a few hours later Churchill returned to the Palace to submit the first list of names of members of the new Government for the King's approval.

During these tense and anxious days Clementine was away from London; her brother-in-law, Bertram Romilly, had died at his home in Herefordshire on 6th May, and two days later, Clementine had travelled north to be with Nellie. It was anguishing for her not to be with Winston during these days; and he, sensing that events were moving towards a climax, telephoned, asking her to return as soon as possible. Accordingly, the day following her brother-in-law's funeral, she travelled back to London, arriving at Admiralty House shortly before Winston left to go to Buckingham Palace to receive the King's command to form a Government. And so they were together to share this strange and grim apotheosis after the years of exile from power and unheeded prophecies. Great events always found Clementine at her best, and at this moment Winston was as calm as he was resolute. 'I felt as if I were walking with destiny,' he wrote, 'and that all my past life had been but a preparation for this hour and for this trial.'[8]

Churchill lost no time in composing his Government, which included members of all the three principal parties, and whose scope was widened to include men of ability and stature from outside the political field. On 13th May Churchill addressed the House of Commons for the first time as Prime Minister, ending his speech with the great peroration which struck the keynote of his leadership:

... I would say to the House, as I said to those who have joined this Government: 'I have nothing to offer but blood, toil, tears and sweat.'

We have before us an ordeal of the most grievous kind. We have before us many, many long months of struggle and of suffering. You ask, what is our policy? I will say: It is to wage war, by sea, land and air, with all our might and with all the strength that God can give us; to wage war against a monstrous tyranny, never surpassed in the dark, lamentable catalogue of human crime ...[9]

That afternoon Germany attacked France across the Meuse, and the next day came the ominous tidings that their tanks had broken through the French line at Sedan, which lay in the gap between the northern end of the Maginot Line and the British-fortified front along the Belgian border. This area, in the thickly wooded region of the Ardennes, had been considered an impassable natural barrier against the advance of large bodies of troops or vehicles. Unhappily this comfortable theory was abruptly disproved as the Panzer units poured through the fatal gap, driving a wedge between the Allied armies.

In the early morning of 15th May, Monsieur Paul Reynaud, the French Prime Minister, telephoned Churchill and told him: 'We have been defeated.'[10] Churchill was not prone to accept so early the idea of defeat, and he flew to Paris the following afternoon. This was the first of five flights he was to make to France in that fatal month; he made three visits to Paris, and after the French Government left the capital, he flew once to Briare, near Orleans, and finally to Tours. On each occasion he tried to encourage and rally our hard-pressed and increasingly demoralised ally and to offer them such practical assistance as lay within our power. He always stressed that Britain would fight on 'whatever happened or whoever fell out'.[11]

Clementine shared to the full Winston's hopes and fears for the French army and nation, and grieved at the growing realisation that not only the military might of France, but also her spirit, was being crushed on this anvil. His journeys to France, decided always on the spur of the moment, caused her sharp anxiety, for they involved a considerable degree of risk. Usually escorted by guardian Spitfires, on one occasion he had to leave France and return without his escort; during this flight his aircraft had to dive down to about 100 feet above sea level to avoid attracting the attention of two German planes which were strafing fishing boats. On his last visit, on 13th June, it was found that a severe bombing raid at Tours airport during the previous night had left large craters in the runways, making landing difficult and dangerous. Although Clementine knew the dangers attending these flights, she never tried to dissuade Winston, nor did she give way to her inner fears. In a favourite phrase of Winston's, she knew how to 'rise to the level of events', and her strongly disciplined nature enabled her at times like these to carry on with all the seemingly petty, but necessary concerns which compose so much of life.

Less than five days after breaking through the French defences the German forces reached the north-east coast of France, thus cutting off the Allied armies in Flanders. On 27th May the order was given to evacuate the maximum force possible. The surrender of the Belgian army on 28th May left the British flank exposed, with no alternative but to make a dash for the sea, through a narrowing corridor held open with desperate heroism. Churchill told the House of Commons on 28th May that it should prepare itself for 'hard and heavy tidings'[12], as the Allied troops fell back fighting all the way to the cruelly exposed beaches of Dunkirk. Now we know that in the course of the next few days over 338,000 British and Allied troops were embarked and ferried across a benignly smooth Channel in vessels that ranged from destroyers and sloops to merchant vessels, pleasure launches and fishing boats. The whole of Britain and the Commonwealth watched and waited and prayed as the saving miracle was accomplished.

On 4th June, my mother and I went to the House of Commons and listened while my father told of this great epic. His speech contained the first warning to the country that we might soon be left alone to face the storm, and he spoke of our determination and ability to 'defend our island home . . . if necessary for years, if necessary alone'. He ended his speech with words that have passed into history:

> . . . we shall not flag or fail. We shall go on to the end. We shall fight in France, we shall fight in the seas and oceans, we shall fight with growing confidence and growing strength in the air; we shall defend our Island, whatever the cost may be. We shall fight on the beaches, we shall fight on the landing-grounds, we shall fight in the fields and in the streets, we shall fight in the hills; we shall never surrender; . . .[13]

Events continued to move relentlessly and swiftly: on 10th June Italy declared war on France and Britain. On 14th June the Germans entered Paris, and eight days later France capitulated. Winston and Clementine, with their long attachment to France and her people, witnessed with intense grief and dismay the downfall of that great country. But if most of the French leaders were at this time lacking in the will to endure, and failed to galvanise their divided and harassed countrymen into a firm and united resolve to continue the fight, the true spirit of France lived on in the person of General de Gaulle who, on the day following Reynaud's resignation and the assumption of power by the ancient and defeatist Marshal Pétain, flew to England, where he raised the standard of 'La France Libre', and called on all French men and women to rally to him.

It is difficult to recapture the atmosphere of those times; there were indeed to be many more days of anxiety, and many hard tidings to bear in the course of the next five years; but never again, I think, did one feel one could scarcely breathe. We got through the days almost automatically, living from news bulletin to news bulletin, and dreading what each would bring.

*

As soon as Winston became Prime Minister, Clementine had to begin the arrangements for their move to No. 10 Downing Street. Throughout the succeeding weeks of oppressive anxiety and unrelentingly disastrous news, she carried on with the necessary plans, and they were installed there by 17th June. 'No. 10' is a charming house, where the Prime Minister can both live and work. On the ground floor are the Cabinet Room and the Prime Minister's Private Office; on the first floor is a series of beautiful and dignified rooms leading one into the other, including a large state dining-room, and a delightful white-panelled passage room, where we always lunched or dined when we were not more than eight people. Upstairs, the bedroom floor with its egg-shell blue passages, cheerful red carpets and pleasantly sized rooms with sash windows, gave the impression of a country house.

During the spring months of this year, Winston and Clementine had been able to spend quite a number of week-ends picnicking in the new Orchard Cottage at Chartwell; but the visits there were to become fewer and fewer, partly on the grounds of safety once the bombing of London started, for Chartwell was on the direct target route, and easily identifiable from the air. But also Winston now had at

his disposal the Prime Minister's official country residence, Chequers, near Aylesbury in Buckinghamshire, a large Elizabethan house, fully staffed and run by a
charming and efficient Scottish curator, Miss Grace Lamont. Winston and Clementine spent their first week-end at Chequers on 1st June, while the evacuation from
Dunkirk was reaching its climax.

The fact that Winston might be in the country made little difference to his programme of work, or his contact with events. Chequers was large enough to accommodate in comfort a skeleton Private Office, two or three telephone operators, the
detectives, chauffeurs and despatch riders, as well as the family and up to eight
guests. Quite soon the pattern for the week-ends took shape: there was nearly always
a nucleus of the family, and occasionally a close friend or two, and superimposed on
these intimates would be succeeding waves of service chiefs, Cabinet colleagues, or
specialists in various subjects, who were bidden to 'dine and sleep'.

Since all week-ends were, as far as Winston was concerned, working week-ends,
the guests were invited on a business basis, and it was rather rare for wives to be
included. Many an overworked general, Civil Servant or government colleague was
reft away from a longed-for, cosy week-end in the bosom of his own family, to
travel to Chequers and spend perhaps a gruelling twenty-four hours. Nevertheless,
the sacrifice was not in vain, for it would be quite impossible to over-estimate the
value of these working week-ends, which often resulted in far-reaching and vital
decisions, or closer understanding, between Churchill and those in whose minds
and hands lay the waging of the war. Chequers was also invaluable for entertaining
important guests from overseas, who particularly appreciated the country-house
atmosphere and the lovely surrounding countryside.

At first the original civilian domestic staff grappled with the almost continuous
succession of week-end parties, but as the war went on, it became impossible to find
servants and, moreover, the requirements of security became increasingly stringent.
It was therefore decided that it would be a proper use of womanpower for Chequers
to be staffed by members of the women's services, and so volunteers from the A.T.S.
(Auxiliary Territorial Service) and the W.A.A.F. (Women's Auxiliary Air Force)
presently took over the running of the house.

*

After the fall of France, this country stood alone. The greater part of our army had
been, almost miraculously, snatched from destruction or captivity, but it had lost
nearly all its arms and equipment in the flight to the sea and the evacuation from the
beaches. From the moment the conquest of France was complete we knew that this
island was in daily increasing danger of invasion by the Germans. The fate of
Poland, and now more recently of the Low Countries and of France, had left people
in no doubt as to what they might expect if our turn came. But the British accepted
this dark prospect with characteristic phlegm; they bent themselves now, day and
night, to supply the neglect of the purblind years, and everywhere preparations
forged ahead to repel an enemy onslaught.

There occurred in early July a sequence of events which, more than any other,
impressed upon the world at large that Britain was in deadly earnest, and would

stop at nothing in her fight for survival. Following upon the collapse of France, the vital question arose as to the fate of the French Fleet. It was a matter of the utmost importance that these powerful ships should not pass into enemy control. Should this have come to pass the balance of power at sea would have been disastrously – perhaps fatally – altered. When all hope had faded that a large part, if not all, of the French Fleet would sail for allied or neutral ports, the War Cabinet took a drastic decision. On 3rd July, the French ships lying in British harbours were taken over by swift, determined action. And at Oran in North Africa the Royal Navy opened fire on the French Fleet; three battleships were destroyed, with the loss of 1,300 lives, and the remaining French ships at Oran and in other North African ports were either destroyed or immobilised.

It must have been just at the time of these searing events – the painfulness of which no one felt more keenly than Winston himself – that General de Gaulle lunched at Downing Street. The conversation turned to the future of the French Fleet, and Clementine said how ardently she hoped that many of its ships and crews would carry on the fight with us. To this the General curtly replied that, in his view, what would really give the French Fleet satisfaction would be to turn their guns 'On you!' (meaning the British). Clementine from the first had liked and respected this dour man, but she found this remark too much to bear and, rounding on him, she rebuked him soundly, in her perfect, rather formal French, for uttering words and sentiments that ill became either an ally or a guest in this country. From the other side of the table Winston sensed that something had gone amiss and, in a conciliatory tone, said to the General: 'You must forgive my wife. *Elle parle trop bien le français.*' Clementine interrupted him, and said in French: 'No, Winston, it is because there are certain things that a woman can say to a man which a man cannot say, and I am saying them to you – General de Gaulle!'[14] After this verbal fracas, the General was much upset, and apologised profusely; and the next day he sent a huge basket of flowers for Clementine. Later on in the war he was to give her a beautiful Lalique cock – the emblem of France – which she greatly treasured.

Throughout the ups and downs of Winston's relationship with this awe-inspiring, brilliant and difficult man, Clementine never wavered in her esteem and liking for him; her sentiments were obviously returned, and their mutual regard for one another lasted on long after the war. Clementine and Madame de Gaulle also made friends; Clementine greatly respected the dedication and dignity of this woman, the circumstances of whose life during the war years were particularly lonely and sad.

Clementine was keenly aware of the demoralised state and unhappy situation of the many French servicemen who now found themselves in this country, many of them having been evacuated with our troops from the Dunkirk beaches. Some joined the newly forming Free French forces straight away; for others the choice was more complicated, and they felt a clash of loyalties. They were offered the alternative of repatriation, and while waiting for arrangements to be made they were accommodated in the White City Stadium, which had been turned into a temporary camp for them. Urged by friends who were trying to help these bewildered and downcast people, Clementine visited White City in August. It made a painful impression on her to see the looks of doubt or despair, and even a few glances of downright hostility, on so many, for the most part young faces. She talked to some of the men, and came home sad and troubled. For the British, life had become very simple: we meant to fight; we thought we would win; but we would fight anyway, and we were spared the agonies of divided loyalties or complicated issues.

It is easy, now that we know the ending of the story, to underestimate the grim burden of anxiety and responsibility that lay on Churchill's shoulders in those days of June 1940. During these bright summer months the world watched, while our fate hung poised in an agonising balance. He never doubted the determination and courage of the British people to endure whatever might come, but he knew the deadly nature of the onslaught which was being prepared just across the Channel; and, above all, he knew our nakedness. It is idle to pretend that the knowledge of all this did not weigh on him. He drove himself, and he drove others with a flail in his desire to prepare the country for the assault which seemed certain to be unloosed. In his determination to drive on through all difficulties he must at this time have become extremely overbearing and tyrannical to many of those who served him, as the following letter from Clementine shows:

10 Downing Street,
Whitehall
June 27, 1940

My Darling,

I hope you will forgive me if I tell you something I feel you ought to know.

One of the men in your entourage (a devoted friend) has been to me & told me that there is a danger of your being generally disliked by your colleagues and subordinates because of your rough sarcastic & overbearing manner – It seems your Private Secretaries have agreed to behave like school boys & 'take what's coming to them' & then escape out of your presence shrugging their shoulders – Higher up, if an idea is suggested (say at a conference) you are supposed to be so contemptuous that presently no ideas, good or bad, will be forthcoming. I was astonished & upset because in all these years I have been accustomed to all those who have worked with & under you, loving you – I said this, & I was told 'No doubt it's the strain' –

My Darling Winston. I must confess that I have noticed a deterioration in your manner; & you are not as kind as you used to be.

It is for you to give the Orders & if they are bungled – except for the King, the Archbishop of Canterbury & the Speaker, you can sack anyone & everyone. Therefore with this terrific power you must combine urbanity, kindness and if possible Olympic calm. You used to quote: – 'On ne règne sur les âmes que par le calme –' I cannot bear that those who serve the Country & yourself should not love you as well as admire and respect you –

Besides you won't get the best results by irascibility & rudeness. They *will* breed either dislike or a slave mentality. (Rebellion in War time being out of the question!)

Please forgive your loving devoted & watchful
Clemmie
[drawing of cat]

This brave letter must have cost Clementine dear to write; indeed, the postscript is most revealing: 'I wrote this at Chequers last Sunday tore it up, but here it is now.' No written answer from Winston survives: none would have been necessary. But he cannot have been enraged, for the letter has survived. Many wives might never have had the perception or the courage to write in such a way: and the letter surely bore fruit, for although Winston could be formidable and, indeed, overbearing, many people who served him at all levels during those hard years have put on record not only their respect and admiration for him as a chief, but also their love for a warm and endearing human being.

On 10th July, the full force of the Luftwaffe was directed against this country. In the first phase the enemy drew our air forces into battle over the Channel and south coast. Then the southern counties, and particularly our airfields, were the object of daily raids by large numbers of aircraft, and finally London itself became the principal target. The Battle of Britain has passed into history; perhaps it will be the last example of war by individual contest. People stood in the summer meadows and watched, while overhead desperate aerial combats raged, fought out by a few hundred young men, many of whom had joined the Air Force for fun, and found themselves the champions of all that free men hold dear.

During August and September, the invasion of these islands was expected by the mass of the population with the same sort of grumbling acquiescence with which farmers anticipate rain and storms to spoil the hay harvest. The daily papers abounded with helpful hints for disastrous contingencies; the cartoonists were never funnier. But what had been a virtually undefended island in mid-June presented a much more formidable proposition by the end of July, and every day our strength increased and our organisation improved. On 7th September, the German Air Force began its series of raids on London; the 'Blitz' had begun, and for fifty-seven nights in succession an average of 200 German bombers attacked London. Despite the toll of death and injury, the destruction of buildings and the general dislocation of daily life, the German objective of making this vast city uninhabitable and of breaking the spirit of its inhabitants remained unachieved. 'London can take it' was the popular slogan. It also became an historical fact.

Soon after we were installed in No. 10, changes had to be made again owing to air-raids, and the extremely unsafe nature of the Downing Street buildings. Below the ground floor of No. 10, on the garden level, were the kitchens, the air-raid shelter, and several offices; these offices were taken over, and after being suitably strengthened by great beams used after the fashion of pit-props, and with steel shutters on the windows, they became a sitting-room and dining-room. They were not without their own charm, giving the impression of a ship's wardroom, and they certainly made it possible for social life to continue in a seemly way, despite constant alarms and not infrequent bombs. These arrangements, however, were soon deemed to be inadequate: the whole fabric of No. 10 was too frail, and the air-raid shelter itself was considered too small and unsafe. This opinion was reinforced by an incident which occurred in mid-October, while Winston was entertaining several colleagues to dinner. An air-raid was in progress and a bomb fell quite close, out on Horse Guards Parade. Winston, on a sudden impulse, left the table and went into the kitchen, where the cook, Mrs Landemare, and her kitchenmaid were working, and he ordered them both to go, with the other servants, to the shelter; this they all somewhat reluctantly did. A few minutes later, a bomb fell very much closer, shattering the great glass window of the kitchen, and the kitchen itself was a shambles of broken wood, fallen plaster and splintered glass.

A secure underground War Room had already been made under the modern, and extremely solid block of government offices next to Storey's Gate. Here there was accommodation for the meetings of the War Cabinet, the Prime Minister's Private Office and a complete subterranean Headquarters, with also a number of rooms for Winston and other people to sleep in. This would have been an ideal 'last ditch' redoubt, but was no solution to day-to-day living, and so offices overlooking St James's Park on the first floor of Storey's Gate, immediately over the War Rooms, were transformed into a flat for Winston and Clementine. At first they and their staff only slept there, entertaining still in the fortified garden rooms at No. 10, while Winston continued to do business as much as possible in the Cabinet Room. But towards the end of 1940, conditions were such that it was both safer and easier to transfer the whole of their life to the 'Annexe', as the new flat had come to be called.

Typically, in a short time, Clementine managed to impress her own taste on the gaunt and unprepossessing rooms; painted in pale colours, and hung with well-lit pictures, and with their own furniture they became almost attractive. The flat had a somewhat public quality about it, since the rooms gave off the main passage which connected various government offices, and embarrassed officials would often encounter Winston, robed like a Roman emperor in his bath towel, proceeding dripping from his bathroom across the main highway to his bedroom. However, 'The Annexe' served very well, and there they lived until July 1945, snug and secure.

Anxieties were also felt at this time for Winston's week-end arrangements. The very fact that he proceeded week-end after week-end to Chequers was thought to hold dangers; moreover, Chequers was not difficult to identify from the air. So an alternative week-end base was sought, and found, in Mr and Mrs Ronald Tree's beautiful house Ditchley, in Oxfordshire, quite close to Blenheim.

Ronnie Tree was half American, but brought up wholly in this country; he had been for many years Member of Parliament for the Harborough division of Leicestershire. Although not until now an intimate friend of Winston and Clementine, he had for long supported Winston's campaign for re-armament; his wife Nancy, also half American by birth, was a beautiful and gifted woman. The Trees welcomed not only Winston and Clementine and their essential entourage, but also their official guests, and whatever members of their family were around. Whenever, therefore, the moon shone brightly, we all repaired to Ditchley. We were becoming so accustomed to the drabness and ugliness of war – khaki, mountains of sand-bags, the blackout, and the dust and desolation of ruined buildings – that one gazed with keener appreciation on elegance and beauty, and glowing, lighted interiors.

★

As soon as Winston became Prime Minister, Clementine's already busy life became busier still. Her field of public activity was no longer mainly departmental, but ranged widely over every aspect of life in wartime England. Her mail-bag doubled; the amount of entertaining she was expected to do increased considerably, and her care and vigilance for Winston, now on this awe-inspiring pinnacle of power, was even more necessary and demanding.

Nor was her vigilance merely for his physical well-being. Clementine's 'antennae' were sensitive to everything that bore relation to him – or through him – to a wider sphere. An example of her watchfulness and the speed with which she was wont to act arose when she learnt that Winston's great-niece – Sally Churchill, the 5-year-old daughter of Jack Churchill's elder son, John Spencer-Churchill – was about to leave the country with a group of other children for the United States. In the early months of the war quite a number of children were sent to America and Canada to be sheltered from the impending storm by kind transatlantic friends or relations. In June 1940, the Government reluctantly introduced it as an official evacuation scheme. Churchill disapproved of it, describing it as a 'stampede from the country'. The scheme came to a tragic end in September 1940 after the *City of Benares* was torpedoed with the loss of seventy-three children.[15]

Sally Churchill's parents were separated, and it seemed by far the best solution when a friend offered to send her with her own daughter to Canada for the duration of the war. Clementine, on hearing of the child's impending departure, realised at once the effect it might have if it became known that a 'Churchill child' had left the country at such a time, and that no amount of reasonable explanations of the circumstances would erase the impression given. Although Sally was on the point of embarkation and the changing of her plans caused great inconvenience and some distress to those who had made the arrangements, Clementine insisted (to the point of having the child's passport withheld) that in no circumstances could she be allowed to depart.

Since Winston trusted her completely, Clementine had an extra responsibility and anxiety to bear; she often knew not only what had befallen, but what was about to befall, or what might befall. This burden of secret knowledge placed a barrier between her and other people. She was not, in any case, a woman of many friends or prone to chattering; but she tended to shun even the few close and trusted friends she had. Sylvia Henley told me how often, during the course of the war, she felt that Clementine literally 'pushed her away'. She did not want to talk banalities with Sylvia, and she was duty-bound not to talk anything else; and she perhaps feared that her tongue might betray her with so intimate a friend. All these pressures and considerations tended to make the small family circle draw even closer together.

Despite the separations and dislocations of war, our family life still revolved around the lodestar of our parents. Our father always rejoiced to see any one of us, whenever we could turn up, but of course he was more than ever preoccupied. My mother kept in touch, gave active help or listened, according to what was needed. Since Goonie Churchill was not well and was living permanently in the country, they had shut up their London house, and so Jack Churchill came to live in Downing Street, and later somewhere was found for him in that veritable warren in the Storey's Gate building. Self-effacing and discreet, Jack was the most loyal of brothers and was always there when he was needed: but he made himself scarce otherwise. Randolph, temporarily home from abroad, was returned unopposed as a Member of Parliament for Preston, in a by-election at the end of September 1940; my mother went to watch him take his seat in the House, sponsored by his father. His wife Pamela was expecting her first child, and she came to Chequers in the middle of September to await the birth in peace and quiet. There, on 10th October, 'little' Winston was born.

Sarah's life at this time was full of problems: her marriage had run into difficulties which were sharpened by the fact that her husband, Vic Oliver, felt he should return to the United States; he was now an American citizen, but Austrian by birth, and a date-line was due to be set shortly with reference to his nationality status. To Sarah, the idea of leaving England and her own family at this moment was an agony, and she found herself torn by a cruel dilemma. During the autumn and winter of this year, she wrestled with this personal and painful problem. She confided her difficulties to her mother, and found support and understanding, if not a solution.

At the end of July, I had gone to Norfolk to stay with Venetia Montagu, whose daughter Judy and I were contemporaries; but my holiday was prolonged into many weeks, for when the Blitz started my mother arranged for me to stay on with my hospitable cousins. I expected to return to London at any time, and start a job. However, my parents were adamant that they did not wish me to live in London while the raids persisted; they had quite enough worries already. So presently I was packed off to Chequers; I was somewhat disconsolate at first, but I soon was very busy working for the Women's Voluntary Service in Aylesbury. I used to look forward to the week-ends when the great gloomy house came to life with the arrival of my parents and their guests.

During this first year of the war, two people came to help Clementine with the demanding new requirements which faced her: one, Grace Hamblin, her Private Secretary, and the other Mrs Georgina Landemare, her cook. Neither were new to her, Grace Hamblin having been with us at Chartwell since 1933; now she left her parents, with whom she lived in the country, and came to work for Clementine in London. She soon was a built-in part of both Clementine's private and official life, and her devotion, tact, efficiency and charm soon became a by-word among all those with whom she had dealings.

Mrs Landemare was a superb cook, combining the best of French and English cooking. She had learnt her craft the hard way, starting as No. 6 in the kitchen over which reigned the French chef, Monsieur Landemare, whom she eventually married. Clementine had come to know and appreciate her talents and her delightful personality during the thirties, when she used to come to Chartwell for special parties or busy week-ends to boost and teach the rather inexperienced cooks or promoted kitchenmaids that Clementine could then afford. When they moved into Downing Street, Mrs Landemare came to cook for Winston and Clementine on a permanent basis. Through all the difficulties of wartime rationing, she managed to produce delicious food. After the war she stayed with us until 1953 when she retired aged seventy.

One aspect of her new role as wife of the Prime Minister was the great number of letters from the general public Clementine received every day, all of which she read herself. Each one, whether complimentary, sensible, abusive or futile, received an answer, either personally dictated and signed by her, or written by Miss Hamblin on her behalf, after they had together discussed what action should be taken or what enquiries made. Clementine set particular store by these letters, and never grudged the time in dealing with them. Through them she felt she had a contact with ordinary people's everyday life, at a time when harassments and aggravations were often caused by a host of rules and regulations. These were often the cause of more grievances than the more horrific or tragic aspects of war. Sometimes nothing could be done, but frequently Clementine was able to sort out some difficulty or injustice by making a personal enquiry to the right Ministry or authority. All this involved a good many hours' work each week, and often several letters were necessary before a final answer could be given. Clementine was greatly helped by Grace Hamblin, who was herself deeply interested in the human problems thus brought to light, and threw herself into the sometimes tedious enquiries with zest and tenacity.

Clementine dealt with most of the problems raised herself, but from time to time she would edit the facts of a case, or of a series of similar cases, and put a business-like memorandum in front of Winston; she was able in this way to draw his attention to conditions or regulations which seemed to be causing dissatisfaction or unnecessary hardship. Winston nearly always took up the cases she put before him; he knew her judgment was usually sound, and that she did not burden him without good reason. While Clementine was ready to enlist Winston's aid over genuine grievances or valid requests, she was also a stout shield between him and the tiresome league of people (usually 'fringe' friends, or distant relations), who wanted special, and usually unsuitable favours, and who thought she would be their advocate and channel. Politely, but quite firmly, she would regret her inability to help. She could even on occasion be quite fierce.

It was in fact through her postbag that Clementine was first alerted to the appalling conditions existing in many of the London air-raid shelters. She received a number of letters on this subject, and the complaints were borne out by one or two people she knew personally who were working in the shelters, who begged her to come and see for herself what the conditions were really like. As early as the end of June 1940, when air-raids had just started sporadically in the provinces, Clementine had sent a minute to Winston's Principal Private Secretary asking him to find out for her what the various arrangements were to shelter people whose homes had been wrecked or damaged in raids, what welfare arrangements existed, whether there was any scale of compensation for injuries, and other pertinent questions. In December she determined to investigate for herself the conditions under which so many people were spending their nights. Accordingly, she made a series of visits to various London boroughs, calling in unannounced on as many of the shelters as she could. Her chief guide and companion on these expeditions was Mrs May Tennant of the Red Cross; she was also often accompanied by Jock Colville, a member of the Private Office, who as the years went on was to become a close friend.

Winston highly approved of Clementine's decision to make these surprise visits, and was eager to hear the results of her investigations. On one occasion when Mrs Tennant called for her, he insisted that they should go in an armoured car as protection should a raid start while they were on their tour. Both Clementine and Mrs Tennant were indignant, but bowed (albeit rebelliously) to 'orders'; however, as soon as they reached the East End, which was their target for that particular night, they abandoned the vehicle which embarrassed them, and made their way on foot to the various shelters.

Clementine was horrified by the conditions she saw in most of the places she visited, and she formed the opinion (reinforced by the views of responsible people who worked in the shelters and by many local authority officials) that, while life in the shelters could never be Ritz-like, there were nevertheless many things that needed to be done, and that could be done, to improve the standards of hygiene and comfort. When she had inspected a representative cross-section of shelters, she submitted a series of memoranda to Winston.

Her suggestions give a vivid and horrifying picture of the conditions which many thousands of Londoners endured for nights on end, in addition to the risk and fear of death, injury, and the loss of their homes, and they also show her practical approach to problems:

Making Waterproof. Every shelter should be water-proof. In several instances the water was dripping through the roof and seeping through the walls and floor . . .

Lice. Lice must spread . . . if the present overcrowding continues and if the bedding in the shelters is not regularly stoved. To avoid offence on this subject it should be pointed out to those using the shelters that war entails lice. No soldier in the trenches in the last war was offended at being asked to go to the de-lousing station . . .

Stoving. All the bedding in the shelters should be stoved two or three times a week. This should be compulsory even though the bedding is private property. I was told of one instance where the local Authorities were afraid of vermin in the bedding, and not having facilities for stoving, insisted on the shelterers taking home their bedding every morning! How can a woman carry her bedding and perhaps two babies – more especially if it were pouring with rain – backward and forward? . . .

Sanitary accommodation. Each shelter should be provided with *adequate* latrines . . . if possible not in the dormitory portion of the shelter itself . . .

In a subsequent memorandum, Clementine came out strongly against the overcrowded sleeping arrangements and poor sanitation:

The more one sees of the 3-tier bunks the worse one feels them to be. They are, of course, much too narrow; . . . They are also too short . . . but the real crime is lack of space perpendicularly. I wonder people do not die of lack of air. Where mothers have their babies sleeping with them it must be quite intolerable, as the baby has to sleep on top of the mother as the bunk is too narrow for it to sleep by her side. I am afraid that a very great number of these bunks have been ordered . . . Would it be possible to stop any further orders on the existing model and have it redesigned?

On the subject of latrines, Clementine urged that

> The latrines should be doubled or trebled in number. This is easy as they are mostly only buckets . . .
>
> The buckets, instead of standing on porous ground, (as they mostly do) could be placed on big sheets of tin with turned-up edges like trays. These tin trays could be washed . . .
>
> Light should be provided over the latrines. The prevailing darkness merely hides and, of course, encourages the dirty conditions . . .
>
> There should be separate latrines for little children, with low buckets and chambers . . .

It was, of course, inevitable that in the first weeks of the Blitz living and sleeping arrangements in the shelters had to be improvised, but these early and rudimentary arrangements were, in too many cases, allowed to remain as the normal conditions. After acquainting herself thoroughly with the problems, Clementine's opinion was:

> It seems to me that the main difficulty in getting things right lies in the number of Authorities concerned, namely Local Authorities, Home Security, Ministry of Health, Ministry of Labour, Ministry of Supply; and the fear of these Authorities of using compulsion where persuasion fails . . .

She also had something to say about Government policy (or lack of it):

> There seems to be general uncertainty as to the Government policy re bad shelters. The reason (or excuse?) given for doing nothing is that the particular shelter is unsafe and that it is not worth while to spend money on it. Meanwhile people continue to live there perhaps fourteen hours out of the twenty-four in really horrible conditions of cold, wet, dirt, darkness and stench . . .

The sustained and close interest which Clementine took in the shelters at this time was largely instrumental in setting on foot rapid and considerable improvements. The chief qualities which characterised her approach to these, as to other, problems were thoroughness, tenacity, and an unwillingness automatically to accept the official answer or explanation, even if it happened to be given by the Minister concerned. Her own knowledge of the problem in hand, combined with a thorough understanding of the workings and weaknesses of government departments and the fallibility of ministers, made any enquiry she initiated all the more effective.

Of course she had the priceless advantage of being able to approach ministers personally; but most of her considered reports were addressed in the first place to Winston, and they went out to the appropriate departments with all the authority and priority which papers emanating from the Prime Minister's Office possessed. Nevertheless, had Clementine's representations been ill-founded or trivial, even Winston's backing would not have got them very far. As it was, her interest in these matters became well known, and soon it was not only long-suffering members of the general public who drew bad cases to her attention: Members of Parliament, social workers, doctors, and officials exasperated at the inertia, indifference, or inefficiency of their own superior authorities appealed to Clementine to exert her influence.

*

At the beginning of November, Mr Chamberlain died; earlier in the year he had undergone a severe operation for a fell disease. Since then he had continued his work with Spartan heroism, but Winston and Mrs Chamberlain together had finally persuaded him to leave London, where the almost continual bombing added to the difficulties of nursing him. Both Winston and Clementine had made friends with the Chamberlains, and had come to like them, and above all to admire, the spirit of patriotism and loyalty which Mr Chamberlain had shown by serving under Winston after so many bitter passages had passed between them in days gone by. Also, Clementine felt a special compassion for Mrs Chamberlain, who had seen her husband the object of fawning adulation at the time of the Munich agreement, only to be cast aside and decried by many who in the palmy days of appeasement had hastened to join the chorus of praise. On Friday, 8th November 1940, Mrs Chamberlain issued a statement to the Press, saying that Mr Chamberlain's strength had been failing and that he was now gravely ill. Clementine wrote to her at once:

November the 9th 1940

My dear Anne,

I was saddened last night when on the wireless I heard your message.

Winston has told me that you were very anxious – But the announcement is a shock to me, as I know it must be to the whole Nation.

I feel for you so much & think of you continually and I pray that the Peace of God is with you both.

Yours affectionately,
Clementine S. Churchill

Neville Chamberlain died on 9th November, and later Mrs Chamberlain wrote Clementine a letter full of affection and gratitude.

When Mr Chamberlain had resigned from the Government in early October, he had also relinquished the Leadership of the Conservative Party, and Churchill had been invited to take his place. Time had indeed brought changes! There were, and maybe still are, two views as to whether he was right to accept this invitation. Churchill himself had no doubt whatsoever; all his experience as a politician made him quite sure that he should grasp with a firm hand the Leadership of the party which held a commanding majority in both Houses of Parliament. The opposing view, which Clementine herself held with passionate conviction, was that Winston had been called by the voice of the whole nation, irrespective of party, at a time of grave national emergency to head a National Government, and that, although he might feel his position to be stronger in Parliament by accepting the Conservative Leadership, he would affront a large body of opinion in the country. Clementine put her view with vehemence, and all her latent hostility towards the Tory Party boiled over; there were several good ding-dong arguments between them. But Winston's view prevailed: he accepted the Leadership of the Conservative Party, and felt sustained through some tough times by the assurance of their solid support.

True to her custom, Clementine accepted her defeat without recriminations. But she never altered her opinion that this step was a mistake, and that it alienated much of the support which Winston derived from the working-classes through the vindication of his pre-war prophecies and his record as a war leader. When about a year later she was invited to head the Red Cross Aid to Russia Fund, she accepted with alacrity, not only because of her wish to do something for the Russians, but also because she felt that in some way this might help to redress the balance.

*

A joyful family occasion lightened the grey winter days of 1940, which were so full of toil, anxiety and trouble: 'little' Winston was christened at Ellesborough Parish Church near Chequers on Sunday, 1st December. Our family party was remarkably complete, and Pamela's parents and her brother came from Dorset. There was a complete muster of godparents on parade: Max Beaverbrook, Lord Brownlow and Brendan Bracken, with Virginia Cowles, the American journalist and author. The christening was held after Matins, and most of the congregation stayed on to join in the simple and touching service with us all. Afterwards we repaired back to Chequers for luncheon, when Winston proposed the toast to: 'Christ's new faithful soldier and servant'.

In just over a week, however, there was cause for more than family rejoicing: the Eighth Army launched an attack in North Africa on 9th December, and by the 15th the Italian forces had been driven from Egypt, with the destruction of five enemy divisions and the capture of 38,000 prisoners. And so, as we gathered for the second Christmas of the war, our hearts were buoyed up with not ill-founded hope and natural jubilation.

Diana and Duncan, Randolph and Pamela, Sarah and Vic, and myself made the tally of children present complete. In addition there was John Martin, one of my father's private secretaries. 'Everyone in good spirits . . . No reports of any air, land or sea activity,' I wrote in my diary on Christmas Eve. And on Christmas Day I recorded that

> This was one of the happiest Christmasses I can remember. Despite all the terrible events going on around us . . . I've never before seen the family look so happy – so united . . . We were complete Randolph and Vic having arrived this morning . . .

Perhaps it is because human beings have this capacity to draw down the blinds, and to shut out the wild, winter weather, and to take comfort and pleasure in the familiar faces in the lamp-light, that mankind has survived at all. At any rate, it was fortunate for us that the Christmas of 1940 proved to be such a happy and peaceful one, for never again during the war were so many of us able to gather together as a family.

TAKING UP THE LOAD

THE YEAR 1940 had seen the over-running of Western Europe by Hitler's hordes, leaving Britain dramatically isolated. But in 1941 the war was to become a world-wide conflict. The battle in the North African desert swung to and fro: Rommel's Afrika Korps pushed the Eighth Army back over the ground they had captured from the Italians, and the Germans invaded Greece and Yugoslavia.

We were still braced for an invasion when, on 22nd June 1941, Hitler hurled his armies against Russia, on a front extending from the Baltic to the Black Sea. Within a month Great Britain and the Soviet Union had signed a treaty of mutual aid, and although the help we could give – or receive – was sorely limited, we were no longer alone in our struggle against Hitler.

Meanwhile succour from a more puissant source began to reach us. In March 1941 Congress passed the Lend-Lease Bill, and each month brought more help from the United States. On 7th December 1941 the Japanese Air Force bombed the American naval base at Pearl Harbour, and the United States entered the war. The days of our splendid isolation were at an end, and as the New Year of 1942 dawned we found ourselves partners in a Grand Alliance, pledged each to each to make both war and peace together.

But throughout the year, the depredations of the German U-boats on our merchant shipping threatened our slender life-line, and in spring 1941 it was the turn of our ports and industrial cities to endure heavy bombing raids: Portsmouth, Merseyside, the Clyde, Hull and Plymouth all suffered grievously in the enemy's attempts to cripple our harbours. And Manchester, Coventry and Bristol sustained heavy attacks, though their ordeal was not so long drawn-out as London's.

Through his frequent broadcasts, Winston Churchill had become closer to the ordinary people of Britain than had any previous Prime Minister. His sombre tones, relieved by shafts of robust, sardonic humour, the total absence of cajolement by facile hopes, and the dogged courage all struck a note in tune with the mood of people of all classes. Through the radio Churchill forged a unique bond with his fellow countrymen and was able to bring them hope and reassurance. He also sought every opportunity to visit places which had suffered severely, or were bearing the brunt of enemy bombardment, and Clementine always tried to go with him. They travelled, with Winston's essential entourage, on the Special Train arranged for this purpose, which not only provided comfortable and restful travelling conditions, but avoided all the difficulties of security which would have been involved by staying in hotels. In addition, secret, 'instant' communication with London was always available, as the train could be plugged in to the nearest telephone line, where a special Top Priority number put it, within a few minutes, in touch with Downing Street.

These tours were often long and tiring. They usually involved trudging through ruined streets, visiting rest centres and canteens, sometimes even scrambling over piles of rubble, but Clementine, despite her not overstrong constitution, stood up to them wonderfully. The scenes they saw and the people they met had a profound effect on them both; Winston was time and again moved to tears by the bravery of the people he saw, and the affection and regard they expressed for him. The effect of these visits to the bomb-battered cities was indescribably moving. He had indeed become the symbol of his country's hope and courage, and under the flail of war the usual reserve of the British character had melted away. Wherever Churchill went, crowds appeared, cheering and clapping; even from the ruins of their own houses people ran to greet him. And many, particularly the women, came to expect, and want to see Clementine at his side.

Indeed Clementine's own personality was now becoming widely known and appreciated, not only because of her habitual presence at Winston's side, but also through her 'postbag', her appeal broadcasts, and through her war work. These things combined in the war years to carve out for her a special place in people's minds.

And it was not only her personality which made its mark: in the dreary, dusty shabbiness of wartime conditions Clementine's lovely appearance and her own distinctive style of dressing added to people's pleasure at seeing her. An observer wrote of her visit with Winston to Plymouth in May 1941:

> There was much pleased feminine comment on Mrs Churchill's striking appearance: snow leopard coat with flounced sleeves, a coloured handkerchief over her head with phrases of her husband's speeches printed on it. Some were surprised Winnie had such a fine, fresh-looking wife . . .[1]

Her elegant, unaffected taste in clothes was perhaps seen at its best during the 'austerity' years of the war, when she managed always to look exceptionally well-dressed, without seeming in the least out of tune with the times. Clementine adopted and popularised a fashion which was a graceful compliment to all the thousands of women factory workers throughout the country. For safety reasons, and also to keep dirt and dust out of their hair, factory girls nearly all tied their heads up 'bandanna' style in head scarves. Clementine disliked hats, and she also thought they looked singularly unsuitable in the context of ruined streets and shattered houses; but, meticulously neat, she did not wish to become dishevelled during the course of a long day's programme. So she adopted the 'turban-bandanna' style, and, using every kind of material – silk, cotton, crepe, tulle and chiffon – she got together a positive library of turbans. Taking trouble to arrange her turban carefully at the start of the day, she scarcely touched it again; it was impervious to wind and weather, and looked equally suitable whether she was visiting a hospital, clambering about in a ship, or lunching with a Lord Mayor in the Mansion House. These turbans, in which she was much photographed, acquired the nature of a distinctive and personal 'trademark'.

Although Clementine took great trouble about her appearance, she never, at any time in her life, allowed clothes to dominate her time or her interest; she gave thought to her dressing, organised it, and then forgot about it. Before the war, she had from time to time 'treated' herself to a dress from Schiaparelli, Molyneux, or some other couturier; but most of her clothes were made by various small dressmakers, usually from paper patterns. Now, with the war, she bought most of her clothes from Molyneux, whose simple and supremely elegant clothes suited her to perfection. As to time spent at the hairdresser, it was practically nil. Clementine went about once every three months to her hairdresser for permanent waving, otherwise she managed her hair entirely by herself, cleaning it every few days (to the family's acute and constant alarm) with neat benzine!

*

In the course of 1941 Clementine undertook two new and large responsibilities in addition to the work with which she was already concerned. In February she became President of the Young Women's Christian Association's Wartime Fund, for which she was instrumental in raising many thousands of pounds. And in October she undertook the Chairmanship of the Red Cross Aid to Russia Fund, thus beginning by far the most formidable job she tackled in either war, and one which was to make enormous demands on her. Clementine began this new work at a moment when her time and energy were, one might have supposed, fully subscribed, but there were several reasons for her undertaking this further major commitment.

When the German onslaught was loosed upon Russia in June 1941 Churchill, despite his life-long hostility to Communism, had at once declared this country's determination to ally herself with the Soviet Union in her struggle against the Nazis, and he had spoken with great feeling of the sufferings of the Russian people in the face of the German advance. Spontaneously a warm wave of sympathy swept through Great Britain, as people learned with mounting horror of the sufferings of the Russian civilian population. The Soviet Embassy in London received hundreds of letters every day expressing friendship and sympathy, and individuals and organisations started to send money to help the Russian war effort. Working-class support was particularly strong; and the Mineworkers' Federation sent the Russian Ambassador a cheque for £60,000 only a few days after the German attack.

These expressions of sympathy in the first few months found no clearly defined organisation which could focus their offers of help and gifts into an effective form of aid to our new and struggling ally. In early October, however, Field Marshal Sir Philip Chetwode, who was the Chairman of the Executive Committee of the War Organisation of the Red Cross and St John, reported that it had decided to form an Aid to Russia Sub-Committee, of which he would be Chairman, and that Clementine had consented to be the Vice-Chairman. A few days later, it was announced that she would also be Chairman of the Aid to Russia Appeal.

Deeply moved herself by the sufferings and heroism of the Russian people in the defence of their homeland, Clementine also understood, and accurately gauged, the strength and volume of the sympathy for the Russian cause among the mass of the population in this country. There was moreover a political aspect which did not escape her notice: from the moment that Russia was set upon by Germany, the Soviet Government appealed loudly and continuously to Great Britain for aid of all kinds, and made imperious demands for British landings in Europe, regardless of our own difficulties or the preparation involved in mounting a Second Front. The British Communist Party, which had hitherto condemned the 'capitalist and imperialist' war, now called for immediate and impossible measures to help the Soviet Union. All over the country 'Second Front Now' was scrawled on walls and hoardings. Churchill lost no opportunity of sending such aid as was possible but, as he commented wryly, 'there was little we could do, and I tried to fill the void by civilities.'[2]

Clementine understood these difficulties very well, and often discussed them with Winston, who later wrote:

> My wife felt very deeply that our inability to give Russia any military help disturbed and distressed the nation increasingly as the months went by and the German armies surged across the Steppes.[3]

And so when Clementine was invited by the Red Cross to head the Aid to Russia Appeal, she eagerly accepted the task. Here was the opportunity to demonstrate in a practical way the genuine desire of this country to render what help it could to Russia, and the fact that the Prime Minister's wife was heading the Appeal showed that the British Government was at one with the feeling in the country, and eager to give expression to it. Moreover, the Joint War Organisation of the Red Cross and St John provided a machine capable of coping with the work involved, which Clementine from the first realised would be tremendous.

A more detailed account of Clementine's war work is given in the next chapter; here it is enough to note that shouldering during 1941 both the Y.W.C.A. War-time Appeal and the Aid to Russia Fund greatly increased her burden of work, and called forth all her reserves of energy and stamina. And amid all these major preoccupations time and thought had also to be found for domestic and family life. Although Clementine's days now were full to overflowing, she always managed somehow to be on hand when Winston wanted or needed her. A more personally ambitious woman, or a more conceited one, would perhaps (albeit subconsciously) have allowed her own personal role and importance to develop into a separate, almost competitive, entity of its own. But her career had always been simply to be Winston's wife, and the fact that she had now become a public figure in her own right did not alter the situation by one whit.

The only time it was normally feasible for Clementine and the family to see Winston was at meal-times, and then there would almost certainly be outside guests. But we all made the most of these opportunities, and any of the children were always welcome to any meal they could manage. Winston's day started when breakfast and his red boxes were brought to him, usually around eight o'clock; he would work in bed, receiving officials or service chieftains, until luncheon-time, unless it was a Cabinet day, or he had some other outside appointment. After luncheon, work again until around six o'clock – then the blessed, life-restoring rest for an hour to an hour and a half. When he awoke, marvellously refreshed, he would bath and change. Soon after the beginning of the war Winston abandoned the dinner jacket in favour of a zip-up 'siren' suit (or 'rompers' as the family disrespectfully dubbed them). Clementine took trouble and pleasure in the designing of these comfortable garments which, made in a variety of materials, remained a key part of his wardrobe to the end of his life. Sometimes as a birthday or Christmas present she would give him a sumptuous version in mulberry or night blue velvet; the family would often weigh in with slippers to match, embroidered with his monogram in gold thread. After dinner, at about ten or ten-thirty, he would say 'good night' and go off back to work, probably till one or two o'clock in the morning.

Clementine was most meticulous not to interrupt or disturb Winston at his work in any way. If she had an urgent message for him that could not wait until they met at a meal, or that it was not possible to discuss in front of guests, she sent him a typed 'memo' (often decorated, like her letters, with a 'kat'). Since Winston also worked solidly throughout the week-ends, and as anyhow there were nearly always guests staying at Chequers, the opportunities for them to be alone together were rare indeed, and precious to them both beyond price. It was unusual for them to be alone at luncheon, but they entertained less in the evenings, and Clementine never let anything come between her and the chance of a quiet, candle-lit evening alone with Winston. She always changed for dinner, and she usually wore one of her ravishing housecoat-cum-dressing gowns made in beautiful materials and glowing colours. She always tried to be, and to look, at her best for him.

On the family front, this year brought its full ration of worries and concerns. Duncan Sandys was seriously injured in a car accident in April. For a while it was feared that one of his feet might have to be amputated; mercifully this was not the case, but the injury was to cause him pain and impediment ever after. Sarah's marriage finally broke up; from the beginning both her parents had feared the worst, but Clementine, in fact, had become very fond of Vic Oliver, admiring his taste and charming manners, though Winston had never got to know him. Both now, however, felt deeply for Sarah. During 1941 Vic and Sarah parted, and a short while after Sarah joined the Women's Auxiliary Air Force. After serving in the ranks, she was commissioned, and was trained in the skilled and exacting work of photographic interpretation. In this arduous, secret work, Sarah sought to forget the sadness and aridity of her life at this time. The unit which carried out this work was at Medmenham in Buckinghamshire, and as this was not very far from Chequers, Sarah was quite often able to go home to visit her parents.

In July, Goonie Churchill died from cancer; she had been ill for some time. Her death brought back to Clementine memories of that other war, when she and her unusual, fascinating sister-in-law had shared a house. Goonie had been her loyal and almost only confidante in the dark and troubled days of the Dardanelles crisis.

I managed to cause a diversion on the domestic front, when I somewhat precipitately became engaged in May to an intelligent, charming and entirely suitable
young man whom, however, I knew very slightly. From the very first my mother
was convinced that I was not really in love at all. Strangely enough, she confided her
fears to Max Beaverbrook:

> . . . It has all happened with stunning rapidity.
> The engagement is to be made public next Wednesday; but I want you to
> know beforehand because you are fond of Mary –
> I have persuaded Winston to be firm & to say they must wait six months –
> She is only 18, is young for her age, has not seen many people & I think she was
> simply swept off her feet with excitement – They do not know each other at all.
> Please keep my doubts and fears to yourself.[4]

My mother not unnaturally did not relish bearing the whole responsibility for
intervening in this delicate matter, and running the risk of being thereafter accused
of 'wrecking my whole life'. But my father was totally preoccupied with events of
national importance, and so my mother had to grapple with this emotional situation
herself. Her views, and friendly counsels from various quarters combined with
misgivings of my own, resulted in the indefinite (and as it proved, permanent)
postponement of the announcement of the engagement. In this matter, as in so
many more, my mother's judgment was right.

It is hardly surprising that the pressure of the work which Clementine had undertaken, combined with the strain of her social and domestic life, was now beginning
to tell; earlier in the year she had suffered from quite a severe attack of bronchitis,
and by the summer she was desperately tired, both physically and mentally. Since
the beginning of the war she had had no holiday, merely an odd week-end here or
there and occasionally a day or afternoon spent at Chartwell. It was not easy,
however, for her to find a suitable moment to 'ease up', and she hated the idea of
leaving Winston, even for a week, in these hard and anxious days. However, in
August 1941 a great event took him far from home. For two years Winston had
corresponded with President Roosevelt, and already a strong and intimate link had
been forged between them, but for some time he had been hoping for an opportunity
to meet the President face to face. Towards the end of July 1941, Harry Hopkins,
the President's personal envoy, told Winston that the President was equally anxious
for a meeting in some secluded place.

Churchill's voyage to meet President Roosevelt in August 1941 was the first of
many journeys across the world he was to make during the war by land, sea and air.
The security arrangements protecting his movements and plans were of course
elaborate, for the risks involved were many and great. Clementine was also somewhat concerned for Winston's health during this journey, and she tried to persuade
him to take with him Sir Charles Wilson (later Lord Moran), who had been
appointed his doctor when he became Prime Minister. She wrote him the following
note on 1st August:

> I feel very strongly that on this all-important journey you should have a Doctor
> with you . . . *Please* take Sir Charles Wilson.

This note is signed with a chubby 'Kat', and overleaf there is this comment: 'Brendan agrees with me.' On this occasion Winston was not to be persuaded; but on nearly all his subsequent journeys Sir Charles Wilson went with him.

Winston and his party sailed on 4th August in the battleship *Prince of Wales*, and arrived at the rendezvous – Placentia Bay, Newfoundland – on 9th August. The announcement of this first meeting of the two statesmen, which lasted three days, reverberated around the world. The outward and visible result of the meeting was the publication of the Atlantic Charter, which gave glimpses of a brighter world to struggling humanity. But the real importance of the occasion was the chance it gave Churchill and Roosevelt to establish the friendship already begun, and to come to understand each other's train of thought. There can have been few meetings which held so much significance for the history of the world.

Clementine took the opportunity of Winston's absence to spend ten days at Dr Lief's health establishment at Tring in Hertfordshire. She made the most of her rest there, and felt truly refreshed. But before she left his care, her doctor warned her that she was driving herself too hard, and he suggested that she should try to have one day in every week set aside as a 'rest day', when not only should no public obligations be undertaken, but she should rest quietly at home, seeing the minimum of people and doing no work of any kind. Clementine agreed that this would be an excellent plan, and for the first seven weeks after she left Tring, 'rest day' is marked down religiously once a week in her diary, but thereafter no mention of it appears again. It just simply was not practicable, and she abandoned it.

But it was a restored and rejoicing Clementine who greeted Winston at King's Cross on the morning of 19th August. The King sent Sir Alexander Hardinge to meet him; Gil Winant (the American Ambassador), Mr Fraser (the New Zealand Prime Minister), and many members of the Government were also on the platform. Although the time and place of Winston's arrival had not been announced, there was nevertheless a large crowd gathered both in and around the station. It was a wonderful welcome home, and it moved him deeply. As he walked down the platform and out to his car, with Clementine on his arm, he was cheered repeatedly.

In early September 1941 my cousin Judy Montagu and I joined the Auxiliary Territorial Service. We had become fired with the idea of serving with one of the new 'mixed' (men and women) anti-aircraft batteries, which were being formed about this time. Our parents understood our wish to go 'a-soldiering' and encouraged us to enlist. So Judy and I set out on what was, for us, a great adventure, our mothers waving us goodbye at Paddington Station.

We went first of all to a Training Centre at Aldermaston, near Reading, for a month's basic army training, and then to a huge camp near Oswestry, in Shropshire, to learn the mysteries of anti-aircraft instruments. I duly regaled my parents with detailed accounts of my life as a private soldier (at 1s 8d a day). While we were at Aldermaston my mother and Venetia Montagu would come down at the week-ends to see their soldier-daughters, bringing vast and delicious picnic luncheons. Judy and I were very nervous lest our mothers should disgrace us by not conforming in the most minute details with the rules and regulations, or by failing to recognise the immense importance in our lives of the Guard Commander (usually a Lance-

Corporal) or such exalted beings as the Company Sergeant-Major. In one of my very first letters home, I begged my mother not to address her letters 'Miss Mary Churchill', but to accord me my full military number and rank: '—— Private M. Churchill A.T.S.'; I also added an earnest request that she should use *plain* envelopes, and not those bearing the incriminating legend '10 Downing Street, Whitehall'. However, my blissful anonymity was preserved only for a little while.

After one of my mother's Sunday visits she wrote to me:

> I did love seeing you yesterday; but I came away with rather a heavy heart – driving away to luxury & comfort & leaving you both to rough it.
>
> My Darling I do love & honour you. I know you have done what is right & that even if it is uncomfortable & rather desolate now you will always all your life be glad you did it & didn't drift into a half & half makeshift job.[5]

She was indeed right; I never regretted for one moment my decision to join up.

Despite all the demands of her life, my mother was a wonderful correspondent, and wrote both her 'active service' daughters long and sparkling letters, of which the following are a few examples:

> 10, Downing Street,
> Whitehall
> Sept. 16, 1941
>
> My own Darling Mouse
>
> Last night, Mr Harriman, freshly arrived from American in a huge Catalina flying boat came to dinner . . . He brought Kathleen [his daughter] with him, looking very pretty. They both asked after you, particularly Mr Harriman who sent you his love & salute. Next time you & Judy go to Reading, do be taken by the local photographer, *together & alone*. It will be such fun to have a picture to put up on my shelf & to stick in my War Scrap Book. And don't forget to ask for a pass for me, becos on Sunday 'I will be right there with bells' – at 2 o'clock.
>
> Papa & I are going to St Paul's Cathedral this morning by special wish of The King. There is to be a Thanksgiving Service for King Peter of Yugoslavia's coming of age. They grow up quickly in the Balkans – I believe he is only 18; but he has shewn an old fashioned Kingly thirst for power by sacking his Prime Minister! I understand he is being told that this is unwise & premature! Then we are to lunch at Buckingham Palace . . .

> 10, Downing Street,
> Whitehall
> September 30, 1941
>
> My own darling Mary
>
> I am thinking of you constantly – I wonder if you & Judy will be a little sad at leaving Aldermaston or if you are full only of excitement & expectation? I shall miss our picnics. As soon as you have a breather do write me all your news . . .
>
> Yesterday I went to my Maternity Hospital & tried to buy a house for a Convalescent Home for the Mothers. But it was too expensive, so I am scratching my

head & wondering what to do next . . . To-day for 3 hours I have been trudging
round the Borough of St Pancras looking at A.R.P. Canteens & decontamination
centres till I thought I should drop. I had to make 3 speeches & grin & look
gracious the whole time! Both my stockings laddered & a heel nearly came off
my shoe! . . .

Chequers
Butler's Cross – Aylesbury
November 2, 1941

My darling Mary

In my last letter describing to you the start & progress of the Russian Fund I
forgot to tell you that the King & Queen lunched alone with Papa & me last
Tuesday.

Mrs Landemare was in a flutter & produced a really delicious luncheon & it
was really all most enjoyable, becos' The Queen is so gay & witty & very very
pretty close up . . . Papa tried to interfere with the Menu but I was firm & had
it my own way, & luckily it was good.

The Queen asked about you & admired a photograph of you scrubbing (the
full face one in the open doorway) . . . The King did not say much – He looked
thin & rather tired . . .

Princess Elizabeth & her sister are being 'educated at Eton'! that is, The
Vice-Provost of Eton & one or two of the most agreeable & brilliant Masters go
to Windsor Castle two or three times a week & instruct them & they enjoy it very
much. I think they have the most amusing lives with lots of dogs (altho they are
only those horrid 'corgies') & poneys [sic] & a delightful Mother . . .

10, Downing Street,
Whitehall
November 12, 1941

My own Mary,

It is three days since we parted, & it feels already like three weeks.

I do hope these coming weeks will not be so strenuous & rushed for you as the
last fortnight . . .

To-day I went to see the King open Parliament – As you know the Lords very
handsomely gave up their Chamber to the Commons when the House of Commons was destroyed; & now the Lords sit in the Robing Room which has been
converted into a miniature, one might almost say toy House of Lords. There is
room for only about 100 Peers instead of 800, the Woolsack has been reduced in
size & the thrones are elegant but tiny. Altogether it is most attractive & cosy.
The Queen looked lovely in plum covered velvet, pearls & sables & the King in
Naval Uniform instead of full Regalia led her in by the hand.

The Russian Fund is staggering – Yesterday £36,000 arrived by one post &
to-day £46,000. We are well over Half a Million Pounds . . .

Yesterday I was taken by Mrs Vincent Massey (the wife of the High Commissioner for Canada) to see the Beaver Club; which is the spot where all Canadian

soldiers congregate – It was packed with magnificent gigantic men nearly all of
them of god-like beauty – And so smart & clean. It is a splendid place with hot
baths & billiards & luscious food & reading-rooms & tailors to mend & press their
clothes & I don't know what else. I thought how nice it would be if I could waft it
all to Oswestry for your use! – pancakes with fresh Butter & maple syrup, home
made doughnuts & all. I think they are horribly spoilt compared with our men
& women . . .

*

Churchill was at Chequers on the evening of Sunday, 7th December 1941, when he
heard the report of the Japanese attack on Pearl Harbour on the nine o'clock news.
It was a fitting coincidence that, dining with him on that momentous evening were
Gil Winant, the American Ambassador, and Averell Harriman, the President's
adviser on Lend-Lease. Clementine too was at Chequers but, feeling exhausted,
she had gone to bed for dinner, leaving the men on their own. As soon as he heard
the news, Churchill put through a call to the White House, and within a few minutes
he was speaking to the President. Churchill recorded his passionate feelings of
relief and sombre rejoicing at the realisation that America, with all her might, was
committed with us to the struggle. There was now no more doubt about how the
conflict would end: 'I went to bed,' he wrote, 'and slept the sleep of the saved and
thankful.'[6]

The entry of the United States into the war made it imperative for Churchill to
see the President again as soon as possible. Accordingly all the intricate and highly
secret arrangements were made, and on 13th December he and his colleagues
sailed for America in the *Duke of York*. The weather was wild, and of all the many
journeys Churchill was destined to make during the war, this voyage set a record
for sheer discomfort. Winston described to Clementine the almost unceasing and
violent gales which delayed their progress. He was not afflicted by seasickness, but
during the voyage he spent the greater part of the day in bed.

> I manage to get a great deal of sleep and have also done a great deal of work in
> my waking hours . . .
>
> We make a very friendly party at meal times, and everyone is now accustomed
> to the motion. The great stand-by is the cinema . . . I have seen some very good
> ones [films]. The one last night, 'Blood and Sand', about bull-fighters, is the best
> we have seen so far. The cinema is a wonderful form of entertainment, and takes
> the mind away from other things . . . Being in a ship in such weather as this is
> like being in prison with the extra chance of being drowned . . .

Winston went over, almost as in a conversation with her, the debit and credit
account of the war at this time, and wrote also of his eagerness to arrive in Washington:

> You can imagine how anxious I am to arrive and put myself in relation to the
> fuller news and find out what is the American outlook and what they propose to
> do . . .

But his thoughts were not only of grand strategy: clothes rationing had been introduced in June, and he added:

I wish particularly to know the length of your stockings, so that I can bring you a few pairs to take the edge off Oliver Lyttelton's coupons . . .

He finished dictating this letter after his arrival at the White House, and added in his own hand:

I have not had a minute since I got here to tell you about it. All is vy good indeed . . . The Americans are magnificent in their breadth of view.
    Tender love to you and all. My thoughts will be with you this strange Christmas Eve.

Your ever loving husband,
W [7]

Back at home, Clementine sat down and wrote to Winston on Friday, 19th December:

My Darling
    You have been gone a week & all the news of you is of heavy seas delaying your progress . . .
    I hope you are able to rest in spite of wind & weather and the anxiety in the Far East – How calm we all are – Hong Kong threatened immediately, Singapore ultimately? perhaps not so ultimately, Borneo invaded – Burmah? to say nothing of the blows to America in the Pacific.
    Here I am bound to my Russian Fund. We have passed the Million Pound target & that without what will come in from the Flag Days, held not only in London but all over the country. I visited many depôts all over London from dawn till dusk. The people came running everywhere. They are so good & sweet especially the old & they all asked about you.
    Yesterday Mary's leave came to an end; I took her & Judy in your car & deposited them as night was falling at their new camp near Enfield. In the gathering darkness it looked like a German concentration camp.
    . . . Well my beloved Winston. May God keep you and inspire you to make good plans with the President. It's a horrible world at present, Europe over-run by the Nazi hogs & the Far East by yellow Japanese lice.
    I am spending Christmas here at the Annexe & going to Chequers on Saturday the 27th.

Tender love and thoughts,
Clemmie

Since Judy and I had only just joined our new battery at Enfield, Christmas leave was of course out of the question; but we enjoyed the cheerful, noisy celebrations organised in our camp. My mother sent us, for the benefit of our 'barrack room', a vast paper cracker, fully four feet long and a foot in diameter; this was a huge success, and greatly added to the fun and merriment. On Christmas Eve she wrote to tell me that the previous afternoon my father had telephoned from the White House:

> He might have been speaking from the next room. But it was not *very* satisfactory as it was a public line & we were both warned by the Censors breaking in that we were being listened to!
>
> 'Nana' and I are all alone this Christmas, but we are not lonely because we feel Papa is saving the World & you & Sarah are also, & are happy in your work . . .

Many thousands of miles away from blacked-out London, Winston spent Christmas in Washington. On Christmas Eve, 30,000 people gathered in the grounds of the White House to see and hear the President and his British guest, and to watch the lighting of the White House Christmas tree.

Clementine's thoughts were not only of Winston, but also of all he was hoping to achieve. 'I have been thinking constantly of you,' she wrote on 29th December,

> & trying to picture & realise the drama in which you are playing the principal – or rather it seems – the only part. I pray that when you leave, that the fervour you have aroused may not die down but will consolidate into practical & far-reaching action . . .

Her hopes were realised, for the 'Arcadia' Conference cemented the merger of the war effort of Great Britain and the United States, and on New Year's Day 1942 the first declaration made in the name of the United Nations – the United States, Great Britain, the USSR and China – pledged that both war and peace would be made together. Churchill had addressed both Houses of Congress on Boxing Day, and then had flown to Ottawa for a three-day visit, including making a speech to the Canadian Parliament, returning to Washington to continue his talks with the President and his advisers.

The pace and pressure of these days were tremendous and telling. In fact, on the night of 26th December he suffered a very slight heart attack; so slight was it that his programme remained unaltered, and not a word was said; but it was an indicative sign. Kindly Mr Stettinius (at this time President Roosevelt's Lend-Lease administrator) offered Winston his house in Florida, and he was able to go there for five restful days. It was his first holiday for nearly three years.

Winston travelled home in a Boeing flying-boat, arriving on 17th January; he had been absent for nearly five weeks, and he was greeted with warmth and relief by his family, his colleagues and the country alike. Upon his return Churchill found a somewhat troubled political situation and a ground-swell of public dissatisfaction. Now that as a nation we were no longer in mortal danger of invasion, the general sense of relief was accompanied by a reawakening of the faculty of criticism. There was a general demand for changes in the War Cabinet, and a feeling that in view of the importance of our relationship with the Soviet Union, the Socialist element should be strengthened. Within the Government itself there were difficulties and personal tensions, particularly between Lord Beaverbrook (then Minister of Supply) and other ministers.

A week after his return there was a debate in the House of Commons; Churchill insisted that the House should divide on a Vote of Confidence, so that the country and the world should see how the National Government stood. The vote brought an overwhelming majority for the Government of 464 to 1. But the discontent within the Cabinet was unappeased, and was reinforced by suggestions from the outside that the time had come for the introduction of 'new blood' into the War Cabinet. An obvious candidate was Sir Stafford Cripps, who had just returned from being our Ambassador in Moscow: he was a man of outstanding intellectual achievements, and a Socialist of unimpeachable integrity and strong views.

Meanwhile Winston was experiencing much difficulty with Max Beaverbrook, who was suffering acutely at this time from one of his recurring bouts of asthma, and who was in a highly tricky and unpredictable frame of mind. Already, while in Washington, Winston had brushed aside an impulsive resignation, and now Beaverbrook was alternating between a deep distaste for the constraints of office and the demand for wider powers as a minister.

The complicated and delicate task of rearranging his team, and placating Max Beaverbrook, whose gifted services he hoped to retain, superimposed on the burden of the daily running of the war, added greatly to the strain of Winston's life. The war news at this time was bad. In North Africa Rommel had launched a new offensive towards the end of January, and the British army was once more driven out of Cyrenaica. In the Far East, the Japanese were advancing through Malaya, and on 15th February the country learned of the surrender of 60,000 of our troops at Singapore: it was the 'largest capitulation in British history'.[8] These were dark and perplexing days indeed. Clementine hated to see Winston so beset on all sides, and resented the extra fret and worry caused by a temperamental colleague. She was often present at meals when all these difficulties were discussed, and she had her own opinions about some of the proposed appointments and re-appointments in the Government.

Since the beginning of the war, Clementine's long-held antipathy to Max Beaverbrook had softened: she was second to none in her admiration for the amazing feats he performed at the Ministry of Aircraft Production; and the exploits as a fighter pilot of his gallant son, Max Aitken, and his father's pride in them, warmed her towards 'big' Max, who also had been charming to her in these dramatic years, and helped her generously with the causes for which she worked. But through this period of 'truce', deep down there slumbered her strong conviction that Max Beaverbrook was a baleful influence on Winston. And now as she saw Winston struggling with tensions and difficulties in his team caused in large part by the contradictory humours of this curious man, she boiled over. During a discussion with Winston about this problem, she became very heated and expressed herself in violent and immoderate terms. Afterwards she wrote him this letter:

Thursday
[no date, but possibly 19th February 1942 or the previous Thursday]
My Own Darling,

I am ashamed that by my violent attitude I should just now have added to your agonising anxieties – Please forgive me. I do beg of you to reflect, whether it would not be best to leave Lord B entirely out of your Reconstruction.

It is true that if you do he may (& will) work against you – at first covertly & then openly. But is not hostility without, better than intrigue & treachery & rattledom [sic] within? You should have peace *inside* your Government – for a few months at any rate – & you must have that with what you have to face and do for us all – Now that you have (as I understand) invited Sir Stafford, why not put your money on him.

The temper & behaviour you describe (in Lord B) is caused I think by the prospect of a new personality equal perhaps in power to him & certainly in intellect.

My Darling – Try ridding yourself of this microbe which some people fear is in your blood – Exorcise this bottle Imp & see if the air is not clearer & purer – You will miss his drive & genius, but in Cripps you may have new accessions of strength. And you don't mind 'that you don't mean the same thing'. You both *do* in War & when Peace comes – we can see. But it's a long way off.

Your devoted
Clemmie

In the event, after much cajoling, Lord Beaverbrook became Minister of War Production, but he suddenly resigned a fortnight later, giving the state of his health as the reason. The reconstructed War Cabinet was announced on 19th February, Sir Stafford Cripps taking the offices of Lord Privy Seal and Leader of the House of Commons, and Mr Attlee becoming Deputy Prime Minister (a new office). The strengthening of the Left Wing in the War Cabinet made the National Government more truly representative, and helped to secure public approval for the stringent controls which the nation was to endure as the war dragged on.

That the combination of bad news from the war fronts, and domestic disagreements within the close circle of his own colleagues, had a wearing effect on Winston is borne out by an entry in my diary for 27th February 1942:

> Luncheon alone with Mummie & Papa at No. 10.
> Papa is at a very low ebb.
> He is not too well physically – and he is worn down by the continuous crushing pressure of events . . .

And in a letter to her sister Nellie Romilly, on 28th February 1942, Clementine wrote:

> These are as you say days of anguish for Winston, so full of strength & yet so impotent to stem this terrible tide in the Far East.
> We must pray that the Country will show patience and constancy & then All may be Well.

Clementine was of course deeply concerned for Winston: she saw every day the toll the weight of the war exacted from him, and he confided to her all his worries and tribulations. With her brave and stoical outlook, she accepted that the strain and burden of the work could scarcely be otherwise. But however and whenever she saw a chance to ease his burden or to spare him extra worry, she did so, and she could be fiercely protective if she thought unnecessary anxieties or problems were added to those it was inevitable he had to bear.

There is an interesting example of how she sought to protect his peace of mind in a family incident that took place in the spring of this hard year.

In April Randolph, who at this time had a Staff job in Cairo, volunteered to join a parachute unit. Strangely enough, when Clementine heard this news, she reacted strongly against Randolph's decision; it was a most uncharacteristic reflex, for she greatly admired spontaneous and brave actions. But the reason for her initial reaction to Randolph's decision is clearly revealed in a letter she wrote to Winston, after an obviously not very happy conversation on this subject:

My Darling,

Please don't think I am indifferent because I was silent when you told me of Randolph's cable to Pamela saying he was joining a parachute unit . . . but I grieve that he has done this because I know it will cause you harrowing anxiety, indeed, even agony of mind.

I feel this impulse of Randolph's . . . is sincere but sensational. Surely there is a half-way house between being a Staff-Officer and a Parachute Jumper. He could have quietly & sensibly rejoined his Regiment & considering he has a very young wife with a baby to say nothing of a Father who is bearing not only the burden of his own country but for the moment of an un-prepared America it would in my view have been his dignified & reasonable duty . . . My Darling – Do you think it would be any use my sending an affectionate cable begging him on *your* account to re-join his Regiment & give up this scheme in which if he begins one feels he must perhaps persevere? . . .[9]

In the event Clementine took no action, and Randolph pursued his intention of joining the Special Air Service. One cannot help feeling that in this matter her judgment went a little astray; but at this time of intense strain her first thought was for Winston.

By June 1942 differing views on grand strategy between the British and American high commands made Churchill anxious to see the President again. Visiting Britain in April, Harry Hopkins and General Marshall had argued in favour of landing an Allied force in Western Europe that very year – a course which Churchill and the British Chiefs of Staff were convinced would be calamitous. Churchill saw a danger that America, if deterred from attacking the enemy in the West, might lend her ear to the powerful 'Pacific lobby' and turn her interest and her strength too much to the Far East. To counter this possibility, and to advocate an alternative plan of action for 1942, in the form of Allied landings along the French North-African coast (Operation 'Torch'), Churchill arranged in mid-June to fly once more to America.

During his ten-day visit to Washington he received the news of the fall of Tobruk. It was a grievous military blow, but worse, it was a humiliation. Ever afterwards Churchill remembered with emotion and gratitude the attitude of the President and Harry Hopkins:

Nothing could exceed the sympathy and chivalry of my two friends. There were

no reproaches; not an unkind word was spoken. 'What can we do to help?' said
Roosevelt.[10]

After concluding satisfactory talks with the Americans, and advancing plans for
the execution of Operation 'Torch' later in the year, Churchill felt he himself must
impart to the Russians the unpalatable tidings that there could be no Second Front
in the immediate future, and he therefore decided that after his return from
Washington he would set off on his journeys once more and combine a visit to Cairo
and Moscow.

On Friday, 31st July Winston and Clementine paid a fleeting visit to Chartwell.
It must have been a precious day for them both; they had so little time together,
and now he was on the brink of another long, fatiguing journey; she did not doubt
its necessity, but she knew, all too well, the risks he must run. Chartwell had a
charm and appeal all of its own during the war. The big house, with shuttered
windows, like blind eyes, stared out gaunt and silent over the beautiful valley. The
grounds, virtually untended, had become like the garden of the Sleeping Beauty.
But the fish were there still, waiting to be fed, and the Canadian goose (which had
earned the name of the 'Naval Aide de Camp', because it would always accompany
Winston on his tours of the lakes) was there to greet them. A few black swans, too,
remained, having survived the depredations of the foxes.

Two days later, Winston flew off to Egypt for a week of conferences and inspections, during which important changes were decided upon in the military hierarchy:
General Alexander was to assume command of the forces in the Middle East; and
General Montgomery was to take over the command of the Eighth Army. Churchill
then journeyed on to Russia, bearing his unwelcome news. 'It was like carrying a
large lump of ice to the North Pole,'[11] he later wrote. The tidings were indeed ill-
received, and the talks threatened to break down: but finally disagreeable reality
was accepted, and comradeship preserved.

Back in Cairo for a few days, Churchill already sensed a new atmosphere per-
meating all levels in the army. On 24th August, his Liberator aircraft touched down
at Lyneham, where Clementine and Randolph were waiting to greet him.

The fruits of Winston's visit to Cairo were not long in ripening. On 23rd October,
the Eighth Army attacked the enemy at El Alamein, launching the heaviest artillery
barrage recorded in the history of war, and on 4th November, after twelve days of
heavy fighting, the Eighth Army inflicted a severe defeat on the German and Italian
forces under Rommel's command; 30,000 prisoners were taken. Here at last was
victory – real, solid and overwhelming. This was the turning-point of the war. 'It
may almost be said,' wrote Winston, ' "Before Alamein we never had a victory.
After Alamein we never had a defeat." '[12]

In his Memoirs, Sir Harold Nicolson gives a detailed description of a luncheon
party he attended on 6th November, two days after these tremendous tidings:

> At 1.15 I stroll across to Downing Street where I am to lunch . . . I go down-
> stairs to the basement where the Churchills are living, since the upper floors*

*They were still actually 'living' at the Storey's Gate Annexe, but when the bombing dimin-
ished they used the basement rooms at No. 10 as much as possible for entertaining.

have been knocked about. They made it very pretty with chintz and flowers and good furniture and excellent French pictures – not only the moderns, but Ingres and David. [The National Gallery had lent them some pictures.]

I find Lady Kitty Lambton and Lady Furness and Clemmie Churchill. We are given sherry. Eddy Marsh comes in, and then the Private Secretary, Martin . . . He tells us not to wait for Winston, as he is late. We go into luncheon: sea-kale, jugged hare and cherry tart. Not well done. In a few minutes Winston comes in. He is dressed in his romper suit of Air Force blue and he carries a letter in his hand . . . He gives the letter to Clemmie. It is a long letter from the King written in his own handwriting, and saying how much he and the Queen have been thinking of Winston in these glorious days. Winston is evidently pleased. 'Every word,' he mutters, 'in his own hand.'[13]

Sir Harold then goes on to give an account of the conversation. Lady Kitty and Lady Furness had just escaped from the South of France; they were old 'fringe-friends', obviously asked for old times' sake.

Winston talks to Lady Kitty and I talk hard to Lady Furness, as she is frightened of the gigantic figure on her right, and Winston is bad at putting people at their ease. Nor does Clemmie Churchill help much . . .[14]

This is a clear example of a luncheon party where the topics of conversation were strictly confined. Both Winston and Clementine knew that, while they were all rejoicing at the wonderful feat of arms in the Egyptian desert, another tremendous operation was impending: 'Torch', the invasion of French North Africa, was planned to take place in two days' time.

Sir Harold continued his description of this occasion by recounting how Brendan Bracken (then Minister of Information) had appeared, and that Churchill told him to arrange for the church bells to be rung the following Sunday.
Some hesitation is expressed by all of us. 'Not at all,' says Winston, 'not at all. We are not celebrating final victory. The war will still be long. When we have beaten Germany, it will take us two more years to beat Japan' . . .[15]

By a strange coincidence, I also recorded the conversation about the church bells in my own diary, because towards the end of this luncheon I arrived from my battery at the beginning of a short leave. I noted that it was a 'very sticky' occasion, and that when
the party broke up, Mummie [was] being violent (quite rightly I thought) with Papa who wanted to have all the bells rung on Sunday.[16]

Since the beginning of the war the church bells had been silent – they were to be the warning that the invasion had started: now those dark days had passed, and Winston wanted the bells to ring out in celebration of the resounding victory at El Alamein. Clementine was more cautious, and fearful lest some reverse should occur which would make nonsense of such a mark of triumph and elation, and she vehemently begged Winston to bide a while; and on this occasion he heeded her arguments. But soon the bells did ring out – joyously and triumphantly – on Sunday, 15th November. By then, the enemy forces in French North Africa had laid down their arms, and the victorious British Army had once more entered Tobruk.

Clementine was particularly busy just now because, at the invitation of the Queen, Mrs Roosevelt had come on a three-week visit to Britain. For the first few days of her visit she stayed at Buckingham Palace with the King and Queen. During her stay in Britain she carried out a full and, to any other woman, totally daunting programme, visiting places as far apart as Glasgow and Londonderry. The main purpose of her visit was to acquaint herself with what the war really meant to the British – and particularly to the women. In addition, she visited United States troops stationed in this country. Winston and Clementine were, of course, most anxious to entertain her, and for the first week-end of her visit, Mrs Roosevelt stayed at Chequers. The following Tuesday, they gave a dinner party for her at No. 10, and Clementine asked some distinguished British women to meet her.

During the course of her visit, Clementine went with Mrs Roosevelt on a good many of her expeditions. The 'First Lady's' pace was too much for her – visibly – on one occasion, when they were touring a W.V.S. clothing distribution centre: Clementine simply sat down on a marble staircase, and joined up with Mrs Roosevelt later! She was not the only one to feel the strain: toughened and younger journalists were worn out by trying to keep up the marathon pace set by the President's wife.[17]

Halfway through Mrs Roosevelt's visit, Clementine wrote a long account of her activities to the President, telling him the effect his wife's presence had 'on our women and girls. When she appears their faces light up with gladness and welcome.' Clementine was much struck by the way Mrs Roosevelt spoke on several occasions to groups of young servicewomen:

Each time she said something significant, fresh and true, and she gave all who heard her a sense of being in the presence of a remarkable and benevolent personality.

Clementine also admired Mrs Roosevelt's handling of a press conference:

I was struck by the ease, friendliness and dignity with which she talked with the reporters, and by the esteem and affection with which they evidently regard her.[18]

At dinner one night, Mrs Roosevelt and Winston had a 'slight difference of opinion'[19] over Loyalist Spain: they never really got on – but each esteemed the other for what they were. Clementine played a neutral, conciliating role, and brought the issue to an end by leading the ladies out of dinner. She liked and admired Mrs Roosevelt, but evidently did not drop her guard, leaving her guest to wonder what sort of a woman was behind the attractive, surprisingly youthful exterior and charming personality observed by Mrs Roosevelt, who commented in her diary:

One feels that she has had to assume a role because of being in public life and that the role is now part of her, but one wonders what she is like underneath.[20]

She knew about Clementine's involvement with aid to Russia, and noticed that she 'is very careful not to voice any opinions publicly or to associate with any political organizations . . .'[21]. She found this also to be true of the wives of all the public officials she met. It was, of course, in strong contrast to Mrs Roosevelt, whose political views and involvements were at times an inconvenience, if not an embarrassment, to the President.

But if at times the British Tory and the New World radical took a tilt at each other, there was no reserve in Winston's praise and gratitude for the effect of Mrs Roosevelt's visit. Clementine came to say goodbye to her on the day of her departure; Winston was at Chequers, but she brought Mrs Roosevelt a letter from him in his own hand: 'You certainly have left golden footprints behind you,'[22] he wrote with grace and sincerity.

Every year, whatever the news, Clementine gathered together a party of the family and closest friends to celebrate Winston's birthday. It was immensely touching to him – and to all of us – how since the war the whole country, and indeed much of the wide world, seemed to want to wish him 'Happy Birthday'. Greetings and presents used to pour in, and despite the rationing and austerity people would send delicacies of every kind. This year of 1942 – Winston's sixty-eighth birthday – we were a small party, only seven apart from my father and mother, who gathered at the Annexe to celebrate: Diana, Sarah, Pamela, Jack Churchill, Venetia Montagu, Brendan Bracken, and myself. My mother arranged a lovely party, as usual, and the rooms looked particularly pretty with so many 'birthday' flowers. We were all conscious of the thousands of people who joined with us in spirit as we drank Winston's health – and this year the bright gleam of victory added lustre and joy to these family rejoicings.

ALL IN THE DAY'S WORK

WHATEVER new preoccupations and commitments came her way as the war ground on, Clementine remained faithful and efficacious as a member of the Committee for the Fulmer Chase Maternity Home, whose cause she had espoused as early as November 1939. There was a real and pressing need for this home. Many officers in all three services made unusually early marriages, many of them were of small means, and few of them had established homes. Their wives for the most part lived with their own families, or 'followed the drum', living in lodgings or rented accommodation; many of them were serving themselves in one of the Women's Services. When the time came for them to have their babies, their husbands might be abroad or at sea; and some of them were already widows. It was felt that it would be a source of reassurance to their husbands to know that there was somewhere where their wives would be looked after skilfully and kindly, and where they could be in comfort and, if possible, safety, when they bore their babies.

A house had already been made available for this purpose by Mrs Edward Baron, who lent her large and comfortable mansion (free of rent and rates) – Fulmer Chase, in Buckinghamshire. As a result of the original appeal letter to *The Times*, it was possible to open the home for thirty patients early in 1940.

From the start, Clementine took the closest interest in the maternity home, and was actively involved in the running of it. Her particular care and interest was the food, and she took endless trouble to ensure that despite the difficulties of staffing and rationing, the patients' and staff's meals were delicious, and appetisingly served.

As the pressure on accommodation at Fulmer Chase increased, the period for which mothers could remain in hospital had to be reduced from three to two weeks, and many of them had to take their babies back to inadequate accommodation. To improve this situation, an anonymous benefactor gave Clementine a sum generous enough to purchase a house, and in February 1942 Fircroft Post-Natal Home (at nearby Gerrards Cross) was opened. It served as an annexe to Fulmer Chase, and here mothers could spend a further fortnight after leaving the maternity home.

Fulmer Chase was not very far from Chequers, and Clementine was therefore able the more easily to attend the frequent meetings of the executive committees of which she was a member. Despite increasing calls on her time, she attended the

Fulmer Chase meetings with regularity, and her association with this cause continued until it was wound up some years after the war.

When I appealed through the Press for material for this book, a large number of the letters containing personal reminiscences of my mother came from women who had had their babies at Fulmer Chase, and who spoke in glowing terms of the care and comfort they had experienced there, and of the pleasure her visits gave. One of them described how Clementine had visited Fircroft in company with Lady Portal, wife of Sir Charles Portal, Chief of the Air Staff, and a member of the Fulmer Chase Committee for many years:

> The visitors arrived . . . inspected our precious babies, made all the appropriate noises, and of course admired them. We then adjourned for coffee, your mother talked to us all about our husbands. She was so very charming to us and after her visit we felt very comforted that she had found time in her very busy life to come and see a handful of mothers who were anxious about their husbands and worried about the future.[1]

*

In February 1941 Clementine became President of the Young Women's Christian Association's Wartime Fund, in succession to Lady Halifax, who accompanied her husband when he became our Ambassador in Washington. During the war, the Y.W.C.A. saw that its principal task lay in providing hostels, clubs, huts and canteens for women war-workers, and particularly for the ever-increasing numbers of young servicewomen, nearly all of whom were far from their homes, and many of them serving overseas. In order to provide adequately for their needs it was essential for the Y.W.C.A.'s appeal to be headed by a considerable public personality.

Fund-raising on the scale on which she was now to be engaged was a new venture for Clementine. In nearly every case the first salvo was fired with a letter to *The Times*, to be followed as soon as feasible by a broadcast appeal. Clementine was not an experienced broadcaster, but she was soon to become one; and if her script was of necessity in the main constructed for her so that all the pertinent points were made, she always wrestled with the text herself, to try to make it come to life. As time went on and she acquired more confidence, and more detailed knowledge of the cause in question, her appeal letters and broadcasts became more natural in manner and even more effective. Unaccustomed as she was to making appeals to individuals for money, and although at first very shy, she soon became very good at it, and was delighted by the gratifying response she nearly always received. In her first letter as Chairman of the Y.W.C.A. Appeal, Clementine asked for £30,000, and one of the first people to respond to her letter was Lord Nuffield, who sent £5,000. As with her broadcasts, she took great pains with her individual appeal letters, which were very much 'her own', and her thanks were gracefully and warmly expressed.

Surprisingly, Clementine was not a 'natural' as a public speaker, although on occasion, at political meetings, she could, when aroused (as in the old Dundee days), forget her shyness and launch forth upon what Winston was wont to call 'the unpinioned wing'. Now for her wartime causes she overcame her natural reticence in public, and would welcome any opportunity and face any audience in order to further the purpose in hand. One such occasion was in December 1943, when she visited the London Stock Exchange and appealed for funds to build a Y.W.C.A. hut. The money was duly forthcoming and when in March of the following year she officially opened the hut, Sir Robert Pearson, the Chairman of the London Stock Exchange, said in his speech that he had mentioned Clementine's visit to this essentially and tenaciously male preserve to the Queen, who had commented that she 'was a brave woman'. Her 'audacity' had been generously rewarded.

Gifts came her way from all sorts of unexpected sources, and not necessarily as the result of a direct appeal. Of one such windfall Clementine gave an amusing account from Canada, when she was there with Winston for the Second Quebec Conference in September 1944. Winston had received an honorary degree at McGill University, and in one of her 'round-robin-diary' letters to the family she wrote:

> One of the dignitaries of the University was Mr McConnell. Mary will remember him because he was the kind, generous, but rather tactless man who tried to give me a mink coat last year and Mary a beaver coat, both of which gifts, with true delicacy(!) we reluctantly declined. Mary will remember that instead he gave me £2,000 for the Y.W.C.A. Well, yesterday, after Papa had had his Ll.D., Mr. McConnell pressed a little envelope into my hand saying he wished to give me another present for so good a Cause. On looking inside this time there was a cheque for £5,000. I am really much overcome by so much kindness.[2]

But Clementine did not regard her role as Chairman of the Wartime Appeal as limiting her simply to the task of raising large sums of money; she became deeply interested in the work of the Y.W.C.A., and wanted to have her say in the general policy and standards of the hostels and clubs. Although she in no way ignored the high Christian mission of the Y.W.C.A. movement, she did not see at all why high principles need go hand in hand with low standards of physical comfort; and it was in this field that she saw a real opportunity to make a contribution. Throughout her years of service, first as President of the Wartime Fund, from 1941 to 1947, and then as Chairman of the National Hostels Committee, from 1949 to 1952, she bent all her powers to improving the running and the standards of the association's hostels.

Clementine's approach to this new job was characteristic: find out the facts; grasp the problem; grapple with the difficulties. As with her investigations in the shelters, she would never allow official appraisal of what could be done to discourage her or to deflect her from aiming at the highest standards; only after thorough investigation of the facts would she allow herself, if convinced by the arguments, to lower her sights.

It was, of course, very difficult to get alterations, or repairs, done on the home front, and bomb-damaged housing had priority. Everything was in short supply: labour; materials; hot water; food – in fact almost all the things that contribute to comfort. Nevertheless, Clementine soon formed a clear view of what should be the Y.W.C.A.'s policy in regard to its hostels: it should try to produce the highest standards possible despite all the difficulties. She felt very much that this was owed not only to the girls who used the facilities the association provided but also to the many people who responded so generously to her appeals.

As soon as she had launched her first appeal for the 'Y.W.', Clementine lost no time in visiting as many of their clubs and hostels as possible. Her eagle eye went straight to the essentials: how many baths were there to the number of girls in the hostel? Was the hot-water supply adequate and efficient? What were the mattresses like? (She never hesitated to have the bed-clothes whisked off so that she could judge for herself.) Were there proper facilities for washing and ironing? Were the rooms too crowded? (Unfortunately they nearly always were, owing to the great number of girls who wanted accommodation.) Were there bedside lamps? But Clementine was not solely obsessed with physical comforts, important though she thought them to be. She never under-estimated the vital role played in each hostel by its Warden; and she appreciated that many a hostel had a reputation for being a happy one because of its Warden's personality, even if the living standards left much to be desired.

Whenever she visited a hostel, she liked to meet the local committee, which was in each place responsible for its general running and finances. She learnt to sum them up fairly quickly: like all committees, they varied. Everywhere she tried to instil into them the idea that it mattered very much that the girls who used the hostels and clubs sought some reassurance that all life had not been reduced to barrack-room or canteen standards; and that in coming to the Y.W.C.A. they might hope to find, even in wartime, some degree of privacy, reasonable comfort in attractive surroundings, fastidious standards of cleanliness and good food well served – in fact an oasis in the dreary and arid desert of the war.

All this was not achieved by merely looking gracious and smiling: Clementine loved to forge ahead, and was intolerant of delays; nor could she stand complacency. She cannot always have been easy to work with, as she found it difficult to conceal or dissimulate her opinions and was often sceptical of explanations. But her fellow colleagues and the officials of the Y.W.C.A. who worked with her closely throughout those years have paid generous tribute to her work. And I have received testimony from girls who were residents in various clubs or hostels at the time of one of Clementine's visitations, of how conditions improved rapidly thereafter.

*

The Red Cross Aid to Russia Fund, headed by Clementine, was launched in mid-October 1941. The response was immediate, and contributions flowed in from all over the country. The ever-generous Lord Nuffield gave £50,000 within the first few days, and donations large and small swelled the fund daily. On 28th October, when the appeal was only twelve days old, Clementine in a broadcast was able to announce that the total stood at £370,000. For the first three months of its existence, the Aid to Russia Fund received all of the Red Cross Penny-a-Week Fund and thereafter, for the rest of the war, a quarter. Three days before Christmas, Clementine again broadcast, and she was able to give the almost incredible news that in less than three months, the fund had passed the £1 million mark.

And this was no momentary wave of passing enthusiasm: all over the country organisations, bands of schoolchildren, and groups of factory and office workers set themselves to collect money for this cause on a regular basis. Individual donations also poured in: millionaires and old-age pensioners alike gave, and gave again. Throughout the country, towns and cities held flag days and organised Anglo-Soviet Weeks from which the Aid to Russia Fund reaped a rich harvest. Auctions, exhibitions, and theatrical galas took place; artists donated pictures, actors gave generously of their time and talent – the great pianist Moiseiwitsch giving a series of concerts for Aid to Russia. The proceeds of the Wembley International in January 1942 were devoted to the Fund, and the England *v* Wales football match in February 1943 raised £12,500 for it, at that time the largest sum ever raised for charity by one sporting event.

From across the world in the last days of December 1941, Malaya, already invaded by the Japanese, sent a contribution; Clementine told Winston, who was in America:

In the midst of their own preoccupations Malaya 2 days ago cabled me £25,000 for my Russian Fund. I was much moved . . .[3]

A few weeks before my mother had told me of another gift – smaller in size, but the story of which wrung one's heart:

. . . I have been given to be sold for the Fund the most exquisite clock, made of different coloured enamels the hands & the numerals are in diamonds. But rather than its value & its beauty, it is its history which is arresting. It was given to the Czarina (murdered by the Bolsheviks) by the British Colony in St Petersburg (now Leningrad) on the occasion of her marriage. Now it is going to help the people whose present rulers massacred her, her Husband & her four [actually five] Children.[4]

The great difficulty of making the aid really effective was the vast scale of Russia's need. In 1942, the British Red Cross sent a representative to Moscow to find out exactly what their requirements were: he was given a schedule of gigantic proportions. Some of the items demanded were at first unobtainable but, nothing daunted, the Red Cross set about finding ways and means to procure as many of the things that had been asked for as possible. Several British factories undertook the manufacture of instruments and medical equipment never before produced in this country.

While it was through Clementine's efforts and influence that the nation's sympathy for Russia was translated into a vast and continuing flow of money, the Aid to Russia Committee of distinguished and knowledgeable men and women wrestled with the technical problems and the practical difficulties of delivering the goods, once procured.

The Russians were at times extremely difficult to deal with, chiefly on account of their often unreasonable demands and their pathological suspicions of our motives or actions. However, despite all difficulties and discouragements the work of the fund forged ahead and, by the end of December 1942, close on £2,250,000 had been subscribed. Owing to the scale of Russian demands, and the necessity of placing orders sometimes six months ahead, the Appeal Committee had deliberately allowed the fund to become heavily overdrawn. On New Year's Eve, Clementine made a broadcast; she gave an account of all that had been hitherto subscribed, and she told her listeners of the shipments that had already been despatched. She then announced that the fund was in debt, and gave the reason for it; she added that another justification for spending so much money in advance was that she knew from experience that she could rely on the public to make it good. Her trustful optimism was fully justified: on 20th February, she was able to announce that in response to her New Year appeal she had received £170,000 in donations and that, combined with the contributions from the Red Cross Penny-a-Week Fund, not only had the debt been cleared but also they could now increase the supplies sent to Russia.

By the end of October 1943, two years after the launching of the Aid to Russia Fund, the £4 million mark was reached. In a statement issued by Clementine, she said:

> This sum of money is small compared with the size of Russia, the number of her wrecked cities and of her heroic unconquerable population. But it is a token from the hearts of all the British people all over the world. The rich and well-to-do contribute generously, but the larger part comes from the workers – hundreds of thousands of them give week by week. It is indeed the people's fund, and through it they express to the Russian nation their respect, wonder and admiration for unsurpassed courage, patriotism, and military achievement.[5]

By December 1944 over £6 million had been achieved, and although active collection for the fund ceased in 1945, contributions continued to be received, and by June 1947 the grand total stood at £7½ million.

During the fund's first fourteen months nearly 300,000 tons of supplies were despatched to Russia. Among the items sent were: 150 tons of drugs, 97 X-ray units, 1,500,000 surgical instruments, 500,000 blankets, and over 1,000,000 garments (all new, and collected and packed by the Women's Voluntary Services).

It may be imagined to what extent her work for Russia added to Clementine's labours. Hours had to be spent in committee, wrestling with the lists of requirements, and how to set about supplying them; then all sorts of difficulties arose over shipping the goods to Russia, and in all these matters she took an active part. Clementine also made many expeditions to plants and factories which were turning out special orders for the Red Cross Fund. She was invited to many of the endless succession of functions and events organised all over the country in support of her fund. She tried to go to as many as possible, and this often entailed long, tiring journeys.

Apart from other correspondence connected with the fund, all the gifts and donations were of course officially acknowledged, but many of them were sent especially and personally to her, and she always tried to acknowledge these herself, either in her own handwriting or at any rate with a personally signed letter. It was not only large and splendid contributions which received personal replies: Clementine, for instance, used to take especial trouble to write to thank schoolchildren who had made several small collections for her Fund. As it would have been humanly impossible to acknowledge even a tithe of the letters and money that came rolling in after she had broadcast an appeal, Clementine would then write out in her own hand a warmly worded letter, which was photographically reproduced and sent to the many contributors, who at least could feel that she had taken some trouble herself. The same direct and personal touch which characterised all her public work did not desert her now, when faced with such a mammoth undertaking.

In all this work Clementine's chief link with the Soviet Embassy in London was the Ambassador's wife, Madame Agnes Maisky. She was not an easy woman to deal with, and Clementine had to spend much time and exercise great patience in listening to long lists of imperious demands or complaints from her. Fortunately, however, Clementine was neither small-minded nor easily offended – and she often gave quite as good as she got! But she was soon accustomed to Madame Maisky, and came to like this brusque, intelligent woman, whose fiery patriotism was so clearly evident.

In September 1943, the Ambassador was recalled to Moscow at the end of his mission. Clementine was at that time in America with Winston, and so unable to say farewell to her formidable friend. But Madame Maisky wrote her a warm letter of farewell:

> During my stay here I greatly appreciated our close relations, and your friendliness and kindness to me; but most of all I am grateful to you for all that you have done to send medical aid to my countrymen. This is a great work, and we shall never forget it.

There were other organisations for sending help to Russia: a number of Communist and left-wing bodies started funds; various Trade Union groups raised money for Russia independently; and sums were contributed direct to the Soviet Red Cross. But none of these agencies caught the confidence or the imagination of the British public as greatly as 'Mrs Churchill's Fund'. By April 1945, of the £9 million collected in Britain from all sources for the help of the Soviet Union, the Red Cross Aid to Russia Fund had contributed £6,700,000.[6] Inevitably there arose from time to time various petty irritations and a spirit of unseemly competitiveness between the various funds striving to collect money to aid the Soviet Union. The Red Cross Aid to Russia Fund had three signal advantages: firstly, it was backed by, and enjoyed the advantages of, the organisational power and prestige of the Red Cross, with its special Aid to Russia Committee of able and devoted men and women. Secondly, there is no doubt that the name Churchill, combined with the respect and confidence Clementine herself inspired among all classes in Great Britain, lent the fund a lustre, and fired people's enthusiasm. Thirdly, all the other funds had a political bias. Through the Red Cross Fund, people with no sympathy for Communism could pay their testimony of admiration and gratitude to the people of Russia, whose heroic fight for their native land, and whose terrible sufferings moved all but clay hearts.

The 'rival' fund which attracted the most attention was the Joint Aid to Russia

Aid Committee (Joint Committee for Soviet Aid) under the leadership of Dr Hewlett Johnson, the Dean of Canterbury. This fund had been started almost simultaneously with Clementine's, and the Red Cross had been asked to take it over. However, various difficulties arose, including some members of the Government making it plain that in their view aid to Russia should not be sponsored by someone with such well-known Soviet sympathies as Dr Hewlett Johnson. The Dean himself evidently had similar reservations about amalgamation with the Red Cross Fund, he and his colleagues feeling that the motivation behind it was essentially political. However, both funds co-existed harmoniously, avoiding duplication of effort and competing in a friendly spirit.[7]

In relation to all this, an amusing, light-hearted incident took place in the early spring of 1944. Field Marshal Montgomery was a great friend of the 'Red Dean', and he asked Clementine if she would like to meet him; she said she would welcome an opportunity to do so. A luncheon was duly arranged at the Army and Navy Club and, recorded the Dean,

we had a most amicable talk, during which I said to Mrs Churchill:
'I know you like good painting.' She replied:
'What makes you think so?' I said:
'Because at a London exhibition I thought far the best water colour was a long boat hauled up on the sandbanks – I should have liked to have bought it, but it was sold. I was so interested that I looked up the name of the purchaser and found it was yourself.'
We talked of Russia and later I sent her my book *The Socialist Sixth of the World*. Not long afterwards, a large parcel arrived, which turned out to be the picture I had admired. The following letter came with it:

10 Downing Street,
Whitehall. 16.3.44

Dear Mr Dean,
How very kind of you to send me your book with such a charming inscription. I am planning a few quiet days in the country at the weekend, when I shall read it. I have already looked at the illustrations which I see are the work of your wife, and I think them lovely.
Thank you also for your letter. The work which I have tried to do for Russia has been a most interesting, educating and happy experience. I am glad that there should be several funds, because I do think that every point of view is then covered and all have an opportunity of expressing the admiration which everyone with an understanding heart must feel for Russia.

Yours sincerely,
Clementine S. Churchill

P.S. I am sending you the 'White Boat', as I think we should both share the pleasure it gave us. Quite a communist sentiment – I'm training on![8]

The crowning moment of Clementine's long and arduous work for the Russian Fund came in 1945, when in response to the invitation of the Soviet Red Cross, she and Miss Johnson (Secretary to the Aid to Russia Fund) went to Russia for six weeks, visiting mainly those centres where the goods and equipment provided by the Fund had been distributed. This interesting journey – one of the most thrilling and moving events in Clementine's already not uneventful life – will be told in a later chapter, but here seems the place to describe the meeting of the Executive Committee of the Soviet Red Cross, which Clementine attended while in Moscow, at which a report was read by Colonel Divakov recounting in impressive detail the work of the Red Cross Fund and praising the fund for having reached 'truly significant dimensions'. In its prosaic, pedantic way this report reads as a triumphant and thrilling 'account rendered' of the use made of the vast sum of money subscribed:

> Up to January 1, 1945, 11,600 tons of medical supplies and clothing provided by Mrs Churchill's Fund and valued at £4,000,000 had reached the Soviet Union.
>
> We have received from the British Red Cross over 2,000 tons of medicine in powder form, some 22,000 units of medical equipment including 600 X-Ray installations, 600 autoclaves, approximately 15,000 sterilisers and over 1,000,000 pieces of rubber goods.

Colonel Divakov went on to describe the important and formidable task at that moment being undertaken by the Aid to Russia Fund, which was the assembling of the entire equipment for two large hospitals in Rostov-on-Don which had both been pillaged and partly destroyed by the Germans.

On this occasion a tribute was paid to Clementine for her part in all this work:

> We learn that Mrs Churchill is concerned not only with organising the collection of funds, but also with the rational expenditure of these funds and with the timely shipment of medicine, equipment and materials required by the Soviet Union.

The report had the grace to acknowledge that Great Britain had other, and equally pressing, needs and obligations, a point which had so often been entirely overlooked by Russians when making imperious and unreasonable demands. Colonel Divakov's report handsomely acknowledged that when Russia's requests could not be immediately complied with, 'Mrs Churchill, on the request of the Soviet Red Cross, used her authority and personal influence in an endeavour to meet our requirements.'

Later in the course of this memorable visit both Clementine and Miss Johnson were to receive Russian decorations (Clementine the Order of the Red Banner of Labour, Miss Johnson the Medal of Labour Distinction) in recognition of their work for Aid to Russia. It is therefore strange, and rather sad, that thirty-three years later, one of the few countries which did not send a representative to Clementine's Memorial Service in Westminster Abbey was the Soviet Union.

And in June 1946 Clementine received at the hands of the King at Buckingham Palace the Grand Cross of the Order of the British Empire, the citation being 'for public services'. But greatly gratified though she was by this accolade, which carries the title 'Dame', she would never allow herself to be called 'Dame Clementine' – preferring to remain (until Winston received the Garter) Mrs Churchill G B E.

The work undertaken in the war by women of all ages and classes was truly remarkable in its scope and variety, and Clementine's own efforts can take an honourable place in the records of women's war work. The name she bore, and her position as wife of a powerful Prime Minister, lent strength to her arm; but to these undeniable advantages she brought the unstinted, unwearying offering of her own talents and personality, which reaped a rich return for those causes for which she worked, and was in itself a shining example.

CONFERENCE AND CRISIS

THE YEAR 1943 was one of dearly-bought advance on all fronts: the Russians began the reconquest of their homeland; the Germans were driven from North Africa, and the Allies invaded Italy; while on the other side of the world, the American forces were locked in a deadly grip with the Japanese in the Pacific, and the British battled to defend the Burma Road. It might well have been named the 'year of conferences', for it saw four meetings of great consequence between Churchill and Roosevelt, and the first meeting of the Big Three at Teheran in November. Wide divergencies of view arose between the British and American Chiefs of Staff over the strategy to be adopted once the North African campaign was over. The main argument revolved around the priority to be given between the planning and timing of 'Overlord' (the invasion of Normandy), and the campaign in Italy and the Mediterranean. In order that a united policy might be forged, meetings were vital between Churchill and Roosevelt and their colleagues. Winston also set great store by personal contact with commanders on the spot; he therefore had to undertake many long, exhausting and dangerous journeys. Nowadays, when air travel is a commonplace, safe and comfortable means of transport, it is difficult to grasp just how different were the conditions of flying then. And to the physical discomforts and the much greater technical limitations and hazards was added the ever-present possibility of attack by the enemy.

For my mother, 1943 was a year of almost continual concern for Winston's health. That this was already a cause of worry when the New Year opened is borne out by an entry in my diary for Sunday, 3rd January, when I spent twenty-four hours' leave at Chequers:

Went for a long & lovely walk alone with Mummie after lunch.

We talked entirely of the family – & especially of Papa. It appears that he *might* get a coronary thrombosis – & it might be brought on by anything like a long & /or high flight –

The question is whether he should be warned or not. Mummie thinks he should not – I agree with her . . .

For my mother, the knowledge of this additional and agonising possibility underlaid all the journeys (and particularly the flights) which my father undertook hereafter. Apart from this continuing, gnawing concern for Winston's health, there were also within the bosom of the family anxieties and tensions mainly arising from the break-up of Randolph's and Pamela's marriage. It was made all the more frustrating and painful for Randolph by the fact that during most of the crucial time he was abroad. The main burden of these difficulties had to be borne by Clementine alone; she did her best, but any intervention in such situations nearly always results in bitter reproaches being levelled, and this case proved no exception to the rule. In moments of reflection and calm Randolph appreciated his mother's difficult situation. 'I hope you don't think me unappreciative of your position in all this disagreeable business,' he later wrote to her. 'I know how difficult things have been for you and I do know that you have tried to understand my point of view.'[1]

For much of the time my mother could not discuss these intimate and painful family matters with anyone, for my father was utterly engrossed by the war, and Sarah and I, in whom she used to confide, were for long stretches of time away with our units. Diana, who had left the W.R.N.S., was now expecting her third child, and was deeply absorbed in caring for her family in the difficult conditions of wartime.

The first of the meetings between Churchill and Roosevelt in 1943 took place in Casablanca in January, before the conquest of Tunisia was complete. Winston left England in a Commando plane on 12th January. Once more, the travelling conditions were austere and uncomfortable: the newly-installed heating apparatus was found to be in danger of overheating and causing an explosion, so that it had to be turned off half-way through the night, and the passengers suffered acutely from the cold.

The President and Prime Minister conferred for about ten days at Anfa, on the outskirts of Casablanca, and then Winston prevailed upon his friend to stay for a further day or two so that he might show him Marrakech and the glories of the sunset on the snows of the Atlas Mountains. After the President's departure, Winston lingered for a further two days in this place which so beguiled him, and while maintaining a constant flow of minutes to the War Cabinet, painted the only picture which came from his brush during the war.

On 14th January Clementine had written to Winston from London:

My Darling,
    The 'Annexe' and 'No. 10' are dead & empty without you – Smoky [the cat, a great favourite with Winston] wanders about disconsolate . . .
    Everything is quiet – so far at *this* end 'the secret' is water-tight . . .[2]

Indeed, security arrangements for the meeting had been amazingly successful, and the journalists summoned to a news conference at Casablanca on 24th January were flabbergasted to see 'The Big Two' and even more astonished to learn that they had been there in conclave for nearly a fortnight.

Winston went on to Cairo, and then – having overcome considerable opposition to this plan from the War Cabinet – to Adana, on the border of Turkey and Syria, for talks with the Turkish President. He returned to Africa where, at Tripoli, he witnessed with emotion and pride a march past of two divisions of General Montgomery's victorious Eighth Army; and he finally called at Algiers for talks with

General Eisenhower before flying home. His movements were decidedly *ad hoc* and, necessarily, concealed by the greatest secrecy. Clementine was apprised by the Private Office of all the changes in his programme, and received two long letters from Winston himself, but although she was accustomed to sudden changes of plan, she was particularly anxious at this time because she knew of the Security Service's fear for Winston's safety during these extended travels. Her concern shows through the note she sent by hand to greet him at the airfield on his return on 5th February:

> My Darling,
> Welcome Home. The anxiety & tension has been severe. What an inspiration was the visit to Turkey. And how glad I am you did not allow yourself to be deviated from that extra lap of your journey. I'm thinking of you flying thro' the tenebrous dark & pray you make a good land-fall.
>
> > Your loving & expectant
> > Clemmie
> > [Picture of lovely fat Kat]

But although Winston returned elated by the success of his mission, his journeyings – which might well have wearied a much younger man – had taken their toll. He had travelled thousands of miles in varying degrees of discomfort and experienced sharp changes of temperature; he had slept in luxury villas, trains, aeroplanes and caravans; and wherever he went, day and night, he carried the burden of the conduct of the war. When three days after his return home, he addressed the House of Commons, he was already suffering from a cold and a sore throat. On 12th February he developed a temperature and spent a day or two in bed. On the evening of the 16th, while dining alone with Clementine, he felt ill and found his temperature had soared. Pneumonia was diagnosed the following day.

I came home for the day on Sunday, 21st February and recorded:

> . . . Arrived home. M was ready for church. In her lovely dark cloth coat trimmed with beaver & the flame-coloured scarf bursting out – beaver muff & hat . . .
> We two went to service at the R. Military Chapel – It was rather lovely & comforting.
> M is not *seriously* worried about Papa – but he is pretty ill.
> I was shocked when I saw him. He looked so old & tired – lying back in bed.

The next day I left for an Anti-Aircraft Practice Camp at Whitby, in Yorkshire, and my mother wrote to me on the 24th:

> First of all I write to tell you that Papa is I think really better. The Doctors still give out the 'no change' bulletin because the temperature has not completely gone down, but I can see for myself that he is better. His face looks quite different. He has lost that weary look. I know, my darling, this will relieve you. I have really been very worried about him.
> I am longing to hear how you are, and all you are doing, and how you are settling down. I love detail about everything if you have time.

The entry in my diary, and my mother's subsequent letter, show to what extent Clementine could maintain a calm exterior and conceal her inmost fears even from those nearest to her.

As soon as Winston was well enough the doctors insisted that he should have at least a ten-day convalescence; so he and Clementine retreated to Chequers. Clementine also took the opportunity to have a holiday from her work, and all but the most pressing problems were fended off. During this period she spent one week-end with the Trees, from where she wrote to me:

> As you see I am at Ditchley for the week-end. Papa has got 'Prof' & Uncle Jack who is also having a rest cure — & masses of films – War & Hollywood . . .[3]

Two days later Clementine was back at Chequers, and she gave me this account of her 'quiet' week in the country:

My Darling,

Here are Papa & I living for a whole week at Chequers! Most unusual – By the time it is over I shall have settled down & be quite enjoying it! Papa is progressing very slowly but (I hope & believe) safely through his convalescence to his normal strong state of health.

Yesterday morning, as Papa could not go to his weekly luncheon with the King – the King came here & paid a morning visit in the White Parlour à la Jane Austen. I did not see him as I was motoring back from my week-end at Ditchley . . . I drove through what appeared to be the *whole* of the British Army, that is the male portion of it! In fact I ran into a grand scale military operation called 'Spartan' . . .

The map was just turned round & the South Coast of England was meant to be the North coast of France.

The invading force were presumed to have landed & the body I met between Amersham & Chequers had taken 5 days marching victoriously (it seems) from the Kentish coast! Chequers was taken yesterday afternoon without a struggle . . . I met the Umpire in the lane who turned out to be Col Macnamara M.P. So I asked him to have a bath & some dinner! He didn't know where he was & had just asked the policeman at the gate the name of the big red brick house! . . . Tomorrow night Anthony & Beatrice Eden are coming for the night – Thursday Mr Amery [Secretary of State for India] arrives & Mr Butler (Minister for Education). Friday I go to Nottingham, so you see it's pretty well non stop . . . Sir Stafford & Lady Cripps are bearing down & David Montgomery from Winchester. Papa is going to give him a wonderful portrait of his Father painted by Neville Lewis the same artist who did you when you were a Baby & would not sit properly! We are having the Desert Film for him.

On Monday we return refreshed (!) to London . . .

Your loving but somewhat exhausted
Mummie[4]

At the end of March I was posted to 481 Heavy Mixed Anti-Aircraft Battery which was stationed in the middle of Hyde Park, and where my father would often 'drop in' on us during the course of an air-raid.

I found my father quite restored in health, but my mother was far from well. Once again the pace and strain of her life and work were telling on her and the anxiety she had felt over my father's illness was now taking its forfeit. She developed a painful boil, and had to undergo a series of inoculations and X-ray treatment, which were most exhausting, and for a short period she was virtually laid up. Although the treatments soon resulted in her improvement, Clementine was so obviously in an exhausted and run-down state that her doctor advised her to go away to the seaside.

Much though she hated leaving Winston, and had conscientious qualms about her work, Clementine was feeling so low that she acquiesced and, with Jack Churchill as a companion, she went to Weymouth, where they stayed at the Royal Hotel for about ten days. From there she wrote to me on 24th April:

> . . . This must be a charming old-fashioned sea-side 'resort' in peace time; but now the lovely golden sands are a thick tangle of barbed wire & there are two rows of iron barricades half under water at high tide – all to keep off an invasion. Last night we had an Alert – planes flying over to Birmingham I'm told. It's rather curious & delicious to be quite out of the world & inside knowledge for a bit & very restful tho' dull. I'm horribly tired & can't yet shake it off. The hotel is comfy, but the food dreary, Bird's Custard at every meal! The 'Times' says London had an alarm last night so I expect you were standing to . . .

When Clementine returned, refreshed and revived, from Weymouth, she found that preparations were afoot for Winston's imminent departure for Washington; he had decided that he must see the President again now that the North African campaign was nearing its close. His doctors had taken the definite view that, on account of his illness in February, it would be unwise for him to undertake any long flights just for the present. Winston and his party therefore travelled by sea, in the *Queen Mary* this time, leaving on the night of 4th May.

Less than a year before, Winston had been in Washington when he received the grim news of the fall of Tobruk; now, on 13th May 1943, it can be imagined with what deep feelings he read this triumphant message from General Alexander:

> Sir:
> It is my duty to report that the Tunisian campaign is over. All enemy resistance has ceased. We are masters of the North African shores.

On that same day, many thousands of miles away, Clementine's thoughts were with him: 'My darling Winston,' she wrote,

> How I wish that in this hour of Victory I were with you – so that we could rejoice together & so that I could tell you what I feel about *your* North African Campaign. You must be deeply moved by these events although you planned them & knew beforehand that they could be achieved.[5]

But in her gratification at the victory Clementine's watchful eye had detected an aspect of the conference in Washington that disturbed her, and in the same letter she wrote:

> I'm worried at the importance given by the Press (notably The Times) to the presence of Wavell & his East Indian Naval & Air Colleagues in your Party. I'm so afraid the Americans will think that a Pacific slant is to be given to the next phase of the War – I have cut out the piece of The Times which disturbs me. *Surely* the liberation of Europe *must* come first.

And in an emphatic footnote she added: 'Do re-assure me that the European Front will take 1st place all the time.'

On 13th May the King had sent this message to Winston:

> Now that the campaign in Africa has reached a glorious conclusion, I wish to tell you how profoundly I appreciate the fact that its initial conception and successful prosecution are largely due to your vision and to your unflinching determination in the face of early difficulties. The African campaign has immeasurably increased the debt that this country, and indeed all the United Nations, owe to you.
>
> George R.I

Winston was much moved by this message, and Clementine was so overjoyed to see his part in the victory recognised that on a sudden impulse she wrote to the Queen.

> 10, Downing Street, S.W.1.
> 14th May, 1943
>
> Madam,
>   I venture to write to Your Majesty to say how moved and touched I am by the wonderful message which the King has sent Winston. It made me cry with joy and I should be so grateful if Your Majesty would tell the King how I feel about it.
>   I wish that at this time of thanksgiving & rejoicing that I were not separated from Winston; but I know that it is important & his duty that he should be with the President now that new plans are taking shape.
>   I hope it is not presumptuous in me to have written this letter.
>   I am Your Majesty's devoted & obedient Servant,
>   Clementine S. Churchill

Two days later, Clementine received the following reply from the Queen, written in her own hand:

> Buckingham Palace
> May 15th 1943
>
> My dear Mrs Churchill
>   I have just received your most charming letter, and hasten to send you a line of thanks for what you have said in it. I know the King sincerely feels all that he wrote in his message to the Prime Minister, and we both feel more grateful than words can say for your husband's unfaltering courage and over-the-mountains vision in the anxious days behind us. We look forward to the future battles with the comfortable feeling that we've got the right man as Prime Minister, and the

best and most civilized people in the world to fight those battles – tolerant & brave & humorous. May God give us true victory to build a well governed world for all peoples.

> I am,
> Yours very sincerely,
> Elizabeth R.

Clementine did indeed miss Winston's presence at this triumphant hour. In a letter to me on 14th May she wrote:

> These glorious victories are uplifting but I have been alone – no-one to rejoice & give thanks with – No Papa — No Mouse [Mary] – 'nothink'! So I've been rather low which is very wrong.

To Winston she wrote:

> ... that was a splendid one [telegram] the King sent you. I am so glad about it. I do wish you were here my Darling so that we could jump for joy at this great & glorious Victory . . .[6]

A few days later Clementine went with Mr and Mrs Attlee to St Paul's Cathedral to a Service of Thanksgiving for the Tunisian victory; she described it to Winston:

> ... The Service was short & restrained & the Cathedral was cold as Charity but when we emerged into brilliant sunlight & clanging bells & whirling pigeons & sweet clapping City stenographers who sensing a ceremony had stayed on after their work one's blood began to flow & one's pulses to beat in time with great events . . .[7]

She also had some good family news to report: on 19th May Diana had given birth to her third child, a girl, Celia. Clementine wrote to Winston:

> Diana had her baby in one swift hour. Doctor & Nurse only just in time. She looks lovely & well but such a crashing labour is a bit of a shock & she must be well nursed. She & Duncan are over the moon with joy.[8]

During Winston's absence, Clementine took the opportunity of visiting Chartwell and staying for nearly a week in Orchard Cottage there. There had been a series of night air-raids on London, and during her first night in the 'peace' of the country-side two big bombs fell in the neighbourhood, shaking the little house. She gave Winston all the details she knew he would love about the garden:

> It [Chartwell] was looking lovely – your favourite rhodie was in full bloom, an explosion of colour, there were still azaleas in the wood behind the Wall Garden, the first roses were blooming on the gray walls & the mantle of pale pink clematis was flung over the west wall of the rose garden. The wisteria on the house was shedding its petals. I fed your fish. They flashed about on the surface of the water. There was a heron in the valley immobile & watchful.[9]

Clementine's time at Chartwell did her good, and she returned to her committee work, entertaining, and a fund-raising tour for 'Wings for Victory' week.

Winston left Washington for Algiers – this time in a comfortable flying-boat – and was able to write to Clementine from Gibraltar, where they paused en route.

28th May 1943

My darling Clemmie,

You really have been splendid in writing to me. Hardly a day has passed that I have not had a letter to give me so much pleasure and delight. I, on the other hand, have been most remiss but I really have been hunted altogether beyond the ordinary. Not only have I had all the big business about which I came, but I naturally took advantage of all the time the President could give me, which was a very great deal . . .

Harry Hopkins [the President's personal adviser] and his wife were most agreeable and friendly, and evidently in the highest favour. Mrs Roosevelt however was away practically all the time, and I think she was offended at the President not telling her until a few hours before I arrived of what was pouring down on her [i.e. W S C and his entourage]. He does not tell her the secrets because she is always making speeches and writing articles and he is afraid she might forget what was secret and what was not. No-one could have been more friendly than she was during the two or three nights she turned up.

They all made great complaint I had not brought you with me, and made me promise that next time you must surely come . . .

My friendship with the President was vastly stimulated. We could not have been on easier terms. There is no doubt that the speech I made showing the success which has attended our joint efforts, and his part in it, strengthened his position . . .

The speech to which Winston referred was an address he had made to both Houses of Congress on 19th May, and of which he wrote in the same letter to Clementine:

I took an immense amount of trouble with the Speech and did not think much of it till it was delivered, but it certainly had a most electrifying effect . . . They never had had anything like the kind of accounts I give to Parliament, and were delighted to be so considered on this occasion . . .

Many thousands of miles away Clementine had listened in on the radio, and she congratulated him:

Your address to Congress was grand & a master-piece of 'walking delicately'. It warmed me to hear your voice so strong, resonant & resolute . . .[10]

The next day Winston and his colleagues continued their journey to Algiers, using for the first time the York aircraft – a transport plane taken over by the R.A.F. and specially converted for these long journeys. Winston had a private cabin, but there were also comfortable bunks for the other passengers, and a small galley where proper meals could be prepared.

While he was in Algiers, Winston stayed in Admiral Cunningham's villa on the hills above the harbour. He was delighted by it, and decided to stay on for a few days, resting and working in this pleasant place. Randolph was there for a few days with his father, who was able to report to my mother how well and sunburnt their son looked.[11] Although she longed to have him home, Clementine thoroughly approved Winston's plan to remain for a little longer in Algiers 'in the sunshine and cool breezes'.[12] He arrived home on 5th June; he had been away a month.

Although 1943 was a year of heavy burden and stress, there was no more doubt about which way the war was going, and the truly agonising strain had been, albeit almost imperceptibly, eased. It was in this year that Winston first wielded his brush again; and cards, laid by since the beginning of the war, were found once more, and Winston and Clementine from time to time enjoyed a little bezique. Another great pleasure – the theatre – was also re-discovered, and during this spring and summer Winston and Clementine saw several plays: *Flare Path* by Terence Rattigan, *Arsenic and Old Lace*, a glorious comedy by Joseph Kesselring, which gave great pleasure, and two plays by Noel Coward, a friend whose work Winston had always admired, *This Happy Breed* and *Present Laughter*. Whenever Winston and Clementine took their seats only a few minutes before 'curtain-up', they would be recognised and a ripple of applause, which grew to a thunder, would fill the whole theatre, and one had the feeling that everyone was really glad that they too were having a 'night off'.

It seemed like the apotheosis of the great North African victory when, on 30th June, Winston received the Freedom of the City of London. Sarah and I were able to be with our parents, and drove with them in an open landau from Temple Bar, past shattered buildings, to the Guildhall, where with time-honoured ceremony the Lord Mayor of London conferred on Winston the highest mark of honour the City of London can bestow.

*

By the late summer Winston once more felt the need for personal talks with the President to concert the Allied attack on the mainland of Italy and continue preparations for 'Overlord'. The city of Quebec was chosen for this meeting, and King George VI offered the use of the Citadel, which is a royal residence. On this occasion Clementine was to accompany Winston, and I was given special leave to act as my father's ADC. The whole party totalled about 200 people, and we all embarked on the *Queen Mary* on 5th August, reaching Quebec five days later. The Citadel stands imposingly on the cliffs above the St Lawrence river, overlooking the city; we had arrived late in the evening, and my mother and I stood for quite a long time gazing at the twinkling lights below – it seemed a most marvellous sight after four years of blacked-out Britain.

Despite her holiday at Weymouth in the spring and later some days of rest at Chartwell, the nervous strain under which Clementine had lived for the last four years was exacting its price, and when she embarked for Quebec she was in a state of profound physical and nervous exhaustion; but she hoped that the four days at sea would revive her. Unfortunately, however, during the voyage she suffered from a bout of sleeplessness, and she arrived in Quebec still jaded and fatigued. President Roosevelt invited us all to spend the few days before the opening of the Conference at Hyde Park, his family home on the shores of the Hudson river. Clementine, however, decided to stay quietly in seclusion at the Citadel, in the hope that she would recover her energy and spirits, and be ready for all the activity and demands of the following week, when the Conference would be in full swing. She had Grace Hamblin with her, and Mr Mackenzie King, the Canadian Prime Minister, with whom she had made friends on his visits to England, promised to look after her.

Winston was greatly disappointed that Clementine would not accompany him to Hyde Park, but he realised that she was really at the end of her tether, and that this was the wiser decision; my mother insisted that I should go with my father. On our return to Quebec three days later we found her looking better, but although she had had no public duties, 'quiet little lunches' and long sightseeing drives with kindly strangers are not restful and relaxing to someone like Clementine, whose strict sense of obligation always meant she would appear at her best, and be at her best, however tired she might feel. I realised that the beneficial effect of the last few days was only superficial.

On Tuesday, 17th August, the Governor-General of Canada, the Earl of Athlone, and H.R.H. Princess Alice Countess of Athlone* came from Ottawa, and shortly after them the President and his retinue arrived; and the next day the Conference got going in earnest. My mother and I were kept extremely busy with a mixture of entertaining arising from the Conference itself, and the receiving and returning of hospitality from numerous charming and kindly Canadians, combined with sight-seeing and shopping expeditions. Clementine's programme was full and without respite, but she saw it through with grace and goodwill. In addition she made two broadcasts, one for England, where the Aid to Russia Fund was holding a flag day, and the second an appeal on behalf of the Canadian Young Women's Christian Association. As always she took great trouble with her script, delivering part of the broadcast in French.

When the Conference was over on 24th August my father and mother went into 'retreat' for four or five days as the guests of Colonel Frank Clarke, at his fishing lodge on the Lac des Neiges in the Laurentian Mountains, about sixty miles from Quebec. Our host's log house was marvellously comfortable, and Winston thoroughly enjoyed these days in the beautiful wild woods, and indulged in some fishing. But my mother was by now too overtired for enjoyment, so she and I came back to Quebec ahead of my father. By this time I was greatly concerned by her nervous state, the slightest things causing her perplexity and worry out of all pro-portion to their importance. Our time in Quebec was nearly at an end, but a visit of more than ten days lay ahead of us all in Washington, where once more much would be demanded of her.

In Washington, we stayed at the White House as the guests of the President and Mrs Roosevelt. Outside in the city, the atmosphere resembled a Turkish bath, but the White House was deliciously air-conditioned. Clementine braced herself again and, in fact, enjoyed much of her visit, which included some delightful sightseeing,

*A granddaughter of Queen Victoria.

as well as various obligations such as visiting the Headquarters of the British War Relief Organisation. And on one evening, Lady Halifax (the wife of the British Ambassador) allowed her to give a party in the Embassy for the wives of all the British officials in Washington.

The highlights of our sightseeing were a personally conducted tour by the President of Mount Vernon, George Washington's family home on the shores of the Potomac; and a flying visit to Williamsburg, the wonderfully re-constructed and preserved Colonial capital of Virginia. It was there, on the afternoon of Wednesday, 8th September, while we were in one of the lovely houses, that a strange man suddenly appeared and told us that the unconditional surrender of Italy had just been announced on the radio.

On our last day in Washington, whilst in a bookshop Clementine missed her footing and fell down some steps, cracking her elbow; it was not serious, but very painful and hampering, as she had to carry her arm in a sling. We all left Washington by train on the evening of Saturday, 11th September, travelling once more to Hyde Park to see the President, with whom we spent the following day.

During our visit we had seen a great deal of Mr Roosevelt, and received much kind attention and hospitality from him. One could hardly fail to be dazzled by the magnetic quality of his charm, but Clementine never really fell under 'FDR's' powerful spell, spotting very quickly that his personal vanity was inordinate. However, they got on very well, although she complained to me after an early encounter, that she thought it 'great cheek of him calling me Clemmie'! It was surely meant as a compliment; but my mother always regarded the use of her own, or other people's, Christian names as a privilege marking close friendship or long association. The President was not the only one to earn a straight look over this personal foible of hers.

That Sunday, 12th September, was Clementine's and Winston's thirty-fifth wedding anniversary, and the day passed very happily, my mother confiding to me that my father had told her that 'he loved her more and more every year'.[13] At dinner, the President proposed their health, and afterwards drove us all down to the little railway station near Hyde Park, where we took our leave of him.[14]

The return voyage was made in HMS *Renown*, and our journey home was a happy one. My father was in relaxed and genial form, and my mother managed to get some good nights' sleep. The voyage for me personally was memorable, for I celebrated my twenty-first birthday; and I was also very nearly drowned, when I was swept the full length of the quarter-deck by a vast wave. However, we all eventually arrived safely home on Sunday, 19th September.

*

For some time past both Churchill and Roosevelt had sought to persuade Stalin to join them in their confabulations; and he eventually agreed to meet them in Teheran towards the end of November 1943.

Winston left Plymouth, once more aboard *Renown*, on 12th November, this time taking Sarah with him as his ADC; also included in the party (most fortunately, as it turned out) was Lord Moran. In fact, Winston was far from well when he started out on this journey; he had a heavy cold, and was suffering from the effects of several inoculations, and during the ten-day voyage he remained for most of the time in his cabin.

They disembarked at Alexandria on 21st November, and flew on to Cairo, where preliminary talks were to be held with the President. These meetings were most frustrating to the British party, for Roosevelt was almost entirely occupied with Generalissimo Chiang Kai-Shek, whom he had invited thither, and Chinese and Far Eastern affairs dominated the sessions.

On 27th November Winston flew on to Teheran, and there the 'Big Three' met at last. This Conference was an example of the homely proverb, 'Two's company, three's none', for Roosevelt and Stalin hived off together in a most marked manner. This was naturally wounding to Churchill, whose relationship with the President was so close. But much more than any personal feelings of hurt, he feared for British interests. However, there was one occasion of open amity and comradeship: on 30th November – Winston's sixty-ninth birthday – Roosevelt and Stalin dined as his guests at the British Legation. Sitting between the President of the United States of America and 'the Master of Russia', Winston reflected upon how times had changed: 'I could not help rejoicing,' he later wrote,

at the long way we had come on the road to victory since the summer of 1940, when we had been alone . . . against the triumphant and unbroken might of Germany and Italy . . .[15]

But the meeting at Teheran was, for Winston, a most exhausting conference. He had not succeeded in throwing off his cold, and he was still suffering from a sore throat, and was only prevented from losing his voice by constant spraying. On 2nd December, Winston and his party returned to Cairo, where he had four more days of discussion with the President. Everyone could see that he was exhausted, and Lord Moran tried to persuade him to abandon his intention of visiting the battle front in Italy on the way home. But Winston would not be deflected from his course.

Clementine was kept in touch by telegrams of Winston's movements and the general trend of events; but he obviously had not revealed to her the real state of his health, nor described the mortifications and frustrations of the Teheran Conference, for on 2nd December she wrote to him:

My Darling

I'm overjoyed to get your message that 'things have taken a very good turn'. Allelulia! Allelulia!

Yesterday F[ield] M[arshal] Smuts came to luncheon with me & was in the gayest spirits – He suggested that I should accompany him to Cairo – I thought he was joking but he was quite serious & I had to firmly prevent him from making enquiries & arrangements. It was to be a surprise for you! But Oh – how I should have loved this whole journey . . .

The Field Marshal brings you this letter – Sarah has written me the most delightful & colourful accounts of your doings & hers. She writes beautifully &

unusually. Perhaps she will write seriously one day. Give her my love & kiss her for me in case I have no time to write to her as well.

> Your loving but 'blackout & winter wearied'
> Pussy [Kat]

On the same day she sent a 'chaser' also by hand of the Field Marshal. She was clearly under the impression that Winston meant to return home direct from Cairo: *'Please please* don't fly home,' she wrote, 'but come in the "London" a perfectly good cruiser . . . This brings only my dear love. Clemmie.'

Four days later she wrote again:

Your telegram just came saying you have gyppie tummy & absolute whirl of business. I do hope the tummy will yield to treatment; I fear it can be rather obstinate . . .[16]

On 11th December Winston, ignoring the advice of those around him, left Cairo for Tunis, planning to spend one night on the way with General Eisenhower. From there he intended to go on to see both 'Alex' and 'Monty'. But on arrival at 'The White House' (General Eisenhower's villa near ancient Carthage) he was feeling so ill and weary that he went straight to bed. The next morning, his temperature was 101°F; Lord Moran judged that this was no trivial, passing indisposition, and sent at once for nurses and a pathologist: pneumonia was diagnosed.

Clementine and the Cabinet were informed of the course of events in a series of telegrams which swiftly succeeded one another, often giving contradictory impressions, which was confusing and alarming. But once she learned that Winston had pneumonia Clementine, strongly urged by his Cabinet colleagues, decided that she must fly out to be with him, and arrangements were put in hand at once. The next morning, 16th December, the bulletin was not reassuring; the whole day was filled with packing, and constantly changing times for her departure; Grace Hamblin was to go with her, and also Jock Colville.

While she was rushing to get ready for her journey, the following letter arrived by hand from Sir Alan Lascelles, the King's Private Secretary:

> Buckingham Palace
> 16.xii.1943

Dear Mrs Churchill,

The King and Queen want me to tell you how much they feel for you in your anxiety – which, indeed, we all share. It is cruel that the P.M.'s triumphant journey should end like this; but T.M. [Their Majesties] hope that good may come out of evil, and that, in the long run, this spell of comparative rest may be a blessing in disguise to him. Meanwhile, you have the deep sympathy of the King and Queen, and, if I may say so, of every one of us here.

During the day of the 16th, a thick blanket of fog crept up, and by the early afternoon all the airfields near London were out of action; so at tea-time Clementine and Grace Hamblin, Jock Colville and I set off for Lyneham in Wiltshire, where the airfield was still clear. It was a long, slow, disagreeable drive through swirling fog, but after about four hours we arrived at Lyneham, where we were given dinner in the R.A.F. Mess. Clementine was to have travelled in a heated aircraft, but an hour or so before take-off a fault was discovered, and the only suitable plane available was an unheated Liberator. So after dinner, Clementine and Grace were zipped into padded flying suits, and I went to see them stowed aboard the plane, where I wished them Godspeed; then an officer took me up to the control tower to watch them take off.

My mother wrote to me after their arrival:

The journey out was *horrible*. Icy cold, *no* heat in Liberator . . .

After saying we were going straight thro' we came down *in the dark* at Gibraltar – oh Wow – your cowardly old Mother's knees knocked together. Off again after breakfast. A lovely dawn. We flew right along the African coast. Jock was such a comfort. I did not sleep at all. It was *icy* cold. But the weather was *perfect* & we did not have to fly high.[17]

It may be imagined with what relief and thankfulness we at home received the news of my mother's safe arrival. On 18th December I received a special message: 'Your Mother is here. All is joyful. No need to worry. Tender love. Papa.'

The news of Winston's illness and the fact that Clementine had flown out to be with him were made public on 17th December, thereafter daily bulletins being issued; and soon we were able to rejoice in improving news of my father's health. My mother knew how thirsty we in the family would all be for an inside account, and her letters, written to us individually or as 'round robins', tell the story of Winston's illness and his convalescence.

18th December 1943

My darling Mary

On arrival at this Villa yesterday afternoon at about 3.30 I was taken straight in to see Papa. The joy of seeing him was overcast by the change I saw in him. But when later in the evening I mentioned this to Sarah and Lord Moran they both said that if I had seen him 48 hours earlier I would indeed have been shocked, and they thought that now he was looking remarkably better. This is accounted for by the fact that it is nearly six weeks since I had seen your father. During the whole of this time he has had one little ailment after another, culminating in the illness which I have now ascertained started a week ago . . . I think he is very happy that I am here. After my arrival I stayed with him till six, when he slept for two hours and I rested too. I then had dinner with him. After dinner Sarah and Randolph [who had flown from Cairo] came in and we all talked. At eleven o'clock Lord Moran came in to say 'Good-night' and I then saw that he wanted us all to go; so we did . . . But Papa showed no signs of fatigue, and once or twice when I got up to go to bed, he would not let me go. At one in the morning I saw a light under his door, and went into the passage and saw the night nurse who said: 'He is awake and feeling very cheerful and having beef tea – come in and see him.' So I did, and sat with him for a quarter of an hour, after which he went to sleep and I returned to my bed.

This morning, Sawyers [Winston's valet] came in early and said would I breakfast with Papa at 8.30? So I went in with him at that time and found Lord Moran in his room, and that at 3.15 in the morning he had had another attack of auricular fibrillation.* The doctors are disappointed but not surprised. Papa is very upset about it as he is beginning to see that he cannot get well in a few days and that he will have to lead what to him is a dreary monotonous life with no emotions or excitements. Yesterday morning, before my arrival, because he felt well again, he was as happy as a lark, and began to smoke again, which of course is wrong; but Lord Moran agrees that it is not so bad for him as it would be for most patients. The smoking has of course been quite cut out to-day . . .

I asked Lord Moran how I could help to carry out his wishes and he said that not more than one person should be in the room at a time. So as there has been a constant stream of people all day I have not done more than poke my nose round the corner of the door.

The Courier is going so there is no time for much more. I love you my Darling & wish you were here . . .

Health Bulletin by C.S.C. (not the doctors) for Sunday December the 19th
Papa much better to-day. Has consented not to smoke, and to drink only weak whisky and soda. In fairly good spirits. New cook arrived. Food much better and Papa enjoyed good luncheon and dinner, though appetite is not very good.

19th December 1943
This Villa is on a little promontory right on the sea with terraces leading down. It is only one storey high, and is like a white box . . . Here I should say that this house is the Headquarters of General Eisenhower who is at present I don't know where – I should think in Italy . . . so that here we are, an enormous party, all the guests of the U.S.A. Army.

. . . Sarah sleeps in the Villa, but I have not yet seen her room as I literally have not had time. Tommy [Thompson]† also lives here, but everyone else sleeps out, either at the guest house or in other villas. All these establishments are run by lieutenants – one a mere man, and the other called the 'White lieutenant' who is a W.A.C. [Women's Army Corps]. She is supposed to be a very high class dietician and was fetched in from Tunis to manage the Villa for us. The food, however, is 'vurry' American. Last night we had a partridge for dinner which Sawyers informed us was cooked for an hour and a half! The result was concrete! Sawyers rather rashly informed the American cook that Mrs. Landemare cooks partridges for only fifteen minutes. Your poor father literally cannot eat the food.

Later
Sarah has been and is a pillar of strength. She has been a great joy to your father; but indeed everybody loves her. She has taken so much trouble with

*A slight one.
†Commander C. R. Thompson, R.N., Flag Officer to Churchill when First Lord, remained with him as personal assistant throughout the war.

everybody, and to smooth out any little crossnesses and difficulties which might have arisen. At Cairo, I am told that she was a perfect hostess at the Casey villa when, for instance, Papa gave a big dinner for the Chiang Kai Shek's. In Teheran she handled the rather difficult and delicate problem of being the only woman with perfect tact, and now here she looks after everybody at the Villa. She sits all day in that big room . . . & talks to all the people who are waiting patiently for something or another.

Health Bulletin for Monday December the 20th (C.S.C.)
Papa very refractory and naughty this morning and wants to leave this place at once. All doing our best to persuade him that complete recovery depends on rest and compliance with regulations. Progress continued.

Monday, December the 20th
Yesterday, Sunday, Papa was much better and in very good spirits. I break-fasted, lunched and dined with him in his bedroom and had lovely talks with him . . .
A little gun boat patrols up and down in front of the house in case a German submarine should pop up its nose and shoot up the Villa. Of course if the enemy knew we were here they could wipe out the place with dive bombers from the airfields near Rome. It is less than two hours' flight from here to the toe of Italy & one hour from Palermo in Sicily . . .

Tuesday, December the 21st
Your father has had a very good night so I am told by the night Nurse; but I have not seen him because quite early he sent for Mr. Kinna to dictate some difficult paper . . .

In the afternoons, Clementine and other members of the party often went on various sightseeing expeditions. On one such Lord Moran went with them, Winston being left in the care of Brigadier Bedford (the heart specialist) and Randolph. When they returned after darkness had fallen,

. . . we found Papa sitting up in bed looking very pink and mischievous and announcing he had had a hot bath with Dr. Bedford's consent. Your father has taken a great deal of trouble to seduce Dr. Bedford, and Lord Moran is quite jealous. After the bath he played innumerable games of bezique with Randolph. In spite of all this he was not really exhausted, though when bed-time came he was looking a little pale and wan.[18]

That same afternoon they had visited Longstop Hill, the scene of a violent battle. With them was Bill Harris, a Coldstream officer, who had taken part in it. Clementine described how when he saw 'this terrible hill for the first time after he crawled up it with his hundred men, he could hardly speak'. She went on to describe how

All along the road from Tunis to Longstop and on to Medjez-el-Bab, the fields on either side were littered with war debris – tanks, crashed planes, piles of ammunition, blown up guns, and so on. It is a horrible sight – the stale remains of war. We did not stop to look at the cemeteries, for we had to get back, but Bill says there are several – some British, some German and some where former foes are buried together.[19]

23rd December 1943

My darling Mary

On Tuesday Sarah went into Tunis to have her hair done. John Martin, Lord Moran and I went in to see the sights. We perambulated up and down the dusty streets. It is really a particularly dirty and unattractive town. I do not believe if seven hundred thousand mops 'swept it for half a year, that they could get it clean' . . .

Health bulletin by C.S.C. Thursday, December 23rd
Very good progress. I think the only anxiety is impatience to be well too soon.
C.S.C.

26th December 1943

Yesterday we all of us thought of the party gathered at Chequers, and of Mary in her battery. We had a most extraordinary Christmas Day ourselves. All the, what Americans call 'high ranking Generals and other notabilities' converged here, and Christmas day was spent by them and Papa in a series of conferences . . .

We had a most interesting Christmas luncheon party with all these notabilities assembled, and your father at the end made a charming speech about his distinguished guests . . . This was his first meal outside his bedroom . . .

Early in the morning Sarah and I went to early Church with the Coldstream Guards. The service was held in a corrugated iron shed full of ammunition and stores. It had been cleared in the centre for the Service. Just as the Service was drawing to a close, there was a fluttering of wings, and a little white dove circled round and settled on a ledge just above the altar. I heard a hefty Guardsman behind me whisper to his neighbour: 'Look now, that means peace'. Your father declared that he was sure it was a conjuring trick, and that the padre had released the dove from under his surplice. General Alexander, who was there, hurried quickly back to the house to find out whether Hitler had indeed thrown in his hand. We were much disappointed when we found that this had not immediately occurred, and we settled down to eggs and bacon!

During the morning we went to the 'Parade' service of the Coldstream which was held out of doors. We all sang Christmas Hymns accompanied by a lovely little pipe and flute band . . .

This morning Randolph has gone back to Italy. General Alexander very kindly took him in his plane . . .

Meanwhile back at home a depleted family party gathered at Chequers: Diana and Duncan with their three children, Aunt Nellie, and Uncle Jack.

Everyone combined to make the party go with a swing, and enthusiastic accounts from various pens were sent to Winston and Clementine. Someone had given oranges and lemons (great luxuries); the President had sent a Christmas tree from his own plantation at Hyde Park; there were turkey and plum pudding and presents for everyone – and through all the usual festivities ran the thread of thankfulness and relief.

After this serious illness, the doctors were adamant that Winston must have a proper period of convalescence before returning home. He himself felt so depleted and feeble that for once he did not oppose their wishes. Marrakech seemed the obvious place, and once more the lovely Villa Taylor where he had stayed only a year before with the President after the Casablanca Conference was put at his disposal by the ever-hospitable United States Army. From there Clementine continued to give all of us at home lively accounts of their life:

> Marrakech
> New Years Day [1944]

... We are living in a glorious villa not far from the Mamounia Hotel where Papa and you and Duncan all stayed some years ago. The villa is a mixture of Arabian Nights and Hollywood, and extremely comfortable as regards beds, hot baths, etc., but alas very sunless, as I suppose it is built for protection against the torrid heat of Summer.

First I must tell you about Papa. He is gaining strength every day, but very slowly indeed. He is disappointed that his recovery is slow; but when in the end he is quite well, the slowness of his convalescence may be a blessing in disguise, as it may make him a little more careful when he has to travel. For instance, when we came from Tunis here, the doctors did not wish him to fly above five thousand feet, but he insisted on going up to twelve thousand, to get above the clouds which of course made it safer as we were over mountainous country. He had oxygen and I think really it has turned out all right, but yesterday he said sadly, 'I am not strong enough to paint'. But this morning, New Year's Day, he came early into my room, and said 'I am so happy. I feel so much better'. So don't be anxious, but we must all realise that he really needs great care. He is not staying in bed now more than he does in his ordinary life. This is his day: He works in bed all the morning and gets up just in time to go for an expedition or for lunch in the garden, after which he goes for a drive. Then he goes back again to bed till dinner. We try to prevent him sitting up late, but I am afraid he does ...

The sun is delicious, but the air is very sharp and cold. One needs one's warmest Winter clothes.

We had a great surprise one morning. Max [Beaverbrook] suddenly arrived! I knew he was coming, but we did not know the day, and he walked in at breakfast time, having flown in a Liberator ...

Yesterday there was great excitement. General Eisenhower and General Montgomery arrived for a pow-wow. General Eisenhower has now gone ... but General Montgomery is staying till to-night ...

> 3rd January 1944

We all went for a picnic on New Year's Day, taking General Montgomery with us. On the way out he drove with Papa, and on the way back he came with me. He really is a thrilling and interesting personage – naive and sincere, good tempered, and with the same sort of conceit which we read Nelson had. He has piercing blue eyes and a wirey young figure . . .

After dinner he flew away home, and Sarah who for security reasons has been in mufti since her arrival here, put on her new Austin Reed uniform (22 coupons – not yet raised) to see him off . . .

Yesterday was bad temper day! Everyone was cross – me especially. Sarah was very sensible and said 'Let's have a bad day, and make a fresh start tomorrow'. So that is what we are doing. This morning everyone is smiling and we are going for another picnic.

There is a very nice British Consul-General here – Mr. Nairn. He and his wife are both Scotch. I like them both very much . . . She is an M.A. London University, and was a professional artist before she married. Tomorrow she is going to take Sarah and me to see the Glauie's 'household' (harem) so we shall have to try and make ourselves look tidy.

The following afternoon Mrs Nairn duly escorted Clementine and Sarah to visit the Glauie, and on 5th January, Clementine wrote us an amusing account:

In the afternoon we went for our carefully arranged visit to the Pasha's 'household' . . . To our great disappointment we did not see the Ladies, but only the Glauie or Pasha . . . who fed us with mint tea and all sorts of oriental sweetmeats. We were waited upon by a terrific great giant who looked like Othello. I thought he was a sort of super butler, but he is a very important Kaid, that is some sort of chieftain. I suppose he is the Lord Chamberlain. He was assisted by two lovely black slave girls, not veiled (but I now understand that inside the house they never are veiled) . . . I asked Mrs. Nairn if they were really slaves, and she said 'No, but they think they are, and probably like to think they are, so it comes to the same thing'. They certainly did not look overworked and they really were luscious to look at . . . After tea the Pasha conducted us into every corner of the Palace, all except the harem, the doors of which we passed, but they were bolted . . . He conducted us to the door, and in the outer vestibule there was a row of myrmidons. He took from one of them a green velvet case which he presented to me for Papa with a little speech. It contained a most beautiful dagger in a gold scabbard. Three huge carpets, all rolled up, were then produced – one for Sarah, one for Mrs. Nairn, and one for me.

At the beginning of the party a negroid looking young man appeared in a badly cut flannel jacket and plus fours. He was one of the Pasha's sons who had been to England and spoke fluent English. But when it was discovered that we spoke French he was chased away, to our disappointment. However, he was in the vestibule, and as we drove away he followed the car on a motor bicycle, tooting merrily. I do not think he likes the oriental splendour of the Palace and we are wondering if we cannot take him for a picnic!

Africa
10th January 1944

Since my last letter there has been a great deal of coming and going. All the 'big shots' have been here for a Conference . . . They all arrived one evening . . . Next morning they met again at 9.30, always of course with Papa. All was over at 11.30 and they were airborne back to Algiers, Italy etc. by noon. It was all over in a flash, and I believe everything 'clicked'. They all went away happy having reached complete agreement.

Meanwhile Randolph came back with Fitzroy Maclean. They were brought by General Alexander from Bari. They both stayed an extra day and have now gone back and will soon be operating in their special sphere with Tito in Yugoslavia . . . I think Randolph is well fitted for this work, and I hope it will be a great success. They went off in good spirits.

. . . We have been for several more picnics; in fact we go out every day when it is fine, but we can rarely go any distance because your Father works all the morning. So except on one or two occasions we have not been able to penetrate deep into the Atlas, but just establish ourselves by the side of a stream in the foothills . . .

I think Papa is now really quite himself again. Every day sees an improvement. He simply loves the picnics. He has been reading Jane Austen – Pride and Prejudice first, which Sarah read aloud to him practically non-stop during the two days that he was really ill, and then to himself Northanger Abbey which he did not like nearly so well, but still I noticed he could not put it down. Now I am re-reading Mansfield Park.

Meanwhile a visit from 'the General' impended: 'General de Gaulle has been by way of coming several times,' wrote Clementine,

and his visit has each time been put off generally by himself. I think he really and truly is coming one day soon. I hope there will be no explosions! . . .[20]

Two days before de Gaulle's arrival Duff and Diana Cooper joined the party; he was at this time the British representative on the French Committee of Liberation. And on 12th January the several-times-anticipated visit materialised. Clementine wrote:

To-day we are rather on tenter-hooks because at last General de Gaulle really is arriving by plane from Algiers in time for luncheon. This part of the visit is hush-hush and security, but afterwards he repairs to his local palace and bursts into publicity and military reviews . . . It is expected that he will have a rapturous welcome both from the French and the native population. I am rather nervous and de G. has again perpetrated one of his chronic incivilities by sending Papa (who really has worked for the French at all these Conferences and also to keep the President sweet, who simply loathes de G.) a boorish message. I am trying to smooth Papa down so I hope this function will pass off without further unpleasantness.[21]

The luncheon party and subsequent 'pow-wow' which had been the cause of so much nervous anticipation both passed off much better than had been feared. Diana Cooper described how

> . . . Clemmie has given him [Winston] a Caudle curtain lecture on the importance of not quarrelling with Wormwood. She thinks it will bear fruit . . .[22]

It evidently did.

The guests were General and Madame de Gaulle, Duff and Diana Cooper, Max Beaverbrook, and Mr and Mrs Nairn. The General arrived in the best of humour and insisted on speaking English throughout the meal. 'To make things equal,' wrote Winston, 'I spoke French.'[23] During the afternoon the ladies diverted themselves in the bazaars and the men had a long and serious talk. Despite the fact that many thorny subjects were broached, the conversations ended on a pleasant note, with the General inviting Winston to attend a review the following day of French and Moroccan troops.

Following the review the party went for their last picnic (the eighth). Diana Cooper described how Winston ventured down a steep gorge, and tried to climb on top of the biggest boulder:

> Clemmie said nothing, but watched him with me like a lenient mother who does not wish to spoil her child's fun nor yet his daring . . .[24]

This long and ill-starred journey was now drawing to its end. The party flew from Marrakech to Gibraltar, where they all embarked on the *King George V*; they disembarked at Plymouth and arrived back in London by train early on the morning of 18th January 1944.

Clementine had been a marvellous correspondent, keeping us all at home fed with news of Winston's steadily improving health, and lively, amusing accounts of their doings. Once the intense anxiety about Winston had subsided, she had been able to enjoy the pleasures of sightseeing and the numerous picnics; and she had relished (as she always did) the tinge of the exotic. But underneath her courage and buoyancy there lurked a built-in weariness – the fruit of the emotional and physical strains with which she had now lived for four years or more.

Diana Cooper recounted a 'curious calm and sad conversation' she had with Clementine one evening in Marrakech before dinner:

> I was talking about post-war days and proposed that instead of a grateful country building Winston another Blenheim, they should give him an endowed manor house with acres for a farm and gardens to build and paint in. Clemmie very calmly said: 'I never think of after the war. You see, I think Winston will die when it's over.' She said this so objectively that I could not bring myself to say the usual 'What nonsense!' but tried something about it was no use relying on death; people lived to ninety or might easily, in our lives, die that day . . . But she seemed quite certain and quite resigned to his not surviving long into peace. 'You see, he's seventy and I'm sixty and we're putting all we have into this war, and it will take all we have.' It was touching and noble.[25]

THE LAST LAP

ARLY IN 1944 the enemy once more turned his attention upon the cities of this country, London being the chief target. Londoners accepted this resumption of the air-raids stolidly, but people were just that much wearier; three years of the sheer slog of wartime life since the first Blitz had inevitably taken their toll. During the 'Little Blitz' the noise was truly appalling, most of it being caused by our own, now much more formidable defences, and even a quiet night brought little rest to many thousands of men and women who, after their ordinary day's work, went home to do their stint as Air Raid Wardens or Fire Watchers. As well as using the now extensive and greatly improved shelter accommodation, people took once more to sleeping in the Underground stations, alongside those already rendered homeless in previous attacks. Westminster was not more immune than other parts of London to the 'Little Blitz' – on the night of 20th February 1944, Downing Street and Whitehall once again suffered bomb damage.

During the previous year Clementine had made several extensive tours of air-raid shelters in various areas of London with officials from the Ministry of Health or the Red Cross and other concerned organisations. Since 1940 the entire organisation and administration of air-raid shelters had been continually improved, and in most cases the standards of hygiene and (relative) comfort were as good as could reasonably be expected. Shelter life had become a feature of wartime London, and had developed its own code and folk culture.

Clementine's programme was as full as ever of outside obligations and activities, over and above the ordinary business of keeping her own domestic life running to her own meticulous standard, answering her large postbag, and entertaining the constant stream of official visitors either in London or at Chequers. Luncheon was the principal occasion when visiting notabilities were entertained; Winston also frequently invited the Chiefs of Staff, the Planners, and all sorts of people who were in close contact with him in his work; thus 'business' was conducted before, during and after meals. The evenings were more often the occasion for the last-minute invitation: for the family; for 'The Prof', or Brendan Bracken, or some other close crony. But there were 'arranged' dinners too. During 1944 the King dined at No. 10 six times.* This was a singular and totally unusual sign of honour, and marks the

*There is a plaque commemorating these dinners in the downstairs room at No. 10 now re-converted to an office.

closeness of the relationship that had grown up during these hard years between the Sovereign and his Prime Minister.

The following figures give some idea of the volume of official entertaining undertaken by Winston and Clementine at this period:

Between mid-January and early September 1944, they gave 75 luncheon parties and 19 dinner parties. (These figures exclude any occasions which could be described as 'purely family'.) Of the other evenings during that period, Clementine's diary rather sadly marks only four of them: 'Dinner alone with Winston.'

Despite the charming and efficient housekeeper and a permanent staff of cheerful Servicewomen, the week-ends at Chequers were far from rest cures for Clementine: the war never let up – and nor did Winston. Between January and September 1944, out of a total of thirty-three week-ends, twenty-four of them were all, or partly, taken up with entertaining official guests from abroad, or commanders home for a short while from their theatres of operations, in addition to the many men Winston had constantly around him for the purpose of conducting affairs. Sometimes in one week-end there would be two, and sometimes three 'shifts' of guests; some lunching, others 'dining and sleeping'. This constant coming and going put a considerable strain on Clementine, whose sense of hospitality and code of good manners meant that she was almost constantly 'on duty'. Very often she returned to London to face a full and exacting week, as tired as when, the previous Friday, she had arrived at Chequers.

The year 1944 was not a happy one in personal terms for some members of our family. Sarah was still wrestling with the problems and sadness caused by the breakdown of her marriage; although she and Vic had separated in 1941, they were not in fact divorced until four years later. Meanwhile she gave herself unsparingly to her intelligence work in the W.A.A.F. – a job which was as arduous as it was interesting.

Randolph also had difficult personal problems to resolve between himself and Pamela, and distance from all the people involved made for misunderstandings. Throughout his life an easily aroused and explosive person, Randolph was at this time under considerable strain and, sadly, the brief meetings with either or both his parents were often marked by painful scenes, which left their mark on all concerned.

Randolph had for some time been leading a hectic and hazardous existence. Having in the spring of 1942 given up a Staff job in Cairo to join the Special Air Service, he had taken part in May of that year in an incredibly dangerous raid on Benghazi, then 400 miles deep in enemy territory. When he had visited his father in Marrakech at the end of 1943 he had been awaiting his orders to be parachuted into Yugoslavia to join the British Military Mission which, headed by Brigadier Fitzroy Maclean, was attached to Marshal Tito and his forces. Early in February 1944, Randolph was dropped into Yugoslavia, where he shared the life and vicissitudes of the partisans.

In the intervals between exciting and dangerous episodes Randolph sought to extend the somewhat limited Croatian cuisine, introducing the partisans to such English delicacies as kedgeree and fishcakes made from tinned salmon. Later on he enlisted his mother's help, and asked her to send him a 'really elementary cooking book'.[1] This she did: sending also *Good Food* by Ambrose Heath. Both books were much appreciated.

In mid-July 1944, he had a brush with death when the transport plane in which he was travelling in Yugoslavia crashed on landing and burst into flames; he was among the ten people who escaped alive from the wreckage. Although Randolph, amazingly, was not very seriously injured, he took some time to recover fully from damage to his knees and spine. Ever kind and hospitable, Duff and Diana Cooper invited him to convalesce with them in Algiers after his discharge from hospital in Bari, and he was still staying with them when his father 'dropped in' for a few hours on his way to Italy in August. This meeting was all affection and rejoicing, and Winston wrote to Clementine:

No reference was made by either of us to family matters. He is a lonely figure by no means recovered as far as walking is concerned. Our talk was about politics, French and English, about wh there was plenty of friendly badinage & argument.[2]

Amidst all these disturbances, activities and anxieties Clementine had little time left over for herself. Always a reserved person, the demands of her wartime life and the burden of the secret knowledge which she bore isolated her more and more, even from her closest and most trusted friends. She leant, I think, mainly on Sarah and myself, as people to whom she could unburden herself and with whom she could talk freely. But of course we were often not there because of our jobs; telephone conversations were in carefully guarded language, even letters could not really be regarded as safe or sure, and we were all meticulously 'security' minded. Fortunately she had in Grace Hamblin a constant, steady, and 'padlock' companion.

Among Winston's colleagues, Clementine had some true and 'cosy' friends – such as Sir Peter Portal, Chief of the Air Staff (whose wife, Joan, was also a friend and a co-worker of hers on the Fulmer Chase committee), and 'Pug' (Sir Hastings) Ismay, Chief of Staff to Winston in his capacity as Minister of Defence. And in the members of Winston's Private Office she found a continual source of loyal help, understanding and support in the many problems and vicissitudes of their everyday life in these years.

But the tide of war brought to Winston and Clementine – and indeed to all our family – one very special friend: Gil Winant, the American Ambassador. He had come to Britain in the spring of 1941; he was a brilliant choice for the job, and during his five years' Ambassadorship he made friends with people in every walk of life. He was particularly beloved in the East End of London, where he was often to be seen in the thick of the air-raids. A man of quiet, intensely concentrated charm, Gil very quickly became a dear friend of us all, entering into our joys and sorrows, jokes and rows (in these last, always as a peace-maker). He was particularly fond of Clementine, and understood intuitively her character, and the strains and difficulties in her life.

But for all these loyal friends, in a life crowded with people, Clementine remained a somewhat lonely woman. One of the former W.A.A.F. officers described to me how, from the windows in the Cypher Office in Storey's Gate, she used to watch Clementine

> . . . in her smart London clothes, going for a walk in St James's Park, quite by herself. One would imagine, just to think quietly among the peace of the lake and the trees, very often after a night of bombing. It used to impress me greatly.[3]

*

As 1944 wore on, the whole country was gripped by the consciousness that some time soon the long-awaited, awesome attack on the continent of Europe must be launched. Passing visitors, and Britons returning home during these spring months all had the same impression: the whole country had become a vast assault-craft. England was splitting at the seams with trained men and every road or free space (especially in the south-east) was filled with equipment and vehicles of every type. Very few knew the day or the hour, but the whole nation shared the knowledge that the event was imminent. Both those under military discipline and the population as a whole were equally conscious of the necessity for the strictest general and personal security measures. In all history there can surely be no other example of such a vast secret being so miraculously preserved. From 28th May, when subordinate commanders were informed of the date of 'D Day', 5th June, all the camps holding assault troops and all ports of embarkation were sealed; telephone communications were forbidden and all mail was impounded; foreign embassies could no longer communicate with the outside world. The whole country held its breath.

During these last days Winston was visiting the camps and embarkation ports; he earnestly longed to view at closer quarters the assault from a British warship, to watch over and in some way to share in this tremendous enterprise in whose conception and growth he had played so close a part. Opposition to this idea was strong and almost unanimous from the King downwards. Clementine understood his wish, but thought it totally unpractical. Winston waged a stubborn fight, but was finally compelled to abandon his plan at the direct and strongly expressed wish of the King.

Two days before the planned hour, the whole vast project had to be postponed for twenty-four hours, due to increasingly bad weather conditions. This decision was right, but agonising. All those who held the knowledge and responsibility for the attack knew that if it could not be launched within the next forty-eight hours, a whole fortnight would have to elapse before moon and tide conditions would once more be suitable. The problem of keeping vast numbers of men cooped up in their embarkation 'cages', and the risk run at every day's delay, of the enemy accurately estimating the place and other details of the attack, made the prospect of further postponement a grim one, and was perhaps decisive. However, the weather improved, although much discomfort and some damage and loss was caused among the smaller troop-carrying craft, and the conditions on the approaches to the beaches were difficult.

On 4th June the Allied forces entered Rome after hard months of costly fighting, but even this glorious piece of news was overshadowed by impending events at home.

On Monday, 5th June, Winston was in his official train after making a final visit to Hampshire; the train had been shunted into a siding near General Eisenhower's Headquarters in the woods behind Portsmouth. Clementine had returned to London from Chartwell on the Sunday evening. On Monday morning, before leaving for her usual committee meeting at the Fulmer Chase Maternity Home, she wrote a note to Winston to go down in the official box which was always despatched to him wherever he was.

10 Downing Street
Whitehall
Monday Morning

My Darling,

I feel so much for you at this agonising moment – so full of suspense, which prevents one rejoicing over Rome.

I look forward to seeing you at dinner . . .

Tender love from:
Clemmie [lovely picture of a cat]
Just off to her Hospital

On his return from D-Day Headquarters, Winston and Clementine had one of their few dinners alone together. Afterwards he went to the Map Room to study the final dispositions and plan of attack. Already great convoys were moving in the darkness to their appointed stations off the coast of Normandy. Just before going to bed, Clementine joined him in the Map Room; Winston said to her: 'Do you realise that by the time you wake up in the morning twenty thousand men may have been killed?'[4]

While the attention of the whole country was fixed in absorbed and agonised interest on the progress of the Allied armies in France, in the second week of June those who lived in London and south-east England once more had cause to feel that they too were part of the battle. For in the early hours of 13th June, the Germans launched the first batch of their long-awaited 'Secret Weapons' – pilot-less aircraft carrying a high-explosive warhead. The 'Doodle-bugs' or 'Buzz Bombs', as they were quickly dubbed, were exceedingly frightening and disagreeable, chiefly because one could hear them for quite a long time before the engine suddenly cut out, when one knew that the brutish thing would plunge earthwards; there were then a few agonising moments of silence between the cut-out and the sickening explosion, and the slow rising of a huge cloud of dust. The blast damage was particularly vicious because the bomb usually exploded before penetrating the ground. The flying bombs were fired in batches at intervals throughout the day and night, and the anti-aircraft defences and civil defence services practically never stood down, meals and sleep being snatched when and as possible. Winston and Clementine were anxious about Diana, who was in the thick of it as an air-raid warden, and myself with my battery in the middle of Hyde Park.

During the early days of the flying-bomb raids the south of England was blessed with 'glorious June' weather, and despite the new terror, the streets and parks of London were full of people enjoying the sunshine. Indeed, one evening I telephoned my mother to tell her how our guns in Hyde Park had been in action that afternoon, witnessed by an interested crowd of people who had assembled to watch an American baseball match on a pitch adjoining the gun-site. The *sangfroid* with which people continued to carry on with their normal lives, however, resulted in some calamitous incidents, such as the occasion when a flying-bomb scored a direct hit on the Guards' Chapel in Wellington Barracks on Sunday, 18th June. Morning Service was in progress in the packed church, and among the congregation were many people whose relations were with the Brigade of Guards in the thick of the fighting abroad. The casualties numbered 121 civilians and soldiers killed. My mother had called at my gun-site to leave a note for me, together with some roses and straw-berries from Chequers; my section was on a brief 'stand-down', but within a few minutes of her arrival the guns were firing, and together we watched the fatal plunge to earth of the flying-bomb which caused this ghastly incident.

The first, and most severe phase of the attacks came to its end in the early part of September 1944, with the over-running of the launching areas in north-east France by the Allied armies; but there were further spasmodic attacks from more remote sites. However, the ordeal from the air was not yet over: Hitler's second 'Secret Weapon', the V2 rocket, was hurled upon us for the first time on 8th September, and October and November saw a daily routine of delivery of two to four rockets a day. The 'shelling' lasted for seven months and was costly in casualties.

Between January and mid-March 1945, Clementine visited the sites of rocket-bomb damage in Woodford and Wanstead (Winston's constituency), Westerham, and Fircroft, near Gerrard's Cross (the Convalescent Annexe for Fulmer Chase) – miraculously in this last place no one was either killed or injured. The rockets put people, already wearied, under further great strain. But stolid courage held out, and the advance of the armies and the sure knowledge that we really were now treading a visibly victorious road enabled people in the target areas to grit their teeth to the end. Like everyone else Clementine got on with her everyday life as best she could, accepting untoward interruptions, noise and consequent fatigue as all part of the day's or night's work.

At the end of August there was another, short but real moment of panic about Winston's health. He had been in Italy since 11th August, visiting General Alexander; he had also met, for the first time, the heroic and redoubtable Yugoslavian leader, Marshal Tito; he had watched from afar (too far, so far as he was concerned) in a British destroyer the Allied landings on the Riviera coast; he had had talks with Italian politicians and the Greek Prime Minister, and had been received in audience by the Pope. On Tuesday, 29th August he flew home to England.

My battery, in the general re-deployment of the anti-aircraft defences, had moved several times during that eventful summer and was encamped at Fairlight Cove, near Hastings, under canvas. On Friday morning, 1st September, I received a letter from my mother which told me of my father's sudden illness, which had developed in the last lap of his Italian journey:

I had a great shock on Tuesday. I went to Northolt to meet Papa. The 'York' made a lovely landing & taxied right up to where everyone was waiting for him. Lord Moran emerged & ran across the tarmac to the car where I was sitting & said:— 'He has a temperature of 103. We must get him back quickly & get him to bed.'

Then Papa emerged looking crumpled & feverish. I got him straight into the car & we rushed away leaving everyone stunned & astonished including the special correspondents. But all is well I hope. The two beautiful Nurses from St Mary's Hospital appeared as tho' by magic – Doctor Geoffrey Marshall the lung specialist took blood tests & X rays & gave M. & B.* It *is* a slight attack – there *is* a small shadow on one lung, but in himself he is well & this morning, now 7 a.m. the temperature is normal. I was sick with fright Tuesday night & yesterday. We hope it will not be necessary to publish bulletins & strange to say Lord Moran says that in about 5 days he *can* go to Canada by sea. I shall go with him now, Sarah too. I do wish you could but your job is essential.

Darling – he says he must see you before he goes, so try to come up, ringing me first . . .[5]

Needless to say, I was dismayed by my mother's letter, but a telephone call conducted in veiled language indicated to me that my father was improving. I was allowed a 24-hour leave pass, and I bolted up to London. On my arrival at the Annexe I found my parents having dinner together in my father's room – he was sitting up in bed attired in his glorious many-hued bedjacket, with my mother by his side in one of her lovely housecoats: it was a most reassuring sight, and I enjoyed the loving welcome they gave me.[6]

This very brief, but nonetheless worrying bout of pneumonia had been disconcerting, but no bulletins were issued, and only the smallest circle of people knew he was ill. Gil Winant, writing on 1st September to Harry Hopkins, rightly judged it:

Tonight his temperature is back to normal and he seems on the way to a quick recovery. But each journey has taken its toll and the interval between illnesses has been constantly shortened.[7]

His forthcoming journey was a somewhat anxious prospect, and we were all thankful that my mother could go with him on this trip. Sarah, who was originally intended to be 'on the strength', stayed behind, as her unit was under great pressure of work. As usual my mother was an excellent correspondent, and we could all follow the events of the next few weeks through the 'Diary' account she sent to us all.

The party embarked at Greenock on the *Queen Mary* on 5th September. During the voyage the weather became very hot and sticky – they had taken a southerly course following the Gulf Stream, partly to get good weather, and partly to avoid U-boat packs. Winston, whom Clementine reported as being 'in low spirits and not very well',[8] worked as usual in his cabin most of the morning. On 7th September,

*The sulphonamide drug which was the first effective treatment for pneumonia.

after reading the early news received by ship's radio, Clementine sent this note from her cabin to his:

Darling – How are you this morning?

What a rousing news Bulletin this morning! Calais, Boulogne, Dunkirk, Le Havre, more & more closely invested – 19,000 Prisoners to the poor unnoticed British! Is the Moselle the frontier between France & Germany? because if so we are in the Reich.*

Then side by side with the announcement about the Home Guard the Americans (with an eye I suppose to the Election) announce demobilisation! Wurrup & Allelulia!

[Signed with a fat cat with very alert ears]

Lord Moran had brought with him on the voyage a pathologist (Brigadier Whitby) and a nurse; and in the event he was proved to have acted prudently and with foresight, for Winston sprang a temperature during the last part of the sea journey. Fortunately, however, it disappeared quickly, and there was no return of the dreaded pneumonia; on 10th September Clementine was able to report to us at home that:

This morning he woke up well, and by then we were out of the Gulf Stream, in glorious normal summer weather, with an oily sea, lovely sunshine and a light breeze . . .

The news had got around in Halifax and Papa had the most marvellous welcome. We had a great send-off from the ship which is going on to New York. The taffrails were garlanded with cheering, shouting, waving men, and then crowds came running and gathered round the waiting train. Now we are but two hours on our journey. All along the line people waved in the fields and at a place called Truro there was a tremendous crowd waiting for us and again at Moncton. At Halifax, while there was a prolonged delay before the train started, the crowd all sang songs, 'Tipperary', 'Pack up your Troubles', 'Roll out the Barrel' and 'Canada', ending up with 'God Save the King'. It is thrilling and moving and, oh, how I wish that Sarah *and* Mary were here . . . The train is so luxurious, all done up in peach-coloured paint and different coloured chintzes, that I cannot bear the idea of getting off it to-morrow.

The Conference party were once more staying in the Citadel, and when Winston and Clementine arrived they found the Governor-General and Princess Alice, Mr Mackenzie King and the Roosevelts already there. While the men conferred, Princess Alice looked after Clementine and Mrs Roosevelt. One afternoon they all went for a picnic and a four-mile walk up in the hills along the Jacques Cartier river, getting back to the Citadel just in time for a dinner party for the Chiefs of Staff. Clementine wrote on 13th September: 'There is a gay almost hilarious atmosphere as I understand the military conversations are going very well.'

Clementine was less 'public relations' conscious than Mrs Roosevelt, and was

*The German frontier was actually crossed on 11th September.

somewhat put about when the latter announced her intention of broadcasting to the Canadian people, and told Clementine that she had been invited to do so too. 'I was staggered and reluctant,' she wrote on 14th September. 'First of all I said I could not possibly do it at such short notice and thought I had nothing to say. But finally I was hounded into doing it.' She was helped by a British journalist, Mr Crookshank, and between them they composed a suitable text, part of it being in French. The joint broadcast was delivered that same evening, and pronounced successful; '. . . but in my opinion,' added Clementine, 'the whole thing was a work of supererogation.' The final straw for Clementine was that after they had finished broadcasting,

> . . . we were expected to do bits of it again as a News Reel. It was mortifying and frightful. Mrs Roosevelt throughout was calm and determined to do it all.[9]

Clementine's struggles with the preparation of the broadcast had been severely interrupted by the necessity for her to attend, with Mrs Roosevelt, a luncheon party given by the wife of the Lieutenant-Governor of Quebec. 'I am sorry to confess', Clementine wrote,

> that I was in a filthy temper . . .
> The luncheon party at Lady Fiset's was just like the one that Mary and I attended a year ago, only this time, instead of 24 women round the table, there were 65. I just don't know how they were all got into the dining room. The blinds were drawn, all the electric lights turned on, and there were seven courses:— Pâté de Foie Gras, Chicken Consommé, Oyster Patties, Galantine of Veal, Cheese Fondu, a very elaborate Ice, and then finally Brandy Cherries covered with pink icing. I ate it all! & enjoyed it. There were four wines handed round, and the ladies ended up with several liqueurs, after which we reeled back into the drawing room. The weather was dull, and here again curtains were drawn and full electric light as though it were a dinner party. Mrs. Roosevelt and I then had a few words of conversation with each of the 65 guests, after which Lady Fiset said Mrs. Roosevelt would like to say a few words – which she did. I tried to hide behind a palm tree because I saw what was coming next. But it was no use. When Mrs. Roosevelt had ceased, Lady Fiset said Mrs. Churchill would now like to reply to Mrs. Roosevelt. Mrs. Churchill was fished out from behind the palm tree – and I won't repeat to you what I said because I have forgotten, being under the influence of the luncheon . . .[10]

That evening there was an official Reception and Supper given by Mr Mackenzie King, who with Mrs Roosevelt and Clementine shook hands with more than 700 people. Clementine's account of this hectic day ended on a rueful note of admiration:

> Besides doing all these things which I have described, on top of it all Mrs. Roosevelt wrote her daily column.[11]

This was entitled 'My Day' and was syndicated widely in the American Press.

Back in England her three daughters eagerly awaited these entertaining instalments of our mother's Quebec journal. Sarah commented:

> Poor Mummie they are certainly making you 'work your passage'! But I am sure all the speeches are a great success even if you don't remember them afterwards![12]

The Second Quebec Conference ploughed on its way, each day bringing for Clementine its ample ration of visits to organisations such as the Navy League, the Imperial Order of the Daughters of the Empire, and the Red Cross who, in addition to cherishing their own Canadian forces, generously worked and gave to British funds, military and civilian alike. Every day there was a luncheon, tea or dinner party – or all three – and in the intervals Clementine combed the shops for presents for the stay-at-homes – such rareties as face tissues, nylon stockings, soap and hairnets, quite apart from the odd dress or glamorous négligée.

At the end of the Conference on 17th September Winston and Clementine, as in the previous year, were invited by the Roosevelts to spend a day or two with them at Hyde Park before returning home.

18th September, 1944

The President and Mrs Roosevelt and their charming daughter, Anna Boettiger and her husband, John, came down to meet us . . . She is the eldest child, aged 38, and the only daughter. She is charming, gay and high-spirited. So far as I have been able to observe she seems much the nicest of the large Roosevelt brood . . .

Windsor came to luncheon and had a long talk with Papa. I had not seen him for several years. He is now 51 or 52 and, in the distance, still has a boyish appearance which is rudely dispelled when one sees him close to.

Harry Hopkins also appeared and stayed till the next morning. He seems to have quite dropped out of the picture. I found it sad and rather embarrassing . . . Almost exactly a year ago we were in Washington, and the President seemed hardly to be able to draw breath without him. Harry was then in hospital beginning his long, grim illness from which he has but just recovered. Two or three times during our fortnight's stay at the White House, when things were stuck, he dragged himself out of his bed and came tottering along more dead than alive, and in half an hour the difficulty was resolved. Now it seems that the intimacy has ended, and I cannot but feel that this is a disadvantage to Anglo-American relationship.

We cannot quite make out whether Harry's old place in the President's confidence is vacant, or whether Admiral Leahy [the President's Chief of Staff] is gradually moulding into it. One must hope that this is so, because the President, with all his genius does not – indeed cannot (partly because of his health and partly because of his make-up) – function round the clock, like your Father. I should not think that his mind was pinpointed on the war for more than four hours a day, which is not really enough when one is a supreme war lord.

Last year I was at Hyde Park only for the inside of a day, and Mrs. Roosevelt had flown away on her journey to the Pacific. She loves her meals out of doors and so life at Hyde Park is a succession of picnics. It is rather fun really, and clever, because, when you have a lot of foreign guests whom you do not know planked [sic] down on the top of you, it all fills in the time.

I went for two terrific walks with Mrs. Roosevelt, who has very long legs and out-walks me easily . . .

Winston and Clementine travelled home again in the *Queen Mary*, arriving in London on 26th September. But it was only for a brief 'turn-around' period of ten days, before Winston was off on his travels again – this time flying on 7th October with Anthony Eden to Moscow. Clementine at first thought she might well have to accompany him to Russia, but his health had so much improved that she decided to remain at home, where her family and many other considerations awaited her attention.

During my parents' absence in Quebec my battery had returned to its original base in Hyde Park, and I was now most opportunely due for a week's leave. My mother, reprieved from having to go to Moscow, gave me a wonderful time, and we enjoyed an orgy of theatre-going: *Scandal at Barchester*; *Richard III*; *Pink String and Sealing-wax*; and *The Last of Mrs Cheyney*. We may have gone short of many things in the war, but the quality, variety and number of good plays running at any given moment in London remains clearly in my memory.

For the purposes of security Winston was given an 'alias' on nearly all his journeyings, and for this visit he was 'Colonel Kent', and in the two weeks 'Mrs Kent' received, as usual, a series of cables and a letter. On 13th October Colonel Kent reported by cable: 'EVERYTHING IS GOING WELL HERE AND THERE IS GREAT CORDIALITY . . .' During this visit Winston was able to renew the friendship begun earlier in the war in England with Averell Harriman, who was now United States Ambassador to the Soviet Union. On the evening of 13th October Winston had dined with Averell and his daughter Kathleen, and wrote to Clementine from their house. They had played some bezique, and Winston reported with satisfaction that he had won two 'Rubicon' games. He went on:

This is just a line to tell you how I love you & how sorry I am you are not here . . . I do hope that you are happy w yr dear & *my* Maria. Give her my dearest love. It is wonderful to get the London papers the same day at about 6 p.m. But the couriers also bring heavy bags & in between meals of 12 or 14 courses & conferences of various kinds I am hard at it. I am very well except for a little Indy [indigestion].

The affairs go well. We have settled a lot of things about the Balkans & prevented hosts of squabbles that were maturing. The two sets of Poles★ have arrived & are being kept for the night in two separate cages & tomorrow we see them in succession. It is their best chance for a settlement. We shall try our utmost. I have had very nice talks with the Old Bear [Stalin]. I like him the more I see him. *Now* they respect us & I am sure they wish to work w us. I have to keep the President in constant touch & this is the delicate side.

★The pro-Communist 'Lublin Committee' and the London-based Government-in-Exile.

Darling, you can write anything but war secrets & it reaches me in a few hours. So send me a letter from yr dear hand.

Clementine spent the week-end of 13th October at Chequers, and had all three of her daughters with her, Diana bringing her baby Celia. Uncle Jack, Cousin Moppet and Mr Winant completed a cosy party. On Sunday, 15th October, Clementine heard a description on the news of the rapturous ovation Stalin and Winston had received from the audience when they went to the Moscow Opera, and she wrote to him the same day: 'I wish I could have witnessed this hard-won recognition of your untiring and persistent work . . .'

While Winston was away, Clementine got on with her own very busy life, but the pressure from official entertaining was eased. She must, however, have been feeling the effect of the 'back-log' of fatigue just now, because two separate days in her engagement book have simply 'in bed' written across them; she was just taking this interlude to 'recharge her batteries'.

In early November she felt shock and sadness when the news came of the assassination by the Jewish extremist Stern Gang of her old friend, Lord Moyne, who was at that time Deputy Minister of State in Cairo. Both she and Winston, who greatly esteemed and liked this distinguished and delightful man, went to his Memorial Service. Clementine's mind must have gone back to those sunlit cruises in the *Rosaura* in the years just before the War. She had enjoyed them so much: now her host and friend was brutally dead. Recalling those journeys, in a bleak November in the fourth winter of a gruelling war, must have seemed like dreaming of another life on another planet.

After all the hard, dark times one could not but watch in these last months with mounting excitement the tide of victory, which now was flowing strongly. There were still hard losses to bear, and reverses to sustain, but nothing now could long impede the inexorable, victorious progress of the Allied armies. One great milestone on the road had been marked by the liberation of Paris by General Leclerc's Division at the end of August. Now in November, General de Gaulle invited Winston and Clementine to come to Paris for the commemoration of Armistice Day on the 11th. I was 'in attendance', and so witnessed the unforgettable scenes of emotion, joy and thanksgiving, as the people of Paris applauded their two great heroes of the hour – de Gaulle and Churchill.

My father had spent his last birthday far from us all in Teheran; this year, which marked his seventieth birthday, we had him for ourselves. The passing of a decade always seems 'special', and this year I think our minds were full of all the last twelve months had held; of his serious illness in North Africa; of all his journeyings; of all the moments of historic drama we had all lived to witness and wonder at. There was a glorious dinner-party at the Annexe, which I described in my diary:

Mummie had made the sitting room ablaze with flowers – The guests were Cousin Venetia, Brendan & Max besides the family – the 3 girls – Aunt Nellie, Duncan, Uncle Jack and Nana [Cousin Moppet].

When we were all assembled – the candles were lit on the cake – 70 of them –

Papa looked so pleased and well . . . Dinner was delicious & ended with peaches, birthday cake & real cream (a present!).

All Papa's presents were loaded on a table – and there was a magnificent 'bottle-scape'.

Max proposed Papa's health . . . Papa's reply made me weep –

He said we were 'the dearest there are' – he said he had been comforted and supported by our love –

It was short – but I couldn't see the faces at the end & then very slowly – almost solemnly he clinked glasses with each one of us . . .

In the last month of 1944, this year of such tremendous events, two crises erupted. One was the violent offensive launched by the Germans in mid-December in the Ardennes which, while it could not stop the now inevitable advance of the Allied armies, caused a serious hold-up, and was costly in men, materials and time. The other was the Greek civil war, which culminated over Christmas in a bitter struggle for Athens and the political future of Greece.

The guerrilla forces controlled by the Greek Communist Party had played a pre-eminent part in the long struggle against Germany. As the Germans withdrew from Greece, the Communists prepared to seize political control in the wake of liberation. Churchill was determined to prevent this, and to secure democratic elections. A British force was despatched to Greece in October 1944 to collaborate with the liberating forces and secure the authority of an all-party provisional Government. Just before Christmas violent fighting broke out in the streets of Athens between the Communist and pro-monarchist groups. Churchill thereupon decided that his personal intervention was the only hope of resolving the deteriorating situation and avoiding full-scale civil war. Accordingly, he arranged to fly off to Athens on Christmas Eve, taking Anthony Eden with him.

Clementine had arranged a large gathering of relations and friends for the Christmas week-end at Chequers: Uncle Jack and his daughter, Clarissa; and Aunt Nellie (a sad but gallant figure, with one son, Esmond, killed flying in an R.A.F. bombing raid, and Giles a prisoner in the sinister castle-prison of Colditz). The three Sandys children arrived a day or two ahead of their parents, Diana and Duncan. Sarah and I both had to be with our units over Christmas Day, but were to join the party on Boxing Day. Family apart, there was 'The Prof' and Jock Colville (doubling as a welcome friend and the Private Secretary on duty); Gil Winant was expected on Boxing Day.

This Christmas seemed to have a special atmosphere; the dark, war years were drawing to their end like a long and bitter winter; even the least optimistic could reasonably feel that this, the sixth, was the last wartime Christmas. Everywhere families were making their arrangements, despite gaps in the family, despite the black-out, and despite rationing. Among them, Clementine had taken infinite plans to prepare a glowing Christmas-tide. Nellie Romilly arrived at Chequers at about tea-time on Saturday the 23rd; she found Winston sitting in the Great Hall. He welcomed her, and then, under the seal of secrecy, told her that he was off the next day to Athens; he begged her to go and find Clementine, who was upstairs and 'very upset'. Nellie went to her sister's bedroom and found her in floods of tears. It was so rare for Clementine to give way; she was accustomed to sudden changes of plan, and had, in these last years especially, developed a strict sense of priorities. Somehow this sudden departure of Winston laid her low: but not for long. On the following evening Winston and Jock Colville left the party and flew off to war-torn Athens.

For two days meetings took place under conditions of siege. Churchill established his headquarters in the British cruiser *Ajax*; and while he was ashore, conferring in the British Embassy, the building was shelled and machine-gunned. He met leaders of all parties, including the Communists, and persuaded them to agree to the establishment of a Regency pending a plebiscite on the maintenance of the monarchy. His personal intervention on the spot was undoubtedly the only way in which agreement could have been reached so rapidly.

By the end of January 1945 the German armies were being slowly compressed within their own frontiers, and the end could not be far off; but with victory so near it became imperative for the 'Big Three' to decide on the immediate shape and manner of things when Germany finally surrendered. Once more, therefore, Winston was off on his travels, this time to Yalta on the Black Sea. With his usual colleagues and staff, and with Sarah in attendance as ADC, he set off on 29th January 1945 to meet Roosevelt and Stalin.

During the flight to Malta he produced a sudden high temperature, which fussed everyone considerably; however, he managed to throw it off and revived amazingly quickly. During these days Winston was evidently brooding deeply on the horror and suffering in the world, for Sarah wrote in a letter to her mother on 6th February:

> Last night just before he went to sleep Papa said: 'I do not suppose that at any moment in history has the agony of the world been so great or widespread. Tonight the sun goes down on more suffering than ever before in the world.'

Winston dwelt on the same theme in his letter to Clementine on 1st February:

> I am free to confess to you that my heart is saddened by the tales of the masses of German women and children flying along the roads everywhere in 40-mile long columns to the West before the advancing Armies. I am clearly convinced that they deserve it; but that does not remove it from one's gaze. The misery of the whole world appals me and I fear increasingly that new struggles may arise out of those we are successfully ending.

His long letter, which was dictated, ends with this *envoi*, in his own writing:

> Tender love my darling.
> I miss you very much. I am lonely amid this throng.
>
> Your ever-loving husband
> W

In ending a letter to Winston on 3rd February, Clementine wrote: 'Tender love & grapple close to the President . . .'. This last piece of advice was easier said than done. Churchill's personal relationship with Roosevelt had been, and was close, but

Cannes 1923

St Moritz, January 1937

Playing croquet on the converted tennis court at Chartwell. Photographed by Lord Montgomery 1964

With the Old Surrey and Burstow Hunt, spring 1939

Winston and Clementine on Horse Guards Parade the day they took up residence at No. 10 Downing Street, 28th May 1940

Clementine launching H.M.S. *Indomitable*, March 1940. It was Winston's favourite photograph of her and he later painted this sketch-portrait

Sorting letters and contributions for the Aid to Russia Fund

Visiting bomb-damaged Swansea, 11th April 1941

The visit of H.R.H. the Duchess of Gloucester to Fulmer Chase Maternity Home. *From left:* the Matron, the Duchess of Gloucester, Mrs Edward Baron, Clementine

Nellie Romilly *c.* 1941

Clementine with Sarah in W.A.A.F. uniform

Mrs Eleanor Roosevelt and Clementine make a joint broadcast at the Second Quebec Conference, September 1944

Clementine at Odessa on her visit to Russia, March–May 1945. Wearing Red Cross uniform, she and Miss Mabel Johnson are surrounded by British prisoners-of-war liberated by the Russians and awaiting repatriation

In Quebec for the First Quebec Conference, September 1943. Clementine, accompanied by Mary in A.T.S. uniform, signs autographs for Canadian girls

The christening of Jeremy Soames at St Mary's, Westerham, 1952. Clementine and Winston, Christopher and Mary Soames (holding Jeremy), Emma and Nicholas, and F.M. Lord Montgomery

Diana and Duncan Sandys with Celia in 1953

Sarah, late 1960s

Clementine leaves No. 10 for Westminster Abbey,
Coronation Day, 1953, wearing the petunia mantle and
insignia of a Dame Grand Cross of the Order of the
British Empire. She was suffering at this time from
neuritis and carried her arm in a sling

Fifty Glorious Years. Winston and Clementine celebrate their Golden Wedding on 12th September 1958 at La Capponcina, Roquebrune. With them are Randolph and his daughter Arabella

Clementine walking with Grace Hamblin in Kensington High Street, summer 1964

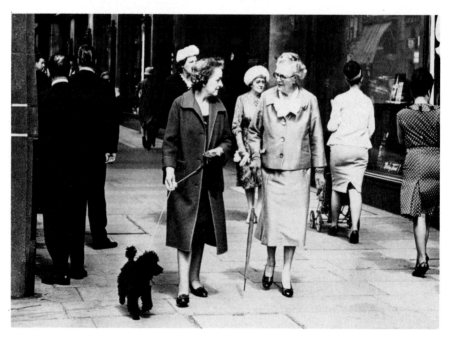

Christopher, Mary and Clementine, January 1965. 'We marched about in the grey chill days – killing time, while time killed him.'

The State Funeral, 30th January 1965. Winston Churchill's coffin arrives at St Paul's Cathedral. To the left Clementine and Randolph lead the family mourners

The Baroness Spencer-Churchill of Chartwell, G.B.E., with her sponsors, Lord Ismay and Lord Normanbrook, The House of Lords, 15th June 1965

The unveiling of Winston Churchill's statue, the work of Oscar Nemon, at Westerham, Kent, 23rd July 1969. Sir Robert Menzies, K.T., with Clementine, who is on two sticks, having broken her hip in the previous April

Sylvia Henley in 1969. A friend and a woman for all seasons

The launching of the Winston Churchill Centenary Appeal at the Banqueting House, Whitehall, 1st April 1974. The three party leaders toast Clementine on her eighty-ninth birthday. *From left:* Minnie and Winston Churchill, Edward Heath, Jeremy Thorpe, Harold Wilson

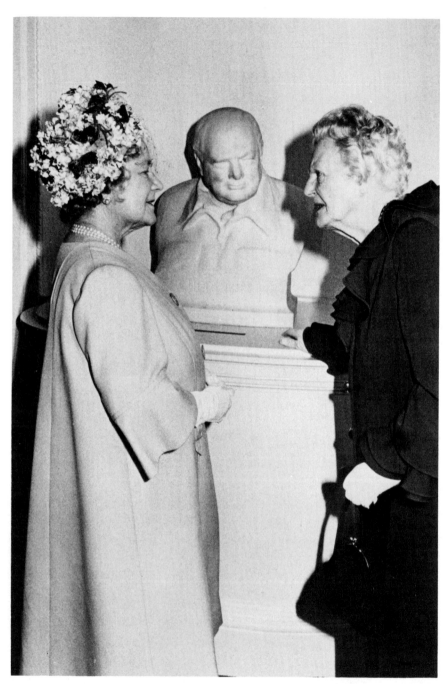

At the opening by Her Majesty Queen Elizabeth the Queen Mother of the Winston Churchill Centenary Exhibition at Somerset House, 9th May 1974

Staying with Winston and Minnie at Broadwater House, Christmas 1975. Clementine with Jack and Marina

Clementine Sylvia Hambro's christening, January 1977. Clementine with Charlotte (Soames) Hambro and her thirteenth great-grandchild. *In background:* Mrs Jocelyn Hambro

Clementine at ninety, photographed by Lord Snowdon
'And calm of mind all passion spent.'

his role at Yalta was delicate and difficult, and Great Britain's bargaining power was weak compared with the strength in wealth, men or materials of either the United States or Soviet Russia. Far more even than at Teheran, Churchill found himself isolated at this last meeting of the 'Big Three'. Roosevelt was already in frail health, and with hindsight one can now see from the photographs taken at the time that he indeed looked a stricken man. The President's inclination to conciliate the Russians on almost every point was cleverly exploited by Stalin. Churchill had to wage a lonely campaign, and came away from Yalta with deep reservations and anxieties about the future.

On his way home, Winston 'dropped in' on Athens, which seven weeks before had been in the grip of civil war; now he was acclaimed by a vast crowd in Constitution Square. From there he flew on to Egypt, and took leave of the President on board the U.S.S. *Quincy*. Winston described Roosevelt as seeming 'placid and frail. I felt that he had a slender contact with life . . . We bade affectionate farewells . . .'[13] It was to be their last meeting.

On 19th February, the day of Winston's return to England, there was a thick fog, and his plane was diverted to Lyneham, whither Clementine set out to greet him. After various changes and counter-changes of plan, they actually met in the Manager's Office of the Station Hotel at Reading, where Clementine described to me how she found Winston ensconced

imbibing whisky and soda. He is marvellously well – much, much better than when he went off for this most trying and difficult of Conferences.[14]

Meanwhile I was on the verge of what was for me personally, and indeed for all of us 'battery girls', a great adventure. Our battery was one of those chosen to go to Europe to form part of the defence of Brussels which, with other cities, was still vulnerable to aerial attack from bases in the interior of Germany. We set out at the end of January via Dover and Ostend, for a snowy (and subsequently extremely muddy) hillock about fifteen miles from Brussels. I wrote my mother long accounts of our daily life, and as usual she kept me supplied with all the news it was discreet to write.

My mother was somewhat frustrated by not knowing my exact whereabouts, my postal address being merely a series of letters and numbers; and I was far too well-trained in security even to indicate whether I was encamped outside Brussels or Timbuctoo. However, on 17th February she informed me triumphantly:

I know exactly where you are. Who do you think told me? Your 'Boss' [Field Marshal Montgomery] who sent Captain Chavasse to look you up. He says 'I sent an ADC (Noel Chavasse) to visit Mary & to ensure that all was well.

Her battery is at . . . . . about 10 miles south west of . . . . ., & they all seem to be well housed & to be enjoying themselves; morale generally is very high, so that seems very satisfactory.

I have not had time to visit her myself; just at the present I am very occupied: on German soil I am glad to say!!'

Winston and Sarah arrived back from their travels on 19th February, and the next day he and Clementine dined at Buckingham Palace; on 21st February my mother gave me this account of the evening:

> Last night Papa and I and Anthony Eden dined with the King and Queen. It really was great fun. The King kept Papa and Anthony a long time in the dining-room, so I had more than an hour alone with the Queen, but it passed like a flash because she is gay and amusing and has pith and point. When the King came in with Papa and Anthony we had a knock-about turn over de Gaulle and his last fit of sulks – the King and Queen and Anthony and myself against Papa who routed the lot of us from the fender where he occupied a commanding post.

*

But Clementine was herself on the threshold of a long and exciting journey: she had been invited by the Russian Red Cross to go to Russia and inspect the use that had been made of the materials sent over the last years by her Aid to Russia Fund. Her departure for Moscow, where she was to spend a week before beginning a tour which would take her many thousands of miles through Russia, was planned for the end of March, and she was to be away for more than a month.

Although Clementine had worked continuously for the Red Cross, she had not up to this moment been a 'uniformed member'; now it seemed best that for the purpose of this journey she should wear uniform; it was also the sensible solution to the otherwise vexing and time-consuming question of 'what to wear'. She was accordingly granted the rank of a Vice-President of County of London Branch, British Red Cross, and had early in the New Year ordered her uniform. I offered some seasoned advice:

> . . . are you having your shirt collars attached – or like a man's – separate? My experience is the latter look better and are in the end more comfortable.[15]

On 11th March she wrote to me:

> I'm getting very near my flight to Russia – another 16 days & I can't get my uniform done. I expect everything will be ready at the last moment. Perhaps when I get back you will be sitting in the ruins of Cologne . . .
>
> Next Thursday I go to Cardiff for a final Y.W.C.A. orgy before disappearing into the Steppes . . .

The uniform continued to be troublesome: 'My uniform does not fit, & makes me look like an elephant!' she complained to me on 20th March. But finally, three days later, she reported triumphantly: 'My uniform will really fit & I've got a Battle top & a Monty beret!'[16]

The Queen invited Clementine to tea on the eve of her departure:

> It was nice of her to send for me just before my great adventure. The King was there. The Queen looked very sweet & soignée like a plump turtle-dove . . .[17]

Although she looked forward to this great experience, Clementine had some pre-occupations: she hated leaving Winston for so long – and they would be so very far apart. she really hated flying, and was as aware as anyone else of the element of risk. That this played on her mind is shown in a letter she wrote me on the day of her departure:

> Darling supposing anything happened to me (e.g. air crash) Do you think you could be released from the A.T.S. on Compassionate grounds to look after Papa? Because he would need it . . .[18]

And to Sarah she wrote:

> . . . look after Papa as much as you can & say a little prayer now & then for your devoted Mother who altho' she keeps up a brave front sometimes feels like a nervous old lady! . . .[19]

Accompanied by Grace Hamblin and Miss Mabel Johnson (Secretary to the Aid to Russia Fund), Clementine flew off on 27th March. Their first stop was Cairo, where they were looked after by the Minister Resident in the Middle East and his wife, Sir Edward and Lady Grigg. Here, bad weather delayed their onward flight for several days; but she was happy and comfortable with the Griggs, and was by no means idle, visiting the principal Y.W.C.A. and three other clubs and hostels, as well as the Military Hospital.

During this enforced pause in her programme, Clementine was assailed by pangs of homesickness; she ended a letter to Winston on 28th March:

> My beloved Winston This is a long separation. Think of your Pussy now & then with indulgence & love.
>
> > Your own
> > Clemmie

The day before Clementine set out Lloyd George had died, at the age of eighty-two; a few days later Winston led the tributes in the House of Commons to his former chief and colleague. Clementine's mind went back, not to the difficult and sometimes embittered moments in the First World War, but to those glorious, crusading days of radical reform, which had left such an undying impression on her mind:

> I loved your speech about Ll.G. It recalled forgotten blessings which he showered upon the meek & lowly.[20]

During her unexpected stay in Cairo, Clementine took the opportunity to write to Field Marshal Montgomery. The crossing of the Rhine by British troops on 23rd March had seemed, as indeed it was, a dramatic milestone on the way to victory. Winston had made a two-day visit to the Field Marshal's Headquarters, traversing the Rhine twice and visiting British troops in advanced positions. Clementine wrote on 28th March:

> My dear Sir Bernard
> I am perched here for 24 hours on my way to Moscow.
> I want to send you my heartfelt & grateful congratulations & rejoicings upon

the Forcing of the Rhine – a glorious Victory which will for ever live in history when we have departed from this earthly scene.

Winston loved his visit to you. He said he felt quite a reformed character & that if in earlier days he had been about with you I should have had a much easier life! referring I suppose to his chronic unpunctuality & to his habit of changing his mind (in little things) every minute! I was much touched & said I had been able to bear it very well as things are. So then he said perhaps he need not bother to improve? But I said 'please improve becos we have not finished our lives yet' . . .

In his reply, Field Marshal Montgomery wrote:

It was a great pleasure to have the P.M. at my H.Q. during the Battle of the Rhine; he was very amenable to discipline and never argued about what was to be done! . . .[21]

Clementine spent her sixtieth birthday on 1st April in Cairo. It was Easter Sunday, and while she was in church the British Ambassador, Lord Killearn, handed her a telegram from Winston. She was so pleased, and wrote to tell him so later in the day.

That evening she and her companions finally got off on the last lap of their journey, arriving at Moscow Airport on 2nd April. Among the government and Russian Red Cross officials there to meet her were Mr and Mrs Maisky, whom she had known in London, our own Ambassador, Sir Archibald Clark Kerr, and Averell Harriman, the American Ambassador. 'This is one of the most inspiring and most interesting moments of my life . . .', Clementine said, with perfect sincerity, in a short speech on her arrival; she had also managed to 'work up' a few apt sentences in Russian, which duly gave pleasure. Since the Yalta Conference, the danger of Soviet domination in Eastern Europe had become an ever more visible threat, and suspicions of Stalin's intentions had led to an increasingly strained relationship between Britain and Russia. Clementine's visit provided a welcome occasion for agreeabilities. Winston cabled her immediately after her arrival:

Lovely accounts of your speech and reception received here. At the moment you are the one bright spot in Anglo-Russian relations.[22]

During the next few crowded and, for Clementine, peripatetic weeks, cables through the British Embassy rather than letters were their mutual means of communication, and hers gave a graphic description of her thrilling and moving journey, while half a world away Winston kept her as up-to-date as he could with events which followed in rapid succession as the tide of victory flowed swiftly forward. Although Clementine was totally absorbed physically and mentally by the demands of her formidable programme, she found it tantalising to be away from the source of instant news, and she minded above all being parted from Winston in these last tremendous days of the struggle they had lived through together, moment by moment, from its beginning.

During her week-long visit to Moscow, Clementine and her companions stayed in the State Guest House. Her programme was a full one: visits to two hospitals, a factory and a children's home were interspersed with official luncheons and dinners, one being given for her by the Molotovs (he was Soviet Commissar for Foreign Affairs); and on two evenings she went to the ballet. Clementine was also received 'most amiably' in private by Mr Molotov in the Kremlin. In a cable to Winston she reported that 'He referred to present difficulties, but said that they would pass and Anglo-Soviet friendship remain.'[23]

Winston, in a cable to her, told her that he had asked the Ambassador to show her Foreign Office telegrams, and with reference to her contacts with the Russians he added:

Please always speak of my earnest desire for continuing friendship of British and Russian peoples and of my resolve to work for it perseveringly . . .[24]

On 6th April Clementine attended a Meeting of the Praesidium of the Executive Committee of the Soviet Red Cross. It was during the course of this meeting that she was awarded, 'amidst stormy applause' (in the words of the official report), the Distinguished Red Cross Service Badge. Among the tributes paid to the work of the Aid to Russia Fund and her own personal contribution, the appraisal of Professor Sarkisov, the Soviet Red Cross representative in London since 1943, and the words of appreciation from Mrs Maisky must have particularly warmed her heart; for their praise was not merely polite, but was based on first-hand knowledge of the work and the problems with which Clementine and her committee had wrestled so doughtily and perseveringly.

However, the highlight of these days in Moscow was her visit to Marshal Stalin, who received both her and Miss Johnson at the Kremlin on the afternoon of 8th April. They were shown into a vast room, at the far end of which Stalin was sitting at a writing desk. Speaking through an interpreter, the Marshal expressed himself graciously about the work of the Fund. Clementine then presented him with a gold fountain-pen from Winston, as a souvenir of their meetings during the war. 'My husband wishes me to express the hope that you will write him many friendly messages with it,' she said.[25] The graceful acceptance of presents was evidently not a prime trait in Marshal Stalin's character, for although he took the pen with a genial smile, he put it on one side saying, 'But I only write with a pencil.' He also added: 'I will repay him.'[26] Clementine, who was now quite inured to Russian ungraciousness, was unabashed and much amused.

Between the 6th and 9th April, Winston dictated a twelve-page letter to Clementine. In it he ranged over a wide field of events and thoughts: the war, the political scene, and likely future developments there, and domestic details from their 'home front'. Indeed, the letter reads more like a conversation than a literary exercise:

My darling Clemmie,
    Since you were swirled away into the night, I have had the most exacting time. What with looking after Bernie Baruch and all the Dominion Premiers, as well as overwhelming toil, I have not found a minute to write. It is now Friday, and I have just finished my sleep and am going down to Chequers, where Smuts is

spending the week-end with me . . . I arranged for Sarah to attend on me for week-ends on duty while you are away, to help me with our various official guests . . .

With the advance of the Allied armies, the danger from air attack was diminishing daily; in reporting to Clementine that there had been no 'bombs or bangs' for a whole week, Winston told her:

. . . I have moved the Cabinets back to No. 10, and have also had one or two meals there. I am giving orders for the rehabilitation of that dwelling, otherwise we shall not be able to use it this year. If you have any strong views about this, pray write to me, so that I can have them carried out. The garden has become very nice now. The lawn is in good order, the herbaceous border is fully stocked and the little magnolia tree is at its best . . .

He had received messages from Roosevelt through Mr Baruch, and he was already aware that the President's strength was failing:

. . . now that Harry [Hopkins] is ill and Byrnes [U.S. Director of War Mobilization] has resigned, my poor friend is very much alone, and according to all accounts I receive, is bereft of much of his vigour. Many of the telegrams I get from him are clearly the work of others around him . . .

Winston was gravely disturbed about the difficulties over Poland and Roumania, for Russia had already violated agreements made only three months before at Yalta.

On the political front at home, with the approach of victory, party politics were beginning to revive. Some colleagues were making speeches in a hostile vein, and Winston told Clementine that

. . . there is very little doubt that the Government will break up shortly . . . I expect the General Election about the middle of June . . .

He had some gratifying news for her about the success of her visit:

There is no doubt that your visit is giving sincere pleasure. Gousev [the Soviet Ambassador to London] called at the Foreign Office yester-day, as Anthony thought, to begin a long attack, but instead he spent a long time in conveying a message from his Government in praise of you and your work, and asking whether they might offer you the Order of the Red Banner of Labour . . .

He had also heard from the British Ambassador that her visit was doing '. . . the utmost good at a most difficult time . . .' But he was anxious lest she should become exhausted:

I do hope you will be sensible and not overdo it. Insist upon days of leisure. They will understand. Otherwise you may be killed with kindness . . .

Clementine was due to leave Moscow for Leningrad and far distant parts of the Soviet Union; Winston knew well how much she set store by knowing the news, but he warned her that once she left Moscow their telegrams to each other would be *en clair*, and that all private information would perforce cease:

> You will not have a cypher, and much of this stuff is dynamite. The same is true of letters. I do not feel able to write freely because I do not know how letters will be forwarded from Moscow . . .

Although this letter, like nearly all of Winston's in these later years, was dictated and typed, he added the ending in his own hand:

> My darling one I think always of you . . . Yr personality reaches the gt masses & touches their hearts. With all my love & constant kisses
>
> I remain ever your devoted husband
> W
> [Charming drawing of a pig]

On the night of 8th April Clementine and her party boarded the special train provided for them by the Soviet Government, which was most roomy and comfortable, and in order that the visitors should be able to enjoy the scenery, the train travelled at sightseer's speeds. Throughout their journeyings Clementine and her companions were accompanied by an interpreter, Madame Kislova, Mr Zinchenko (head of the Press Department of the Foreign Office), as well as by Professor Sarkisov – a real and tried friend. They reached Leningrad late on the afternoon of 9th April, and were installed in a comfortable villa in the suburbs. 'Think Leningrad is the most beautiful city I have ever seen,' she cabled Winston the next day.

Clementine's visit lasted three days, and she genuinely enjoyed it and was greatly touched by the warmth and spontaneity of the welcome she was accorded. Leningrad had been blockaded for nearly two and a half years, and much of the population had suffered from the effects of prolonged starvation. One of Clementine's visits was to a scientific institute and hospital where there were many children being nursed back to health and strength. Here she received a particularly warm welcome from the nurses, who gathered round the British visitors clapping enthusiastically.

The Chairman of the City Council had been most attentive, calling upon Clementine and later escorting her to the ballet. On the last night of their visit, Clementine and her party were entertained again by the Chairman and his wife, who gave a dinner and musical entertainment, which sounded very jolly:

> We ended the evening with community singing. I think our Russian hosts were astonished that we were so familiar with the Song of the Volga Boatmen![27]

It was at this dinner that it was announced that Clementine had been awarded the Order of the Red Banner of Labour, and Miss Johnson the Medal of Labour.

Their next destination was Stalingrad, and on the way the train had to pass through Moscow. Only a very short stop there had been scheduled on the afternoon of 13th April, but as the train drew in to the station Clementine saw that a large silent crowd was waiting on the platform, and in the front were the Molotovs; they boarded the train. 'We come with bad news,' said Mr Molotov. 'President Roosevelt is dead.' Clementine was stunned by this grievous news: she at once understood its import to the course of events, and knew also what a deep and personal loss the President's death would be to Winston. But she collected herself instantly, and suggested to the Molotovs that they should sit in silent recollection for a few minutes in the railway carriage; this they did. Because of this news Clementine remained a few hours in Moscow, and was able to speak to Winston from the British Embassy.

Then they headed south for Stalingrad. The siege of this great city had lasted for six months, and every house had been fought for in this fierce ordeal. Even amid all the other horrors of the war, the eyes of the world had been fixed upon this savage and searing episode, and now, two years later, the ravaged city made an indelible impression on Clementine, who was later to write:

> What an appalling scene of destruction met our eyes. My first thought was, how like the centre of Coventry or the devastation around St Paul's, except that here the havoc and obliteration seems to spread out endlessly . . . The imagination is baffled by the attempt to encompass calamity on so vast a scale.[28]

Clementine was shown the vast rebuilding operations in progress; factories, hospitals and schools (the latter working in two shifts), and a prefabricated wooden village which was being built to house 20,000 people. She was deeply impressed:

> They are rebuilding their city with the same spirit of determination with which they fought the Germans house to house until there was not one left intact . . .[29]

Between 17th and 19th April Clementine visited three spa towns in the Caucasus: Kislovodsk, Essentuki and Pyatigorsk. From Kislovodsk she cabled Winston on 18th April, describing how they had been to the local theatre:

> The audience were rapturous in their welcome and threw bunches of violets from the gallery. This morning we spent visiting sanatoriums full of severely wounded Red Army soldiers. The whole town turns out to greet us every time we go out and I am continually amazed and moved by so much enthusiasm. We have been here only a fortnight but we have travelled through this great country from North to South and I want you to know that this tremendously warm feeling seems universal.

It is always interesting, and sometimes humbling, to see one's own life and preoccupations from afar and through other people's eyes, and during her journey through Russia Clementine realised how far away, how very far away indeed, Europe was to the Russians. The immensity of their own sufferings as a nation, the progress and losses of their own army, and the immediate problems of reconstruction with which they were grappling with so much determination, absorbed all their thoughts, emotions and energies. They were genuinely grateful and appreciative of the wish to help, and for the solid help provided through the British Red Cross Aid to Russia Fund but, as Clementine herself wrote: 'I could not honestly say that I found a great deal of curiosity about British life or affairs . . .'[30]

On 21st April the party arrived at Rostov-on-Don, which was really the focal point of their visit, for it was in this city that the Aid to Russia Fund was undertaking the complete re-equipping of two large hospitals, which had both suffered severe damage at the hands of the Germans.

It had been proposed to equip the two hospitals with 500 beds each, but when Clementine and her party saw the need and potentialities there, it was decided to increase the provision to 1,500 beds.[31] This on-the-spot revision highlights the practical value of Clementine's visit, quite apart from the goodwill it engendered. In a cable to Winston en route from Rostov to Sebastopol she said:

. . . I am happy that our hospitals are in this town [Rostov] in which . . . thousands of citizens were put to death, many other thousands of women and children deported to Germany and the remainder stood the brunt. It must have been a lovely city once and stands high overlooking the Don which is stiff with delicious fish. We were mobbed by friendly crowds. Everywhere we see smiling faces and even in the hospitals grievously sick people sit up and say greetings to British women.[32]

Thousands of miles away at home Winston tried to keep Clementine level with major events, but things were moving at hectic speed, and now that she was so far from Moscow their cables to and fro took longer to arrive and often crossed with each other. As the liberating armies swept forward they discovered the terrible camps, the stark reality of which now became apparent to all, and the grisly truth, displayed by photographs, appalled even a world accustomed to tales of cruelty and horror. Winston wrote on 21st April:

. . . Intense horror has been caused by the revelations of German brutalities in the concentration camps. They did not have time to cover up their traces . . .

The next stage of Clementine's journey was four days spent in the Crimea. Sebastopol made a particularly sad impression on her:

. . . it presented so melancholy a spectacle . . . Before the Nazis destroyed it in their blind rage, it must have been a dream of beauty, as lovely as a poem, with its many pillared and frescoed houses.[33]

In Yalta Clementine and her party stayed in the Vorontzov Palace, and she slept in the room Winston had occupied during the Yalta Conference. Here they all had a 'day off', and apart from visiting various institutes, and a 'Young Pioneers' Camp' at Artec, their hosts had thoughtfully included some less arduous engagements as well – visits to Chekhov's house, the Botanical Gardens, and the cellars where all the Crimean wine was stored.

On 20th April the Russians had entered Berlin, and three days later the United States and Russian armies met at Torgau, south of the city. This splendid news percolated to Simferopol on 28th April, where Clementine was spending the last day of her Crimean visit; she at once cabled to Winston:

I have just heard the glorious news of the meeting of the Red Army with the Allies and by your statement on the wireless it seems the end is near. I long to be with you in these tremendous days and I think of you constantly.

All my love   Clemmie

Clementine's next stop was Odessa, the great port on the Black Sea; here she spent two days. She toured the city, visited two hospitals, went to the opera and, on 1st May, witnessed a parade. But of especial interest to her and her companions was that there were in Odessa about 250 British prisoners-of-war who had been liberated by the Red Army and were in a camp awaiting repatriation. Clementine was taken to visit them, and also another camp in which were French, Belgian and Dutch ex-prisoners, many of them having been deported to Germany for slave labour, and who now were on the threshold of their return home.

Meanwhile dramatic news crowded in almost hourly: Mussolini had been executed by the Italian partisans; the German forces in Italy had surrendered; and on 30th April Hitler had shot himself in the air-raid bunker of the Chancellery in Berlin while the sounds of the Russian guns grew ever nearer.

As she heard the news of these events in disjointed telegrams and press reports, triumphant joy and relief were mingled for Clementine with an almost overpowering desire to get home to England and to Winston.

But her journey was not finished yet. Although it was not originally in the programme, Clementine had during her tour received an invitation from the Chairman of the Kursk City Council, Madame Maslennicova, and so it had been arranged for her to go to Kursk after Odessa. She was later to write:

I was stirred to witness that in this city whose civic chief is a woman, thousands of women have volunteered to help in its rebuilding. I saw them working with a will among the ruins. I am sorry they had only spades with which to clear away the rubble – I wished they could have had bulldozers.[34]

On 5th May, Clementine and her companions arrived back in Moscow; Winston had sent a cable to greet her:

Delighted with all your telegrams. Skymaster [the aeroplane used for all Winston's long flights] starts for you tonight with many papers and messages . . . Several crises are coming to a head, and as you see both our great enemies are dead . . . My hours are shocking but I am very well . . .[35]

On 4th May Winston had sent Clementine a second, much longer telegram – now that she could receive news safely through the Embassy he felt free to confide to her his gnawing anxieties:

You seem to have had a triumphant tour and I only wish matters would be settled between you and the Russian common people. However there are many other aspects of this problem than those you have seen on the spot . . . It is astonishing one is not in a more buoyant frame of mind in public matters. During the last three days we have heard of the death of Mussolini and Hitler; Alexander has taken a million prisoners of war; Montgomery took 500,000 additional yesterday and far more than a million to-day; all north-west Germany, Holland and Denmark are to be surrendered early tomorrow morning . . . and we are all occupied here with preparations for Victory-Europe Day . . . I need scarcely tell you that beneath these triumphs lie poisonous politics and deadly international rivalries. Therefore I should come home after rendering the fullest compliments to your hospitable hosts . . .

As soon as she read all the telegrams, Clementine cabled to Winston:

. . . I am full of joy at the overwhelming victories of Alexander and Montgomery. I long to be with you but have some necessary engagements to fulfil and some loose ends to tidy up after which I shall joyfully fly home by Malta leaving at dawn on the 11th. In the midst of all this military glory I know you are having harassing and sometimes sad experiences . . .[36]

These last few days in Russia were full of engagements: Clementine visited a school, several hospitals and the Moscow Metro; she attended receptions given in her honour; she gave a press conference, and went to a concert and the ballet. She and Miss Johnson received their decorations at the Kremlin from the hands of the First Vice-Chairman of the Supreme Soviet of the USSR and, at a luncheon given two days before their departure by the Soviet Government in honour of the visiting British party, Mrs Molotov presented Clementine with a most beautiful diamond ring as a token of 'eternal Friendship'.

Her journey had been a tremendous success: it had been 'laid on' officially at the highest level wherever she had been, but there is no doubt that her own personality and open, intelligent approach had played a major part in turning an official exercise in public relations into a genuine two-way expression of gratitude, appreciation and friendship between the British and Russian peoples.

But it must not be supposed that the wonderful welcome she had received everywhere she went in Russia, or the gilded hospitality, had entirely blinded Clementine's eyes to the true state of things, or that, when the need arose, she was not able to make firm representations. During her journey one of the few letters forwarded to her was from Miss Eleanor Rathbone, the Independent Member of Parliament for the Combined English Universities and a woman of great distinction. She was on the Parliamentary Committee for Refugees, and the previous winter had made a speech in the House of Commons drawing attention to the fate of the vast numbers of Poles who were being deported by the Russians to labour camps in distant parts of the USSR. When Miss Rathbone heard of Clementine's visit she asked her, if at all possible, to make some kind of representation about these unfortunate Poles. After her return home Clementine wrote the following letter, which shows so well her directness, her instinctive reaction in favour of some immediate action, and her clearsightedness.

28th May 1945

My dear Miss Rathbone,

I was glad to have your letter with me in Russia, but alas, I was not able to do any good. I saw Mr Maisky several times during the two periods when I was in Moscow, and I did let him know that I was acquainted with some of the facts concerning the Polish deportees. Actually he started the subject in rather a school-masterish lecturing manner! After listening as patiently as I could I am afraid I rather flew at him and said that I was kept informed by our Ambassador of the telegrams which were passing between the Foreign Office and the Kremlin, and that I would not discuss the matter with him as I was afraid it would make me very angry. So he beat a diplomatic retreat.

From my small and limited experience I am convinced that the only hope is that the English-speaking world should act together and go so far as to inform the Kremlin that if they do not mend their ways we may have to break off Diplomatic relations with them.

I am terribly grieved at the progressive deterioration in the relationship between our countries. When one has been in Russia, only for a few short weeks, one cannot help loving the people, and one must always separate them from their Government which is mysterious and sinister, and terribly strong.

Yours sincerely
Clementine Churchill

[She added this postscript in her own handwriting, referring to her suggestion about breaking off diplomatic relations:]

Winston would disapprove! I am sending you an article I have written on my journey.

*

Tuesday, 8th May was Victory-in-Europe Day: early in the morning Clementine sent Winston this short cable:

All my thoughts are with you on this supreme day my darling. It could not have happened without you.

Arrangements were quickly made by the British Embassy for a service of thanksgiving; there was no official Chaplain, but an R.N.V.R. officer who was a Methodist minister conducted the service. A day or two before, Dr Hewlett Johnson, the Dean of Canterbury (the 'Red Dean'), had arrived in Moscow on a visit in connection with his Russian Aid fund, and at Clementine's suggestion he was invited to give the Address.

At luncheon at the British Embassy that day (where Mr Frank Roberts, the Chargé d'Affaires acted as host in the absence of the Ambassador) the guests included General Catroux, the French Ambassador, and Monsieur and Madame Herriot. Monsieur Herriot had been President of the Chambre des Députés at the fall of France, he and his wife having later been deported to Germany; they had both just been released by the Russians. Later in the afternoon they all listened to Winston's broadcast from London. Monsieur Herriot wept; he said to Clementine:

'I am afraid you may think it unmanly of me to weep. But I have just heard Mr Churchill's voice. The last time I heard his voice was on that day in Tours in 1940 when he implored the French Government to hold firm and continue the struggle. His noble words of leadership that day were unavailing. When we heard the French Government's answer, and knew that they meant to give up the fight, tears streamed down Mr Churchill's face. So you will understand if I weep to-day, I do not feel unmanned.'[37]

The next evening Clementine broadcast over Moscow Radio a message from Churchill to Marshal Stalin:

... It is my firm belief that on the friendship and understanding between the British and Russian peoples depends the future of mankind.[38]

On her last night in Moscow, Clementine was taken to the ballet to see *Swan Lake*. She described the scene at the end of the performance in her own words:

At the fall of the curtain the prima ballerina, with exquisite grace, turned the applause from herself to our box. She wheeled towards us, clapping and smiling, the whole company followed her, and then the great audience took up the applause.[39]

This graceful and heart-warming scene made a perfect ending to her memorable journey.

In his cable to Clementine of 2nd May, Winston had told her:

... You should express to Stalin personally my cordial feelings and my resolve and confidence that a complete understanding between the English-speaking world and Russia will be achieved and maintained for many years, as this is the only hope of the world.

Now, on 11th May, the morning of her departure from Moscow, Clementine put this message in her own words in a handwritten letter:

My dear Marshal Stalin,
   I am leaving your great country after a wonderful & unforgettable visit.
   I have seen with sorrow some of the ravages caused by a wicked & ruthless Enemy & observed the dignity, courage & patience of your people.
   I have enjoyed the most warm hearted hospitality & everywhere I have been welcomed with the greatest kindness & enthusiasm. And my happiness has been crowned by being received by you & by the decorations which you have bestowed upon Miss Johnson & myself.
   I know of the international difficulties which have not been surmounted, but I know also of my Husband's resolve & confidence that a complete understanding between the English Speaking World & the Soviet Union will be achieved and maintained as this is the only hope of the World.

Yours sincerely,
Clementine S. Churchill

I count myself fortunate to have been in your country in these days of Victory, and to have seen the Sun of Peace rise in Moscow.

Soon after her return, Clementine wrote a small booklet entitled *My Visit to Russia*, which was sold for the benefit of the Aid to Russia Fund. She described the welcome she had received, and the impression made upon her by all she saw, and the people she met. The oft-repeated expressions of friendship on either side, and the pious hopes for a new dawn of amity and understanding between the Russian and the British people now of course have a somewhat hollow ring. Even at the time we see that Winston and, sharing his knowledge, Clementine, had realistic reservations and anxieties which were to be only too dismally fulfilled. But in reading the account one must try to recapture the atmosphere of that time. The British people had been awestruck by the heroism and sufferings of the Russians, our allies in a tremendous and agonising struggle. The extent of that admiration was expressed in the sustained and amazing support for the Aid to Russia Fund from people of all classes. Much that soon became common knowledge was then unrevealed, and the journey from admiration and hopeful aspirations to grey dis-illusion and suspicion was a long-drawn-out process. The efforts of those who once hoped for better things should not be the object of a superior latter-day cynicism.

Leaving Moscow in Skymaster on the Friday, Clementine, Miss Johnson and Miss Hamblin had a swift and safe flight home, arriving at Northolt early on the morning of 12th May. Winston was determined to go and meet her himself, but he did not leave Storey's Gate quite in time, and Skymaster had to make a few extra tours round the airfield to allow a loving but tardy Winston to be on the tarmac to welcome home his Clemmie.

Although Winston had tried to keep her abreast of events (private and national) during her long journey some of his cables had, in fact, only met Clementine on her return to Moscow, and there was much of course that she could only learn from him upon her return home.

In the family circle, Winston had been deeply anxious for his brother Jack, who had sustained a heart attack, and who had for a number of days been seriously ill; now, happily, he was on the road to recovery. Clementine's sister, Nellie Romilly, had been in agony for the safety of her son Giles who, with Lord Lascelles (son of the Princess Royal), Earl Haig, and other *prominenti*, had all been removed from their camp a few hours before the liberating Americans arrived and taken off to an unknown destination, no doubt as potential hostages. After a period of acute anxiety, however, she had received the joyful tidings that he, and his companions, had been freed. Sarah was well, but during her mother's absence her divorce from Vic Oliver had been granted; it was the final milestone on what had been an increasingly unhappy road.

My battery was now encamped outside Hamburg, and I had some leave just at the time of my mother's return. My parents took me with them when they went to St Paul's Cathedral, to a moving and wonderful service attended by King George and Queen Elizabeth. 'This is such a national thanksgiving as never was before', said the Archbishop of Canterbury in his address, 'for everyone from greatest to least has borne his share of suffering and toil.'

Only those who lived through those years can understand the emotional relief, joy and gratitude which the proclamation of victory in Europe inspired. Now we know the disillusions of the years that came after. Yet a vile tyranny had been laid low, and proud countries liberated from a hideous yoke by the years of sustained endeavour and sacrifice. All were entitled to their hour of unclouded rejoicing.

THE TWO IMPOSTORS

'If you can meet with Triumph and Disaster
And treat those two impostors just the same'
RUDYARD KIPLING

'AFTER THE WAR' had seemed a far-off, golden period – the recurring theme of many contemporary songs; but few people had time or energy to dwell upon it in detail. Sufficient to the day was very much the sweeping up of last night's shattered glass, or queueing for too few oranges. Now peace was upon us, and the end of the war illuminated deep disagreements in the nation which had been obscured while our survival was at stake. It is true that political discords had never been far below the surface, but the three main parties had honoured the electoral truce. The Coalition Government had remained united, and had been sustained by an overwhelming and unfaltering parliamentary majority. But by the end of 1944 unity within the Government and in the House of Commons (which still remained unshakeable on matters concerning the defeat of our enemies) was very fragile on all future domestic issues.

In moving the annual Bill to prolong the life of Parliament in October 1944, Churchill made it clear that he foresaw victory in Europe as marking the end of the Coalition Government. If he perceived this situation with realistic clarity, he accepted it with reluctance; he had hoped that national and political unity could be maintained until all our enemies had been defeated. But the present Parliament was ten years old, and Churchill was adamant that the coming of peace must be followed at the earliest opportunity by a General Election in which the people's voice could be heard.

But it was not only politicians and their parties who felt they could now afford the luxury of considering their own interests and of casting their minds forward to the return of normal times; families and individuals also started making plans for the future, and among them, Clementine took prudent thought for the morrow. During the winter of 1944–5 she started quietly looking around for a new London house. Her thought (to which her deepest wishes were certainly the father) was that at the end of the war and the dissolving of the Coalition Government, Winston would retire. This idea never formed part of his own personal post-war plan: his mind was totally dominated by the war and the problems which would soon confront the victorious allies and a prostrate Europe. Nevertheless, although Clementine did not involve him in her discreet house-hunting, he was in favour of their acquiring a London home, whatever might befall in the near future.

Early in the New Year of 1945 Clementine saw a charming house in Kensington, 28 Hyde Park Gate; it was secluded and quiet, and had a delightful garden; she thought this would be just right for them. She had told me about her discovery, and in one of her first letters to me in Belgium she wrote:

> Yesterday afternoon I took Papa to see the little house I covet. He is mad about it, so now I must be careful not to run him into something which is more than he can afford.[1]

Their life at Chartwell was also a subject for thought and planning. Clementine knew that this would always be the place Winston was happiest in and would truly think of as home; but if the running of it had been a burden and an anxiety in the palmier days between the wars, the contemplation of managing it in the aftermath of the war was daunting. Winston too must have had his doubts about it all, for in a letter to me on 30th January my mother wrote:

> Papa & I have decided as soon after the War as possible to build a tiny Baby Chartwell on the other side of the lakes on the slope just below the Gainsborough Road*. The old house will be made into a Churchill Museum! What do you think?

The theme of a golden life at Chartwell after the stormy years was much in all our minds this spring, and although these first tentative plans did not materialise in their original form, Chartwell was to remain their home for the rest of Winston's days; it sheltered children and grandchildren, and afterwards became the museum both Winston and Clementine had envisaged.

But Clementine's mind was not solely preoccupied with thoughts for their own domestic arrangements in the early months of 1945. Her letters to Winston while he was away at the Yalta Conference show that she was most attentive to conditions both in this country and on the Continent. In February, Joan Portal had been staying with a French Service family in France, and had been shocked by the want and cold among their civilian friends and relations. On her return to London, she and her husband had lunched with Clementine, who wrote to Winston on 12th February, recounting what Lady Portal had told her, adding

> Both 'Houses' are working up steam & the Press is writing some moderate & some exaggerated articles. At least I hope they are exaggerated . . . There is, it seems, a great deterioration since November the 11th [1944] when we saw Paris exalted . . .

She enclosed with her letter a 'snip' from the same day's *Daily Mail* headed 'CATS – 30s Each in Paris', in which it was stated that 30,000 cats had 'disappeared' in Paris since the Liberation and that 'Acute food supply difficulties have produced a systematic cat hunt in the city. A cat is now worth 30s.' Clementine begged Winston

---

*This was a cart track running down between the woods into the fields, and so named by my parents because of its romantic aspect.

to 'influence General Marshall or the President to release enough lorries to *distribute* the food & coal already in France . . .' The cold and misery were to be widespread throughout Europe that icy winter. The wonderful, saving 'Marshall Plan' was not to get going for over two years.

Before Winston had left for Yalta on 29th January, a crisis had arisen in this country over the distribution of coal, due to lack of man-power combined with some very severe weather. From their letters it would seem that Clementine had the simple, straightforward idea that soldiers could be used to help out with coal deliveries in this critical situation. On 30th January, she ended a letter to Winston:

> The radio announced this morning that coal distribution by Army lorries begins today! It didn't mention who thought of this.

And in Winston's letter of 1st February, which must have crossed with hers, he wrote:

> Keep your eye on the coal shortage as long as it lasts, and keep prodding at them to give the necessary military lorries etc. . . .

*

A fortnight after Victory Day in Europe, on 23rd May 1945, Churchill tendered his resignation to the King, the Labour Party having refused to continue the Coalition until after the defeat of Japan. In all fairness it must be remembered that the swift collapse of the Japanese after the bombing of Hiroshima in August could not then have been foreseen. The King charged Churchill with the formation of an interim administration, and the 'Caretaker' Government, as it was called, held the fort for the few weeks remaining until the dissolution of Parliament.

It was widely thought in this country, and certainly generally assumed abroad, that the Conservative Party would win the election – if only on the prestige and record of its leader. Yet there were signs to the contrary for those few who read them aright. Several important by-elections since 1940 had been won by Independent candidates, and since 1942 the Gallup Poll (a then fairly new device in this country and not widely published) had shown that Labour consistently led the Conservatives in public popularity. The Conservatives' opponents were always quick to emphasise that in the years before the war Tory Governments had failed to prepare the country for the coming conflict – a failure which of course Churchill had continually condemned. The Conservatives' lack of sympathy for the victims of the Depression, and their methods of dealing with the economic situation, were also constantly held up to contumely.

Electioneering began as soon as Polling Day was fixed for 5th July. Winston and Clementine lost no time in making a tour of his constituency, which had changed, owing to the growth and movement of population from the near-country seat of Epping, into the populous borough of Woodford. By chivalrous agreement, none of the opposition parties nominated candidates to stand against him; he was however opposed by a middle-aged eccentric, Mr Alexander Hancock, who decided to stand as an Independent.

Due to his still being Prime Minister, and the need also for him to undertake speaking tours covering the whole country, Winston was of necessity somewhat of an absentee-candidate. Clementine, however, did several tours on his behalf, making short speeches and visiting supporters and campaign workers.

The *Woodford Guardian* of 6th July described how, 'Dressed in a black wool costume, with a bright red scarf and a chiffon turban, and standing on a low wooden platform . . .', Clementine had addressed an open-air gathering:

> A cross against his [Churchill's] name, she said, would mean they were glad he had been head of the Coalition Government and had approved of its conduct of the war and that they had confidence in him for the future.
>
> She thought that the election had come as a grief and disappointment to many. After the cooperation of the war years they were flying at each other's throats. 'But we must not allow ourselves to be depressed, for after the election I am sure we will all work harmoniously together for the good of our country . . .'

On the eve of Polling Day, while Winston toured the South London area, she addressed no fewer than six meetings in Woodford, and on the day itself she accompanied Winston on his traditional tour of the constituency.

Winston did not relish the return to party political electioneering. It was, for him, a traumatic change of gear from being the nationally accepted leader of a united nation, working with tried and trusted colleagues regardless of party affiliations, to find himself overnight the leader of a faction, and of necessity cast in a contentious and divisive role. But although it was a very real effort to plunge once more into the maelstrom of party politics, he was a pugnacious animal, and a doughty champion of his party. As for Clementine, she had never made any secret of the fact that, in her view, Winston should, at the victorious conclusion of the war, resign from office and not seek re-election at all. Having led a Coalition Government and a united nation, she felt very strongly that he should retire rather than become the leader of one-half of the nation against the other. To this view Winston was wont to retort that he was not yet ready 'to be put on a pedestal'.[2]

Churchill launched his national campaign in his first party broadcast on 4th June. He reproached the Labour and Liberal parties for withdrawing from the Coalition, and for putting party before country, and he also delivered a forceful attack on Socialism, in which he suggested that, to bring about a Socialist order of things, the Labour Party '. . . would have to fall back on some kind of Gestapo, no doubt very humanely directed in the first place'. These words were ill-received by thousands of his listeners. Clementine, to whom he had shown the script of his broadcast, spotted this unfortunate sentence at once, and she had begged Winston to delete the odious and invidious reference to the Gestapo. But he would not heed her.

During the campaign, Clementine was once more to deplore the political influence of Lord Beaverbrook, who, both as a platform speaker and through his newspapers, did vigorous battle for Winston and the Tory Party (although, as some wit was to remark, he greatly preferred 'the jockey to the horse'). But the jocular and overbearing tone adopted by the Beaverbrook Press was out of tune with the serious mood of the electorate. Clementine sensed all this, and she was also anxious about the advice Winston received privately from Max Beaverbrook and from Brendan Bracken, both of whom had constant access to him. She thought much of their counsel was ill-judged, and their outlook rashly optimistic. Her view was shared by several of Winston's colleagues, and the Beaverbrook–Bracken influence was much commented upon in hostile criticism from the Opposition.

There is a revealing sentence in a letter my mother wrote me just before my father was to make the third of his four election broadcasts; it shows that he himself was not happy with his own performance or judgment:

Papa broadcasts tonight. He is very low, poor Darling. He thinks he has lost his 'touch' & he grieves about it.[3]

The Socialists cleverly and effectively presented two images of Winston to the public: one was 'Churchill the Great War-time Leader', who had led the nation to victory; the other was 'Churchill the Party Leader': irresponsible, out of touch with ordinary people, subject to the malign influence of Lord Beaverbrook, and not to be trusted in peacetime. The result was that thousands of people who turned out to cheer him in the streets, silently voted against him in the polling booths.

The Opinion Polls pointed a trend to the Left, but none forecast the coming landslide. The Services vote was one unknown quantity: three million men and women in the Forces were entitled to vote by post or proxy, and as they were scattered far and wide and the votes had to be gathered in, a space of twenty-one days was arranged between Polling Day and the counting of votes. It is now generally assumed that the Forces vote (which could not be represented in the Opinion Polls) was strongly Labour.

The Conservatives' early predictions of the outcome of the election were cautious, but after Winston's tour of the Midlands, the North of England and Scotland at the end of June, the Tory pundits took a more sanguine view of their prospects, and Winston's own spirits revived. His tour was a triumphal progress: in four days, he made about forty speeches and travelled over a thousand miles. Clementine was with him for most of the time and, as Winston was still directing the war against Japan, he was able to use his official train with its mobile Communications Centre. Everywhere he went he was received by dense, cheering crowds, who had often waited many hours for his cavalcade to arrive. The tour was an overwhelming personal triumph, and at its end, gruelling although it had been, Winston was re-vivified and full of hope. But Clementine, although she had rejoiced to see him so tumultuously received, had her own private doubts. She had noticed from time to time, as she sat beside him in the open car, that, four or five rows back in the crowds, there were watchful and even hostile faces.

The election campaign was now entering its last stages, and in the run-up to Polling Day Winston visited many constituencies in London. Here for the first time in the campaign he encountered active and vigorous opposition. At Walthamstow Stadium, on 3rd July, before an audience of 20,000 people, he was almost prevented from making his speech because the heckling and booing were so intense, while at Tooting Bec, on the eve of the poll, a squib was thrown at him, all but exploding in his face. However, Winston was too seasoned a campaigner to take much notice of such incidents, and most of his critics at these meetings appeared to be youths below voting age.

The fight over, there ensued the uncanny and tantalising three-week pause between Polling Day and the Declaration of the Poll. Winston and Clementine took advantage of this space to go to France for a brief holiday. Through the good offices of Bryce Nairn (the newly appointed British Consul at Bordeaux, and a friend from the days of Winston's convalescence at Marrakech in January 1944), they were offered hospitality by General Raymond Brutinel at the Château de Bordaberry, near Hendaye, a seaside resort close to the Spanish frontier. The General was an agreeable and unusual man; of Scottish–French descent, he was a naturalised Frenchman who had served in the Canadian Army; he and Winston got on famously. I had saved up my leave, and so was able to join my parents in the first holiday we had shared since just before the war. Our party also included Lord Moran, 'Tommy' Thompson and Jock Colville.

Winston at first was low and tired, but the magic of painting soon laid hold of him, absorbing him for hours on end, and banishing disturbing thoughts of either the present or the future; he also enjoyed the sea bathing enormously. Although Clementine unfortunately stubbed and cracked her toe during the course of the visit, she all the same enjoyed this much-needed respite.

Their holiday could only last a week, for grave matters awaited Winston, and he flew off from Bordeaux on Sunday, 15th July, to Potsdam, where the three allied victors were to determine the future of Europe, and much else. As always he wanted Clementine to go with him, but she was committed to report to the Women's British Soviet Committee on her journey to Russia, and she was also anxious to press on with her plans for opening up Chartwell against Winston's return; so she returned to London, confiding him to my care.

From the Conference area on the outskirts of Potsdam (an area soon earning the title 'Babelsburg') I wrote her almost daily accounts of our life there. My father had been allocated a handsome house of rose-pink stone, with a lawn sloping down to a romantic-looking lake. Of course my mother was eager to hear about his first meeting with, and impression of, President Truman, up to now a new and unknown quantity. I was able to send her a 'news-flash' on 16th July:

> This morning Papa paid his first visit to President Truman, who is installed in a monstrously ugly house about 400 yds down the road . . . Papa remained closeted for about two hours – during which time Anthony [Eden] joined them . . .
>
> When Papa at length emerged we decided to walk home. He told me he liked the President immensely – they talk the same language. He says he is sure he can work with him. I nearly wept for joy and thankfulness, it seemed like divine providence. Perhaps it is F.D.R.'s legacy. I can see Papa is relieved and confident.

The conference was due to continue beyond the date of the result of the election, and Winston had therefore invited Mr Attlee to accompany him to Potsdam, on the basis that, in the event of a change of government, there would be continuity of knowledge and thought. While grappling with all the work of the conference, there was not much time to dwell on the secret hidden in the ballot boxes; but none of us could banish the cloud of uncertainty over the future. On 17th July I reported:

> Papa is well, although experiencing tiresome bouts of indigestion every now & then. Last night he was in bed quite fairly early – nor do I think he will stay up late tonight.
>
> Isn't it agony not knowing the results of the election? & it will be awful when we do . . .

However, this mood of pessimism did not persist; Max Beaverbrook's forecasts were mainly optimistic; both Conservative and Labour quarters estimated that the Tories looked like having the lead; the Gallup Poll showed a swing to the left, but it was thought (no doubt wishfully in our circle) that this would only diminish, but not destroy, the anticipated Conservative majority. Even Stalin entered the Forecasting Stakes, and told Winston that his sources confirmed his own belief that the Conservatives would be returned by a majority of about eighty.[4]

Two nights before the British contingent were to leave for home, Winston gave a dinner party for the President and Stalin; I did what I could to help with the arrangements; and the following day I wrote an account of the evening to my mother, describing how the house had, about an hour before the party, been surrounded and laid siege to by what appeared to be half the Red Army.

> At last the guests started to arrive . . . then a fleet of cars swooped up & out skipped Uncle Joe attended by a cloud of minions . . .
>
> Uncle J. wore the most fetching white cloth mess jacket blazing with insignia. Close on his heels the President arrived, having walked from his house.[5]

I did not dine with them, but at my father's suggestion returned later to the diningroom and, from the vantage point of a stool behind his chair, witnessed the end of the dinner:

> The party appeared to be a wild success – and presently Uncle Joe leapt up and went round the room autograph hunting! The evening broke up about midnight, in a general atmosphere of whoopee and goodwill.
>
> Tomorrow I shall be home. I long to see you, darling Mummie.

We all flew back to London on Wednesday, 25th July. In the mood of confidence which now prevailed in our party, Winston and his colleagues made farewells at Gatow airport of a distinctly 'be-seeing-you-again' nature. Clementine met us at Northolt on our return, and that evening we dined en famille at the Annexe. Randolph was full of confidence, and left soon after dinner to go back to Preston for the end of the count there. Diana and Duncan, however, who came in after dinner, were gloomy about Duncan's fate in Norwood. Next morning, when I breakfasted in my mother's bedroom, as I always did when I was at home, she told me that during the night my father's own confidence had vanished – he later described it in his own words:

> . . . just before dawn I woke suddenly with a sharp stab of almost physical pain. A hitherto subconscious conviction that we were beaten broke forth and dominated my mind . . .[6]

Since he had to be at the centre of events throughout the day, Winston did not attend the count in his own constituency; Clementine went down to represent him, and took me with her. We arrived quite early, and as the count proceeded my mother spotted that Winston's somewhat 'crack-pot' opponent was amassing a considerable number of votes, which disquieted her, for although Winston was returned with a majority of over 17,000, she realised this could not bode well for the way things would go in the rest of the country. As soon as she was able to, Clementine telephoned the Private Office, and was told that early reports showed 44 Socialist gains to 1 for the Conservatives.

We were both rather silent on our drive back from Woodford, and as soon as we arrived at the Annexe we went to the Map Room, where all had been prepared to tabulate the results. On our way we met Jock Colville, looking grave. ' "It's a complete debacle," he said, "like 1906 . . ." ' [7] In the Map Room we found my father, David Margesson (former Chief Government Whip and minister) and Brendan Bracken; the results were rolling in, showing Labour gain after Labour gain. It was now one o'clock, and it was already quite clear that the Conservatives were defeated. Every minute brought news of the defeat of friends, relations and colleagues; Randolph and Duncan were both out; everyone looked dazed and grave.

> We lunched in Stygian gloom – David Margesson – Brendan (himself just defeated) – Uncle Jack . . .
> Sarah arrived looked beautiful & distressed –
> We both choked our way through lunch.
> M. maintained an inflexible morale . . .
> Papa struggled to accept this terrible blow – this unforeseen landslide . . .
> But not for one moment in this awful day did Papa flinch or waver.
> 'It is the will of the people' – robust – controlled –
> The day wore very slowly on – with more resounding defeats.
> All the Staff and all our other friends looked stunned & miserable . . . [8]

But even in these bleak hours my father's sense of irony and humour did not desert him. During the day my mother had said: 'It may be a blessing in disguise', to which my father replied: 'Well, at the moment it's certainly very well disguised.'

During the afternoon of this day, which seemed interminable, Winston sat on in the Map Room, where he had so often studied the ebb and flow of our fortunes on the seas and battlefields; now he watched the tale of resounding political defeat. Clementine had accepted the situation, and did not particularly want to watch the death throes, so, feeling she could be more useful later, she retired to rest.

The final count showed that with 393 members of the new House, the Socialists had a majority of 146 over all other parties and groups. [9] It was a tremendous victory. At seven o'clock that evening Churchill drove to Buckingham Palace to submit his resignation to the King, and to lay down the burden he had shouldered in darker times. Shortly afterwards Mr Attlee was received by the King, who invited him to form a government.

That night we were ten for dinner, all family and faithful friends. Uncle Jack, still looking thin and ill; Venetia Montagu, battered by the course of a mortal illness, but stalwart to the end; Brendan, Anthony Eden, Diana and Duncan, Sarah and myself. Dinner was a somewhat muted affair, understandably so; with everyone trying to help and say the right thing. My father still maintained his courageous spirit, and I described my mother as 'riding the storm with unflinching demeanour . . .'[10]

The next few days were, if anything, worse than that dreadful Thursday. After years of intense activity, for Winston now there was a yawning hiatus. The whole focus of power, action and news had been transferred to the new Prime Minister. The Map Room was deserted; the Private Office empty; no official telegrams; no 'red boxes'. True, letters and messages from friends and from countless members of the general public started pouring in, sweet and consoling, expressing love, indignation and loyalty. But nothing and nobody could really soften the bitter blow.

My mother, I noted in my diary on 27th July, 'for the first time looks tired & shattered'. But at least she had something to do: namely – pack up, move out, and start their new life. She did not delay, and started in on the organising with Grace Hamblin at once. The ensuing days were made more painful, too, for both Winston and Clementine by many leave-takings: the Chiefs of Staff and the Private Secretaries, who were off back to Potsdam with the new Prime Minister to take up the threads of the conference, and Winston's personal detectives. His Private Office had been more than usually close to their Chief and his family, with all the crises, and the journeyings, and week-ends 'on duty' at Chequers or elsewhere. Saying goodbye and thank-you to them was not easy.

Although they were seriously considering the house in Hyde Park Gate, no firm decision had been taken as yet, and Clementine was pushing on with the plans to make Chartwell inhabitable once more. With the advent of peace Clementine knew that Winston would yearn to move back into the big house again, instead of perching in Orchard Cottage, as had been their wont. Realising that it would be extremely difficult to get domestic help, Clementine decided not to use the ground floor and basement rooms at all, but to organise their life on the top two floors. But at this moment, the work entailed in carrying out this sensible plan had only just begun.

Winston and Clementine were therefore at this moment homeless. They wanted to get out of No. 10 and the Annexe at Storey's Gate with all possible speed, both for the convenience of the Attlees and because these places had now become hateful to them. This urgent problem was solved for them by the swift and warm-hearted gesture of Diana and Duncan, who within forty-eight hours of the election results offered to lend Winston and Clementine their lovely flat in Westminster Gardens until they found somewhere to live.

Winston had been to see 28 Hyde Park Gate in January, but it was only now that he concentrated his mind upon it; another visit impressed him with its charms and possibilities. During the last few months they had visited various other houses, but now the decision was taken in favour of No. 28, and negotiations put in hand forthwith.

Winston and Clementine spent the week-end immediately following the election at Chequers, to take leave of the staff there and to collect their things. They gathered round them for this last visit all the family, and in addition Lord Cherwell ('The

Prof'), Gil Winant, Brendan Bracken, Tommy Thompson and Jock Colville came for all or part of the week-end. It would, in other circumstances, have been a very cosy jolly party; but it was certainly quieter than usual with such a gathering of the family, and although everyone tried to be gay, we were all still rather stunned by the events of the previous week. Winston made valiant efforts to be cheerful; he played cards, and there was croquet (which he liked watching, especially admiring Clementine's expertise and strategy), and neighbours called in to say their goodbyes. After dinner there were films; Clementine quite firmly went to bed before the cinema; she was exhausted, and always found the film sessions over-long at the best of times. The hardest moments were when, after the film, Winston came downstairs; normally, then he would get all the latest news; there might even be a 'box', brought down by despatch rider with some urgent and secret communication. Now there was nothing. We saw with near desperation a cloud of black gloom descend. Tommy and Sarah and I played gramophone records for him: Gilbert and Sullivan (usually top favourites) were unavailing now, but French and American marches struck a helpful note, and finally 'Run, Rabbit, Run' and 'The Wizard of Oz' had a cheering effect. Finally, very late, he felt sleepy, and we all escorted him upstairs to bed.

On Sunday, 29th July, we sat down fifteen to dinner, and before we went to bed we all signed the Chequers Visitors Book. My Father signed last of all, and beneath his signature he wrote: 'Finis'. We know now that it was no such thing, but that is how he and my mother and all of us felt then.

*

While Clementine addressed all her energy to moving out of the Annexe and No. 10, Winston divided his time between the penthouse suite at Claridges (while Diana and Duncan made haste to move into a furnished flat) and Chartwell. Orchard Cottage was once more a haven, and our devoted Cousin Moppet took on the cooking. The gardens were a wilderness, the roses all a-tangle and the grass knee-high, but Winston roamed through them, and found them peaceful and beautiful

The night before I left to rejoin my unit, my parents took me to see a revival of Noel Coward's *Private Lives*. It was a complete contrast to the events and emotions through which we were passing; my father simply loved it, and we all roared with laughter. To our moved amazement, on his entering and leaving the theatre, the whole audience cheered and clapped, and the principal actor, John Clements, came forward and made a most charming speech. During the following days and weeks there were many such heart-warming incidents.

It was a beautiful, pearly morning on 3rd August, when my mother walked very early with me across the park to the assembly point from where I was to start my journey back to Germany, after a leave I was not likely to forget. Soon after my return to my battery we were inspected by Field Marshal Montgomery, and my first letter home described how

. . . just before he climbed back into his minute 'plane he talked to me. He was charming and kind and wanted to know how Papa was, & he asked specially about you. He really was kind & said that should you need me it could be arranged for me to be flown back. So I thanked him and said I would remember what he said in case of need.

And then he flew off.[11]

During these difficult weeks everyone they knew seemed to want to help Winston and Clementine. A warm-hearted friend, Audrey Pleydell-Bouverie, who years before, in 1931 after Winston's serious accident in New York, had lent them her house over there, once more came forward with the generous offer of her house in the country, pending Chartwell's rehabilitation. Clementine's reply illustrates her feelings at this time:

Now that again we have suffered another unexpected shock, once more you offer to take us in. It is sweet of you, dear Audrey, and I shall never forget it. But actually I think it is best to struggle into Chartwell and re-adjust our lives . . .[12]

But that it was a struggle is amply shown in the long letter my mother wrote me from Chartwell on 14th August:

My darling Mary,

Time crawls wearily along. It's impossible to realize that it is not yet three weeks since your Father was hurled from power. He is lion-hearted about it . . .

We have settled into Westminster Gardens & I shall never forget Duncan & Diana's prompt & generous action in lending it to us. Now Nana & I are struggling to get the flat down here ready. Our 'married couple' on whom we pin great hopes arrive tomorrow, & all yesterday Nana, Miss Hamblin & me scrubbed and polished their rooms – they are still not ready. But I must be truthful & say that I was not allowed to scrub & polish as it seems I am too old & inefficient – I merely heaved furniture about which you know is one of my favourite hobbies – And I opened hampers stuffed full of old curtains, rejoicing when I found some long-lost treasure & despairing when I discovered that mice (I repeat mice) have nibbled holes in some lovely old rose damask covers & made nests everywhere. As for the moth!!!

'Lay not up for yourselves treasures upon this earth . . .'.

But these are not treasures but necessities becos you can't buy 'nothink' [clothing and household fabrics were still rationed] . . .

I hope I shall be able to organise a comfortable & happy home for Papa; but the truth is that it is silly to have two homes just now (London & Country) because of the rations which get all eaten up in one place & becos' of servants – Rich people now-a-days have a small house in the country & when in London have permanent rooms in an hotel . . . I blush to think that I who organised the Russian Fund, the kitchen in Fulmer Maternity Hospital & who complained about the organisation of the Y.W.C.A. am stumped by my own private life. But I think I shall learn to do it. The difficulty is that Papa is unpredictable in his movements & altho' I'm used to that, I still find that very tiring to cope with . . . Nana has been cooking for us & has been sweet to Papa, who feels her kindness very much just now.

'Now mind during these last months to keep your conduct & morale as high as it has been during the whole war,' says your old Mother who is dropping to pieces herself!

Your devoted Mummie

Please, [I begged in my reply] on *no* account push/heave or lift grand pianos, thereby straining yourself. I am appalled by your account of the moth/mouse Fifth Column activities. It's too much to think humans have been rationed, while they have gorged themselves on our curtains . . .[13]

But, if Clementine opened her heart to me about her domestic trials, she was well aware that many thousands of people were facing greater difficulties in finding homes and adjusting their lives, and only those close to her knew of her harrassments. Both she and Winston were too dignified and too proud to present anything other than a stoical and urbane aspect to the curious, albeit sympathetic, eyes of the world at large.

*

Winston did not lurk long licking his wounds; when Parliament reassembled on 1st August, less than a week after the election results, he took his new place on the Opposition front bench. The Conservatives started singing 'For he's a jolly good fellow' as he walked to his place; the mass of the Socialist members rejoined by singing the 'Red Flag', which was on the whole thought to be ungracious, considering the magnitude of their victory. But not all parliamentary exchanges were to be on this level; Japan surrendered unconditionally on 14th August 1945, and two days later Mr Attlee, the new Prime Minister, paid a generous tribute to Churchill's leadership in the House of Commons:

. . . In the darkest and most dangerous hour of our history this nation found in my Right Honourable friend the man who expressed supremely the courage and determination never to yield which animated all the men and women of this country. In undying phrases he crystallized the unspoken feeling of all . . . His place in history is secure.[14]

Winston also spoke in the same debate, and on 18th August my mother wrote to me from Westminster Gardens:

Papa made a brilliant moving gallant speech on the opening of Parliament. He was right back in his 1940–41 calibre. The new house full of rather awe-struck shy nervous members was rivetted & fascinated – On V.J. Day many people gathered round this block of flats to see Papa & cheer him & he got mobbed in Whitehall by a frenzied crowd. These friendly manifestations have reassured & comforted him a little. He says all he misses is the Work & being able to give orders.

The crowds shout 'Churchill for ever' & 'We want Churchill'. But all the King's horses & all the King's men can't put Humpty Dumpty together again . . .

This letter, with its trace of bitterness, was followed on 26th August by a sad and despondent one written from Chartwell. After saying she had got a letter from me, and commenting on various aspects of my army news, my mother continued:

But what really excited & relieved me was that you say you [my regiment] may soon be disbanded & that you will apply for a post in England. Now my Darling please ask for a job at the War Office, so that you can live at home in your lovely bed-sitting room at Hyde Park Gate. Because I am very unhappy & need your help with Papa.

I cannot explain how it is but in our misery we seem, instead of clinging to each other to be always having scenes. I'm sure it's all my fault, but I'm finding life more than I can bear. He is so unhappy & that makes him very difficult. He hates his food, (hardly any meat) has taken it into his head that Nana tries to thwart him at every turn. He wants to have land girls & chickens & cows here & she thinks it won't work & of course she *is* gruff & bearish. But look what she does for us. I can't see any future. But Papa is going to Italy & then perhaps Nana & I can get this place straight. It looks impossible & one doesn't know where to start . . .

Then in a few days we shan't have a car. We are being lent one now. We are learning how rough & stony the World is.

I was much disturbed by this letter, for I realised that the adjustment from the wartime tension and tempo of their life was bound to be painful and difficult for both of them. For although they had lived for over five years on an exhaustingly heroic level, they had not suffered the physical shortages and domestic difficulties which had been the lot of ordinary people. Because they had to entertain so many people officially, they received 'Diplomatic Rations'; Chequers was staffed by the Women's Services, and civilian staff had been available for London; cars and petrol were always at hand. Now, of course, all these comforts and facilities disappeared. I understood how, in their emotionally and physically exhausted state, the combination of petty problems with the hurt and bewilderment of Winston's political downfall could produce tensions and flare-ups between them. Although I did not want to leave my unit before the regiment was actually disbanded, I felt a new priority had appeared and that, in the circumstances, I could ask for a home-posting. A short time later, on 31st August 1945, I was able to write with some good news:

My darling Mummie,

I was so grieved to read in your letter, which arrived yesterday, of all your worries and desolations. I feel for you and Papa more deeply than I can say; and I know only too well, how much of the burden weighs on you.

I asked at once for an interview with the 'Queen AT' over here, and today I drove down to Headquarters . . . (we are about 120 miles away from them) and saw her . . . and explained everything. She was kind and very helpful. A posting to England (London) is going to be arranged for me. So darling Mummie, I hope so much to be with you perhaps within a month . . .

True to their word, the Army authorities arranged for me to be posted as an Administrative Officer to a War Office Holding Unit in London, in Radnor Place. I did not live at home, but as my parents' new house was just the other side of Hyde Park from my billet, even a few hours off meant I could visit them easily and often.

On 7th September, just before I left my unit in Germany, my mother had written

me a much more buoyant letter which also contained some sagely maternal
advice:

> Tomorrow week you will be twenty-three, a perfect age, & a perfect springboard
> from which to leap into married life! But I hope you won't think of it for a year
> after you get home! because I am sure it will take you a little while to adjust
> yourself to civilian life after being a soldier for so long. (I'm finding it damned
> hard to adjust myself!)

Meanwhile, in early September, Winston went to Italy for a holiday, where he
stayed in a house on the shores of Lake Como lent to him by Field Marshal Alexander. It would have done Clementine good too, for she was exhausted, and of course
Winston wanted her to go with him. But with all she had to do at Chartwell, and
with the new London house to be arranged, she preferred to stay at home. Also, it
is quite clear from her letters to me and to Sarah that she was in a tense and unhappy state, and one has to be in the right mood, even to enjoy blue skies and sunshine. 'Cast care aside,' Winston was wont to say when Clementine was wrought up,
but with her nature, that was easier said than done. Fortunately, Sarah was able to
get leave to accompany him, and Lord Moran went too. The thoughtful Field
Marshal assigned two young officers from Winston's old regiment, Major John
Ogier and Lieutenant Tim Rogers, to look after Winston and to see that all went well
with the arrangements. Not only did they do that, but they also proved to be delightful and cheering companions – brave and young and full of fun – they appealed to
Winston in every way. The day after his arrival, 3rd September, Winston wrote to
Clementine:

> This is really one of the most pleasant and delectable places I have ever struck. It
> is a small palace almost entirely constructed of marble inside. It abuts on the lake,
> with bathing steps reached by a lift . . . Every conceivable arrangement has been
> made for our pleasure and convenience.
>   . . . Yesterday we motored over the mountains to Lake Lugano, where I found
> quite a good subject for a picture . . . I have spotted another place for this after-
> noon . . . These lakeshore subjects run a great risk of degenerating into 'choco-
> late box', even if successfully executed.

The letter was dictated, but at the end he added in his own writing:

> I have been thinking a lot about you. I do hope you will not let the work of
> moving into these 2 houses wear you down. Please take plenty of rest. With fondest
> love,
>
>   Your devoted husband,
>   W
>   [There is a little pig at the bottom of the letter]

The same day Sarah wrote a most understanding letter to her mother:

> . . . I wish you were here with us. I was so distressed to see you so unhappy and
> tired when we left, and so was he. We never see a lovely sight that he doesn't say

'I wish your mother were here'. Wow! You know, I expect you will feel a little low and tired and oppressed by the million domesticities that will now sink down upon you, for a bit. Six years is a long time to live at such a high tempo, knowing as fully as you did all the moments of anxiety and worry, and decisions. You are bound to feel a reaction – as he does, and will for some time.

Sarah then went on to give a lively and vivid description of their surroundings and daily activities:

. . . I really think he is settling down – he said last night – 'I've had a happy day'! I haven't heard that for I don't know how long!

In a P.S. Sarah added:

He really is distressed about you – wow – He has just prowled round my room, and tried to read my letter! He says I'm to say – he's good. He really is!

On 5th September, Winston wrote to Clementine:

We have had three lovely sunshine days, and I have two large canvasses under way, one of a scene on the Lake of Lugano and the other here at Como. The design is I think good in both cases, and it has been great fun painting them . . .

Alex arrives tomorrow, and I am looking forward very much to seeing him. I cannot say too much for the care and authority which he has bestowed on making my visit pleasant . . .

It has done me no end of good to come out here and resume my painting. I am much better in myself, and am not worrying about anything. We have had no newspapers since I left England, and I no longer feel any keen desire to turn their pages. This is the first time for very many years that I have been completely out of the world. The Japanese War being finished and complete peace and victory achieved, I feel a great sense of relief which grows steadily, others having to face the hideous problems of the aftermath. On their shoulders and consciences weighs the responsibility for what is happening in Germany and Central Europe. It may all indeed be 'a blessing in disguise'.

But although these were soothing, sunlit days, Winston continued to miss Clementine, and that she was often in his thoughts is borne out in a long epilogue, in his own hand, to one of his letters:

My darling, I think a great deal of you & last night when I was driving the speed-boat back there came into my mind your singing to me 'In the gloaming' years ago. What a sweet song & tune & how beautifully you sung it in all its pathos. My heart thrilled in love to feel you near me in thought. I feel so tenderly towards you my darling & the more pleasant & agreeable the scenes & days, the more I wish you were here to share them & give me a kiss.

You see I have not forgotten how to write with a pen. Isn't it awful my scribbles?[15]

The original plan was that the whole party should return about the 20th September, but Winston was so relaxed, and so beguiled by sunshine days, that he decided to drive along the Riviera to Monte Carlo, and spend a little time in that part of France where he had spent so many happy pre-war holidays. Sarah had to return to her unit, and Lord Moran to his other patients, so with his two ADCs, now the firmest of friends, his valet Sawyers, and his detective Sergeant Davies, he set off. He told Clementine of his intentions in a letter on 18th September:

> I hope you will not mind my change of plans. The weather has been so good and the prospects seem so favourable that the opportunity of having another four or five days in the sunshine was too tempting to miss . . .
>
> I really have enjoyed these 18 days enormously. I have been completely absorbed by the painting, and have thrown myself into it till I was quite tired. I have therefore not had time to fret or worry, and it has been good to view things from a distance. I think you will be pleased with the series of pictures . . . which I have painted. I am sending them home by Sarah, who will give you all our news . . .
>
> Sarah has been a joy. She is so thoughtful, tactful, amusing and gay. The stay here wd have been wrecked without her.

When Winston and his party arrived at Monte Carlo, they stayed at the Hôtel de Paris for a day or two, until Ike (General Eisenhower) most hospitably pressed them all to go and stay in his own villa at Cap d'Antibes, although he himself was not there. Winston hoped that he could prevail on Clementine to join him during this last lap of his holiday; Alex's plane would have wafted her to him, but she preferred to wait for him at home. As always, when he could not persuade her, Winston was a little rueful: 'Naturally I am vy sorry you cd not come out by Alex's plane,' he wrote (in his own hand) from Eisenhower's villa, on 24th September. 'It would have done you good to bask in this mellow sunshine for a space . . .' On the same day Winston also dictated a long letter to her, full of his painting expeditions, plans for his return, and (having read a whole batch of English newspapers) his comments on world and home events. He ended this last 'holiday' letter:

> There will be no lack of topics to discuss when we all come together again. Meanwhile, this rest and change of interest is doing me no end of good and I never sleep now in the middle of the day. Even when the nights are no longer than 5, 6 or 7 hours, I do not seem to require it. This shows more than anything else what a load has been lifted off my shoulders.

While Winston was away, Clementine had been able to get to grips with the alterations and rearrangements necessary to make Chartwell a viable proposition. Fortunately, little was needed to be done at Hyde Park Gate, other than some redecoration. In the immediate post-war period there were shortages of everything, and with so many houses to be repaired as a result of bomb damage, and the requirements of the new house-building programme, materials and labour were both scarce and restricted. However, when Winston arrived back early in October, Clementine had just managed the move in time to welcome and install him there.

Gradually the new arrangements at Chartwell took shape. The large kitchen, scullery and pantry in the basement were abandoned for ever as such, and much smaller and labour-saving kitchen arrangements were organised in a former staff bedroom on the top floor, with a service-lift to the floor below, where the 'Best' Visitors' room took over as the dining-room. Clementine's beautiful azure-coloured bedroom with the 'barrel' ceiling made a lovely sitting-room, with views over the gardens and lakes. Clementine herself ascended to the top floor, and made her bedroom in the Tower Room, which was a charming self-contained suite. Winston's study-bedroom remained unchanged, and the large drawing-room on the ground floor made a most handsome studio. The 'Office' on the ground floor remained as such, and the secretaries (still two of them) lived in Orchard Cottage. In 1946 Sir Alexander Korda gave Winston the most modern film projector and screen, and the old dining-room was turned into a cinema. This rearrangement of Chartwell lasted for several years, and made it possible for Winston and Clementine to live there despite all the difficulties of the post-war years.

In 1946, a group of Winston's friends, who chose to remain anonymous, bought Chartwell from him, and presented it to the National Trust, with the proviso that Winston and Clementine could live there for their lifetime. This generous and far-sighted act meant that not only could Winston enjoy without care his beloved Chartwell to nearly the end of his days, but that this house and grounds, with all their memories and links with him and the years so fateful for our country, would be forever part of Britain's heritage.

Clementine crowned this gift, after Winston's death, by giving to the house, in perpetuity, not only a large number of his pictures, but also the greater part of the furniture which had always been there.

The gardens, fields and woods at Chartwell were, of course, in a shaggy and neglected state after the war years. But gradually their condition was restored. Clementine had to fight some brisk battles with Winston, who, as in years gone by, would distract the gardeners from their proper work by taking them off to help with tree-felling, brushwood clearance or wall and fence repairing, to all of which activities he attached a high priority and the organising and supervising of which afforded him hours of carefree pleasure. Clementine, however, attached much more importance to velvet lawns, and the re-making of the flower garden, and the production of vegetables. Winston therefore acquired his own personal 'work-force', which consisted of a part-time old-age pensioner (Kurn, who in days gone by had helped him with his bricklaying), and another less venerable helper. A little later two German prisoners-of-war came to work full time. This team did valuable works of reclamation, excavation and reconstruction, and the garden staff were left to their province, much to Clementine's and the Head Gardener's relief.

Their pre-war attempts to farm on a small scale had, it will be remembered, not been a signal success, and Clementine dreaded starting once more on schemes similar to those which had been such a constant source of vexation and expense in the past. Winston, however, was determined to live in a pastoral and patriarchal way, and of course it was highly advantageous to produce one's own food in the bleak years of rationing, which were to be prolonged for several years after the end of the war. Max Beaverbrook started them off on their post-war 'smallholding' economy by sending them as a present a flock of hens. They arrived while Winston was away in Italy, and Clementine wrote gratefully and enthusiastically to Max about his handsome present on 14th September 1945:

> My dear Max,
>   I must tell you about your lovely hens & their companion, that glorious cock. They are the admiration of all beholders – they are looked after by my cousin Marryot Whyte [Cousin Moppet] who is thrilled by them. They are laying, not very freely yet, but the numbers of eggs are increasing & they have a most delicate flavour . . .

Clementine gradually warmed to the idea of 'home-producing', and the old beehives (occupied by unsupervised and sleepy bees) were galvanised into renewed life, and increased output. There was an exciting development when the Royal Jersey Agricultural Society presented Winston with a beautiful Jersey cow, called May Belle of the Isles, which arrived at Chartwell in the autumn of 1946. To wait upon May Belle (and a companion cow which joined her later) the services of a land-girl were procured, and Chartwell truly became a land flowing with milk, honey and eggs.

Although the alterations at Chartwell, the outside operations and the advent of livestock, caused Clementine some worry, she was not further harassed by anxieties as to the financial consequences of these undertakings. For now, for the first time in their lives, Winston was rich. He had always kept his family by his pen, and now, in the years he was to be in opposition, he would write six volumes of *War Memoirs*. And his writings, both past and present, now commanded sums far exceeding anything they could have dreamed of in times past. Chartwell would always have its problems, but it was never again to be the monster worry of former times. In 1946, the farm adjoining Chartwell, but lower down the valley, came up for sale; Winston bought it, with its herd of Shorthorn cows. Farms and farming were wise investments just then, but these activities also suited Winston's inclinations. In the following year he also bought a market garden at French Street, near Westerham, and another neighbouring farm, Bardogs, at Toy's Hill. Presently, at Bardogs, he established a Jersey herd, and later Landrace pigs. In all he farmed about 500 acres.

Winston now had, if not a veritable kingdom, at least a principality, the governing and welfare of which were a constant interest and pleasure to him. The Grand Tour by Land-Rover, accompanied by family and guests, became a regular feature of Chartwell life. When he was away he liked to have detailed reports about everything, and he, in turn, kept Clementine posted in her absence. A typical Chartwell 'bulletin' from one of his letters to her reads:

> The harvest is proceeding with tremendous vigour and in perfect weather. Most of the fields are already cut and stooked and some have been put up on tripods . . . The lettuces in the walled garden were sold for £200, though they cost only £50 to grow . . . The hot-houses are dripping with long cucumbers. The grapes are turning black and a continuous stream of peaches and nectarines go to London. I have one a day myself – 'le droit du seigneur'.[16]

But for Winston, all these new acquisitions and interests were, of course, only pleasurable sidelines. As he took up the challenge as Leader of the Opposition, politics involved him as much as ever. Soon the writing of his Memoirs also occupied many hours, and, 'in the holidays', travelling and painting were captivating. Although the strains and exertions of the war years had undoubtedly left their mark, yet Winston revived astonishingly rapidly from his immediate post-war fatigue; and as he became more and more engrossed in his new, and former occupations, he ceased to brood at any length on the hurt and humiliation of his political overthrow.

But it took Clementine much longer to 'get her wind', both physically and mentally. The problems with which she had to grapple were essentially dreary as well as difficult, and she had not got the outlet that Winston's many 'toys' gave him. Although she acquiesced in the developments at Chartwell, she derived more worry than pleasure from them. Moreover, she was not really reconciled to the fact that Winston was determined to battle on in politics. She had longed, and she still longed, for him to retire. All her life her energy had been in excess of her stamina, but like many others, during the crisis years, Clementine had 'kept going': now accumulated exhaustion was catching up on her. Throughout the autumn and winter of 1945 her health was only middling, and she suffered from depression and nervousness. The build-up of her worries, which her fatigue served to enlarge, made her often impatient and irascible with Winston; and he, for his part, could be demanding and unrealistic. These months saw a series of scenes between them. After any quarrel both suffered pangs of remorse, and both were always anxious to make it all up. But these were difficult days for them both.

One unexpected problem arose when Clementine realised that 28 Hyde Park Gate, while being a delightful house for private life, was inadequate when it came to providing the necessary office room to accommodate a secretariat. Subconsciously, I suppose, when she was house-hunting, she had had in her mind a home for an old, retired couple, happily and honourably released from long years of active service: the real facts were different. The public part of both their lives seemed scarcely abated. Hardly a potentate or distinguished visitor came to London without wishing to call, or to leave some delicate offering; old wartime comrades and colleagues were faithful, and there was the constant come-and-go of active political life. The amount of 'general public' mail was still amazing; it used to grow to flood proportions at Winston's birthdays, when extra staff had to be enlisted. And if the press gave out that he had a cough or cold (let alone a real malady), kind letters advising (and often accompanied by) remedies would pour in. And in addition to all this was Winston's literary work. Consequently four full-time private secretaries were needed – three for Winston's work, and one for Clementine's – and this secretariat required considerable room-space.

Clementine had always visualised the necessity for an office, but the room in No. 28 which she had in mind was not at all adequate to the actual situation and took up a much-needed extra sitting-room. She felt desperate, and at a loss to know how to solve this knotty and urgent problem. Fortunately, at the crucial moment the next-door house came on the market; for a while Clementine hesitated, as it seemed to her a monstrously extravagant way to acquire more office space – to buy a complete house with a garden! However, it really was the only solution, and No. 27 was duly bought. And eventually Clementine's Scottish prudence was appeased when it was found possible to create a charming maisonette on the top two floors, which was let.

Now that the war was over, many people wished to express their gratitude and admiration to Winston; here, in Great Britain, towns and cities proffered him their highest honour – the freedom of their boroughs. Foreign countries, and particularly those which had suffered enemy occupation, sent pressing invitations to him to visit them. France had received Winston and Clementine officially in November 1944, only a short time after the liberation of Paris; now, in the winter of 1945, the Regent of Belgium and his Government invited them both to Brussels. Sadly, when the time came, Clementine did not feel up to going, and so to me fell the chance to see my father received with overwhelming love and enthusiasm in Brussels and Antwerp, and given many honours at the hands of the Belgian Government and people.

A few weeks before the Belgian visit, on 20th October 1945, Clementine, however, had shared in an honour which was accorded to them both, when they received together the Freedom of the Borough of Wanstead and Woodford. That she was made a Freeman in her own right was a true and graceful tribute to the part Clementine had played in the affairs of Winston's constituency, and the place she had won in their affections in the twenty-odd years Winston had represented them in Parliament. In her brief speech she said:

My dear Friends,
I feel this to be a significant and most honourable day in my life. It has been my privilege often to visit you when my Husband would have wished to come but has been prevented by the fact that his duties have been, not only to his own constituency, but to the whole country. On these occasions you have always been very kind to me and never allowed me to feel I was a mere substitute.

When we first came to you in 1924, we had been through rough political waters, and I remember that, at the first meeting of women I attended, in replying to a very kind welcome, I said I hoped we would be with you 'for keeps'. It has turned out to be so, and when the tale is told it will be seen that our association with you is woven into the pattern of our lives in rich and happy colours.

But although this was for her a gratifying and happy day, and although she looked beautiful and smiling – yet, on this occasion, as on many others, her appearance belied her true state. Her morale at this moment was very low, and I must have been particularly worried about it, for on the day after their sunshine day of cheers and prizes I wrote my mother a long letter:

My dearly beloved Mummie,
I felt I had to write to tell you how much my thoughts are with you. I hate to see you so hedged round with so many tedious vexations – and I grieve that you feel so low and exhausted in spirit . . .
It is difficult to put down on paper all I want to say. But I do understand that these days for you are not smiling ones. That in addition to the depressing scenes

around and before us all, you have many sadnesses and disappointments and mortifications which are made harder to bear by physical fatigue.

You spoke yesterday in your lovely speech about 'the pattern of our life'. Turn your eyes from the intricate, tiring, vexing piece you have got to now, and rest them by dwelling on all you have accomplished already. I gaze at it with so much love and admiration.

It seems to me such a triumph that after so many events – which have all of them left their marks on your own private life and experience you and Papa should have come through still loving each other and still together.

To me – it is one of the most wonderful and admirable rocks to which I cling amid the daily evidences of ship-wrecked marriages – & so many of them not even ship-wrecked – but just deserted.

For despite all his difficultness – his overbearing – exhausting temperament – he *does* love you and *needs* you so much.

I know you often feel you would gladly exchange the splendours and miseries of a meteor's train for the quieter more banal happiness of being married to an ordinary man . .

But one of the ingredients of your long life with Papa is the equality of your temperaments. You are both 'noble beasts'.

Your triumph is that you really have been and are – everything to Papa. Many, many great men have had wives who ran their houses beautifully and lavished care and attention on them – But they looked for love and amusement and repose elsewhere. And vice versa. You have supplied him with all these things – without surrendering your own soul or mind . . .[17]

So as not to tax any further her nerves and energy, Clementine wisely took her doctor's advice, and severely restricted the number of engagements or obligations she accepted for some time. And her spirits revived, as slowly but surely, her domestic life assumed organised shape. No. 27 took the strain off No. 28, and the new arrangements at Chartwell were finally completed during November.

This year saw the first of Winston's peace-time birthday parties, one of many such for us all, glowing and glorious occasions. And in order to gather as many of the family together as possible, Winston and Clementine decided to spend Christmas in London. It was quietish, but very pleasant, with Diana and Duncan, Sarah, myself, Uncle Jack and Aunt Nellie, all mustered. It made a quiet and peaceful ending to a year that had seen such cataclysmic events for the world, and had been full of drama in our own personal lives as well.

SWORDS INTO PLOUGHSHARES

WINSTON AND CLEMENTINE spent most of the first three months of 1946 in the United States. Lord Moran had told Winston that it would be wise for him to be out of Britain during the bleakest months, and that a long rest would do him nothing but good. With 'resting', Winston combined a number of public and private engagements. He was officially received in Cuba; he conferred in Washington with President Truman; he addressed the State Legislature in Richmond, Virginia; he received honorary degrees from the universities of Miami and Columbia. He made a detour to visit Hyde Park, the family home of President Roosevelt, where he laid a wreath on the grave of his old friend and comrade. In New York he was accorded a civic welcome and the city's Gold Medal, and was received by cheering crowds and ticker tape.

But the most important event of his transatlantic visit was at Westminster College, Fulton, Missouri, on 5th March 1946 when, at the invitation of President Truman, and in his presence, Winston made a speech which has since assumed historical importance. In the course of his address he coined a phrase that has passed into the bleak phraseology of the political history of our time, when he referred to the 'iron curtain' which had descended 'from Stettin in the Baltic to Trieste in the Adriatic', behind which now lay 'all the capitals of the ancient states of Central and Eastern Europe . . .' As with his warnings between the wars, this realistic, forward-looking speech was received with much disapproval in some quarters, and he was considerably scolded for pointing out the fact that Soviet Russia was successfully establishing an iron grip on all the countries within its orbit.

On nearly all these varied occasions Winston was accompanied by Clementine; and Sarah, who had been demobilised from the W.A.A.F. shortly before Christmas, flew out to join them at Miami. Apart from these numerous visits and functions, they also had several weeks of sea and sunshine, staying with Colonel Frank Clarke (their Canadian friend from the First Quebec Conference days) at his house at Miami Beach. From there on 18th January 1946 my mother wrote to me:

We arrived here 48 hours ago in tropical heat, rather much but delicious – And lo & behold in the same night it changed & we are shivering among rustling palm trees & grey skies . . . Papa has not yet settled down to painting, and is a little sad and restless, poor darling. I hope he is going to begin writing something.

Later in the day. The weather has slightly improved and Papa has now started a picture of palms reflecting in the water. I visited him, and draped a knitted Afghan round his shoulders as he was sitting under a gloomy pine tree in a particularly chilly spot . . .

Very likely as a result of sitting and painting in the shade, Winston caught a slight chill, which caused everyone some anxiety – the fear of pneumonia always lurked in the background – but happily this was only a passing indisposition, and on 22nd January my mother wrote again:

Papa, thank God, has recovered or nearly so. We had a wretched 36 hours when we telephoned to Lord Moran & the temperature, tho' not very high simply would not go down & poor Papa was very nervous about himself, & yet very obstinate & would either take no remedies at all or several conflicting ones at the same time.

But today he bathed! & loved it. The weather is now perfect but tropical. Crickets chirp all night – there are lovely flowering hedges of hibiscus pink lemon & apricot . . . The sea is heavenly – water about 70° . . .

Papa has learnt a new card game 'Gin Rummy' & plays all day & all night in bed & out of bed. He has started 2 not very good pictures.

Tender love (I must fly Papa is calling)
from your devoted
Mummie

That letter made all of us at home feel much relieved. The family security service had been efficient, and this health scare went unobserved by the Press.

From my unit in Radnor Place I was able to keep an eye on the home fronts, and in a series of long gossipy letters to my parents I kept them in touch. At Chartwell things were going ahead despite hard winter weather. On 23rd January I reported: '. . . the German prisoners are hard at work. Great wood chopping operations . . . the wood shed is three-quarters full . . .' At No. 28 the secretaries and staff had all been laid low with influenza, but were recovering:

I miss you and Papa so much; I often go home – but the little Victory House seems very deserted and solitary . . .[1]

Just before they were due to return home I had some personally exciting news which I related to my mother on 12th March:

I'm longing to see you all again – and joy oh joy – your birthday and my demob: will *both* be on April the First! I feel quite light headed with the dual excitements of your return and my 'liberation'.

The *Queen Mary* docked on the evening of 26th March, and I went to Southampton to greet them. And I was not the only one – in my diary I recorded that

Right through S'hampton & way out into the suburbs there were groups of people waiting to welcome Papa home. And there was a little crowd waiting in the chilly darkness round the door of No. 28.

April 1st, this year of 1946, was, as I had written to my mother, rather 'special' for us both. I went through the official process of demobilisation in the morning, and later drove home to Chartwell with Sarah and Mrs Landemare, bearing my mother's birthday cake.

> Arrived at Chartwell we fêted Mummie and she seemed pleased with our presents.
> The 'flat' is looking lovely, and it was full of flowers – branches of forsythia and pots of magnolia stellata . . .[2]

We were a small, but loving company: my parents, Sarah, Nana and myself. After dinner, when we all 'drank her health & ate her cake',[3] the family fell to playing 'Oklahoma' – another new card game of the moment.

Now that I was an ex-servicewoman, I turned my mind and energies to civilised and civilian pleasures and occupations; first among them being the task of trying to catch up on a raggedly finished education. During this spring and summer my mother and I went together to many galleries, museums and exhibitions. At the week-ends we nearly always headed for Chartwell. Life there was beginning to pick up in an enjoyable way: the alterations for living which had been made were proving a great success, and consequently Clementine could take pleasure in being there. The tennis court had been rehabilitated, and her interest in the garden was reviving.

During these next few years, honours and distinctions were showered on Winston, and there were many moving and heart-warming occasions when countries, cities and official bodies expressed their affection and gratitude for all he had done and for all he stood for. On many of these gala occasions Clementine went with him, and almost invariably she came in for an 'honourable mention'; it was clear that her role in his life, and her wartime activities, were recognised by everyone. But she also was the recipient of several outstanding honours individually, and in her own right. This was gratifying to her, and made Winston beam: 'A little bit of sugar for the bird', he would say with pleasure and pride. The first, and the greatest, was heralded by a letter from the Prime Minister, Mr Attlee, marked 'Confidential', and dated 20th May 1946.

> My dear Mrs Churchill,
> I feel very sincerely that it would not be fitting if the Victory Honours Lists, of which the forthcoming List is the last, did not include your name. I hope, therefore, that you will allow me to submit your name to His Majesty for appointment as a Dame Grand Cross of the Order of the British Empire in recognition, not only of your work for the Aid to Russia Fund, and for the promotion of Anglo-Russian understanding, but also of those other many services which made so marked and brave a contribution during the years of the war. I hope this will be agreeable to you, for I am sure it would be an Honour which would be widely acclaimed.
>
> > Yours sincerely,
> > C. R. Attlee

It could not have been more gracefully or more handsomely put; it touched

Clementine very much, and in writing to thank Mr Attlee for his proposal to submit her name for this honour, she added:

I also thank you for the terms of your letter and it makes me happy that you feel that I was able to help a little in these last terrific years when we all fought together in heart and mind.

Her name duly appeared in the Birthday Honours List on 13th June 1946, and she received her decoration at the hands of King George VI at an Investiture in July, proudly watched by Sarah and myself.

During this same summer, two universities offered her honorary degrees: Glasgow and Oxford. In presenting her to the Principal of Glasgow University on 19th June 1946, for a degree of Doctor of Laws (*honoris causa*), the Professor of Scottish History, touching on the great services performed by women in the war, said the university wanted to honour her 'not only as a symbol of the great debt which we owe to our women, but also and chiefly, for her own great merits'. He then went on to refer to her work for the Aid to Russia Fund, and finally to her role as a wife:

There are times when the fate of the world seems to depend on the life of one man. Such a time we have known. And we can but remember with gratitude what it meant to Mr Churchill that there stood beside him in the evil days one who added womanly grace and womanly wisdom, a power to achieve, a faith to persevere, and a full measure of the courage which, as we like to think, reflects the ancient valour of a Scottish ancestry.

In her reply, Clementine took this opportunity to speak of her thoughts and feelings on Anglo-Russian relations at the present time:

Of my journey to Russia I would here say just one thing. During that to me ever-memorable visit I learned how different an event seems when you view it from Moscow instead of in London or Washington . . .

I mention this because now that there are widening rifts and cooling estrangements and dark suspicions we must sometimes try to transport ourselves in thought across the crashed continent of Europe and imagine what a Russian would feel, isolated after the 1917 Revolution for twenty-five years; then drawn into partnership by terrible necessity and, now that the Nazi monster is laid low, reverting to his loneliness. But *we* do not want to be cut off from one-sixth of the human race, and however queerly the Kremlin may behave, I am sure the Russian people – if we could only get into human touch with them – want to be friends. The life-line which the British Red Cross threw to the Soviet Red Cross in 1941 still holds fast. If it is to be severed, the fault must not lie with us.

Finally, Sir, you have mentioned me as the wife of my husband. This is really the reason why I am here among you. But if, as in your courtesy, you say I have contributed to any of his achievements, any faith to persevere, or any of his courage – then I am proud and glad, and deeply moved by your appreciation and the honour you do me today.

At Oxford, where later in the summer of 1946 Clementine was made a Doctor of Civil Law at the first Encaenia there since the end of the war, Winston (who had himself received an honorary degree from the University many years before) walked in the procession headed by the Chancellor of the University, Lord Halifax, and witnessed the conferment of her degree. He heard the Public Orator, who had praised her war work, end his oration (which was all in Latin) by reminding himself, and the assembled company, that their Honorary Graduand was married –

... And how great a man her husband is! But I'm not concerned with him now as the Pilot of our Empire's destinies, or as the 'Father of his Country' (*pater Patriae*). I'm concerned with him as the man about the house ... he's a perfect volcano, scattering cigar-ash all over the house (... *totas aedes Coronarum favillis conspergi*)!

I present to you the very Soul of Persuasion, Guardian Angel of our country's guardian, Mrs Clementine Churchill ... Let her assume the same silks as her husband and take her customary place – at his side.

Between 1944 and 1951, Winston was received officially in their capital cities by the Heads of States and Governments of seven European countries: France, Belgium, Holland, Luxembourg, Switzerland, Norway and Denmark. Great and famous cities also welcomed him – among them Antwerp, Rotterdam, Metz, Strasbourg and Nancy, Geneva and Zürich. On many of these occasions Clementine was with him, and shared in his triumph. Each country or city bestowed on Winston their highest honours and presented them with beautiful presents. But above all gifts and honours was the tribute paid by the great, cheering crowds of ordinary people, who greeted him wherever he went in all these places – crowds that stood for hours, often in the cold and wet, to acclaim the man, and the country and cause, which he had come to embody. These scenes have left an indelible memory in the minds of any of us, his family, who were with him on any of these occasions. Although Winston Churchill had suffered electoral defeat in his own homeland, yet he was beloved and admired there, but none of us had realised all he had signified and, in the occupied countries above all, how much his voice alone had meant – to thousands of human beings. In the cold and dangerous darkness of their imprisonment, his words had been like a beacon of hope.

*

On 20th November 1947 Princess Elizabeth married Lieutenant Philip Mountbatten R.N., newly created H.R.H. the Duke of Edinburgh. Winston and Clementine were invited to the ceremony in Westminster Abbey, and to other functions arranged around the wedding. In a letter Clementine wrote to Horatia Seymour, who was spending that winter in South Africa, we have a sparkling account of this event which shook us all out of the doldrums of post-war dreariness:

... we are now entering the long tunnel of Winter & it's too soon to see the gleam of spring at the end of it.

Still we have had the Royal Wedding which lifted our hearts & our feet off the ground. It really seems too good to be true – but true it is which is a shining miracle – The Ceremony itself was beautiful; and we went to an Evening Party at Buckingham Palace which was really gay & brilliant – The beauty of the Queens is like a fairy story. Our Queen's dazzling & magnetic charm the Queen of Denmark as beautiful as Princess Patricia in her youth and with a gentle, thoughtful & intelligent face – & the Queen of the Hellenes lovely gay & sprightly like a tortoiseshell kitten. Then they were most beautifully dressed, our Queen & the Greek Queen shimmering gleaming & sparkling, the Queen of Denmark in pale lacey [sic] romantic clothes. The most beautiful & sumptuous of all was the Duchess of Kent. Her gown for the Wedding was pale silvery damask with a pattern of soft pink feathers.

The bridesmaids are not really very pretty girls but they were beautifully turned out & their wreaths were romantic & unusual. (This letter is getting like the 'Tatler'!) . . .

Over in London for the Royal Wedding were many notabilities. Clementine knew Horatia would be interested:

Smuts is here & we have seen him several times. He really cares for Winston & is a source of strength & encouragement to him. Then there is your Friend Mackenzie King as unchanging as a Chinese image & then General Marshall, the hope of Mankind . . .

*

During these years, when Winston was in Parliament, but out of office, he and Clementine (usually with one or other of the family) spent some agreeable holidays abroad. They always sought sunshine, and good painting grounds. During this 'interim' period Winston, on the recommendation of his doctor, tried to be in a warmer climate during the worst of the British winter months. He was mainly faithful to the places he knew, Marrakech and the Côte d'Azur – with a diversion in January 1950, when they both went to Madeira, from where Winston had to return ahead of schedule because of the dissolution of Parliament prior to the General Election. These winter holidays were not only productive of pictures, but also of chapters, for during these weeks he devoted many hours to writing.

Clementine set great store by being at home at Christmas-time; moreover, she had exhausted the tourist delights of Marrakech and the Riviera. So, on the occasions when Winston longed to be away to the sunshine with his paint-box and his book as soon as possible after Parliament had risen for the Christmas recess, Clementine used to remain at home, joining him later on. Although he missed her, he was never lonely, as a change-of-guard of pleasant companions had always been arranged. Every few days Winston would write her an account of how he passed his time, always including a (really incredible) tally of his literary output. On 18th December 1947 he wrote from Marrakech:

I have been working very hard, rather too hard, in fact. My routine is: Wake about 8 a.m., work at Book till 12.30, lunch at one, paint from 2.30 till 5, when it is cold and dusk, sleep from 6 p.m. till 7.30, dine at 8, Oklahoma with the Mule

[Sarah] . . . At 10 or 11 p.m. again work on Book. Here I have been rather naughty; the hours of going to bed have been one o'clock, two, three, three, three, two, but an immense amount has been done and Book II is practically finished. I am not going to sit up so late in the future.

To a letter from Marrakech on Christmas Day 1950 he added in his own writing:

. . . I came here to Play, but in fact it has only been *Work* under physically agreeable conditions . . .

Clementine was always a little fearful on Winston's account of the treacherous winter climate of Morocco, because she knew that he was always loath to leave his painting, and used to stay out after it was wise to do so. On Christmas Eve 1947, Winston wrote to reassure her of his prudence in this respect:

The weather continues to be cloudless and lovely. The air is cold, and in the shade or when the sun goes down it is biting. I am very careful to wrap up warmly and never paint after 5 o'clock . . .

Despite this, he did catch a cold in the New Year, which developed into bronchitis; fortunately the attack was not long or serious, but Clementine, accompanied by Lord and Lady Moran, arrived on 3rd January to supervise, pet, and scold him.

The long parliamentary summer recess gave ample opportunities for some lovely sunlit holidays, in places which were a pleasure also to Clementine, and as they nearly always invited some of us children for part, or all of the time, she had companions, while Winston painted to his heart's content. One most enjoyable holiday was made possible by a group of generous Swiss admirers, who placed at Winston's and Clementine's disposal a beautiful and secluded house on the shore of Lac Léman, halfway between Geneva and Lausanne, where they stayed for nearly three weeks in the summer of 1946; Diana and Duncan and I stayed with them too. During this visit Clementine searched out her old governess, who lived in Lausanne – Mlle Elise Aeschimann, whose kindness and tenderness to her as a small child she had never forgotten. Clementine had always kept in touch with her, and a few years after this was able to help Mlle Elise financially, when she fell on straitened times.

This restful holiday would have been perfect for Clementine, whose health had been far from good this year, except for a most unfortunate accident in a speedboat. She was standing up watching my most inexpert attempts at water ski-ing when the speedboat made a sudden turn, causing her to fall; she struck herself violently against part of the boat's wooden structure, bruising herself badly and breaking several ribs. For at least a week she was in great pain, and under heavy sedation. At the end of their lakeside holiday, Winston and Clementine were due to be received in Berne by the Swiss Government, and in Geneva and Zürich by the cities' authorities. Sadly, she had to miss all these occasions, and it was many weeks before she was fully recovered. It was at Zürich that Churchill, on 19th September 1945, had made his famous speech, calling on Europe to unite, and laying the foundation stone of the European Movement.

In the summer of 1948, Winston and Clementine stayed for several weeks in Aix-en-Provence; I had married Christopher Soames in 1947, and we were both included in this lovely holiday. We all stayed in the Roi René Hôtel at Aix, the weather was perfect, and almost every day we used to set out, equipped with a delicious picnic, to spend the day in some lovely and 'paintatious' place. Les Calanques, Les Baux, the Roman arch at St Rémy, and the Fontaine de Vaucluse (where we cooled our wine by hanging the bottles with string round their necks in the icy, aquamarine river that wells from a gulf in the earth) – these were some of the places we visited. While Winston painted under his great umbrella, the rest of us went for leisurely walks, or visited the local museum, or just sat and gazed at the beautiful summer scene.

In the summer of 1949, Winston and Clementine went for their summer holiday to Italy, staying at an hotel on the shores of Lake Garda; the pleasant memories of this place, from his visit just after his defeat in 1945, had remained. They stayed here for nearly a month, Winston, as usual, combining hours of painting with hours of writing. On 10th August they both went to Strasbourg, where Winston was to attend the Inaugural Session of the Consultative Assembly of the Council of Europe; he took part in several debates, and addressed a mass meeting of the European Movement. On 15th August, applauded by large crowds, he was made a citizen of the city of Strasbourg. After this, Clementine flew home, while Winston went to stay with Max Beaverbrook at his villa, La Capponcina, near Monte Carlo.

It was during this visit that Winston suffered his first stroke. It occurred, while he was playing cards in the early hours of 24th August. The arrival of Lord Moran the next day was spotted at the airport, and the Press were immediately on the alert. Since, happily, the stroke was slight, and the effects began to wear off quite quickly, a bulletin was put out to the effect that Winston had caught a chill while bathing, and would have to spend a few days in retirement, resting. The only change of plans was that he had been due to return to Strasbourg for the final stages of the European Consultative Assembly's session – and this was cancelled. Clementine, who had of course been kept informed about Winston's condition, although anxious, remained at home, as her sudden arrival would certainly have aroused suspicions that he was suffering from something more than a chill. He made a wonderfully quick recovery and was able to fly home on 1st September.

Apart from the journeys and holidays Clementine shared with Winston, she also made some independent expeditions on her own, taking with her for company either one of us, or a close friend or two. These jaunts were usually rather short, as Winston minded very much if she absented herself for long. She usually chose periods such as the Easter recess, when he would be installed contentedly at Chartwell, with work, waterworks and painting to occupy him; and she always made sure there would be a succession of children and friends to keep him company. One of the most successful of these holidays was at Easter 1950, when she went to Venice for a week, taking with her as a companion, Penelope Hampden-Wall, her delightful young secretary, who had taken over the London side of life, while Grace Hamblin concentrated on Chartwell. Clementine greatly enjoyed this Venetian jaunt; she had some agreeable friends there, and she was able to indulge in some intensive sightseeing. Winston wrote to her (in his own hand) from Hyde Park Gate, whither he had returned from Chartwell after the Easter recess on 18th April:

> I am so sorry that you have had disappointing weather. I do hope that you have enjoyed the change of scene & the relief of household cares, & that you will come back refreshed . . .
>
> I have thought much about you my sweet darling, and it will be a joy to have you back. Your flowers are growing beautifully on the Chartwell balcony, & here [Hyde Park Gate] the cherry tree is a mass of bloom. All yr arrangements have worked perfectly in yr absence, and no one *cd* have been more comfortable than
>
> yr P [pig].

Attached to this letter was the 'Chartwell Bulletin' – a four double-sided-page edition – which contained the most detailed account of every aspect, animal, vegetable and mineral, of the situation there. He also reported on book progress:

> I have completely turned off politics these last ten days in a struggle to deliver Volume IV in good condition on May 1 . . .

On her way back, Clementine visited Verona, Mantua and Milan, where she spent a few days, with the intention of visiting the Brerà Picture Gallery. On her arrival she discovered that the gallery had not been re-opened since the war, but that Milan was crowded with people from nearly every European country who had come to visit the Annual Milan Fair. Disappointed in her hope of seeing the Brerà Gallery Clementine decided to visit the Fair, where she was disgusted by the low standard of the British exhibit. In fact, when she arrived home four days later she was still boiling over with indignation, for on the day after her return, she dictated a burning memorandum on the subject:

> After a general tour round the Pavilions, where I noticed the magnificent displays by France, Western Germany and Spain, and useful realistic contributions from Eastern Germany, Poland and Czechoslovakia and also Canada and South Africa, I asked if Great Britain was taking part. My guide, an Italian businessman who had spent several years in India as a Prisoner of War, seemed embarrassed and said 'Oh yes, I will take you there.' In a remote position on the top floor Great Britain was sandwiched between the Philippines and a Television Stand. Our contribution consisted of a desk in an open space flanked by a few photographs of the BBC and a British miner. Behind a partition there was a poor exhibition of English books. I felt mortified . . .

Clementine had planned to leave Milan the following day, but she was so incensed by what she had seen that she postponed her journey home for a day in order to make more thorough enquiries. The British Consul told her that the Fair was an extremely important one from the point of view of trade, as it attracted buyers from all over Europe, and that the low standard of the British exhibit was the subject of much unfavourable comment, and that 'Britishers' in particular were mortified by their country's pathetic showing. Clementine, in her Memorandum, reported all this and added:

The impression gained from a visit to the British stand was that we were down and out and never going to recover.[4]

Winston sent this fiery document to the President of the Board of Trade (at that time Mr Harold Wilson), with a covering letter in which he observed mildly:

Of course I am all for economy, but these Fairs are our shop windows . . . At any rate it seems to me depressing that we should be so hopelessly put in the shade by countries whom we have defeated or rescued . . .[5]

Winston was deeply concentrating during the spring and summer of 1950 on getting ahead with his *Memoirs*. The General Election in February of that year had left the Labour Government with their majority sliced to five, and it was obvious that their days in power were running out. He therefore decided to stay at home to concentrate both on politics and the Book. There was no combined family summer holiday this year, and Clementine made another expedition abroad in June, this time to Spain, taking me with her. We stayed at the Ritz in Madrid, and indulged in a veritable orgy of sightseeing. Johnny and Peregrine Churchill (Winston's nephews) and Mary, Johnny's wife, were in Madrid at the same time, and we joined forces on several occasions. Although it was an entirely private visit, my mother was treated with great consideration and courtesy by the Spanish Government, who provided cars, detectives (apparently deemed necessary) and other facilities. The Head of State Tourism, Señor Bolin, and his wife made themselves most agreeable and helpful. From the British Embassy a kindly wing was extended by Charles and Natasha Johnston, the First Secretary and his wife, who greatly added to our enjoyment, and were a fount of valuable information and guidance on a number of topics and personalities.

We had one very grand Spanish contact, who showed us much kindness and hospitality – the Duke of Alba. In a remote, romantic and historical way he was Winston's kinsman, being descended from James Fitzjames, Duke of Berwick, who was the natural son of James, Duke of York (afterwards James II of England) by Arabella Churchill, the sister of the great Duke of Marlborough.

It was on this visit that Clementine made friends with a delightful woman, the Marquesa de Casa Valdes, her husband and her family. Much of the pleasure of this visit was due to them, and an affectionate and enduring bond was formed between us all, and Clementine subsequently stayed with them in Paris. One of our most enjoyable days was spent visiting their beautiful and patriarchal estate at Guadalajara. Another expedition was to the Escorial, and we launched several attacks on the Prado, from which we emerged exhausted, though not defeated. I went to a bullfight: my mother hated them, and very sensibly preferred to go for an artistic promenade with the Duke of Alba.

Unfortunately we rather overdid the programme of sightseeings and expeditions, and my mother was too tired to go to either Avila or Toledo, which was disappointing, but she insisted that I should not miss seeing these two beautiful places before we returned home. This visit as a whole had been a great success, and had whetted her appetite for the beauties and splendours of Spain, and the following Easter she made another expedition. This time she went to Seville, where she stayed through-out Holy Week to watch the world-famous processions. As delightful companions she had Bill and 'Pussy' Deakin. In the thirties Bill Deakin had helped Winston with *Marlborough*; now, after a brave and brilliant war, in which he led the first British Military Mission to Yugoslavia and was awarded the D.S.O., he had re-turned to Oxford. At this time he was Warden of St Antony's College, and also directed all the research for Winston's *War Memoirs*. Both he and his wife were great personal friends.

In Seville they stayed at the Hotel Alfonso XIII, and throughout her visit my mother wrote me long and detailed accounts of all they did and saw. Reading her accounts one feels the tug between the Puritan/Protestant element in her nature and her sensitivity to the great beauty and emotional appeal of much she saw. And her radical instincts made her suspicious of official Falangist explanations. Here are some extracts from her letters:

Monday, 19th March 1951

Yesterday, being Palm Sunday, the great Religious Processions began . . .

The whole population of Seville is in the streets & chairs for hire are provided everywhere. Each church has its procession which wends its way by circuitous routes to the Cathedral. The procession is formed round the particular treasure of each Church which is carried in triumph on a decorated (very baroque & splendid) platform . . . The focal point is in front of the Town Hall where there are boxes for 'distinguished' guests (Actually, you can buy one (like for Wimble-don) for about £8. We have one.) In the middle there are two sumptuous red armchairs, & yesterday a rumour flew round that Franco & his spouse were coming. But no – the Mayor in tails & white gloves & the Head of the Falange in Seville occupied the fauteuils, & from time to time were relieved by under-studies.

We saw 3 of the 7 processions . . . The figures are life-size in plaster & very well modelled . . . Magnificently clad Virgins with beautiful sad pensive faces . . .

The crowds chattered gaily & noisily, but here & there you saw people moved with deep emotion. It's a great pagan carnival but it shews Holy Church trium-phant over pain, corruption, tyranny & unbelief.

Watching processions of penitents, where the acolytes were in black, bearing great black candles or crosses, and the series of religious tableaux, Clementine herself was deeply moved. On 20th March she wrote:

All the time I'm watching the Processions, lines from hymns run in my head. 'Take up thy cross the Saviour said, if thou would'st my disciple be . . .' 'Watch as though on thee alone hung the issue of the Day, pray that help may be sent down . . .'

The Bolins, whom she had met the previous year in Madrid, turned up, and Clementine accompanied them to the church of the 'Macarena' (the most popular & beautiful of the innumerable Seville virgins). Señor Bolin was to be installed into the 'Brotherhood' of the Virgin.

He knelt down & made his bows & was blessed, & in the Vestry afterwards I saw a fat bundle of notes being handed over. Bill says the Church of the Macarena is a Falange 'Cell'. The doctrine is this fantastic idolatry and very reactionary politics.[6]

However, it was not only Spanish politics and Roman Catholic idolatrous customs which made Clementine give vent to some critical sniffs; after describing how many of the houses in the plazas were Consulates, 'double fronted & important . . .', she went on:

But our Consul, Alas! is a depressed person & his office is in a dingy set of rooms in a dingy building. He is miserable & hates Seville & was not going to bother about the Processions; so we have invited him & his Wife to our Box, hoping he will be noticed by the Mayor. So far he has received not the slightest civility from any official.[7]

The state of the Anglican church was also a subject of her somewhat wry comment:

There is an English church here (quite deserted & neglected) & the Charwomen are prevented by their Confessors from scrubbing it out. I told the Consul's wife that I thought the 10 English Protestants here might scrub it themselves![8]

Clementine wrote more about the carnival atmosphere in Seville, on 20th March:

I have been hailed in the streets as 'Clementina' which is a welcome change from 'Oh my Darling Clementine'!
   The Hotel is packed with Americans & there are one or two 'croyants' French families who have brought their children . . .
   So far, no sign of 'our cousin' the Duke of Alba . . .
   Meanwhile 10 bulls are on their way here for Easter Sunday. A queer re-action to the Resurrection of our Lord.

And on 23rd March:

During Holy Week the population of Seville seem to live on shrimps & rusks. These are sold from hand-barrows & no-one goes home for a meal, except vulgar tourists like us. The shrimps are delicious (when fresh!).

Clementine was most struck by the beautifying effect of the mantilla; 'I must tell you all about the Mantillas,' she wrote on 25th March:

The women of Seville did not seem to me particularly beautiful. The middle-classes are dressed in loud ugly colours & their clothes are badly cut & truthfully they look rather common. (Not so the poor who are like animated skeletons & have a haggard dignity.) But on Holy Thursday – What a transformation! All women are in black, some in long dresses, & they wear their mantillas over very high transparent tortoiseshell combs. Everyone has a crimson carnation tucked into her bosom or in her hair. I was rather surprised at the carnations on this day of fasting, prayer & mortification. But I was told it signified the Blood of Christ. The rich also wear long twinkling ear-rings . . . They looked really ravishing.

In a PS Clementine added: 'We have got mantillas (little modest ones) but no combs; But we had carnations.'

These engaging accounts of Clementine's travels were duly circulated throughout the family. It was the 'consolation prize' for not actually sharing the holiday – to be able to enjoy it vicariously.

*

At the end of the war Diana, Randolph and Sarah were respectively thirty-six, thirty-four and thirty-one years old, and, like everyone else of their generation, they set about picking up the threads of their interrupted lives. Diana was much occupied by her three children, the youngest of whom was two. Although Duncan Sandys' parliamentary career was temporarily suspended by his defeat in 1945, he was never out of political life, concentrating on the European Movement in which he was, in this country, one of the prime movers. Winston esteemed and liked Duncan very much, and their family bond was reinforced by their mutual concern for the cause of European unity. It was not long before Duncan was adopted for another constituency, Streatham, which he fought and won in 1950, and which he was to hold until he resigned in 1974; he held office continuously from 1951 to 1964. Diana, therefore, with her growing family and a husband in active politics, had a very full life. She and Duncan came often to Chartwell and later on to Chequers, and her relationship with her father was always warm and affectionate. But between her and her mother there seemed too often to be an atmosphere of watchfulness and carefulness, rather than ease or cosiness.

Randolph led his own rampaging existence: lecturer, journalist, author and politician – he always had lances to break, and hares to start. Although blazingly loyal and demonstratively affectionate, he was not a 'comfortable' person to have around, and too often was in the mood when he would – all else failing – pick a quarrel with a chair. Unhappily the emotional and angry scenes which had so often marked his brief times at home in the war had left lasting scars on his relationship with both his parents. At no time, however, was the bond of loyalty severed, or the desire to 'try again' blunted. But hurts and misunderstandings were, alas, frequent.

Clementine could not bear the sheer commotion and noise of arguments with Randolph. Except on the rare occasions when she actually 'blew up' herself, she more often simply retreated into a chill silence, or removed herself from the scene altogether. Yet whenever Randolph did try to please her, it made her truly happy, and he greatly appreciated all the very real practical help she was able to bring to his financial difficulties, as Chairman of the Trust set up by Winston after the war for his children and grandchildren. Yet so often neither of them seemed to be able to 'get through' to the other. A letter from me to my mother (undated, but probably in September 1948) is revealing about the situation between them.

My Darling Mama,

When I dined with Randolph I sat next to him, and he said how very sweet you had been to him about all his difficulties . . .

He spoke in warm, loving and grateful terms of you. He said you had spared him much humiliation. And I can see he is full of admiration and *true* gratitude of the way you are treating him in these painful affairs.

I then said that you had told me how happy you were made by his gentlneess & affection to you.

I thought you would like to know this – because I know a little of the grief and perplexity you have gone through on his account, & because of his manners towards you.

Please burn this letter.

I am glad now that my mother forgot my injuction, because so many years later this letter has cast a gentle beam of light on the so often strained situation that existed between her and Randolph.

In his relationship with his father – which, I believe, he prized above all else – what Randolph failed to perceive was that, after the passage of the war years, Winston had lost much of his own relish for polemics in private. In days gone by he had enjoyed verbal knockabout turns – giving as good as he got (although he hated real rows). Now he was so many years – and a whole exhausting war older, and it upset him to hear present or erstwhile colleagues berated or vilified by Randolph. And what stores of energy and strength remained to him were precious, and were not to be squandered in mock battles of words, but reserved for the tasks that still lay ahead. Randolph's insatiable appetite for controversy, unabated by time, was undoubtedly the main reason why his father sought less of his company than in days gone by, and was more reserved in his confidences. Randolph was conscious of this change, and it grieved and embittered him. But both he and his father were too warm-hearted to maintain distances or hostile positions for long periods, and through all the ups and downs of their relationship Winston's loyalty to Randolph was only equalled by Randolph's loyalty to his father.

When Randolph's marriage with Pamela Digby ended in divorce in December 1945, both Winston and Clementine had been saddened, as they had become very fond of their daughter-in-law, and they were devoted to 'little Winston', who had been born in 1940. As in the war, Clementine used to reap, quite unjustly, Randolph's displeasure at times, because she maintained affectionate relations with Pamela (which, incidentally, greatly facilitated the making of holiday arrangements and so forth for their child). Many people will recognise this as a 'copy-book' situation, which is beset with difficulties, and is a breeding ground for misunderstandings. However, as time went on Randolph grew to be less suspicious and touchy, and 'little' Winston visited and stayed with his Churchill, as well as his Digby, grandparents very often.

In November 1948 Randolph married June Osborne. Both Winston and Clementine welcomed her warmly into the family and earnestly hoped that now Randolph might find some measure of domestic peace and happiness. There was in his life an unassuaged loneliness, combined with a touchingly patriarchal sense of family. Yet with his many gifts and great heart, he does not seem to have possessed the aptitudes for marriage. A beautiful child was born, Arabella, in 1949, and largely because of her, Randolph and June persevered with a relationship that was both unhappy and tempestuous. But they soldiered on for thirteen years, finally divorcing in 1961.

Winston and Clementine always grieved very much about the shipwrecks of their children's marriages. Winston could never quite understand why the 'young people couldn't-make-it-up-and-have-another-try'. He knew what he owed to his own rock-like marriage, and he took the simple view that you fell in love, married and lived happily ever after. Clementine was more comprehending of the emotional tangles and entrenched attitudes that grow up in unhappy relationships. Although her own standards for married life were very strict, I was often struck by how un-censorious she was, and how fair-minded, when it came to the marital mishaps and difficulties of her own children or friends. The draft of a gentle and understanding letter to June survives; it must have been sent in reply to a long and very sad letter from her daughter-in-law written in March 1950. Clementine wrote:

Dearest June,

I was very sad after I had read your letter and seen Randolph. Marriage strikes deep roots, and I pray that with you both in spite of storms these roots may hold. Do not hesitate to come and see me if you think I could help.

Your affectionate
Clementine S.C.

Soon after her demobilisation Sarah took up once more her stage career, about which she had been constant in mind ever since she made her debut as one of 'Mr Cochran's Young Ladies' in 1935. Now it was not vaudeville, but the straight stage to which she bent her energy and talents. In the summer of 1946 she played the lead in a Victorian thriller, *Gaslight*, and both Winston and Clementine went to see her in it. That autumn she went to Rome, having signed a contract with an Italian film company, but soon after she started working there she fell ill, and when it became evident that it was more than a passing indisposition, Winston and Clementine despatched me to Rome to keep Sarah company, and to see that she was taking proper care of herself.

I was naturally delighted, both at the prospect of an unexpected jaunt and at being with Sarah. However, this journey coincided with a fateful moment in my own private life. On a recent and very brief visit to Paris with my father I had met Christopher Soames, an officer in the Coldstream Guards, and an assistant military attaché at the British Embassy. Despite distance and duty, our friendship was budding, and at the very moment of my departure for Rome to join Sarah, Chris-topher was due to come to London for some leave. He hastily changed all his plans and accompanied me to Rome instead. Fortunately my sister Sarah has an iron constitution, for although I came to Rome with the sole intention of nursing her tenderly back to health, I arrived in a high state of emotion with a good-looking young man in tow. However, despite all this, she made a complete though slow recovery. During the short time Christopher Soames could stay in Rome before his leave expired we became engaged. My letters home were, in consequence, a jumble of bulletins on Sarah's health combined with explanations of my own heart's state, which must have been confusing and unsatisfactory to all concerned, more particularly so since neither Christopher nor I had met each other's parents.

Like most people in love, Christopher and I were blissfully and egotistically oblivious to all reactions which might contain an element of doubt or reserve on our families' part. On the whole both sides took the sudden news of our engagement with stoicism laced with hopefulness, and Sarah from her sick-bed wrote moving pleas for confidence and understanding to my mother. Both my parents had many misgivings because of my precipitate action, and my mother in particular was extremely anxious. But both she and my father made only welcoming and affectionate noises when Christopher and I arrived home.

From their very first meeting my father and Christopher took to each other. It was the beginning of a warm – a moving relationship, which grew in affection and trust. It had an enormous effect on Christopher's personality and life, and their real friendship added to the happiness I found in my marriage. And if my father gave much to Christopher – Christopher also was able to bring the breath of fresh air from outside, from a younger generation, to my father. His ebullient, cheerful personality brought fun back into my father's life, revived old enjoyments, and added a new one – racing. And once launched in politics himself, Christopher was able to perform a very real service in being a link between Winston and a younger generation of politicians on both sides of the House of Commons.

My mother, however, was not such an easy conquest, and although in her more formal way she was welcoming and affectionate to Christopher, and expressed no immediate or open opposition to our engagement, she nursed deep doubts about this 'stranger' who had suddenly arrived on our family scene. She also, not unreasonably, in view of my (up-to-now) changeable affections, wondered if I really was settled in my mind and my heart. Six years before, when I had become seriously romantically entangled, my mother had not hesitated to use all her influence with me to break off my engagement, for she was convinced that I was not really in love, that I was too young, and had had very little experience in these matters. Now the situation was different – I was twenty-four, and I had been out and about in the world; and when she saw that I had the 'bit between my teeth', and was determined to marry Christopher, she acquiesced gracefully, and did everything to help us both. But we were both aware that her attitude was less enthusiastic than my father's.

During the latter part of this autumn Clementine was not well; the accident on Lac Léman during the summer holidays had thoroughly shaken her, and her ribs were painful for a long time afterwards. She became progressively more exhausted, and finally in early December, on her doctor's advice, she cancelled all her engagements, and had a complete rest: that is, as much rest as it is ever possible to have in one's own house, with, moreover, a daughter's wedding in the offing. We spent Christmas very quietly at Chartwell; my marriage was only a few weeks away, and in the middle of my excitement and happiness I suddenly felt very aware, as all children must who have happy and close ties with their parents, that marriage must perforce bring a change in one's relationship with them. On Christmas Eve I wrote a letter to my mother, to try to express what I knew I would find it hard to say.

Mummie darling,

As I write to you so many memories of Christmasses spent together come to my mind. Here, at Blenheim, at Admiralty House. Then those unforgettable, exhausting homesick Christmas Days in the army – and now this last one together again.

But although I ardently long for my wedding day – I find it hard to leave you both – and today especially the thread of childhood memories and my life's association tug very hard upon my heart . . .

Darling Mama, this brings you all my love and Christmas wishes – How much I wish and hope you will gain in strength and find peace and happiness in the New Year.

I do truly grieve to grieve you – and wish my joy and the fulfilment of my life did not leave you rather alone.

I look ahead already to the fun we shall have again together. How I long to welcome you in our home wherever it will be. And how often and often we shall meet and do things together.

Tender, loving, grateful thoughts from your
Mary

Christopher and I were married in February 1947, at St Margaret's, Westminster where my parents had started out on their long road together. It was a bitter winter, and the country was in the grip of a major fuel crisis. We left a gloomy, freezing London for our honeymoon in snow and sunshine in Switzerland. On the Sunday after our wedding, my mother wrote to me from London.

My Darling and beloved Mary,

I addressed the envelope first, and writing your new name for the first time gave me a sensation of anguish and satisfaction – anguish that your life at home is ended, satisfaction that you are founding with the man you love your young own home with all its hopes & joys and experiences.

Your jubilant telegram thrilled us all & we are in imagination sharing the blue sky & dazzling sunshine & in reality your blissful happiness. It is agonisingly cold here & in this completely electric house we are feeling the 5 hour daily switch off. But I got a doctor's certificate for Papa's bedroom as he can really not work in the icy cold. We have pulled his bed near the window so he can see without a lamp . . .

My darling Mary. I am quite numb & I have not begun to miss you yet. I went once into your deserted bed-room, but not again. But what sun-lit vistas open before me in the future – of you and your children & you & Christopher both so young battling victoriously and happily through this grave new world . . .

Diana has just been in. She sends you her love. She was very sweet & relaxed & I enjoyed her visit . . .

Papa did not go to Chartwell this week-end becos' of the biting cold & I think he has been quite happy here. He sends you his dear love & messages to Christopher.

Jock [Colville] came to luncheon & I thanked him for all the trouble he took. He really is the King Pin of Ushers.

. . . Goodbye Darling for now. Give Christopher one kiss from me if you can spare it from yourself!

Your devoted Mummie[9]

During our honeymoon Christopher was taken suddenly very ill with a duodenal ulcer, and we were stranded somewhat forlornly at St Moritz. My mother flew out to be with us, thereby causing a slight sensation and some amused comment about mothers-in-law among the other hotel guests! As usual, she was ready with a practical suggestion: it was clear that Christopher would have to leave the army, and my mother suggested that we should come and live in the charming farmhouse at Chartwell Farm, which my father had very recently bought. This wonderful solution to our housing problem was warmly approved of by my father, who further suggested that Christopher (who was making a steady recovery) should take on the management of the farms. So began an idyllic, pastoral period in our lives; and during the next ten years we lived (with our growing brood) at the bottom of my parents' garden. Christopher and Clementine quickly grew to know and appreciate each other, and 'The Chimp' (as my parents affectionately called him) was soon a built-in part of the family, and a trusted confidant in all matters. Years later, when Christopher, my mother and myself were enjoying a cosy and comfortable evening together, he taxed her jokingly with her original lack of confidence and liking: 'Yes, darling,' she said, patting his hand, 'but I've made up for it since.'

Sarah was almost completely immersed in her stage and film career, and she spent the summer and autumn of 1949 in America playing the lead in a touring production of *The Philadelphia Story*, in which she had a great success. Some time previously, in London, she had met Antony Beauchamp who, after serving as an official war artist with the 14th Army in Burma, was busy establishing himself as a photographer. As their relationship developed Sarah had brought him to meet her parents and they had all been in Monte Carlo together in early January 1949. During that spring, after Sarah had returned to America for her work, Antony came several times to see them; unfortunately, neither Winston nor Clementine took to him. Clementine did try, but she never came to like or trust him. And although she endeavoured to make things easier between them, Winston remained resolutely hostile.

Later that year Antony went to America to join Sarah, and laid strong siege to her. She had earlier written to her mother that she felt she was 'very near now to taking the plunge . . .'[10] So Winston and Clementine certainly knew that a decision was imminent. However, Sarah wavered for some little time more. But between her summer and autumn season with *The Philadelphia Story* she and Antony went for a short holiday to Sea Island, Georgia, and there Sarah made up her mind to marry him. She wrote at once to tell her parents of her final decision. 'Thank you, darling Mummie,' she wrote on 14th October, 'for your patience and forbearance through these difficult months while I had to sort my mind and heart out . . .'

Although when she wrote, the date and place of their marriage had not been fixed,

Sarah and Antony subsequently decided to be married then and there, on 18th October 1949, on Sea Island, while Sarah had two or three days more of holiday left. The arrangements were made swiftly, and cables informing their families sent. Unfortunately the news broke in the Press before Winston and Clementine had received any word, either by letter or cable, from Sarah. The shock and hurt of hearing of the marriage first from the Press greatly upset both Winston and Clementine – but particularly Clementine, who took it very hard indeed. And despite ruinously long telephone calls, and fully explanatory, distressed and loving letters from Sarah, she retreated into a hurt silence, broken only by a few telegrams – some of them about business affairs.

During that autumn Sarah wrote several letters home, describing her hectic life on tour, and always begging her mother not to be 'hurt'. She wrote a special and loving letter to her father for his birthday. In mid-December Antony wrote a long, and in part severely reproachful, letter to Clementine, saying how deeply unhappy her long and chill silence was making Sarah, and he said that the exhaustion of her theatrical tour, combined with her distress at not hearing from home, was having an effect not only on Sarah's spirits but also on her health, and he begged her mother to write to her.

Clementine's long silence, and her unspoken reproach, are a little difficult to understand, although her original reaction to the way the news of the wedding had reached her and Winston is comprehensible. But it certainly bit deep, and it may have been her sense of foreboding that the marriage would not be happy one, which combined to make writing to Sarah so hard for her. However, Antony's letter had the salutary effect of goading her into action, and she wrote both to him and to Sarah almost immediately long letters couched in reconciliatory terms. She assured Antony:

> There was no displeasure or coldness. But Absence and distance & circumstances have perhaps clogged natural impulses.[11]

About her long silence she wrote to Sarah:

> . . . I confess I felt numb. I felt able only to telegraph to you from time to time. I am glad Antony's letter arrived & galvanized me. Again I am sorry and you must forgive me and believe in my love and care for you . . .
>
> We have made friends with Antony's father and mother [Mr and Mrs Entwistle – she was Vivienne, the photographer] and we had an agreeable luncheon all together . . .[12]

Thus, the long and wounding 'freeze-up' was ended.

Sarah and Antony came back to London for a brief visit the following May, between working engagements. They were, of course, greeted with open arms. Clementine gave a large dinner party uniting both the families at Hyde Park Gate, and at the week-end Sarah and Antony came down to Chartwell just before leaving to return to America. It was all a great success, and everyone was overjoyed to see everyone else. Clementine was able to tell Sarah that she had been doing some house-hunting for her and Antony against their return home to England, and that a 'choice' house was in the offing. When Sarah and Antony flew back to America a few days later, the dark clouds of estrangement and misunderstanding had been blown away, and the sunshine warmth of Sarah's relationship with her parents shone out once more.

*

One of Winston's chief satisfactions in his old age was the provision he was able to make for his family and descendants, through the Trust he had set up. He made Clementine the Chairman of the Trustees. Two of these were 'The Prof' and Brendan Bracken, who between them combined worldly wisdom with a thorough knowledge of the family. It interested and delighted Clementine to think up ways in which to help each child in the particular way he or she needed. But although sympathetic and swift in action to rescue any of us from the results of unwise budgeting, or even downright fecklessness, Clementine always felt a pang to see what was the fruit of Winston's genius and generosity being poured, as it were, down the drain. It was natural that she should think of their own early impecunious years, and what an alleviation to their constant anxieties about money such a beneficent Trust would have been to her and Winston in days gone by.

But helping any of us in a constructive way filled her with interest, enthusiasm and pleasure. A house or flat was needed – she was indefatigable in helping to search for one, and her practical eye often prevented the acquiring of some seductively pretty 'bijou residence' with perhaps a disastrously inconvenient lay-out for modern living and maybe no damp-course. She was ever ready to recommend to her fellow Trustees that the children should be helped with some basic domestic improvement such as a new kitchen floor, or a service lift, or a modern boiler, or just a wonderful windfall to help towards furnishing, curtaining and carpeting our home-sweet-homes. There is a file of grateful letters from various children and grandchildren thanking for divers blessings, of which Winston was the source, but in which Clementine's practical and imaginative thought is always apparent.

A WOMAN'S WORK IS NEVER DONE

ITH THE END OF THE WAR, two of the causes for which Clementine had worked so unremittingly – the Fulmer Chase Maternity Home and the Aid to Russia Fund – had come to a natural conclusion, although there was some lengthy and intricate winding-up to do in both cases, which Clementine, with characteristic thoroughness, saw through to the end.

Fulmer Chase had been a real success story. When the home closed in 1945, it had three branches – a pre-natal home, Fulmer Chase itself for the confinements, and (from 1942) Fircroft, the post-natal home where the mothers went for a fortnight. Over 2,500 babies were born at Fulmer Chase, and there had been no maternal deaths. The standards of nursing, care and comfort had been such that they had been described in *The Midwife*[1] as 'beyond praise'. It had been indeed a satisfying and satisfactory bit of work, and Clementine had loved her share of it.

In March 1947 Clementine resigned from the Presidency of the Y.W.C.A. War and National Fund. In a farewell broadcast appeal on 23rd March 1947, she asked for continued support and help for the Y.W.'s work in providing yet more hostels for

> ... girls released from war service, girls from factories and offices, government employees and students – a continuous stream from all parts of Britain of girls with jobs but nowhere to live.

As a result of this broadcast a good sum of money rolled in, but Clementine also received some letters she must have greatly valued from people she had worked with, either at the Y.W.C.A. headquarters or in the regions, who all spoke with regret that she was resigning, and expressed appreciation for what she had done in those war years for the organisation, both in raising money and improving standards in the hostels. One colleague wrote:

> ... I am sure others are feeling as I do tonight – a real sadness that this will be your last *official* public act for us! You have been so good and understanding, so practical & stimulating that we shall miss you sorely ...[2]

That they did miss her, and had valued her work, was amply proved when nearly two years later the association sought her help once more, and in January 1949 Clementine was elected Chairman of the National Hostels Committee. It was a compliment and a challenge she accepted with real pleasure and interest. Between the wars she had never relished committee work, nor had she been gripped emotionally or intellectually by any one particular cause or social theme. But the last war had changed all that. Her position as the wife of the Prime Minister had, of course, given her a certain power and influence which, as we have seen, she learned to wield with effect. But this was not the whole story: Clementine had acquired the taste for doing a real job of work and grappling with policies and problems 'in depth', as opposed to the amiable surface interest – genuine though it may be – which the wives of men in public life are expected to take in causes probably not of their own choosing, and in which they may have only a peripheral interest. Clementine's wartime involvement in the Y.W.C.A.'s work, and in particular that part of it which dealt with hostels, had really gripped her interest, and when she accepted the Chairmanship of the National Hostels Committee she felt she knew something about the work and its problems already, and had a very clear idea of the goal towards which the committee should strive.

A very few weeks after becoming Chairman, Clementine found herself taking the chair at the yearly Hostel Wardens' Conference at Southsea. Afterwards, in her official report of the Conference,[3] Clementine remarked upon the fact that the programme dealt almost exclusively with the religious and social aspect of the Y.W.C.A.'s work, and admitted that she was surprised that all the manifold practical difficulties of managing hostels had not been examined in detail. She acknowledged that the course of the conference had made her understand 'the other point of view – namely that Man cannot live by bread alone'. Nevertheless she concluded with a firmly expressed hope that the programme for the next conference would allow '. . . several sessions to deal with the physical standards of well-being, and with the practical details of administration'.

When it came to a discussion on actual living standards in the hostels, she was bluntly outspoken: she avowed she had been:

disgusted at the conditions that I saw when I visted the hostels. The war was being made an excuse. Now that the war is over it is still being made an excuse.[4]

She had clear ideas about what should be a 'minimum standard', and she spelt them out in detail, ending with a fiery declaration of intent:

We must exert ourselves and get out of the state of squalor and sordidness . . . I have joined the National Hostels Committee to see if we can try and make the hostels more comfortable.[5]

Clementine set about this task with energy and assiduity. She regularly attended the committee meetings at Headquarters, and she had endless small private meetings with people concerned with the work; during the three years of her Chairmanship she made a series of tours, visiting hostels in every part of the country. From these visits, by which she set great store, she got an up-to-date picture of the state of things, and saw the problems and difficulties that had to be mastered – nor did she underrate them.

After every tour Clementine made detailed notes on the various hostels. A random sample reads:

This Hostel has just been redecorated and is in very good condition. Well-equipped bedrooms with good built-in cupboards. Ablutions of great interest because each washbasin is in a separate cubicle with door ... Shelves and hooks provided ... Excellent small laundry. Young, happy residents of various occupations.

Another hostel in the same area was not up to the same standard:

All bedrooms whether single or double are small and cramped, so much so that most of them cannot take a gas or electric fire without danger. Not enough cupboards or chests of drawers, and nothing like enough W.C.s, bathrooms or washbasins in the main building. Inadequate laundry arrangements, although space available to have good one at small cost.

After another visit she wrote:

We had a delicious meal here and I spent half an hour reading the menu book. I have seldom seen such a variety of interesting dishes.[6]

As well as these notes, which were for her own and Headquarters' guidance, there are always, relating to every tour, copies of the letters Clementine wrote to the Chairmen of the local committees and the wardens of the hostels she had visited, taking up in great detail all she (and whoever had accompanied her from Headquarters) had observed. The letters show an amazing grasp of practical detail, and understanding of the problems. They contain praise (but only, obviously, where it was due), and understanding and encouragement where people were struggling with intractable houses, lack of staff and funds. Where she had criticisms to make, they were invariably constructive. After visiting hostels in Birmingham soon after her appointment, she wrote on 22nd February 1949 an appreciative letter to the local organiser, ending on a humble and endearing note:

I am finding my work connected with the Y.W.C.A. most interesting, but rather difficult. I hope in a year or two I shall be a more satisfactory Chairman.

Judging from the answers to her letters, her remarks, albeit sometimes critical, were appreciated rather than resented. After a round of visits to hostels on Merseyside in May 1950, the Organising Secretary of the Central Council, Miss W. A. Gorick, wrote:

... Residents, Committee Members and Wardens alike have been deeply touched by your concern that the work of the Association should be of the highest quality and your delightfully apt, amusing and yet practical comments have been taken very much to heart.[7]

A former resident in a Glasgow Y.W.C.A. recounted how, at the time of a visit by Clementine:

... I and many of the residents were ex-servicewomen and therefore rather cynical about visits by 'high heid yins' [high-ups]. We were consequently terribly surprised, and pleased, when as a result of your mother pronouncing our beds too hard and the facilities for doing our washings [sic] not good enough, these matters were remedied . . .[8]

After her first few tours, Clementine saw clearly that the only way to improve the general standard of the hostels on a national basis was for there to be some sort of guide-book setting out minimum living standards, for the use of all local committees and wardens. Her idea was adopted enthusiastically by the National Committee, and work was started on producing *The Hostels Handbook*. It was ready in time for the Wardens' Conference in March 1950, and it covered in detail every aspect of running a hostel, including keeping the accounts; scales of staffing; the furniture and equipment desirable in every bedroom was specified (it is even noted that 'Two wastepaper baskets are necessary in a room with four beds'): scales of the minimum numbers of lavatories, washbasins and bathrooms; the provision of washing and ironing facilities; the amount of linen required, and a note on how often the sheets should be changed! Not all the recommendations could be put into force by all hostels, but the *Handbook* was warmly received and studied, and it set up standards which became accepted as those which must be striven for.

Although as Chairman of the National Hostels Committee fund-raising was not her province, Clementine was in fact a champion collector for the work that gripped her so much. People would quite often give her money 'for a favourite charity', and as she longed to have a source from which she could help hostels with equipment or special improvements which fell outside the scope of their normal budgeting, she started collecting the donations which were given to her into a special fund for this purpose – it became known as 'Mrs Churchill's Special Hostels' Fund'. In 1950 the McConnell Foundation sent her £3,000 specifically for hostels (this was at the instigation of the generous Canadian, Mr McConnell, who already way back in the war had commuted an offer of a mink coat into a handsome donation to the Y.M.C.A.). Mr Giraudier, a warm-hearted Cuban gentleman, was another regular contributor. In 1949 Winston had given one of his pictures to be auctioned in aid of the Y.W.C.A., the proceeds of which swelled her Special Fund, as did successive sums from the yearly openings of the gardens at Chartwell. From this Fund Clementine rejoiced to be able to make substantial grants towards the improvements she had so much at heart.

There was once, however, an unfortunate misunderstanding about a quite large sum which had been allocated from her Special Fund. Clementine duly received a grateful letter from the hostel in question, but she was much displeased when she read that the handsome gift had been spent on what she considered to be an expensive piece of 'eye-wash' (such as pictures or flower vases) instead of its having been used to do something basic, such as renewing all the mattresses, or putting an immersion heater in the tank to boost the hot water supply, or buying electric irons and ironing boards. She never allowed such a thing to happen again, and thereafter she personally had to approve the use of any allocations made from her Fund.

Soon after Winston became Prime Minister again in 1951 Clementine realised she would not be able to continue her regular work for the Y.W.C.A., and it was with real regret that she wrote resigning from the job to which she had really given the cream of her thought and energy for nearly three years, and which had given her great satisfaction. The President, Mrs Newhouse, in her letter accepting her resignation, wrote on 4th January 1952:

> . . . Not only have you raised the standard of our hostels all over the country, but you have given so much to the whole Association . . .

Clementine never severed her links with the 'Y.W.', and indeed remained on as a Vice-President of the Association, and was a member of the Executive and Finance Board (which for a long time she attended when matters concerning the hostels were discussed). For many succeeding years there are quite fat files of correspondence concerning 'Y.W.' matters. A regular entry in her engagement diary was the two-day Annual Fair held in London in aid of Y.W.C.A. funds, which she actively supported and attended.

When the new Y.W.C.A. National Headquarters (which included a hostel for 100 girls) was ready in March 1953, Clementine was invited to open it. Of all the many 'openings' she had performed in her life, this one must have surely given her the most satisfaction, for she had been involved in the plans from the start, and the hostel accommodation incorporated so many of the features and facilities she had striven for in the past. It was not inappropriate that there was in this 'model' hostel a 'Clementine Churchill Wing'.

*

After the Second World War, as in the twenties and thirties, Clementine's political activities were centred on Winston's constituency. She was his chief 'liaison officer' with the Divisional Association in Woodford, and she kept in constant and close touch with them. She studied most carefully the programmes for Winston's visits to the constituency, to make sure that they were not overloaded or too demanding: she could wax quite fierce – but she evoked not only respect and loyalty but also true affection from the leading men and women in the Conservative Association. Every year her engagement diary shows a regular series of visits to the Woodford area. Quite often on a Friday or Saturday she would attend some afternoon or evening meeting or social function in the constituency, driving to Chartwell afterwards to join Winston. It was quite a long and tiring expedition for her.

As wife of the Leader of the Conservative Party, Clementine was of course much in demand all over the country to address meetings or open bazaars but, with very rare exceptions, she resolutely declined to accept political engagements outside Winston's constituency. She had too many other obligations (not least her Y.W.C.A. work), and she knew her stamina would not be equal to it. There were of course a few major exceptions to this rule – she nearly always accompanied Winston to the Annual Conference of the Conservative Party, and she always tried to attend some of the sessions of the Conference of the Conservative Central Women's Advisory Committee, which was held in London in the spring of each year. She always received a heart-warming welcome from the delegates, who came from every part of the country, and whom she once described as representing 'the greatest, grandest constituency in the world. You represent the women of Britain . . .'

Clementine was nearly always on these occasions, as at constituency functions, called upon to speak; and occasionally she had to make a 'full dress' speech, which she prepared most carefully, often submitting it to Winston to 'vet'. Although all her married life she had had to make speeches – and one recalls the accounts of her fiery campaigning in the old Dundee days – yet, in these later years, political speaking was not really to her taste. She usually read her speeches, and indeed someone who often heard her speak in Woodford described her as a 'nervous speaker'. But where she excelled was when she had to make an impromptu speech, probably at the end of a meeting – then her charm of manner and naturalness shone out, and she never forgot to thank people by name for what they had done. During elections Clementine was still a doughty campaigner, and did her share of speaking, and unprepared occasions often found her at her lively best. But she shouldered making speeches as a necessary duty, not a pleasure. Clementine's real contribution in the constituency was her genuine interest in local and association affairs; her true appreciation of what individuals did in different ways for the organisation; and her willingness to spend time, and to take trouble with people.

As the Party Leader's wife, Clementine, when making a speech, had to wield official facts and figures, and follow the 'Party' line. Comparing the drafts of some of her political speeches with those on other subjects, one is immediately struck by the difference: many of the political ones seem stilted, and the Central Office handout touch is easily recognisable; but the drafts are copiously corrected in her own hand, and no doubt 'came alive' as she spoke. But where she was speaking to her own brief on subjects such as Aid to Russia, maternity care, and the problems, policies and goals for Y.W.C.A. hostels – all causes which had caught her enthusiasm and in whose work she was personally absorbed – the difference in style is very striking. Even on paper they have life and appeal.

*

When Peace had returned to a war-shattered Europe, and a battered, rather weary Britain, she had not been accompanied by her traditional companion Plenty. Many of the shortages and difficulties which confronted people in their everyday life in the immediate aftermath of the war continued in varying degrees for months and years. Clothes were rationed until the spring of 1949, and some foodstuffs were still rationed as late as 1953. During a series of economic crises bread and potatoes were actually rationed for the first time, and petrol rationing was re-introduced for a period. Perhaps the worst single problem was the acute housing shortage, which weighed heavily on young families and brought a crop of heartbreaking social problems.

For a time these hardships and hassles were accepted as being the obvious legacy of the war, but gradually people's patience and acceptance wore thin, and while dire predictions of an egalitarian, doctrinaire Socialist state proved to be fanciful exaggerations, equally the benefits of nationalisation and a more centrally organised economy were not blazingly apparent. From the nadir it had reached in the rout of the 1945 election, the Conservative Party in these years, with Churchill as its Leader, Lord Woolton as Chairman, and Mr R. A. Butler as its leading philosopher, passed through a period of renaissance in organisation, thinking and morale. By February 1950, the credibility and popularity of the Government was seriously eroded, and in the General Election held in that month Labour's majority was reduced to five.

During this period, while ordinary people in every country struggled to remake their personal lives, the outlook on the international scene dashed the bright optimism of those who had expected the dawn of a new age of harmony among the nations. The critical voices that had been raised by Churchill's warning in his Fulton speech of Russia's intentions were soon silenced, as the grip of the Kremlin tightened on Eastern Europe. The reaction to this threat was to make the Western powers – both allies and erstwhile enemies – draw closer to each other, and to the United States.

But world events seemed to lurch from crisis to crisis, and overall there brooded the mushroom shadow of nuclear power: a new, sinister and terrifying element, to the presence and implications of which the whole world had to adjust its thinking and its actions.

Still in the midst of public life, and in close contact with the most informed circles, Winston and Clementine now, as always, lived with the reality of events. The feeling of contrast between the preoccupations of daily life and the natural relief of 'getting back to normal', with the tensions and uncertainties caused by recurring crises in world affairs, is reflected in a letter Clementine wrote to Queen Elizabeth on 7th April 1948, after she and Winston had stayed at Windsor Castle:

> . . . I can truthfully say that I have not enjoyed a week-end Party so much for what seems an immeasurable space of time.
>
> After 'Clumps', which I had not played for forty years, (or more) & then in a much more sedate fashion, I felt nearly forty years younger.
>
> It was moving and stimulating to feel the pulse of Life beating strongly in Your Majesties' family, delightful to see the wonderful treasures all in their places again, and to feel 'here firm though all be drifting' –

During these five years when the Conservatives were in Opposition, life at Chartwell, which had taken a little time, and a great heave, to get going once more, truly blossomed and flourished anew. There was hardly a week-end when Winston and Clementine were in England that they did not spend there, with usually one or two people staying; and particularly in the spring and summer, family, friends and colleagues would come down for the day.

One of the new features of life at Chartwell was the warm and sunny relationship which soon developed between the Churchills and the neighbourhood. Before the war, although from time to time one or other member of the family was in demand as a foundation-stone-layer or bazaar-opener, there was little other involvement in parochial affairs. Winston never went to church except on State occasions, and although Clementine usually did at the great festivals, church-going was never a feature of our family life. Many people in the thirties had regarded Winston with mixed feelings, and some had looked upon him as an outright *enfant terrible*, while as far as the local shops were concerned, the Churchills had a bad reputation when it came to paying bills. But now all that was changed: the neighbourhood took a pride in having Winston Churchill in their midst, and Winston and Clementine themselves were more accessible and outgoing.

A great feature of summer life in these years was to be the annual openings of the gardens to the public. Literally thousands of people came to visit Chartwell on these occasions. Starting in 1948 with one opening, in succeeding years the gardens were opened always twice, and in 1951 there were four open days. The regular beneficiaries of the considerable proceeds were the Y.W.C.A. and local charities. Since Chartwell is situated mid-way between Westerham and Crockham Hill, the proceeds of the open days devoted to local causes were divided between the two communities. So too was the organisation of these occasions, which brought Clementine in particular into pleasant contact with her neighbours. These Garden Days, and Winston's and Clementine's attendance from time to time at such local functions as the Westerham Whit Monday Gala Day and the Edenbridge Agricultural Show, did much to cement the now warm and friendly relationship they enjoyed with the neighbourhood.

Now that the house was easier to run, and she was no longer haunted by financial nightmares, Clementine began to enjoy Chartwell as she had never done in the bygone years. Croquet replaced tennis as the summer game, and the tennis court made a quick transformation into a 'regulation' croquet lawn. Clementine played very well, and most of all she liked 'real' croquet, but nearly all her friends (and certainly her children) preferred the shorter, more immediately rewarding Golf Croquet to the scientific longueurs of the classic game. She happily acquiesced in this compromise, and many pleasant afternoons were passed in this way. New recruits were found in the growing grandchildren, and although Winston did not play himself, he was an attentive spectator, and particularly enjoyed seeing 'Monty' (a frequent and faithful visitor) out-manoeuvred as a strategist.

Both Winston and Clementine enjoyed their grandchildren, and they quite often came, with or without their parents, to stay, and Christmas-time once more saw real family gatherings. Because we lived literally at the bottom of the garden in the Farm House, the Soames grandchildren saw a great deal of their grandparents, and had an easy, uninhibited relationship with them both, which has remained a glowing memory. From quite an early age the children could trot up unescorted to the 'big house' to pay unannounced social calls. It was a ritual in the summer that, as the nursery party wended its way with Nannie, the pram and attendant dogs to the swimming-pool, a child would be despatched to tell Grandpapa and Grandmama, and one or both of them would almost invariably come down to the pool with any guests to watch or join in the aquatic fun, often staying to share nursery picnic tea. Winston was now always a spectator, as he had been persuaded not to swim except in really warm water, and since the war the pool, although crystal clear, was unheated. My mother described a typical afternoon to me when Christopher and I were away in Scotland in August 1952:

After luncheon we converged with your babies [Nicholas aged 4, Emma nearly 3 and Jeremy 3 months] upon the swimming pool & although it was by no means very warm, Sarah plunged in with Nicholas & Emma who screamed with delight

& excitement. I had on the beautiful taffeta bathing suit which you gave me, but at the critical moment I flinched & stayed on the verge warmly wrapped up in a bathing robe! Papa came down & afterwards we all went to your house to tea in the Day Nursery. Giuseppe [our Italian cook] made the most delicious miniature doughnuts & some twirley whirley things made of the same mixture. Nicholas & I devoured the whole plate between us . . .[9]

Whenever we were away, holidaying or electioneering, my mother kept a fond and grandmotherly eye on our nursery, writing us lively and reassuring reports, such as this one:

You will have heard from Nannie that your babies are well, beautiful & happy – They have been to tea here twice & are coming back tomorrow. It's such fun . . .[10]

It rejoiced my heart then, as now, to feel that life at the Farm House was a source of pleasure and joy to both my parents, because for us all, those were golden, unforgettable years.

A totally new interest and diversion for Winston, inspired and largely contrived by Christopher, was racing. In 1949 he registered in his own name Lord Randolph's colours, and soon acquired a grey French colt, Colonist II, which won thirteen races for him, and large sums in prize money, before he was sold to stud in 1951. He soon had several other horses in training, which afforded him great pleasure, as well as being financially successful. He also owned a small stud at Newchapel Green, near Lingfield, which being quite near to Chartwell he was often able to visit. Winston was much gratified to be made a member of the Jockey Club in October 1950.

Clementine at first greatly disapproved of this new enterprise: but nothing succeeds like success, and when she saw what enormous pleasure Winston derived from his racing activities and that, moreover, they more than carried themselves financially, she became reconciled to this new foible. But she never could work up any real interest in racing herself, and only went on 'star' occasions to the races, or visited the stud, in order to please Winston. She wrote to Ronnie Tree (who had become and remained a great friend since the wartime week-ends at Ditchley) in May 1951:

Have you seen about his horse Colonist II? He has won about 10 races in a year & is now entered for the Gold Cup. I do think this is a queer new facet in Winston's variegated life. Before he bought the horse (I can't think why) he had hardly been on a race-course in his life. I must say I don't find it madly amusing![11]

*

After the General Election in February 1950 it was clear to everyone that the Labour Government would not be able to hold out for long with such a fragile majority. Opposition hopes and spirits were high, and inter-party strife was marked by its keenness and acerbity. During the summer of 1951 the Conservatives forced several all-night sittings with constant divisions upon the House; Winston took his part in these marathons, and in every way demonstrated his vitality and capacity to continue to lead his party. He was now seventy-six, and his health had been comparatively good in these last years. He had made a good recovery from an operation for hernia in 1947, and the slight stroke (which had passed un-publicised) had left no obvious effects on him. He was increasingly troubled by deafness, and eventually had to resort to a hearing aid, which he found most tiresome.

Clementine's health had also been quite good and, as we have seen, she had undertaken quite a considerable load of work for the Y.W.C.A. since 1949, on top of her other obligations. But one of the underlying causes of the bouts of exhaustion, which from time to time laid her low, was an internal trouble. She had staved off the inevitable for quite a time, but in May 1951 she had to undergo a major 'repair' operation. She was in St Mary's Hospital, Paddington, for three weeks, and suffered all the pain and lowness of spirit which are inseparable from such an illness.

Clementine spent the greater part of her convalescence at Chartwell, and then she and I went off at the end of July to Hendaye, near Biarritz, where we had all holidayed after the 1945 election. We spent a fortnight leading a quiet seaside life, with plenty of bathing, which did her a great deal of good. We both joined Winston and Christopher in Paris in the middle of August, and went all together to Annecy. From there Winston and Clementine went to Venice, returning home in early September, all prepared for the forthcoming fight. On 4th October Parliament was dissolved, and the second General Election campaign within twenty months began.

Clementine held the fort in Woodford, as before, while Winston travelled to various key centres to speak. He also held several large meetings in his own constituency, but he did not undertake quite so intensive a programme as in previous campaigns. There were several new features in this election: it was, for instance, the first where television played a major role. In the interests of presenting a united anti-Socialist front, Conservative candidates stood down in some seats to allow a free run to Liberals; and reciprocally Liberals gave way in neighbouring seats to Tory candidates. The *Daily Mirror* ran an odious campaign on the theme: 'Whose finger do you want on the trigger? . . .' – inferring that war was more likely under Churchill's leadership. It may have been as a result of this 'war-monger' campaign that the opinion polls showed a marked recovery in Labour support during the last few days of the election. When the results started to come in late on 25th October, early trends showed only a slight swing to the right, and it was not until the late afternoon of the 26th that a Conservative victory was certain, their final overall majority being 17. The King summoned Churchill to Buckingham Palace that evening and invited him to form a Government.

While Winston addressed himself to the formation of his first and only all-Conservative and peacetime Government, Clementine prepared to move back, once more, into No. 10. She must have felt – for his sake alone – some sense of satisfaction after the bitter defeat of six years before: but of elation she felt none. Nothing that had happened had changed the conviction she held in 1945, namely, that Winston should have retired at the end of the war. Nevertheless – here they were again, and she set about reorganising their life yet once more. Ronnie Tree had written to her after the election, and in her reply on 4th November she wrote:

I do hope Winston will be able to help the country. It will be up-hill work, but he has a willing eager heart . . .

By contrast, her spirit was one of dogged, somewhat weary determination, rather than of enthusiasm. Physically she was only six months from a major operation, and as always when her morale was low, difficulties loomed large. One event, however, that caused her (and indeed everyone in our circle) great pleasure and reassurance, was the return of Jock Colville to the Private Office as Joint Principal Private Secretary. After 1945 he had for two years been Private Secretary to Princess Elizabeth, and had since 1949 been at the British Embassy in Lisbon as Head of Chancery. In 1948 he had married Lady Margaret Egerton – Meg – who became as dear and trusted a friend to Winston and Clementine as was Jock himself. During these years of Winston's last Prime Ministership, when there were many private anxieties and problems, it was a wonderful support to have someone at hand who knew the public and the private side of it all. He understood Clementine very well, and he was a friend and confidant whose sense, loyalty and humour never failed.

Within a week of the election results, Clementine and Grace Hamblin (recalled from Chartwell to help with the 'second innings') went to see what the form was at No. 10. The Attlees when they took over in 1945 had, very sensibly, arranged a self-contained flat on the second floor of the house, only using the first floor State Rooms for large parties, when the staffing and catering were all done by Government Hospitality. It was into these pleasant, unpretentious apartments that Winston and Clementine moved on 19th November – Clementine had marked it 'D-Day' in her engagement diary.

From the start Winston longed to move back into the whole house, but Clementine stalled – servants were difficult to get, and the kitchen arrangements for the downstairs dining-rooms were ill-devised and labour-consuming. However, as time went on, and the Coronation of Queen Elizabeth was in the offing, and with the prospect of an even increased number of guests, Clementine, after some prodding from Winston, made a plan with the Ministry of Works, which was submitted to Winston. He commented in a Memorandum to Clementine, dated 'July 1952':

> I think it [the plan] is a brilliant conception and should be done in the public interest, as it is a great pity these rooms are not available for use. We really ought to have them for Coronation Year. Look at all the distinguished people I have had to entertain in our poor little attic. I am sure they are surprised at the difference between the accommodation and the menu . . .

Although Clementine was obviously rather dragging her feet about moving from their 'perch' aloft, she soon was herself persuaded, and the plan was duly carried out to everyone's satisfaction.

One aspect of their translation back into Prime Ministerial life which presented no complications was Chequers. Still staffed by servicewomen, and now, since the retirement of Miss Lamont, under the direction of Mrs Hill, Winston's secretary for many years until 1946, Chequers was to be again both a haven and the perfect place for the dispensation of official hospitality. But Winston could not bear the thought of abandoning Chartwell. Much though he appreciated Chequers – Chartwell was always home, and where he would rather be than anywhere else in the world. The house in Hyde Park Gate was let, and of course it would have been much simpler from every point of view if Chartwell could have been shut up for 'the duration' and all their life concentrated in the two official houses. But throughout these last years of office they spent many more week-ends at Chartwell than at Chequers, and invariably they were at Chartwell for Easter and Whitsuntide, and for long spells during the summer holidays. Nevertheless Chequers was the ideal place for entertaining larger numbers of people and for giving a 'rest' to Chartwell; and from the family point of view Chequers will always be remembered for the four successive Christmases we all spent there. The great, rather gloomy house truly seemed to come to life and glow on those occasions, with blazing log fires, miraculous decorations made by Mrs Hill, a towering Christmas tree in the Great Hall, and above all the wonderful jumble of generations.

One of the major strains imposed on Clementine during these last years for Winston as Prime Minister was a constant, gnawing anxiety about his health, which undoubtedly preyed on her own nerves. Towards the end of February 1952 Winston suffered from a brief period of aphasia, the result of a spasm of the cerebral arteries, which caused him temporary confusion in his speech. This occurrence worried him very much, and of course raised for him, and for the strictly limited circle who came to know about it, the whole question of his ability to carry the burden of work required by a Prime Minister. This question was to recur during these last years of office, and it always posed the same painful conundrum: Winston felt he still had things to do for his own country and the world that only he, with his unique position in international affairs, could do – and he was not alone in this view. But he knew the risk he ran by continuing in office, and he dreaded, not dying in harness – that would have been his chosen way – but sudden or gradual incapacity.

At his best Winston was still amazing, both in public and in private, but it was all achieved at a high expenditure of his stock of energy, both mental and physical; and there were times now when he could not cope with the long detail of problems. Lord Moran understood Winston thoroughly, and he was indeed fortunate he had as his doctor a man who understood not only the medical considerations and risks to his patient, but one who was also fully aware of the implications, with regard to the office he held, of his condition at any time. Lord Moran moreover understood the relationships between, and with, Winston's colleagues, and where one could expect loyalty, understanding, and total discretion – and where one could not.

For a few weeks after this minor, but disquieting incident, the people (mainly his closest colleagues) who knew about it, apart from his immediate family, considered ways to lighten Winston's burden, without his giving up being Prime Minister. The consensus of their opinion was that in his unique position he could conceivably continue as Prime Minister from the House of Lords. Winston toyed with this idea, but soon he felt better, and confidence returned, and no more was heard of the matter. Clementine, who always reacted calmly and with sense to the reality of events, understood the implications of the 'aphasia'. But she had accepted, however reluctantly, Winston's determination to soldier on, and it was not at moments such as these that she battered him with admonitions: it was at these times she surrounded him with tenderness and understanding.

In September 1951, just before the General Election, King George had undergone a major operation. The tour he and Queen Elizabeth had planned to make to Australia and New Zealand later that autumn was cancelled; but Princess Elizabeth and the Duke of Edinburgh set off on a Commonwealth tour early in the New Year. Although the King was known to be in a fragile state of health it came as a great shock to everyone when he died in his sleep at Sandringham in the early hours of 6th February 1952. None among his subjects felt sadder than Winston, who not only cherished the memory of the close relationship which had developed between Sovereign and Prime Minister during the war years, but was genuinely personally devoted to the King. Now the accession of the young Queen Elizabeth II aroused in him every instinct of chivalry.

The late summer of 1952 saw a family event which created a considerable stir both inside and outside our family: Clarissa Churchill, Winston's only niece, became engaged to Anthony Eden, whose first marriage had been dissolved in 1950. Although he and Clarissa had known each other for some time, their intention to get married had been a well-kept secret. In early August, Clarissa wrote to her aunt, who was holidaying on Capri with Sarah and Antony, to tell her the news, and saying she wanted Clementine to be the first person to hear it. A few days later she and Anthony dined at Chartwell and told Winston of their engagement. Clementine and Winston were at one in wanting Clarissa to be married from No. 10, and to give the wedding breakfast there afterwards. Clementine had to bustle on her return from Italy to make the arrangements, for only a week later, on 14th August, on a glorious summer's day and amid considerable public interest, the marriage took place. Scarcely a year later, when Anthony was struck down by illness, Winston and Clementine were once more able to spread a sheltering wing, by inviting them both to stay at Chequers for nearly three weeks in quiet seclusion, so that Anthony could gather his strength after two operations, and before setting out to undergo a third in Boston.

In the New Year of 1953 Winston went to the United States to visit General Eisenhower, the new President-elect, and also Mr Truman, the outgoing President; it was planned to combine these visits with a holiday in Jamaica, where a house had been offered to him. Here was a prospect of a short breather before the crowded year ahead for both Winston and Clementine, and they took Christopher and me with them. We all boarded the *Queen Mary* on New Year's Eve, and apart from my parents and ourselves, the party was composed of Jock Colville, two secretaries, a detective, a valet and a maid and '100 pieces of luggage'![12] My parents both enjoyed Atlantic crossings in the 'Queens'. The five days always passed so agreeably and restfully, with a sense of isolation from the world.

Arrived in Jamaica, we all stayed in the house, with its lovely garden and paradisal beach near Ocho Rios, which Sir Harold and Lady Mitchell had lent Winston and Clementine. Apart from a visit to Kingston, where Winston was officially received by teeming, tumultuous crowds, the fortnight was private and off-duty. We bathed and sunbathed; my father painted three pictures; my mother and I made expeditions and visits to the agreeable friends who had properties in the neighbourhood – Noel Coward, Edward Molyneux, the Brownlows, and Max Beaverbrook. After this golden holiday we all headed for home again on the *Queen Mary*, arriving at Southampton at the end of January.

Clementine was quickly into the collar again on her return, and almost her first engagement was a proud and glorious one – she launched the aircraft-carrier H.M.S. *Hermes* at Barrow-in-Furness on 16th February. In stark contrast to this glamorous event was the tour she made shortly afterwards of areas in East Anglia which had suffered severely in the unprecedented floods, which had inundated wide areas from the Humber to the North Foreland, causing several hundred deaths and rendering thousands homeless at the beginning of February. When Clementine toured the areas, the floods had subsided and people were struggling to make their homes once more habitable. She met many of the people who had shared in the rescue work, and visited rest centres, a clothing distribution centre and a feeding centre.

After the 1945 election the King had wished to make Winston a Knight of the Garter. The Garter is one of the oldest orders of chivalry, and it is in the personal gift of the Sovereign. Raw and mortified by his defeat, Winston had then declined the King's offer. Now, in the year of her Coronation, Queen Elizabeth offered him once more this most special distinction, and Winston, moved and gratified by her gesture, accepted. Letters of congratulation from people in all walks of life poured in – many of them addressed to Clementine. The Princess Royal (for whom Clementine had the highest regard) wrote charmingly: 'I am very delighted about this particularly as I know how much the King wished him to have it . . .'[13] A fishmonger from Blackpool wrote:

Permit me please to add my warmest of congratulations . . .
I am not able to express what we all feel towards this wonderful person.
Have, however shown a little material appreciation by sending you today the best halibut that I could find . . .[14]

Both Winston and Clementine were invited to dine and sleep at Windsor Castle on 24th April, when the Queen invested him with the Order. He was installed as a Knight the following year at the beautiful traditional service always held in St George's Chapel, Windsor.

Even before the many functions arranged around the Coronation had begun, Winston and Clementine had been involved in a good deal of entertaining, when Marshal Tito of Yugoslavia in March, and Dr Adenauer, Chancellor of the German Federal Republic in May both made official visits to London. Now, at the end of April, Churchill's burden of work was made the heavier by having to shoulder responsibility for Foreign Affairs for several months, Anthony Eden having become seriously ill. The Foreign Secretary had been due to give a dinner at Lancaster House on 5th June for the Queen and all the Heads of States and Governments attending the Coronation. In Anthony Eden's absence Winston and Clementine presided, and Clementine assumed a measure of responsibility for the arrangements for this very large and important party, in addition to her own considerable load of entertaining. Luncheons, dinners and receptions succeeded each other. Government business still had to be done, and Winston attended all the plenary sessions of the Commonwealth Conference which took place also at this time.

Coronation Day, 2nd June, was a splendour, despite cold, wet weather; nothing could douse the enthusiasm of the vast, drenched crowds. Winston and Clementine made a splendid pair – he in the Garter Robes worn over the uniform of the Lord Warden of the Cinque Ports, and Clementine looking outstandingly distinguished and beautiful in the petunia satin robe of the Order of the British Empire; a friend had lent her a tiara. Winston and Clementine rode in a coach in the procession, with a mounted escort of his own first regiment, the 4th Queen's Own Hussars. At No. 10 a large party of the grandchildren, nannies and various relations spent the day watching the procession from windows in the Treasury buildings in Whitehall and the service on television.

But the combined strain of junketings with an overload of work and responsibility were not slow to take their toll. It happened towards the end of a large dinner at No. 10 on Tuesday, 23rd June, given in honour of Signor de Gasperi, the Prime Minister of Italy, and his wife: there were about thirty-eight people to dine, including Christopher and myself. In proposing his guest's health, Winston made a singularly delightful and witty speech, but as the company was leaving the dining-room Christopher suddenly noticed that his father-in-law was having difficulty in standing up. Christopher helped him out of his chair, and with Clementine, who had seen from across the room that something was amiss, escorted him to a chair in the State drawing-room. I only realised my father's plight a short time later, as I was busy entertaining the guests. Christopher told me to try and 'guard' him from the people, as he was having difficulty with his speech; I did my best, but it was not very easy; my father looked unhappy and uncertain and was very incoherent. Christopher managed to convey to Signor de Gasperi that Winston was very much over-tired, and the Italian Prime Minister, with kind understanding, soon took his leave, the other guests following his example. A few had noticed the slur in Winston's speech and his unsteadiness, but attributed it to his having had a little too much to drink; nobody guessed the real reason – that he had sustained a stroke. Meanwhile Jock Colville tried, unsuccessfully, to contact Lord Moran, but finally had to leave a message asking him to come to No. 10 in the morning. We escorted my father upstairs to his bedroom, and there he seemed to feel, and to be, much better.

Lord Moran came early the next morning and diagnosed a stroke; and he called into consultation Sir Russell Brain, the distinguished neurologist. Although there were visible signs of the stroke, Winston seemed better, and, amazing as it seems, he presided at Cabinet that morning, where none of his colleagues noticed that anything was amiss; although Harold Macmillan later said that 'Churchill looked very white and spoke little'.[15] There were no guests for luncheon – only my mother, Christopher and myself – which was fortunate, as by that time Winston was extremely tired, and once more had difficulty in getting up from his chair. Clementine was quiet calmness personified, but she was of course deeply worried. Winston had intended to answer Questions in the House that afternoon, but Clementine and Christopher persuaded him at luncheon not to do so, adding their weight to the doctors' warning that he might risk breaking down completely if he did.

My mother and I had been going to Wimbledon, but this was cancelled, and we all awaited developments with anxiety. Meanwhile the closest secrecy was maintained. It was of paramount importance that no rumours circulated, one of the chief reasons being that plans had already been announced for a meeting to take place in Bermuda, in the middle of June, between President Eisenhower and the French and British Prime Ministers. There was much comment and interest throughout the world at the prospect of this top-level conference, and pending a decision to the contrary, arrangements for it went ahead. Winston was due to leave for Bermuda on H.M.S. *Vanguard* in a week's time – on 30th June.

On Thursday, 25th June, the effects of the stroke were rather more pronounced. When I went round to see him that morning I was painfully struck by his appearance, and found him very despondent. In the circumstances, it was thought better that he went down to Chartwell, where privacy could be more easily achieved, and he duly drove there later in the morning, accompanied by Jock Colville.

On the way, Winston asked Jock to tell nobody what had happened: this was a request which it would have been wrong, and indeed impossible, to obey.[16] Fate was kind – Winston had been able to walk unaided to his car at Downing Street, but by the time he reached Chartwell he needed considerable help getting out of the car; but there were no outside or curious eyes to witness this.

During the next two days the paralysis increased, and it became quite clear that Bermuda was out of the question. Indeed on Friday, 26th June, Lord Moran told Jock Colville that he thought it unlikely that Winston would live through the weekend.[17] On Saturday afternoon the following announcement was made:

> The Prime Minister has had no respite for a long time from his very arduous duties and is in need of complete rest. We have therefore advised him to abandon his journey to Bermuda and to lighten his burdens for at least a month.
>
> (Signed) Moran
Russell Brain[18]

The quiet, private agony of those succeeding days had faded even from my memory. Reading my diaries, written in the anxiety and sadness of the moment, has revived it:

> Saturday, 27th June 1953
> Saw Papa – felt wretchedly gloomy. There are nurses now, and he cannot walk, or use his right hand much. In the afternoon he had a fall – but beyond the jolt – no damage.

> Sunday, 28th June 1953
> Today he is gayer . . . Lord M. says there is a distinct improvement. It's so difficult to tell people when they ring up – Because when he's down – we're down – And when he's cheerful our spirits, too, revive . . . Mama is truly marvellous – tender, considerate, thinking of everyone's comfort. Unblinded by hope or fear – she teaches us all.

During these days his closest family and friends, and some colleagues, came in succession to visit him: Max Beaverbrook; Brendan Bracken; 'The Prof'; Lord Camrose; Sir Norman Brook (Secretary to the Cabinet); Harold Macmillan;

'Monty'; the Salisburys. On Saturday, 27th June, Randolph and June came to luncheon, and a day or two later he wrote to his mother:

> I do want you to know how much I am thinking of you at this sad and difficult time. I thought you were magnificent on Saturday & doing everything possible to maintain Papa's morale. So long as that persists no miracle is impossible . . .[19]

Sarah flew back from America – she told the Press that her current television series was over, which was true too. When she and Antony came to Chartwell on Monday, 29th June, Winston had had a good day, and Lord Moran had found him distinctly improved, but I wrote in my diary:

> She [Sarah] was distressed. It made me realise how used to it we have become, and how *low* we were – for today we feel almost gay – he seems so improved. But of course it is only comparative.

The Press and the public seemed to accept the explanation for the 'need to rest'; even Sarah's arrival, and the cancelling of a Chartwell 'open' day, which was to have been on 1st July, were received without much comment. As the days went by Winston's condition improved, but there were bad days and good days. Statements were issued to the Press – it was known that he was seeing quite a number of people, and reading papers, and generally keeping in touch with affairs. But inevitably there were rumours and speculation, and reports circulated in the foreign Press that Winston was completely paralysed. This particular lie was laid when he was photographed on the doorstep at Chartwell on 24th July before leaving to drive to Chequers, where he stayed for the next week or two, to give the staff at Chartwell a much-needed rest. Nearly a month later the *Daily Mirror* gave great prominence to a report in the American Press that Winston had had a stroke, and although he had made an astonishing recovery, it was not thought likely he would be able to resume active leadership.

On 18th August, Winston presided at his first Cabinet meeting since his illness: it went very well, and he grappled vigorously with a long agenda, but it tired him very much, and the next day, on his return to Chartwell, he looked dazed and grey.

But from the very earliest days of his illness, the great and anguishing question mark, 'Can he go on?', hung over us all. He brooded on it all the time. Nearly all of us who saw him constantly could not believe that his recovery would be complete enough for him to wrestle again with public life. We must have been a loving, but defeatist band, I fear.

In the early days of his affliction, Winston's goal was to hang on until the autumn, when Anthony Eden would be recovered enough to take over the succession. Then there was a further horizon – the Queen was due to go on a prolonged tour of the Commonwealth, leaving England towards the end of November, and returning in May 1954 – he would hold the fort till then. But as his strength increased, the 'holding on' theme was more and more superseded by the idea of 'carrying on'. During these long weeks Winston suffered untold frustration; he felt power had been snatched from him just when he might have made moves of vital and lasting importance in the field of international relationships.

Stalin's death in early March 1953 had led to changes in the chemistry of Soviet policy. Churchill had warned the world about the 'Iron Curtain': now he felt his last task was to assist the 'thaw' in international relations. He felt quite simply, and without conceit, that he could play a unique part in this process. These were agonising weeks for Clementine. She saw, all too clearly, that Winston meant to battle on; she did not doubt the need for his presence in the counsels of the world, nor that he had a unique gift to offer – she simply could not bear to contemplate the prospect of the slow diminution of his powers, nor the possibility of a public breakdown. She bore up wonderfully well throughout this time, although she herself had a fall and cracked some ribs. She scarcely left Winston for more than a few hours at a time, and she gave him unwavering love, comfort and companionship. But he knew her views without asking – and Clementine knew the depths of the dilemma in which Winston found himself.

Lady Violet Bonham Carter visited them both at Chartwell, and writing afterwards, on 13th August, she paid Clementine a just tribute:

> I must tell you darling, what *intense* admiration I felt for your courage, wisdom & dispassionate judgment, when your emotions must have been so deeply involved –
>
> I cannot imagine anything more difficult & agonising than these last weeks must have been for you – with all their conflicts of hope, fear, anxiety & decisions for the future . . .

If Churchill was to return to his job as Prime Minister, various deadlines had to be met. The first one had been the Cabinet meeting on 18th August – all had gone well. But the real test would be the Conservative Party Conference in early October at Margate, when he would have to speak for at least forty minutes to a large meeting, and endure the keen scrutiny of the Press. Meanwhile, he started to lead a more normal life; he diverted himself with a little croquet; saw more people and read an increasing number of official papers. While Christopher and I were away in Scotland, my mother wrote from Chequers on 5th September about my father's progress:

> I am sad about Papa; because in spite of the brave show he makes, he gets very easily tired & then he gets depressed – He does too much work & has not yet learnt how & when to stop. It just tails off drearily & he won't go to bed. He *is* making progress, but now it is imperceptible. If no setback occurs the improvement can continue for 2 years . . . I expect you have seen from the newspapers the tremendous 'va-et-vient' of ministers. Papa enjoys it very much. Incidentally they are even more tired than he is by the sitting over the dinner table till after midnight! . . .

A week after this letter, Winston and Clementine travelled to Doncaster, where the Queen had invited them both to watch the St Leger from her box, and then to travel on up with her in the Royal Train to spend the week-end at Balmoral. Winston had accepted this invitation a month before – it was a target, and a test. The day of the Leger, Saturday the 12th, was Winston and Clementine's forty-fifth wedding anniversary. Everyone from the Queen and her family downwards made much of them, and Winston had a wonderful welcome of his own from the crowd.

The two days at Balmoral were most agreeable, and when they returned home Winston was refreshed and encouraged.

Max Beaverbrook had offered the loan of La Capponcina at Cap d'Ail, and Winston, Christopher and I flew out there on 17th September. Clementine did not come with us – Winston was now so much better she felt she could entrust him to us, and she and Nellie went off for a few days sightseeing and theatre-going in Stratford. From La Capponcina I reported truthfully, if rather sadly:

Papa is in good health – but alas, low spirits – which Chimp and I are unable to remedy. He feels his energy and stamina to be on an ebb tide – He is struggling to make up his mind what to do. I'm sure you know the form – you have been witnessing it all these months . . .

He thinks much of you & wonders what you are doing . . .

Chimp & I are having a lovely time – bathing – reading – cards & we love being with Papa – Only we yearn to be able to do more than be the mere witnesses (however loving) of his sadness . . .[20]

Winston wrote several long letters to Clementine, in his own hand – the writing is surprisingly clear; it was evident how much he missed her, and how unsettled he was still in his own mind about the future. On 21st September he wrote:

My darling One,

The days pass quickly & quietly. I have hardly been outside the garden, & so far have not had the energy to paint in the sunlight hours . . . I do not think I have made much progress, tho as usual I eat, drink and sleep well. I think a great deal about you & feel how much I love you. The kittens [Christopher and myself] are vy kind to me, but evidently they do not think much of my prospects. I have done the daily work and kept check of the gloomy tangle of the world, and I have dictated about 2000 words of a possible speech for Margate in order to try & see how I can let it off when it is finished to a select audience. I still ponder on the future and don't want to decide unless I am convinced . . .

This letter, which went on to describe in a quite lively way the various guests he had entertained at the Villa, ended: 'Ever your loving & as yet unconquered W. [with a very debonair pig]'. When we returned, a few days ahead of him, we brought my mother another letter, in which he wrote that he had got going with his painting and certainly felt

. . . the necessary vigour & strength to be as bad as I used to be . . .

I do hope my darling, you have found the interlude restful and pleasant. I must admit I have had a good many brown hours. However the moment of action will soon come now . . .

That letter was written on 25th September. Winston returned to England at the end of the month, and on 10th October he addressed the Conservative Party Conference. It was a great ordeal, and Winston knew, and Clementine knew, just how much depended upon his performance, which would be judged and commented upon, not only by the large audience in the hall, but by a host of unseen witnesses and interested commentators. We were all tensed up for this formidable test. It was an unqualified success – *The Times* wrote of a 'triumphant return to public life'. Doctors, closest colleagues, loving relations – all of us had been confounded. As we looked back over the harassments and anxieties of the past months, it seemed miraculous.

There was no more talk, for the present, of resignation or retirement, as Winston once more took up the normal load of his work as Prime Minister. But Clementine, deeply thankful though she was at the return of his health and strength, knew that he was working, if not living, on borrowed time, and that at any moment he might be struck down again. She had had an exhausting summer, and in response to a warm invitation, she went to Paris for a week in October to stay with Lord and Lady Ismay (he being, at that time, Secretary-General to NATO). She greatly enjoyed this short 'breather'. Winston wrote to her three times during this short absence – in his 'own paw'. There was a new kitten at No. 10 (called Jock, after its donor) which was

> . . . behaving admirably & with its customary punctilio! Rufus [the poodle] is becoming gradually reconciled . . .[21]

He reported quiet on the domestic front (which must have been a great relief to Clementine). There was also the pleasant and gratifying news that Winston had been designated as that year's winner of the Nobel Prize for Literature. But despite public and private preoccupations, Winston's loneliness without Clementine emerges in every letter:

> I was lonely last night but Pitblado [Joint Principal Private Secretary] dined. I am reading 'The Dynasts' & getting into it.[22]

Three days later, just before leaving London for a brief visit to Chartwell, he wrote:

> I am writing in the Cabinet room, & the little cat is holding the notepaper down for me. I miss you vy much. One night I had dinner in bed as I did not want anyone but you for company. I do hope you are enjoying yourself and finding the days interesting.[23]

The postponed Bermuda Conference was now arranged to take place in the first week in December. Lord Moran accompanied Winston, and Christopher was also of the party in his official capacity as Winston's Parliamentary Private Secretary*. The new date for the Conference unfortunately coincided with the date of the presentation of the Nobel Prizes, which takes place every year in Stockholm in early December, and King Gustav Adolf and Queen Louise had invited Winston and Clementine to be their guests at the royal palace for the occasion. When a Nobel prize-winner is unable to receive the prize personally, it is customary for the Ambassador of the recipient's country to receive it on his or her behalf. It was therefore unusual, and a signal honour, that Clementine was invited to represent Winston on this notable occasion, and to accept the Prize for Literature on his behalf. The King renewed his invitation to her, and also invited me to come as a companion to my mother. And so it was that we spent four unforgettable days in Stockholm.

*Christopher Soames had entered politics in 1950 as Conservative M.P. for Bedford, a seat he was to hold until 1966.

The social occasions and festivities which form the annual programme surrounding the actual ceremony of presentation of these world-famous prizes are most beautifully and imaginatively organised, and the Press and population of Stockholm take a keen interest in all the events and personalities involved. Although the Swedes were disappointed that Winston could not himself come to Stockholm, the reason for his absence was completely understood, and Clementine arrived on the evening of Tuesday, 8th December, to be received as his most welcome representative, surrounded by the reflected aura of her husband's great reputation; for even here, in neutral Sweden, Winston Churchill had a unique standing. But if she came to Stockholm as a substitute, she quickly became accepted and acclaimed in her own right. Her first engagement was a party for the Press given at the British Embassy by the Ambassador, Mr (now Sir) Roger Stevens. Here she made a great hit: and the combination of a natural manner, friendliness and her looks (which stunned them) made a good start to the visit. The Swedish Press thereafter paid detailed attention to all she said and did and wore. It was delightful staying at the Palace, as nothing could have exceeded the King's and Queen's hospitable kindness. King Gustav Adolf and Clementine got on extremely well together; the King was a great savant and very interested in a number of subjects. Queen Louise was also most charming, and there was an immediate bond in that she was a sister of 'Dickie' Mountbatten.

The presentation of the Nobel Prizes, of which five were at that time awarded in any one year, took place in the great concert hall in Stockholm, and afterwards at a banquet for over 900 people Clementine read Winston's speech of thanks for this exceptional honour. After the banquet the company moved to the great Blue Hall, where a ball took place. During the evening nearly a thousand students entered the hall wearing their white caps and carrying banners. The student choir sang folk-songs, and then, as the dancing was in progress, suddenly the band broke into the time-honoured strains of *My Darling Clementine*, the words being taken up by the students. Clementine was quite overcome by the charming tribute, and received loud applause as she waved from the balcony where she was sitting with the royal party and the prize-winners and their families. When my mother and I arrived back in England on Saturday, 12th December – a day after the return of the Bermuda party – there was a great reunion, and we had a golden account to give of those last few days, and Winston was thrilled and gratified by the wonderful reception his 'darling Clementine' had received.

But for all the high days and holidays, and for all the perks and privileges that go with high official position and general public esteem – Clementine was finding the going hard and heavy. Her heart had never been in this second term of office, and although she would always put on a good show in public, her morale was often desperately low in private. She found the constant entertaining during the week in London, often followed by week-end parties at Chequers, a great strain. Christopher and I had a room at No.10, and nearly always went to Chequers if there were official guests, in order to help, and so I was often the distressed witness of my mother's moments of weariness and depression. But although her spirits were often desperately low, I never ceased to be amazed at the way in which she could snap out of the doldrums in order to do whatever had to be done. I remember just before one large evening reception at No. 10 her being in an extremely agitated state, to such an extent that I begged her to allow us to say she was not well, and for her to go to bed; she agreed, and I went to tell my father. The first guests were just about to arrive when suddenly my mother appeared, looking beautiful, not a hair out of place, dripping with diamonds and decorations and, taking command of the whole situation, carried on through the evening without one betraying sign that half an hour before the party she had been in a state of nervous, and near hysterical collapse.

When she was driving herself hard, Clementine became difficult to live with and to work for. Towards the secretaries and the servants, to whom she was normally polite and considerate (and most understanding of any personal problems), she would become, when under strain herself, super-perfectionist and cuttingly cold. To her family she would be generally 'tricky' and demanding. Nervously restless, she would fuss endlessly over what seemed to one to be trifling matters. Above all when she was 'down', the present held no enjoyment, and the future loomed with problems great and small. It was at these times also that she would be most difficult and sometimes quite aggressive with Winston – producing objections to any proposals he made, and making it quite clear to him that everything was a great burden.

It is idle to pretend that Winston himself was not, at times, maddening. He could, on occasion, behave like a spoilt and naughty child. A loyal and affectionate staff often managed so that these usually brief outbursts passed unnoticed. Most of Winston's colleagues were indulgent, but Clementine used to become enraged if the incident happened before other people. She would (usually) restrain her feelings at the time, but they would burst forth as soon as they were in private. Moreover, if there were casual witnesses, she felt humiliated and embarrassed both for him and for herself. She was absolutely unafraid of him, and she used to rate him thoroughly. But for all that he sometimes deserved her scoldings, there were periods now when she really harried him too much – and without regard to the load he himself was bearing, and finding heavier all the time.

Strangely enough, although there were sometimes explosive scenes, Winston endured a good deal with remarkable patience. He knew that he had imposed this extra mileage on her against her own wishes for herself, and her judgment of what was right for him, and he saw how exhausting she was finding her life. Clementine herself was often conscious that she had been too abrasive, and she suffered remorse and unhappiness when she felt she had been unkind or unreasonable. Both were always eager to make up any quarrel. This touching 'olive twig' survives among Winston's papers; it is not dated, but belongs to the 1954 period – it speaks for itself. It was probably pushed under Clementine's door:

Darling
   Fondest love. I am so sorry I was awkward at dinner.
   My heart was full of nothing but love, but my thoughts were wayward.

Your ever devoted
W

But Clementine's reproaches were not always harsh and acrimonious. The following missive survives, written in September 1954 in her 'own paw' on Chequers writing-paper. Winston had evidently monopolised the White Parlour with some of his colleagues.

A Petition from the CAT [drawing of cat]

The 'White Parlour' is the ladies' Bower & the *private* sitting room of the Wife of the Prime Minister.

Would it be possible for the Prime Minister when he confabulates with men to use: –

1) 'The Prime Minister's Study' (opposite dining-room)
   or
2) the Long Gallery upstairs?

This note is signed with another fat feline, beside which appears in Winston's handwriting the following comment:

I was only trying to catch a fat mouse for the Cat. [Drawing of mouse.] I will not trespass again. W

Looking back, it is not difficult to trace the causes of Clementine's change of demeanour and attitude during this last period at Downing Street. The most continuing reason was to be found in her own state of health and strength. It must be remembered that when Winston returned to office at the end of October 1951, Clementine had only just finished her convalescence after a major gynaecological operation. She threw herself into all that her side of the job entailed, but already in December there is a weary note in a letter she wrote to 'Streetie':

It's just over 6 weeks since the Election & the heavy going has not started yet; just a reconnaissance so far . . .

I am well now, but hope to be stronger later. Its now six months since the operation & some people say it takes a year! So it's really better to have it before one is 66![24]

In obedience to the instructions of her doctors, who were adamant that she must go right away from the strains and worries of home life, Clementine went for a fortnight to Montecatini (an Italian health resort) in early July 1952, in company with Mary Marlborough, who always greatly benefited from the cure there; and later she joined Sarah and Antony in Capri. Winston, as usual, was an excellent correspondent, and tenderly solicitous for her health and progress, but he missed her sorely. Writing on 11th July, he told her:

Another week of toil is over & I am off to Chartwell in an hour. How I wish I was going to find you there! I feel a sense of loneliness and miss you often and wd like to feel you near. I love you vy much my dear sweet Clemmie. But I am sure you needed the 'Off Duty' break to recover buoyancy & resilience. I am most anxious to get yr report.

Later on, in September, Winston and she went together to La Capponcina at Cap d'Ail, lent to them by Max Beaverbrook. Before their visit, on 17th August 1952, Clementine wrote to Max:

It is indeed kind and thoughtful of you to have lent us your lovely home & garden. We look forward to the sunshine, the peace & the rest.

I am much better, but my doctor was vexed that I came home after a month as he wanted me to stay longer than that . . . Now I can resume my 'rest cure' in wonderful surroundings. I hope Winston will paint. He says, 'There are a 1000 pictures to be painted from Max's garden!'

The autumn found her much restored, and she started taking up public engagements again, but, on her doctors' advice, she now limited her commitments. For most of 1953 Clementine's health was fairly good, but the extra strain of Coronation entertaining and then Winston's grave illness put her under pressure, and towards the end of the year she started having trouble in her right arm and shoulder from what was eventually diagnosed as neuritis. This painful and extremely wearing affliction dogged her for a long time. During March and April 1954 the condition became acute, and she was in severe pain. Several doctors and treatments were tried, and she had to wear a surgical collar for some weeks. Apart from it being disagreeable to wear, she hated being seen in it, which made her shun company which might otherwise have cheered her. One fellow-sufferer was Max Beaverbrook, and they had a lively correspondence on symptoms, doctors and remedies. He sent her some flowers one day with a little note saying: 'From one victim of neuritis who deserves it, to another victim who does not deserve it. Max.'[25] He could be irresistible.

In a bid to conquer the neuritis Clementine took a three-week cure at Aix-les-Bains, Grace Hamblin (who had rheumatic trouble) going with her as a companion and fellow-patient. The treatment there did her some good, but the trouble still recurred from time to time. One way and another Clementine was tussling with indifferent health throughout Winston's last tenure of office and, in addition, the plain fact was, she was getting older – and feeling it.

During these years also there were other causes of strain for Clementine apart from those relating to her health. In 1953 Diana suffered a severe nervous breakdown, which continued to affect her over a considerable period of time. Both Winston and Clementine grieved deeply for her, and saw with dismay the great unhappiness this illness caused Diana, and the difficulties and anguish it brought into her life. As is often the case in such illnesses, those who are nearest and dearest are sometimes the least well equipped or able to help. The relationship between Clementine and Diana had for many years been a fragile construction, and now there were moments when it came near breaking-point. Yet also, there were times when Diana was most tender and loving towards her mother, and the rift of incompatibility and mutual misunderstanding was bridged. But Clementine suffered not only the temporary pain from harsh, but forgivable verbal wounds; she must also have had the heart-searchings that all parents feel as they see a child in the grip of a bewildering illness, the root causes of which may well go back to adolescence and childhood. Strangely enough, although Winston found psychological troubles and their explanation quite beyond his ken, he nearly always had a calming and soothing influence on

Diana in her moments of distress; and she found in him tenderness and rock-like stability.

For the greater part of these years Sarah was in America, where she had plenty of work both in the theatre and on television. Clementine missed her very much, for she and Sarah were close to each other. Diana and Sarah were always devoted friends, and Sarah was often able to be a helpful and mediating influence whenever she happened to be in England. Sadly, from about 1953 her own marriage began to run into serious difficulties, and for a good deal of the time while she was working in America, Antony was in London. After periods of temporary separation, they finally parted for ever in 1955. Although Clementine had never really liked Antony, and had forebodings from the beginning, she naturally grieved deeply for this further unhappiness in Sarah's life. Sarah's own letters home are full of references to long and understanding letters from her mother, which were a life-line of comfort and support to her through the hectic and emotionally arid months during which she was touring in America and wrestling with painful personal problems.

Finally, there was a sad personal loss for Clementine to bear. In July 1954 it was discovered that her sister Nellie was suffering from inoperable cancer. In August and September she was at intervals in St George's Hospital having massive doses of ray treatment, which made her feel dreadfully ill and weak. Clementine had her driven down to Chartwell at the week-ends, and cherished her tenderly. When she went away for a fortnight's holiday with Rhoda Birley to the south of France, Nellie continued to come to Chartwell, where she and Winston kept each other company, and she wrote Clementine gay and gossipy letters with all the Winston and Chartwell news. Throughout that autumn and winter Nellie was constantly either at Chequers or Chartwell whenever she felt strong enough. But although she made a brave appearance at Winston's birthday party, at Christmas she was not up to joining the big family gathering at Chequers. In the New Year it was clear she had not much longer to live, and Clementine made it possible for her to be nursed at home. She died aged sixty-six on 1st February 1955.

The two sisters had totally different temperaments and characters, and the circumstances and course of their lives were in sharp contrast. Nellie's life from the time of her marriage to Bertram Romilly was full of difficulties. He always suffered from fragile health as the result of the head wound he had sustained in the First World War, and they were very badly off financially. Nellie loved her two sons, Giles and Esmond, with a blind devotion, standing loyally by them through a series of adolescent peccadilloes. Bertram died in 1940, and throughout the war she had a sad and lonely time, with Giles a prisoner-of-war, and Esmond being killed flying. But despite all her trials and tribulations she remained gay, gallant and undaunted. Of the two sisters, Nellie had a much happier, easier-going temperament than Clementine; and with her winning charm and gregarious nature, she made a host of friends in all walks of life. Her natural optimism and her capacity for friendship may well have made up for much in her life. The two sisters were devoted to each other, but from time to time there would be mild tiffs; and Nellie used sometimes to earn a good scolding from Clementine for her perennial propensity for gambling. But there was never a rift, and when she died, the very great number of letters which Clementine received were not only a true tribute to Nellie, but also showed that people realised the gap which would now be left in Clementine's life.

*

The highlight in my parents' personal lives in 1954 was Winston's eightieth birthday, in which event interest began to be evinced several months beforehand. Private people and public organisations alike conspired to make it perhaps one of the most widely celebrated birthdays on record. Both Houses of Parliament decided to make Winston a joint and all-party presentation on this occasion – to take the form of a portrait of himself by Graham Sutherland. The House of Commons were to give him a handsomely bound book recording the gift, and containing the signatures of all those of his fellow members who had joined to make this generous and imaginative gesture: only a very few members refused to participate. Sittings for the portrait started in mid-August at Chartwell, and both Winston and Clementine took at once both to Graham Sutherland and his charming wife. On 1st September my mother wrote to me (Christopher and I were in Scotland):

> Mr Graham Sutherland is a 'Wow'. He really is a most attractive man & one can hardly believe that the savage cruel designs which he exhibits, come from his brush. Papa has given him 3 sittings & no one has seen the beginnings of the portrait except Papa & he is much struck by the power of his drawing . . .

There were several more sessions at Chartwell, and in mid-November the Sutherlands spent a week-end at Chequers for the final sitting.

On 13th November, Winston visited Harrow (for the fifteenth year in succession) to take part in 'Songs'; a new verse had been added in his honour to 'Forty Years On', and the boys presented him with a cigar cabinet. During the weeks immediately preceding and following his actual birthday, individuals and organisations continued to shower him with wonderful presents. Thousands of people both in Britain and overseas sent contributions to a 'Winston Churchill Eightieth Birthday Presentation Fund', and on the day itself Lord Moynihan, on behalf of the fund, presented Winston with an 'interim' cheque for £150,000. When the fund was closed a year later the total subscribed by over 300,000 people came to £259,000. Winston made this amazing present into a Trust Fund from which he was able during the ensuing years to make handsome contributions to various causes, and in May 1958 he gave £25,000 from this Trust towards the founding of Churchill College, Cambridge.

When, on his actual birthday, Tuesday, 30th November, Winston went to Buckingham Palace for his usual Tuesday night audience with the Queen, she gave him four beautiful silver wine coasters, engraved with the ciphers of herself and the Duke of Edinburgh and the other members of her family who had joined to give this handsome present. During the day presents and greetings from all over the world poured into Downing Street – the telegrams and cards numbered over 23,000. It seemed that the love and regard in which Winston was held by all sorts and conditions of men and women welled up and spilled over. Both Winston and Clementine were deeply moved, and quite taken aback by these demonstrations.

On the morning of 30th November itself took place the moving, and in parliamentary history unique, ceremony, when both Houses of Parliament assembled in Westminster Hall to salute Winston Churchill, and to give him their presents – jointly the Sutherland portrait and (from the House of Commons) the commemorative book. The State Opening of Parliament by the Queen had taken place earlier in the morning, and afterwards members of both Houses and their wives proceeded to Westminster Hall for the presentation and addresses. The speeches, made by the Speaker, Lord Salisbury, the 'Father of the House' – Mr David Grenfell (who presented the book on behalf of the Commons), and Mr Attlee, were all felicitous, moving, and shot through with shafts of humour in true parliamentary vein, and transcending all barriers of political partisanship. Winston, who made his speech after the portrait had been unveiled, remarked of it with wryness: 'The portrait is a remarkable example of modern art. It certainly combines force and candour . . .'

But the picture itself had already become for him a source of deeply wounded feelings. Although he had seen some of the early sketches, he did not see the work again until it was finished, about a fortnight before his birthday – and he then took an instant loathing to it. He felt he had been betrayed by the artist, whom he had liked, and with whom he had felt at ease, and he found in the portrait causes for mortal affront. Clementine too was shocked by it – she thought it was a cruel and gross travesty of Winston, showing all the ravages of time, and revealing nothing of the warmth and humanity of his nature. They were both deeply disturbed by it, but when she realised the violence of Winston's reaction – to the extent that he even considered refusing to accept the picture, she threw her influence into calming his wounded sensibilities, and tried to make him concentrate on the feelings which the commissioning of this portrait represented, to which indeed he was very much alive, and to which he paid warm and heartfelt tribute in his speech. But all this made a great and emotional upset behind the scenes in the days prior to the presentation.

All shadows, however, were banished on the day, by the warmth of the ceremony, and by the tributes from political friends and foes alike, and by the acclamation of the great assembly as, at the end of the proceedings, Winston and Clementine (who was looking quite beautiful and radiant) walked slowly down the centre aisle. The thunderous applause seemed to envelop them both as they passed out of the great historic hall into the November sunshine, where more cheers awaited them from the crowds in Parliament Square.

Our own family celebration had to wait until the evening of the following day, when Clementine gave an after-dinner party for all the family, and for close friends and colleagues: about 170 people. It was at once cosy and splendid; with champagne, and hugs all round, and some sentimental tears. Round the intricate pink and white edifice of the birthday cake was a banner, upon which were inscribed the Shakespearian words:

> Take him all in all he is a man. We shall
> not look upon his like again.

*

A postscript to these wonderful days is provided in my diary for the ensuing week-end, which my parents spent at Chartwell:

> Mama has collapsed with fatigue and a streaming cold; and we all feel flat and stale and tired – WSC is fresh as a daisy, and enjoying mulling over his presents and letters![26]

DOES THE ROAD WIND UP-HILL ALL THE WAY?

FROM THE MOMENT of Winston's taking office once more as Prime Minister in the autumn of 1951, there lurked in the background of many people's minds the question: 'How long can he last?' In those early days he told his own intimate circle that he thought he would only stay in office for a year. By the end of that year, however, imminent resignation was far from his thoughts. During his serious illness in the summer of 1953 the idea of his retirement from office was widely discussed, and in some quarters, advocated. But then there had been his vigorous return to public life, dating from his speech at the Conservative Party Conference in October.

From that time on, however, until his resignation some nineteen months later, there not unnaturally continued to be speculation from time to time, either openly in the House of Commons and in the Press, or privately and in political circles. Winston took all this in his stride, and Clementine realised that as long as he continued in office there was bound to be comment and criticism, which neither surprised nor upset her. But she felt only contempt and disgust (as did many people) for the snide comments on the level of an exceptionally unchivalrous cartoon in *Punch* (3rd February 1954), where the effects of a stroke on Winston's face were clearly indicated. Although she was ever of the same mind about his 'second innings', which was certainly known by those in their immediate circle, Clementine was intensely loyal, and gave no encouragement to the voicing of similar views by others.

Winston realised perfectly clearly that the stroke he had sustained, despite his amazing recovery, had left its effects. In a letter to Clementine (who was at Aix-les-Bains) on 25th May 1954, he wrote in reference to an important speech he had shortly to make:

This is a toil which lies ahead of me and I do not conceal from you that original composition is a greater burden than it used to be, while I dislike having my speeches made for me by others as much as I ever did.

But periods of worrying about his capacities and feeling a lack of confidence alternated with a stubborn resolve to continue in office. When talking about the question of his possible retirement, Winston was wont to remark cheerfully that he meant to carry on until 'either things become much better, or I become much worse'.

That Clementine was perfectly able to take a realistic and unemotional attitude when dealing with the difficult question of Winston's resignation was demonstrated in an incident that took place in the middle of July 1954, shortly after Winston had returned from a visit to the United States and Canada. There was unrest in the Cabinet, which demonstrated itself in various ways, but involved Clementine when Mr Harold Macmillan (then Minister of Housing) asked to see her privately at No. 10. He told her that he came on behalf of himself and several close colleagues in the Government, to say that they thought Winston should retire in favour of Anthony Eden. Clementine listened attentively, and said she would of course convey this information to Winston. Immediately Mr Macmillan left her, Clementine sent for Jock Colville and recounted what had happened. This was during the course of the morning, and Winston and she were lunching alone together that day. Clementine begged Jock to join them, as she felt his presence would be helpful. Jock noticed that Clementine seemed very ill at ease at the beginning of luncheon, which was unusual, as she was never afraid of Winston, and could normally broach thorny questions without demur. But she must have been fully aware of the importance of Harold Macmillan's action, and that he would never have taken such a step but for real and valid reasons, and that the existence of such feelings in the heart of the Cabinet was, of course, of utmost significance.

Presently, however, Clementine took the plunge, and told Winston what had happened. She did so admirably – with calm detachment – merely giving the facts of the interview, and refraining from any comment. Winston took it rather well, and with complete calm; he merely asked Jock if he would go and telephone Mr Macmillan's office to say that the Prime Minister would be grateful if the Minister of Housing would 'step round' in the course of the afternoon.

During the ensuing interview, it appears that Winston was most urbane, but that he told Harold Macmillan that he thought he would soldier on, as there were several matters on hand that he would like to 'see through' – but of course, if the Tory Party wanted to get rid of him, they were at perfect liberty to do so.[1] Winston knew very well that he commanded not only the loyalty of the Tory Party as a whole, but also that his prestige transcended party barriers, and that neither his own party, nor the country as a whole, would look kindly upon a 'palace revolt' of discontented or impatient colleagues.

One of the reasons for the feelings of frustration and irritation (despite their undoubted admiration and affection for him) of his colleagues was the fact that, during the last twelve months before he finally resigned, Winston was continually changing his mind and his programme of timing. His own health and energy, combined with events, made it a difficult as well as, for him personally, an agonising decision. Churchill had a genuine and deep desire to see accomplished, or at least set on their way, a few major objectives. First among these was the rebuilding of that close and special relationship between the British Prime Minister and the President of the United States which had been so vital in the war, and which he thought held as great a significance now, in this time of uneasy peace.

Churchill had been the first to point to the silent, sinister encroachment of the power of Russia over Eastern and Central Europe, but after Stalin's death in 1953 he looked for any opportunity to make a fruitful contact with the new regime, despite the unhelpful orientation of American policy at that time.

Finally, when in February 1954 details of the American tests of the hydrogen bomb became known, Churchill at once grasped the immense gulf in power that now yawned between the atomic and the hydrogen bombs, and its sinister import for mankind. He sought another opportunity to visit President Eisenhower, specifically to discuss these matters: a fruitful meeting took place in June – it was to be his last as Prime Minister. And it was due largely to Churchill's realistic appraisal of the changed nuclear situation that the implications of the hydrogen bomb were faced and thought through in the British Chiefs of Staff paper on Global Strategy, which had an influence on American thought and policy.

These objectives which Churchill hoped so earnestly to achieve before laying down the burden of power and responsibility were not unworthy: nor was he wrong in feeling that, to them all (if time and strength were granted him) he could make a unique contribution. But also there was, of course, the reluctance of an old man to relinquish power. He cherished no illusions – there could never be a 'next time'. His long, varied and splendid public life would be over, and he did not relish the prospect of brooding over the cooling embers.

The uncertainty of Winston's intentions was not only an inconvenience to his colleagues in the Government: Clementine too found it perplexing in terms of their domestic arrangements. The Cuban Ambassador and his wife, who had been the tenants at 28 Hyde Park Gate, left early in 1954 at the conclusion of their lease. Unwilling to let the house again for a long period, Clementine managed to find a tenant who wanted a house for the summer months only; thereafter the house was not let again.

During the summer of 1954, Winston continued to be in a state of indecision. On the eve of the parliamentary recess I wrote in my diary, on 29th July:

> . . . W S C is a marvel & a mystery. And none of us *really* know what his intentions are – Perhaps he doesn't himself!

A month later the whole question must have been in the balance, for in a letter to my mother on Sunday, 29th August from Scotland, where Christopher and I were staying, I wrote:

> Papa rang up Chimp, & told him all had gone well on Friday [there had been a Cabinet meeting]. We are so glad. I'm sure indecision was the worst of all possible climates to live in for everyone – & liable to breed unrest.
>
> I'm afraid Papa's decision to stay must in some ways be a blow to you – I only hope that you are feeling better from yr neuritis & more rested, and that the winter ahead will not be too burdensome . . .

There was no more wavering for quite a little time after this, and indeed in the middle of October Winston made several important changes in Cabinet appointments. On 26th October 1954 I wrote in my diary:

> I've just been reading my journal of about a yr ago –

How fantastic it now seems that one actually thought & believed that Papa *must* retire!

He is in full flight now – having re-shuffled his government.

But everyone knew that the final decision could not be far off now, and only the right moment had to be found. It was perfectly clear to us all, as we assembled at Chequers for Christmas, that this would be the last one there. It seems appropriate that the record number staying in the house-party was reached that year, with the twenty-two signatures in the Visitors' Book, showing a complete muster of children and grandchildren.

In the New Year of 1955 Churchill realised that his hope of a summit meeting with the Russians would not be realised in a near foreseeable future. The present Parliament was in its fourth year, and he knew he had not the strength in him to fight another General Election as Prime Minister. He now faced up to the fact that he must fix on a definite date to resign. The first week in April seemed to be the most suitable, but up to the last possible minute the day itself was still uncertain. On 1st March 1955 he made a momentous and magisterial speech on the hydrogen bomb in the House of Commons. It was a month before his final resignation, and it was his last great pronouncement as Prime Minister.

During the week-end of 18th March, Christopher and I were at Chequers, and the date – 5th April – had been fixed, but was still not public knowledge. My father was in low, sad spirits that week-end, and bitter at moments. Clementine's neuritis had returned with a vengeance a little while before, and she had retreated to Chequers for a fortnight to rest and to try to throw it off. Although she was intensely relieved that the decision had at last been taken, she understood with deep compassion how dark a moment this was for Winston. In my diary for Saturday, 19th March, I wrote:

From now till the 'day' it will be hard going. He minds *so* much. It is sad to watch –

Mama too feels it – she said 'It's the first death – & for him, a death in life'.

When I wrote to my mother to thank her for our visit, I ended my letter:

I do think of you so much darling Mama – especially during these last days of Papa's public life – It must seem like the end of a long, long journey, full of harassments & trials – & triumphs & bitter-sweet joys and anxieties. But what a story! And I know it would not have been such a splendid one if you had not been there.[2]

For nearly a month from 25th March there was a major strike in the newspaper industry, and during that period London national newspapers ceased publication. But in the provinces the *Manchester Guardian* continued to appear and provided a running commentary on the events leading up to Winston's resignation. The strike meant, from a private and personal point of view, that we were spared the full pressure of press comment and speculation which would have been inevitable in these last few weeks, and which would have made life for Winston, his close circle and his government colleagues, that much more difficult. As it was, the programme as finally arranged took place with a measured dignity which did credit to everyone.

The week-end of 25th–27th March was their last week-end at Chequers. On Saturday, the 26th, Winston visited Woodford to open the Sir James Hawkey Memorial Hall; Clementine was unwell and remained quietly at Chequers. He gave no indication as to his immediate intentions. The rest of the week-end was spent very quietly, with just a few members of the family staying. Clementine's rest in the country had done her good, and they returned to London on the Monday for the 'last lap'.

On Tuesday, 29th March, Winston answered Prime Minister's Questions in the House of Commons, and later had his usual Tuesday evening audience with the Queen. Clementine had a busy week, making personal preparations, but 'business as usual' was very much the order of the day for her and for us all. On her seventieth birthday, Friday, 1st April, there was a party in the evening at No. 10 – a mixture of family and friends, including the Attlees, the Macmillans and the Morans. Winston and Clementine both stayed in London for that last week-end, Winston going down to Chartwell on the Sunday for the day. But Clementine remained at No. 10, garnering her strength.

On Monday, 4th April, the Queen and the Duke of Edinburgh came to dinner at No. 10. The occasion had been arranged quite some time before, and it had then been envisaged as a small party of not more than ten or twelve guests. But when it was realised that the date would, in fact, be on the very eve of Winston's resignation, it was felt that a small dinner party was no longer appropriate, and it was expanded to about fifty guests. Arranged somewhat hurriedly, the party was composed of an inspired jumble of Winston's several lives: the Speaker, the Leader of the House of Lords (Lord Salisbury) and other close colleagues in the Cabinet, including, of course, his successor, Anthony Eden; the Leader of the Opposition, Mr Attlee, and the Liberal Leader, Lord Thurso (Archie Sinclair) – all these among others, with their wives. The military glories of the past were remembered in the presence of Alex and Monty; Mrs Neville Chamberlain (a graceful touch), and the Duchess of Westminster, Nancy, the widow of Winston's great old friend, Bendor. The faithful 'in the wings' friends – Brendan and 'The Prof', and Winston's two Principal Private Secretaries, David Pitblado and Jock Colville and their wives, who had borne loyally and discreetly the heat and burden of many days. And lastly his closest family, Diana and Duncan, Randolph and June, Christopher and myself; but, sadly, no Sarah, who was in America.

Despite the absence of London newspapers there had been in the last few days a general sense of expectancy – and there was nearly always a crowd watching the comings and goings in Downing Street. Of course everyone at the dinner party knew or guessed its significance. It was splendidly done. Clementine sailed through it all, looking beautiful and calm. Winston, in proposing the Queen's health, made a touching, graceful and debonair speech, reminding the company that it was a toast

which I used to enjoy drinking during the days when I was a cavalry subaltern in the reign of Your Majesty's great-great-grandmother, Queen Victoria . . .

and he spoke of

> the wise and kindly way of life of which Your Majesty is the young and gleaming champion.

When he sat down, the Queen rose and with infinite charm proposed the health of 'My Prime Minister'. The next morning, Tuesday, 5th April, Winston presided over his last Cabinet, and in the afternoon he went to Buckingham Palace and tendered his resignation as Prime Minister to the Queen.

The following day there was a tea-party of about a hundred for all the staff at No. 10 – the private secretaries, the telephonists, the messengers, the drivers – so that he and Clementine could thank them and take leave of them all. Winston then left for Chartwell; Clementine remained behind in London as she had many things to arrange. He was cheered away by his staff, who lined the long corridor that leads from the Cabinet Room to the front door.

When he arrived in the gloaming at Chartwell there was a small crowd at the gates to welcome him back. Christopher and I both dined with him. He was in quite good form, and messages were flowing in. So all had been accomplished with fitness and, as Winston had said to a press reporter on the steps of Chartwell, 'It's always nice to come home.'

*

The week-end following Winston's resignation was Easter. Fortunately no one was staying, for Clementine was quite exhausted and the wicked neuritis had returned; so she spent a good deal of time in her bedroom. However, on Easter Sunday the Sandys family came down in force for luncheon, as well as three or four old friends and colleagues. The combination of family and friends was very welcome, and Winston was in buoyant form. Two days later he and Clementine flew off to Sicily, with Jock Colville and 'The Prof' for company. They were there a fortnight, and for Clementine the holiday was a failure: she had little respite from pain, and in addition the weather was cold and grey. Although Chartwell and Hyde Park Gate were both at this moment uninhabitable because of alterations and decorations, she was only too glad to get back to England, and they both stayed for a short time at the Hyde Park Hotel.

While they had been away the date of the General Election – 26th May – had been announced. Winston came back eager to help the Government in some way; but no suitable suggestion was made. It was quite natural that the new Prime Minister should wish to stand on his own feet, and not seem to be leaning on Winston's prestige: but it was hurtful. Winston took it rather more philosophically than all of us – who seethed. Anyway, he had his own seat to fight, and he addressed a few meetings outside his own constituency – one of them in Bedford, where he spoke for Christopher.

Churchill was once again elected at Woodford by a large majority. Throughout the country the election campaign was remarkable for its lack of excitement, and the Conservatives were returned with an increased majority. In the new Parliament

Churchill took the place he had habitually occupied in the thirties – the first seat below the gangway on the government side.

With the election over, Winston and Clementine had to settle down to a new tempo of life. All their family and closest friends were deeply concerned for Winston in this period, when the active and fascinating part of his public life had been sliced off for ever, and there remained none of the stimulation that the prospect of a return to the fray had previously always provided. Everybody rallied round to keep him company and to try to divert him. The gallant buoyancy of the days immediately following his resignation did not last, but was succeeded by long periods of depression, boredom and lethargy. On 11th June he had a 'spasm' – a mild one – but it made us all anxious.

For both Winston and Clementine the summer of 1955 was a dark valley to pass through. The strain of the uncertainty and the anxiety of the last months of Winston's tenure of office had left Clementine wrung-out. And with the removal of the stimulus which the multitude of her obligations had provided, she gave way to low spirits. Sarah and I worried about her. In a letter to her mother in Sicily, Sarah wrote:

Don't be sad – I cannot believe that all the sparkle and gaiety & care that you have given cannot in some little measure be given back – . . .[3]

At the end of July I wrote in my diary:

I am oppressed by the sadness of old age . . . CSC I know suddenly feels old & done for. And him – He just seems slower & sleepier every day . . .[4]

Although Clementine had longed for Winston to resign, and was particularly glad personally, in view of her own ill-health, to be relieved of entertaining and official obligations – in fact, the problem of adjustment to a more leisured way of life was, ironically, much more acute for her than for him.

For when his spirits revived – which they did – and when he was in reasonable health, life for him still had pleasures and many occupations. He now took up the completing of the four volumes of his *History of the English-Speaking Peoples*, started before the war, and laid aside ever since. Painting kept him occupied for many happy hours, and the resources of Chartwell never failed. His racing activities continued to prosper, and afforded him many pleasurable outings; there were cards; reading; and the affection and company of family and friends. And everywhere he went he was showered with loving, admiring attentions, which greatly touched and gratified him.

But for Clementine the problem was more difficult. Firstly, her poor state of health, which was to persist for a long period, coloured her whole outlook on life. Secondly, she had for so long lived a life of dedication to Winston and her public duty, that her capacity to enjoy herself (which had never been in any case a strong ingredient in her make-up) seemed to have withered – like a muscle that atrophies through lack of use.

Clementine had no hobbies such as gardening – that great solace and refuge for countless Englishwomen. For her it was more a matter of administration – not an absorbing or satisfying occupation; and her own active involvement stopped after dead-heading roses and irises. Nor did tapestry, knitting or embroidery – those other excellent forms of occupational therapy – appeal to her. Although she had driven a car in the past, during the years of their official life Clementine had a chauffeur, and she had lost the habit of driving. Now, when she tried to grapple once more with gears, and the increased volume and buzz of traffic, she found herself unequal to it. And so (to the barely concealed relief of her nearest and dearest) she abandoned driving. In these financially more palmy days she could always have had the services of a chauffeur, but to drive oneself gives a blissful measure of independence and flexibility in plans.

Social life as such, depending on charming fringe-friends, had never held anything for her, and her highly developed critical faculty combined with the puritanical streak in her character made her often at odds in the gilded temples (or villas) of Mammon. Clementine's splendid independence of mind, which so characterised her views and actions throughout her life, and which saved her from being a 'yes' woman to a dominating personality, did not extend into the territory of her own life and pleasures. If she had been more egotistical, more pleasure-loving or more personally ambitious, she might have been less at a loss when the calls of duty ceased to be so imperious and consuming. But if she had been any, or all of these things, the history of her relationship with Winston, and her influence over him, would certainly have been different. And so, to some extent, might have been the history of our times.

*

After Winston's resignation Clementine was determined to grapple seriously with the neuritis which had been plaguing her since the end of 1953. In May there is a record of a series of appointments with a new doctor. Then in early June she fell and broke her left wrist; she had to wear a plaster for many weeks, and the pain was so continuous and wearing that her doctors prescribed injections of pethidine, which she learnt to administer to herself every few hours.

Quite apart from her own health, this period was a sad and worrying one for Clementine on the family front: Winston had a 'spasm' in June; Diana was nervously ill again; and Sarah and Antony were in the throes of parting for good. There seemed to be no respite for her from pain or anxiety. Although she was loath to leave Winston at this time, she decided to go to St Moritz in August, where there was a centre for treatment which had been recommended to her. She was determined to get well herself, so as the better to look after him. She went to St Moritz for a month, staying at Suvretta House; and for part of the time I was able to be there with her.

In her own personal life, this was the first gleam of sunshine for a long time. The bracing mountain air, a spell of good weather, and encouraging results even after a few days of treatment, all combined to raise her spirits. Winston's care and anxiety for her is reflected in his constant flow of letters, nearly all of them written in his 'own paw', which always pleased her. 'Do write to me & don't give up hope', is how he ended a letter on 8th August, written shortly after her departure. He thought about her constantly, and I reported to her on 9th August (for I did not join her until later in the month):

> Darling Papa really does seem in distinctly better form these last five days. He was awfully worried & low about you, & I think knowing you had safely arrived & having had a letter – he feels much better about everything.

Clementine found one or two people she knew in or near St Moritz, and she made the acquaintance of a courtly and erudite old widower, Mr Lewis Einstein, who was also staying there. He was agreeable company, and we all trundled about in his large and comfortable car viewing panoramic sights. Nor did Clementine want for reading material, for Winston kept her supplied with his revised and polished chapters for *The English-Speaking Peoples*, which was engrossing his whole attention just now. He liked to know what she thought of them, and on receiving her comments on the early chapters he wrote, on 17th August:

> I am so glad you like it, and what you say about it is a great encouragement to me . . . I am delighted at what you say about helping a lot of people to read history . . .

When Clementine returned to Chartwell early in September, she was in better spirits. Later in the month both she and Winston went to La Capponcina (once more lent to them by the generous Max), taking Christopher and me with them. This visit proved a great success all round. Winston wrote and painted away, while Clementine had us both for company. Christopher was a great enlivener of Winston: making him laugh; playing cards with him; and, at times, teasing him affectionately. Winston and Clementine were lent a comfortable yacht, which was anchored at Monte Carlo, and in which we could all go for expeditions, which Clementine particularly enjoyed. She stayed in France for a whole month; while Winston remained on until the middle of November.

But, alas, the improvement in her health was not of long duration. As the autumn advanced the pain returned, and with it bad nights and despair of spirit. The pethidine brought periodic relief, but cured nothing; and in the sleepless hours, dark thoughts and cares multiplied. A Roman Catholic friend sent her a rosary, which she tried to learn to use. Her distress was obvious, and yet one did not seem to be able to help.

Sarah, who with Diana had gone out to France to be with their father, wrote on 9th November:

> I wish all was better for you – When you hold your rosary at night – do not wish for sad things – hold it for comfort – or pray we can all yet be happy – I am powerless & incapable in front of your despair – but I thank you for sharing it with me – it makes me feel closer to you. I love you very much
>
> > Your ever loving child.   Sarah

Sarah came very close to her mother in these dark days. She herself was going through the mill of personal unhappiness with the final break-up of her marriage, and she stayed quite a lot at Hyde Park Gate that winter, and was able to be with her mother more than usual. Diana was walking a narrow tightrope of nervous and physical health, and being close to them both, Sarah was able to play a healing and helpful role between Diana and her mother.

Christmas, which Winston and Clementine spent at Chartwell (as they were to do for the next six years), brought a more cheerful interlude. Sarah had to go back for a while to America, but Randolph and June came down, bringing with them Arabella, now aged six, who stayed with us and our brood at the Farm. Both the 'big' house and the 'small' combined continually in entertaining each other; all the Sandys family descended on Boxing Day, and a day or two later there was a lovely Christmas party for all the family and estate children.

Clementine had borne up over Christmas, but the New Year found her at a low ebb, and early in January 1956 she went into University College Hospital for a complete overhaul. It was expected that she would be there for not longer than three or four days, but unluckily she caught a streptococcal infection and became quite ill, only fending off pneumonia with antibiotics. Winston meanwhile, before Clementine became so ill, left for the South of France, as had been planned, where he stayed with his friend Mr Emery Reves at Roquebrune. Clementine was glad for him to be out there, and knew he was happy and well looked after. As usual, Winston wrote to her every two or three days, and was in daily touch with her doctors. At one point he very nearly returned home to be with her, but we persuaded him that she really was improving, and that he was better in the sunshine.

Clementine was in hospital for three weeks, and even when she was allowed home again she was still so tired that it was over a week before she wrote her first letter to Winston since she had been in hospital. On 29th January she wrote:

My darling, I am ashamed that this is my first letter to you. But I have been so sick & weary that I have not been able to hold a pen or read a book. But now I am really better . . .

'Sick and weary' she may have been, but the state of the world had not passed her by, and a sure sign of her improved health is shown in the spirited PS to this letter; commenting on the grave crisis in Cyprus, she wrote:

I am shocked that the Government mean (perhaps) to 'jam' Athens Radio. I can't imagine anything more ineffective. And all the time we have been scolding Russia for 'jamming' us – It's lucky the Government have got a long term before them or I think Gaitskell [Leader of the Socialist Opposition] would get them out . . .

During Clementine's imprisonment in hospital a plan for her convalescence was devised. It was arranged that she and Sylvia Henley (who had herself been far from well) should go by sea to Ceylon. This was an ideal plan for Clementine, as it would combine a long sea voyage, a warm climate and wonderful sightseeing, all of which things she enjoyed. In addition she would have the bracing company of Sylvia Henley, to whom she was devoted, and with whom she was totally at ease. Winston thoroughly approved of this plan, and he came home from France so as to be with her, returning to Roquebrune after her departure. From there he wrote her frequent accounts of his days, which were pleasantly divided between agreeable company, painting, writing, and house-hunting (of which latter activity more will be recounted later).

Clementine was a much less good correspondent, and although she had written or cabled from various stops on the outward journey, there was evidently a long gap, for Winston wrote rather reproachfully on 17th March (a month after her departure from home):

> My darling One – NO news from Ceylon by letter or telegram! I do hope this is because you and Sylvia are enjoying yourselves.

They were; and in fact letters were on the way: one with a description of a visit they had made to one of the great 'buried' cities of Ceylon, which had thrilled and interested them. Clementine and Sylvia returned home from their eight-week journey on 13th April, and as she wrote to Sarah on 1st May:

> We set out two old crocks & have returned quite set up again. I still tire very easily but, Thank God, the neuritis has faded away & both my arms feel equal . . .

With the improvement in her health, her spirits and her capacity to enjoy things also revived. Just over a month after she returned from her long journey, Clementine went off for a week's jaunt to Paris, staying with her 'St Moritz' friend, Mr Einstein. They went to four plays and visited the Louvre, the Carnavalet Museum, Malmaison, St Germain-en-Laye and Versailles. They also attended three dinner parties, and lunched at the British Embassy with the Ismays: a packed week, which she thoroughly enjoyed. During that summer life was quite busy at Chartwell, with a good many visitors coming and going, including the President and Mrs Truman, who came to luncheon towards the end of June. In early July Winston and Clementine gave a garden party for a large contingent of Winston's constituents; an occasion which became an annual event for several succeeding years.

During August, Clementine again returned to St Moritz. Despite the previous winter's relapse, she felt the cure there had done her great good. This time she stayed at the Palace Hotel, to be more in the centre of things and nearer her treatments. Unluckily, a day or two before she left home Clementine had a bad fall, and arrived, hobbling, in St Moritz covered with bruises; fortunately she had her maid with her (as she generally did now when she travelled). Most opportunely her crony, Mr Einstein, was once more taking the mountain air, and the trundles in the big car were more than ever a welcome diversion.

Meanwhile the Suez crisis was brewing. In early June Egypt declared that the Suez Canal Company's concession would not be extended, and had ordered British troops to leave the Suez base. Subsequently Colonel Nasser, the newly elected President of Egypt, nationalised the Canal, and the following month, August, he boycotted the London Conference on Suez and rejected the American proposals for the future international use of the Canal. Clementine followed all this as best she could from the newspapers and the radio. Winston was kept informally in touch with the situation, but he explained to her on 3rd August: 'As I am well informed, I cannot in an unprotected letter tell any secrets . . .' My mother described to me in a letter on 9th August, how she and some English acquaintances in the hotel had been

... breathless & ears cocked round the Wireless trying to hear Anthony Eden. We gathered most of what he said (altho' we were told that Russia was jamming). Everybody was rather disappointed – I was loyal and said it was excellent –

Clementine came home to Chartwell towards the end of August and we all rejoiced to see her at last in very much better health. It had been such a long, hard grind, and now she really did seem to have made strides towards recovery. Winston and she remained at Chartwell together until the middle of September, when Winston went off to Roquebrune, Clementine staying on only a short time at Chartwell before going to London, where she indulged in a positive orgy of theatre-going. All Winston's letters from France spoke of his joy and relief at her recovery. On 24th September he wrote:

My darling One, It is such a pleasure to receive your letters. The handwriting is so strong and you can dash them off with a vigour wh shows your troubles and their consequences are now steadfastly relegated to the background.

*

Soon after Winston's resignation, Anthony Montague Browne, who had been in the Private Office at No. 10 since 1952, came to look after Winston's affairs. Anthony had been a pilot in the R.A.F. during the war, and had been awarded the D.F.C. After the war he had entered the Foreign Service, and in due course became one of the Prime Minister's Private Secretaries. He had, during his time there, gained the esteem and confidence of both Winston and Clementine, and when Winston resigned Anthony was seconded by the Foreign Office to work for him. In ceasing to be Prime Minister, Winston remained until the day of his death a world figure, and it was essential that his affairs, public and private, should be watched over and handled by someone trained in the tradition and ways of the public service. It would be impossible to overrate the service which Anthony rendered Winston in the last ten years of his life. Winston confided all his affairs to him, and Clementine too depended much on him for help and advice in many matters. Giving up his prospects of a promising career in the Diplomatic Service, Anthony remained to help Winston long after there was any glamour or excitement in the job. And in those last years of slow, sad decline he never failed in his loyal and devoted service and companionship to Winston, and became a trusted friend of all of us in the family. It was indeed fitting that on the last cold, grey morning he would be with us all.

*

For several years, Winston (in those moments when he contemplated life in retirement) had toyed with the idea of buying a villa in the South of France. Clementine had viewed this project with dismay from the start: she had quite enough trouble running two establishments. But the idea of a house of his own on the Riviera took deep root in Winston's imagination. He had always loved that sunshine region, and the thought of being able to spend months on end there, installed in his own sur-roundings, painting and writing and sitting in the sun, glowed in his mind. With his resignation the scheme became a matter for active and immediate consideration. Because Winston had so set his heart upon a house in France, Clementine really tried to consider the proposition with an open mind. But the more she thought about it, the larger loomed all the difficulties. First, to find a really nice property, then the enormous cost of the purchase and subsequent alterations, and finally (and for her most worrying of all) how to staff and run it. Many of her objections could be (and were) swept aside, but two remained immovable: her dread of having a third establishment to run, and the fear that although Winston was now much better off than at any other time in his life, yet this project might well over-stretch him financially in the long run, and she dreaded the prospect of a return to their economic cliff-hanging of former years. In her view, the only real advantage she saw in Winston having his own house was that it would remove the necessity of accepting hospitality on a large scale from very rich and, in her opinion, not always very suitable people. This last consideration carried real weight with her.

Winston pooh-poohed Clementine's prudent and practical objections with an airiness which greatly irritated her, and the 'Villa' discussions could become ex-plosive. The family was somewhat divided in their views and sympathies over this thorny question. We could see both sides of it, but one sometimes had the feeling that Clementine made too much of the difficulties, and it was easy to sympathise with Winston's wish for a holiday home in the sun.

But Winston was not to be easily put off, and from 1955 for two years he was seldom in the South of France without making enquiries, and sending out recon-naissance parties to view prospective villas. The regional newspapers daily reported details of his search, and, of course, once it was known that 'Monsieur Churchill' was looking for a residence, villas appeared from behind every cactus, at double the asking price! Winston did not conceal from Clementine that he was house-hunting, but when she was with him he wisely refrained from sending her on hot and tiring expeditions. He just hoped something lovely would 'turn up' and that she would be charmed by it. When she was in England, he would send her accounts of 'Hunt-the-Villa', always reassuring her that nothing precipitate would be done. But these activities caused poor Clementine much anxiety, which was well under-stood by Sarah who, while staying with her father in France in November 1955, wrote to her mother:

> . . . we have been going to see villas (mostly monstrous!) with vague plans of buying – don't worry – he would never without you – I don't think he even wants to really – but he does love the sun so . . .[5]

Notwithstanding the elusive nature of the 'Dream Villa', Winston, after his resignation, spent great chunks of the year abroad. He could have gone to hotels; and he could now afford the very best ones. But to people of that generation the charm and seclusion of 'private life' in private houses, with private service, was very powerful. Moreover, to anyone of Winston's eminence, a private domain is the only protection from prying eyes, whether they are admiring, malicious or merely curious. Winston was blessed in his friends, and he had found in the past and now, hospitable havens, where he could be undisturbed.

Since 1949 Winston and Clementine often stayed at La Capponcina. Sometimes Max Beaverbrook would be there himself, and at other times he would lend them the house with its charming housekeeper, excellent chef and smiling staff. Winston loved staying there, and Clementine, for her part, disliked being at La Capponcina less than anywhere else on the Riviera. Indeed, she had some very happy visits there, especially when any of us children, or Anthony Montague Browne and his wife Nonie, of whom she was very fond, were staying. She had no qualms about Winston accepting princely hospitality from such an old friend, and she and Max had long since called a truce in their warfare. In these last years Max showed all his winning charm to her and, when challenged, Clementine had to admit that she had become quite fond of him. Winston was of course greatly gratified to see the end of hostilities, for not only was Max Beaverbrook a friend of fifty years' standing, but, as others slipped away, he became the survivor of them all.

In 1956 Winston went to stay for the first time with Mr Emery Reves at his home near Roquebrune. La Pausa is a large house standing high on the shoulder of the mountainside above Cap Martin, commanding sensational views towards Menton on one side and Monte Carlo on the other. Emery Reves, by origin a Hungarian Jew from Budapest, came into Winston's life before the war when he handled the foreign rights of many of his newspaper articles. In 1940 he had become a British subject; during the war most of his family in Europe were liquidated, and he himself was badly wounded in a London air-raid. After the war Mr Reves acquired the foreign-language rights in Churchill's *War Memoirs* and the *English-Speaking Peoples*, making thereby a great deal of money both for his client and for himself. Emery Reves lived mainly in the United States, and he also owned this house on the Riviera, which he filled with his remarkable collection of chiefly Impressionist pictures. And it was here that he hospitably invited Winston and Clementine and members of their family, on many occasions and for long periods in the fifties. The châtelaine of La Pausa was a beautiful woman, a good deal younger than Emery, Wendy Russell, a former New York model.

In January 1956, when Winston paid his first visit to La Pausa, Clementine was ill in hospital, going very shortly afterwards to Ceylon to convalesce. Winston therefore went without her to Roquebrune, accompanied by Anthony Montague Browne, and being joined later by Diana. Winston's letters to Clementine were full of the beauties and comforts of the house, and of the care, kindness and thoughtfulness of his hosts. During this visit Winston was seriously searching for a furnished villa to rent, and Emery and Wendy accompanied him on several inspections. But it was due to their hospitable blandishments and to the fact that he was then, and on successive visits, so comfortable and happy in their house, that he abandoned the search for a villa of his own.

Clementine paid her first visit to La Pausa later that year, joining Winston there on 1st June after her whirlwind week in Paris. She could only stay five days as she had to get back to England, where she had engagements. During the next few years Winston was to make some ten visits to La Pausa, staying often for many weeks at a time. But Clementine was there with him on only four occasions, and (except in the early spring of 1958, when Winston was seriously ill) she made her visits as short as was compatible with politeness. Emery and Wendy repeatedly invited her, and to their welcoming motions Winston added his pleading. But the fact was that Clementine did not enjoy herself there. She found life at La Pausa claustrophobic. Not having a car, it always meant hiring one specially; and to take a walk outside the villa grounds was difficult, as the mountainside was very steep. Winston worked all morning in bed, and after luncheon painted or rested; in the evenings he liked to play cards for a while; he loved her being there, but he was not companionable. Emery and Wendy were full of care for Winston, and solicitous for all their guests' pleasure, but Clementine found she was really the prisoner of kindness and of other people's plans. And although it was mostly smiles and pleasantness on the surface, there was very little she and her hosts had in common. Seeing therefore that Winston wanted for nothing at La Pausa, and was surrounded by care for his every need, she preferred to stay in England or to make some other plan for herself.

It must also be remembered that Clementine had a long and abiding dislike of the Riviera and all it stood for. When, after 1959, Winston took to staying at the Hôtel de Paris in Monte Carlo, she usually went out to keep him company for at least part of his visits: but it really was a sort of penance. In a letter to Sarah from there in January 1960, she burst out: 'God – the Riviera is a ghastly place. I expect it's all right if you keep a flower shop or if you're a waiter!'[6] And in the autumn of that year, staying again in Monte Carlo, she wrote to me: 'I am suffocated with luxury & ennui as you feared . . .'[7]

Presently, however, a new feature of sunshine holiday life developed which was to prove pleasurable to both Winston and Clementine. During Winston's first visit to La Pausa he made the acquaintance of Mr Aristotle Onassis, the Greek shipowner and millionaire. Winston wrote to Clementine, who was in hospital, on 17th January 1956 that:

> Randolph brought Onassis (the one with the big yacht) to dinner last night. He made a good impression upon me. He is a vy able and masterful man & told me a lot about Whales. He kissed my hand!

A little while later the villa party were all invited to dine aboard the *Christina* with Mr Onassis and his wife Tina. Winston told Clementine that Ari Onassis had offered to lend them the yacht, which offer Winston did not accept, but he told Clementine in his letter of 8th February, 'It [the yacht] is the most beautiful structure I have seen afloat.' The following February, when both Winston and Clementine were at La Pausa, they lunched on board the *Christina*, and Clementine also had the opportunity of meeting this compelling and most unusual man and the lovely Tina. These were the beginnings of a friendship which was to bring much enjoyment and pleasure to Winston and Clementine, for at the end of September 1958 Ari Onassis invited them both for a ten-day cruise in the Mediterranean. They had been staying at La Capponcina, where they had celebrated their Golden Wedding. Both Winston and Clementine enjoyed the cruise, and it made the perfect epilogue to the golden summer.

In the next two years they were the guests of Ari and Tina on four more journeys, one being a three-week cruise in Greek waters in the summer of 1959. And in March 1960 they embarked at Tangier for nearly a month's journey which took them to the West Indies. Clementine, who had visited many of these islands before the war with Lord Moyne in the *Rosaura*, particularly enjoyed this cruise. She was able to re-visit Nelson's Harbour in Antigua, in raising funds for the restoration of which she had been most active a few years before. Clementine had always loved sea journeys, and now here were holidays they could share. Ari and Tina were the epitome of thoughtfulness and kindness, inviting as well as Winston and Clementine people whom they knew would be a pleasure to them. 'Cruising' was a new thing in Winston's life, and in these luxurious circumstances, and with such delightful hosts, it is not surprising that he found the journeys highly agreeable. Moreover, as the years slid by and Winston became less mobile, this was the ideal holiday for him.

They were both very sad when Ari and Tina parted and, shortly afterwards, in 1961, were divorced. Although Tina was a much younger woman, her charming manners, her gaiety and her kindness always made life on board the *Christina* enjoyable for everybody. Clementine said she missed her very much after her departure. They were, however, to meet each other again in a different context quite soon, for in 1961 Tina married Winston's cousin, Sunny Blandford. But after 1960 Clementine did not go with Winston for any of the three cruises that remained to him in the *Christina*.

*

Reading old diaries and letters reminds one strongly how much one lives life from day to day. It is only on looking back over a span of years as a whole that patterns emerge in such things as holidays, habits and health. During the ten years of life that were left to Winston after his resignation, he weathered numerous minor incidents of ill-health, as one would expect in someone of his age, which varied in degree from the odd bronchial cold, annoying 'tickles' and such-like passing in-dispositions, to the more worrying 'dizzy spells', and the occasional 'spasm', which were significant, and always exacted a toll, however slight or imperceptible. Hanging over him was the possibility of another major stroke, which might kill or, worse, disable him. In this last decade of his life Winston also survived one serious bout of pneumonia, and two bad falls. As a result of the first he broke a bone in his neck in November 1960; in the second, two years later aged eighty-eight, he broke his hip in a fall in the Hôtel de Paris at Monte Carlo, having to be flown back to London, where he was in hospital for nearly eight weeks.

Even after his retirement from public life, the Press throughout the world kept a constant watch on Winston's general health, and the smallest indisposition (if noticed) aroused their interest, and also their suspicion that there might be 'more to it' than was given out in any statement. The solicitude of the public for his well-being continued, letters and enquiries from all over the world literally pouring in when he suffered some publicised illness or accident. But this interest and solicitude were somewhat overpowering to deal with, and Clementine and the rest of the family were at considerable pains therefore not to draw attention to Winston's minor indispositions, which so often passed off in a day or two. In the case of rumours circulating, or during any of his graver illnesses, statements or regular bulletins were always made to the Press. And it was at times like these that Anthony Montague Browne's efficiency, judgment and calm were invaluable.

Looking back over those years one can see that Winston had reasonably good health for about two and a half years after his resignation. Clementine, and all of us, were always watchful and anxious – sometimes perhaps too anxious. But what one sees now to have been a passing and maybe trivial episode, could have been the start of a grave, or even of the final illness. In retrospect the two features of Winston's pattern of health seem to have been (I speak of course as a layman) bouts of melancholy or lethargy, and increasing deafness. After the few sad months which succeeded his resignation his interest in life and all his 'toys' and occupations revived. But in these latter years he did tend from time to time to sink into periods of silence and gloom; from which he would often emerge with startling suddenness – rather like a sinking fire which suddenly burns up bright and clear.

By 1955 Winston was becoming increasingly deaf, and like most people he put up an obstinate resistance to the idea of wearing a hearing-aid. Clementine sometimes scolded him quite fiercely about the need for him to do so, not only for his own sake but for other people's. Winston gradually came to realise his need for a device; but it was a necessity he loathed, and he often had to be prodded into wearing it.

In the middle of January 1958 Winston went to stay at La Pausa. Clementine planned to join him there for a week later on in February. The latter end of the previous year had not been good for her healthwise; a minor foot operation had necessitated a week in hospital, and in December she had been laid low with two recurring attacks of influenza, which had a debilitating effect. Now in the New Year disturbing news came from America about Sarah. In August 1957, Antony Beauchamp had taken his own life by an overdose of sleeping pills. He and Sarah had been separated for nearly two years, but his death came as a tremendous shock to her; and suicide leaves such a cruel legacy of unanswered, often unanswerable questions. During the winter Sarah went back to America, where she had plenty of work on offer, and in the New Year she was living all alone in a house on Malibu Beach near Los Angeles, while she was working on a television programme.

On 14th January 1958 it was reported in the British Press that Sarah had been arrested and charged with being drunk. There were of course distressing photographs and accounts of the episode. In the subsequent court case, she pleaded guilty and was fined. Clementine was of course deeply distressed for Sarah, and also made wretched by the blazing publicity which inevitably attended the affair. On this occasion, as when there were other similar incidents, Winston minded very much and grieved for Sarah, but he always took it less hard than did Clementine. As he grew older he seemed to acquire a degree of insulation from sad or unpleasant news about those he loved, which is perhaps one of the kinder gifts Time bestows. But, of course, there were no shut doors. When Sarah arrived back from America in early February Winston was staying at La Pausa, and she went straight there to be with him. Ten days later her mother flew out to join them. Sarah was in France with them both for two or three weeks, writing to her mother after she left:

. . . I was so grateful for your sweetness and reticence with me – . . . Thank you both – you and Papa for being so gentle and understanding – [8]

In mid-February, Winston became ill with a chest cold which developed rapidly into pneumonia. By coincidence, Clementine had arrived for an already planned visit the same day as the first bulletin saying Winston was 'indisposed' was issued on 18th February. But the one week's visit she had envisaged turned into a month. Lord Moran flew out the next day; Winston was really quite ill, but he responded well to the treatment, and was after about ten days in a fragile, but convalescent state. He was due to go to America in the third week of April, and up till now was determined to stick to his plans; but on 15th March my mother wrote to me:

Papa, for the first time shews hesitation about going to America –
I think Alas – he feels definitely weaker since his illness – He certainly made a marvellous recovery, but without the mass use of antibiotics he would have sunk and faded away . . . If Papa does go to America . . . would you go with him in my place? I don't feel strong enough, I am ashamed to say; but I think a member of his family should go . . . Of course – *I* hope he won't go – If he does not make one or two speeches & television appearances, the visit will be a flop as regards the American People – who . . . want to see and hear him. Then if he lets himself be persuaded to make public appearances it will half kill him. Monty, the dear creature has just arrived & thinks Papa is crazy to contemplate the idea . . .

Monty's visit had been most opportune, and a comfort to them both. A few days later, on 18th March 1958, my mother wrote to me: 'Monty returns to Versailles [his HQ as Deputy Supreme Commander, Europe] this morning. His visit has been a great tonic . . .' One day he and Clementine visited Menton: 'We went into a beautiful old church & burnt 2 candles for Papa.' In his illness Winston felt more than ever that he wanted Clementine there. She knew this, and although these weeks must have seemed very long, there was no question of her not staying with him: 'I shall stay & return with Papa, even if he lingers on after recovery', she told me in the same letter.

At about this time Winston had a relapse, which proved rather worrying. On top of the recurrence of the pneumonia, he was also suffering from jaundice. There were more bulletins, and his return home, which had been planned for the end of the month, was postponed. Lord Moran, who had returned home after Winston's first improvement, leaving him in the excellent care of a local British doctor, now returned to take stock of the new situation. After a few days, Winston again improved, and this time did not look back. But of course the illness and relapse had left him in a weak state.

He was finally well enough to return home on 3rd April, two days after Clementine's seventy-third birthday, and in time to spend Easter at Chartwell. He had made a remarkable recovery, but good sense prevailed, and about a week later an announcement was made of the cancellation of his intended visit to the United States. It is hardly surprising that this long and tiring illness should have definitely affected Winston's health, and it was soon after his return from France that it was thought he needed more continual care than could be given him by a valet who had other duties in the household as well. A full-time nurse, Roy Howells, was therefore engaged, who looked after him in every way with devotion and kindness until Winston's death.

One realises in retrospect that it was from the time of this illness that Winston started to decline generally. But the twilight was long, and as after a glorious day the beams of the sun linger on, lighting parts of the slowly darkening landscape – so it was to be with Winston's last years.

*

This year of 1958 which had started so badly had, however, a happy and glorious finale. On 12th September Winston and Clementine celebrated their Golden Wedding. They were staying with Max Beaverbrook at La Capponcina and spent the day quietly, but very happily. Messages of affectionate congratulation poured in: and one of Winston's horses, Welsh Abbot, had enough sense of occasion to win a race at Doncaster. Of the family, only Randolph and Arabella were able to be there; but (aided by Arabella, who recited reams of a classical poem, 'The Garland of Meleager', for the edification of her grandparents) Randolph gave them on behalf of all their children a token of our present, which was a border of golden roses for Chartwell. Since the summer months are not the time for planting borders, Randolph had conceived the wonderful idea of asking a number of famous artists and friends each to paint one of the roses that would be in the border. Paintings, engravings and drawings in great variety were contributed by (among others) Augustus John, Ivon Hitchens, Duncan Grant, Vanessa Bell, Cecil Beaton, John Nash, Oliver Messel, Adrian Daintry, André Dunoyer de Segonzac and Sir Matthew Smith. Gifted friends and relations also added their offerings, making a dazzling and unique 'catalogue' of roses. The pictures had all been sumptuously bound in a large album, and the script and the illuminations were exquisitely done by Denzil Reeves of Colchester. Later that year the border was duly planted. It runs like an avenue through the centre of the kitchen garden, circling the sundial where the Bali dove lies buried. It was a romantic idea, and soon looked lovely in reality, and I believe it gave our parents pleasure.

I minded dreadfully not being able to be with my parents on this glorious day, but a combination of children, domesticities and politics held me in England. However, I wrote to my mother:

> . . . we thought & spoke about you & Papa *so* much over the Glorious Golden 12th and had such loving telegraphic exchanges; . . . What moving and touching tributes! I felt so proud & so gratified that your great achievements, & all your long years together should receive the praise due. You see now what you *both together* mean to hundreds & thousands of people . . .[9]

Sarah, writing from London, echoed the same thought:

> I wonder if you know how many people share in the joy & pride of today? And what another aspect of radiance you both have shed upon daily life by the way you have led your private lives . . .[10]

One final gleam of glory in this year was in November, when General de Gaulle (as Head of the French Government) invested Winston with the Cross of the Liberation. This is the highest award designated for those who served with the Free French Forces or in the Resistance. It was a signal honour, and a gesture which moved Winston and Clementine deeply. They both stayed at the British Embassy with Sir Gladwyn and Lady Jebb, and on 6th November Clementine watched the ceremony of the Investiture by General de Gaulle in the garden of the Hôtel Matignon. Whatever had been the differences between these two men over the years, only the strong link which bound them – a fierce love of liberty and of France – was remembered on this day.

After the ceremony, Winston and Clementine lunched with General and Madame de Gaulle at the Hôtel Matignon. One cannot help wondering if Clementine told the General that she had a few months previously won a bet on his account. On 29th May 1958 de Gaulle had been voted into power by the French people after growing unrest in Algeria, and a series of short-lived governments in Paris. Always a strong supporter and admirer of the General's, Clementine had 'backed her fancy'. In early June, in a letter to Max Beaverbrook, she had added this delightful post-script:

I've won £50 over General de Gaulle. Someone 3 months ago bet me he would never be in public life again! I took it at once.[11]

The General was to confirm her good judgment even more, when six weeks after he had so signally honoured Winston, he was overwhelmingly elected as President of the French Republic.

TWILIGHT AND EVENING BELL

CLEMENTINE's health had been better for about a year after she had finally thrown off the accursed neuritis. But from the summer of 1958 she started to suffer from shingles, which affected her face, eyelid and eye. Shingles is a painful, lowering and persistent complaint, and although it developed slowly and fitfully, it all but ruined a delightful holiday in Morocco in August 1958. She had been invited by Bryce and Margaret Nairn to stay with them in Tangier; this was a friendship which brought Clementine much happiness and pleasure over the years. After their first meeting at Hendaye in the summer of 1945 they had next all met up at Madeira, where Winston and Clementine had spent the New Year of 1950, and where again the Nairns were *en poste*. Now, Bryce Nairn was Consul General at Tangier, and Clementine went out to spend three weeks with them at the British Legation. Apart from the shingles, which was a harassment, she had a most enjoyable time with the Nairns, and flew back to France just in time to join Winston for their Golden Wedding celebrations.

In the New Year of 1959, Winston and Clementine went back to their old haunt, Marrakech, staying at the Mamounia Hotel. Since their last visit there eight years before, Morocco had become independent, and Clementine noticed changes. The hotel was in a rather dilapidated state, and there seemed to be hardly any tourists. The Nairns came up from Tangier, and the Churchill party had also imported its own fun, as my mother reported to me on 28th January:

> The first ten days were enlivened by Jock, Meg and Biddy Monckton – When Papa heard that Biddy was coming without Walter, he was rather sulky . . . But soon he took to her like a house on fire & kissed her tenderly on departure. As for Meg, she & Papa flirted outrageously & almost romped . . . When they all went away poor Papa fell into the doldrums – He is better now & has started a picture from the terrace outside his bed-room.

Most of the party had been ill part of the time with one minor affliction or another, but, my mother continued:

> . . . Thank God Papa is blooming in his health. His memory fails a little more day by day & he is getting deafer. But he is well. I have learnt to play poker & enjoy it very much . . .

Their visit to Marrakech lasted a month, and on 19th February they boarded the *Christina* at Safi, joining the hospitable Ari Onassis for a cruise in the Atlantic which took them to the Canary Islands.

Winston's health was such that he was able to undertake a visit to the United States in May of that year. He had not been well – he had circulatory troubles – just before the journey, and both Lord Moran and Clementine were anxious lest the strain of the visit should be too much for him: but he was determined to go. Clementine had not planned to make this journey, nor would Winston allow Lord Moran to accompany him; he hated to appear an invalid. So off he flew with Antony Montague Browne to Washington, where he was warmly received by General Eisenhower, and stayed with him at the White House. During the course of his visit, Winston made a speech at a dinner. From Washington he flew to New York, and stayed a day or two with Bernie Baruch. After this stimulating but tiring week in the United States he returned home safe, if only fairly sound, to England; he had 'got away with it' again.

Clementine was plagued by shingles for a year, but at last it abated, although it left her with a drooping eyelid. Fortunately this could be put right: and at the end of August 1959 she was operated on by Sir Benjamin Rycroft, who completely cured the blemish. It was while she was recovering from the operation at the Queen Victoria Hospital, East Grinstead, that Sir Benjamin took her into a large ward and told her that a great number of the patients there could have their sight restored if only there was enough corneal tissue available. Clementine was so struck by this that she forthwith willed her eyes to Moorfields Eye Hospital for therapeutic purposes.

With Winston's resignation in 1955, the load of public obligations had been greatly reduced for Clementine, and in the succeeding eighteen months, in consequence of her poor health, she undertook only the minimum of engagements. But as her health improved she once more started to accept invitations in connection with various causes which either appealed to her personally or with which she already had some link either through Winston, or on her own account. Her diary in the succeeding year or two shows a sprinkling of plaque-unveilings, hospital ward or department openings, and other similar functions. And, of course, she was ever faithful to Winston's constituency. But in these latter years she avoided engagements far from London, as she found the travelling too long and tiring.

Winston and Clementine were included in nearly all great State occasions, such as royal weddings, and State banquets for visiting potentates. They both went regularly to the Garter Service at Windsor every June until 1960, after which Winston found the long procession and service too exhausting. And a feature of their winter programme which Clementine enjoyed as much as Winston was their annual visit to Harrow for 'Songs'.

In these later years Clementine took part in two major public appeals. In the course of World Refugee Year she made a radio appeal at Christmastime 1959, which brought in £48,000. The following year Winston gave one of his pictures to be auctioned at Sotheby's in aid of refugees, and during the summer one of the Chartwell garden openings was in aid of the same cause.

Two years later Clementine lent her name to, and followed with interest, the appeal for the buildings of New Hall, Cambridge, the University's third college for women. Ever since her Berkhamsted days, when Miss Harris had fired her with a desire to go to university herself, Clementine had kept a strong sense of the necessity for the opening up, and levelling up, of opportunities for women. Now, because of her age and health, she felt unable to do more than lend her name. But the Chairman of the Council of New Hall assured her that her support and backing would be a tremendous help. A year or two previously she had used her influence to ensure that Churchill College, Cambridge, would open its doors to women. At one of the early meetings of the Trustees, Winston had said that 'My wife thinks women should be admitted to Churchill . . . and I think so too . . .'[1] And Churchill became the first college in Oxford or Cambridge to receive women students on the same terms as men, and living in the same college.

But as throughout all her married life, Clementine's first priority had been to run her home. Her standards of perfection never altered, nor her attention to minute detail. Her right hand in all her domestic arrangements was, as ever, Grace Hamblin. Good servants were not easy to find: there were the true stalwarts like Mrs Landemare, who had been in our lives for over twenty years; Vincent, the Head Gardener, who remained and stayed on after the National Trust took over Chartwell; and Bullock, the chauffer, who was with them until Winston's death. But these lynchpins apart, other members of the household tended not to stay for very long. They nearly all disliked the shuttling to and fro between Chartwell and Hyde Park Gate, which must indeed have been tiring and restless. Although 'time off' was meticulously planned (and Clementine's diary is full of little notes as to whose day off it was), the entertaining in both houses, although no longer on an official scale, was almost continuous, and there were also the secretaries and nurses (two now) to be fed. Of course there were quite long periods when Winston was abroad, but it was rare for both houses to be shut, as Clementine spent so much more time at home than Winston. Considering that she was now in her seventies and in fragile health, it is hardly surprising that she often felt daunted by the demands life made on her both inside and outside her home. No wonder she had jibbed at the thought of another household in France!

After 1955, when Chartwell had once more become their only country base, Winston and Clementine spent a larger proportion of the year there than in London. Until 1962 (in the summer of which year Winston broke his hip), Christmas and the New Year were always spent at Chartwell, as were most of the Easter and Whitsun recesses. Although, as time went on, Winston used to go for longer and more frequent visits abroad, especially during the first dark dreary months of the year, when he was in England week-ends at Chartwell were sacred. And as time went on 'the week-end' became longer and longer, Friday-to-Monday soon becoming Thursday-to-Tuesday. June, July and August saw them almost continuously at Chartwell; September was a favourite 'cruising' or 'abroad' month. October, November and December were again 'week-ends at Chartwell' months.

The reconciliation between Clementine and Chartwell, which had its beginnings soon after the end of the war, blossomed in these last ten years of their life there into a period when she took increasing pleasure and satisfaction in this place which had always represented an earthly paradise to Winston, and up to now had afforded her mainly worry and fatigue.

The relief from gnawing financial care was a major factor in this change in her attitude, and the knowledge that Chartwell would one day be open in perpetuity to the public gave her an incentive, and a longer perspective than she had ever had before. In the gardens and grounds she now planned with an eye to the future. In the past she had so often tried to dissuade Winston from undertaking large-scale works, but now the boot was on the other foot! Clementine conceived and carried out several major improvements, while Winston made demurring noises – although he nearly always admired and approved the final result. The most successful (and the most expensive) of all her projects was the wholesale removal of the ratty old greenhouses, dilapidated frames and potting-sheds from the site they had hitherto occupied, and the erection of a splendid range of glass in a much better place, where the buildings were concealed behind a wall. The space made vacant by the sweeping away of the old greenhouses was transformed into a wide and sunny terrace, which looks out across the vegetable garden and away over the Weald of Kent.

But Clementine had always found the gardens too spread out and exhausting to cope with; and now that she was older this was even more the case. The parts of the garden she liked the best were the croquet lawn, where she spent many happy hours, and the grey-walled rose garden, which was not too far from the house, and on a scale she could manage and enjoy. About 1949, she moved her bedroom from up aloft in the Tower Room suite (whither she had ascended in the first wave of post-war alterations) down onto the ground floor, converting the blue sitting-room into a charming bedroom, which gave out onto the pink terrace. Here Clementine made a 'trough' garden, where she loved to sit out with her guests. In the spring the deep wooden troughs and tubs were filled with white tulips, forget-me-nots and polyanthus; while in the summer they spilled over with single white geraniums, cherry pie, fuchsias and verbena.

The frequent openings of Chartwell gardens to the public made her intensely 'garden proud', and Vincent and his gardeners found it a considerable challenge to produce the standard they all aimed at two, three or four times in the summer. Clementine liked to be there on the open days, and took a keen and competitive interest in the numbers of people who came (often as many as 6,000), and the amount of money raised for various good causes.

In these later years Clementine happily spent more and more time at Chartwell, particularly in the spring and summer, even when Winston was away. The fact that Christopher and I and our children lived at the bottom of the garden undoubtedly made a difference to her life in the country. Our plans were carefully concerted, and hardly a day went by without some contact. And if Clementine was away and Winston alone at Chartwell, she confided him to our care, and we dined or lunched with him, or he with us, almost daily.

By the time Christopher and I had four children Chartwell Farm was really bursting at the seams, and so we had to look for a larger house. It was a great wrench for us all when we moved away in 1957 to Hamsell Manor at Eridge Green near Tunbridge Wells. It was about forty minutes' drive from Chartwell: but although 'dropping-in' was no longer possible, the to-and-fro between Chartwell and Hamsell was frequent. My parents would often come over to luncheon or dinner, bringing their guests with them, and vice versa. During the considerable time the alterations and decorations were in progress at Hamsell, my mother often visited the scene of operations, picnicking with us amid the dusty chaos. Every detail fascinated her, and she had many practical suggestions and ideas. She always thought of lovely presents for house or garden: camellias; white iron Victorian garden seats; and one year, having noticed the howling winds on our Sussex hilltop, a revolving summer-house to bask in. Whenever my mother came to stay with us, she entered into our life, greatly enjoying meeting our friends in the neighbourhood.

Christopher and Clementine now had a most affectionate relationship; and she relied upon his judgment in many things. She followed his political career with keen interest, thoroughly appreciating his vicissitudes first as a Junior, and then as a Cabinet Minister. She had a sensitive understanding, and when Christopher's father – with whom he had had a difficult relationship – died, she felt instinctively that the purely conventional expressions of sympathy would not strike the right note. In a letter full of comprehension Clementine wrote:

My dearest Christopher,
    You are much in my thoughts.
    I know that it has been a deprivation that you never knew your Father well – Winston had the same experience with his Father, and like you, minded very much.
    Although he did not shew it, I feel your Papa must have been proud of what you have made of your life and of what you are –
    It's not the same thing I know, but you have a sure abiding place in Winston's heart and mine

Your loving Mama in law
Clemmie[2]

Both Winston and Clementine enjoyed their role as grandparents, and counted the steadily rising tally with great satisfaction. By 1959, with the birth of our Rupert, the total of ten was complete: two Churchills, three Sandys, and five Soameses. In 1962 Edwina Dixon (Sandys) produced their first great-grandchild, and Winston and Clementine were delighted with their new, positively patriarchal standing. The arrival of a new baby in the family always thrilled Clementine, and she would hasten to see it as soon as possible. She was always troubled that modern mothers were, in her view, 'hounded' out of bed in a most barbaric fashion – in her time, three weeks in bed without a toe to the floor was the normal thing – and although she conceded that medical practice in this field had progressed since her day, she still thought we all did too much too soon. When she worked for Fulmer Chase Maternity Home during the war, one of her dearest ambitions for it was achieved when the annexe 'Fircroft' was opened; there the mothers could have a further respite before facing the demands of ordinary life again.

While we were living at Chartwell Farm, three of our children were born, and both my parents were usually in close attendance to encourage before, and to rejoice afterwards. My mother always insisted I should telephone her, whatever the hour, the moment the baby showed any sign of starting. She would come down the hill at once, always disappearing discreetly at exactly the right moment, taking Christopher away with her to be distracted and fed. When Jeremy was born in 1952, I see from my diary that I telephoned my mother at five in the morning and that 'She arrived like lightning looking too soignée & pretty for words'.[3]

Clementine was a much-loved grandmother – with an aura of glamour; and as their grandchildren multiplied and grew, Winston and she loved to see them. In the summertime several of them usually came to stay; and as babies, our 'country bumpkins' often had a short London season, staying with their grandparents at Hyde Park Gate. The various Nannies liked her very much, partly because she was so considerate for their comfort and happiness if they were staying, and partly because she never interfered. Until the farms were sold in 1957 there was the Christmas party at Chartwell for all the children on the estate and as many of her own grandchildren as could be mustered. Thereafter she organised a mass family outing to a Pantomime in London; the highlight of these annual treats being in 1958, when we all went in force (including Winston) to see Sarah as Peter Pan.

As well as giving parties, Clementine also loved to be invited to them, and from the grandchildren's earliest years attended their birthday parties. As they grew older and outdoor sports took over from nursery games or conjurors, she was a keen spectator at their home-made 'Sports Galas' or cricket matches (being always in demand afterwards to present the prizes). As the children's tastes became more sophisticated, it diverted her very much to be included in their teenage parties, and when Edwina Sandys came out in 1957 her grandparents gave a dance for her at Claridge's. As well as taking the minutest interest in all the details of the arrangements, Clementine enjoyed herself enormously on the night.

*

One of the penalties of longevity is that some of the dearest and most familiar faces depart, leaving gaps which cannot be filled. Winston and Clementine had a great community of friendship in those who had known, and borne with them, the storms and struggles of the thirties. Among these, Venetia Montagu had died of a cruel illness in 1948. But her elder sister Sylvia Henley marched on, ramrod straight, defying time's statistics, and proving the truest of the true to both Winston and Clementine. There was Violet Bonham Carter, with whom they shared so many memories of past triumphs and disasters. Not supplying the close friendship a woman-friend can give, but there – in the foreground of her life's canvas – were 'The Prof' and Brendan Bracken. They had both been part of the tapestry for over thirty years. 'The Prof' died in July 1957, and Brendan thirteen months later of an agonising illness. It is true that Clementine had long mistrusted this flaming-haired friend of Winston's, but in these latter years no one more than she had appreciated his valiant friendship, or was more grateful for his wise and humanly understanding advice in our family's affairs.

She had never been an easy person to get to know well, and for long periods the need for total discretion had added an outer defensive wall for would-be friends to breach in addition to the ones already constructed by her own innate reticence and shyness. But in these years after the war Clementine made new friendships, and revived some old ones which were to give her much happiness, and which let fresh air into her life which might otherwise have been too inward-looking and claustrophobic. Among the older generation was her own Ogilvy cousin, Lady Helen Nutting, a beautiful, intelligent and original woman, who came a great deal to Chartwell in these later years. Horatia Seymour, pale and frail-looking but still the ghost of a great beauty, was another friend from their long past. She presently came to live in Tunbridge Wells, and nearly always saw Clementine during her visits to us at Hamsell.

A consideration of all Clementine's closest friends reveals that they all had at least one thing in common – Winston liked them too. Among latter-day friendships which they shared were two (most unalike people), the beautiful and gifted Rhoda Birley (the widow of Sir Oswald Birley, the painter) and the irrepressible Monty. He was devoted to Clementine, and accepted with good grace some not undeserved scoldings from her from time to time for various 'Montyish' lapses. He was to prove in sadder years an assiduous and faithful friend to them both.

But Clementine's friendships were not confined to those from long ago, or of an older generation. She very much liked the company of younger people – they cheered her up, and gave her hope. Among these, the Colvilles, the Montague Brownes, the Deakins and the Rowans* all spring at once to mind. And in her charming young secretaries she found delightful companions for expeditions of all sorts. She greatly admired the way younger people grappled with their lives, and she always loved to know details of their housekeeping arrangements, children, boyfriends or husbands. Through her own children she also made some friends she greatly enjoyed, and who would bring glimpses of quite differing worlds and generations.

For a woman in her seventies with fragile health and long exhausting years behind her, Clementine's life in this last decade which remained to Winston and her together was still a full and demanding one. But there were many pleasurable and interesting aspects to her life, and no lack of true friends to give her companionship and affection. But Clementine's capacity to relish all these was directly linked to her own state of health and spirits, which were in their turn closely bound up with her preoccupation over Winston's well-being. Her life still revolved entirely around him. As in earlier days she could always brace herself to meet her obligations, so often leaving only the lees of her energy for her own friendships, interests and pleasures.

*

In ceasing to be Prime Minister, Winston still remained what he had been for half a century – a Member of the House of Commons; and for forty years the same constituency had faithfully returned him to Westminster. He cared greatly for his

*Leslie Rowan had been Winston's Assistant and later Principal Private Secretary 1941-5.

role as a Member of Parliament, although after 1955 he was not so constant an attender at the House's deliberations, largely owing to the long periods he spent abroad. He made very few speeches at all after he ceased to be Prime Minister, and in fact the first time he spoke in the House after his resignation was on 30th November 1959, when he thanked the House for their congratulations and wishes on his eighty-fifth birthday. But although he may have been a silent presence in Parliament, he followed events very closely, and Anthony Eden, and then Harold Macmillan, always kept him well informed. When Anthony Eden resigned through ill-health early in 1957, the Queen sent for Churchill, among others, and sought his advice on the succession of the Prime Ministership.

He rarely now made a speech in his constituency, but he always acquainted his electors of his views on crucial issues in the form of letters to the Constituency Chairman which were released to the Press. Any Parliamentary Questions which needed to be raised on behalf of Churchill's constituents were looked after by the Conservative Member for the neighbouring seat of Walthamstow East, Mr John Harvey, himself one of Winston's constituents and a former Chairman of the Woodford Conservative Association – this was true and loyal neighbourliness. Constituency correspondence certainly did not suffer: it was dealt with with extreme care by his Agent, Colonel Barlow-Wheeler, a most able and dedicated man, and his own secretariat. But the main task of visiting Woodford and of attending functions fell (as it had always done) on Clementine. She also, through her close and friendly contacts with the officers of the constituency party, kept a vigilant eye on its affairs.

There were from time to time rumblings of discontent among the younger elements of the local party, who felt the constituency was not properly represented, and that Winston's constituents did not get their fair share of attention. But these murmurings were subdued, if not entirely silenced, by the steadfast loyalty and affection the senior party members felt for Winston, and by Clementine's assiduous attentions. Most people in Woodford were undoubtedly proud to have him as their Member of Parliament.

As the time drew near once more for a General Election there was speculation as to whether Churchill intended to contest his seat again. At a meeting in London in early January 1959 of the Executive of the Woodford Conservative Association he made a vigorous speech, but let fall no hint of his intentions. On 20th April of the same year, however, at the end of a 22-minute speech to a crowded meeting in Woodford, he told the audience that he would be ready once again to offer himself as their candidate;[4] this announcement was received with tumultuous applause. And so in October 1959 Winston and Clementine (aged eighty-five and seventy-four) fought yet another election: it was their fifteenth campaign together.

Clementine for some time now had held the view that Winston was too old to go on in politics, and that while the House of Commons would continue to accept him with proud and tolerant affection, sooner or later Woodford would become restive, despite the loyalty of the local party. Winston knew what she thought, but she did not engage in any strong private campaign of dissuasion. She knew it was the last stimulus left to him in life, and that he hoped to die, as he had for so long lived –

the Right Honourable Member for Woodford. As in former years the decision was his, and she loyally, albeit somewhat wearily, braced herself for this last fight.

Winston made two speeches in his own constituency, and the only occasion on which he spoke outside Woodford was at a meeting for John Harvey at Walthamstow. Two days before Polling Day, which was on 8th October, Winston made his usual open-car tour of the division, Clementine following in another open car. They were received with loyal affection and enthusiasm. The Conservatives were returned with an overall majority of 100 seats; Winston himself, although winning by a majority of more than 14,000 over his one Labour opponent, did less well than in 1955. It may well be that the feelings of discontent among some of his own supporters were reflected in this result.

★

When Winston had fallen at Hyde Park Gate in mid-November 1960, breaking a small bone high up in his neck, he had made an astonishingly good recovery. Inevitably the accident had left its mark, however, and he was not able to go to Edwina Sandys' wedding to Piers Dixon a few days before Christmas. Nevertheless, he made his reappearance in the House of Commons towards the end of January 1961. In April he visited the United States – it was to be for the last time – during the course of a month-long voyage in the *Christina*. It was a purely private visit, and while in New York he saw again his old friend, Bernie Baruch. During 1961 he paid four visits to the Riviera, went to the races to see his horses run, and in November he and Clementine attended their granddaughter Celia Sandys' coming-out dance at Quaglino's Restaurant.

After she had thrown off the shingles in 1959, Clementine's health had been quite good for a while. But in early March 1961 she retreated to St Mary's, Paddington, for nearly a month, for a complete rest and thorough check-up. The previous year had been a busy one for a woman of seventy-five: she had been particularly active in the constituency, where she tried to compensate for Winston's absence. Together with Winston, and alone, she had also attended quite a number of 'gala' occasions, such as the functions surrounding General and Madame de Gaulle's State Visit in April. During the course of the few crowded days they were in England, the General and Madame de Gaulle paid a private visit to Winston and Clementine at Hyde Park Gate – a gesture which had touched them greatly. Later that same month they had both attended Princess Margaret's wedding in Westminster Abbey; and yet one time more they were at Windsor for the Garter Service in June.

In that winter of 1960, when Winston had his fall, there was for Clementine all the worry and strain of the succeeding weeks. They spent Christmas and the New Year at Chartwell; Clementine was feeling exhausted, but she fended off her mounting fatigue with a course of injections. Winston was due to go for a spring cruise in the *Christina*, and the doctors now insisted that Clementine should go into hospital. Winston's absence meant that she at least had no worries for his care or comfort, and this in itself represented the lifting of a burden, for the organisation of their domestic life was still a perpetual harassment to her.

After the inevitably dreary weeks in hospital, my mother came down to spend

Easter at Hamsell. When she left us, she went on to stay in Brighton at an hotel, for the doctors were most anxious that she should have as long a break as possible from all the frets and worries that over the months had contributed to her exhaustion of body and spirit. The seaside always suited her and, as Horatia Seymour was then living at nearby Hove, she had pleasant company. When Winston arrived home, he found Clementine much restored, and her 'batteries recharged' for the next lap.

Winston's health and mental alertness were slowly declining, but there were still bright moments, and still sources of enjoyment. Although he always showed pleasure when any of his close family were around, old friends stimulated him often more than 'nearest and dearest'. Backgammon and bezique (especially the latter) were daily pleasures: Clementine, Sylvia Henley and Anthony being the most regular players, meticulous count being kept of the 'debts'. After years of official papers, novels (mostly historical), old and new, now absorbed him by the hour. All his outings and public appearances were carefully prepared and stage-managed so that, impeccably attired, he gave a debonair impression. He was always attended by Anthony, or at the Other Club dinners by Christopher, who also, with a kind Member, Rolf Dudley-Williams, escorted him on both sides during his visits to the House.

And so the months went slowly on. But it is noticeable from her engagement diary that from 1961 Clementine was always at home when Winston was in England, making a few brief visits away only when he was comfortably and safely in the Hôtel de Paris in Monte Carlo, where he now habitually stayed, or with the kind and protective Ari Onassis in the *Christina*.

The fall in the Hôtel de Paris the following summer of 1962, in which Winston broke his hip, necessitating two operations and a prolonged recovery period, marked another definite stage in his slow decline. His mobility was considerably affected, and while he was in the Middlesex Hospital Clementine, who had been in close consultation with the doctors, set about making alterations at Hyde Park Gate which would enable Winston to lead his life without negotiating stairs. The Office, which had hitherto occupied the whole of the main reception room of No. 27, was turned into a lovely bedroom for him. It was a quiet room, with bay windows looking out over the garden. Through in No. 28 a lift was installed from the ground floor to the dining-room on the lower ground floor, so that Winston could still come down to meals, and also have easy access to the garden, where he so loved to sit. Although he was nearly two months in hospital, it was a great rush to get all the work done. On his return home Winston was much pleased with the new arrangements, and particularly liked his new bedroom.

After this last accident it was a whole year before he went to Chartwell again. As Winston climbed slowly yet one more time up the steep slope of recovery, Clementine was hardly ever absent from his side. During the whole of the summer of 1962 she did not stir from London. It was a long vigil. Violet Bonham Carter wrote to her on 27th October 1962, with sympathy and true perception:

My Darling Clemmie, I must write you a line (*not* to be answered) to say *how* moved I am, whenever I see you, by your amazing courage under this long strain,

& by your gaiety & tenderness to beloved W. It is as though you alone could reach him with comfort & amusement. Your 'private line' with him has remained intact. Most people can be brave in short spasms – but the steadfast endurance of the 'long haul' is attained by few. You have had *so* many years of – sometimes intermittent, sometimes continuous – anxiety & strain with never a let-up – & now W needs you & claims more from you than ever before. I am filled with admiration & emotion when I see you together . . .

Lady Violet understood also that if Clementine was to last the course, she must have periods of let-up, and in this same warm and understanding letter she told Clementine that she would brush up her bezique, so that she could come and play with him from time to time. She was as good as her word, and with Sylvia Henley and Sybil Cholmondeley* formed an unofficial 'committee' who would in turn come to dine and play cards with Winston, while Clementine had a 'night off', going to the theatre or just dining out quietly with friends.

Christmas 1962, like the two more that remained to Winston, was to be spent in London. Clementine contrived to make it a true feast, and she wrote in gallant vein to Sarah, who was in Spain:

Yesterday, Christmas Day we had a Patriarchal luncheon – Four generations, Papa & me, – Diana, Edwina & Piers – & Mark (5 weeks old). Papa was photographed by Fritz [the Swiss chef] holding Mark in his arms – We had poor Lord Moran whose wife is still very ill though better . . . Last week I took all Mary's children and Arabella to the Circus – It was great fun & we were much feted by Coco the Clown . . .[5]

But now not only was Winston physically less strong, but mentally he had become more lethargic. Gradually the silences became longer, and he was content to sit gazing into the fire, finding faces in the quivering glow; or in the two summers that were left to him he would lie on his 'wheelbarrow' chair contemplating from the lawn the view of the valley he had loved for so long. If he were not in good form, meals could be conducted in almost total silence. He rarely initiated a subject, and his deafness was an added and most daunting barrier to communication. But he hated to be alone, and indeed he hardly ever was. Sometimes after a long silence he would put out a loving hand, or say apologetically: 'I'm sorry I'm not very amusing today' – which wrung one's heart. He still loved to play bezique, but the games were now more drawn out, and he sometimes became confused with the score. This natural, but infinitely sad decline was slow and uneven. There would be bright clear spells, and then dull and rather hazy days. Life held little for him now, and after the announcement in May 1963 that he would not contest the approaching election, the last stimulus was taken from his life.

Faithful as were old friends, and loyal and assiduous the entourage, the main burden of companionship fell, of course, on Clementine. Her devotion never failed, but sometimes her spirits flagged. She herself was now in her late seventies, and

*Marchioness of Cholmondeley: sister of Sir Philip Sassoon. She and her husband were lifelong friends of Winston and Clementine.

although she was glad for a slowing of the day-to-day pace of life, she was ten years younger than Winston, and her mind, accustomed to the brisk mental barter and exchange of political affairs, at times fretted (albeit unconsciously) at the increasingly sluggish flow of thought and conversation. The process of increasingly silent meals, the effort of communication, and even the temperature of the house itself, all contributed to a claustrophobic atmosphere which over a long period was chafing to her sensitive and highly-strung nervous constitution. We, in the family, and her close friends became increasingly aware of this, but there was no easy solution.

In family terms the years 1962 and 1963 brought a full quota of joy and – alas – tragedy. After so much unhappiness and loneliness, Sarah married Henry Audley (the 23rd Baron Audley) in April 1962; he was a charming, sensitive and gifted man, with somewhat fragile health. He was nearly fifty (almost the same age as Sarah), and they met each other early in 1962 in Marbella in Spain, where Sarah was staying, and where he had a house. Writing to her mother on 22nd March 1962, telling her that she was going to be married, Sarah wrote:

> I never ever believed I would ever find anyone ever again who could make me take heart and believe that happiness & love were yet ahead of me . . .

Shortly after this they both came back to England, and Henry was presented to the family. Clementine liked him very much and Winston, although now rather too old to really 'take in' new personalities, rejoiced for Sarah in her new-found happiness, as did we all. They were married in Gibraltar on 26th April, and Diana flew out to be with them. There is a series of happy letters from both Sarah and Henry to Clementine during their Moroccan honeymoon, and later from Marbella, where they planned to live for most of the time.

The year 1963, however, was to be one of heavy tidings. In early July, while Sarah and Henry were staying in Granada, he was suddenly struck down by a massive coronary and died. They had been married less than fifteen months, and Sarah's new-found happiness and the promise of security in which she had hardly dared to believe were thus brutally shattered. Diana, who had been the witness of their joy, now flew out to sustain Sarah, and they were together when Henry was buried in the British Cemetery at Malaga.

During the summer of 1963, Clementine began once more showing signs that the heat and burden of the long day were indeed too much. Nervous tension and fatigue slowly built up, and she had real cause for anxiety on Winston's account when in mid-August he had a vascular stoppage just above his left ankle. Circulatory troubles always rang a warning bell, and he had to go to bed, which made him low and sad. It was school holiday time, and I was away with my family in France. But I received worrying accounts from Chartwell from both Grace Hamblin and from Monty, who had been to stay with my parents and who gave me a detailed report on them both. Winston was evidently improving physically, and his circulation was restored. 'But, as you know,' Monty wrote on 1st September 1963,

> he can't now read a book or a paper; he just lies all day in bed doing nothing.
> This has been a great strain on Clemmie, and she finally collapsed under it all

and took to her bed the day after you and the children looked in on your way to France. She really is worn out. Winston dislikes being left alone all day with his nurses, and dislikes having meals alone; Clemmie found it a strain having to talk loudly to make him hear.

Since I have been here I have been with him all day, trying to interest him in things and showing him photographs of us two in the war. He is now definitely on the mend. He will recover. My view is that Clemmie is now the problem; she is worn out and needs rest . . .*

Subsequently Clementine was examined by several doctors; they could find nothing specific, but all agreed that she was exhausted in mind and body.

I was greatly concerned, but could be of little help until the school holidays were over. But on 20th September my mother came to stay for what was meant to be a nice long restful visit with agreeable local distractions. But quite soon I realised, to my dismay, that she was really ill. Our local doctor confirmed that her state of nervous exhaustion and mental anxiety were such as to be quite beyond ordinary sympathetic care – she needed expert attention. So her visit to us at Hamsell was unhappily curtailed, and she was admitted to the Westminster Hospital, where she remained, receiving proper treatment, for over three weeks. It was while Clementine was in hospital, on the night of 19th–20th October, that Diana took a massive over-dose of sleeping tablets, and died.

After she had parted from Duncan some time in 1956–7, Diana had settled in a charming house in Chester Row, S.W., where she lived with her daughters, Edwina and Celia. The misery her bouts of nervous ill-health had caused her had been accentuated by the break-up of her marriage. Diana and Duncan had been married nearly twenty-five years when they were divorced in 1960: they had three children, and had known great happiness together in earlier days. The ending of their marriage was a grievous and deeply felt experience for Diana. In April 1962 Duncan married again, to Marie-Claire, Viscountess Hudson, and around that time Diana made it officially known through her solicitor that she wished in future to be known as 'Mrs Diana Churchill'.

Undoubtedly the lack of understanding between herself and her mother was a cause of deep insecurity and unhappiness to her, but in this last period of her life Diana and her mother became, if not close to each other, at least on warmer and more understanding terms. Clementine felt deeply sympathetic to her in the break-up of her marriage, and Diana and her children were often at Chartwell, either for the day, or at week-ends, and invariably at Christmas-time. Diana also went on several occasions to the South of France or on the *Christina* to keep her father company. Now, during the distressing and perplexing illness which Clementine suffered in September and October 1963 Sarah was in Spain, and Diana and I had kept closely in touch about our mother's condition and the treatment she was undergoing. Diana was a source of wise counsel and compassionate understanding:

*It must be remembered that Winston's state varied very much, and this was a particularly bad period following on the specific circulatory trouble in his foot; he was by no means continuously bedridden.

she knew, all too well, the labyrinthine miseries of nervous and spiritual fatigue and despair.

From about the middle of 1962 Diana had started to work in a voluntary capacity for the 'Samaritans', the organisation which gives instant and round-the-clock help to anyone in despair or on the brink of suicide. The work had gripped her enthusiasm, and she devoted many hours a week to it. Another source of satisfaction to her was Edwina's marriage, and later, the birth of her first grandchild. Indeed, during the summer of 1963 she seemed in better spirits, and in a calmer and more robust state of mind than she had been for a long time.

Diana had a great gift for friendship, and there were in particular three or four people to whom she could, and did, normally turn, in moments of depression or worry. In the family, her closest relationship was with Sarah. Together they had faced much, and each would always rush to the other's rescue in moments of crisis. As ill-chance would have it, at the time she took her life her main 'props-and-stays' were all away from London, and Celia also was staying in the country over that week-end. Edwina had seen her mother on the afternoon of Saturday, 19th October, and had found her in good spirits. Diana was due to lunch with her mother at the hospital the following day, and to dine with her father on that same Sunday evening. And so the dreadful news, when it broke upon us all, was not only totally unexpected, but seemingly inexplicable.

Both Winston and Clementine, although through different causes, were spared the sensations of extreme shock and grief that such a sudden and tragic event must normally bring. The lethargy of extreme old age dulls many sensibilities, and my father only took in slowly what I had to tell him: but he then withdrew into a great and distant silence. Despite her illness, it was absolutely necessary for my mother to know about Diana without delay, for she always listened to the news on the radio, and usually read the newspapers. Owing to the nature of her illness, she was under fairly heavy sedation, and so what I had to break to her was mercifully filtered and softened. I went to see her every day, and little by little she took it all in. But it was a merciful dispensation that they were both spared the necessary, but chill formalities and details of the inquest.

Clementine was enough recovered to return home the day before Diana's funeral, but neither of her parents was well enough to go to the service. However, both were present at the crowded and moving Memorial Service which was held the following week in St Stephen's, Walbrook, the church in the City of London the crypt of which houses the headquarters of the Samaritans. Diana's ashes lie near her parents' grave at Bladon.

*

From the time of the 1959 General Election everybody concerned with the matter, and who knew Winston's true state of health, realised that he could not fight another election campaign. He had said himself before the 1959 campaign that if the Socialists were victorious he would fight them again next time, but that if the Conservatives won, he would give Woodford a by-election. However, as the months succeeding the election went by, no mention was made of this, although in private conversation

Clementine put forward her view that, even if Winston meant to stay on as Member, he should let the association know that he did not intend to fight the seat again, so that they could look round for a suitable successor. Clementine often discussed this delicate problem with Christopher, who completely shared her view, and he quite often raised the subject with Winston, who usually resisted discussion of the question and turned an obstinately deaf ear to these reasonable, but to him distasteful arguments. The Woodford Executive was too loyal to make an issue of the question themselves, but of course they hoped that a decision sooner rather than later would be forthcoming.

Towards the end of 1961 Clementine began to put pressure on the Woodford Executive Council to take the initiative, and themselves to raise with Winston the question of his continuing as their Member. But the Council were very loath to make the first move. Their Chairman at this time was Mrs Doris Moss, a most able and charming woman, devoted to both Winston and Clementine, and greatly liked by both of them. She was fully aware of the delicacy and difficulty of the situation, and she had said to Winston privately, and in public on many occasions, that while she was Chairman, the Council would never ask for his resignation. However, both she and her colleagues continued to hope that Winston would make the first move, or that Clementine would raise the subject with him afresh. But writing to Mrs Moss in early February 1962, Clementine told her that it was extremely unlikely that they could expect the first solution and that she, for her part, was not prepared to be the go-between in this matter, which was so painful to Winston and the discussion of which he so assiduously avoided.

In all the record of their long life together, this is the first example I can find of Clementine lacking the will and the nerve to raise and argue a matter with Winston which she deemed to be of vital importance. Her realistic appraisal of the situation in the constituency, her pride in him and for him, and her standards of perfection-ism made her view with dismay the alternative prospect of a slow and perhaps humiliating decline. Any hint of patronising pity or kindly forbearance in people's attitudes was agony to her; as was the constantly lurking fear that Winston might fail or collapse in public.

Clementine had never before shirked an issue, but now she knew that in urging him to resign his seat she would be counselling him to cut finally the last link between himself and the ebb and flow of public life which had for so long been the throbbing impulse of his own. Enfeebled by age and the illnesses he had so marvel-lously survived (and although he was now an infrequent attender at Westminster), he still drew strength and satisfaction from being a Member of the House of Commons. The question of his final retirement had been discussed between them from time to time, but always inconclusively, and usually, unhappily.

But now, Clementine could not bring herself to urge Winston to sever this main artery with life. They were both old, and more and more dependent on each other's company as friends departed, and life bustled on. She dreaded to cast over their relationship the shadow of what she knew Winston would regard as a cruel, indeed, a disloyal suggestion. Whenever she discussed the infinitely painful subject with me, she always said that she could not bear for Winston to be estranged from her.

And so for a while, an impasse having been reached, the situation remained unchanged. Clementine continued to hold the fort in the constituency, and often Anthony Montague Browne would go down with her to help, and quite often she invited visiting speakers to address meetings, at which she was nearly always present herself. But although she soldiered on, she was sensitive about the situation there, and it made her ill-at-ease. The summer garden party at Chartwell to which Winston and Clementine annually invited a large contingent from Woodford had to be cancelled in 1962, when Winston broke his hip; and naturally enough, during the weeks of his illness and slow convalescence, the whole matter remained in abeyance.

But early in 1963 another General Election was only at most eighteen months off, and Mrs Moss and her colleagues on the Divisional Executive realised that the issue of Winston's resignation must be grasped and resolved, whatever anybody's feelings. This time Mrs Moss herself raised the matter with Winston; Clementine invited her, with her husband, to luncheon at Hyde Park Gate on 10th April. At the end of luncheon, by previous arrangement, Clementine and Mr Moss withdrew, leaving Mrs Moss alone with Winston. After talking to him in general terms about the situation, she left with him (it was Clementine's suggestion) a carefully reasoned memorandum, setting out the whole problem and its urgency. No decision was arrived at on that occasion.[6]

The next day Winston left London to spend Easter at Monte Carlo, taking Anthony and Nonie Montague Browne with him for company. Clementine remained in England, coming down to us at Hamsell for the Easter week-end. The whole Woodford problem was troubling her greatly, and she talked to both of us about it. On Easter Day, Christopher wrote a long letter to Winston putting forward once more, with necessary but stringent candour, all the arguments which had already over the past months been advanced, and urging him to accept the fact (however unpalatable) that the time had come when he really must give Woodford a decision – and that there could be only one.

In a later exchange of affectionate letters between Winston and Clementine, he did not mention the painful question, but it is clear from Clementine's letter to him on 19th April that she knew he was still turning over in his mind the possibility of actually contesting his seat at the next election, despite his now very real physical frailties. 'I hope, Darling,' she wrote,

> you are thinking carefully about the letter Christopher wrote to you – He read it to me before he despatched it & I agree with all he says.
>
> I don't see how you can stand next year without campaigning & fighting for your seat. And it would be kind to let your Executive Council know now, before they become too restive . . .

Winston flew home on 25th April, and the following day Mr and Mrs Moss again came to luncheon. Clementine had been struck down by a virus, and was in bed, but Anthony Montague Browne, who was also present at the luncheon, gave her a full account of what had passed. It had been painful and difficult; but Mrs Moss had been admirable in the handling of the situation. However, there had been no positive response from Winston whatsoever. But if he had not wished to commit himself at the luncheon, only a few more days passed before he brought himself to take the, for him, infinitely depressing decision. On 1st May Clementine wrote to Christopher:

> ... In tomorrow's newspapers you will see Winston's letter to his Chairman telling her that he will not stand again at the next General Election.
>
> I feel your excellently reasoned letter was a contributory cause to it being written *at last*!
>
> I am much relieved as the situation at Woodford was becoming increasingly uneasy ...

The tension and anguish of this long-drawn-out dilemma may well have contributed to Clementine's illness later in the summer of 1963. But this sad and difficult episode had a dignified and seemly epilogue in the following year. The Government and Leaders of the Opposition wished to mark in some special way Churchill's departure from the House of Commons, and they decided to do so by the moving of a vote of thanks and appreciation of his services just before the House rose for the summer recess. This had been, until early in the century, the manner in which the House paid tribute to distinguished and victorious senior officers in the Services, and to Speakers and servants of the House. The custom had fallen into disuse, and it was proposed to revive it for Winston Churchill. It was felt by everyone concerned that it would be too testing for Winston to reply to the Vote of Thanks in the House, especially with the emotion such an occasion would obviously engender. It was proposed, therefore, that the Resolution should be moved in his absence, and that a special Committee from the House should then call at Hyde Park Gate to hand him a copy of the Resolution. Winston would then thank them, and hand them a written speech of thanks which at a convenient moment could be read out to the House.

Clementine was in entire agreement with the course proposed. She however incorporated the suggestion in a short memorandum which she gave to Winston on 18th April, and asking him if such a procedure would be 'agreeable' to him. She sent a copy of the memorandum to Christopher with a covering note:

> Dearest Christopher,
>
> Yesterday I gave Winston this little note. At first he seemed to pretend not to understand it, but later on said he thought it would be very suitable. You will notice that I have carefully left out any suggestion that he could possibly be in the House when the Vote of Thanks is proposed. I did not show him the wording of the Resolution.
>
> Later on in the afternoon he seemed very sad and depressed.
>
> Yours affectionately,
> Clemmie[7]

Christopher, who in all this was the chief link, had sent a copy of the proposed Resolution to Clementine. It read as follows:

> That this House offers to the Right Hon. Gentleman the Member for Woodford, its grateful thanks in deep appreciation of his outstanding service to the nation and expresses its sincere regret that the Right Hon. Gentleman, after a Parlia-

mentary career so long and so distinguished, will not seek to be re-elected to this House.

This somewhat banal effusion touched off an immediate and fiery reaction in Clementine. On 18th April she wrote:

My dear Christopher,
   This is what Mr. Speaker said to the Duke of Wellington when he was thanking him for his services:
   'My Lord,
      Since last I had the honour of addressing You from this place, a series of eventful years has elapsed; but none without some mark and note of your rising glory.
      The Military Triumphs which your valour has achieved upon the banks of the Douro and the Tagus, of the Ebro and the Garonne, have called forth the spontaneous shouts of admiring nations. Those Triumphs it is needless on this day to recount. Their Names have been written by your conquering sword in the Annals of Europe, and We shall hand them down with exultation to our children's children.'
   As a tribute compare this with the mangy resolution you enclosed with your letter.

                                                             Yours affec.ly
                                                            Clementine S.C.

The essence of this broadside was tactfully communicated to the right quarters, and presently a re-drafted Resolution was sent to Clementine, who signified that she liked the new version very much better.

Winston Churchill was present for the last time in the House of Commons on 28th July 1964. He had been a Member almost continuously for over half a century. The following day, in the afternoon, Sir Alec Douglas-Home, the Prime Minister, accompanied by the Opposition Party Leaders Mr Harold Wilson and Mr Grimond, and the Leader of the House, Mr Selwyn Lloyd, together with the two 'elders' of the House, Sir Thomas Moore and Mr Shinwell, called at Hyde Park Gate to present to Winston the Resolution which had been carried earlier in the day in the House – 'nemine contradicente'. The words of the Resolution were:

That this House desires to take this opportunity of marking the forthcoming retirement of the right honourable Gentleman the Member for Woodford by putting on record its unbounded admiration and gratitude for his services to Parliament, to the nation and to the world; remembers, above all, his inspiration of the British people when they stood alone, and his leadership until victory was won; and offers its grateful thanks to the right honourable Gentleman for these outstanding services to this House and to the nation.[8]

This private but historic ceremony took place in the dining-room at Hyde Park Gate. Clementine had asked some of us children to be present with her to witness this rather sad, muted occasion. But it made a dignified end to a long, proud chapter.

29

PORT AFTER STORMY SEAS

THE TRAGIC DEATHS of Henry Audley and Diana in 1963, and Clementine's distressing illness, combined to make that winter a particularly quiet one. After she came out of hospital, she needed a little while to adjust herself to life once more. And the manner of Diana's death left for her, as for all of us, a legacy of painful thoughts and questions. But Clementine now seemed much more able to accept the slow tempo which Winston's infirmities imposed on his own life, and upon those who lived with him. And now that his impending retirement from the House had been settled and announced, a whole weight of worry and fret had been lifted from Clementine. She continued to keep in touch with the constituency, but she was no longer harassed by embarrassment, or a sense of fatiguing obligation.

After 1963, Winston did not go abroad again. But he was not totally inactive. He faithfully attended the Other Club dinners, where old and younger friends and former colleagues all joined to make him feel the glow of their affection and regard. During the months left to him as the Member for Woodford, he went on several occasions to the House of Commons. Indeed, towards the end of February he caused surprise and pleasure when he attended the House one night, staying to vote in more than one Division.[1]

Winston and Clementine went down to Chartwell for the first time that year for Easter, and two days later, on 1st April, Clementine's seventy-ninth birthday, they lunched with us at Hamsell, bringing with them Sylvia Henley and Monty and one of his godsons, Nigel Hamilton, who were staying with them. In addition to a quiverful of Soameses, we had invited 'Cousin Moppet' and Horatia Seymour (both of whom lived nearby). It was a happy feast: and I am so glad I did not know it was the last time my father was to be at Hamsell.

In early June they went back to London again, and there on 9th June they received news of Max Beaverbrook's death. Winston was greatly saddened and depressed. Since Clementine had 'laid up her sword', her relationship with Max had been mellow; his kindness in these last years had touched her heart. It must also have moved her to have received this 'accolade' from him, less than a year before his death, written in his own hand on the occasion of Winston's eighty-ninth birthday the previous November:

My dear Clemmie, What a burden you have borne over so many years – and with what charm & dignity. How much the Nation & the World owes to you for all your labours. And on this *89th birthday* I send you this message. Many many intimates sending Winston messages of love & devotion will think of you. Max. Churchill's birthday 1963.

Winston and Clementine stayed in London until the end of July, when after Winston had made his formal leave-taking of the House, and received their Resolution of Thanks, he and Clementine returned to Chartwell. There they remained tranquilly for nearly three months. They enjoyed visits from friends and relations, and Clementine made one or two brief expeditions to London.

In mid-October they packed up, and went back to winter in London. And Winston left, for the last time, the place which, for over forty years, had given him happiness, occupation and peace of mind.

Throughout 1964 Clementine's health was mercifully in general much better; although she did have some trouble with her eyes, and she too began to find the need of a hearing aid – which necessity she disliked as much as had Winston. But apart from these tedious but minor troubles, she seemed to be on a much more even keel, notwithstanding the fact that, apart from two week-ends spent with us at Hamsell (one in February and one in July), and three days in Paris in October, she had no holiday, and was constantly at home. Undoubtedly she could have done with more 'time off', but she felt Winston needed her more than ever, as slowly but perceptibly his health and spirits declined. Clementine, like all of us, was conscious that the sands were gently running out.

However, she had distractions, and friends rallied round either to divert Winston, or to take her out. She loved the theatre, and exhibitions were as ever a great pleasure and interest. As usual, during Wimbledon fortnight she was a regular spectator, the Committee always giving her tickets in the Royal Box. She used often to take a grandchild with her, and these Wimbledon outings were regarded by them as beautiful treats.

During this year she undertook one or two public engagements. On 13th May she attended the opening of Howard House, a home for retired nurses. The previous year she had signed a letter with Lord Moran appealing for support for this home; it was a cause she cared about – she always realised that nursing was a hard and exhausting career.

But there were two particularly outstanding occasions for Clementine in 1964. Churchill College, Cambridge, founded by Winston in 1958 (and to which he had subscribed a great part of his 80th Birthday Fund), was now a living, working entity, and the formal opening by the Duke of Edinburgh took place on 5th June. Winston was not well enough to attend such a long and, of necessity, tiring event. But Clementine represented him, and all the family was invited. It was of course a thrilling day for all of us to see this brainchild of his old age so gloriously launched on its useful and significant career.

And in the latter part of the year there was another occasion to which Clementine also went with pleasure. A lawyer, Mr Alan Spiers, had presented to the British

Embassy in Paris a bust of Winston by Oscar Nemon, and on 21st October Clementine unveiled it. She wrote Sarah, who was in Rome, a lively account:

> I have just got back from spending 3 days in Paris – I went to unveil a bust (by Nemon) of Papa which is placed in the British Embassy. It is extremely good. I lunched with General de Gaulle which I enjoyed very much. He was very mellow. I stayed at the British Embassy with Edwina's parents-in-law, Sir Pierson & Lady Dixon. Edwina was there & we did sightseeing together . . .[2]

On the family front the year had been variable, but fortunately less tragic and dramatic than 1963. Although Randolph had a lung operation and was seriously ill during March, he made a good recovery. While he was in hospital his mother visited him frequently. And in early August, on the eve of our departure for a family holiday abroad, Christopher had a riding accident and injured his pelvis, and had to spend ten weeks in hospital. My mother at once offered practical help, by having Nannie and the younger children to stay at Chartwell, so that I could spend my time with Christopher.

But the most important family event, and one which gave true joy and pleasure to both Clementine and Winston, was the marriage of Randolph's son, Winston, to Minnie d'Erlanger. Although his grandfather was unable to go to the ceremony and the reception, Winston and Minnie and their parents all went to No. 28 to greet and be greeted by him.

Winston's ninetieth birthday brought an avalanche of good wishes. The Queen sent him flowers, and many people gathered in the street outside No. 28 on the eve of his birthday and on the day before, when, carefully dressed and looking benevolent, Winston appeared at the open window of the drawing-room so that the Press could take some birthday photographs. The little crowd of well-wishers cheered and clapped and sang 'Happy Birthday to You'. Before luncheon on the actual day Clementine arranged for all his secretarial, nursing and domestic staff to gather in his bedroom to drink his health in champagne. She took this opportunity to thank them all for their loyal and devoted care. Clementine's present to him was a small golden heart enclosing the engraved figures '90'. It was to hang on his watch-chain, and joined the golden heart with its central ruby 'drop of blood' which had been her engagement present to him fifty-seven years before. During the afternoon the Prime Minister called to bring Winston good wishes from the Cabinet.

That evening there was the usual hallowed family dinner party: Randolph, Sarah, myself and Christopher; Winston and Minnie, and Arabella, Julian Sandys, Edwina and Piers Dixon, Celia Kennedy (Sandys); and Cousin Sylvia. The only guests not members of the family were Jock and Meg Colville, and Anthony and Nonie Montague Browne. Monty had been invited but was himself ill in hospital. The house glowed with candlelight and flowers, and we were united yet one more time in drinking first Winston's health and then Clementine's. But this birthday evening had for us all a poignant quality – he was so fragile now, and often so remote. And although he beamed at us as we all gathered round him, and one felt he was glad to have us there – in our hearts we knew the end could not be far off.

*

On Monday, 11th January 1965 my four elder children and I were due to go up to London to see my parents, and to dine and go to the theatre with my mother. During the morning my mother telephoned me at Hamsell to say that my father was far from well, and seemed to have had another 'spasm'. Lord Moran had been to see him on the previous day, and was bringing Lord Brain, the neurologist, to examine him. She insisted that our plans should not change, so the children and I went to No. 28 that evening as arranged. My mother told me that in the doctors' opinion Winston had suffered a stroke, but that it was not possible at this stage to judge its gravity. I went in to see my father, who was in bed. He was silent, and I do not think he recognised me. We all went to the theatre, but our minds were full of anxious thoughts.

During the next day I visited my parents. My father's eyes were open, but he seemed very remote and said nothing. He was still eating a little, but was having to be fed. Christopher came to see him during the afternoon, and was alone with him. Desperately trying to kindle a spark, he said: 'Wouldn't you like a glass of champagne?' Winston looked at him vaguely. 'I'm so bored with it all,' he said. These were, I think the last coherent words he spoke to any member of the family. During that afternoon I had seen Lord Moran. He seemed gloomy. 'Is this it?' I asked. 'I'm afraid so,' he replied.

During the next days the effects of the stroke became gradually more pronounced, with paralysis affecting his left arm and hand. At this stage there was still an element of doubt as to whether he might, yet once more, recover. But it was an anguishing prospect, for Lord Moran warned us that he would be gravely impaired, and would not even regain the level of existence of the last sad months. The question had at once to be faced as to whether a bulletin should be issued. It was decided that nothing should be announed at the present time, but that should my father's state change decisively, or if there were to be rumours and specific press enquiries – then a statement should be made at once. Meanwhile only those members of the family and friends who were closest and could be easily contacted were told.

For the next two days there was not much change in his condition. He was semiconscious at times, and even when he slipped into unconsciousness, the strength of his grasp, as one sat holding his hand, was warm and strong. On Thursday, 14th January, he seemed a little worse. Although I had been coming to the house every day, I now moved in, so that I could be close at hand if needed. To pass the time and to get some fresh air and exercise, my mother and I went for walks, and, on one bitter afternoon, we paced the long galleries of the Victoria & Albert Museum in a somewhat distracted way. As these days went by without rumours, we marvelled at our luck. We all felt that there was everything in favour of keeping the secret for as long as possible, for it seemed perfectly clear that whatever the course of my father's illness might be, it was likely to be a long-drawn-out ordeal, and that nothing would be the same again once the news was known to the public.

Friday, 15th January was a cold, grey day, but my mother and I went for a brisk walk in Hyde Park during the morning. As we returned home and were approaching the top of Hyde Park Gate, we saw Anthony Montague Browne coming quickly towards us, and the same thought flashed instantly through both our minds – he was coming to tell us that Winston had died. But Anthony was hastening to warn us that the news was out, that there had been several enquiries from the Press, and that an interim bulletin had been issued. We hurried on home, and a few minutes before we got into the house, the first cameramen and reporters were arriving. By the middle of that afternoon No. 28 was in a state of siege, and the street was crowded. During the afternoon a bulletin was put out signed by Lord Moran and Lord Brain. It said: 'After a cold, Sir Winston has developed a circulatory weakness and there has been a cerebral thrombosis.'

From now until, at Clementine's personal request, some five days later the Press withdrew to the end of the street, we were completely hemmed in, not only by reporters, cameramen and television crews, but by numbers of the general public, calling to deliver notes and flowers, or just standing quietly in the chilly street. It was quite difficult getting in and out of the house. Reporters were, without exception, kind and courteous, and once it became clear that a steady flow of informed, official bulletins would be issued, one was not stopped and questioned. An account was published daily of the comings and goings at No. 28; people were asked – through the medium of the Press – to refrain from ringing up for news and to wait for the bulletins, as the two telephone lines in the house would otherwise have been completely drowned by the flood of enquiries.

My mother said she would like a priest to come, and I telephoned Philip Hayllar, the vicar at Eridge, whom my mother had often met on her visits to Hamsell, and whom she liked very much. He slipped into the house, unremarked, on the Friday evening. My mother and I knelt on either side of my father's bed while Philip Hayllar said some simple prayers and blessed him. Winston was now unconscious, and slipping gradually into deeper sleep. We knew in our hearts that he was dying.

During that evening, the Prime Minister called. My mother, although quite calm, was exhausted, and had gone upstairs to rest, so I received Mr Wilson on her behalf. Throughout his illness, Buckingham Palace and Downing Street kept in close touch with Winston's condition. The following week a delegation bearing a personal message from the Pope called, and Clementine with several members of the family received them. Messages poured in from all over the world. Anthony Montague Browne and the secretaries were on duty almost round the clock. The nursing team, headed by Mr Howells, was increased to four.

Sarah arrived back from Rome in the early hours of Saturday, 16th January, and went straight to the house to see her father. Every day children, grandchildren and closest friends called, and through all their visitations Winston slept tranquilly. His room became the heart and centre of the house, where we all slipped quietly in and out, to sit just a little while more with him. It was such a peaceful scene – the gently lighted room full of flowers; the quiet form in the big bed, with the beautiful hands spread on the quilt. Our children came up to say farewell to their so dearly loved grandfather – they were rigid and apprehensive until they had been into that peaceful room, where their grandmother was sitting quietly by their grandfather's side holding his hand, and with the marmalade cat he so much loved curled up at his feet. Afterwards I found Jeremy (aged twelve) in tears in the passage, and mur-

mured some banal words of comfort: 'Oh, I know that!' he said almost roughly. 'But it's just seeing *them* together, for the last time.'

As the last days of their long journey together were thus drawing to their gentle end, Clementine seemed to withdraw into an inner remote quietness. Although Anthony Montague Browne and I dealt with as many problems and queries as possible, all major points were of course addressed to her. She saw a great number of the messages, letters and telegrams that poured in every day, and dealt with many of them personally. Clementine looked immaculate at all times, and the house continued to be impeccably run: there had never been any room in her life for slipshod ways.

Almost every day we went out for a drive or a walk, or visited in a somewhat robot-like trance the National Gallery and the Wallace Collection. It was, however, quite an ordeal, running the gauntlet of the crowd at the door, and in public places one could feel people's loving but curious sympathy reaching one in waves. So, on the whole, we marched about the parks in the grey chill days – killing time, while time killed him. Clementine never liked to be out for long, for although Winston was sinking slowly, there were one or two crisis moments when we thought the end was coming.

Public concern throughout the world never lessened through all the days Winston lay dying. On Sunday, 17th January, prayers were offered for him in churches of all denominations throughout the country. The Morning Service was broadcast from St Mary's, Westerham, and my mother and I listened, sitting in her bedroom. It seemed quite natural that together we knelt to join in the prayers. Meanwhile the state of siege in which we were living was becoming a great trial. The reporters and cameramen were keeping a 24-hour vigil. Nearly every time someone called, or Lord Moran gave out the bulletins, or made a visit (sometimes twice or three times in the twenty-four hours), the crowd pressed closer round the front door and the television arc-lights were turned on. Clementine's bedroom was on the first floor, and directly over the front door; and on the ground floor the drawing-room windows gave directly onto the street. Although the crowd was as quiet as possible, its presence penetrated even inside the house. The strain was considerable, and particularly so for Clementine. She was also very conscious of the great inconvenience inevitably caused to other residents in the street (which is a cul-de-sac) by the constant presence of so many people, clustered on the pavements and often spreading over the roadway as well. On Tuesday, 19th January, after consulting with Anthony Montague Browne, the following request was issued on her behalf:

Lady Churchill expresses her true thanks to members of the press who have shown great kindness and restraint. However, she would be most grateful if the press, radio, T.V. and film representatives could withdraw from Hyde Park Gate. The numbers have grown to such an extent that the cameras' floodlights and inevitable disturbance have become a severe strain, apart from obstructing the street. In future, medical bulletins will be issued over the telephone at the news agencies and not read aloud at the front door.

This most courteous request met with an immediate response – within about half an hour of the statement being issued all reporters and cameramen had withdrawn from around No. 28, and from now on they posted themselves at the top of the street. Their instant co-operation and understanding were greatly appreciated by Clementine (and, indeed, by all of us living and working in the house), and rendered less arduous the four days of the long vigil that were left.

During all this time Clementine's demeanour was calm and quiet. I only saw her break down once – briefly. Once, she said to me: 'I don't know where all my tears have gone.' Members of the family kept her company at meals, and Sylvia Henley came often to lend her unfailing strength. Apart from our walks, she went out rarely; but one day she lunched quietly with Christopher and me at our flat. During the day she would go and sit with Winston, either alone or with one of us; sitting for long periods holding his hand. The nurses told me that, even after Winston had sunk into a deeper level of unconsciousness, they were convinced he was aware of her presence; and sometimes Clementine found it quite hard to withdraw her hand from his clasp. Just before she went to bed Clementine would always go to say 'good-night', and to sit with him for a little while. She nearly always woke during the night, and at one or two in the morning she would come downstairs to see how Winston was.

While she was resting on the evening of Friday, 22nd January, Randolph came round with the happy news that Minnie, young Winston's wife, had given birth to a son. Not wishing to disturb his mother, Randolph left a note for her – adding at the end: '. . . in the midst of death, we are in life.'

The bulletins about Winston's condition continued to be published at least twice a day, although there was often nothing new to report. On the evening of 20th January the bulletin noted: 'The weakness of Sir Winston's circulation is more marked.' Two days later: 'Sir Winston has had a restful day, but there has been some deterioration in his condition.' On 23rd January: 'The deterioration in Sir Winston's condition is more marked.'

I woke up at half-past five on the morning of Sunday, 24th January and went downstairs. I met Nurse Huddleston (who was on duty with Mr Howells) coming up to wake me – my father's condition had deteriorated, and she told me she did not think 'he could go on very long'. We decided however not to wake my mother for a little while. About half-past six I was just going up to fetch her when she appeared. Lord Moran was sent for, and I started telephoning the other members of the family and Anthony Montague Browne. My mother and I sat one on each side of my father. About a quarter-past seven Randolph and young Winston arrived and, soon after, Sarah and Celia (with whom Sarah was staying). They all joined Clementine in Winston's room: Lord Moran and Anthony were also there.

Clementine did not move from Winston's side all this time, but sat by the bed holding his right hand. Once she looked up at me: 'Go and tell Mrs Douglas we shall be . . .' she broke off to count those around her – '. . . eight for breakfast.' She then turned again to Winston, and concentrated her whole thought upon him. When I returned from carrying her message I sat at the foot of the bed. Clementine was, throughout, on Winston's right, and young Winston at his left: the others had gone into the drawing-room for a while. Sitting exactly opposite my father, I suddenly noticed a change in him – his breathing seemed to alter. Through the open door I signalled to one of the nurses, who observed the change, and instantly ran along the passage to fetch the others. We knelt around him, Sarah, Celia and I at the foot of the bed, Randolph stood near the pillow by his son, Lord Moran was on his right by my mother. I was dimly aware that at the back of the room the two nurses and Anthony had fallen to their knees. There was absolute silence – Winston gave two or three long, long sighs – nobody moved or spoke. Presently Clementine looked up at Lord Moran: 'Has he gone?' she asked. He nodded. Presently, one by one we got up and silently left the room. I went back and remained with my mother for some little time. Then we both kissed his hand and then his brow and left him.

At half-past eight that morning the news was given to the Press:

SHORTLY AFTER 8.0 THIS MORNING, SUNDAY, JANUARY THE 24TH, SIR WINSTON CHURCHILL DIED AT HIS LONDON HOME. MORAN.

Some of the family went quickly away, those of us remaining had breakfast (rather chokily) with Clementine. We listened in as the news the world had been waiting for was broadcast. Clementine then went upstairs to dress and when she came down again she went to the candlelit room. Death had smoothed all wrinkles away – there was no sign now of feebleness or age. The alabaster-like presence distilled around it a majestic sense of peace and finality. During that day my mother and I spent long periods sitting there, in silent contemplation and recollection. Otherwise Clementine remained most of her time in her room. She was perfectly calm, and addressed her mind to those matters which had to be discussed or decided. Anthony, who had through all these long days been a tower of strength, continued now to take an immense burden off Clementine, and dealt with the enquiries and messages which once again were at flood-tide.

It was hard indeed to tear ourselves away from that great and peaceful presence, but presently Clementine too took her very last farewell. Later, she sent me down to see the undertakers, and to assure myself that all was seemly, and to instruct them to close the coffin.

*

Seven years before, the Queen had told the then Prime Minister, Mr Macmillan, that in the event of Churchill's death she wished him to be accorded a Lying-in-State, followed by a State Funeral – a signal and rare honour to be accorded to a commoner, and the first since the Duke of Wellington. The Queen's wish was in due course transmitted to Winston, who was deeply touched and gratified by this gesture from the Sovereign whose family he had so long served, and for whose person he had such a great regard and deep affection. A myth has taken root that Winston took a detailed interest in the planning of his own funeral, down to the choice of hymns: this is not true. Although I myself once heard him express the hope that there would be 'plenty of bands', the matter did not greatly occupy his thoughts. He was more than content to leave these arrangements to others.

From the moment of Winston's quiet end, 'the plan' took over. There had for some time been a discreet liaison between the Earl Marshal's office and Anthony Montague Browne, and he in his turn had consulted Clementine on various points or communicated to her such information as was timely and necessary without being distressingly cold-blooded. At every step her feelings, and those of Winston's family, were taken into consideration.

On Monday, 25th January, the Houses of Parliament paid their tributes to Winston. Clementine did not go to the House of Commons, but various members of the family went, and Sarah and I watched and listened from the Speaker's Gallery while political friend and foe alike recalled what Winston Churchill had been to the House and to his country. His old place – the seat below the gangway on the government side – had been left symbolically empty. Many of the speakers made especial reference to Clementine, and to her constant and steadfast role at Winston's side.

Winston lay in his room at 28 Hyde Park Gate from the Sunday morning on which he died until the evening of the Tuesday. During those two days his room was still the centre of the house, and Clementine and all of us would go and sit there very often. On the evening of Tuesday, 26th January the closest members of the family gathered at No. 28, and at nine o'clock the Lord Chamberlain, Lord Cobbold, arrived to escort the coffin to Westminster Hall where Winston was to lie-in-state until the State Funeral on the following Saturday. From the moment his body left his home, he, and all of us, became integral parts of a great pageant of state, upon which were fixed the interest and emotions not only of his own countrymen, but of people throughout the world. The coffin, covered by the Union Jack, was driven in a motor hearse, and we all followed in other cars. Although it was a dark and cold night, there was a crowd outside Westminster Hall. At the door the Bearer Party formed by the Grenadier Guards took the coffin into the vast gloom of the historic hall. The small family group followed, led by Clementine (in black and veiled) and Randolph. When the coffin had been placed on the catafalque, the Archbishop of Canterbury said some prayers and gave a benediction. Then the first four officers from among those from all three Services who were to find the guard during the days and nights of the Lying-in-State, took up their positions by the catafalque. And guarded thus, we left him.

During the next three days Westminster Hall was open twenty-three out of the twenty-four hours so that people could come and pay their respects. In the bitter cold weather the queue was often a mile long, and people had to wait for up to two hours to reach the hall. When the doors were finally closed to the public early on the morning of Saturday, 30th January, the day of the funeral, over 320,000 people had passed by the catafalque.

For Clementine these days were spent mostly in seclusion at home; but every day she went to spend some time at the Lying-in-State, usually taking me with her. Members of the family were allowed in by a side-door, and we were able to stand at the side of the hall without disrupting the flow of people. It was an amazing, an unforgettable sight. The only gleam of light in that vast place seemed to come from the great cross at the head of the catafalque, and from the candles round the flag-covered coffin, on which reposed the Insignia of the Order of the Garter. The guarding officers stood like statues, heads bowed, hands clasped on the hilts of their naked swords. The change-of-guard, which took place every twenty minutes, was performed without a spoken command and in almost total silence. Carpeting had been laid, and so the stream of people who passed in on both sides of the catafalque without interruption were equally noiseless – and as one stood and watched it had the mesmeric effect of a river flowing past.

Although all the arrangements were made by the Earl Marshal (the Duke of Norfolk) and his officials, there were, of course, many points on which Clementine was consulted. One of her earliest expressed wishes was that there should be no flowers sent, other than those from the family. The cathedral authorities sought her views as to what hymns should be incorporated in the Order of Service. She in her turn consulted with some of us, and between us we chose hymns that had been Winston's lifelong favourites: 'Fight the good fight'; Bunyan's 'He who would valiant be'; 'O God, our help in ages past'; and the great Battle Hymn of the Republic – 'Mine eyes have seen the glory of the coming of the Lord', the words of which Winston knew from start to finish. We also asked that the beautiful prayer of the Knights of the Order of the Garter might be incorporated in the service.

For a long time it had been Winston's wish that he should be laid at Chartwell, and then a few years before he died, after a visit to Blenheim, when he visited Bladon churchyard (which is in sight of the Palace, just outside the park walls), where his parents and brother Jack were buried, he suddenly changed his mind and told Clementine that he would like to lie with them there; and these wishes were expressed in his last will. Accordingly it was arranged that following the Funeral Service at St Paul's his coffin would be borne by river to Waterloo, and from the station by train to Long Handborough, near Bladon.

The flood of letters and telegrams from all over the world was overwhelming. Anthony Montague Browne helped Clementine to draft answers to Heads of State and Governments and official bodies. Now, and during many weeks to come, she herself wrote many letters; and three or four secretaries grappled with many hundreds more. However, on 27th January, Clementine made an announcement through the Press on behalf of herself and her family, expressing our gratitude for so many people's thoughts.

... The kindness of all those who have expressed their sympathy at this time means much to them.

They hope that the senders will understand if they do not receive personal replies as the numbers are so very great.

The following month Clementine sent through the British Embassy in Washington a separate and special message to the thousands of Americans who had written or cabled their sympathy and appreciation of Winston.

During the days before the funeral few people other than members of the family came to see her, out of consideration and delicacy. There was one exception, however: the faithful friend and valiant colleague of Winston's, Sir Robert Menzies, Australia's Prime Minister, called on the morning of Friday, 29th January. His was a warm and consoling presence, and Clementine was glad to see him. Immediately after the funeral he made a moving broadcast from the crypt of St Paul's, and at the end he referred to Clementine: 'A great and gracious lady in her own right. Could I today send her your love, and mine?'

Although Saturday, 30th January was bitterly cold, it was a fine day, and sometimes a gleam of pale sunshine broke through the leaden grey sky. An official car took my mother and me to Westminster Hall, where the procession assembled; we met the rest of the family there. We all stood by the catafalque as the coffin was lifted down and carried by the Bearer Party found by the Grenadier Guards to the waiting gun carriage, drawn by naval ratings. Immediately behind the gun carriage walked Randolph and Christopher, followed by other male members of the family and Anthony Montague Browne. Clementine and the rest of us rode in five of the Queen's carriages. In the first carriage were Clementine, with Sarah and myself sitting opposite her. We had been given rugs for our knees, and each of us was handed a small hot-water bottle for our hands. This was typical of the detailed thoughtfulness which marked all the arrangements. The processional journey to St Paul's was to take an hour, and we would indeed have been very cold but for this kindly and practical provision. As Big Ben struck a quarter to ten, the Funeral Procession led by the Duke of Norfolk set out. We were very silent in the carriage; it swayed gently and creaked a little, like a small boat at sea. The music of the bands and the throb of the drums only reached us faintly. From St James's Park came the crash of the 90-gun salute – one for each year of Winston's life. Near the Cenotaph we noticed the crowding banners and faces deeply marked by emotion of the French Resistance groups, come to take leave of one whose voice alone had given them heart and strength. The way was lined by great, silent crowds – all sorts and conditions of men, women and children. Through the large uncurtained windows of the carriage one could see clearly the expressions on people's faces. I was deeply struck by how noble – often how beautiful – is the human countenance in recollection, gravity or sorrow.

Up the Strand, up Fleet Street, past a City church where the priest and his white-robed choir crowded out onto the church steps, golden cross held aloft in hope and blessing, and – at last – into the forecourt of St Paul's. The Bearer Party once more shouldered their heavy burden, and moved slowly and painfully up the great stone steps. Randolph, who all the day was to care tenderly for his mother, gave her his arm, and together, followed by the rest of us, they followed the coffin up into the shining vastness of St Paul's.

There were, one was afterwards told, about three thousand people in the cathedral. Our impression, as we entered, was almost one of solitude. The organisation had been so perfect, so timed to the second, that even the official ushers were still as stone. The vast congregation had already risen to its feet. Ahead of us, swaying gently, went the shoulder-high coffin, and there seemed to stretch before us a limitless vista of pale blue carpet. And somewhere, beneath the shimmering cupola, the piercingly beautiful voices of the choir sang the words that dignify and lend hope to the humblest as to the greatest of funerals: 'I am the Resurrection and the Life'.

The Queen had broken all custom in attending the funeral; and had laid aside her usual precedence. She and her family, already in their places, awaited the arrival of her greatest commoner. The coffin was laid on a catafalque in the chancel, and we took our seats on the right. Opposite to us were the Heads of States and Governments. Among them, General de Gaulle stood out, distinguished by his great height and the pallor of his gaunt countenance. The service was inexpressibly beautiful, but in a grandly simple way – the matchless words of the liturgy and of the 'old' Bible alternating with the hymns that are the family heritage of the Church of England. There was indeed 'None here for tears' – only for honourable pride and loving, grateful recollection. Ever since his death we had realised that he belonged as much – perhaps more – to others than he belonged to us, and that we were only a small part of the laying-to-rest of Winston Churchill.

The coffin was embarked, after the service, at Tower Pier in the Port of London Authority launch *Havengore*. Massed pipe bands wailed him aboard, and there was a 17-gun salute. As the launch drew away from the pier the band played 'Rule Britannia'. As *Havengore* turned upstream and headed for the Festival Pier, the cranes on the shore opposite slowly dipped their giant-giraffe necks. Overhead, Lightnings of Fighter Command flashed by. The river was lead and pewter, and on the deck of the launch the coffin was still guarded by Grenadier Guardsmen.

The nation now handed Winston Churchill back to his family. At Waterloo a new Bearer Party took over, found by the regiment with which Winston had first served – the 4th Hussars (now the Queen's Royal Irish Hussars). During the nearly two-hour journey to Long Handborough, Winston lay, once more, 'In State' – in the rattling luggage-van – where, even here, soldiers of his old regiment kept watch around him.

One felt one had touched the outer limits of emotion – yet, in some ways, what those of us in the train saw now was most moving of all. There were groups of people on the platforms of the station through which the train rumbled, waiting to take their leave of him too. A Thames lock-house keeper all alone at his post, coming to attention and saluting. The winter fields had little groups of people – families with their children and dogs, a farmer, taking his cap off; children on shaggy ponies – all waiting in the chill of a winter's afternoon, to watch Winston Churchill's last journey home.

From the earliest announcements of the arrangements for the funeral, stress had been laid on the strictly private nature of the Burial Service at Bladon. To the official statements Clementine added her own personal request that there should be no press or TV coverage for the last part of the journey and the interment. And her wish was respected in the most remarkable way. Bladon village was sealed off from outsiders by the police, but there is a limit to what can be done by official restraint in our country, and there were press representatives from all over the world in London, sent expressly by their papers to obtain the fullest possible story and detailed picture-coverage; and restraint and respect for privacy on such occasions are better understood by the British Press than by others. All I know is, that if there were spying eyes and lenses or uninvited persons in the churchyard, they were not noticed by any of us. Mostly local people lined the sides of the road from Long Handborough Station to the entrance to Bladon village, and those whose houses directly overlooked the churchyard behaved with kind and touching discretion.

The coffin, still borne by soldiers of his regiment, was met at the lych-gate of St Martin's Church by the Rector, the Rev. J. E. James, who led the way to the grave-side. Apart from members of the family, the only others with us at this act were Anthony Montague Browne, Jock Colville, Leslie Rowan, Lord Moran and Grace Hamblin. And last, but not least, the man who had, at the Queen's command, directed the whole of this unique happening – the Duke of Norfolk. He stood, a dignified and watchful figure, at the head of the grave, presiding over the last details of this sad, but infinitely proud day.

After the Committal and the lowering of the coffin into the grave, Clementine first of all, and then all of us one by one, filed past and bade our last farewell. The whole ceremony took only a little while. Before we left, two wreaths were placed on the grave: Clementine's red roses, carnations and tulips, bearing a card, 'To my Darling Winston. Clemmie.' And a wreath of exquisite spring flowers from the Queen, with a card in her own hand, 'From the Nation and Commonwealth. In grateful remembrance. Elizabeth R.'

Twilight was falling as we made our way back in silence to the cars, and to the train, which carried us back to London. Clementine had not faltered throughout this long day – one would not have expected her to. Now on the homeward journey she talked to some of those who had come on this last lap. Bernard Norfolk came and sat by her, and she thanked him for all the arrangements, so perfectly carried out in every detail. When he got up to leave her, he suddenly bent over and kissed her hand.

We were very tired when we got back to No. 28. It had been a long, long day. My mother and I and Grace Hamblin had an early dinner together, and after Grace left us we watched for a while part of the replay of the funeral on the television. Then my mother got up to go to bed, and I busied myself switching out the lamps. As she reached the door she paused, and turning round said, 'You know, Mary, it wasn't a funeral – it was a Triumph.'

30

AFTERWARDS

A DAY OR TWO AFTER the funeral, my mother came down to us at Hamsell for a fortnight. She had not sustained the trauma of shock, but she bore the burden of the back-log of the fatigue of many years, and the strain of the prolonged emotion of these last weeks. Clementine did not collapse; her mood was one of proud and loving recollection; and only slowly did the great void that now gaped in her life assume its inescapable dimension. As well as resting a good deal, she continued to answer great numbers of the letters she had received. One was to the Prime Minister – Mr Harold Wilson; his consideration touched her particularly in the matter of Anthony Montague Browne, whom he suggested should remain on the Foreign Office strength, but stay on with her for a few months more to help and advise on the many matters which would arise immediately after Winston's death. But she was also conscious of the great back-up of sympathy and support she had received from official quarters in many ways, and she wrote to Mr Wilson:

> May I express to you my true and heartfelt thanks for the wonderful and sustaining way in which many Government Departments have helped me in recent days? I am thinking not only of the State Funeral, but of many other matters. I know that much of this is due to your personal sympathy.[1]

In these first weeks after Winston's death, Clementine took two major decisions. She was quite clear that, although she had a perfect right to live at Chartwell for her life, she would hand it over straight away to the National Trust. Secondly, after some consideration, she decided to sell both the houses in Hyde Park Gate. She had been left comfortably off, but her practical good sense did not desert her. Even the original No. 28 would be too big for just one person, expensive, and a 'business' to run. Soon, she would look for a flat. Most of these plans were decided by her during her visit to Hamsell. After she left us to return to the empty shell that now was No. 28, she wrote me a letter I have always treasured:

February the 15th 1965

My darling Mary,

I shall never forget your strong loving help to me during this last month. I have felt comforted and supported by you.

Hamsell has been my refuge and resting place this last fortnight & I feel revived –
Your devoted
Mama

Kind friends and relations stretched forth helping hands at this moment. Ronnie and Marietta Tree* invited Clementine to Heron Bay, their romantic and lovely house on the seashore in Barbados, and the Duke of Marlborough sent a warm invitation to visit him and his family at his house Woodstock near Montego Bay in Jamaica. In both these invitations Christopher and I were included. It was an ideal plan, and would make the necessary change and break before Clementine started to remake her life.

A few days before we left my mother visited Chartwell, taking Grace Hamblin and me with her to meet representatives of the National Trust, and to make preliminary plans for the take-over. It was, naturally, a rather muted occasion. Neither my mother nor I had been to Chartwell since she and my father had left there for the last time. The sensitive understanding of both Robin Fedden and Ivan Hills of the National Trust helped her, but she was calmly fixed in her mind about her intentions, and she at once addressed herself to the main theme of her thoughts concerning Chartwell's future. By the terms of the original sale of Chartwell in 1946, only the house and grounds were designated for the National Trust. There was no commitment about furnishings; the house could have been handed over an empty shell. But from the beginning both Clementine and Winston felt that the house should be 'so garnished and furnished as to be of interest to the public . . .'[2] This intention Clementine now reaffirmed to Mr Fedden and Mr Hills, telling them at the same time that she wished the house to be seen as it was in its heyday during the twenties and thirties, rather than in its latter-day practical, but rather topsy-turvy arrangement. My mother delegated to Grace Hamblin and me the task of working closely with the National Trust in carrying out all the details which the takeover and readaption of the house would involve.

Shortly before she left for the Caribbean, Clementine received a warm and understanding letter from Randolph, who was spending the winter months in Marrakech, working on the official biography of his father. He wrote:

I have been thinking so much about you, dearest Mama, and am very glad to hear that you are going to the Barbados and to Jamaica. I know what a terrible time you have had in the last ten or fifteen years and trust that you have realised my understanding of this. When you have had a good holiday and rest you must try to create a new life for yourself. To begin with you will probably feel a vast void . . .[3]

We left Southampton in the *Queen Mary* on 24th February, bound for New York, on our way to Barbados, where we spent ten days with the Trees. Clementine was very tired, but this was a perfect and peaceful interlude. From there we flew to Jamaica, where Clementine stayed with Bert Marlborough's eldest daughter, Sarah Russell, while Christopher and I stayed with her father. The houses were quite

*Ronnie and Nancy Tree had been divorced, and he had married Marietta Fitzgerald in 1947.

close, and we made daily plans together. But through these weeks, despite great kindness and solicitude, blue skies and sunshine, Clementine, although ever pleasant and appreciative, seemed to be living in a world of her own, remote from us all. She arrived home towards the end of March only somewhat rested and refreshed by her month-long holiday. And of course, once home, decisions and problems awaited her. She also began at once looking for a flat, and starting life anew – and alone.

*

It was during the voyage to New York that my mother told Christopher and me that the Graham Sutherland portrait of my father was no longer in existence. We were both flabbergasted. We knew the picture had been sent to Chartwell not long after the presentation, and had been stored away there. But the information Clementine now imparted to us was a total surprise. She told us that Winston's deep dislike of the picture, and the bitter resentment at the manner in which he had been portrayed, weighed more and more on his mind during the months that followed its presentation in November 1954, to such an extent that Clementine told us she had promised him that 'it would never see the light of day'. As far as I know, she consulted no one about her intention, and it was entirely on her own initiative that some time in 1955 or 1956 she gave instructions for the picture to be destroyed. I do not believe Clementine ever specifically told Winston the steps she had taken: but her original pledge calmed him, and reassured him that the actual portrait which he so heartily loathed would not be seen by generations yet unborn. (But of course photographs had been taken of the picture.)

As time went by there were spasmodic, but persistent enquiries about the portrait, and requests for it to be exhibited on permanent loan or for specific exhibitions. These enquiries were at first easily parried, both Winston's and Clementine's dislike for the picture soon becoming a well-known fact. The very small number of people who came to know of its fate were all of the same mind – namely, that whatever the enquiries, or the speculation, the facts should not be revealed in Clementine's lifetime. It was therefore inevitable that from time to time a few of us were forced to be less than candid when questioned on the subject. Clementine herself simply refused to discuss the matter at all, except with those of us who knew the story. And even with us, it was not a topic frequently touched upon.

Within a month of Clementine's death in December 1977 her Executors, of whom I was one, issued a statement telling the bare facts of what had befallen the portrait. I had written a personal letter to Mr Sutherland, making sure he had received it before the statement was released. When the storm of controversy blew up, as, indeed, we had anticipated, those of us who had known the facts for so long were glad we had consistently advised my mother not to allow the story to be revealed in her lifetime.

Although a small number of people probably guessed that the Sutherland portrait had been destroyed (among them, the artist himself), the news came as a complete surprise to the public. To generalise: the artistic world had the vapours; some of the Press were governessy; and there was some valid criticism. But as far as one can judge from the consensus of the letters published in the correspondence columns of the newspapers, and from those received by members of our family, a poll on the subject would have shown an overwhelming endorsement of Clementine's right to dispose of a picture of her husband which they both regarded as offensive.

There is, however, one point about which some doubt has been expressed, and which should be cleared up. The idea circulated that it had always been the intention of the Members' Parliamentary Committee that, in time, the picture should be returned, and hung somewhere in the Palace of Westminster in perpetuity. It was claimed by some, therefore, that Clementine did not have the right to cause it to be destroyed, since it was not in fact Winston's outright property. On investigation, it seems the idea that the picture should eventually revert to the House of Commons did form part of the Committee's thinking at an early stage. But this condition was certainly not formulated in any document that I know of; nor was the idea mentioned in any of the speeches at the presentation of the picture. There was no question in the minds of those in close contact with Winston and Clementine at this time or later, that the Sutherland portrait was anything other than an outright gift. Moreover, there exists a document drawn up and signed on behalf of the Members' Parliamentary Committee assigning the 'sole and exclusive copyright' of the portrait to Winston Churchill.[4]

It is right that the destruction of the Sutherland portrait should be put in its proper context. It was not an isolated case of 'destructivitis' on Clementine's part. Fiercely protective of Winston's honour, she had all along been the ruthless guardian of his 'image', in all senses of the word.

Although Clementine greatly admired Sickert's work, and although he was a friend from her girlhood days, this had not deterred her from putting her foot through a sketch he had done of Winston some time around 1927* which she disliked. And seventeen years later, in September 1944, when Clementine and Winston were staying with the Roosevelts at Hyde Park after the Second Quebec Conference, she wrote home:

> I paid a visit to the President's Museum and managed to hook out of it a horrible caricature of your Father by Paul Maze. I boldly told the President I did not like it and he said, 'Nor do I'. So I said, 'May it come out?' and he said, 'Yes' and so now it is destroyed.[5]

In fact the picture was not a 'caricature', although she regarded it as such: it was, as far as I can remember, a charcoal sketch.

However, Clementine appears to have been in quite good company. There is in the National Maritime Museum at Greenwich a portrait of Queen Elizabeth I. Below the picture is a notice which says that the Queen must have liked this portrait, since, according to Sir Walter Raleigh, those of which she did not approve 'she knockt in pieces and cast into the fire'![6]

---

*In all probability this may have been one of several studies for the oil painting Sickert did of Winston Churchill *circa* 1927, which now hangs in the National Portrait Gallery. Two studies are extant: one in the Walker Art Gallery in Liverpool, and one in a private collection in London. (Information concerning the last two studies comes from *Sickert* by Wendy Baron, London, 1973.)

After I learned about the fate of the Sutherland, I reminded my mother that she had told me that she had at first disliked the tragic, haunting portrait Orpen had painted of my father in 1915, just after he had resigned as a result of the catastrophe of the Dardanelles. Later she had come to think it the best portrait ever done of him. Would she not perhaps have changed her mind about Graham Sutherland's picture too? But she was adamant that nothing would have altered her opinion in this latter case.

Clementine's strong dislike of Graham Sutherland's portrait was not an instantaneous reaction. She had quickly 'taken to' both Mr and Mrs Sutherland, and although his paintings which she had hitherto seen struck her as 'savage cruel designs'[7] she was pre-disposed to view this 'state' portrait of Winston favourably. She first saw the finished picture at the end of October 1954 when lunching with Sir Kenneth and Lady Clark, who were old friends, at Saltwood Castle, near Hythe; Mr Sutherland had deposited the picture with the Clarks, hoping that they would show it to Clementine. I was present too, and Sir Kenneth (now Lord Clark) has reminded me that my mother's first reaction was not unfavourable. She studied the picture for some time, and then spoke of it with approval, and praised its truthfulness. I certainly remember that her antipathy was not immediate: but it worked up pretty quickly. I think in her heart of hearts the picture probably rather stunned her, and when she realised how much Winston hated it, his views coloured her own. But, as her whole life shows, she was perfectly capable of taking an independent view, and so I think her early approval of the picture was not very whole-hearted; and when she saw how deeply Winston felt, she herself came to hate the picture too.

Lord Clark has told me that he never thought Winston would be pleased with the picture; he wrote to me:

. . . He had come to accept an image of himself, which had become an international symbol; & this Graham had completely disregarded . . .[8]

Whatever her views, however, Clementine still had a friendly contact with Mr Sutherland. Early in December 1954, shortly after the presentation of the portrait, he sent her a sketch of a hand he had made during the sittings. In her reply Clementine wrote: 'I am touched that you should have given me the sketch of Winston's hand. Thank you very much indeed.'[9] That was all; she gave no hint of her own or Winston's feelings.

In October 1957 Clementine wrote to thank Max Beaverbrook for inviting them both to Nassau. Lord Beaverbrook was a great admirer of Graham Sutherland's paintings, and, from her letter, it looks as if they had discussed his work, and Winston's portrait in particular, for she went on:

. . . I visited the Tate Gallery last week & contemplated the two brilliant and ferocious portraits of Madame Rubinstein – I must say I should hesitate to have my face lifted by her! I'm afraid that if I have any say in the matter, Winston's portrait by Mr Sutherland will never see the light of day. This gift which was meant as the expression of the affection and devotion of the House of Commons caused him great pain & it all but ruined his 80th birthday – It wounded him deeply that this brilliant . . . painter with whom he had made friends while sitting for him should see him as a gross & cruel monster.[10]

The portrait of course had been destroyed some two years before she wrote this letter. But it is a complete and personal record of how Winston had felt, and of how she herself had come to feel. It suffices to add that Clementine never regretted what she had done, and indeed only a few months before her death she confirmed that she had not changed her mind on this subject by one iota.

*

A few days after her return from the Caribbean Clementine celebrated her eightieth birthday. Randolph organised a splendid luncheon party for her at the Café Royal, attended by an almost complete muster of children and grandchildren. It was like a launching into that new life which Randolph had so rightly said she must carve out for herself.

Within a short time she found herself a flat at 7 Princes Gate, S.W.7. It was only about half a mile from Hyde Park Gate, so she would not be moving out of her neighbourhood. The flat was on the sixth floor of a handsome apartment block: it was large and sunny, all the main rooms looked southwards over gardens, and there was a wide and pleasing panorama of buildings and rooftops. Clementine began at once on the necessary alterations and redecorations. But although she had herself, without prompting, decided not to continue living at Hyde Park Gate, the wrench of leaving it was, understandably, severe. She moved into her new home early in September, and the Hyde Park Gate houses were sold at auction late in October.

But happily for her, Clementine did not start her new life bereft of all domestic continuity. From Hyde Park Gate came with her Nonie Chapman, her private secretary, and Mrs Lily Douglas, her cook. Nonie had been Clementine's secretary since April 1964; she was to be with her now until her death. Nonie veritably 'structured' her life. Apart from dealing with Clementine's considerable volume of correspondence, she organised the household, and drove my mother about. But the companionship she gave Clementine, and the unfailing and tender devotion Nonie showed towards her, contributed more than it is possible to evaluate to the large measure of happiness and serenity Clementine was to know in these last twelve years of her life.

Mrs Lily Douglas had come as cook to Hyde Park Gate in 1964, and now, giving up the hierarchical set-up of a large domestic staff, Mrs 'D' followed Clementine into her new flat and new life, in which she became a great feature, not only as an excellent cook, but because she was an interesting and highly intelligent person. She was devoted to Clementine, and shouldered the responsibility of watchfulness, especially at week-ends, when Nonie was away. There was a succession of mainly sweet and kind Filipino maids, but continuity and security were assured by the presence of Nonie Chapman and Mrs Douglas. It was a great grief to Clementine (and indeed to us all) when dear Mrs D died in March 1976 of cancer.

This year of 1965 saw Clementine involved in many things flowing from the aftermath of Winston's death. On 5th April, Clementine and Randolph lunched with the

Queen at Windsor. In a private ceremony, Randolph handed back to the Queen in the customary fashion his father's Insignia of the Order of the Garter. In the afternoon, Clementine, Randolph and several other members of the family attended the beautiful and moving service held over Winston's Banner, which always takes place in St George's Chapel, Windsor Castle, after the death of a Knight. After the service, the Banner was handed over to Clementine, and it now hangs from the great oak beam in his study at Chartwell.

Later in the year, at the twenty-fifth Battle of Britain Service in Westminster Abbey on 19th September, Clementine and more than forty members of our family were present, and after the service we watched the Queen unveil a memorial stone laid between the great west door of the Abbey and the Unknown Warrior's tomb. It bears the inscription: 'Remember Winston Churchill.' Every year thereafter, on the anniversary of Winston's birthday and of his death, Clementine would lay flowers on this memorial.

Within a month of Winston's death, Field Marshal Alexander launched an appeal to form the Winston Churchill Memorial Trust, the purpose of which would be to fund Travelling Scholarships for men and women from all over the English-speaking world. The idea had been discussed with Winston and Clementine, and now it had her full blessing and support. Nearly three million pounds were raised, and 1966 saw the first batch of over sixty Churchill Scholars. During the succeeding years Clementine kept a lively interest in this 'living' memorial to Winston.

In May 1965 an event occurred which caused her much pleasure and gratification. On the recommendation of the Prime Minister, Mr Harold Wilson, the Queen conferred a Life Peerage on Clementine. She assumed the title of Baroness Spencer-Churchill of Chartwell, and her introduction into the House of Lords took place on 15th June; her sponsors were Lord Normanbrook and Lord Ismay. We were all so proud and overjoyed for her, and felt this would be a new outlet and interest. Clementine herself was full of enthusiasm. She took her seat on the 'cross-benches', which caused astonishment in some quarters, but certainly not among those who knew her well. In 1965 she attended the House thirteen times, voting for the Abolition of the Death Penalty Bill on 20th July. The following year seven attendances for her are recorded, but she did not vote again, and she never made a speech. It was a great disappointment to her that after 1966 her deafness was such that she could not hear the debates, which of course rendered her attendance pointless.

During the last year of Winston's life, Clementine had been very loath to leave him for any length of time. Now, we all felt it was important for her health and spirits that she should come away as often as possible from London and her endless preoccupations with house-moving and other matters. She made five week-end visits to Hamsell, and started the (for us joyful) ritual of spending Christmas with us: which she did for eight consecutive years. Randolph had a beautiful house and garden – Stour, at East Bergholt, Suffolk, and here she would make 'day-trips' to see him, which she very much enjoyed. Young Winston and Minnie, with their enchanting and growing family, lived near Haywards Heath in Sussex, and here too was a frequent port of call. Staying with other than relations Clementine found something of an effort; but during these next few years she made several visits to old friends. And in August 1967 she went to Scotland, staying first with Captain and Lady Victoria Wemyss at Wemyss, and going on to Airlie Castle to stay with her cousins, Lord and Lady Airlie. This was a pleasurable and nostalgic journey into the long-distant past.

In London her social life quickly revived: old friends invited her out, and she now started entertaining in her new home. Her diaries are sprinkled with details of small luncheon parties, in addition to the numerous occasions when her family came to see her. Evening engagements she already found tiring; they were few and far between, and after 1966 the only people other than her immediate family who dined with her were Jock and Meg Colville, Sylvia Henley and Grace Hamblin. Sylvia Henley was a frequent luncheon and dinner guest, and her devoted friendship supplied a continuity of companionship right to the end of Clementine's road. They played a running tournament of backgammon, with the small stakes meticulously recorded and paid up. Sylvia's always keen and active mind was a stimulus, and she often accompanied Clementine to exhibitions and on expeditions. Horatia Seymour, the other close surviving friend of her youth, she would always see on her visits to us, for Horatia lived in Tunbridge Wells. Clementine was greatly saddened by her death in November 1966.

Clementine also carried out a considerable number of public, or quasi-public engagements. From now to the end of her life, if she was in London and well, she always made a point of attending the annual Battle of Britain Service at Westminster Abbey; and Harrow Songs, so long a feature of her life with Winston, now became a regular feature of her winter programme.

Churchill College, Cambridge, was a continuing source of pride and interest to her. She had visited the college with Winston in the early stages of its building, in 1959, when he planted two trees; and in June 1964 she was present to see the Duke of Edinburgh formally open the college.

After his father's death, Randolph had suggested to her that Churchill College would be the most appropriate place for Winston's treasured collection of Napoleonic books, most of them beautifully bound; Clementine agreed and presented the college with some 150 books in early December 1965. Some years later she gave the Bevin Library at Churchill the copies of General de Gaulle's speeches, inscribed by him. But her greatest benefaction (with the agreement of the Churchill Archives Settlement) was to arrange the deposition of the eighteenth-century tortoiseshell casket enclosing 630 original manuscript letters from John Churchill, first Duke of Marlborough, to Antonie Heinsius, the Grand Pensionary of Holland. This priceless collection of letters had been the gift of the Netherlands Government in 1945, Queen Wilhelmina having flown over to England to present them to Winston herself, as a thank-offering for his services in the war to her country and to the world.

Winston, as Chairman of the college Trustees, had once told them that Clementine thought women should be admitted to Churchill; he had added that he was in full agreement with her view. This was certainly a result of her influence, for Winston could scarcely be termed an advocate of feminism. In 1969, Churchill College decided to admit women – they were the first 'Oxbridge' college to do so; although it was not until October 1972 that women were actually admitted to Churchill.

Clementine greatly enjoyed visiting Churchill College, which she did from time to time after Winston's death. She was always received with the utmost warmth and kindness by the Master, Fellows, students and staff.

It was most unfortunate that just when her health and spirits were beginning to revive after Winston's death Clementine should have had an accident. In mid-October, 1965, she was walking alone in Hyde Park, on a path which runs alongside a football pitch. A high ball in its descent struck her on the side of the head, throwing her down and breaking her right shoulder. Although the injury was not severe in itself, it shook her badly, and she endured several weeks of pain. The boys who had been playing were deeply concerned and apologetic, and brought her round a lovely bunch of flowers. One of her younger grandsons, hearing about his grandmother's misfortune, remarked that he was so very sorry about Grandmama, but he didn't actually know she played football!

The highlight of 1966 for Clementine was the opening of Chartwell to the public towards the end of June. She was thrilled by this event, and in the year it had taken to prepare the house and gardens for a continual flow-through of people, and to re-make the rooms as once they were, she had taken a keen supervisory interest. Colours, chintzes and upholsteries had been as faithfully copied as possible and the original furniture had been put back as before. The main change was in the pictures: many of them were Clementine's own favourites – such as two exquisite Nicholson paintings of the black swans and some of Winston's canvases. But there were no empty spaces on the walls, for she loaned Churchills to fill all the gaps, and a goodly number for the studio as well. Many of these she ultimately left to Chartwell.

Earlier, in May, prior to its opening to the public, the National Trust gave a large luncheon party at Chartwell, in honour of the original donors and of Clementine. All her family and some of her closest friends were also invited. It was a lovely oc-casion, and to the eyes of my mother, Randolph, Sarah and me, the Chartwell of yesterday had miraculously been revived before us. During the years to come Clem-entine loved to visit Chartwell several times in the spring and summer. Everything interested her, from the flower arrangements to the lavatories. She kept a keen eye on the garden where, under the aegis of Mr Lanning Roper, much of her own original planting and taste are perpetuated. She wholeheartedly approved any necessary alterations, and admired the improvements and additions he made. Vincent, her own former Head Gardener, was still there, and she enjoyed at first walking, and then later being pushed round the gardens with him as guide.

The first Administrator of Chartwell was Grace Hamblin, and Clementine wanted to know the details of the successes and also the teething pains of the first season or two; the admission figures were regularly telephoned to her. That Chartwell was immediately, and in the longer term too, a success with the public is shown by the figures: in the thirteen seasons from 1966 to 1978 an average of 155,513 people passed through the gates yearly. When Grace Hamblin retired in 1973, her successor Mrs Broome continued to keep Clementine in touch. I truly believe that my mother had more real pleasure and satisfaction from Chartwell in these last twelve years of her life than in all the forty she lived there up to my father's death.

*

In May 1966, Lord Moran published a book about Winston Churchill, whose doctor he had been for twenty-five years. The work – entitled *Winston Churchill: The Struggle for Survival 1940/65* – had been serialised the previous month in the *Sunday Times*.

At once a storm of controversy arose, based mainly on the ethical point which finds its basis in the Hippocratic Oath. When, in addition to the waiving of this traditional and basic rule of confidence, it became known that Clementine's and Winston's closest family were in total opposition to the publication of Lord Moran's book, the fires of public argument were further fanned.

Despite press statements (mainly at the time of Winston's last illness) that the two men were intimate friends, this was not the case. A friendly atmosphere – and, on Winston's part, perfect trust – certainly existed between them, such as is not uncommon in doctor–patient relationships. But while Lord Moran's skill and devotion to Winston have at no point been in question, they were never 'great' friends. The two men's natures, and their outlooks, were too dissimilar. Lord Moran's relationship with Winston was essentially a professional one, and his presence in our house and on many journeys stemmed from this.

In 1964 Clementine learned that Lord Moran intended to publish a book based on his relationship with Winston: she was much upset, and she raised the matter *viva voce* with Lord Moran himself. A letter to him, marked 'Private and Confidential' and dated 30th July 1964, puts the matter clearly:

> I am seriously disturbed by our conversation yesterday. I think that you should have told me of your intentions: it was only through the matter having been mentioned in the Press that I found out you intended to write a book about Winston, and I subsequently raised the matter with Jock.
>
> I had always supposed that the relationship between a doctor and his patient was one of complete confidence.
>
> Had you been writing your own biography, with passing references to Winston, it would have been underst ndable, though I would have hoped that you would tell us what you intended to say. But I do not see how you can justify your present course. An impartial observer would, I think, consider that your career had been a successful one and had not been damaged by your association with Winston, and I think he has not shown himself ungrateful to you.
>
> ... I do urge you to reconsider your intentions.

To this letter Clementine received no reply. In the months that followed she asked on more than one occasion that she might be allowed to see the proofs of the book. All her requests were ignored.

When Clementine had learned of Lord Moran's intention, she did not raise the subject with Winston. At this time (some seven months before his death), his health had deteriorated to a point where it would not have been feasible to discuss such a matter with him in any detail, and she did not want to arouse anxieties, and so disturb his peace of mind in this last phase of his life.

In January 1966, a year after Winston's death, Lord Moran wrote blandly to Clementine asking her permission to use a photograph of the Orpen portrait of

Winston in his book. Quite a time back, he had asked Winston if he could have the Orpen picture photographed for himself, because he liked and admired the picture so much. Winston had given his permission, and the photograph had been framed, and had stood thereafter on Lord Moran's mantelpiece. To his letter of 20th January 1966, requesting Clementine's permission for him to use the Orpen photograph for his book, Clementine the next day replied:

> . . . With regard to the Orpen picture, I would rather that you had not asked my permission to publish this painting in your book, for I regret very much that you should write about Winston. You will no doubt remember that I asked if I might see the proofs more than a year ago, but you ignored my request. I am very sorry about this, but I think you should know my feelings.

This letter, at least, received a reply. On 24th January 1966, Lord Moran wrote Clementine a long, diffuse letter covering various points. About his not having sent Clementine the proofs, he pleaded that most writers are averse to having incomplete versions of their work examined; and he expressed the hope that when she read the book in its final form she would not disapprove of it.

As to the doctor–patient relationship, Lord Moran based his argument on the approval – nay, encouragement – he had received from the eminent historian, Professor G. M. Trevelyan, who had taken the view that everything would eventually become known about such an historical figure as Winston Churchill. Lord Moran also averred that both Field Marshal Smuts and Brendan Bracken had given him strong encouragement to write the book.

In addition Lord Moran explained to Clementine how he had sought to do justice to Winston and to portray the physical odds against which he battled, particularly after his major stroke in 1953.

Finally, he returned to his request that he might be allowed to use the Orpen picture for his book. There is a short note attached to the correspondence, dated 25th January 1966, stating that Clementine had telephoned Lord Moran to tell him that as the portrait now belonged to Randolph, the matter was out of her hands. The Orpen portrait is not included among the illustrations in Lord Moran's book.

The publication of the serial and the book caused Clementine real distress, although she did not intervene herself in the long-drawn-out argument which raged in the correspondence columns, and in the Press generally. But Randolph was a doughty champion; and from Winston's own close entourage Jock Colville and Anthony Montague Browne also took up the cudgels. Two of his secretaries, and a former detective, made further telling points in the series of letters. Randolph's letter to *The Times* (26th April 1966) took up specifically the point Lord Moran had made (*The Times*, 25th April), in which he related how he had sought the advice of Professor G. M. Trevelyan (who had, incidentally, died in 1962), who had told him: 'This is history, you ought to get it on paper.' Randolph commented:

> Professor Trevelyan did not say: 'You ought to publish it'; certainly not within 15 months of his patient's death, and against the wishes of his family . . .

In a further letter (*The Times*, 3rd June 1966), Lord Moran took up some points which had been raised in the numerous letters. He stated that the book had Winston's knowledge and approval, and that Brendan Bracken, at Winston's request, had arranged a meeting for Lord Moran with his lawyer, Mr Anthony Moir, about a certain business aspect of the book. The following day (*The Times*, 4th June) Mr Moir, Winston's lawyer for twenty-three years, replied that

> Lord Moran sought my advice on a literary matter in 1958 but according to my own recollection, supported by the note which I made immediately after the interview, which was confirmed by a letter to him on the following day, no mention was made of a book to be solely based upon a part of Sir Winston's life and no reference was made to any approval having been given by him to any book.

As to Lord Moran's declaration in the same letter that he had had Winston's permission and approval to write the book, Anthony Montague Browne wrote (*The Times*, 6th June):

> He claims that he obtained Sir Winston's approval for the writing of his book. Why did Sir Winston not inform Lady Churchill, from whom he had no secrets, of his blessing on this somewhat unusual medical procedure? Why did Lord Moran not inform her himself?
>
> I served Sir Winston for the last 12 years of his life. He was meticulous in keeping his Private Office informed of decisions taken in their absence: he warned none of us of this one.
>
> Moreover, we know from Mr Anthony Moir, Sir Winston's solicitor (June 4), that at the meeting described by Lord Moran there was no mention of a biography of Sir Winston, nor of any permission having been given for one. Might it not have been prudent of Lord Moran to have confirmed his remarkable release from the Hippocratic Oath to just one member of Sir Winston's family, just one of his advisers or staff, by reference to Sir Winston during his lifetime?

Winston's own attitude to the possibility that a member of his entourage might write about him was described by Mr Evan M. Davies (*The Times*, 28th April 1966):

> In 1948, a month after I was posted to Sir Winston as his personal security officer, he was sitting in the grounds of Chartwell and, following a long silence, he asked: 'Are you going to write a book about me?' I told him nothing was farther from my mind and I assured him I would never do so. 'In that case I can relax', he said.
>
> I remembered this on the several occasions when publishers made approaches to me.

My mother said to me of Lord Moran's book: 'It shows Winston in a completely false light.' She, as did all of the family, bitterly resented the wholesale quoting of Lord Moran's conversations with Winston and others close to him, certainly without Winston's permission, and in a great number of cases without the consent of the other persons quoted. Several of them complained that, not only had their permission not been sought, but that Lord Moran had, on occasion, quoted the conversations totally out of context, and in some cases with the wrong date attributed to them.

The account of Winston's conversations, procured largely during the discharge of

Lord Moran's medical duties, tends to show that Winston had at times a nervous preoccupation with his health, and gives the impression that he was almost perpetually ill. But eminent people, as well as more ordinary folk, chiefly seek interviews with their medical advisers when they are concerned about their state of health, and not in order to discuss with them such things as war strategy and politics.

Clementine was also deeply sceptical about Lord Moran's claim that he had Winston's approval for writing the book. With Anthony Montague Browne, she wondered greatly that Winston had never mentioned this to her or to others close to him; and she was amazed that, in the circumstances, Lord Moran had not done so himself.

But ultimately the real and unchanging objection to Lord Moran's book that Clementine and her family held, which was shared by many others in all walks of life, including many doctors, was founded on the simple proposition that – prince or pauper, prime minister or ploughman – a person should be able to repose complete trust in the inviolable confidence of his priest, his lawyer and his doctor.

It was at Clementine's express wish that a collection of essays entitled *Action This Day: Working with Churchill* was published in 1968. Written from different angles by six people* who throughout the course of the war had worked in close contact with him, the essays show Winston in all his strength, diversity and charm, without blinking his faults or denying his weaknesses. Clementine felt that this book helped to redress the false picture painted by Lord Moran.

*

In these latter years, and especially since Winston's death, the relationship between Randolph and his mother had become less strained. He made efforts to please her; and she, in her turn, after Winston's death sought, and often accepted, his suggestions and advice. After the writing of his father's official biography had been entrusted to him in 1960, Randolph had bent his energy and his brilliant, tempestuous mind to the accomplishment of this great work – the task he cared for above everything else in his life. But, tragically, his health began to fail, and after a lung operation in 1964, although he seemingly made a good recovery, he cannot have felt that time was with him. Nevertheless, he battled on, and the first two volumes of *Winston S. Churchill* were published in 1966 and 1967 respectively.

On 6th June 1968, Randolph died suddenly at Stour; he was fifty-seven. Although his health had been visibly deteriorating for some months, yet his death came as a shock. As always in sorrow, Clementine had little to say. Now, of the five children she had borne, only Sarah and I survived. At Randolph's funeral at East Bergholt, and later at the crowded Memorial Service in St Margaret's, Westminster, she remained a mute, dignified figure.

But despite the penalty that Time inexorably exacts from those who live on, in terms of family and friends; despite occasional gusts of controversy, or hurtful

*The contributors were: Lord Normanbrook; John Colville; Sir John Martin; Sir Ian Jacob; Lord Bridges; Sir Leslie Rowan. It was edited by Sir John Wheeler-Bennett, who also wrote the Introduction, and was published by Macmillan. All the royalties from *Action This Day* were given by the contributors to Churchill College, Cambridge.

slaps at Winston's departed greatness; in the face of increasing deafness and failing sight, and the toll which two falls (in which she broke first one and then the other hip) took of her strength – looking back over Clementine's last decade, one sees what a long and glorious sunset it was.

Since Winston's death, Clementine truly lived in the glow of what so many people throughout the world had come to feel for him. The awe and admiration of what he had been as a man, and of his long life's extraordinary story; gratitude beyond the grave for what he had meant to the history of our country, and indeed to that of civilisation; love, for this very lovable and human human being – these feelings now found expression in touching solicitude for the woman he had loved so dearly, and who, by her single-minded love for him, her loyalty, and her tenacious, fierce integrity, had made also for herself a special place in people's affection and esteem.

Even now in her old age many demands were made upon her: to visit this; to open that; to launch a ship; to approve a bust or picture of Winston (tricky ground here). Her considerable correspondence made her address her mind to many different things. Reading the newspapers (wearing white cotton gloves to protect her hands from the grubby newsprint) and listening to the radio news, were sacred rituals. The radio gradually had to be turned to shouting pitch, and presently Nonie Chapman had to read her the papers: but she was astonishingly well informed. The correspondence columns of *The Times* particularly interested her; and every now and then she would quite spontaneously fire off a letter herself – always signed in the old-fashioned way: 'I am, Sir, your obedient servant . . .'.

Nor did she react only through the post to events or matters which roused her interest, her indignation or her pity. In April 1970, the German Ambassador to Guatemala was kidnapped and shot. A book was opened at the German Embassy for people to sign as a mark of their sympathy, and the then German Ambassador to London told me how the Embassy staff were as astonished as they were moved to recognise Lady Spencer-Churchill in the rather frail old woman who, helped by her young secretary, slowly climbed the Chancery steps to record, in the only way she could, her revulsion and disapproval of such a barbarous act.

Through all these last years, Clementine maintained her contacts with societies with which she had long connections. The Y.W.C.A. kept her informed of any aspects of their work which they knew would particularly interest her. It was not until 1966 that her Special Fund to help hostels with their improvements was finally exhausted. She was to remain their Honorary Vice-President for life, and she was a regular visitor and supporter of their mammoth Christmas Fair.

In the same way, Clementine kept in close touch with Winston's former constituency. She was to remain their Conservative Association's President until the end of her life. Although she no longer attended meetings or functions in Woodford, every year the Chairman of the Association would write her a long and detailed letter putting her in the picture as to the affairs of the Association. In her reply, she always picked up various points which were of greatest interest to her.

Clementine did not take on many new obligations, but two are of note. In 1966 she became one of the Trustees of Lord Attlee's Memorial Foundation; and in 1968 she actually took a small part in a film made to raise funds for the Appeal. As late as 1972 she accepted the Presidency of the National Benevolent Fund for the Aged. To her last years she continued to try to make whatever contribution it was in her power still to do.

Her family in all its several generations was to be an abiding source of interest and stimulation to her. She loved to attend their weddings, christenings and confirmations. We were all ever welcome at Princes Gate, where her old standards of hospitality and delicious food were still maintained. The company of her grandchildren she found revitalising, and their jobs, examinations, friends and ambitions were all interesting to her. My daughter Emma, nearly seventeen, had dined with her in January 1966; and my mother wrote to me:

> . . . She seems to love her school. She told me she was learning German. I think she should be learning Russian & in turn her children Chinese! so as to keep up with the trend . . .[11]

*

In the autumn of 1968, my husband was sent as Ambassador to Paris. His appointment had come as a complete surprise to everyone, including ourselves. He had lost his seat in Bedford at the General Election of 1966, and in early 1968 he was busy looking for a new parliamentary seat to fight, when Mr Harold Wilson, the Prime Minister, and Mr George Brown, the Foreign Secretary, offered him this challenging job as Ambassador, with the special mission of helping to bring about Great Britain's entry into the Common Market. When my mother learned from Christopher of this new and surprising turn in our lives, she was not only delighted for us, but from the first absolutely certain that Christopher was right in accepting this new assignment, although it removed him for the time being from the domestic political scene.

Excited though I was from the beginning by the prospect of this new adventure in our lives, and of Christopher's job in which I would have a share, I was concerned that it would of necessity make me less immediately available for my mother. She had, in fact, nine more years to live, but at the time of our going to Paris she was already eighty-three. Sarah was often in America, and I knew that my mother to some extent depended on me. But never at any moment did she allow this thought, which was with us both, I think, to cloud the natural excitement and anticipation she shared with us. And on the wet September morning when we set out from Victoria on the Golden Arrow, there on the chilly platform to bid us 'Godspeed' were my mother and Sarah.

During the next four years a regular feature of Clementine's life, and ours, were her visits to us in Paris. Always staying for a week, and eschewing the speed and easy comfort of the air, she invariably travelled by the overnight Train Ferry. We felt at the time that she really did enjoy herself, but now, reading her 'thank-you' letters again, I have wept happy and grateful tears.

The British Embassy in Paris is a glorious mid-eighteenth century house, which later became the home of Pauline Borghese, Napoleon's sister. It must be among the most beautiful and historic houses in Europe. And if one has a large family, this glittering, romantic house has room for all, and responds to all the demands of both diplomatic and family festivities. At Christmas we would try to assemble all our own children, Christopher's mother (Hope Dynevor), his sister and her family, and my mother. Clementine, although getting older and deafer, fitted in perfectly, and enjoyed the hurly-burly of the different generations. On New Year's Day 1971, she wrote to me from London:

> Darling, this is the third Christmas I have spent with you in Paris. All equally delightful. It is something to look forward to all the year . . .

When she came to stay at other times, usually in the spring, I tried to choose a relatively quiet patch, so that I could 'concentrate' on her. My mother had known and loved Paris all her life; now we re-visited many famous and favourite sights. After she broke her hip in 1969, walking long distances was out of the question. But, luckily, she had no false inhibitions about using a wheelchair for expeditions. And with a 'gardien', or more usually with me, pushing her, we bowled through kilometres of galleries and exhibitions. We became quite ambitious, and with my Nannie to help as 'pusher', we managed parks and gardens as well: once narrowly avoiding calamity, when we nearly capsized my mother over an obstinate tree root in the gardens of Le Petit Hameau at Versailles.

Apart from the expeditions, Clementine took great interest in all the political aspects of Christopher's job, about which he would talk to her at length, and she enjoyed meeting her old friends and ours, and other Embassy guests. And, needless to say, she wanted to know every detail of my now rather glossy housekeeping arrangements.

On 9th November 1970, General de Gaulle died very suddenly at his home, Colombey-les-Deux-Eglises. Clementine had just returned home from a visit to us. Always an admirer and a believer in this great man, she was much saddened. Ever since the war she had kept up a spasmodic, friendly but formal correspondence with both General and Madame de Gaulle, and twice she had sent him messages at moments of political crisis: once in 1953, at the time of his Rassemblement du Peuple Français, and again during the weeks of end-April/early-May 1969 when, after the Referendum which resulted in his narrow defeat, he resigned on 28th April, as he had vowed he would. To this last message of hers, the General replied:

> Il n'y a pas de message qui m'ait touché plus que le vôtre. En le recevant de votre part, il m'a semblé qu'il me venait, au même temps, au nom du grand et cher Winston Churchill. Je vous en remercie de tout coeur.[12]

On the first anniversary of Winston's death, Clementine had received a letter from General de Gaulle, then President of France, which moved her deeply:

> Voici venir le triste et émouvant anniversaire. Laissez-moi vous dire, qu'en portant en cette occasion ma pensée sur la grande mémoire de Sir Winston Churchill, je ressens, mieux que jamais la dimension de sa personalité, l'étendue de

son oeuvre, enfin la force et la qualité des liens qui m'attachaient à lui et qui, à travers nous deux, unissaient l'Angleterre et la France. Je voudrais que vous sachiez aussi de quel coeur ma femme et moi-même partageons le chagrin où vous a laissée, ainsi que les vôtres, la disparition de votre si cher et si glorieux mari.[13]

Now, in November 1970, she had been staying with us in Paris, and within twenty-four hours of her return home she learned of the General's sudden death. In her thank-you letter to me, dated 10th November, she wrote:

. . . I have just heard of the death of General de Gaulle; & although it is true that at times he was no friend to England, it saddens me very much – It is the end of an epoch . . .

I wrote to her a week or two later, describing the solemn Requiem which had been held in Notre Dame, and to which Great Britain had sent a splendid representation headed by the Prince of Wales and the Prime Minister (Mr Heath) and no less than three former Prime Ministers. I described to my mother how I had been to Notre Dame although Ambassadors' wives had not been asked, as a generality, and also how Clarissa Avon (Eden) and I had both been specially invited to President Pompidou's reception later that same day.

. . . So I felt Papa's memory had been honoured as well as the General's – As you say a whole epoch seems to have ended with his death – [14]

*

A faithful and constant friend in all these last years was Edward Heath. Clementine followed his fortunes – and misfortunes – with an affectionate, almost maternal eye. He, for his part, was never failing in charming attentions. He would sometimes give a luncheon party for her, at Albany, and later at No. 10 Downing Street; and he lunched with her from time to time. One year he accompanied her to Harrow Songs, and in the summer of 1972 he took her to see the Tutankhamen Exhibition.

One very agreeable occasion was in November 1971, when Edward Heath, then Prime Minister, invited Clementine and a small family party to luncheon at Chequers, to inspect in its new surroundings a picture by Winston which Clementine had given to Chequers. During Mr Heath's Prime Ministership, he had presided over some major changes in the decoration and arrangement of Chequers. Needless to say, Clementine was much interested to see these alterations: and she found them a great improvement on the rather gloomy décor she had known in her day. She was also able to inspect the progress in growth of the avenue of beech trees which Winston and she had presented to Chequers after his resignation in 1955, to commemorate their time there.

*

Although, as the years went on, Clementine found staying away for holidays an effort, and she did not like flying or complicated journeys to get to a chosen destination, in 1970 and 1971 she found a very good solution: taking Nonie Chapman with her, she embarked on 'cruise' life. In September the first year, she went on the *Andes*, a ship of the Royal Mail Lines, for a three-week cruise in the Mediterranean. It was a great success. She made some agreeable shipboard acquaintances, and towards the end of the cruise she took part in a Fancy Dress Competition, appearing as 'A Lady in Black'. To the warmly expressed delight of the other competitors, and Clementine's great surprise and unconcealed pleasure, she was awarded First Prize. Her trophy was an enamelled powder case, which she often used thereafter.

The following year she repeated her holiday plan, and set out on another enjoyable Mediterranean cruise. But in 1972 she contented herself with a visit to us in Paris. In November of that year Clementine had her second fall, which resulted in a broken hip: this really did slow her down very considerably, and thereafter no cruises were undertaken. But they remained a pleasant memory.

There were some very special highlights in these last twelve years of Clementine's life. In December 1969, she unveiled a statue of Winston in the House of Commons. Executed in bronze by Oscar Nemon, the statue stands on the left of the Churchill Arch, through which Members of Parliament pass as they enter or leave the Chamber. When the Chamber of the House of Commons was rebuilt after being destroyed by bombing in the Second World War, Winston had suggested that the archway leading into the Chamber should be left with all its battle scars upon it, to remind future generations of the perils through which free democratic institutions had passed in those terrible years. It had been thereafter known as the Churchill Arch.

In 1970, the Lord Mayor of Westminster launched a public appeal for funds to commission and erect a statue of Winston Churchill on a site in Parliament Square made available by the Government. The statue, chosen by the Royal Fine Art Commission from a number submitted, was by Mr Ivor Roberts-Jones. It combines a sombre likeness with considerable allegorical allusion. Some months before the unveiling, the Queen's Private Secretary had written to Clementine saying that the Queen would so much like her actually to unveil the statue: Clementine was greatly touched. The occasion itself, on 1st November 1973, was moving and memorable. It was a fine, grey day, and a great concourse of people gathered in Parliament Square. As well as the Queen, Queen Elizabeth the Queen Mother attended the ceremony, as did the Prime Minister, and four former Prime Ministers, and a great number of notabilities. Of our family, more than twenty were present, representing four generations. There were some very nice touches to the proceedings: the Band of the Royal Marines played some of Winston's favourite tunes – from the Edwardian music-halls, Gilbert and Sullivan, and the Harrow song, 'Forty Years On'. The bells of St Margaret's, Westminster, rang out, and among the bell-ringers were two who had rung the peal at Winston's and Clementine's wedding sixty-five years before.

At the end of her speech, the Queen said:

For more than fifty eventful years, Lady Churchill was his deeply loved companion and I think it would be right, therefore, for her to unveil the statue of her husband.

And, turning to Clementine, the Queen handed her the silken cord which would release the Union Jack shrouding the statue. And so it was that, in the presence of his revered Sovereign, Winston Churchill's statue was unveiled by his beloved 'Clemmie'.

The year 1974 was the centenary of Winston's birth. It was chiefly marked by the launching of an appeal for a Churchill Centenary Trust, from which both the Winston Churchill Memorial Trust (Churchill Fellows) and Churchill College, Cambridge, were both to benefit. The Appeal was launched at a large party attended by, among others, the three party leaders, at the Banqueting House, Whitehall. It coincided with Clementine's eighty-ninth birthday. After the reception at Banqueting House, the family whisked her away and gave her a birthday luncheon at Claridge's.

In May, Clementine was present when the Queen Mother opened a large and fascinating 'Churchill' Exhibition at Somerset House. In the lovely rooms of that eighteenth century 'palace' was displayed every kind of Churchilliana, and the long pageant of his whole life was vividly recorded. Clementine was thrilled by the exhibition, and made several visits to it.

The culmination of Winston's Centenary year for the family was on 30th November – the hundredth anniversary of his birth. A large number of members of his family, in their several generations, and some of his closest friends, attended a commemoration service at St Martin's, Bladon. It was all arranged by Sunny Marlborough, who had succeeded to the dukedom on the death of his father in 1972. The church service was, for us all, deeply moving, and afterwards Winston pushed his grandmother to her husband's grave in the churchyard, where she laid some flowers and sat for a little while in contemplation. She said to Winston: 'I hope I shall not be long now.'

Clementine had not, since her youth, been a great church-goer; but in these later years, she 'took' to it again. When she was settled at Princes Gate, she made a regular habit of walking every Sunday to nearby Holy Trinity, Brompton. As her deafness increased, she would sit right at the back of the church, slipping out, with the kindly help of the verger, before the sermon. After her first hip accident in 1969, when she could no longer go out unaccompanied, her expeditions to Holy Trinity ceased. But whenever she stayed with her family, we shepherded her carefully to and from church. Later, both at Christmas and Easter, if she was in London, the Vicar from Holy Trinity would bring Holy Communion to her.

Clementine never talked much about her inner feelings, but I am sure she thought about her death, and was quite prepared to receive her summons, whenever it might come. She would often talk to me in a brisk, practical way about various arrangements, and her wishes for her possessions: and I, coward that I am, would shy away from such 'tomb talk'. Clementine thought much about Winston: one evening in the year before her death, when I had been dining with her, she said: 'I do miss Papa so . . . really more than I did just after he died.'

*

In the summer of 1975, Clementine received yet another sign of appreciation of herself as an individual personality. During the July Congregation of Bristol University, of which Winston himself for more than thirty years had been Chancellor, Clementine was awarded the Honorary Degree of Doctor of Laws. She was greatly gratified, but she did not feel strong enough herself to go to Bristol to receive this honour, and she deputed me to receive it on her behalf.

In these last years I came to realise fully just what a special place my mother had carved for herself in the minds and hearts of all sorts of men and women. After her several accidents, two of which resulted in her becoming gravely ill, and which were widely reported, I helped to answer the letters and messages which poured in from the general public. I saw then how her devotion as a wife, her steadfast adherence to her ideals and high standards, and her tenacious struggle with all life had confronted her with, had been recognised, and that people seemed to have found in her an example and an inspiration.

*

To celebrate Clementine's ninetieth birthday in April 1975, her granddaughter, Celia, and her husband, Dennis Walters, lent their house, and the family gave a party in her honour. To this party came a great gathering of children, grandchildren and great-grandchildren, as well as cousins and her greatest friends. She enjoyed it very much.

But now the rhythm of her daily life was perceptibly slowing. Her great deafness made it difficult for her to hear, or join in, general conversation; and although she had many people to luncheon, she usually only had them one or two at a time. But in this summer she made three expeditions to Chartwell, and gave a tea party at Princes Gate for all the Chartwell guides and helpers.

After Christopher and I returned from Paris, we were in England only a few months before in January 1973 we went to Brussels, where he took up his post as one of the first two British Commissioners to the European Economic Community. The tour of Commissioner lasts four years, but since I was not needed 'in the shop', as I had been when Christopher was Ambassador, and thanks to his understanding and generosity, I was able to come home a good deal to England, and stay for longer periods than when we had been in Paris. I was very glad of this, because now my mother's health did from time to time cause us all anxiety: one felt that slowly the clock was winding down. Although we always came home to England for Christmas with our children, we had sold Hamsell, and now lived in a much smaller house, Castle Mill House, near Odiham, in Hampshire, where, sadly for us, we could no longer have my mother to stay: so she used to make 'day-trips' to see us. But Winston and Minnie made three out of the four remaining Christmases of Clementine's life happy and joyful with them.

For some little time, those of us who had the knowledge and responsibility for Clementine's financial situation had become increasingly anxious about it. When she went to live at Princes Gate, she could afford her way of life. But inflation, and, as time went on, the need for more and more nursing, wrought ravages in Clementine's personal economic situation. After considerable discussion and consultation, she decided to sell several pictures, including two of Winston's. When Clementine's intentions became public knowledge, there was a loud and, for the greater part, sympathetic outcry in the Press. Most touching letters began to arrive at Princes

Gate, with offerings from pensioners, retired officers, and many other people. Nonie Chapman was kept very busy expressing Clementine's deep thanks, and returning these infinitely generous contributions. Inevitably politics and public argument combined to make the whole thing embarrassing. In 1972 the Heath Government had enacted legislation providing pensions for the widows of Prime Ministers, Cabinet Ministers and Members of Parliament, but it was not retroactive, and so Clementine had not benefited from it. There were suggestions, both in the Press and in Parliament, that special provision should be made for her by Parliament, and a kindly disposed individual wrote to *The Times* with the idea of launching an appeal to alleviate her circumstances. Clementine was, predictably, horrified, and immediately issued a statement to the effect that while she was deeply touched by the motives which prompted these suggestions, she would greatly deplore any legislation or appeal being initiated on her behalf. Although she was rather sad to have to part with some treasured possessions, Clementine was always eminently practical, and did not make 'heavy weather' over it.

When, several weeks later, the pictures were sold by Christie's, they realised an astonishing sum. Clementine was stupefied – and delighted – by the result. One of the pictures, a charming little oil-painting of Clementine by Lavery, showing her in a sunbonnet, holding Sarah as a baby on her lap, was bought by Mr Roy Miles, who gracefully returned it to her for her life-time, so that she should not be deprived of its enjoyment. It is now in the National Portrait Gallery.

For some time Clementine had felt real anxiety about her future, but now the worries were lifted from her brow. As to Winston's pictures, he had left them all to her unconditionally. And it would have given him great satisfaction to know that 'my little daubs', as he called them, would help one day to secure for her comfort and dignity to the end of her days.

*

Clementine now led a real 'old lady's life'. She rested more, and had good days and less-good days: but her twilight was a happy one, lit by a golden haze of love and esteem. The serenity so long attributed to her had come at last, and a stoical acceptance of those dreary companions of old age – deafness and loss of sight.

The disciplines of a long lifetime remained. Her house was well run; the food was delicious – she and the cook conferred most days. Her appearance was as lovely and as immaculate as ever: even when dining alone Clementine always changed into one of her ravishing housecoats.

Being read aloud to, or listening to her Talking Book formed an important part of her daily routine. When she was well, and consequently her concentration good, she enjoyed biographies, memoirs and histories. It was a treat for her when Martin Gilbert came to Princes Gate to read her some chapters of Winston's official biography, the writing of which he had taken up when it fell from Randolph's hand; and she managed to read the greater part of the volumes published up to her death.

The progress of her own biography greatly interested my mother, and she read all the earlier chapters, including some of the First World War period, and supplied useful corrections of fact. When I found old letters or papers which I thought would divert her, I always sent them to her. Her memory became patchy – but the remembered episodes and personalities were clearly lit.

When Clementine was feeling tired, she fell back on light romances and historical novels, the works of Georgette Heyer and Barbara Cartland alternating agreeably with the more serious works already mentioned. And, of course – every day – the newspapers.

Most afternoons she would set forth, often with Sylvia Henley, in her red Rover driven by Nonie Chapman, with the wheelchair in the boot, for a drive. As Clementine's sight failed, exhibitions and galleries lost their point; but the public parks remained to the last a pleasure. She became quite an expert upon them – comparing their states of maintenance and planting. Bushey Park was a favourite, as were Isabella's Plantation in Richmond Park at azalea time and (as she ceremoniously called it) 'The' Regent's Park, particularly when the roses were out.

But Clementine's most continuing pleasure right to the end of her days was to see her family and friends. Perhaps these years of her widowhood were the first period of her life when she had ever had the leisure to cultivate her friends. And she now discovered how many she had, and how true and constant they were, as she picked up the threads of old – and newer – acquaintance.

Clementine suffered many of the almost inevitable inconveniences of great old age. Apart from her publicised illnesses, there were bouts of pneumonia (they always made us very anxious) and odd high fevers; and less serious aches and pains, which nevertheless are a burden towards the end of a long day. And it made one's heart ache after any illness to see how painfully slow and wearying was the climb back up-hill to the plateau of her now fragile, normal health.

But among her blessings – and she did count them – was that she always had company, and did not therefore suffer what must be one of the worst horrors of old age – loneliness. And although Clementine could not pass the hours by watching television, or by reading, yet there was for her, in addition to her family and friends, the boon of Nonie Chapman by day, and a faithful team of nurses at the week-ends and by night. Those long, weary, dark hours, when soul and body seem to be at the lowest ebb, were made lighter for her by, not only the skill, but above all by the companion-ship of her nurses. I believe they kept her in touch with the throb of life; and that they came to have a real affection and regard for her was testified to again and again in the letters I received from them after my mother's death, and by their presence, almost without exception, at both her funeral and Memorial Service.

Clementine's interest in her children, grandchildren and great grand-children continued undimmed. Unless prevented by illness, she would never fail to attend a gifted granddaughter's – Edwina Sandys's – highly successful exhibitions of paint-ing and sculpture. Sarah, to acting, writing, reciting poetry and singing songs, had now added the wielding of brush and pen, and her mother always visited the galleries where her work was being shown. And she could often be counted upon as an early visitor to a family cocktail party, leaving only when the crowd and the noise really became too overpowering. When our Charlotte, married at nineteen to Richard Hambro, gave birth to a daughter – Clementine the second – her great-grandmother, very frail now, attended her christening in a freezing church on a freezing January day in 1977. Later that year her last, and fourteenth, great-grandchild was born – Julian and Elisabeth Sandys' youngest son – Roderick.

Nor was it only for the family that Clementine, now over ninety, would 'get herself on parade'. When the French President and Madame Giscard d'Estaing came to London in June 1976 on a State Visit, at the President's request time was carved out of his programme of official engagements for him and Madame Giscard d'Estaing to call upon Clementine. It was a graceful gesture, and Clementine was complimented and pleased. However, she took it very calmly, summoning Winston and Minnie, and Christopher and me to be with her when she received the President and his wife. The time allowed for the visit was five to ten minutes: the visitors stayed nearly half an hour, the President and Clementine sitting conversing agreeably on the sofa. She presented him with the volumes of Winston's life; and when a few months later another volume was published – she remembered to send it to him.

Other enjoyable, if less ceremonious occasions were when, in the winters of 1975 and 1976, Harrow boys came to Princes Gate to sing for Clementine the songs Winston had taught her to love, but which she could no longer go to Harrow to hear for herself. She greatly enjoyed the boys' visits, and made sure there was a large tea, with plenty of rich chocolate cake.

One of Winston and Clementine's oldest friends, Lord De L'Isle, having tea with her early in 1976, asked if she had ever met Mrs Margaret Thatcher: Clementine replied that she had not, but would very much like to do so. Shortly afterwards, Lord De L'Isle brought Mrs Thatcher to see Clementine. They talked about the suffragette days, and how Clementine, unlike Winston, had been strongly in favour of 'Votes for Women'. My mother told me about their meeting later; she had been much pleased and interested to meet Mrs Thatcher, who may soon make history by becoming Britain's first woman Prime Minister.

But there were sad occasions when, with a great sense that she stood there for Winston too, Clementine made dignified 'actes de présence'. On 1st April 1976 – her own ninety-first birthday – Clementine attended the military funeral of Field-Marshal Lord Montgomery – Monty. She had not been in touch with him for some time: his health had been such that he had lived the last years of his life in seclusion. War had forged strong links between Winston and Clementine and this great but bizarre man, and he had been a faithful friend in the sadder years. It was quite a long expedition for her to go to St George's Chapel, Windsor, and a very long wait. She could not hear the splendid hymns nor see (although she was seated in honour, quite close by) the touch of panache in the placing of his famous 'beret' on the great commander's coffin.

Nearly a year later, Clementine mourned the death of a man who had been a part of the tapestry of her life with Winston for over forty years – Anthony Eden, Earl of Avon. After the tragic débâcle of the end of his career through illness, his wife Clarissa, Winston's niece, had cherished him through more than a decade of fragile health. Now he was among the last of Winston's political and wartime comrades and friends to depart. And in the previous summer, charming, cultivated, sympathetic Ronnie Tree died. It is one of the heavier penalties of great longevity that the muster of contemporaries dwindles away, leaving an emptier scene: '*Could* auld acquaintance be forgot – How light the heart would be . . .'

Clementine attended the Battle of Britain Service at Westminster Abbey for the last time in September 1976. Her presence at this annual commemoration had become a looked-for feature of this service which had such a particular significance for people. Wearing her medals Clementine was gently shepherded from her car, and wheeled down the long aisle of the thronged Abbey. The previous year, Miss A. M. Johnson, one of Clementine's friends in this last period of her life, had accompanied her to the Abbey, and she wrote to me:

> Last Sunday I went with Lady Churchill and your sister to the Battle of Britain Memorial Service. I always go to it anyway, – but this year it was particularly poignant . . . It was very moving indeed to see the rapturous welcome of the crowd when Lady Churchill came out of her car, – & – the gasp of admiration as the entire congregation within the nave rose instantly to their feet as she entered the Abbey . . .[15]

*

Towards the end of January 1977, my husband had a major coronary by-pass operation. It was a success, but he had long weeks of pain and weakness. My mother was full of tender enquiries, sending flowers, and 'baby' bottles of champagne – which cheered us both! And Christopher was well enough for us to give a small luncheon party at our flat to celebrate Clementine's ninety-second birthday on 1st April. The family included, of course, dear Cousin Sylvia, herself ninety-five, and still ramrod straight. Also there to drink my mother's health were Nonie Chapman, Grace Hamblin and Meg Colville. It was a loving 'demonstration', which I believe she enjoyed. But even small, intimate parties were now really too much for her.

Life went on for her like a gentle stream – but it flowed much more slowly now. Hearing, even with an aid, was a great effort, and as my father had done, she would withdraw sometimes into great and distant silences. But on 'good' days there were still pleasures and interests. It was Jubilee Year, and Clementine was glad she had lived to see so happy and glorious the young Queen whose first Prime Minister Winston had been. In May, Prince Charles opened an exhibition of Winston's pictures at Knoedler's Gallery in aid of the Jubilee Appeal. Clementine was much disappointed that she was not well enough to go herself. But a few days later she had a private viewing 'after hours', and although she could not see the pictures in detail, we described each one to her. Mostly lent by the family, she remembered nearly all of them. They had been beautifully lit, and she received the impression of how jewel-like they looked, hung against the grey velvet walls of the gallery.

In mid-June, Clementine made an expedition to Chartwell. It was all looking lovely: attendance figures were up, and the takings from the souvenir shop were booming. It all gave her great satisfaction; she enjoyed her luncheon in the restaurant, and returned home laden with flowers. A few weeks later, my mother drove down to lunch with us at Castle Mill: and this made another happy day.

On 26th July, Clementine was suddenly taken ill, and rushed to King Edward

VII Hospital, where she was quickly operated on for an abdominal stoppage. Amazingly, she weathered the operation, which was a success, and revealed nothing sinister. But it was a stiff ordeal for her to suffer. Her own nurses, and Pat and Matilda (her dear and devoted Filipino maids) scarcely left her: they gave her confidence, and knew all her little ways. Among the loveliest of the flowers she received was a bouquet from the Queen Mother, with a personally written note of sympathy and encouragement. Clementine improved enough for her to be brought home, with gentlest care, about a fortnight after the operation.

But then followed weeks of desolating weakness and fatigue. However, slowly, she began to pick up: she started eating better, and enjoying company more; gradually she resumed a gentle routine of a guest or two to luncheon; and she started her afternoon drives again. But we all realised this last illness had taken a heavy toll of her. However, my mother was well enough for me to feel I could go to America in November to visit my daughter Charlotte and her husband (who were living in New York) and to see the 'new' Clementine.

Ever an early Christmas shopper, Clementine started arranging all her presents with Nonie, giving her usual detailed thought to what everyone would like best; and Nonie was busy as usual with discreet enquiries. But, for the first time this year, she did not send any Christmas cards. Clementine always chose a reproduction of one of Winston's pictures to send, and her Christmas card list for 1976 had shown 100 names. Writing in all of them herself, she used to do batches of them on her 'good days' throughout the autumn months. In the last year or two the message and signature were quavery, and sometimes ran off the card . . . but: 'Keep right on to the end of the road . . .'

On 30th November, the anniversary of Winston's birthday, Winston and Minnie invited Clementine to luncheon with them at the Berkeley. It was the first time she had actually been out to a meal since her operation in the summer, and she enjoyed herself very much. Winston and Minnie had again asked her to stay with them for Christmas, and they talked about the plans: she was looking forward to it.

I liked it best of all now, when I lunched or dined alone with my mother; sometimes we did not speak very much – but that did not matter. Even as a middle-aged woman I rejoiced, and felt sustained to be received as a beloved child. I saw my mother for the last time when I lunched alone with her on 6th December. She was in rather good form, and she gave me her usual open-arm loving welcome. She still looked beautiful, but drawn and frail now. Above all, I dreaded for her another test of pain or wearying weakness: but Death was to come kindly.

On Monday, 12th December, she was feeling pretty well. Nonie Chapman always lunched with Clementine on Mondays and, the day being fine, they decided they would go out for a drive afterwards. Clementine's coat, gloves and scarf were ready in the front hall. At luncheon, which she was quite enjoying, Nonie suddenly noticed a change in her breathing: she called the maids, and between them they got her to her bedroom. There in a few minutes more Clementine died peacefully and without pain.

*

Messages and letters – official and public, personal and private – came flooding in for Clementine's family from all over the world. The tributes and appreciations in the Press, and on radio and television, were moving and remarkable. We had felt her death would evoke a response from many people, but the reality of the expressions of love and esteem for her far exceeded any expectation we could have had.

The Service of Thanksgiving for Clementine Spencer-Churchill's life was held in Westminster Abbey on 24th January 1978, the thirteenth anniversary of the death of Winston Churchill. The Queen and the Royal Family sent representatives; the Prime Minister, the Speaker, the Leaders of the Conservative and Liberal Parties, and many Members of both Houses of Parliament were there. There were sixty countries represented either by their Ambassadors, their High Commissioners or other representatives. People from many aspects of civic and official life, and organisations for which Clementine had worked or had connections with sought to be present. Winston's old regiment, the Queen's Royal Irish Hussars (4th Hussars) were there, helping to show people to their places, as were officers and men from the submarine H.M.S. *Churchill*. Applications for seats had poured in – and there was room for all. And, apart from those who had received tickets, there were a great number of people – they filled the nave – who had come simply and anonymously, to join with us all, to remember, and to give thanks.

Our family made its way up to places in the Lantern near the High Altar, where we paused so that Sarah and I could place a wreath of white flowers for them both on the great marble slab which bears the words: 'Remember Winston Churchill'. The long, gleaming procession of clergy with the Dean and Chapter, the Archbishop of Canterbury, and the Apostolic Delegate, moved up the aisle, and the service began. It was moving and splendid; and sad, and above all, triumphantly thankful.

We prayed the prayer of St Ignatius Loyola, which asks for '. . . a steadfast heart which no unworthy affection may drag downwards . . . an unconquered heart which no tribulation can wear out . . . an upright heart which no unworthy purpose may tempt aside . . .'

It reminded me so much of her.

The former Dean of Westminster, Dr Eric Abbott (a friend of Clementine's), read from the *Epistle to the Corinthians* of the Love that 'beareth all things . . . hopeth all things, endureth all things. Love never faileth.' And that reminded me of her too.

And young Winston read an extract from the sermon preached by old Bishop Welldon nearly seventy years before in the Church of St Margaret's, Westminster, at the marriage of Mr Winston Churchill to Miss Clementine Hozier:

The sun shines upon your union today; the happy faces of your friends surround you; good wishes are lavished upon you; many prayers ascend to Heaven on your behalf. Will you suffer me to remind you how much you may be to the other in the coming days? There must be in the statesman's life many times when he depends upon the love, the insight, the penetrating sympathy and devotion of his wife. The influence which the wives of our statesmen have exercised for good upon their husband's lives is an unwritten chapter of English history, too sacred to be written in full . . . In the sunny hours of life, in the sombre hours, if they, too, come, may you recall the feelings and the resolves that were yours when you knelt today before the altar of God. So it is with deep feelings that I commend you to the blessings of the Eternal and Supreme. May your lives prove a blessing each to the other and both to the world, and may you pass in the Divine mercy from strength to strength and from joy to joy.

As we came out into the gusty winter world, the bare branches of the trees were blowing about against a leaden sky. Away across Parliament Square, Winston Churchill's statue was trudging forward, doggedly, into whatever future may be, and somewhere, far above us, the bells of the Abbey were ringing out – full peal.

NOTES AND SOURCES

The whereabouts of the correspondence between Winston Churchill (WSC) and Clementine Churchill (CSC) is indicated in these notes by an asterisk or a dagger mark, denoting that a letter forms part of the Spencer-Churchill Papers (*) or the Churchill Papers (†). The letters RSC are an abbreviation for Randolph Spencer Churchill. In all letters quoted the original spelling has been retained so far as possible and [sic] inserted where appropriate. Some punctuation has been amended slightly for easier comprehension.

Chapter 1 FORBEARS AND EARLY CHILDHOOD

1 James Quinn, S.J., *Cavalier of Christ*, p. 18
2 The Author is indebted for many of these details concerning Lady Airlie to *Thatched with Gold: the Memoirs of Mabell, Countess of Airlie*
3 See the notes prefixed to the lyrics in W. S. Douglas, *Kilmarnock Edition of the Poetical Works of Robert Burns*, Part 1, p. 294. Glasgow, 1938
4 D. E. W. Gibb, *Lloyd's of London: A Study in Individualism*, p. 152
5 CSC wrote *circa* 1930 some 'sketch'

chapters about her childhood entitled '*My* Early Life', from which account this quotation and much subsequent information have been taken. Unfortunately the account ceases in about 1904
6 Letter from CSC to Giles Romilly, 2 Jan. 1957
7 Earl of Airlie to Blanche, Countess of Airlie, 29 Dec. 1890
8 *Census of Scotland*, Edinburgh 685/1, vol. 7, schedule 30. MS, New Register House, Edinburgh

Chapter 2 DIEPPE AND AFTERWARDS

1 Simona Pakenham, *60 Miles from England (The English at Dieppe, 1814–1914)*, pp. 179–80
2 This story and many other details of their Dieppe life have been taken from the papers of Nellie (Mrs Bertram Romilly)
3 Wendy Baron, *Sickert*. Also Simona Pakenham, *Pigtails and Pernod*

4 From CSC, '*My* Early life'
5 CSC to Miss Beatrice Harris, 8 Oct. 1942
6 Lady Cynthia Asquith, *Diaries 1915–1918*, p. 494. Entry in Index
7 Sir Alan Lascelles to the Author, 26 Nov. 1964

Chapter 3 TO THINE OWN SELF BE TRUE

1 Mabell, Countess of Airlie, *Thatched with Gold*, p. 125
2 RSC, *Winston S. Churchill*, vol. II, p. 252
3 Letter dated 22 Oct. 1906 from Lady Blanche Hozier to her brother, Hon. Lyulph Stanley, who lived in Colorado, U.S.A.
4 WSC to CSC, 16 Apr. 1908*
5 CSC to Nellie Hozier, undated, but probably 13–15 Aug. 1908
6 Mabell, Countess of Airlie, *op. cit.*, p. 125
7 From the Blunt Papers (British Library). Quoted in Churchill companion vol. II, p. 803
8 WSC to CSC, undated, written at Blenheim, probably 13 Aug. 1908*
9 CSC to WSC, undated, written at Blenheim, probably 13 Aug. 1908*
10 Mabell, Countess of Airlie, *op. cit.*, p. 125
11 *idem*
12 CSC to WSC, undated letter written from Batsford Park, Aug. 1908*
13 WSC to CSC, undated letter but must have been written immediately after their engagement*

Chapter 4 EARLY DAYS TOGETHER

1 Wilfrid Scawen Blunt, *My Diaries*, vol. II, p. 222
2 Edward Marsh, *A Number of People*, p. 154
3 Violet Bonham Carter, *Winston Churchill as I Knew Him*, p. 219
4 Beatrice Webb, *Our Partnership*, p. 416. Entry for 16 Oct. 1908
5 WSC to CSC 28 Apr. 1909 [WSC writes 1910]*
6 CSC to WSC, 4 Nov. [1909]*
7 WSC to CSC, 12 Sept. 1909*
8 CSC to WSC, 12 Sept. [1909]*
9 CSC to WSC, 11 Sept. [1909]*
10 CSC to WSC, 16 Sept. [1909]*

Chapter 5 HOME OFFICE TO ADMIRALTY

1 CSC to WSC, 18 Sept. 1909*
2 *The Times*, 9 Dec. 1909
3 *The Times*, 4 Feb. 1909. At a meeting in Dundee
4 *The Times*, 15 Nov. 1909, and CSC's personal account
5 WSC to CSC, 10 Nov. 1909*
6 WSC to CSC, 19 Dec. 1910*
7 CSC to WSC, 21 Sept. 1910*
8 CSC to WSC, 19 Dec. 1910*
9 Wilfrid Scawen Blunt, *My Diaries*, vol. II, pp. 279–80. Entry for 5 Sept. 1909
10 *ibid.* p. 294. Entry for 25 Nov. 1909
11 CSC to WSC, dated 'Saturday evening' [3 June 1911]*
12 WSC to CSC, 29 June 1911*
13 *ibid.*

Chapter 6 AT THE ADMIRALTY

1 WSC, *The World Crisis 1911–1914*, p. 119
2 Neville Lytton to Nellie Hozier, 4 Sept. 1911
3 CSC to WSC, dated 'Tuesday Evening' [16 Jan. 1912]*
4 CSC to WSC, 7 Feb. [1912]*
5 Sir Edward Grey to CSC, 18 Feb. 1912
6 *Belfast Weekly News*, 15 Feb. 1912
7 Lord Riddell, *More Pages from my Diary, 1908–14*, p. 37
8 *ibid.*
9 *The Times*, Special Correspondent, 8 Feb. 1912
10 CSC to WSC, 25 Mar. [1912]*
11 Violet Bonham Carter, *Winston Churchill as I Knew Him*, p. 265
12 CSC to WSC, dated 'Sunday' [14 July 1912]*
13 CSC to WSC, dated 'Monday Evening' [22 July 1912]*
14 CSC to WSC, wrongly dated 'Wednesday the 23rd' [24 July 1912]*

15   CSC to WSC, 23 July [1912]*
16   CSC to WSC, 24 July [1912]*
17   CSC to WSC, dated 'Tuesday Evening' [30 July 1912]*

18   *The Times*, 14 and 17 Aug. 1912
19   *The Times*, 13 Sept. 1912
20   CSC to WSC, 4 Nov. [1913]*
21   WSC to CSC, 1 Feb. 1913*

Chapter 7   THE SANDS RUN OUT

1   CSC to WSC, 31 Jan. [1913]*
2   CSC to WSC, 6 Apr. [1913]*
3   Mrs Asquith to WSC, 10 Feb. 1910†
4   H. H. Asquith to Venetia Stanley, 27 Apr. 1915
5   *ibid.* 30 Mar. 1914
6   *ibid.* 10 Jan. 1915
7   *ibid.* 26 Jan. 1915
8   *ibid.* 1 Feb. 1915
9   *ibid.* 7 Mar. 1915
10   Neville Lytton to Nellie Hozier, 8 Feb. 1911
11   WSC to CSC, 23 July [1913]*
12   WSC to CSC, 23 Apr. 1914*
13   WSC to CSC, 27 Apr. 1914*
14   CSC to WSC, 19 Sept. [1913]*
15   CSC to WSC, undated, but headed 'In the train to London, 7 p.m.' [20 Oct. 1913]*
16   CSC to WSC, 23 Oct. 1913*
17   The account of this whole incident has been pieced together from CSC's own recollections, and the accounts given

to the Author by Margaret, Countess of Birkenhead (then Mrs F. E. Smith) and the 10th Duke of Marlborough (Sunny's son Blandford)
18   WSC to CSC, 3 Nov. 1913*
19   CSC to WSC, dated 'Wednesday the 22nd' [April 1914]*
20   CSC to WSC, 24 Oct. [1913]*
21   Quoted in RSC, *Winston S. Churchill*, vol. II, p. 703
22   CSC to WSC, 24 April [1914]*
23   CSC to WSC, 4 June [1914]*
24   CSC to WSC, 5 June [1914]*
25   CSC to WSC, 6 July [1914]*
26   WSC to CSC, 13 July 1914*
27   WSC, *The World Crisis 1911–1914*, p. 190
28   *ibid.* p. 197
29   CSC to WSC, undated*
30   WSC to CSC, 28 July 1914*
31   CSC to WSC, 29 July [1914]*
32   CSC to WSC, 31 July [1914]*

Chapter 8   ALL OVER BY CHRISTMAS

1   CSC to WSC, undated but almost certainly just before 26 Sept. 1914. See Martin Gilbert, *Winston S. Churchill*, vol. III, p. 92*
2   WSC to CSC, 26 Sept. 1914*
3   CSC to WSC, 9 Aug. [1914]*
4   CSC to WSC, 12 Aug. [1914]*
5   CSC to WSC, 14 Aug. [1914]*
6   CSC to WSC, 14 Aug. [1914] (2nd letter)*

7   H. H. Asquith to Venetia Stanley, 5 Oct. 1914
8   Violet Bonham Carter, *Winston Churchill as I Knew Him*, p. 332
9   Figures taken from British, French and German Official Casualty Returns – WSC, *The World Crisis 1916–18*, Appdx I

Chapter 9   THE DARDANELLES

1   Lord Hankey, *The Supreme Command*, vol. I, pp. 265–6
2   WSC, *The World Crisis 1911–1914*, p. 73
3   Violet Bonham Carter, *Winston*

Churchill as I Knew Him, p. 362, from which also the account of the review is taken
4   H. H. Asquith to Venetia Stanley, 26 Feb. 1915

5 WSC, *The World Crisis 1915*, p. 252
6 Martin Gilbert, *Winston S. Churchill*, vol. III, p. 431
7 WSC, *The World Crisis 1915*, p. 353
8 Violet Bonham Carter, *op. cit.* p. 393
9 H. H. Asquith to Venetia Stanley, 14 May 1915
10 H. H. Asquith to WSC, 21 May 1915. Gilbert, *op. cit.* p. 464
11 H. H. Asquith to Venetia Stanley, 22 May 1915
12 WSC, *The World Crisis 1915*, p. 803
13 Gilbert, *op. cit.* p. 473
14 See A. J. P. Taylor, *English History 1914-1945*, p. 31, fn. 3
15 H. H. Asquith to Venetia Stanley, 22 May 1915
16 Gilbert, *op. cit.* p. 472 [ex Montagu MSS]
17 *ibid.*
18 WSC, *Painting as a Pastime*, p. 18
19 E. Ashmead-Bartlett, *The Uncensored Dardanelles*, p. 121. Diary entry 10 June 1915

Chapter 10 THE PLACE OF HONOUR

1 Lord Beaverbrook, *Politicians and the War*, vol. 2, p. 74
2 Violet Bonham Carter, *Winston Churchill as I Knew Him*, p. 429
3 WSC to CSC, 18 Nov. 1915*
4 CSC to WSC, 19 Nov. [1915]*
5 CSC to WSC, 21 Nov. [1915]*
6 WSC, 'With the Grenadiers' in *Thoughts and Adventures*, [1932] p. 101
7 CSC to WSC, 22 Nov. [1915]*
8 WSC to CSC, 25 Nov. 1915*
9 WSC to CSC, 27 Nov. 1915*
10 *ibid.*
11 WSC to CSC, 1 Dec. [1915] (3rd letter, marked 'Later still')*
12 CSC to WSC, 28 Nov. [1915]*
13 CSC to WSC, 19 Nov. [1915]*
14 CSC to WSC, 25 Nov. [1915]*
15 CSC to WSC, 28 Nov. [1915]*
16 WSC to CSC, 1 Dec. 1915*
17 *ibid.* (2nd letter, marked 'Later')*
18 *ibid.* (3rd letter)*
19 *ibid.*
20 WSC to CSC, 3 Dec. 1915*
21 *ibid.*
22 WSC to CSC, 1 Dec. 1915 (3rd letter)*
23 WSC to CSC, 23 Nov. 1915*
24 WSC to CSC, 25 Nov. 1915*
25 WSC to CSC, 27 Nov. 1915*
26 WSC to CSC, 4 Dec. 1915*
27 WSC to CSC, 8 Dec. 1915*
28 WSC to CSC, 12 Dec. 1915*
29 WSC to CSC, 4 Dec. 1915*
30 *ibid.*
31 *ibid.*
32 *ibid.*
33 CSC to WSC, 6 Dec. [1915]*
34 CSC to WSC, 28 Nov. [1915]*
35 CSC to WSC, 6 Dec. [1915]*
36 *ibid.*
37 *ibid.*
38 WSC to CSC, 8 Dec. 1915*
39 CSC's words in her letter to WSC of 4 Dec. 1915
40 WSC to CSC, 8 Dec. 1915*
41 CSC to WSC, 9 Dec. [1915]*
42 *ibid.*
43 WSC to CSC, 10 Dec. 1915*
44 CSC to WSC, 12 Dec. [1915]*
45 WSC to CSC, 12 Dec. 1915*
46 WSC to CSC, 18 Dec. 1915, from which letter the ensuing quotes and account of the 'Brigade' drama is drawn in general*
47 Hansard, *Parliamentary Debates: Commons*, vol. 78, 2218
48 WSC to CSC, 15 Dec. 1915 (2nd letter)*
49 *ibid.*
50 CSC to WSC, 17 Dec. [1915] (1st letter)*
51 WSC to CSC, 18 Dec. 1915*
52 *ibid.*
53 *ibid.*
54 *ibid.* 'Later'
55 *ibid.*
56 *ibid.*
57 WSC to CSC, 20 Dec. 1915*
58 *ibid.*
59 *ibid.*
60 *ibid.*

Chapter 11   WAITING IN SILENCE

1   WSC to CSC, 2 Jan. 1916*
2   WSC to CSC, 1 Jan. 1916*
3   CSC to WSC, New Year's Day 1916†
4   WSC to CSC, 3 Jan. 1916*
5   WSC to CSC, 5 Jan. 1916*
6   CSC to WSC, 7 Jan. 1916†
7   CSC to WSC, 9 Jan. 1916†
8   WSC to CSC, 13 Jan. 1916*
9   CSC to WSC, 16 Jan. 1916†
10 WSC to CSC, 6 Jan. 1916*
11 WSC to CSC, 10 Jan. 1916*
12 WSC to CSC, 7 Jan. 1916*
13 CSC to WSC, 11 Jan. [1916]†
14 WSC to CSC, 16 Jan. 1916*
15 WSC to CSC, 7 Jan. 1916*
16 CSC to WSC, 10 Jan. 1916*
17 WSC to CSC, 17 Jan. 1916*
18 WSC to CSC, 19 Jan. 1916*
19 WSC to CSC, 7 Jan. 1916*
20 WSC to CSC, 19 Jan. 1916*
21 CSC to WSC, undated, marked
    'Later' [16 Jan. 1916]†
22 CSC to WSC, 18 Jan. [1916]†
23 CSC to WSC [16 Jan. 1916]†
24 CSC to WSC, 20 Jan. [1916]†
25 WSC to CSC, 22 Jan. 1916*
26 WSC to CSC, 24 Jan. 1916*
27 CSC to WSC, 21 Jan. [1916]†
28 ibid.
29 CSC to WSC, 24 Jan. [1916]†
30 CSC to WSC, 5 Jan. 1916†
31 WSC to CSC, 26 Jan. 1916*
32 WSC to CSC, 20 Jan. 1916*

33 CSC to WSC, 24 Jan. [1916]†
34 WSC to CSC, 27 Jan. 1916*
35 CSC to WSC, 30 Jan. [1916]†
36 CSC to WSC, 27 Jan. 1916†
37 WSC to CSC, 27 Jan. 1916*
38 ibid.
39 CSC to WSC, 31 Jan. [1916]†
40 CSC to WSC, 2 Feb. [1916]†
41 CSC to WSC, 31 Jan. [1916]†
42 WSC to CSC, 31 Jan. 1916*
43 WSC to CSC, undated [1 Feb. 1916]*
44 CSC to WSC, 4 Feb. 1916†
45 ibid.
46 ibid.
47 WSC to CSC, 4 Feb. 1916*
48 CSC to WSC, 9 Feb. [1916]†
49 WSC to CSC, 6 Feb. 1916*
50 WSC to CSC, 10 Feb. 1916*
51 CSC to WSC, 23 Feb. [1916]†
52 WSC to CSC, 14 Feb. 1916*
53 WSC to CSC, 20 Feb. 1916*
54 WSC to CSC, 22 Feb. 1916*
55 CSC to WSC, 16 Feb. 1916†
56 CSC to WSC, 25 Feb. [1916]†
57 CSC to WSC, 27 Feb. 1916†
58 CSC to WSC, 12 Feb. [1916] (a
    continuation of a letter begun on 11
    Feb. and continued at 5 a.m. the next
    morning)†
59 CSC to WSC, 21 Feb. [1916]†
60 CSC to WSC, 25 Feb. [1916]†
61 CSC to WSC, 27 Feb. 1916†

Chapter 12   DAY MUST DAWN

1   Violet Bonham Carter, Winston
    Churchill as I Knew Him, p. 449. And
    the Author verified this story with
    CSC
2   Martin Gilbert, Winston S. Churchill,
    vol. III, p. 722
3   CSC to WSC, 14 Mar. [1916]†
4   ibid.
5   ibid.
6   CSC to WSC, 13 [14] Mar. [1916],
    7 p.m.† [wrongly dated by CSC]
7   CSC to WSC, 15 Mar. [1916]†
8   WSC to CSC, 13 Mar. 1916*
9   WSC to CSC, 19 Mar. 1916*
10 WSC to CSC, 21 Mar. 1916*

11 CSC to WSC, 22 Mar. [1916]†
12 CSC to WSC, 24 Mar. [1916]†
13 ibid.
14 CSC to WSC, 22 Mar. [1916]†
15 CSC to WSC, 24 Mar. [1916] (2nd
    letter)†
16 WSC to CSC, [22 Mar. 1916]*
    [WSC writes 22.1.16 but CSC was
    sure it was March.]
17 CSC to WSC, 25 Mar. [1916]†
18 ibid.
19 WSC to CSC, 23 Mar. 1916*
20 WSC to CSC, 28 Mar. 1916*
21 CSC to WSC, 1 Apr. 1916†
22 CSC to WSC, 4 Apr. 1916†

23 CSC to WSC, 6 Apr. [1916]†
24 WSC to CSC, 10 Apr. 1916*
25 CSC to WSC, Monday 27 [Mar. 1916]†
26 WSC to CSC, 7 Apr. 1916*
27 CSC to WSC, 12 Apr. [1916]†
28 ibid.
29 CSC to WSC, 14 Apr. [1916]†
30 ibid.
31 WSC to CSC, 15 Apr. 1916*

32 Dundee Advertiser, 27 July 1917
33 CSC to WSC, 16 Feb. 1916†
34 RSC, Twenty-One Years, p. 15
35 CSC to WSC, 23 July 1918†
36 CSC to WSC, 15 Aug. 1918†
37 WSC to CSC, 17 Aug. 1918*
38 CSC to WSC, 15 Aug. 1918†
39 ibid.
40 CSC to WSC, 29 Oct. 1918*
41 WSC to CSC, 12 Sept. 1918*

Chapter 13 BLEAK MORNING

1 Martin Gilbert, Winston S. Churchill, vol. IV, p. 166
2 H. Pelling, Winston Churchill, p. 242
3 Gilbert, op. cit. p. 173
4 RSC, Twenty-One Years, p. 19
5 CSC to WSC, 9 Mar. 1919*
6 ibid.
7 CSC in personal recollections to the Author
8 CSC to WSC, 31 Mar. 1920†
9 WSC to CSC, 30 Mar. 1920*
10 RSC, op. cit. p. 12
11 WSC to CSC, 27 Jan. 1921*
12 CSC to WSC, 13 Feb. 1921†
13 ibid.
14 ibid.
15 WSC to CSC, 14 Feb. 1921*
16 WSC to CSC, 27 Jan. 1921*
17 WSC to CSC, 6 Feb. 1921*

18 CSC to WSC, 21 Feb. 1921†
19 WSC to CSC, 14 Feb. 1921*
20 WSC to CSC, 21 Feb. 1921*
21 WSC to Lord Curzon, 29 June 1921
22 Sarah Churchill to CSC, undated but obviously Aug. 1921
23 Told to the Author by WSC
24 The Autobiography of Margot Asquith, vol. I, p. 23
25 WSC to CSC, 19 Sept. 1921*
26 CSC to WSC, 22 Sept. 1921†
27 ibid.
28 ibid.
29 WSC to CSC, 29 Dec. 1921*
30 ibid.
31 WSC to CSC, 4 Jan. 1922*
32 CSC to WSC, 4 Jan. 1922†

Chapter 14 THE TWENTIES

1 CSC to WSC, 3 Feb. 1922†
2 CSC to WSC, 17 Aug. 1922†
3 CSC to WSC, 4 Aug. 1922†
4 WSC to CSC, 10 Aug. 1922*
5 CSC to WSC, 18 Feb. 1921†
6 Quoted in Martin Gilbert, Winston S. Churchill, vol. IV, p. 878
7 Dundee Courier, 8 Nov. 1922
8 WSC, 'Election Memories' in Thoughts and Adventures [1932], p. 213
9 Recounted by H. Pelling in Winston Churchill, p. 292. The source is S. Salvidge, Salvidge of Liverpool, p. 275

10 CSC to WSC, 29 Jan. [1916]†
11 CSC to WSC, 11 Mar. 1925†
12 CSC to WSC, 20 Mar. 1926*
13 CSC to WSC, 25 Mar. [1926]*
14 WSC to CSC, 28 Mar. 1926*
15 CSC to WSC, 21 Apr. 1924*
16 WSC to CSC, 22 Mar. 1925*
17 WSC to CSC, 3 [Aug.] 1929* (The letter is clearly dated, in WSC's hand, '3.9.29', but this must have been a mistake.)
18 WSC to CSC, 8 Aug. 1929*
19 WSC to CSC, 19 Sept. 1929*
20 CSC to WSC, 8 Feb. 1921†

Chapter 15 CHARTWELL

1 CSC to WSC, 11 July 1921†
2 CSC to WSC, dated 'Wednesday' [between 16–18 July 1921].†
3 Sarah Churchill, *A Thread in the Tapestry*, p. 22
4 WSC to CSC, 27 Jan. 1923*
5 CSC to WSC, 29 Jan. [1923]*
6 CSC to WSC, Thursday [1 Feb. 1923]*
7 WSC to CSC, 2 Sept. 1923*
8 CSC to WSC, dated 'Thursday the 26th' [Mar. 1925]†
9 CSC to WSC, Memorandum*
10 CSC to Margery Street, 14 July 1933
11 WSC to CSC, 25 Sept. 1928*
12 WSC to CSC, 2 Feb. 1937*
13 CSC to Margery Street, 14 Jan. 1934

Chapter 16 HERSELF AND OTHERS

1 CSC to WSC, 31 Mar. 1920†
2 RSC, *Twenty-One Years*, p. 25
3 Diana Churchill to CSC, 28 [Nov. 1923]
4 Diana Churchill to WSC, 4 Dec. 1923
5 RSC to CSC, 21 May 1926
6 Diana Churchill to WSC, 6 Oct. 1926
7 Diana Churchill to CSC, 19 Nov. 1926
8 RSC, *Twenty-One Years*, p. 86
9 *ibid.*
10 WSC to CSC, 8 Apr. 1928*
11 CSC to WSC, 13 Apr. 1928*
12 RSC, *Twenty-One Years*, p. 104
13 CSC to RSC, 21 Dec. 1930
14 CSC to WSC, 17 Feb. [1931]*
15 *ibid.*
16 CSC to WSC, 22 Feb. 1935*
17 WSC to CSC, 2 Mar. 1935*
18 *ibid.*
19 CSC to Margery Street, 30 Nov. 1933
20 *ibid.*
21 CSC to Margery Street, 9 June 1933
22 *ibid.*
23 CSC to Margery Street, 18 Sept. 1934
24 CSC to Margery Street, 21 Aug. 1935
25 CSC to Margery Street, 7 Dec. 1935
26 CSC to WSC, 29 Dec. 1935*
27 CSC to Margery Street, 30 Dec. 1935
28 CSC to WSC, 31 Aug. 1929*
29 CSC to Margery Street, 18 Sept. 1934
30 CSC to WSC, 1 Jan. 1936*
31 CSC to WSC, 11 Jan. 1936*
32 CSC to WSC, 23 Jan. 1937*
33 CSC to WSC, 29 Jan. 1937*
34 Violet Bonham Carter, *Winston Churchill as I Knew Him*, p. 218
35 Robert Rhodes James, *Churchill: A Study in Failure*, p. 292
36 Andrew Boyle, *Poor Dear Brendan*, pp. 15–18
37 CSC to RSC, 18 Jan. [1931]
38 CSC to WSC, 10 Sept. [1926]†
39 CSC to WSC, 29 Jan. 1927. From Lou Sueil in the South of France*
40 CSC to WSC, dated 'Friday the 30th' [Mar. 1928]*
41 WSC to CSC, 4 Apr. [1928]*
42 WSC to CSC, 15 Mar. 1925*

Chapter 17 HOLIDAY TIME

1 CSC to RSC, 12 Jan. 1932
2 *ibid.*
3 CSC to WSC, 22 Dec. 1934*
4 WSC to CSC, 23 Jan. 1935*
5 WSC to CSC, 1 Jan. 1935*
6 WSC to CSC, 2 Mar. 1935*
7 CSC to WSC, 17 Jan. 1935*
8 Maryott Whyte to CSC, 16 Jan. [1935]
9 Sarah Churchill to CSC, 22 Jan. 1935
10 Sarah Churchill to CSC, 17 Feb. 1935
11 CSC to WSC, 20 Jan. 1935*
12 *ibid.*
13 CSC to WSC, 22 Feb. 1935*
14 CSC to WSC, 26 Feb. 1935*
15 *ibid.*
16 WSC to CSC, 30 Jan. 1935*
17 CSC to WSC, 26 Mar. 1935. Continuation of letter begun on 18 Mar.*
18 Information kindly supplied by Lord

Zuckerman, President of the Zoo-
logical Society of London, from the
Zoo's Archives
19 CSC to the Author
20 *ibid.*
21 CSC to WSC, 1 Apr. 1935. Further
continuation of letter begun on 18
Mar.*
22 WSC to CSC, 9 Mar. 1935*
23 CSC to WSC, 2 Apr. 1935*
24 WSC to CSC, 10 Mar. 1935*

25 WSC to CSC, 5 Apr. 1935*
26 WSC to CSC, 13 Apr. 1935*
27 WSC to CSC, 11 Apr. 1935*
28 WSC to CSC, 10 Mar. 1935*
29 WSC to CSC, 5 Apr. 1935*
30 WSC to CSC, 13 Apr. 1935*
31 CSC to Margery Street, 21 Aug. 1935
32 From a poem by W. P. Ker. The lines
were suggested to Clementine by
Freya Stark

Chapter 18 THE THIRTIES

1 CSC to WSC, 7 Jan. 1936*
2 From the official report of the conference
3 See Charles Lewis Broad, *Winston
Churchill, The Years of Preparation*,
pp. 352–3
4 *'Chips': the Diary of Sir Henry (Chips)
Channon*, ed. Robert Rhodes James.
Entry for 26 Feb. 1937
5 John G. Winant, *A Letter from
Grosvenor Square*, p. 98

6 WSC to CSC, 2 Feb. 1937*
7 CSC to WSC, 19 Jan. 1939†
8 CSC to Margery Street, 6 Apr. 1939
9 CSC to WSC, 13 Dec. [1938]†
10 CSC to WSC, 24 Dec. 1938†
11 CSC to WSC, 1 Jan. 1939†
12 WSC's letter of 29 Dec. 1938*
13 CSC to WSC, 19 Jan. 1939†
14 From *Fare Well* by Walter de la Mare

Chapter 19 YEAR OF DESTINY

1 WSC, *The Second World War*, vol. I,
p. 363
2 *ibid.* pp. 363–4
3 *ibid.* p. 365
4 *ibid.*
5 CSC to Nellie Romilly, 20 Sept. 1939
6 WSC, *op. cit.* vol. I, p. 375
7 Diana Cooper, *Trumpets from the
Steep*, p. 37
8 WSC, *op. cit.* vol. I, p. 601
9 Hansard, *Parliamentary Debates: Commons*, vol. 360, 1502
10 WSC, *op. cit.* vol. II, p. 38

11 *ibid.* p. 100
12 *ibid.* p. 87
13 Hansard, *Parliamentary Debates: Commons*, vol. 361, 796
14 The account of this incident was given
to the Author by CSC; and the facts
were confirmed and amplified by the
Hon. Mrs Averell Harriman (Pamela
Churchill), who was present at the
luncheon
15 Norman Longmate, *How We Lived
Then*, p. 74

Chapter 20 TAKING UP THE LOAD

1 Tom Harrisson, *Living through the
Blitz*, p. 214
2 WSC, *The Second World War*, vol.
III, p. 345
3 *ibid.* p. 421
4 CSC to Lord Beaverbrook, 10 May
194[1]. Dated 1942, but this is clearly
an error
5 CSC to Author, 15 Sept. 1941

6 WSC, *op. cit.* vol. III, p. 540
7 WSC to CSC, undated but headed
'At Sea but now White House' [21
Dec. 1941]*
8 WSC, *op. cit.* vol. IV, p. 81
9 CSC to WSC, 11 Apr. 1942*
10 WSC, *op. cit.* vol. IV, p. 344
11 *ibid.* p. 428
12 *ibid.* p. 541

13 Harold Nicolson, *Letters and Diaries 1939–45*, pp. 257–60
14 *ibid.*
15 *ibid.*
16 Author's diary, 6 Nov. 1942
17 From account of the visit in Joseph P. Lash, *Eleanor and Franklin*, pp. 661–3

18 CSC to Franklin D. Roosevelt, 1 Nov. 1942
19 Diary of Mrs Roosevelt, quoted in Lash, *op. cit.* p. 663
20 Lash, *op. cit.* p. 664
21 *ibid.*
22 WSC to Mrs Roosevelt, quoted in Lash, *op. cit.* p. 668

Chapter 21 ALL IN THE DAY'S WORK

1 Letter from Mrs Jean Pegg of Chelsea, dated 1 Dec. 1964
2 CSC to family, 17 Sept. 1944
3 CSC to WSC, 29 Dec. 1941*
4 CSC to Author, 12 Nov. 1941
5 Statement issued by CSC from 10 Downing Street, 28 Oct. 1943, as quoted in *The Times* the following day
6 Figures taken from statement made by

Col. Divakov at the Meeting of the Presidium of the Executive of the Union of Red Cross and Red Crescent Societies of the USSR, held in Moscow on 6 Apr. 1945
7 Dr Hewlett Johnson, *Searching for Light*, pp. 193–4
8 *ibid.*

Chapter 22 CONFERENCE AND CRISIS

1 RSC to CSC, 4 July 1944
2 CSC to WSC, 14 Jan. 1943*
3 CSC to Author, 7 Mar. 1943
4 CSC to Author, 9 Mar. 1943
5 CSC to WSC, 13 May 1943*
6 CSC to WSC, 15 May 1943*
7 CSC to WSC, 20 May 1943*
8 *ibid.*
9 CSC to WSC, 17 May 1943*
10 CSC to WSC, 20 May 1943*
11 WSC to CSC, 29 May 1943*
12 CSC to WSC, 30 May 1943*
13 Author's diary, 12 Sept. 1943
14 *ibid.*

15 WSC, *The Second World War*, vol. V, p. 339
16 CSC to WSC, 6 Dec. 1943*
17 CSC to the family, 18 Dec. 1943
18 CSC to the family, 21 Dec. 1943
19 *ibid.*
20 CSC to the family, 10 Jan. 1944
21 CSC to the family, 12 Jan. 1944
22 Diana Cooper, *Trumpets from the Steep*, p. 179. Letter to Conrad Russell dated 12 Jan. from Marrakech
23 WSC, *op. cit.* vol. V, p. 401
24 Diana Cooper, *op. cit.* p. 181
25 *ibid.* p. 182

Chapter 23 THE LAST LAP

1 RSC to CSC, 13 Jan. 1945
2 WSC to CSC, 'In the air over Algeria', undated but certainly 11/12 Aug. 1944*
3 Reminiscence from Mrs Jean Hale of Barbados to Author, 3 Jan. 65
4 Incident recounted in Gerald Pawle, *The War and Colonel Warden*, p. 302
5 CSC to Author, 31 Aug. 1944
6 Author's diary, 1 Sept. 1944
7 Robert E. Sherwood, *The White House Papers of Harry L. Hopkins*, vol. II, p. 806

8 CSC to family, 8 Sept. 1944
9 CSC to family, 14 Sept. 1944
10 *ibid.*
11 *ibid.*
12 Sarah Churchill to CSC, 20 Sept. 1944
13 WSC, *The Second World War*, vol. VI, p. 348
14 CSC to Author, 21 Feb. 1945
15 Author to CSC, 18 Feb. 1945
16 CSC to Author, 23 Mar. 1945
17 CSC to Author, 27 Mar. 1945
18 *ibid.*
19 CSC to Sarah Churchill, 29 Mar. 1945

20 CSC to WSC, 30 Mar. 1945*
21 F. M. Montgomery to CSC, 8 Apr. 1945
22 WSC to CSC, 2 Apr. 1945*
23 CSC to WSC, 5 Apr. 1945*
24 WSC to CSC, 6 Apr. 1945*
25 CSC, *My Visit to Russia*, p. 17. Much of the account of her journey is taken from this short book, written on her return
26 This was recounted to the Author by Mrs Whitfield of Warminster, Wilts., to whom Miss Johnson told the story. CSC confirmed that it was true

27 CSC, *op. cit.* p. 26
28 CSC, *op. cit.* pp. 28–30
29 CSC to WSC, cable dated 18 Apr. 1945*
30 CSC, *op. cit.* p. 34
31 CSC, *op. cit.* p. 36
32 CSC to WSC, 24 Apr. 1945*
33 CSC, *op. cit.* pp. 37–8
34 CSC, *op. cit.* p. 48
35 WSC to CSC, 2 May 1945*
36 CSC to WSC, 5 May 1945*
37 CSC, *op. cit.* pp. 56–7
38 WSC, *op. cit.* vol. VI, p. 477
39 CSC, *op. cit.* p. 59

Chapter 24   THE TWO IMPOSTORS

1 CSC to Author, 28 Jan. 1945
2 The Author is obliged to Lord Duncan-Sandys for this reminiscence
3 CSC to Author, 21 June 1945
4 WSC, *The Second World War*, vol. VI, p. 549
5 Author to CSC, 24 July 1945
6 WSC, *op. cit.* vol. VI, p. 583
7 Author's diary, 26 July 1945
8 *ibid.*
9 Facts and figures concerning the election taken from McCallum &

Readman, *The British General Election 1945*, ch. 2
10 Author's diary, 26 July 1945
11 Author to CSC, 6 Aug. 1945
12 CSC to Mrs Pleydell-Bouverie, 9 Aug. 1945
13 Author to CSC, 18 Aug. 1945
14 Hansard, *Parliamentary Debates: Commons*, vol. 413, 97
15 WSC to CSC, 8 Sept. 1945*
16 WSC to CSC, 13 Aug. 1947*
17 Author to CSC, 21 Oct. [1945]

Chapter 25   SWORDS INTO PLOUGHSHARES

1 Author to CSC, 20 Jan. 1946
2 Author's diary, 1 Apr. 1946
3 *ibid.*
4 CSC, Memorandum, 'The Milan Fair', 25 Apr. 1950
5 WSC to President of Board of Trade, 27 Apr. 1950
6 CSC to Author, dated 'Saturday, 25th March' but clearly 24 Mar. 1951

7 CSC to Author, 20 Mar. [1951]
8 CSC to Author, undated but *c.* 17 Mar. 1951
9 CSC to Author, 16 Feb. 1947
10 Sarah Churchill to CSC, 29 Aug. 1949
11 CSC to Antony Beauchamp, 20 Dec. 1949
12 CSC to Sarah Churchill, 20 Dec. 1949

Chapter 26   A WOMAN'S WORK IS NEVER DONE

1 *The Midwife*, 21 Dec. 1942
2 Lady Procter to CSC, 23 Mar. 1947
3 Y.W.C.A. Hostel Wardens' Conference 28 Jan.–1 Feb. 1949. *Official Report*
4 CSC, speech at Y.W.C.A. Hostel Wardens' Conference, 1949
5 *ibid.*
6 Extracted from report by CSC on

visit to East Midland Division Y.W.C.A. 22–4 May 1950
7 Miss W. A. Gorick to CSC, 11 May 1950
8 Mrs Eva K. Mackenzie of Glasgow to the Author, 25 Nov. 1964
9 CSC to Author, 31 Aug. 1952
10 CSC to Author, 26 Aug. 1952
11 CSC to Ronnie Tree, 28 May 1951

12 Author's diary, 31 Dec. 1952
13 H.R.H. the Princess Royal to CSC, 26 May 1953
14 W. H. Cartmell to CSC, 27 Apr. 1953
15 H. Pelling, *Winston Churchill*, p. 605. See also H. Macmillan, *Tides of Fortune*, p. 516
16 Told to the Author by Sir John Colville
17 *ibid.*

18 *The Times*, 29 June 1953
19 RSC to CSC, 30 June [1953]
20 Author to CSC, 22 Sept. [1953]
21 WSC to CSC, 13 Oct. 1953*
22 *ibid.*
23 WSC to CSC, 16 Oct. 1953*
24 CSC to Margery Street, 9 Dec. 1951
25 Lord Beaverbrook to CSC, 22 Mar. [1954]
26 Author's diary, 3–5 Dec. 1954

Chapter 27   DOES THE ROAD WIND UP-HILL ALL THE WAY?

1 The Author is indebted to Sir John Colville for the details of this incident
2 Author to CSC, Thursday [24 Mar. 1955]
3 Sarah Churchill to CSC, dated 'May' [1955]
4 Author's diary, 26 July 1955
5 Sarah Churchill to CSC, 9 Nov. 1955

6 CSC to Sarah Churchill, 14 Jan. 1960
7 CSC to Author, 7 Oct. 1960
8 Sarah Churchill to CSC, 12 Mar. 1958
9 Author to CSC, 19 Sept. 1958
10 Sarah Churchill to CSC, 12 Sept. 1958
11 CSC to Lord Beaverbrook, 5 June 1958

Chapter 28   TWILIGHT AND EVENING BELL

1 Told to the Author by Sir John Colville
2 CSC to Christopher Soames, 6 July 1962
3 Author's diary, 25 May 1952
4 *The Times*, 21 Apr. 1959
5 CSC to Sarah Churchill, 26 Dec. 1962

6 The Author is much indebted to Mrs Doris Moss, O.B.E., for many details concerning this period
7 CSC to Christopher Soames, 19 Apr. 1964
8 Hansard, *Parliamentary Debates: Commons*, vol. 699, 1237

Chapter 29   PORT AFTER STORMY SEAS

1 *The Times*, 20 Feb. 1964

2 CSC to Sarah Churchill, 24 Oct. 1964

Chapter 30   AFTERWARDS

1 CSC to Mr Harold Wilson, 9 Feb. 1965
2 WSC to Mr Charles Nicholl of Messrs. Nicholl, Manisty, Few & Co., 11 Apr. 1946
3 RSC to CSC, 14 Feb. 1965
4 Dated 30 Nov. 1954
5 CSC to family, 18 Sept. 1944
6 The Author is indebted to her nephew, Winston S. Churchill, M.P., for a letter to him from Mr Elliot Evers of Malvern, Worcs., containing this interesting and apt piece of information
7 CSC to Author, 1 Sept. 1954

8 Lord Clark, O.M., C.H., to Author, 10 Aug. 1978, to whom she is most grateful for other details
9 CSC to Mr Graham Sutherland, O.M., 4 Dec. 1954
10 CSC to Lord Beaverbrook, 13 Oct. 1957
11 CSC to Author, 24 Jan. 1966
12 General de Gaulle to CSC, 19 May 1969
13 President de Gaulle to CSC, Jan. 1966
14 Author to CSC, 21 Nov. [1970]
15 Miss A. M. Johnson, now Matron of the Star and Garter Home, Richmond, to the Author, 28 Sept. 1975

SELECT BIBLIOGRAPHY

Manuscript Sources

Baroness Spencer-Churchill Papers
Churchill Papers (Churchill College, Cambridge)
Mary Soames personal papers and diaries
Diaries of Blanche, Countess of Airlie
Beaverbrook Papers

Printed Sources

Airlie, Mabell, Countess of, *Thatched with Gold*, London, 1962
Airlie, 12th Earl of, *The Bonnie House of Airlie*, ed. Katherine Thomasson, privately
    printed, Brechin, 1963
Ashmead-Bartlett, E., *The Uncensored Dardanelles*, London, 1928
Asquith, Lady Cynthia, *Diaries 1915–18*, London, 1968
Asquith, Margot, *Autobiography*, 2 vols, London, 1920, 1922
Baron, Wendy, *Sickert*, London, 1973
Beaverbrook, Lord, *Politicians and the War*, 2 vols, London, 1928; reprinted 1966
Birkenhead, 2nd Earl of, *F. E.*, London, 1959
Blanche, Jacques-Emile, *Cahiers d'un artiste*, 6 vols, Paris, 1915–20. vol I
Blunt, Wilfrid Scawen, *My Diaries*, 2 vols, London, 1912, 1920
Bonham Carter, Lady Violet, *Winston Churchill as I Knew Him*, London, 1965
Boyle, Andrew, *Poor Dear Brendan*, London, 1974
Broad, Charles Lewis, *Winston Churchill: The Years of Preparation*, London, 1963
Butler, D. Edgeworth and Freeman, J., *British Political Facts 1900–1960*, London,
    1963
Cambray, P. G. and Briggs, G. G. B., *Red Cross and St John War Organisation
    1939–47*, London, 1949
Churchill, Clementine S., *My Visit to Russia*, London, 1945
Churchill, Randolph S., *Twenty-One Years*, London, 1965
——*Winston S. Churchill*, vols I and II, London, 1966, 1967; also *Companion*

Volumes I and *II*, London 1967, 1969. (For later vols see under Gilbert, Martin)

Churchill, Sarah, *A Thread in the Tapestry*, London, 1967

Churchill, Winston S., *Painting as a Pastime*, London, 1948

——*The Second World War*, 6 vols, London, 1948–54

——*Thoughts and Adventures*, London, 1932

——*The World Crisis*, 6 vols, London 1923–31

Cooper, Lady Diana, *Trumpets from the Steep*, London, 1960

Cross, Colin, *The Liberals in Power 1905–1914*, London, 1963

Gibb, D. E. W., *Lloyds of London, A Study in Individualism*, London, 1957

Gilbert, Martin, *Winston S. Churchill*, vols III–V, London, 1971, 1975, 1976; also *Companion Volumes III* and *IV*, London, 1972, 1977

Hankey, Lord, *The Supreme Command*, 2 vols, London, 1961

Hansard, Parliamentary Debates: Commons, various dates

Harrisson, Tom, *Living Through the Blitz*, London, 1976

James, Robert Rhodes (ed.), *'Chips': the Diary of Sir Henry (Chips) Channon*, London, 1967

James, Robert Rhodes, *Churchill: A Study in Failure 1900–1939*, London, 1970

——'Churchill the Outsider', series of four articles in *The Observer*, 4th–25th September 1966

Jenkins, Roy, *Asquith*, London, 1964

Johnson, Dr Hewlett, *Searching for Light*, London, 1968

Keesing's Contemporary Archives, various dates

Lash, Joseph P., *Eleanor and Franklin*, London, 1972

Lavery, Sir John, *The Life of a Painter*, London, 1940

Leslie, Anita, *Jennie: The Life of Lady Randolph Churchill*, London, 1969

Lloyd George, David, *War Memoirs*, 6 vols, London, 1933–6

Longmate, Norman, *How We Lived Then*, London, 1971

McCallum, R. B. and Readman, A., *The British General Election of 1945*, London, 1947

Maclean, Fitzroy, *Eastern Approaches*, London, 1956

Macmillan, Harold, *Tides of Fortune*, London, 1969

Magnus, Sir Philip, *King Edward VII*, London, 1964

Marsh, Sir Edward, *A Number of People*, London, 1939

Minney, R. J., *No. 10 Downing Street*, London, 1963

Moran, Lord, *Winston Churchill: The Struggle for Survival 1940–65*, London, 1966

Nicolson, Harold, *Letters and Diaries 1939–45*, London, 1967

O'Brien, Terence, *Civil Defence* (Official History of the Second World War series), HMSO, London, 1955

Pakenham, Simona, *Pigtails and Pernod*, London, 1962

——*60 Miles from England: The English at Dieppe 1814–1914*, London, 1967

Pankhurst, E. Sylvia, *The Suffragette Movement*, London, 1931

Panter-Downes, Mollie, *London War Notes 1939–45*, London, 1972

Pawle, Gerald, *The War and Colonel Warden*, London, 1963

Pelling, Henry, *Winston Churchill*, London, 1974

Quinn, James, S. J., *Cavalier of Christ: John Ogilvie, Priest and Martyr*, Glasgow, 1976

Riddell, Lord, *More Pages from my Diary 1908–1914*, London, 1934

Sherwood, Robert E., *The White House Papers of Harry L. Hopkins*, 2 vols, London, 1948–9

Steen, Marguerite, *Pier Glass: More Autobiography*, London, 1968

Taylor, A. J. P., *English History 1914–1945*, London, 1965

The Times Diary and Index of the War, London, 1921

Tree, Ronald, *When the Moon was High*, London, 1975

Tunney, Christopher, *Biographical Dictionary of World War II*, London, 1972

Webb, Beatrice, *Our Partnership*, London, 1948

Wharton, Edith, *A Backward Glance*, New York and London, 1934

Wheeler-Bennett, Sir John (ed. and Introduction by), *Action This Day: Working with Churchill*, various contributors, London, 1968

Wilson, W., *The House of Airlie*, 2 vols, London, 1924

Winant, John G., *A Letter from Grosvenor Square*, London, 1947

Woods, Frederick, *Bibliography of the Works of Sir Winston Churchill*, rev. ed., London, 1969

Young, Kenneth, *Churchill and Beaverbrook*, London, 1966

Newspaper Sources

Principally *The Times*, but most national papers consulted at various dates; also, among others, *Belfast Weekly News*; *Dundee Advertiser*; *Dundee Courier*; *Woodford Guardian*; *Woodford Times*, for specific reports.

INDEX

The following abbreviations have been used for members of the family: CSC (Clementine Spencer Churchill); DC (Diana Churchill); MC (Mary Churchill); RSC (Randolph Spencer Churchill; SC (Sarah Churchill); WSC (Winston Spencer Churchill). Other abbreviations are: C (Churchill); H (Hozier); WWI/WWII (First and Second World Wars).

References to Churchill family correspondence will be found under the sub-heading 'Letters' in the entry for each individual; letters between members of the family and other persons are included in the entries for their correspondents.